# Contemporary Critical Discourse Studies

# Contemporary Critical Discourse Studies

## EDITED BY

## CHRISTOPHER HART AND PIOTR CAP

Bloomsbury Academic
An imprint of Bloomsbury Publishing Plc

# BLOOMSBURY

LONDON · NEW DELHI · NEW YORK · SYDNEY

**Bloomsbury Academic**

An imprint of Bloomsbury Publishing Plc

| | |
|---|---|
| 50 Bedford Square | 1385 Broadway |
| London | New York |
| WC1B 3DP | NY 10018 |
| UK | USA |

**www.bloomsbury.com**

**BLOOMSBURY and the Diana logo are trademarks of Bloomsbury Publishing Plc**

First published 2014

**British Library Cataloguing-in-Publication Data**
A catalogue record for this book is available from the British Library.

ISBN: HB: 978-1-4411-4163-7
ePDF: 978-1-4411-6077-5
ePub: 978-1-4725-2704-2

**Library of Congress Cataloging-in-Publication Data**
Contemporary critical discourse studies / edited by Christopher Hart, Piotr Cap.
pages cm
ISBN 978-1-4411-4163-7 (hardback) — ISBN 978-1-4725-2704-2 (epub) –
ISBN 978-1-4411-6077-5 (epdf) 1. Critical discourse analysis. 2. Cognitive grammar.
I. Hart, Christopher (Linguist) editor of compilation. II. Cap, Piotr, editor of compilation.
P302.C62193 2014
401'.41—dc23
2014009527

Typeset by RefineCatch Limited, Bungay, Suffolk
Printed and bound in Great Britain

# Contents

**Introduction**   *Christopher Hart and Piotr Cap*  1

**PART ONE**   Dimensions of Discourse  17

**History**  19

**1**   *Historia Magistra Vitae*: The Topos of History as a Teacher in Public
Struggles over *Self* and *Other* Representation  19
*Bernhard Forchtner*

**2**   Metaphor in the Discourse-Historical Approach  45
*Andreas Musolff*

**Argumentation**  67

**3**   Argumentation Analysis and the Discourse-Historical Approach:
A Methodological Framework  67
*Martin Reisigl*

**4**   It Is Easy to Miss Something You Are Not Looking for: A Pragmatic
Account of Covert Communicative Influence for (Critical) Discourse
Analysis  97
*Steve Oswald*

**Social Cognition**  121

**5**   Discourse-Cognition-Society: Current State and Prospects of the
Socio-Cognitive Approach to Discourse  121
*Teun A. van Dijk*

**6**   Applying Social Cognition Research to Critical Discourse Studies:
        The Case of Collective Identities 147
        *Veronika Koller*

## Conceptualization 167

**7**   Construal Operations in Online Press Reports of Political
        Protests 167
        *Christopher Hart*

**8**   Expanding CDS Methodology by Cognitive-Pragmatic Tools:
        Proximization Theory and Public Space Discourses 189
        *Piotr Cap*

## Corpora 211

**9**   'Bad Wigs and Screaming Mimis': Using Corpus-Assisted Techniques
        to Carry Out Critical Discourse Analysis of the Representation of Trans
        People in the British Press 211
        *Paul Baker*

**10**  Digital Argument Deconstruction: An Ethical Software-Assisted
        Critical Discourse Analysis for Highlighting Where Arguments Fall
        Apart 237
        *Kieran O'Halloran*

## Sound and Vision 281

**11**  Critical Discourse Analysis and Multimodality 281
        *Theo van Leeuwen*

**12**  Sound and Discourse: A Multimodal Approach to War
        Film Music 297
        *David Machin*

## PART TWO   Domains of Discourse 319

### Political Discourse 321

**13** 'American Ways of Organizing the World': Designing the Global Future through US National Security Policy 321
*Patricia L. Dunmire*

**14** 'Yes, We Can': The Social Life of a Political Slogan 347
*Adam Hodges*

### Media Discourse 365

**15** Media Discourse in Context 365
*Anita Fetzer*

**16** Media Discourse and De/Coloniality: A Post-Foundational Approach 385
*Felicitas Macgilchrist*

### European Union 407

**17** Discourse and Communication in the European Union: A Multi-Focus Perspective of Critical Discourse Studies 407
*Michał Krzyżanowski*

**18** The Discursive Technology of Europeans' Involvement: EU *Culture* and Community of Practice 433
*Elena Magistro*

### Public Policy 461

**19** The Privatization of the Public Realm: A Critical Perspective on Practice and Discourse 461
*Gerlinde Mautner*

**20**  Pushed out of School: A Critical Discourse Analysis of the Policies and
Practices of Educational Accountability 479
*Rebecca Rogers*

## Race and Immigration 501

**21**  Immigration Discourses and Critical Discourse Analysis:
Dynamics of World Events and Immigration Representations
in the British Press 501
*Majid KhosraviNik*

**22**  Race and Immigration in Far- and Extreme-Right European Political
Leaflets 521
*John E. Richardson and Monica Colombo*

## Health 543

**23**  Critical Studies of Health and Illness Discourses 543
*Nelya Koteyko*

**24**  Public Health in the UK Media: Cognitive Discourse Analysis and its
Application to a Drinking Water Emergency 559
*Olivia Knapton and Gabriella Rundblad*

## Environment 583

**25**  Ecolinguistics and Erasure: Restoring the Natural World to
Consciousness 583
*Arran Stibbe*

**26**  Values, Assumptions and Beliefs in British Newspaper Editorial
Coverage of Climate Change 603
*Cinzia Bevitori*

Index 627

# Introduction

## *Christopher Hart and Piotr Cap*

Critical Discourse Studies (CDS) is a transdisciplinary, text-analytical approach to critical social research (Fowler et al., 1979; Hodge and Kress, 1993; Fairclough, 1989, 1995; Chouliaraki and Fairclough, 1999; Reisigl and Wodak, 2001; Weiss and Wodak, 2003; Van Dijk, 1999, 2003, 2006; Wodak and Chilton, 2005; Wodak and Meyer, 2009; Wodak, 2012; amongst others). It is not confined to any specific methodology or particular area of analysis but, rather, CDS is and always has been multifaceted, dealing with data of very different kinds and applying a broad base of methodologies sourced from across the humanities, social and cognitive sciences (see e.g. Breeze, 2011 for a comprehensive overview). Both the 'discourse' and the 'studies' in its designation thus mean something different to different researchers.[1] Discourse is a multidimensional, multimodal and multifunctional phenomenon. Discourse must be 'unpacked' with reference to different dimensions of context (linguistic, intertextual, historical, social and situational). As a practice, it also involves both cognitive and linguistic or other semiotic, including audio and visual, dimensions. Functionally, discourse is used (simultaneously) to represent, evaluate, argue for and against, and ultimately to legitimate or delegitimate social actions. In this way, discourse is socially constitutive as well as socially conditioned (Fairclough and Wodak, 1997; Wodak, 2011, etc.). That is, on the one hand, discourse is shaped by the situations, institutions and social structures which surround it. At the same time, however, discourse itself constitutes these situations, institutions etc., as well as the social identities and relationships between their members/participants. In respect of the latter, discourse thus functions in creating, sustaining and/or transforming the social status quo.

Since this dialectical relationship between discourse and social reality is quite evidently complex, different researchers in CDS focus on different aspects of this relationship, working at different locations on the continuum that links the 'micro' (the linguistic) with the 'macro' (the social) (Lemke, 1995; Benke, 2000). Some practitioners, for example, are more concerned with the macro-level social structures which facilitate or motivate discursive events whilst others focus more on the micro-level, looking at the particular chunks of language that make up these events. These preferences are, of course, never mutually exclusive but are a matter, purely, of analytical emphasis.

Finally, there is – at the meso-, socio-pragmatic level (Fetzer and Bull, 2013) – a plethora of studies focused on how discourse is used in different communicative genres, how it traverses communicative channels (viz. the new media), and how it is subject to continual recontextualization and hybridization along the way (Cap and Okulska, 2013). Methods of *studying* discourse are similarly diverse, depending naturally on the domains and dimensions of discourse under consideration, as well as the theoretical goals of the researcher. Different macro- and micro-level theories provide more or less appropriate tools depending on the task at hand. At the micro-level, for example, Hallidayan linguistics has proved especially useful in analysing the ideological assumptions enshrined in written texts (Fowler, 1991; Hodge and Kress, 1993). Conversely, Conversation Analysis allows for a consideration of the rearticulation and negotiation of power in (institutionalized) talk exchanges (Atkinson and Heritage, 1984; Drew and Heritage, 1992, etc.). And a combination of the two offers a fruitful framework for analysing computer-mediated communication (Ten Have, 2000; Giltrow and Stein, 2009; Yus, 2011). Needless to say, anyway, that this diversity and fluidity makes CDS a difficult discipline to pin down.

Perhaps the best way of defining CDS is therefore by the 'critical' in its designation. Here, CDS is often characterized as a perspective, position or attitude (e.g. Van Dijk, 2009: 62). The concept of critical in CDS, however, is understood in as broad a fashion as the concept of discourse. Some, for example, work with a neo-Marxist notion of critique (Fairclough, 1995; Chouliaraki and Fairclough, 1999) while others orient themselves more to the Critical Theory of the Frankfurt School (Wodak, 2001; Reisigl and Wodak, 2001).[2] In both cases, critique presupposes a particular political stance on the part of the researcher and is intended to be instrumental in bringing about social change. For others still, critique comes not so much from a particular political perspective but is concerned more with abuses of language per se and the cognitive and linguistic mechanisms involved.[3] At the same time, there are long-standing traditions in discourse analysis, e.g. post-structuralist discourse analysis, which adopt a critical perspective (e.g. Slembrouck, 2001) but which would not normally be thought of as falling under the banner of CDS. Criticality, then, is in some sense or another a necessary condition for defining CDS but it is not a sufficient condition. What seems to set CDS apart from other forms of critical discourse research is a (constantly growing) focus on the micro-level analysis of attested data – texts. To this extent, CDS relies heavily on the field of linguistics, although to different degrees in different works. Here, although CDS is a complex domain which is, in principle at least, without boundaries both methodologically and in terms of the type of data it targets, clear traditions *can* be identified. These traditions may be delineated either in terms of particular methodological 'schools' or 'approaches' (e.g. Wodak and Meyer, 2009) or in terms of the discourse domains and genres targeted (e.g. Cap and Okulska, 2013; Bhatia, 2004; Martin and Rose, 2008). These alternative demarcations represent two possible vantage points in CDS: looking from a theoretical/methodological point of view toward the range of data that a given model is equipped to handle or looking from the point of view of particular data-types toward the range of theories and methodologies that one would need to properly account for them. These complementary perspectives are depicted in Figure 0.1.

As represented by the bold outline in Figure 0.1, the majority of attempts to date at mapping the field of CDS have been made from the perspective of particular methodological approaches, which carry out their analyses against distinct theoretical backdrops and tend to be concerned with particular dimensions or features of discourse as a linguistic, cognitive and social practice. Several volume-length treatments have represented CDS along these lines (Wodak and Meyer, 2009; Weiss and Wodak, 2003; Wodak and Chilton, 2005; Chilton and Schäffner, 2002; Van Dijk, 2008; among others).

In one of the more recent and most comprehensive attempts at taking stock of the field, Wodak and Meyer (2009) distinguish six approaches to CDS.[4] We will not describe each of these approaches again here, nor provide a detailed historical overview of the trajectory of CDS. We assume that the reader is at least familiar with the CDS landscape as it has hitherto looked.[5] Otherwise, the reader is directed to Wodak and Meyer (2009) for a detailed outline. Wodak and Meyer present these six approaches in relation to their specific 'theoretical attractors' on the one hand and the extent to which they proceed deductively or inductively on the other (2009: 20). A diagrammatic representation of their delineation is reproduced in Figure 0.2.

The outline presented by Wodak and Meyer is useful. However, there is, of course, more than one way to carve up the field of CDS and there are a number of things that the representation in Figure 0.2 fails to capture. In the first place, it does not recognize the interconnectedness of particular approaches. For example, the discourse-historical and socio-cognitive approaches are both related in their focus on argumentation, although the discourse-historical approach deals with argumentation in more detail. Similarly, the discourse-historical approach borrows heavily in its outline of 'referential strategies' from the social actor model (Reisigl and Wodak, 2001: 46–56). And the social actor model, although the categories within it are socio-semantic rather than purely grammatical, is presented as a grammar in the format of a Hallidayan functional network (Van Leeuwen, 1996). The social actor model thus owes much to other systemic functional approaches such as critical linguistics (not represented) and the dialectical-relational approach.

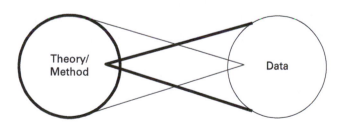

**FIGURE 0.1** *Perspectives in CDS.*

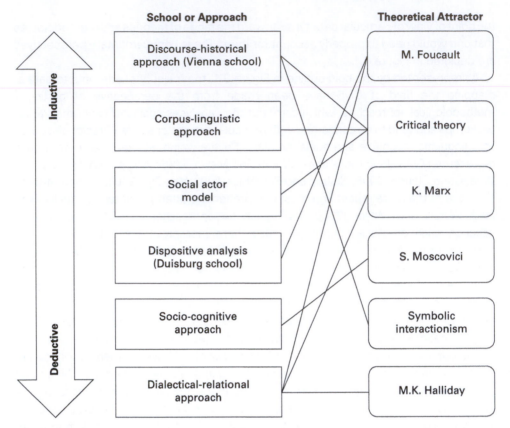

**FIGURE 0.2** *Approaches and macro-level theoretical attractors* (reproduced from Wodak and Meyer, 2009: 20).

In the second place, CDS is a heady mix of social and linguistic theory and whilst different approaches can be mapped out according to the social theories they are influenced by, they may equally be distinguished by the linguistic fields that provide for their micro-level text-analytical methodologies. Here, Halliday's systemic functional grammar (Halliday, 1985, 1994) has been particularly influential, especially in critical linguistics and the dialectical-relational approach but also across much of the rest of CDS (Wodak, 2001; Chilton, 2005). Historically, this is owed to the development of CDS from critical linguistics. Critical linguistics, or the 'East Anglian' school (Fowler et al., 1979; Fowler, 1991; Hodge and Kress, 1993), then, is an historical precursor to CDS. However, it is still widely practised such that it can be considered a major approach in CDS (Fairclough and Wodak, 1997).

Since the 'breaking out' of CDS from critical linguistics the field has developed in exciting new directions drawing on a broader range of linguistic theories. The discourse-historical approach, for example, draws on the theory of pragma-dialectics presented by van Eemeren and Grootendorst (1992) and in particular on the notions of topoi and fallacy. The corpus linguistic approach has developed on the back of Corpus Linguistics, a recent innovation in linguistics (Stubbs, 2002, 2004; Partington, 2006; Baker, 2006; Baker at al., 2008; O'Halloran, 2010).[6]

Corpus linguistics, of course, is not the only significant development in linguistics which CDS has been quick to react to. Indeed, CDS has grown exponentially in the last few years and several new schools or approaches have arisen which are not included in Figure 0.2. We see this rapid expansion as, in part, a response to recent advances in linguistics and other communication sciences – not just for the sake of it but because such advances make it possible to address certain criticisms raised against CDS and/or because contemporary programs in linguistics and communication science provide new tools which can shed fresh light on the ideological or persuasive potential of discourse. Looking from the data perspective as depicted in Figure 0.1, we also see new frameworks as being developed or refined in response to new discourses and genres. The corpus linguistic approach, for example, helps to answer criticisms pertaining to bias and representativeness in data selection as well as to the statistical significance of findings (cf. Stubbs, 1997; Widdowson, 2004). It is, however, not just a 'problem solver' which can be applied in conjunction with other approaches to ensure against subjectivity and overgeneralization (cf. Wodak and Meyer, 2009: 27). The corpus linguistic approach comes with its own unique analytical techniques, such as collocation and prosody analysis, which can reveal ideological properties of texts that have otherwise remained beyond the radar of CDS (Baker, 2006). Finally, the corpus linguistic approach can also be seen as having developed in order to enable a proper handle on digital genres in the 'information age'.

Intriguingly, the fertility of the corpus linguistic approach is only to a relatively minor extent recognized in Wodak and Meyer's (2009) collection. Apart from its inclusion in the delineation they present, they acknowledge, we believe, only a part of what the corpus approach contributes to CDS. The primary role of corpus analysis, as presented, is to ensure an acceptable balance between theory- and data-driven analysis. Compared to other corpus-based analyses (e.g. Baker and McEnery, 2005), however, this constitutes a very limited view of what a corpus linguistic approach can do.

The panorama presented by Wodak and Meyer (2009), at least in so far as it is intended to capture the complete CDS landscape, suffers a further shortcoming in light of recent developments in CDS. We see at least four contemporary approaches which are not acknowledged at all. These increasingly influential paradigms can be identified as: critical metaphor studies[7] (Charteris-Black, 2004; Koller, 2004; Musolff, 2004, 2010; Zinken, 2007, etc.); the cognitive linguistic approach (Hart, 2011a/b/c, 2013a/b; Marín Arrese, 2011); the legitimization-proximization model (Cap, 2006, 2008, 2013; Chilton, 2004, 2011b; Dunmire, 2011; Kopytowska, 2013); and the 'Neuchâtel/ Fribourg' school of critical cognitive pragmatics (Saussure and Schulz, 2005; Maillat and Oswald, 2009, 2011; Lewiński and Oswald, 2013).[8]

The need to include these four additional approaches in an up-to-date assessment of the CDS landscape is, we believe, essential. Each of these new agendas represents, like most strands in CDS, an individual yet interdisciplinary research programme. Moreover, in line with other schools in CDS, each of them constitutes a nuanced line of inquiry illuminating otherwise unexplored features of the social-linguistic interface. Critical metaphor studies, for instance, has shown the fundamental role that metaphor plays not only in our *understanding* of the socio-political world we inhabit but also in the way we argue about socio-political issues. It has, in addition, shown that metaphorical expressions in language cannot be treated as isolated entities but has demonstrated, instead, that they are manifestations of integrated knowledge networks in the form of conceptual metaphors, which provide structure and coherence to our very experience. It is in this way, for critical metaphor studies, that language reveals traces of ideology (Goatly, 2007).

The cognitive linguistic approach moves beyond metaphor (Hart, 2011b/c) to consider the ideological import of other linguistic (lexical and grammatical) structures in terms of the conceptual processes they invoke. These processes are, in accordance with findings from Cognitive Linguistics, seen as instantiations of non-linguistic, domain-general cognitive processes. The cognitive linguistic approach therefore provides a typology of conceptual processes, including categorization, metaphor, modality and deixis, which are reliant on broader cognitive systems and which bring into effect a range of ideological discursive strategies. The legitimization-proximization model is more focused on the context-specific functions of a particular conceptual operation – proximization – and the different forms of realization (spatial, temporal, axiological) which, in response to changing states of affairs in global politics, come to be the most stable strategy for a given speech event type at a given moment of time. Finally, the Neuchâtel/Fribourg school presents an almost exclusively explanatory framework in which the manipulative facility of language, as manifested in fallacious arguments, is theorized as a kind of cognitive illusion or cognitive misdirection. This form of manipulation is made possible by the fact that 'people are nearly-incorrigible "cognitive optimists"' (Sperber et al., 1995: 11) who take for granted that their spontaneous cognitive processes are highly reliable and that the output of these processes does not need double checking (Maillat and Oswald, 2009). What all these recent approaches have in common is that they do not treat the ideological, persuasive or manipulative potential of discourse as a property of language itself but of the cognitive processes which language is able to mobilize.

As we see it, then, from a theoretical/methodological perspective, the current landscape in CDS can be laid out as in Figure 0.3.[9] In this representation, approaches are presented in relation to their micro-level linguistic-analytical attractors rather than their macro-level social-theoretical attractors. Some approaches, as can be seen, have their feet in more than one field representing the interdisciplinary nature of contemporary programmes in CDS. Each field also provides methodological sources for more than one approach. This does not mean that approaches necessarily draw on the exact same theories within those fields or that they are concerned with the same set of linguistic features. From the field of pragmatics, for example, only critical cognitive pragmatics draws explicitly on Relevance Theory. The discourse-historical approach and the socio-cognitive approach also draw on pragmatics but are more concerned with topoi, which is not a feature of critical cognitive pragmatics. These three approaches do all, though, draw to a lesser or greater extent on the theory of pragma-dialectics. The legitimization-proximization model, by contrast, adopts a more traditional linguistic-pragmatic stance, in the sense that meanings, derived from cognitive categories of space, time and value, are seen as being put to work strategically in service of various *speech act functions*. One thing they all have in common, though, is that somewhere within their purview is a concern with argumentation. The constellations in the diagram therefore link approaches by common objects of analysis, though alternative approaches may come at these from slightly different angles.

The various approaches to CDS can also be arranged along a number of axes representing more general epistemological orientations. Wodak and Meyer recognize

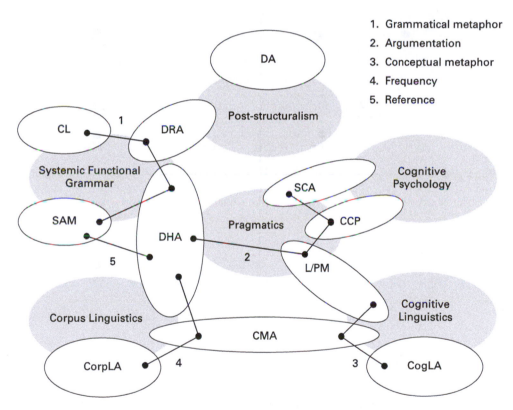

1. Grammatical metaphor
2. Argumentation
3. Conceptual metaphor
4. Frequency
5. Reference

**FIGURE 0.3** *Contemporary CDS: Approaches and methodological attractors.*

CL: Critical linguistics; DRA: Dialectical-relational approach; DA: Dispositive analysis; SAM: Social actor model; DHA: Discourse-historical approach; SCA: Socio-cognitive approach; CCP: Critical cognitive pragmatics; L/PM: Legitimization-proximization model; CogLA: Cognitive linguistics approach; CMA: Critical metaphor analysis; CorpLA: Corpus linguistics approach.

this and present a topography in which the six approaches they identify are positioned (i) according to the degree of agency or intention they attribute to (powerful) producers of discourse or the extent to which they see discourse as determined by social or institutional structures; and (ii) according to the amount of linguistic detail presented in their analyses (or put another way, the extent to which alternative approaches are reliant on specific theories in linguistics). We see at least two further axes along which approaches in CDS could be located relative to one another: the extent to which they are concerned with linguistic content or structure (syntagmatic, paradigmatic, cohesive, conceptual); and the extent to which they focus on the cognitive or functional dimensions of discourse. Figure 0.4 presents a topography along these lines. The positions of different approaches should not be taken as absolute but as idealized locations along two continua.

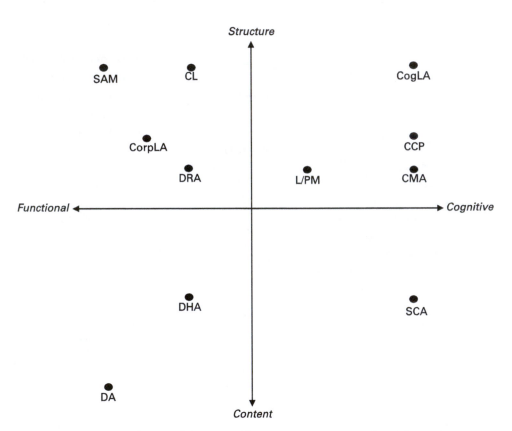

**FIGURE 0.4** *Approaches to CDS arranged by content>structure and social>cognitive.*

CL: Critical linguistics; DRA: Dialectical-relational approach; DA: Dispositive analysis; SAM: Social actor model; DHA: Discourse-historical approach; SCA: Socio-cognitive approach; CCP: Critical cognitive pragmatics; L/PM: Legitimization-proximization model; CogLA: Cognitive linguistics approach; CMA: Critical metaphor analysis; CorpLA: Corpus linguistics approach.

The diagrams in Figures 0.3 and 0.4 are not intended to suggest that particular approaches are entirely discrete, closed off from one and other. CDS is a fluid paradigm and different approaches can be combined in different ways to yield new, useful synergies (e.g. Baker et al., 2008). This book presents a number of such cross-fertilizations: a combination of discourse-historical, corpus linguistic and cognitive linguistic approaches in the study of metaphor (Musolff); a combination of insights from the social actor model and the socio-cognitive and discourse-historical approaches in analysing collective identity (Koller); and the incorporation of the legitimization model within the discourse-historical framework (Dunmire); amongst others. Neither are we suggesting that the most established approaches (such as the dialectical-relational and discourse-historical approaches) have stagnated or been superseded. Far from it, as papers in this volume attest. In Fetzer's chapter, for example, Fairclough's conceptualization of discourse is seen to be merged with more recent work on context and the production-reception dynamic in media discourse. New synergies are constantly being developed in productive ways. Approaches are also evolving within themselves (often in light of competing views). In this volume, for example, the notion of *topos* – a key concept in the discourse-historical approach – is further elaborated by Forchtner and, in response to recent views which define topos in the more formal sense of Classical Rhetoric (Žagar, 2010), by Reisigl. In van Dijk's text, an up-to-date and revisited version of socio-cognitive analysis, 'CGA', is outlined in order to demonstrate the continuing explanatory advantage of the socio-cognitive framework over competing decontextualized, 'form-autonomous', models. These examples are just some of the specimens we could point to; throughout the book the reader will be able to identify many more mergers, synergies and dialogues – often polemical but always productive – between established CDA voices and more emerging traditions.

Technically, the book is organized in a way that reflects the two alternative perspectives in Figure 0.1.[10] Chapters in Part I represent, collectively, the most important approaches in CDS (including the eleven approaches identified in Figures 0.3 and 0.4) which have been developed and applied in relation to different dimensions, functions and modalities of discourse (history, argumentation, cognition, conceptualization, corpora, sound and vision). Part II takes a converse perspective and includes studies of those discourse domains currently of most concern in CDS, arguing in each case for the most feasible model or models to adequately theorize and analyse these discursive domains. Thus, Part I and Part II can be described as theory- versus data-driven, respectively. Needless to say, though, that there are (inevitable) overlaps between the two parts. These overlaps are indicative of the fact that this division merely reflects alternative perspectives. Many of the chapters in Part I, for example, illustrate their frameworks through analyses of discourse domains theorized in more detail in Part II. Likewise, many of the chapters in Part II appropriate aspects of the models elaborated in greater detail in Part I.

There are also overlaps within the two parts. O'Halloran, for example, although concerned primarily with developing a corpus-informed methodology, does so with respect to argumentation analysis. And Musolff, in his chapter, traces the reoccurrence of a particular metaphor, as a form of conceptualization, within its intertextual, historical context. Similarly, in Part II, the discourse domains presented are not to be taken as mutually exclusive. The boundary between what constitutes political and what constitutes media discourse, for example, is notoriously and increasingly difficult to define. At the same time, other discourses, such as those of immigration or the EU, are examples of political and media discourse. And there is then, of course, an interdiscursive blurring between domains such that discourses of the EU, for instance, draw on or 'speak to' discourses of immigration, and vice versa. Again, these are only indicative cases. The reader will find many more connections between the chapters. In the later chapters of Part II, the book considers new discourses (of 'Health' and 'Environment') which have only recently come under the analytical lens of CDS and are consequently missing from other CDS anthologies. These discourses may similarly occur as examples of political and media discourse but they can also be seen to instantiate a scientific or pseudo-scientific discourse.

The volume is made up, in both Part I and Part II, of a series of 'blocks' containing two chapters each. The rationale for this arrangement is different in the two parts. Part I includes blocks in which the first chapter assumes, in principle, a broader perspective than the second chapter. The second chapter, on the other hand, tends to be more restricted in scope; it often follows up on one or selected aspect(s) of the framework surveyed in the first chapter and puts this to use in a more specific case study. Van Dijk, in his chapter, for example, presents a bird's-eye view of the way societal structures and discourse structures enter into different kinds of relationships and of how these relationships are (necessarily) cognitively mediated. The second chapter in this block, from Koller, focuses on specific relations between social and discourse structures in the narrower context of collective (and conflicting) identities within discourse communities. There is no comparable pattern within the blocks in Part II, where the rationale for including two chapters is intended instead (i) to illustrate some of the alternative analytical angles that one may take with respect to these discourse domains; and (ii) to reveal some of the internal complexities of these domains. As a whole, however, starting from the assumption that all discourse is ultimately political and all politics is ultimately discursive (Chilton, 2004), Part II can be read as getting gradually narrower in focus and responding to new forms of discursive politics.

In recognizing the innovations, interconnections and fresh motivations in contemporary CDS, then, it is our intention in this collection to provide a snapshot in time of a discipline which is constantly evolving, reacting to the world around it, reassessing the validity of its methods, and extending into new territories. We hope that it will remain an important reference work for CDS in the future but recognize the clear need to continue to take stock of an ever-changing field.

# Notes

**1** See Breeze (2011) for an in-depth discussion of different, often geographically and historically motivated, conceptions of the term 'discourse' and 'discourse studies'. Our aim is not to add another rock to the pile. Rather, we acknowledge the multiplicity of possible approaches and argue that, given such multiplicity, defining CDS by reference to 'discourse' and 'discourse studies' is insufficient.

**2** The extent to which critique as sometimes understood in CDS is an inherently westernized version of critique has recently been raised as a potential problem for CDS (Chilton, 2011a).

**3** This is the position of critical cognitive pragmatics (e.g. Saussure and Schulz, 2005).

**4** They in fact label the field 'Critical Discourse Analysis' (CDA) in accord with the tradition of the last 25 years. The term CDS, however, has recently come to find favour in place of CDA (Van Dijk, 2009; Hart, 2011a). For van Dijk, this relabelling is motivated by the fact that critical discourse research is not restricted to *applied analysis* but incorporates also *theoretical development* (2009: 62). We strongly agree with this position and opt for 'Critical Discourse Studies' ourselves. In addition, the label Critical Discourse Analysis (CDA) is often used metonymically to refer to one or other of the more prominent individual approaches, identifiable as critical linguistics, the dialectical-relational approach and the discourse-historical approach (Titscher et al., 2000), rather than in the more general, inclusive sense that was originally intended. For these reasons also, then, we prefer the less restricted term CDS.

**5** The corpus linguistic approach (Baker et al., 2008; Gabrielatos and Baker, 2008; Mautner, 2007) is a relatively new addition to the landscape. It was not present, for example, in Wodak and Meyer (2001).

**6** It should be stressed at this point, that approaches in CDS do not simply borrow and apply ready-made frameworks from linguistics. Rather, CDS adapts and re-thinks linguistic theories abductively in response to data and operationalization (Wodak and Meyer, 2009: 30). In this sense, we are cautious about characterizing CDS as an area of *applied linguistics*.

**7** Arguably the most developed and the most methodologically rigorous of the 'new approaches'.

**8** Nor does Wodak and Meyer's typology include Critical Linguistics in the first place. This can be explained by the fact that most of the analytical techniques of Critical Linguistics have been incorporated by other approaches (Billig, 2008; O'Halloran, 2003). We believe, however, that Critical Linguistics still merits inclusion as an independent model.

**9** Although this book includes a section explicitly devoted to multimodal discourse, we do not propose a separate 'multimodal approach'. Research in multimodality, including its applications in CDA, has been on the increase in the last two decades (e.g. Kress and Van Leeuwen, 1996; Van Leeuwen, 1999, 2000, 2005; Ventola et al., 2004; Norris, 2004; Richardson and Wodak, 2009; Stocchetti and Kukkonen, 2011). The results indicate that multimodality, in theoretical terms, is best described as a *perspective*, which involves an integrated account of the use – in various configurations and ratios – of language, image, sound and music. Such a perspective could be assumed within each of the schools/approaches listed. This is not to say, however, that a multimodal perspective would not require tailored additions to and/or realignments of analytical apparatuses within these frameworks designed specifically to account for the nature of multimodal data.

**10** We shall refrain here from providing a synopsis of each of the 26 chapters, although some of the chapters/authors have been (or will be) referred to in order to illustrate the most important of the book's programmatic points and structural features.

# References

Atkinson, J. and Heritage, J. (eds) (1984), *Structures of Social Action: Studies in Conversation Analysis*. Cambridge: Cambridge University Press.

Baker, P. (2006), *Using Corpora in Discourse Analysis*. London: Continuum.

Baker, P. and McEnery, A. (2005), 'A corpus-based approach to discourses of refugees and asylum seekers in UN and newspaper texts'. *Journal of Language and Politics*, 4(2), 197–226.

Baker, P., Gabrielatos, C., KhosraviNik, M., Krzyżanowski, M., McEnery, T. and Wodak, R. (2008), 'A useful methodological synergy? Combining critical discourse analysis and corpus linguistics to examine discourses of refugees and asylum seekers in the UK press'. *Discourse & Society*, 19, 273–306.

Benke, G. (2000), 'Diskursanalyse als sozialwissenschaftliche Untersuchungsmethode'. *SWS Rundschau*, 2, 140–62.

Bhatia, V. (2004), *Worlds of Written Discourse. A Genre-Based View*. London: Continuum.

Billig, M. (2008), 'The language of critical discourse analysis: the case of nominalization'. *Discourse & Society*, 19(6), 783–800.

Breeze, R. (2011), 'Critical discourse analysis and its critics'. *Pragmatics*, 21(4), 493–525.

Cap, P. (2006), *Legitimization in Political Discourse: A Cross-disciplinary Perspective on the Modern US War Rhetoric*. Newcastle: Cambridge Scholars Press.

—— (2008), 'Towards the proximization model of the analysis of legitimization in political discourse'. *Journal of Pragmatics*, 40(1), 17–41.

—— (2013), *Proximization: The Pragmatics of Symbolic Distance Crossing*. Amsterdam: John Benjamins.

Cap, P. and Okulska, U. (eds) (2013), *Analyzing Genres in Political Communication: Theory and Practice*. Amsterdam: John Benjamins.

Charteris-Black, J. (2004), *Corpus Approaches to Critical Metaphor Analysis*. Basingstoke: Palgrave.

Chilton, P. (2004), *Analysing Political Discourse: Theory and Practice*. London: Routledge.

—— (2005), 'Missing links in mainstream CDA: modules, blends and the critical instinct', in R. Wodak and P. Chilton (eds), *A New Agenda in (Critical) Discourse Analysis*. Amsterdam: John Benjamins, pp. 19–51.

—— (2011a), 'Still something missing in CDA'. *Discourse Studies*, 13, 769–81.

—— (2011b), 'Deictic Space Theory (DST): the fundamental theory and its applications'. *Paper at the 42nd Poznań Linguistic Meeting*, Poznań, 1–3 May 2011.

Chilton, P. and Schäffner, C. (2002), *Politics as Text and Talk: Analytic Approaches to Political Discourse*. Amsterdam: John Benjamins.

Chouliaraki, L. and Fairclough, N. (1999), *Discourse in Late Modernity. Rethinking Critical Discourse Analysis*. Edinburgh: Edinburgh University Press.

Drew, P. and Heritage, J. (eds) (1992), *Talk at Work: Interaction in Institutional Settings*. Cambridge: Cambridge University Press.

Dunmire, P. (2011). *Projecting the Future through Political Discourse: The Case of the Bush Doctrine*. Amsterdam: John Benjamins.

Fairclough, N. (1989), *Language and Power*. London: Longman.

—— (1995), *Critical Discourse Analysis*. London: Longman.

Fairclough, N. and Wodak, R. (1997), 'Critical discourse analysis', in T. van Dijk (ed.), *Discourse as Social Interaction*. London: Sage, pp. 258–84.

Fetzer, A. and Bull, P. (2013), 'Political interviews in context', in P. Cap and U. Okulska (eds), *Analyzing Genres in Political Communication: Theory and Practice*. Amsterdam: John Benjamins, pp. 73–100.

Fowler, R. (1991), *Language in the News*. London: Routledge.

Fowler, R., Kress, G. and Trew, T. (1979), *Language and Control*. London: Routledge.

Gabrielatos, C. and Baker, P. (2008), 'Fleeing, sneaking, flooding: a corpus analysis of discursive constructions of refugees and asylum seekers in the UK press 1996–2005'. *Journal of English Linguistics*, 36(1), 5–38.

Giltrow, J. and Stein, D. (eds) (2009), *Genres in the Internet*. Amsterdam: John Benjamins.

Goatly, A. (2007), *Washing the Brain: Metaphor and Hidden Ideology*. Amsterdam: John Benjamins.

Halliday, M. A. K. (1985), *An Introduction to Functional Grammar* (1st edition). London: Arnold.

Halliday, M. A. K. (1994), *Introduction to Functional Grammar*. London: Arnold.

Hart, C. (ed.) (2011a), *Critical Discourse Studies in Context and Cognition*. Amsterdam: John Benjamins.

Hart, C. (2011b), 'Moving beyond metaphor in the Cognitive Linguistic Approach to CDA: construal operations in immigration discourse', in C. Hart (ed.), *Critical Discourse Studies in Context and Cognition*. Amsterdam: John Benjamins, pp. 171–92.

—— (2011c), 'Force-interactive patterns in immigration discourse: a Cognitive Linguistic Approach to CDA'. *Discourse & Society*, 22(3), 269–86.

—— (2013a), 'Event-construal in press reports of violence in political protests: a Cognitive Linguistic Approach to CDA', *Journal of Language and Politics*, 12(3), 400–23.

—— (2013b), 'Constructing contexts through grammar: cognitive models and conceptualisation in British Newspaper reports of political protests', in J. Flowerdew (ed.), *Discourse in Context*. London: Continuum, pp. 159–184.

Hodge, R. and Kress, G. (1993), *Language as Ideology*. London: Routledge.

Koller, V. (2004), *Metaphor and Gender in Business Media Discourse: A Critical Cognitive Study*. Basingstoke: Palgrave.

Kopytowska, M. (2013), 'Blogging as the mediatization of politics and a new form of social interaction: a case study of "proximization dynamics" in Polish and British political blogs', in P. Cap and U. Okulska (eds), *Analyzing Genres in Political Communication: Theory and Practice*. Amsterdam: John Benjamins, pp. 379–422.

Kress, G. and Van Leeuwen, T. (1996), *Reading Images: The Grammar of Visual Design*. London: Routledge.

Lemke, J. (1995), *Textual Politics: Discourse and Social Dynamics*. London: Taylor & Francis.

Lewiński, M. and Oswald, S. (2013), 'When and how do we deal with straw men? A normative and cognitive pragmatic account'. *Journal of Pragmatics*, 59, 164–77.

Maillat, D. and Oswald, S. (2009), 'Defining manipulative discourse: the pragmatics of cognitive illusions'. *International Review of Pragmatics*, 1(2), 348–70.

—— (2011), 'Constraining context: a pragmatic account of cognitive manipulation', in C. Hart (ed.), *Critical Discourse Studies in Context and Cognition*. Amsterdam: John Benjamins, pp. 65–80.

Marín Arrese, J. (2011), 'Effective vs. epistemic stance and subjectivity in political discourse: legitimising strategies and mystification of responsibility', in C. Hart (ed.), *Critical Discourse Studies in Context and Cognition*. Amsterdam: John Benjamins, pp. 193–224.

Martin, J. and Rose, D. (2008), *Genre Relations: Mapping Culture*. London: Equinox.

Mautner, G. (2007), 'Mining large corpora for social information: the case of "elderly"'. *Language in Society*, 36(1), 51–72.

Musolff, A. (2004), *Metaphor and Political Discourse: Analogical Reasoning in Debates about Europe*. Basingstoke: Palgrave.

—— (2010), 'Political metaphor and *bodies politic*', in U. Okulska and P. Cap (eds), *Perspectives in Politics and Discourse*. Amsterdam: John Benjamins, pp. 23–42.

Norris, S. (2004), *Analyzing Multimodal Interaction – A Methodological Framework*. London: Routledge.

O'Halloran, K. (2003), *Critical Discourse Analysis and Language Cognition*. Edinburgh: Edinburgh University Press.

—— (2010), 'How to use corpus linguistics in the study of media discourse', in A. O'Keeffe and M. McCarthy (eds), *The Routledge Handbook of Corpus Linguistics*. Abingdon: Routledge, pp. 563–76.

Partington, A. (2006), 'Metaphors, motifs, and similes across discourse types: corpus assisted discourse studies (CADS) at work', in A. Stefanowitsch and S. Gries (eds), *Corpus-Based Approaches to Metaphor and Metonymy*. Berlin: Mouton de Gruyter, pp. 267–304.

Reisigl, M. and Wodak, R. (2001), *Discourse and Discrimination: Rhetorics of Racism and Anti-Semitism*. London: Routledge.

Richardson, J. and Wodak, R. (2009), 'The impact of visual racism: visual arguments in political leaflets of Austrian and British far-right parties'. *Controversia*, 6(2), 45–77.

Saussure, L. de and Schulz, P. (eds) (2005), *Manipulation and Ideologies in the Twentieth Century: Discourse, Language, Mind*. Amsterdam: John Benjamins.

Slembrouck, S. (2001), 'Explanation, interpretation and critique in the analysis of discourse'. *Critique of Anthropology*, 21(1), 33–57.

Sperber, D. (1995), 'How do we communicate?' in J. Brockman and K. Matson (eds), *How Things Are: A Science Toolkit for the Mind*. New York: Morrow, pp. 191–9.

Stocchetti, M. and Kukkonen, K. (eds) (2011), *Images in Use*. Amsterdam: John Benjamins.

Stubbs, M. (1997), 'Whorf's children: critical comments on critical discourse analysis', in A. Ryan and A. Wray (eds), *Evolving Models of Language*. Clevedon: Multilingual Matters, pp. 100–16.

—— (2002), 'Two quantitative methods of studying phraseology in English'. *International Journal of Corpus Linguistics*, 7(2), 215–44.

—— (2004), 'Language corpora', in A. Davies and C. Elder (eds), *Handbook of Applied Linguistics*. Oxford: Blackwell, pp. 106–32.

Ten Have, P. (2000), 'Computer-mediated chat: ways of finding chat partners'. *M/C*, 3(4), 1–18.

Titscher, S., Meyer, M., Wodak, R. and Vetter, E. (2000), *Methods of Text and Discourse Analysis*. London: Sage.

Van Dijk, T. (1999), 'Critical Discourse Analysis and Conversation Analysis'. *Discourse & Society*, 10(4), 459–70.

—— (2003), 'Critical discourse analysis?', in D. Schiffrin, D. Tannen and H. Hamilton (eds), *The Handbook of Discourse Analysis*. Oxford: Blackwell, pp. 352–71.

—— (2006), 'Discourse and manipulation'. *Discourse and Society*, 17(3), 359–83.

—— (2008), *Discourse and Context: A Socio-Cognitive Approach*. Cambridge: Cambridge University Press.

—— (2009), *Society and Discourse: How Social Contexts Influence Text and Talk*. Cambridge: Cambridge University Press.

Van Eemeren, F. and Grootendorst, R. (1992), *Argumentation, Communication, and Fallacies. A Pragma-Dialectical Perspective*. Hillsdale, NJ: Lawrence Erlbaum.

Van Leeuwen, T. (1996), 'The representation of social actors', in C.R. Caldas-Coulthard and M. Coulthard (eds), *Texts and Practices: Readings in Critical Discourse Analysis*. London: Routledge, pp. 32–70.

—— (1999), *Speech, Music, Sound*. London: Palgrave.

—— (2000), 'Visual racism', in M. Reisigl and R. Wodak (eds), *The Semiotics of Racism – Approaches in Critical Discourse Analysis*. Vienna: Passagen Verlag, pp. 35–56.

—— (2005), *Introducing Social Semiotics*. London: Routledge.

Ventola, E., Charles, C. and Kaltenbacher, M. (2004), *Perspectives on Multimodality*. Amsterdam: John Benjamins.

Weiss, G. and Wodak, R. (2003), *Critical Discourse Analysis: Theory and Interdisciplinarity*. Basingstoke: Palgrave.

Widdowson, H. (2004), *Text, Context, Pretext: Critical Issues in Discourse Analysis*. Oxford: Blackwell

Wodak, R. (2001), 'The discourse-historical approach', in R. Wodak and M. Meyer (eds), *Methods of Critical Discourse Analysis*. London: Sage, pp. 63–95.

—— (2011), 'Critical linguistics and critical discourse analysis', in J. Zienkowski, J.-O. Ostman and J. Verschueren (eds), *Discursive Pragmatics*. Amsterdam: John Benjamins, pp. 50–70.

Wodak, R. (ed.) (2012), *Critical Discourse Analysis* (4 volumes). London: Sage.

Wodak, R. and Chilton, P. (eds) (2005), *A New Agenda in (Critical) Discourse Analysis*. Amsterdam: John Benjamins.

Wodak, R. and Meyer, M. (eds) (2001), *Methods of Critical Discourse Analysis*. London: Sage.

—— (eds) (2009), *Methods of Critical Discourse Analysis* (2nd edn). London: Sage.

Yus, F. (2011), *Cyberpragmatics: Internet-Mediated Communication in Context*. Amsterdam: John Benjamins.

Žagar, I. (2010), '*Topoi* in critical discourse analysis'. *Lodz Papers in Pragmatics*, 6(1), 3–27.

Zinken, J. (2007), 'Discourse metaphors: the link between figurative language and habitual analogies'. *Cognitive Linguistics*, 18, 445–66.

# PART ONE

# Dimensions of Discourse

# HISTORY

# 1

# *Historia Magistra Vitae*

# The Topos of History as a Teacher in Public Struggles over *Self* and *Other* Representation[1]

*Bernhard Forchtner*
Humboldt University of Berlin

## 1 Introduction

In *De Oratore*, finished in 55BC, Cicero (1959: II, 9, 36) famously stated that history 'sheds light upon reality, gives life to recollection and guidance to human existence'. Indeed, it was long assumed that such 'guidance' could be provided by studying the past and following its example. However, from a perspective interested in discourses, representations and their consequences, the focus shifts to how this topos of *historia magistra vitae* (in the following 'history as a teacher') and subsequent claims to know 'the lessons' from the past, for having learnt, and for being able to offer guidance, give meaning to contemporary actors, events, objects and processes and demarcate *us* from *them*. Discourse analysis, in particular its critical branch, thus raises questions such as 'what pasts and presents does this topos of history as a teacher define?' and 'what conclusions does the use of this topos in public struggles over demarcating *us* from *them* facilitate?' The relevance of these questions can be easily illustrated by turning briefly to two quotes taken from a debate on the then looming attack on Iraq in the European Parliament on 29 January 2003.

Political torment plagued Europe in the last century. The ideologically 'legitimised' obsession with power on the part of dictators created millions of victims. They certainly did not spare their own citizens. Is the parallel with the loathsome regime of Saddam Hussein not obvious here? [. . .] Do the Member States of the European Union want to have this on their consciences, particularly given their own painful experiences during the last century? [. . .] Recent European history should show government leaders their responsibility in this regard.

America should listen to old Europe, this wise old lady, covered in blood and tears [. . .]. Let America listen to her! This old lady would say: choose security through international law, bow to the decisions of the UN, agree to another UN meeting, which we must demand, for another resolution.

These two examples illustrate not only conflicting uses of the topos of history as a teacher, but also difficulties in judging the appropriateness of the conclusions it facilitates. While the first quote by Bastiaan Belder, MEP from the *Europe of Freedom and Democracy* group, mobilizes the past in order to *support* the war in Iraq, the second speaker, Bernard Poignant, a MEP from the *Party of European Socialists*, draws on the very same past in order to justify his *opposition*. Of course, listeners and readers will have their preference; but it seems to be the case that both narrations of past and present cannot simply be discarded. In other words, it is indeed difficult to identify the past's 'true nature', history's lesson, and thus I argue (probably rather uncontroversially) that discourse analysts should focus on the construction of actors and their identities, of events and their significance, of objects and their mobilization, and of processes and their meaning, in and through uses of this topos.

Accordingly, this article asks how *historia magistra vitae* is used in discursive struggles over the 'right' lessons and the construction of *others* as misguided. I am thus interested in the persuasive character of language use and aim to make transparent 'the possible means of persuasion' (Aristotle, 1982: I, 2, 1) with regards to this topos. More specifically I will conceptualize four possible uses of this topos based on different premises and facilitating different conclusions. In short, I am interested in how narratives of the past serve as backgrounds for arguing for particular lessons in the present. However, instead of including references to lessons from, e.g., memories of national glory and heroism, these conceptualizations will be limited to lessons from past wrongdoings such as the Holocaust as the paradigmatic crime against humanity. That is, I will conceptualize and exemplify what I call *rhetorics of judging, rhetorics of failing, rhetorics of penitence* and *rhetorics of judge-penitence*.[2]

Firstly, rhetorics of judging facilitate a mode of assimilating collective memories into collective identity by pointing to past wrongdoing not committed by the in-group while nevertheless claiming to have learnt present-day 'lessons' from this wrongdoing, and subsequently to reject out-group actors and actions as not being 'in the know'.

Appeasement arguments are probably the most significant example and have featured prominently in public struggles over, e.g., the Cold War and the Iraq war in 2003. These arguments identify a past wrongdoing ('naïve pacifists appeased Hitler'), formulate lessons ('stop dictators sooner rather than later') and direct them against an external *other* ('today, the left is appeasing again'). Secondly, rhetorics of failing too, emphasize past wrongdoing, which is not committed by the respective in-group. However, the claim to know the lesson is now directed against the present-day in-group as being in need to self-critically examine itself in the light of this past. References to past events now widely accepted as 'being wrong', e.g. the Holocaust and the Vietnam War, are likely to feature prominently in this type of rhetoric. Thirdly, rhetorics of penitence frame *our* past as wrong and, more or less explicitly, emphasize the on-going necessity to demarcate the contemporary in-group from its past wrongdoing. The current wave of public apologies by states and non-governmental organizations, e.g. the speech by the French president François Hollande (2012) discussed below, to commemorate the detention and deportation of French Jews in 1942, applies such rhetoric. And although these speech acts are often problematic, they are not per se a fad but potentially enable a more inclusive and open reconstruction of communal identities. Rhetorics of judging, failing and penitence are familiar structures in discourses on the past. In contrast, I fourthly draw on Albert Camus' last published novel, *The Fall* (2006), to offer an original conceptualization of rhetorics of judge-penitence. Here, claims for having learnt the lessons are based on in-group admissions of past wrongdoings in order to ultimately present *us* as morally superior vis-à-vis an external *other*.

A focus on uses of the topos of history as a teacher is timely, given that past decades saw memories of the past – in particular past wrongdoings – as 'replacing progress and revolution as the master metaphors of history' (Giesen, 2004: 10). In the course of this development, memory turned 'into a new secular religion' (Müller, 2002: 19). It is thus the specific context of our time, 'the age of apology' (Gibney et al., 2008), which renders possible a variety of uses of *historia magistra vitae*. Furthermore, the discursive construction of communal identities, in particular national identities, in relation to the past has been one of the central areas in critical discourse studies (cf. among many Heer et al., 2008; Wodak et al., 1990, 1994, 1998, 2009; Wodak and De Cillia, 2007; Reisigl, 2007). In these studies, the focus rests primarily on traditional, heroic and self-complacent constructions of past events and subsequent anti-Semitism and chauvinism. However, also in these constructions, we find uses of *historia magistra vitae* which serve to construct particular identities and legitimize these positions.

The benefits of my conceptualization are twofold: first, by providing an abstract reconstruction of uses of *historia magistra vitae*, I offer a comprehensive taxonomy. Of course, empirical examples will never resemble pure types; yet, their reconstruction will illuminate their workings and functions. Second, and I will only indicate this in passing, these types might be useful in strengthening CDA's critical agenda by serving as a social mechanism for un/blocking collective learning processes, that is enabling more open/closed symbolic boundaries of the respective community.

Section 2 clarifies the notions of discourse, (mnemo)history, and 'narrativization' (White, 1980) in relation to each other and to critical discourse studies (CDS), in particular the discourse historical approach (DHA). This is followed by a discussion of the concept of *topos* in general as well as the topos of history as a teacher in particular. By drawing, among other things, on Stephen E. Toulmin's model of argumentation, Section 4 conceptualizes and exemplifies this topos by introducing rhetorics of judging, rhetorics of failing, rhetorics of penitence and rhetorics of judge-penitence. I close by summarizing my findings, the possibility to evaluate these four types and making some final remarks on the problem of demarcating these rhetorics.

## 2 From discourse, (mnemo)history and narrativity to . . .

In the following, I draw primarily on the DHA in CDS although the main points articulated in this article are not restricted to the former's framework. This concerns in particular the concepts of discourse and context, to which I turn first before addressing further theoretical concepts.

Following Martin Reisigl and Ruth Wodak (2009: 89), I view discourse as a cluster of context-dependent semiotic practices related to a macro-topic, as being 'socially constituted and socially constitutive' and 'linked to the argumentation about validity claims [. . .] involving several actors who have different points of view'. Discourses are thus not viewed as 'mono-perspective', as in other approaches in CDS (Reisigl, 2013: 79), but defined by their topic-relatedness, e.g. discourses *on* the war in Iraq. The benefit of such an empirically-orientated notion is of course that it points to opposing positions within discourses, such as conflicting claims over 'the lessons' from the past. These claims establish diverse intertextual and interdiscursive links to other texts and discourses (Reisigl and Wodak, 2009: 90–93), which implies that semiosis is heavily context-dependent. The DHA's notion of context has four dimensions, ranging from the co-text, to intertextual and interdiscursive relationships, the specific 'context of situation', and the wider socio-political and historical context (2009: 93). Consequently, familiarity with the historical context is paramount for discourse historical analysis in order to understand (and possibly criticize) meaning and its (re-) production.

This emphasis on the historical context is critical. However, given that discourse analysis is not primarily interested in the past per se but rather its uses, the DHA should be (and indeed largely is) less interested in a positivist notion of history and historical truth but in what Jan Assmann (1997: 8f) summarized as 'mnemohistory': '[u]nlike history proper, mnemohistory is concerned not with the past as such, but only with the past as it is remembered'. In order to understand public struggles for legitimacy and related discursive processes of demarcating *us* from *them*, it is thus necessary to understand collective memories (for a seminal overview, cf. Olick et al., 2011). These memories are not about the aggregation of individual memories, in whatever kind of collective subject, but the social frame in and through which individuals recollect past events. To paraphrase Karl Marx, individuals have their own memories, but they do not have them just as they please. In line with this, Maurice Halbwachs (1985: 31) famously described 'each individual memory as a "viewpoint" on the collective memory' and emphasized their selective constructedness and primary function of guaranteeing a sense of communal continuity.

As such, collective memories must be understood as stories which circulate in specific networks and thereby demarcate groups (Tilly, 2002). I would thus argue for a more explicit incorporation of narrative analysis, in particular the structural analysis of narratives, into CDS (cf. Barthes, 1977; Greimas, 1983 and 1987; I am not able to discuss relevant concepts here but cf. Viehöver, 2011). Such an incorporation of narratology is not only meaningful in empirical terms but also concerns the issue of (mnemo)history in discourse analysis. Arguably, it is in and through narratives that arguments are proposed. That is, while narratives employ arguments they also serve as arguments for particular kinds of actions. Furthermore, narrative is a key ontological category. It was particularly Paul Ricoeur (1988: 241) who made the point that 'temporality cannot be spoken of in the direct discourse of phenomenology, but rather requires the mediation of the indirect discourse of narration'. Notwithstanding Ricoeur's understanding of discourse, narrative here becomes the organizational principle of social life (cf. also Barthes, 1977; White, 1980). As such, every reference to the past is mediated through narrative form, what Hayden White referred to as the 'narrativization' of the past. Such narrativizations are about the choice of events, an event being defined as an action causing a change of state, and the choice to arrange them according to the fundamental schema of beginning (prior state)–middle (event)– ending (new state). The force of narrative derives exactly from this practice of arranging (selected) events in a unified plotline, including the closure of this sequence. In other words: a 'good story' is one which has 'a "point"' (Van Dijk, 1980: 14). Similarly, White (1980: 24) speaks of the 'moral meaning' every narrative conveys due to the very fact that the act of narrativization – and not the past itself – selects and arranges historical events in a particular way. In a similar vein, Ricoeur (1988: 249) states that no narrative can be ethically neutral. This does not imply that historical events themselves cannot be shown to be factually true or not; why should we be unable to say what happened on 9 November 1989 (the fall of the Berlin wall)? Rather, it concerns the fact that events that occurred in the past do not determine their representation in the present, a process which depends on its necessarily selective storying in this very present. This feeds back into the understanding of *historia magistra vitae*, as well as into the function of reconstructing the historical context of a particular discourse. Not only should analysis be aware of the inherent and irreducible perspectivity of historical reconstruction but, and this is the reason for talking here about a moral point every narrative conveys, this does away with ideas of 'objective lessons'. Instead, attention is necessarily directed towards the agenda of these narratives and how they are linguistically realized.

# 3 . . . the topos of history as a teacher

From a historical perspective, the study of memories, i.e. the substance of narrative boundaries, and rhetoric is interwoven. While the art of memory was arguably perfected in the Middle Ages, Cicero (1959: II, 84, 352) stated that 'the science of mnemonics' goes back to the Greek lyrical poet Simonides of Ceos (556–468BC). Simonides allegedly identified members of a banquet, which he had just left before they were crushed by a collapsing roof, through the orderly arrangement of his memories. That is, he 'inferred that persons desiring to train this faculty [memory] must select *localities* and form mental images of the facts they wish to remember and store those images in the *localities*' (1959: 354; italics added). Memorizing a speech thus meant to pass through a series of 'places' or *topoi* (Cicero used the Latin term *loci*).

In Aristotle's work, these topoi are part of both dialectic as well as rhetorical argumentation and, in the full Aristotelian scheme of rhetoric, belong to the stage of finding arguments (*heúresis* or *invention*, cf. Kienpointer, 1995: 454). For Aristotle (1982: I, 2, 8), a topos in a 'rhetorical syllogism' denotes a salient, yet usually implicit, premise on which persuasive performances rely (1982: I, 2, 21–2). While Aristotle saw topoi mostly as abstract or general elements (e.g. the *topos of more or less* which might be realized as 'if not even the gods know everything, hardly can men'; 1982: I, 23, 4), Cicero, in contrast, provided the concept of *locus communis*. Such loci are material, 'ready-made arguments' (Rubinelli, 2009: 106), which can be used only in comparable cases or contexts.

Similarly, Stephen E. Toulmin introduced the concept of *warrant* in terms of established ways of linking *data* (the ground on which the claim or conclusion is based) and *conclusion* (the point of arrival) within specific fields. Warrants are 'statements indicating the *general ways of arguing* being applied in each particular case and *implicitly relied on* as ones whose *trustworthiness* is well established' (Toulmin et al., 1979: 43). Martin Wengeler (2003: 67) views topoi as content-related 'figures of thought in approaching a political issue'. Following this line of argument but being more open concerning whether or not topoi are formal or material, Reisigl and Wodak (2001: 74f; cf. also Kienpointer, 1995: 454) view topoi as rules that connect data with conclusions. They are:

> [. . .] highly conventionalised parts of argumentation which belong to the obligatory elements of argumentation and take the form either of explicit or inferable premises. They are more or less formal (for example *locus a minore*) or content-related (*topos*

*of external constraints*) warrants or 'conclusion rules' which connect an argument or arguments with a conclusion, a claim. As such, they justify the transition from an argument or arguments to the conclusion.

(Wodak et al., 1999: 34)

In sum, while there are differences concerning their formal (paradigmatically represented by Aristotle) or material (paradigmatically represented by Cicero) character, topoi are always seen as building blocks on which actors must draw in order to persuade (or convince) the listener, i.e. in order to tailor their performances successfully to knowledge shared by their audience.

Moving to the topos of history as a teacher, we turn again to Cicero's *De Oratore* (1959: II, 9, 36) and the statement that history 'sheds light upon reality, gives life to recollection and guidance to human existence'. The conceptual historian Reinhart Koselleck (2004: 36) argued that, concerning historiography, this topos had long presented certain memories of the past as guides for present-day action and self-understanding, but vanished in the course of the Enlightenment's 'discovery of the uniqueness of historical processes and the possibility of progress'. According to Koselleck, the rise of modernity ended previously held certainties rooted in a Christian space of experience and horizon of expectation – thus making the topos outdated. However, this does not imply that its rhetorical use in political dramas has not prevailed. Yet, to my knowledge, there is no study which has recently focused primarily on the public use of this topos. Interestingly though Walther Kindt (1992: 202) briefly refers to *historia magistra vitae* in his analysis of German texts on the 1991/2 Iraq war, noting that this topos might facilitate the negative representation of *the other* as obstinate and ignorant. Even more relevant is Wodak et al.'s (1998: 205; 2009: 86; cf. also Reisigl Reisigl 1998: 240) analysis of Austrian national identity which identifies the topos as, e.g., 'playing down and trivializing the past' because it serves as a 'collective cognitive-emotional buffer zone', via which the in-group ultimately loses sight of the victims. As such, these authors (as well as others) have analysed particular uses of this topos but have not offered a more abstract typology. What Reisigl and Wodak (2001: 89), however, provide is a neat definition of the topos of history (they view the topos of history as a teacher as a subtype of the topos of history). In the following, I will simply draw on their definition of the topos of history when talking about the topos of history as a teacher which is defined as: 'because history teaches that specific actions have specific consequences, one should perform or omit a specific action in a specific situation (allegedly) comparable with the historical example referred to' (2001: 80). Transferring Reisigl and Wodak's definition into a simplified Toulmin scheme, the following reconstruction emerges (Figure 1.1). By narrativizing a particular past ($A_1$, the data), the warrant (or topos) of history as a teacher justifies the conclusion, i.e. to act in a certain way ($A_2$) towards a certain result ($X_2$). This argumentation scheme might apply to micro-arguments as well as to larger units, even entire narratives.

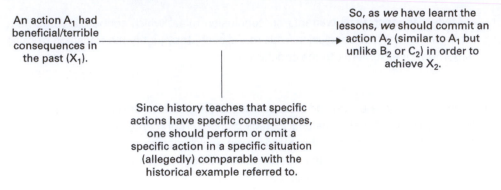

**FIGURE 1.1** *Reconstruction of the topos of history as a teacher.*

# 4 The past in the present: Conceptualizing four uses of the topos of history as a teacher

Having discussed this topos, I finally turn to its uses. By drawing on the Toulmin scheme discussed above, I will conceptualize and discuss four extracts in order to exemplify the empirical realization of rhetorics of judging, rhetorics of failing, rhetorics of penitence and rhetorics of judge-penitence. These examples serve only illustrative purposes and are taken from different contexts – Denmark in 2003, the United Kingdom in 2009, France in 2012 and, finally, Europe more generally; yet, in all cases, past wrongdoing facilitates 'the point' made by these interventions. In doing so, I draw on the DHA's notion of discursive strategy (Reisigl and Wodak, 2009: 94) as more or less conscious or automated acts and point to their linguistic realizations which enable particular *self* and *other* representations. Thus, I examine the ways in which nominations and predications (as well as mitigations/intensification and perspectivization) of actors, events, objects and processes are linked to and form the basis of arguments.

## 4.1 *Rhetorics of judging*

Probably the most prevailing use of the topos of history as a teacher occurs in what I call rhetorics of judging. As mentioned above, the topos links the data (a past wrongdoing committed by an out-group) and the conclusion (that similar actions proposed today by *others* should be avoided). That is, although rhetorics of judging do not deny a past wrong, this does not include a critical stance towards this past as *our* past or as being relevant for *our* present. Thus, rhetorics of judging rest on a double exclusion of both *our* wrong past (or at least its backgrounding/silencing) as well as *the other* as not knowing the lessons from the past (Figure 1.2). While *our* past is not problematized, learning from *the* past is nevertheless claimed so that an external *other* and her/his actions can be delegitimized.

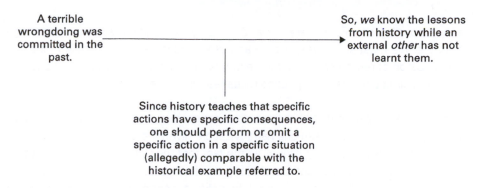

FIGURE 1.2 *A reconstruction of rhetorics of judging by others.*

In order to exemplify this, I turn to Denmark during the debate over the Iraq war in 2003 (for more details, cf. Kirchhoff, 2004; Kaae and Nissen, 2008; Farbøl, 2011). As in other (non-)European countries, the war was heatedly debated whereby a centre-right government, headed by Prime Minister Anders Fogh Rasmussen (*Venstre*, the Liberal Party), decided to join the *Coalition of the Willing*. This stance was initially justified via the apparent danger from Iraqi weapons of mass destruction (WMDs). Given the collapse of this argument in mid-2003, Rasmussen increasingly legitimized Danish participation in the Iraq war through linking the war against Iraq with criticism of the country's policy of cooperation with Nazi Germany between 1940 and 1943. He thereby contradicted the basic Danish post-war narrative according to which the national subjects had heroically resisted the German occupiers. In fact, the Danish political and economic elite (as well as broad sections of the general population) had cooperated with Germany, which only stopped in 1943 due to a popular uprising.

Elsewhere, I (Forchtner, 2013) discuss the subtleties of Rasmussen's main speech delivered in August 2003. Here, however, I want to point to the main, although less sophisticated, rhetorics applied by his supporters. The following extract is taken from a newspaper article by the then Conservative (*Det Konservative Folkeparti*) Minister for Culture, Brian Mikkelsen (2003), entitled 'We should never again fall into the trap of neutrality'.

[. . .] we have suffered a veritable plague of social-democratic-liberal neutrality and a kind of universal head-in-the-sand politics in which the peace movement has successfully blindfolded a good many young people.

Now, in particular, as we look back to August 1943 with respect, we must remind each other that the very things we should avoid are the pitfall of neutrality and the action of sidestepping dictators and despots as rotten eggs on whom we turn our backs. Instead, we should stand up against them, and stand up against them again. It is the spirit of 1943 that should light our way, not that of 1940 or 1968.

The past, just as the present, will continue to play one trick after another on us. This is why it is important that we keep remembering and recalling as best and as precisely as we possibly can. For we are not at the mercy of history. History is not stronger than we. We must simply respect it – and use it. Each generation should thus pass on the baton of remembrance to the next. It is the only way to combat forgetfulness and to minimise the risk of repeating mistakes which we could have avoided.

It is immediately apparent that Mikkelsen does not perform a self-critical narrative of *our* past failing. This could have been one narrativization, given the cooperation between the Danish state and Nazi Germany, as well as the fact that the Conservative Party was part of the national unity government too (Among the four parties which formed the unity government and were thus responsible for the policy of cooperation – the conservatives, the liberals, the social-liberals and the social democrats – Mikkelsen's party was, however, most critical of cooperation. Cf. Birkelund, 2003: 119). Instead, Mikkelsen, in this final part of his essay, assigns the role of the villain most explicitly to the wider left, aligning them with past mistakes, while claiming that present-day heroes are characterized by combatting 'forgetfulness' and, consequently, Saddam Hussein's dictatorship.

If this is the basic story told in this article, it becomes compelling due to the linguistic means utilized. Focusing on linguistic nomination and predication, there is a gulf created between an unspecified but homogeneous in-group and a negative, more specifically nominated, out-group. The former is realized through the repeated use of deictic expressions such as 'we' and 'us' which denote the 'good' part of the Danish people as the piece was published in a national newspaper (with a primarily bourgeois readership). The gulf is further emphasized by representing this social actor as either the passive victim of *the other* ['we have suffered'] or deontically activated through 'must'/'should'. Similarly, and with regard to how this in-group is linked to events and processes, the consequences of war such as violence and (civilian) suffering are hardly elaborated in the text (besides a reference to 'tragic deaths and terrorists', 'fanaticism and blood frenzy'). Instead, what should be done is described via uncontroversial lexis and playful metaphors, such as sidestepping rotten eggs and lightening our way. The latter does not only background the questioning of what policies the 'spirit of 1943' might exactly suggest in concrete circumstances, but also implies a breaking free from and leaving behind a dark past – one that, however, 'we' (the affirmed in-group of 'good Danes') are not responsible for.

In contrast, *the other* and related events and processes are described much more specifically. First, these actors are identified via ideological anthroponyms (at least, these terms are likely to be negatively connoted by readers of this newspaper and the government's clientele): 'the left', 'liberals' and 'the peace movement'. The latter is especially interesting as the author proposes an argument in order to justify its inclusion in the category of villains. Mikkelsen does this through use of the topos (or fallacy) of innocent and naïve youth, explaining the rejection of the war by many young people by the ruthless seductive ability of the peace movement (the fact that anti-war arguments often referred to mass demonstrations and popular opinion might have caused this move by Mikkelsen). By mentioning 1968 (another 'ideological' nomination), interdiscursive reference is furthermore made to the left and liberals. After all, Denmark too experienced a series of debates in the 1960s due to, e.g., the emergence of the New Left (but also various liberal groups). This included anti-nuclear weapon initiatives and criticism of NATO membership, as well as the USA's Vietnam War – which all led to conflicts with the Conservative Party (DIIS, 2005). Second, the reader learns of events and processes in terms of, e.g., 'plague', 'the pitfall of neutrality', 'head-in-the-sand politics' and 'sidestepping dictators', which are all connoted negatively. This interpretation is argumentatively transformed into authoritative, 'true' historical knowledge through the call for 'remembering and recalling as best and as precisely as we possibly can', thereby making rejection of the data an immoral and irrational act.

Against this background, the topos of history as a teacher connects the data that past mistakes were (and are still) made by the left and liberals with the conclusion that, only implicitly voiced in this extract but made explicit in previous sections of the article, avoiding these mistakes demands action against Saddam Hussein (Figure 1.3). In line with Kindt, this kind of intervention into public struggles simply claims that *we* know the true lessons, thereby attempting to delegitimize *the other* and her/his actions as being obstinate and morally inferior.

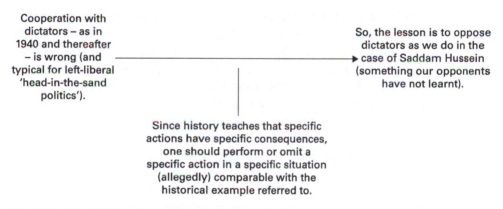

**FIGURE 1.3** *Mikkelsen's rhetoric of judging.*

## 4.2 Rhetorics of failing

In contrast to the traditional way of linking past and present wrongdoing, and the double externalization via which this takes place in rhetorics of judging, I now move to a more self-critical form of utilizing the past. In rhetorics of failing, the past wrongdoing (data) remains that of an out-group; yet, the lesson which is supposedly drawn, the conclusion, is not any longer directed against *others* but serves as a warning to the in-group not to repeat these wrongdoings. To know the lessons and to learn from the past thus demands criticism of *our* present-day (or potential) wrongdoing, i.e.: the in-group's constant alertness (Figure 1.4).

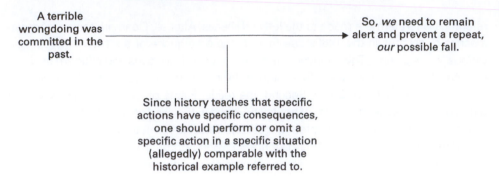

**FIGURE 1.4** *A reconstruction of rhetorics of failing by others.*

The following extract is taken from an article by the British journalist Robert Fisk (2009) in the United Kingdom newspaper *The Independent*. The piece deals with the post-9/11 military intervention in Afghanistan, was entitled *America is performing its familiar role of propping up a dictator* and was published on 4 November 2009.

Could there be a more accurate description of the Obama-Brown message of congratulations to the fraudulently elected Hamid Karzai of Afghanistan? First the Palestinians held fair elections in 2006, voted for Hamas and were brutally punished for it – they still are – and then the Iranians held fraudulent elections in June which put back the weird Mahmoud Ahmadinejad whom everyone outside Iran (and a lot inside) regard as a dictator. But now we have the venal, corrupt, sectarian Karzai in power after a poll far more ambitiously rigged than the Iranian version, and – yup, we love him dearly and accept his totally fraudulent election. [. . .]

*The March of Folly* was Barbara Tuchman's title for her book on governments – from Troy to Vietnam-era America – that followed policies contrary to their own interests. And well may we remember the Vietnam bit. As Patrick Bury, a veteran British soldier of our current Afghan adventure, pointed out yesterday, Vietnam is all too relevant.

Back in 1967, the Americans oversaw a "democratic" election in Vietnam which gave the presidency to the corrupt ex-General Nguyen Van Thieuman [sic!]. In a fraudulent election which the Americans declared to be "generally fair" – he got 38 per cent of the vote – Thieu's opponents wouldn't run against him because the election was a farce. [. . .]

But it's part of a dreary pattern. US forces were participating in a civil war in Vietnam while claiming they were supporting democracy and the sovereignty of the country. In Lebanon in 1982, they claimed to be supporting the "democratically" elected President Amin Gemayel and took the Christian Maronite side in the civil war. And now, after Disneyworld elections, they are on the Karzai-government side against the Pashtun villagers of southern Afghanistan among whom the Taliban live.

Where is the next My Lai? Journalists should avoid predictions. In this case I will not. Our Western mission in Afghanistan is going to end in utter disaster.

Let me first address the data of rhetorics of failing, i.e. past wrongdoing committed by *others*. Actions linked to 'Vietnam-era America' are continuously identified as the event from which actors should have learnt. The fact that American actions committed during this event are narrated as being wrong, is all too clear as the war is linked to, among others, '*The March of Folly*', 'the Americans' support for a 'corrupt ex-General' in 1967, a 'fraudulent election' which 'the Americans' approved, a 'dreary pattern' of 'US forces' being involved in civil wars as well as a reference to the My Lai massacre. The second paragraph establishes the Vietnam War's significance explicitly ('And well may we remember the Vietnam bit'). This is strengthened by basing it on a 'veteran British soldier['s]' account (*argumentum ad verecundium*) who 'pointed out' Vietnam's relevance. Importantly, and I will return to this later, this 'British' authority characterizes the current wrong, the war in Afghanistan, as 'our (. . .) adventure'.[3]

Moving to present-day wrongdoing, the reference to 'Obama-Brown' (the then President of the United States Barack Obama and the then Prime Minister of the United Kingdom Gordon Brown) and 'governments', which are criticized for being hypocritical in their support of Hamid Karzai and not following their interests respectively, might suggest a split between an in-group ('the innocent people') and a 'morally corrupt' political elite solely responsible for repeating past mistakes. Furthermore, the USA is attributed a 'familiar role of propping up a dictator' and, in the final paragraph, Fisk states that 'they are on the Karzai-government side'. However, while rhetorics of judging are thus activated in this article as the United States too is represented as today's *other*, a persistent wrongdoer, there is more to it because the lessons are also made relevant to the present-day British in-group.

This is visible right at the beginning where it is not simply 'Obama-Brown' who are criticized but the in-group ('we') is also spoken of as 'loving him [Karzai] dearly and accept[ing] his totally fraudulent election'. Even if this personal pronoun is not understood as standing for the wider population's complacency with regards to its government's stance, latter uses of, e.g., 'our' ('our current Afghan adventure') open up the potential for perceiving the in-group as co-responsible. That is, by narrating the 'adventure' as *ours* – irrespective of whether or not this was intended by the author – the text at least allows for the possibility of relating the lessons from past wrongdoing to *us* because *we* currently take part in wrongdoings. Most clearly, this is visible in the article's dramatic climax, Fisk's prophecy, in the final sentence: '[o]ur Western mission in Afghanistan is going to end in utter disaster'. As such, 'we' (the British and the wider West 'we' are part of), and not only *others* as in rhetorics of judging, are narrated as co-responsible for present-day wrongs and are the addressees of the identified lesson.

As such, the example illustrates how the topos of history as a teacher links a representation of *their* past wrongdoing to the conclusion that *we* are currently failing too; or – to be more precise – 'utter disaster' is looming if *we* do not learn (Figure 1.5).

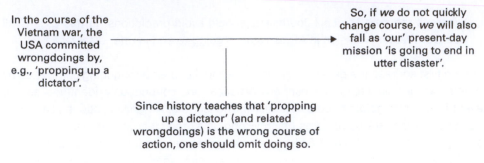

**FIGURE 1.5** *Fisk's rhetoric of failing.*

## *4.3 Rhetorics of penitence*

I now move to what I conceptualize as rhetorics of penitence. Here, I draw especially on findings in the interdisciplinary field of memory studies, which has prospered partly due to an increase in self-critical 'public rituals of confessions of guilt' over recent decades (Giesen, 2004: 130; for collections of cases, cf. Cunningham, 1999; Barkan and Karn, 2006; Gibney et al., 2008).

In rhetorics of penitence, such admissions (data) justify claims to know the lessons, which are coupled with calls for the continuous facing up to *our* past wrongdoing (conclusion). The contemporary self is thus imagined by demarcating itself from its own past wrongdoing (and attempts to silence this wrongdoing) while at the same time remaining part of what *we* are (Figure 1.6). That is, an internalized past is rejected in order to construct an internal *other*; subsequently, no once-and-for-all redemption is possible. As long as knowing 'the lesson' and learning from the past is represented as an on-going process in and through which *we* define what *we* do not want to be vis-à-vis *our* past, this is not even necessarily contradicting a cautiously positive self-image as being the process of becoming a reformed subject (indeed, it seems impossible to imagine an actor whose self-image is entirely negative).

Turning to a recent admission of past wrongdoing, it is widely accepted that, as in Denmark and most other European countries, post-war France experienced a 'decades long difficulty of acknowledging what had really happened during the war and the overwhelming desire to block the memory or else recast it in a usable way' (Judt, 2007: 808). In France, this concerned the so-called Vichy Syndrome (Rousso, 1984), i.e. the silencing of collaboration between the Vichy regime and the German occupiers, including the former's anti-Semitic policies. This 'syndrome' developed from the Gaullist myth of an almost universal resistance, to silence during the presidencies of Georges Pompidou and Giscard d'Estaing, and the refusal to apologize by François

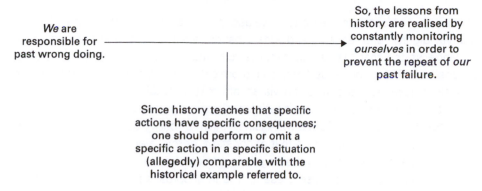

*We* are responsible for past wrong doing.

So, the lessons from history are realised by constantly monitoring *ourselves* in order to prevent the repeat of *our* past failure.

Since history teaches that specific actions have specific consequences; one should perform or omit a specific action in a specific situation (allegedly) comparable with the historical example referred to.

**FIGURE 1.6** *A reconstruction of rhetorics of penitence.*

Mitterrand (Golsan, 2006: 78–84). It was only under the presidency of Jacques Chirac that France officially apologized, on the 53rd anniversary of the rounding up of 13,152 Jews at the Vélodrome d'Hiver, in 1995. Yet, although a breakthrough, it has been suggested that even Chirac's speech enabled an affirmation of France (cf. the intriguing analysis by Carrier, 2005: 74–80).

In 2012, on the 70th anniversary of the rounding up, the then French President, François Hollande, gave a speech at the site of the demolished velodrome which illustrates the working of rhetorics of penitence (the first paragraph is from the beginning, the second from the middle and the third from the final section of the speech).

> We've gathered this morning to remember the horror of a crime, express the sorrow of those who experienced the tragedy, and speak of the dark hours of collaboration, our history, and therefore France's responsibility. [. . .]
>
> The truth is that French police – on the basis of the lists they had themselves drawn up – undertook to arrest the thousands of innocent people trapped on July 16, 1942. And that the French gendarmerie escorted them to the internment camps. The truth is that no German soldiers – not a single one – were mobilized at any stage of the operation. The truth is that this crime was committed in France, by France. [. . .]
>
> We must never let our guard down. No nation, no society, nobody is immune from evil. Let us not forget this verdict by Primo Levi on his persecutors. 'Save the exceptions, they were not monsters, they had our faces.' Let us remain alert, so that we may detect the return of monstrosity under its most harmless guises.

Hollande's construction of France's past, present and future revolves around the nation's tragic failure (despite of the acts of 'the Righteous', 'General de Gaulle', 'the Resistance', 'the Free French Forces' and 'Jewish institutions, like the Oeuvre de secours aux enfants') to live up to its values, principles and ideals ('laïcité', 'freedom', 'human dignity' and 'equality and emancipation' are mentioned in the text; indeed, Hollande states that 'Jews had become fully fledged citizens for the first time in Europe' in 1791 – he adds that 'this promise' was 'trampled underfoot'). While Mikkelsen justified his conclusion via an affirmative reading of *us* and *our* heroes, Hollande avoids separating a heroic resistance from, e.g., a small group of civil servants who collaborated with Germany. Against such a background, the only position contemporary France can take is that of constant 'heroic' alertness.

This is clearly reflected in the linguistic choices made. Although the beginning of the speech addresses those present, it is in accordance with the genre that the nomination of the actor as 'we', 'our' and 'us' is not limited to those in attendance but includes the entire nation. This actor is asked to do a variety of things, such as to 'remember', 'express the sorrow' and 'remain alert' – all indicating the significance of the past as a wrong. The event too is nominated without any hedging: 'the horror of the crime', 'the tragedy', 'dark hours of collaboration, our history' – which is linked to 'France' itself and explicitly marked as *our* responsibility. This conclusion, based on what we might call the *topos of responsibility* (if someone does something, s/he is responsible for its consequences), is based on a number of explicitly stated reasons. Thus, already at the very beginning of the speech, we find an acknowledgement of responsibility. As mentioned above, the in-group takes the position of the villain. And like the event, their role is not relativized. This is most evident in the predication of both the police and the gendarmerie as 'French', as well as in the intensification of their agency via 'not a single one [German needed to be mobilized]'. This second paragraph is perhaps the most explicit passage of the entire speech, and by employing anaphora (the repeated use of '[t]he truth is') forcefully foregrounds the wrong. Similarly, the reference to Primo Levi constitutes an *argument from authority* which, I argue, does not commit a fallacious appeal to authority (for arguments from an expert opinion, cf. Walton et al., 2008: 15). After all, it is neither the only support for Hollande's wider argument nor does it suggest a clear-cut processing of information by offering a straightforward solution (as if the villains were monsters and thus ontologically different from *us*). Instead, it raises difficult questions for the contemporary in-group.

In line with this, the text does not point to an external but an internal *other* and consequently, Hollande calls for commemorations, Holocaust education and a fight against anti-Semitism in France. Although his speech does not include an offer to make amends, it exemplifies rhetorics of penitence by admitting full responsibility, a renunciation of the act, and a call to refrain. In short, and as Figure 1.7 illustrates, *historia magistra vitae* facilitates a very different conclusion than in the case of Mikkelsen. Here, the data are about the unambiguous representation – not its silencing – of the in-group's wrong past which justifies the conclusion that *we* must never let *our* guard down.

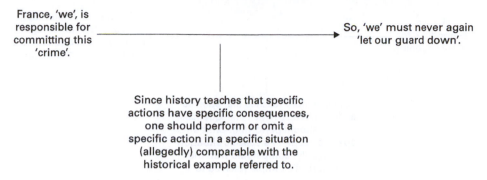

France, 'we', is responsible for committing this 'crime'.

So, 'we' must never again 'let our guard down'.

Since history teaches that specific actions have specific consequences, one should perform or omit a specific action in a specific situation (allegedly) comparable with the historical example referred to.

**FIGURE 1.7** *Hollande's rhetoric of penitence.*

## 4.4 Rhetorics of judge-penitence

Transcending these three modes and the widespread perception of 'bad silence' versus 'good admissions of wrongdoing', I finally turn to a counter-intuitive way of utilizing claims for having learnt the lesson. That is, *we* admit *our* past wrongdoing (data) in order to present *us* as morally superior vis-à-vis an external *other* (conclusion). Here, I draw on a figure in Camus' last published novel, *The Fall* (2006; cf. also Finkielkraut, 2004: 123). The latter's motto – '[t]he more I accuse myself, the more I have a right to judge you' – indicates how the increasing legitimacy of admissions of wrongdoing renders possible projecting the in-group as a penitent sinner who can, implicitly or explicitly, claim to know the lessons, and thus to be morally superior. In consequence, *others* can be depicted as morally inferior exactly because a self-humbling stance towards *our* painful past elevates *us* above *them* (for more details on judge-penitence, cf. Forchtner, 2014).

Kindt as well as Reisigl and Wodak have pointed to self-legitimizing aspects of *historia magistra vitae*. This observation seems especially relevant concerning rhetorics of judging but I argue that there is more to rhetorics of judge-penitence which, strictly speaking, mobilize two warrants. Besides the topos of history as a teacher, its force rests on a by now secularized but initially Judeo-Christian cultural structure best summarized by one of Jesus' parables aimed at those who are sure of their own goodness: 'everyone who exalts himself will be humbled, and whoever humbles himself will be exalted' (Luke 18: 14). I am not debating here theological dimensions of this quote but the fact that due to this cultural structure (a topos!), admissions of one's own wrongdoing create legitimacy. In a second step, this legitimacy can then be 'spent' – which is exactly what happens in rhetorics of judge-penitence (Figure 1.8). Such legitimacy might similarly be created in the case of rhetorics of penitence; yet, it is only here that it ultimately justifies the 'othering' of an external *other*.

The extract below exemplifies this fourth way of utilizing the topos of history as a teacher, requiring, as we shall see, less contextualization than previous examples. It is

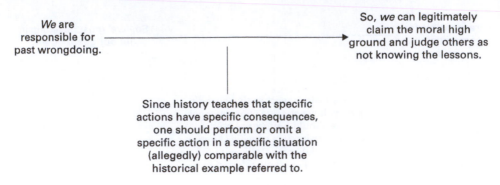

FIGURE 1.8 *A reconstruction of rhetorics of judge-penitence.*

taken from the end of a book on Europe and the United States, by the Swiss lawyer and politician Gret Haller (2003: 227), which was published by a German publisher. The book discusses different relations to state, nation and religion, whereby its main concern are experiences made by the author in the former Yugoslavia.

> Europe has such a long and guilt-laden history, not only within its own continent but also in the colonised areas of other continents, so that it – definitely after the Second World War – had to start anew and so no longer has a claim to do missionary work with others for its own convictions. If Europeans participate in aid and development projects, they are furthermore deterred by something else from considering only one (their own) approach as being possible and right. It is the experience of inner-European pluralism. Not so for the US-Americans who have a pronounced awareness of their sense of mission [*Sendungsbewusstsein*].

At first sight, what Haller conveys seems to mirror Hollande's text. After all, Europe's past is neither presented in heroic and glorious terms nor is she silencing *our* wrongdoing. Instead, this wrong is made explicit. However, she then moves away from a self-critical characterization of the past. Instead, 'Europe' becomes an actor who faced her dark past and thus emerged as a reformed character. Hence, 'Europe' now faces an external *other*, a new villain: the United States of America.

Concerning the nomination of the in-group, a lack of personal pronouns such as 'we' (in comparison to the above cases) is evident. Whilst this is due to the different genres, it is interesting to notice the effect of this: while 'we' at least provides the reader with the possibility to opt out of collective responsibility, 'Europe' and 'Europeans' hardly allow for such a move, thus making the construction quite rigid. In a similar vein, *the other* is, without any mitigation, nominated as 'the US-Americans', avoiding any differentiation. Thereby, a fallacy of hasty generalization is committed, to the effect that a sharp boundary between the actors is established. The naming of events and processes (colonialism, 'the Second World War') aids Haller's initial characterization of

'Europe' as having a 'long and guilt-laden history'. Applying what might be called a fallacious *argument from necessity* (because something was exceptional, it must have certain consequences), Haller then states, without any discussion, that 'Europe' 'had to start anew' and lost its missionary zeal. Note that this is not simply a normative statement but presented as an outcome (this interpretation seems justified due to 'furthermore' in the following sentence). In contrast to Hollande's warning not to let our guard down, for Haller, the work seems to be done as 'Europe' is represented as a reformed character.

Looking at the predication of *the other*, the German *Sendungsbewusstsein* (for 'sense of mission') is a pejorative term, often referring to religious fanaticism. It thereby aids a construction of *the other* as even uncivil – and certainly very different. And indeed, Haller continues her argument on the following page by referring to religion, claiming that 'broad sections of the United States public' perceive their convictions as absolute. What is important here is not so much whether or not this is factually true (firstly and similar to claims over 'the right lessons', religion too can be mobilized – with good reasons – in favour of very different conclusions; secondly, the degree of secularization varies enormously even within the European Union and is not always more advanced than in comparison to the US; cf. Baldwin, 2009: 163–72), but that this statement is intensified by using the adjective 'pronounced' which, again, widens the gulf between Europe and 'US-Americans'.

In sum, the use of the topos of history as a teacher here facilitates the conclusion that *we* are reformed subjects while *they* lack this learning process, a conclusion warranted by both *historia magistra vitae* and the cultural pattern 'everyone who exalts himself will be humbled, and whoever humbles himself will be exalted'. By initially foregrounding Europe's 'long and guilt-laden history', i.e. an admission of wrongdoing, Haller generates legitimacy, which she utilizes to construct the in-group as being superior vis-à-vis a morally impoverished *other* and her/his actions (Figure 1.9).

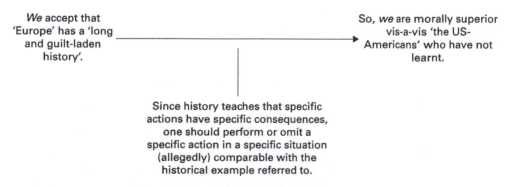

**FIGURE 1.9** *Haller's rhetoric of judge-penitence.*

# 5 Conclusion, or: critiquing uses of the topos of history as a teacher?

I started from the assumption that discursive struggles draw increasingly on interpretations of past wrongdoing instead of visions of future progress. I thus turned to *historia magistra vitae* and conceptualized four uses of this topos (rhetorics of judging, rhetorics of failing, rhetorics of penitence and rhetorics of judge-penitence), which all imagine particular pasts, present and futures. In the course of this, I have emphasized the logic of narrative; and as the past is narrativized, the very possibility of its objective representation is lost. This does not imply that truth claims concerning individual events cannot be assessed anymore; e.g. claims concerning what happened on 9 November 1989. However, it does imply that the past, as far as it is narrativized, should neither be the (sole) basis for evaluating discourses in general nor of uses of the topos of history as a teacher in particular.

For instance, Mikkelsen's argument could be questioned from a historiographical position, saying that, e.g., his party was part of the cooperating government, that his party, as part of this government, unconstitutionally detained Danish communists and that the uprising in 1943 was not of conservative origins. This criticism might be historically accurate – yet, the question remains to what extent such a positivist perspective is suitable when dealing with the workings of deep-seated cultural structures and (national) narratives. The situation is similar when turning to rhetorics of judge-penitence, the cultural structures it draws on and debates over, e.g., whether or not there are differences between the US and Europe, which and how substantial they are, and if Europe indeed started anew. However, rhetorics of judging and rhetorics of judge-penitence, due to their structural composition, are likely to facilitate a very constrained processing of information.

Instead of drawing on historiography or rejecting the analysed argument per se, a critique of these rhetorics might thus point to the sort of bias which prevents some balance in the speaker's argument as well as critical distance from his/her own argument (I refer here to only two of five characteristics proposed by Walton, 1991: 19). In other words, the strong narrative coherence – Jerome Bruner (1991: 9) speaks of 'narrative seduction' – characterizing most stories which affirm the self vis-à-vis a negative external *other* prevent a rather open and inclusive proceeding of the arguments they put forward.[4] Sure, rhetorics of failing and rhetorics of penitence too propose particular representations. Yet, they tend to contradict their own 'bias' by raising self-critical questions about the community's past and/or (crucially) present and thereby enable a more inclusive and open reconstruction of the in-group's current symbolic boundary. This brings to mind a brief note by Jürgen Habermas (1998: 10) who insists that learning from the past, if at all, can today only be triggered by disappointments and acceptance of past failures. Accordingly, the cognitively demanding acceptance of one's own past wrongdoing (or the explicit acknowledgement that past wrongdoing – even if committed by someone else – is a warning to the present-day in-group) can become an instrument of self-enlightenment by opening the in-group's horizon to the *other*'s experiences. By being confronted with the other's suffering *we* were, are or might be, responsible for and the recognition of wrongs being (potentially) part of the in-group, the latter's perspective might be de-centred. Such storying of *our* past can become the foundation of collective learning processes (for the notion of collective learning processes, cf. among others Eder, 1999; Miller, 2002; Habermas, 2003).

That is, and returning to the four types conceptualized above, rhetorics of judging and judge-penitence silence internal doubt as a motor of learning as fully constituted, present-day identities are claimed (more forcefully of course in the case of rhetorics of judging than in rhetorics of judge-penitence as the latter includes memories of *our* failing). Thus, collective learning processes tend to be blocked. In contrast, rhetorics of failing and penitence avoid such final closure as they remain open to voices by *others* and *our* discomfort (rhetorics of penitence more radically so in comparison to rhetorics of failing as the former points to the in-group's past and potential present-day wrongdoing). The subject narrated here remains at least partly fragmented and as such, collective learning processes tend to be unblocked. Besides contributing to the study of how the topos of history as a teacher works in public discussions through offering a comprehensive taxonomy, this line of thought offers a second benefit in that it views these uses in terms of social mechanisms which un/block collective learning processes, that is which facilitate more open/closed symbolic boundaries.

In addition to the critiquing of these rhetorics – which I was only able to touch upon briefly here – these four types are not as neatly separable as my conceptualization might suggest. Texts are heterogeneous entities, including different arguments which might facilitate different subject positions. This is illustrated by Fisk but also, by Hollande, whose closing sentences – '[i]t is by being clear-sighted about our own history that France, thanks to the spirit of harmony and unity, will best promote her values, here and throughout the world. Long live the Republic! Long live France!' – drift from rhetorics of penitence to judge-penitence. I do not mind the positive reference to France and her spirit here – as I have said, one cannot expect to find solely negative constructions of self. However, by turning outwards ('promote her values [. . .] throughout the world'), Hollande's admission of wrongdoing runs the risk of becoming instrumental in the (implicit) 'othering' of external *others* as less morally developed (for similar cases on the EU-level, cf. Forchtner and Kølvraa, 2012). Given the rather unambiguous linguistic construction of *us* as guilt-laden, the especially strong calls for alertness and the unspecific character of this final sentence, I doubt that many understand this speech as a call for moral superiority. Yet, this final detail illustrates that in an age in which the past is omnipresent, the mobilization of its 'moral meaning' in public struggles must be scrutinized.

# Notes

1 This research was funded by a DOC-fellowship from the Austrian Academy of Sciences and an ESRC studentship at the Department of Linguistics and English Language at Lancaster University. I am thankful to Ruth Wodak and Raimundo Frei for their comments on an earlier version of this article. All mistakes remain, of course, my own.

2 Drawing on the discourse-historical approach in critical discourse studies, I could have spoken about these four structures of communication in terms of different discursive strategies of self and other representation. While my notion of rhetorics resembles this notion of strategy as being 'more or less intentional' (Reisigl and Wodak, 2009: 94), I nevertheless prefer the term rhetorics here as it does not link my conceptualization to a particular framework. These rhetorics are furthermore viewed as diverse, the plural indicating the variety of possible realizations (cf. also Forchtner and Kølvraa, 2012; Forchtner, 2014).

3 It is against this background that a brief reference to *our* past wrongdoing ('the 19th-century British colonial army') in a paragraph not included here, does not affect the status of the US-war in Vietnam as being *the* past wrong from which lessons should be drawn.

4 An understanding of how such processes work, might be provided by Didier Maillat and Steve Oswald's (2011: 71) notion of manipulation as forcing the interpretation of information 'within a limited context' and blocking 'access to any alternative contextual assumption' as well as Andreas Musolff's (2004: 173–7) idea of open and closed metaphor scenarios. While the former are open to criticism, the latter facilitate the closure of thinking (for more on possible notions of critique in CDS and the DHA in particular, cf. Reisigl and Wodak, 2001: 32–5; Forchtner, 2011; Forchtner and Tominc, 2012).

# References

Aristotle (1982), *The 'Art' of Rhetoric*. London: Heinemann.

Assmann, J. (1997), *Moses the Egyptian. The Memory of Egypt in Western Monotheism*. Cambridge: Harvard University Press.

Baldwin, P. (2009), *The Narcissism of Minor Differences. How America and Europe are Alike*. Oxford: Oxford University Press.

Barkan, E. and Karn, A. (eds) (2006), *Taking Wrongs Seriously. Apologies and Reconciliation*. Stanford: Stanford University Press.

Barthes, R. (1977), 'Introduction to the structural analysis of narratives', in S. Heath (ed.), *Image, Music, Text*. London: Fontana Press, pp. 79–124.

Birkelund, P. (2003), 'Samarbejde eller brud? Det Konservative Folkepartis store dilemma', in J. Lund (ed.), *Partier under pres – demokratiet under besættelsen*. Copenhagen: Gyldendal, pp. 95–129.

Bruner, J. (1991), 'The narrative construction of reality'. *Critical Inquiry*, 18(1), 1–21.

Camus, A. (2006), *The Fall*. London: Penguin.

Carrier, P. (2005), *Holocaust Monuments and National Memory Cultures in France and Germany since 1989*. New York: Berghahn.

Cicero (1959), *De Oratore. Books I and II*. London: Heinemann.

Cunningham, M. (1999), 'Saying sorry: the politics of apology'. *Political Quarterly*, 70(3), 285–93.

DIIS (2005), *Danmark under den kolde krig. Den sikkerhedspolitiske situation 1945–1991. Bind 2: 1963–1978*. Copenhagen: DIIS.

Eder, K. (1999), 'Societies learn and yet the world is hard to change'. *European Journal of Social Theory*, 2(2), 195–215.

Farbøl, R. (2011), 'Irakkrigen og den historiske ulegitimering'. *Slagmark. Tidsskrift for Idéhistorie*, 60, 73–85.

Finkielkraut, A. (2004), 'Im Namen der Anderen. Reflexionen über den kommenden Antisemitismus', in D. Rabinovoci, U. Speck and N. Sznaider (eds), *Neuer Antisemitismus. Eine globale Debatte*. Frankfurt/Main: Suhrkamp, pp. 119–32.

Fisk, R. (2009), 'America is performing its familiar role of propping up a dictator'. *Independent*, 4 November. Available at: http://www.independent.co.uk/voices/ commentators/fisk/robert-fisk-america-is-performing-its-familiar-role-of-propping-up-a-dictator-1814194.html (accessed 12 October 2013).

Forchtner, B. (2011), 'Critique, the discourse–historical approach, and the Frankfurt School'. *Critical Discourse Studies*, 8, 1–14.

Forchtner, B. (2013), 'Nazi-collaboration, acknowledgements of wrongdoing and the legitimation of the Iraq war in Denmark: a judge-penitent perspective', in P. Cap and U. Okulska (eds), *Analyzing Genres in Political Communication: Theory and Practice*. Amsterdam: John Benjamins, pp. 239–65.

—— (2014), 'Rhetorics of judge-penitence: claiming moral superiority through admissions of past wrongdoing', *Memory Studies*, 7(4), in press.

Forchtner, B. and Kølvraa, C. (2012), 'Narrating a "new Europe": from "bitter past" to self-righteousness'. *Discourse & Society*, 23(4), 377–400.

Forchtner, B. and Tominc, A. (2012), 'Critique and argumentation: on the relation between the discourse-historical approach and pragma-dialectics,' in *Journal for Language and Politics*, 11, 31–50.

Gibney, M., Howard-Hassmann, R. E., Coicaud, J.-M. and Steiner, N. (eds) (2008), *The Age of Apology. Facing up to the Past*. Philadelphia: University of Philadelphia Press.

Giesen, B. (2004), *Triumph and Trauma*. Boulder: Paradigm.

Golsan, R. J. (2006), 'The legacy of World War II in France. Mapping the discourses of memory', in R. N. Lebow, W. Kansteiner and C. Fogu (eds), *The Politics of Memory in Postwar Europe*. Durham: Duke University Press, pp. 73–101.

Greimas, A. J. (1983), *Structural Semantics. An Attempt at a Method*. Lincoln: University of Nebraska Press.

—— (1987), *On Meaning. Selected Writings in Semiotic Theory*. Minneapolis: University of Minneapolis Press.

Habermas, J. (1998), 'Can we learn from history?', in S. Rendall (ed.), *A Berlin Republic: Writings on Germany*. Cambridge: University of Nebraska Press, pp. 5–13.

—— (2003), 'Rightness versus truth: on the sense of normative validity in moral judgements and norms', in B. Fultner (ed.), *Truth and Justification*. Cambridge: MIT Press, pp. 239–75.

Halbwachs, M. (1985), *Das kollektive Gedächtnis*. Frankfurt/Main: Suhrkamp.

Haller, G. (2003), *Die Grenzen der Solidarität. Europa und die USA im Umgang mit Staat, Nation und Religion*. Berlin: Aufbau.

Heer, H., Manoschek, W., Pollak, A. and Wodak, R. (eds) (2008), *The Discursive Construction of History: Remembering the Wehrmacht's War of Annihilation*. Palgrave: Basingstoke.

Hollande, F. (2012), 'The crime committed in France, by France'. Speech given on 22 July. Reprinted in *The New York Review of Books*. Available at: http://www.nybooks.com/articles/archives/2012/sep/27/crime-committed-france-france/ (accessed 5 October 2012).

Judt, T. (2007), *Postwar. A History of Europe Since 1945*. London: Pimlico.

Kaae, M. and Nissen, J. (2008), *Vejen til Iraq – Hvorfor gik Danmark i Krig?* Copenhagen: Gads.

Kienpointer, M. (1995), 'Rhetoric', in J. Verschuren, J. O. Östman and J. Blommaert (eds), *Handbook of Pragmatics. Manual*. Amsterdam: John Benjamins, pp. 453–61.

Kindt, W. (1992), 'Argumentation und Konfliktaustragung in Äußerungen über den Golfkrieg'. *Zeitschrift für Sprachwissenschaft*, 11(2), 189–215.

Kirchhoff, H. (2004), *Samarbejde og Modstand Under Besættelsen – En Politisk Historie*. Odense. Syddansk Universitetsforlag.

Koselleck, R. (2004), 'Historia Magistra Vitae: the dissolution of the topos into the perspective of a modernized historical process', in R. Koselleck (ed.), *Futures Past. On the Semantics of Historical Time*. New York: Columbia University Press, pp. 26–42.

Maillat, D. and Oswald, S. (2011), 'Constraining context: a pragmatic account of cognitive manipulation', in C. Hart (ed.), *Critical Discourse Studies in Context and Cognition*. Amsterdam: John Benjamins, pp. 65–80.

Mikkelsen, B. (2003), 'Aldrig mere i neutralitetens fælde', *Berlingske Tidende*, 30 August, 8.

Miller, M. (2002), *Some Theoretical Aspects of Systemic Learning*. Available at http://www.sozialwiss.uni-hamburg.de/Isoz/isoz/miller/miller/systemic_learning.pdf (accessed 3 September 2013).

Müller, J.-W. (2002), 'Introduction', in J.-W. Müller (ed.), *Memory and Power in Post-War Europe: Studies in the Presence of the Past*. Cambridge: Cambridge University Press, pp. 1–35.

Musolff, A. (2004), *Metaphor and Political Discourse. Analogical Reasoning in Debates about Europe*. Basingstoke: Palgrave.

Olick, J. K., Vinitzky-Seroussi, V. and Levy, D. (2011), 'Introduction', in J. K. Olick, V. Vinitzky-Seroussi and D. Levy (eds), *The Collective Memory Reader*. Oxford: Oxford University Press, pp. 3–62.

Reisigl, M. (1998), '"50 Jahre Zweite Republik" – Zur diskursiven Konstruktion der österreichischen Identität in politischen Gedenkreden', in O. Panagl (ed), *Fahnenwörter in der Politik – Kontinuitäten und Brüche*. Wien: Böhlau, pp. 217–51.

—— (2007), *Nationale Rhetorik in Fest- und Gedenkreden. Eine diskursanalytische Studie zum "österreichischen Millennium" in den Jahren 1946 und 1996*. Tübingen: Stauffenburg.

—— (2013), 'Critical Discourse Analysis', in R. Bayley, R. Camerron and C. Lucas (eds), *The Oxford Handbook of Sociolinguistics*. Oxford: Oxford University Press, pp. 67–90.

Reisigl, M. and Wodak, R. (2001), *Discourse and Discrimination: Rhetorics of Racism and Anti-Semitism*. London: Routledge.

—— (2009), 'The discourse-historical approach', in R. Wodak and M. Meyer (eds), *Methods of Critical Discourse Analysis* (revised edn). London: Sage, pp. 87–121.

Ricoeur, P. (1988), *Time and Narrative – Volume 3*. Chicago: The University of Chicago Press.

Rousso, H. (1984), *The Vichy Syndrome: History and Memory in France since 1944*. Cambridge: Harvard University Press.

Rubinelli, S. (2009), *Ars Topica. The Classical Technique of Constructing Arguments from Aristotle to Cicero*. Berlin: Springer.

Tilly, C. (2002), *Stories, Identities, and Political Change*. Oxford: Rowman & Littlefield.

Toulmin, S., Rieke, R. and Janik, A. (1979), *An Introduction to Reasoning*. New York: Macmillan.

van Dijk, T. A. (1980), 'Story comprehension: an introduction'. *Poetics*, 9(1–3), 1–21.

Viehöver, W. (2011), 'Diskurse als Narration', in R. Keller, A. Hirsel and, W. Schneider and W. Viehöver (eds), *Handbuch Sozialwissenschaftliche Diskursanalyse. Band 1*. Wiesbaden: VS, pp. 193–224.

Walton, D. (1991), 'Bias, critical doubt, and fallacies'. *Argumentation and Advocacy*, 28, pp. 1–22.

Walton, D., Reed, C. and Macagno, F. (2008), *Argumentation Schemes*. Cambridge: Cambridge University Press.

Wengeler, M. (2003), 'Argumentationstopos als sprachwissenschaftlicher Gegenstand. Für eine Erweiterung linguistischer Methoden bei der Analyse öffentlicher Diskurse', in S. Geideck and W.-A. Liebert (eds), *Sinnformeln. Linguistische und soziologische Analysen von Leitbildern, Metaphern und anderen kollektiven Orientierungsmustern*. Berlin/New York: de Gruyter, pp. 59–82.

White, H. (1980), 'Narrativity in the representation of reality'. *Critical Inquiry*, 7, (1), 5–27.

Wodak, R. and de Cillia, R. (2007), 'Commemorating the past: the discursive construction of official narratives about the "Rebirth of the Second Austrian Republic"'. *Discourse & Communication*, 1(3), 337–63.

Wodak, R. and Meyer, M. (eds) (2009), *Methods of Critical Discourse Analysis* (2nd revised edition). London: Sage.

Wodak, R., de Cillia, R. Reisigl, M. and Liebhart, K. (2009), *The Discursive Construction of National Identity*. Edinburgh: Edinburgh University Press.

Wodak, R., Menz, F., Mitten, R. and Stern, F. (1994), *Die Sprachen der Vergangenheit. Öffentliches Gedenken in österreichischen und deutschen Medien*. Frankfurt/Main: Suhrkamp.

Wodak, R., de Cillia, R., Reisigl, M., Liebhart, K., Hoffstätter, K. and Kargl, M. (1998), *Zur diskursiven Konstruktion von nationaler Identität*. Frankfurt/Main: Suhrkamp.

Wodak, R., Nowak, P., Pelikan, J., Gruber, H., de Cilla, R. and Mitten, R. (1990), *Wir sind alle unschuldige Täter. Diskurshistorische Studien zu Nachkriegsantisemitismus*. Frankfurt/Main: Suhrkamp.

# 2

# Metaphor in the Discourse-Historical Approach

## Andreas Musolff
## University of East Anglia

## 1 Introduction

**(1)** So long as there has been a body politic to host them, parasites have feasted on its blood. (*The Independent*, 7 December 2011; regarding a scandal about lobbyists who had claimed to be able to 'sell' contacts to British government ministers.)

**(2)** [. . .] a visit to [the US] Congress, the Japanese Diet or the Strasbourg parliament elicits the same sense of a body politic that has given itself over to squabbling on a scale that makes it incapable of long-term decisions. (*The Observer*, 30 December 2012.)

The English phrase *body politic*, which appears in the above-quoted examples, belongs to a group of metaphors in English that refer to political entities in terms of bodily organs and functions, such as *head of state, head of government, long arm of the law, organ (of a party)*.[1] As a lexical unit, *body politic* seems to have originated in the early sixteenth century in English through a loan translation from medieval Latin *corpus politicum* (also: *corpus mysticum*), which had previously been used to describe the political role of the king as opposed to his physical identity and by extension, the monarchical state in England (Charbonnel, 2010; Hale, 1971: 43–50; Kantorowicz, 1997: 7–23; Koschorke et al., 2007). Examples (1) and (2) above demonstrate that the phrase *body politic* is still employed today in British media discourse. As part of a larger research corpus that is still being added to, a sample of 176 texts from British media in the period 1991–2013 has been assembled, which currently total over 76,000 words. Comparative samples have been collected for the German press, with 160 texts (137,917 words) from the 1950s to today and, for the French press, of 45 texts (41,503 words) for the last decade.[2] Between them, they include over 90 *body*-related concepts that are currently applied to politics in the respective national discourse communities (see: Table 2.1). Due to the differing sizes and periods of coverage of the three samples, no statistical conclusions can be drawn; however, some main usage patterns that seem to be typical for the three national discourse communities can be identified. In this chapter, I propose a discourse-historical motivation for the usage patterns of the phrase *body politic* in English and its French and German cognates. The findings and methodology will be related to the predictions about semantic variation made within Cognitive Metaphor Theory, in order to gauge their theoretical significance and assess the contribution the discourse-historical analysis can make to the investigation of metaphor in general.

## 2 Present-day usage of *body politic*, of *corps politique* and *corps social*, and of *Staatskörper* – *Volkskörper*, *nationaler Körper*

Linguistic expressions of metaphorical concepts are universally 'translatable' in the sense that their meanings can always be paraphrased if necessary, but that does not mean that their lexical manifestations stand in a one-to-one relationship across different languages. English *body politic* can thus be 'roughly' translated into other languages by combining the respective 'matching' lexical items (cognates) in accordance with the syntactic and morphological rules of each language, e.g. German, *politischer Körper*; French, *corps politique*; Italian, *corpo politico*; Dutch, *politiek lichaam*; Russian, политическое тело; Greek, Πολιτική Σώματος; etc. These are, however, only rough and ready translations, not exact matches. French and German, for instance, each have several terms or phrases instead of one idiomatically fixed construction such as *body politic*.

In German, the phrase *politischer Körper*, which most closely resembles *body politic*, can be found in the present-day corpus sample but it competes against (and seems to be outnumbered) by other expressions: *Staatskörper* (and its morphological variant *Körper des Staates*; literally, 'state body'/'body of the state'), *Nationalkörper* (lit., 'national body'), and *Volkskörper* (lit., 'people's body'), as shown in the following examples:

> **(3)** Die Empörungsfähigkeit ist die Immunabwehr des politischen Systems. Wenn sie verlorengeht, verfällt der *politische Körper*. (*Der Spiegel*, 22 December 2011; 'The ability to be appalled [by political scandals] is the immune defence of the political system. When this ability is lost, the *body politic* degenerates.')[3]

**(4)** An der Berliner Humboldt-Universität hat die Regierung eigens ein 'Kompetenzzentrum' eingerichtet, in dem acht Wissenschaftler darüber wachen, dass Gender Mainstreaming korrekt in den Staatskörper eingepflanzt wird. (*Der Spiegel*, 30 December 2006; 'At the Humboldt University in Berlin, the government has just set up a special "expert centre" of eight scientists who check that *Gender Mainstreaming* is correctly implemented in the *state body*.')

**(5)** [Theaterkritiker] sprechen vom 'Bühnenkörper' und vom *'nationalen Körper'* – Gesellschaft ist *der große Leib*, über den sich das Theater beugt. (*Die Zeit*, 19 May 2005; 'Theatre critics speak of the "stage body" and the "*national body*"; it's society's *great body* that is being scrutinized by the theatre.')

**(6)** Kein Atom im *Volkskörper*. [= headline] Die Anti-AKW-Bewegung in Österreich streitet derzeit heftig. Denn einige Gruppen [. . .] pflegen einen unkritischen Umgang mit rechtsextremen Umweltschützern. (*Jungle World* [Austrian magazine], 25 August 2011; 'No nuclear pollution of [literally: no atomic power in] the *people's body*! The anti-nuclear movement in Austria is sharply divided, for some groups have a cosy relationship with right-wing extremist environmentalists.')

The different expressions that combine the notions of POLITICS and BODY in these German examples are closely related in terms of etymology, morphology and semantics but are by no means exchangeable. *Staatskörper/Körper des Staates* (lit. 'state body'), which accounts for 33 per cent of all 85 metaphor instances that contain the lexical unit *Körper*, seems to be the most neutral, ideologically unmarked expression, which targets any kind of political (state) entity,[4] as does *politischer Körper* ('state body') which has only four occurrences in the sample.[5] *'Nationaler Körper'* has just one occurrence in the sample and it seems to express mainly the concept of SOCIETY as distinct from STATE (example (5)). By contrast *Volkskörper*, as in example (6), accounts for more than 50 per cent of the sample (46 occurrences) and is a highly marked form: almost all of its post-1965 uses in the sample refer to extreme right-wing and/or xenophobic discourse in present-day usage or, historically, to Nazi-jargon (where it played a central role in 'justifying' the Holocaust by depicting Jews as *parasites* on the German *people's body*).[6]

In the majority of examples, the term *Volkskörper* is quoted or referred to from a critically commenting position, as evidence that its 'primary' (actual or potential) users are comparable to, if not like, the Nazis themselves, i.e. have similar racist prejudices. Thus, the journalist Katharina Rutschky criticized certain participants in post-war debates about demographic decline in Germany as echoing Nazi-propaganda by exhibiting an 'injured soul in the sick *people's body*' ('Im kranken *Volkskörper* steckt eine verletzte Seele', *Die Welt*, 11 April 2006). But even when no explicit historical link to the Nazi-period is made, readers are expected to be aware of the historical association in order to understand the use of *people's body*, e.g. example (6), where it is used in the headline as an ironically 'quoted' motto of suspected Neo-Nazis. (No actual reference is given and it is unlikely that the motto has been quoted verbatim, so, strictly speaking, we are dealing with an imagined motto but that does not affect the power of the metaphorical allusion). To translate *Volkskörper* in present-day German texts simply as *body politic* would be misleading because any uncritical use of *Volkskörper* is taken as indicating either an extreme right-wing stance or political naivety on the part of its original utterer.

In present-day French political discourse we find three lexicalized variants of the STATE-BODY metaphor, i.e. *corps politique*, *corps électorale*, and *corps social*:

(7) L'atomisation des individus sous le choc de la crise et la divergence du *corps social* trouvent une traduction directe dans la vie publique avec la radicalisation et la poussée des populismes. (*Le Figaro*, 4 May 2012; 'The atomization of individual citizens under the shock of the [economic] crisis and the splits in the *body of society* translate directly into radicalization and the surge of populisms in public life.')

(8) La classe politique, droite libérale et gauche socialiste confondues, a malmené depuis plus de vingt-cinq ans *le vieux corps social français*. (*Le Figaro*, 9 November 2010; 'For more than 25 years, the political classes, both the liberal right and the socialist left, have mismanaged the ageing *body of French society*.')

(9) [. . .] le président [= Nicolas Sarkozy] [. . .] entraîne *le corps politique français* dans une consternante régression. (*Le Nouvel Observateur*, 1 May 2012; 'The President pulls the *body politic* into a regression that gives reason for concern.')

(10) Mitterrand à Sarkozy: une irrésistible érosion de la fonction présidentielle et du *corps politique*. (*Le Monde*, 5 March 2011; 'From Mitterrand to Sarkozy – an unstoppable decline of the presidential office and the political system.')

(11) A noter un chiffre peu souligné lors de la soirée électorale, à savoir les 2,14 millions de votes nuls et blancs, soit 5,8% du *corps électoral*, un niveau extrêmement élevé, qui correspond sans doute à une part de l'électorat frontiste du premier tour. (*Éco121*, 7 May 2012; 'To note a figure that was not highlighted during the election night, i.e. the 2.14 million void votes, 5.8 per cent of the whole electorate, which represents an extremely elevated level that is doubtless owed in part to the *Front National* voters of the first round.')

The meanings of the phrases *corps politique*, *corps électorale*, and *corps social* are not identical but very closely related: the social, electoral and political *bodies* are all aspects of the same referent, i.e. the politically active part of the French populace. Examples

(7) and (8) depict French society that has to be cared for by the political classes, lest its problems lead to a disintegration of the nation. This 'social body' is not to be confused with the political classes themselves; rather, it is the foundation of the nation as a 'political body' (which, perhaps, is closest to the 'body politic' meaning in English). The nation's actual political incarnation, as it were, are the voters in the national election (even if they spoil their votes, as is suspected of far right wing sympathizers in example (11)). The 'electoral body' is thus the concrete manifestation of the 'political body' of the nation, which in turn is the politically active manifestation of the 'body of society'. Such mutually defining uses of *corps politique, corps électorale*, and *corps social* can be found many times over in the French sample but have few counterparts in the English and German samples. Which discourse tradition can they be linked to? A commentary in the leftist newspaper *Libération* can help us here, which highlights the STATE-BODY metaphor in its title: '*Le corps politique, un malade à la recherche de sa thérapie*' ('The body politic: a sickly patient in search of a therapy'). Its author, the writer Philippe Boisnard, argues that the political classes must rethink their fundamental political assumptions, in particular the notion that French society and state are based on the notion of absolute obedience to the sovereign general will, which dates back to Rousseau's *Social Contract* (1762):

(12) [. . .] *de penser la dimension politique à l'image d'un corps*, il n'y aurait qu'à relire Rousseau, [. . .] *Du contrat social*, [. . .] Cette métaphore n'est pas anodine, elle suppose que ce *corps* soit dirigé par une seule unité intentionnelle [. . .] et que tous les *membres* de la société ne soient plus considérés que comme *organes* de celui-ci. ('In order to think of the political sphere in terms of the *image of a body* should require no more than to reread Rousseau's *Social Contract*. This metaphor is by no means neutral; it supposes that this *body* is directed by a singular unity of intention and that all *members* of society are only to be considered as its *organs*.')

(Boisnard, 2005)

It is impossible to provide here a detailed discussion of Boisnard's interpretation of Rousseau's philosophy of state but one quotation from *Du Contrat Social* (Book II, Chapter 4: *Des Bornes du Pouvoir Souverain*) may be quoted that appears to support Boisnard's main point:

(13) Comme la nature donne à chaque homme un pouvoir absolu sur tous ses *membres*, le pacte social donne *au corps politique* un pouvoir absolu sur tous les siens, et c'est ce même pouvoir qui, dirigé par la volonté générale, porte [. . .] le nom de souveraineté. ('Just as nature gives each man absolute power over all his *limbs*, the social pact gives the *political body* absolute power over all its *members*; and [. . .] it is the same power, directed by the general will, that bears the name of sovereignty'; Rousseau, 1990: 120, for the English translation, Rousseau, 1994: 67.)[7]

If we follow Boisnard's reading, the relationship between the 'political' and 'social bodies' of the nation, which seems to underlie examples (7)–(10) can be traced back to the theoretical framework of the French enlightenment thinker. Such an explication does not entail that every politician or journalist who uses the terms *corps politique* or *corps social* today has got to be aware of their conceptual linkage in Rousseau's philosophy. However, it seems plausible to assume that thanks to Rousseau's prominent role in French education and public discourse since the Enlightenment these definitions have become commonplace to this day. In this context it is relevant that the French press sample, in contrast to the English and German ones, contains several interventions by public intellectuals, such as the philosophers Alain Renaud, Giorgio Agamben and Bernard Henri Lévy and the politician/writer Régis Debray.[8] If intellectuals' and philosophers' voices play such an eminent role in public discourse, it is not surprising that key arguments and metaphors from philosophical texts and traditions play a greater role in French debates than in other national discourses. This philosophically oriented 'habitus' (Bourdieu, 1990) of the French public sphere seems to shape the conceptual and argumentative focus of the metaphor as much as the historically minded (and perhaps to some extent still guilt-obsessed) habitus of the German public sphere, which harks back to the catastrophe of National Socialist rule.

So what about *body politic* in British English discourse?[9] In the first place it can be observed that this phrase is a semantically and morphologically marked form, due to the archaic use of *politic* in the meaning of 'political' and its positioning after the noun, which is not typical for present-day English but was productive in early modern English (Hughes, 1988: 186). Of course, present-day speakers of English need to know as little about the origins of *body politic* terminology as French speakers using *corps politique* need to know of Rousseau's philosophy. Nevertheless, English users must have acquired the construction as a fixed expression; otherwise it would have disappeared together with other modern early English constructions and Britons would only be talking of a *political body*. This latter phrase can in fact be found in current discourse but is chiefly used to designate specific political institutions, groupings and business 'corporations' but not the whole of society/state,[10] i.e. it is not exchangeable with *body politic*.

One aspect that seems to stand out in the British discourse about the *body politic* by comparison with the French and German samples is the frequent occurrence of wordplays on its 'double entendre' as referring to an individual's status in the political hierarchy and his/her specific physical characteristics, usually in an ironical sense. The following examples are representative of more than 20 per cent of all instances of usage of *body politic* in the British sample:

(14) *Body politic:* [. . .] In what is perhaps the ultimate betrayal of the Celebrity 'Cool Britannia' culture he embraced upon entering Downing Street, *Heat* this week prints a long-lens snap of Blair resplendent in his Caribbean holiday

podge – *a sort of 'ripples and nipples' look.* (*The Independent*, 14 August 2007.)

**(15)** Sorry, Gordon [= Gordon Brown, British Labour Prime Minister], but *your body politic* doesn't match Putin's. (*The Observer*, 1 November 2009.)

**(16)** Just last week [the pro-conservative magazine *The Spectator*] landed yet another bruising punch on [British Labour Prime Minister] Blair's *solar plexus, a part of the body politic* that Iain Duncan Smith [= then the Conservative Opposition Leader] has notably failed to reach. (*The Independent*, 7 July 2002.)

In (14) and (15), two former Labour Prime Ministers are being ridiculed ostensibly for non-photogenic body features, but in the respective historical political context this irony could be understood also as extending to their perceived political weakness (in Blair's case, as an outgoing Prime Minister, in Brown's case as a caretaker Prime Minister who had not won a general election). In example (16), however, the context is different and the BODY PART concept of *solar plexus* is embedded in a special scenario. Prime Minister Blair, then at the height of his popularity, is depicted as a boxer who cannot even be touched by his official parliamentary opponent but is still vulnerable to attacks from the pro-conservative media, specifically the magazine *The Spectator*. It would be absurd to assume that anything happened to Blair's real physical solar plexus, so it can only be his 'political body' that has been targeted.

A kind of 'reverse' version of the political BODY PART concept in (16) can be found in the Conservative politician Boris Johnson's repeated ironical self-deprecation as a 'mere toenail in the British body politic'.[11] The presupposed *body* is the *nation's body*, and Johnson presents himself as a 'lowly' body part within it, thus apparently showing modesty regarding his own standing. However, contextual knowledge, which British hearers/readers would have had in 2005 and 2009 (i.e. about his influential role as Conservative MP and editor of the pro-conservative magazine *The Spectator* until 2005, and as the Mayor of London since 2008), suggests an ironical reading. Assuming that the audience of his statements knew him as an important/ambitious Tory politician, Johnson could describe himself as a lowly part of the *body politic* for them to infer that his opinion was in fact far from unimportant. He could thus achieve the rhetorical effect of appearing both funny and modest but not unambitious at the same time.

Taking the English examples (1, 2, 14, 15, 16 and Johnson's uses) together, we find that the BODY source concept in *body politic* can target different aspects of politics in present day British English: a) the state or the whole national political sphere, b) a specific institution or grouping, c) a politician's standing. It is thus to some extent polysemous. In order to disambiguate the meaning of a particular instance of use and select its 'optimally relevant' (Sperber and Wilson, 1995) interpretation in the context,[12] readers have to activate popular-scientific and practical knowledge about bodies and their parts, which can be evaluated on various criteria (e.g. medical, aesthetic, sports-related). These criteria provide the basis for a graded system of evaluations ('healthy body = better than sick body', 'head = more important than toenail', etc.), which targets notions of social and/or political hierarchies.

From a historical perspective, this evaluative system can be found in earlier uses of the *body politic* metaphor that date back to the Middle Ages, which conflated the ancient tradition of describing the state as a body-internal hierarchy from head to toe (Nederman, 1992, 2004; Musolff, 2009) with the theologically derived notion of the *King's Two Bodies*, i.e. the distinction between a mortal/vulnerable body and the eternal 'mystical'/political body of the sovereign, as analysed by E. H. Kantorowicz and others (Kantorowicz, 1997; Bertelli, 2001; Horten, 2009). This latter topic is not exclusive to the English/British History of Ideas, but it received its terminological fixation in the pair *body natural – body politic* in English. The intricacies of late medieval and Renaissance debates about how to separate the crown's status and property from the monarch's 'personal' body (and property) are of course today largely forgotten, but an awareness of the double meaning of *body* in the political sphere seems to have survived in the public consciousness in Britain and still plays a significant role in present-day discourse, as is shown by the fact that it makes up one fifth of the British sample occurrences.[13] By contrast it figures only marginally in the public discourses of France and Germany, and where it occurs is referred to as a topic of scholarly research. Wordplays on its *double entendre* are by far more typical for the British public sphere than for the French and German media discourses.

## 3 Discourse history as motivation for topical metaphor use

Our hypothesis concerning the motivatedness of the STATE-BODY metaphor in British, French and German media discourses may be summarized in this way: the metaphor of the 'political body' was first borrowed and translated from medieval Latin into the European vernacular languages during the early modern period as a cross-lingually shared concept; since then it has branched out into divergent, though still interconnected, discourse traditions. These traditions are anchored in 'national' political cultures insofar as these include typical historical experiences, myths and famous/infamous precedents, which are understood by members of the respective national discourse communities, whereas they have to be given extra explanation/paraphrasing when translated.

The main theoretical challenge of providing an explanation of these historical developments lies in the modelling of the long-term semantic development of metaphors. Conceptual Metaphor Theory (CMT) in its early phase (roughly, from *Metaphors we live by* through the 1980s) did not make historical investigations its foremost concern. Even if the historicity of conceptual metaphor systems such as that of the *Great Chain of Being* was acknowledged in principle, as in Lakoff and Turner's volume on poetic metaphors, *More Than Cool Reason* (1989), the main emphasis was on the synchronic study of the metaphor as a quasi-universal mapping that 'occur[red] throughout a wide range of the world's cultures' (1989: 167). When CMT broadened to include cognitive 'embodiment' theory, the role of the body as a universal basis of human experience and conceptualization was further emphasized, with special regard to neurophysiological structures (e.g. so-called 'mirror neurons') and to ontogenetically 'primary' experiences that were regarded as the basis of metonymies and 'primary metaphors'; these were in turn considered to be the building blocks of all complex metaphors (Johnson, 1987; Lakoff and Johnson, 1999; Grady and Johnson, 2003; Gibbs, 2005; Lakoff, 2008). The explanatory model thus remained essentially the same as in early CMT, with the main modification that now a certain degree of semantic variation could be allowed for. However, this variation was still only acknowledged as a 'surface' phenomenon that was derivative of 'underlying' primary conceptual structures. The latter were still seen as universal, whilst inter- and cross-language variation was derived from differing combinations of primary metaphors and metonymies (Kövecses, 2005: 63–4; Yu 2008: 259).

Within this universalist and essentially ahistoric model, the STATE-BODY metaphor can be motivated at a very abstract level, i.e. as the combination of a general metaphor COMPLEX (SOCIAL) SYSTEMS ARE BODIES[14] and the ubiquitous metonymy BODY/BODY PART FOR PERSON.[15] All uses of the STATE-BODY metaphor appear in this perspective as instances of one and the same universal metaphor; variation phenomena are explained as products of differential combination and ordering of primary metaphors and metonymies. Whilst such an analysis is consistent with the general assumptions of Conceptual Metaphor Theory and accounts for some cross-cultural differences of the conceptual architecture (e.g. as regards emotion metaphors),[16] it leaves more finely grained distribution patterns such as those found in our corpus data unaccounted for. The question of a possible discourse-historical motivation for such variation is not even raised in this perspective because the universal experiential basis is considered sufficient to motivate all the semantics of all BODY-based metaphors, including those in public political discourse.

Among the more recent cognitive approaches, Croft (2000) and Croft and Cruse (2004) have made attempts to 'historicize' CMT. In his monograph on *Language Change*, Croft proposes a refinement of an evolutionary ('memetic') approach to the development of thought and language by presenting a two-step model of diachronic linguistic variation as (i) innovation or 'altered replication' – in analogy to biological 'mutation' – and (ii) selection or 'differential replication' (Croft, 2000: 23–9). It is the latter aspect that is relevant for the discursive 'entrenchment' of linguistic structures in the socio-communicative context (2000: 38), and in particular to the 'life history' of metaphors as told in Croft and Cruse (2004):

When [a metaphor] is first coined, the only way to interpret it is to employ one's innate metaphorical strategy, which is subject to a wide range of contextual and communicative constraints. Once a metaphor takes hold in a speech community and gets repeated sufficiently often, its character changes. First, its meaning becomes circumscribed relative to the freshly coined metaphor, becoming more determinate; second, it begins to be laid down as an item in the mental lexicon; third, it begins a process of semantic drift, which can weaken or obscure its metaphorical origins. [. . .] As time passes [. . .] the sense of the expression's metaphorical nature fades and eventually disappears.

(2004: 204–5)

In contrast to the model of metaphor emergence in terms of universal experiential grounding proposed by the Lakoff-Johnson school, this model of *innovation* and *selection-propagation* helps to differentiate between the creation of metaphors and their diffusion and entrenchment in specific discourse communities. It is the latter aspect that seems the most promising for modelling divergent discourse traditions that emerge from a previously shared conceptual metaphor, as in the case of the concept of the 'political body'. It is only in communicative, i.e. socio-culturally embedded contexts, that new metaphor variants are accepted or rejected, which implies that every replication of an utterance is in itself a re-creation, and thus a subtle innovation, of concepts. The discursive history of *body politic* imagery and of other 'durable metaphors' is therefore unlikely to follow a linear path of change but instead it develops as a 'complex adaptive system' (Frank, 2009; Gonthier, 2010), where meaning changes are neither random nor teleological but are expressed in shifting usage/distribution patterns that are influenced by socio-economic factors. The cognitive approach on its own thus seems unable to provide a comprehensive model of diachronic meaning change; it needs complementing by an account of how differentially disseminated variants emerge across diverse discourse communities.

The most promising model of diachronic variation to fill this gap in accounting for the dissemination and entrenchment of metaphors seems to be the discourse-historical analysis (DHA) (Reisigl and Wodak, 2001; Wodak, 2007, 2009), which focuses on the historically situated, ideological/argumentative dimension of discourses as 'bundle[s] of simultaneous and sequential interrelated linguistic acts, which manifest themselves within and across the social fields of action as thematically interrelated semiotic, oral or written tokens' (Wodak, 2009: 66). In addition, DHA attempts to 'transcend the pure linguistic dimension' by including 'the historical, political, sociological and/or psychological dimension' in order to 'triangulate' their research findings by collecting 'a variety of different empirical data' from social science viewpoints as well as from hermeneutic and corpus-base methodologies (Reisgl and Wodak, 2001: 35).

The divergent discourse traditions in the use of the STATE-BODY metaphor that we have outlined can be understood as 'bundles' of linguistic acts in the DHA sense, i.e. as representing usage patterns that are indicative of attitudes and ideological orientations in specific cultural communities of practice. The historical resonance of *Volkskörper* in German with its echoes of Nazi jargon, the interdependence of *corps politique* and *corps social* in French, and the *double entendre* of the *body politic/natural* in British English can be viewed as examples of such discursive traditions. The empirical basis for their 'discursive reality' is in the first place the observable evidence in the distribution patterns of corpus data, both at the synchronic level and as a diachronically ordered series of cross-referential texts. Ideally, such corpus evidence should be both genre-comprehensive as well as statistically validated in order to count as the result of a 'corpus-driven' approach (Deignan, 2005, 2008). The corpus samples for *body politic* and its cognates in other European languages that have been collected so far fall short of these ideals and constitute only 'corpus-based' evidence but by comparison with other data collections in the research literature, they seem to be the largest and most wide-ranging sample on *body politic* metaphors available at the moment. Within the corpus, the distribution patterns, i.e. relative frequencies of terms, phrases and their collocations, yield the primary data for both quantitative and qualitative analyses. Syntactic contexts and genre-specificity may turn out to provide further important research avenues (Deignan, 2008: 284–5, 287–9).

To reach a full discourse-historical 'triangulation', we would also need detailed evidence from social science and historical research on the socio-historical context, which could only been hinted at here. However, even in the absence of a fully comprehensive interdisciplinary analysis, the corpus-based evidence can go a long way in reconstructing a plausible version of the discourse traditions in question, as it also includes meta-communicative and intertextual relationships of metaphoric texts. Allusions, referenced or unattributed quotations and comments provide evidence for discourse-historical explanations by the users, provided they are critically assessed for their representativeness and accuracy. In the German and French samples, for instance, references to discourse-precedents such as Nazi-jargon or famous philosophical works are relatively frequent. By comparison, British politicians' and journalists' wordplays on the physical/virtual *body politic* may remind some hearers/readers of famous precedents but hardly ever mention historical models. A special case is that of loan metaphors such as *the sick man of Europe*, which dates back to the eighteenth century as a reference to the Ottoman Empire, but is nowadays routinely used to evaluate the relative political and economic strength of EU member states (Musolff, 2004: 134). Its use is often accompanied by more or less correct historical explanations, even in the British press.[17]

Lastly, the analysis of the argumentative exploitation of metaphors, which is particularly prominent in political discourse, provides a further layer of evidence for the recurrent use of discourse-specific 'metaphor scenarios'. Scenarios are a subtype of cognitive schemas which, in addition to an 'event structure' based on the SOURCE-PATH-GOAL-SCHEMA (Kövecses, 2002: 134–6; 2005: 43–7), contain sufficient conceptual material to form a mini-story and suggest a preferred or default goal/solution (Lakoff, 1987: 285–6; Musolff, 2006; Semino, 2008: 219–22). BODY-based metaphors of state/society typically invoke a scenario with at least one participant, i.e. the imagined body/person entity, plus an event structure that presupposes a goal of self-preservation of that entity. This goal provides the yardstick to evaluate fundamental propositions about the *body politic*'s STATE OF HEALTH, its FREEDOM TO MOVEMENT and COHERENCE OF ACTION. It is here where the discourse-historical evidence of antecedent metaphor uses becomes particularly important. Allusions to the problematic status of *Volkskörper* in current German public discourse, for instance, would be incomprehensible if the audience were wholly unaware of the associated, highly charged scenario in Nazi propaganda, which depicted perceived political/racial enemies as *parasites on the people's body*. The Nazi-preferred 'therapeutic' solution to this threat was the elimination of such *parasites*, which was literally enacted in the form of genocide (Musolff, 2007, 2010a). The shared knowledge of that 'final solution' and its historical impact makes uses of *Volkskörper* in mainstream German public discourse problematic to this day. Similarly, the interdependence of social, political and electoral body in the French data is not just a re-'instantiation' of philosophical concepts used by Rousseau and other Enlightenment thinkers but it reopens the arguments in their debates about the relationship between state and society. As the author of the comment in example (12) explicitly states, the STATE-BODY metaphor in its Rousseauan version 'is by no means neutral' because it presupposes the notion of a 'singular unity of intention' of the political body's will (see also example (13)). It follows that in order to retain the ability/freedom to act, the whole body must obey the will of the body's *mind/brain*.[18] If any part of the body is threatened, the whole of society and electorate must act as one. Thus conceived, the STATE-BODY metaphor again contains a strong argumentative bias suggesting a specific course of action (i.e., unquestioning obedience to the state authorities, which is what the author of (12) asks his readers to reflect critically, in order to understand better the present-day changes in French society).

Even the seemingly playful punning on the *double entendre* of the English phrase *body politic* as designating physical and political standing/appearance, which we found as a prominent pattern in British discourse, has an argumentative and narrative logic that favours a specific evaluative conclusion. Examples such as (14) and (15) which ostensibly ridicule a politician's physique only make sense if one assumes that a successful politician should also have an attractive body appearance. Examples such as (16) and Johnson's self-mockery as a *toenail in the body politic* rely on the assumption that the politician as a *part of the body politic* needs to be strong (in order to survive a *punch* to the *solar plexus*) or a *valuable limb* (in contrast to mere *toenail-* or *pustule-* status). In all these cases, an idealized BODY concept is presupposed, against which other body-forms can be judged. Whilst such judgements and their underlying assumptions about 'ideal bodies' would probably be considered sexist, ageist, racist and offensive, were they publicly applied to 'real-life' bodies, they seem to be acceptable when used metaphorically.

The fact that these presuppositions are ultimately based on universally shared body experience in no way reduces their socio-cultural 'constructedness'. The pre-scientific, folk-theoretical nature of such assumptions about the body does not entail that they are simple, unmediated reflections of physically measurable facts. All publicly articulated knowledge about the body, whether scientific or pre-scientific, is culturally mediated, historically situated and differentially distributed in discourse communities:

there is thus no universally identical concept BODY but at best a range of stereotypical assumptions that are ordered around salient BODY prototypes (Lakoff, 1987). It would be a fascinating further study to analyse which precise BODY prototypes are invoked as source concepts in different discourse traditions and whether they can also be related to historically prominent shared experiences. To do this, it would be necessary to study the full range of source concepts for each discourse community.

# 4 Conclusions

The analyses presented here provide only a small glimpse of a comprehensive comparison of usage patterns of the STATE-BODY metaphor in English, French and German public discourses. Nonetheless, some tentative conclusions can be drawn as regards the hypothesis of discourse traditions shaping the emergence of divergent pathways of political imagery in national cultures. We have related the patterns in the semantic variation of this shared conceptual metaphor across usage data from three languages to prominent historical model formulations that go back decades or even centuries. The main explanatory basis for making this linkage is the assumption that the lexical, collocational and textual data from the research corpus echo certain salient formulations from the respective national discourse cultures. It is not claimed that present-day users are necessarily aware of these precise formulations; explicit referencing to specific texts is only typical in certain discourse registers, such as quasi-scholarly comment articles in the quality press. However, it is claimed that members of the respective communities do have at least an approximative awareness of the discourse-historical status of phrases such as *body politic, corps politique* or *Volkskörper*, as not just being metaphorical but also connected to popular political memories, mythologies and famous (and infamous) formulations of ideologically charged concepts. In order to be at all accessible for a wider discourse community, these awareness and knowledge structures have to be non-expert, over-simplifying and may even be factually wrong. They are semantically represented in the form of an allusive or associative meaning aura with extremely 'fuzzy' conceptual boundaries, rather than as well-defined categories – the latter may well feature only in expert sub-cultures, such as the community of Conceptual Historians. For this reason, it is only to be expected that their public users, e.g. politicians or journalists, will try to deny these associations if they sense that they have made a discourse-tactical mistake. Thus, when the former Finance Senator of Berlin and member of the Board of Directors of the Federal German Reserve Bank, Thilo Sarrazin, came under attack for using the scenario of the 'people's body (*Volkskörper*)' in his bestselling book against immigration into Germany,[19] he denied all allegations of closeness to Nazi jargon and ideology.[20] A critically oriented discourse-historical approach can expose such defences as hypocritical by identifying the specific antecedents of such metaphor use and demonstrating their enduring relevance for topical discourses.

**Table 2.1** Main concepts of metaphor field centred on THE STATE IS A (HUMAN) BODY in British English, French and German media discourses

| Super-categories<br><br>Body | Categories | Samples<br><br>English | French | German |
|---|---|---|---|---|
| | 1. Body | X | X | X |
| | 2. Organism | X | | X |
| | 3. Immune system | X | X | |
| | 4. Vitality | | | X |
| - *life-death* | 5. Birth | X | | |
| | 6. Life | X | | X |
| | 7. Death | X | X | X |
| - *monster* | 8. Monster | X | | |
| **Anatomy-physiology** | | | | |
| | 9. Anatomy | | | X |
| | 10. Arm | | X | |
| | 11. Arteries | X | | |
| | 12. Blood | X | | X |
| | 13. Brain/mind | | X | X |
| | 14. Capillaries | | | X |
| | 15. DNA | X | | |
| | 16. Foot | | | X |
| | 17. Gall-bladder | X | | |
| | 18. Hand | X | | |
| | 19. Head | X | X | X |
| | 20. Heart | X | | |
| | 21. Leg | | X | |
| | 22. Limb/member | | X | X |
| | 23. Liver | X | | |

| | | | |
|---|:---:|:---:|:---:|
| 24. Lung | | | X |
| 25. Muscles | X | | |
| 26. Organ | | X | X |
| 27. Root canal | X | | |
| 28. Skeleton | | X | |
| 29. Nerves | | | X |
| 30. Solar plexus | X | | |
| 31. Toenail | X | | |
| **State of health** | | | |
| *- good state of health* | | | |
| 32. Healthy | X | X | |
| 33. Immunity | X | | |
| 34. Virility | | X | |
| *- bad state of health* | | | |
| 35. Allergy | X | | |
| 36. Boil | | | X |
| 37. Bump | | | X |
| 38. Blood clot | X | | |
| 39. Cancer | X | X | X |
| 40. Canker | X | | |
| 41. Cirrhosis | X | | |
| 42. Coma | X | | |
| 43. Cyst | X | | |
| 44. Disease | X | X | |
| 45. Epidemic-pandemic | X | | |
| 46. Fever | X | | X |
| 47. Gangrene | | X | |
| 48. Heart attack | | | X |

(*Continued*)

**Table 2.1**   Continued

| Super-categories | Categories | Samples | | |
|---|---|---|---|---|
| State of health | | English | French | German |
| | 49. Influenza | X | | |
| | 50. Infection | X | | X |
| | 51. Neuralgia | X | | |
| | 52. Pain | X | | |
| | 53. Paralysis | X | | |
| | 54. Pathology | X | | |
| | 55. Plague | X | | |
| | 56. Rot, disintegration | X | X | |
| | 57. Sclerosis | X | | |
| | 58. Sick man | X | | |
| | 59. Symptom | X | | X |
| | 60. Temperature | | | X |
| | 61. Tuberculosis | | | X |
| | 62. Tumour | X | | X |
| - agent of disease | | | | |
| | 63. Alien body | | X | X |
| | 64. Bloodsucker-leech | | | X |
| | 65. Contagion | X | | |
| | 66. Microbes | | | X |
| | 67. Parasite | X | X | X |
| | 68. Poison | X | | X |
| | 69. Splinter | | X | |
| | 70. Tentacles | X | | |
| | 71. Vermin | | X | |
| | 72. Virus | X | | X |
| | 73. Zit | X | | |

| *- injury* | | | |
|---|:-:|:-:|:-:|
| 74. Bruise | | | X |
| 75. Disembowel | X | | |
| 76. Dismember | X | | |
| 77. Fracture | | X | |
| 78. Germ warfare | X | | |
| 79. Wound | X | X | X |
| *- therapy* | | | |
| 80. Amputation | | | X |
| 81. Cleansing | | | X |
| 82. Diagnosis | | | X |
| 83. Doctor | | | X |
| 84. Diet | X | | |
| 85. Infusion | | | X |
| 86. Life-support machine | X | | |
| 87. Medicine | X | X | |
| 88. Operation | X | | X |
| 89. Probe | | | X |
| 90. Relief | X | | |
| 91. Root canal tratment | | | X |
| 92. Sex change | | | X |
| 93. Therapy | X | X | X |
| 94. Vaccinate | | X | |
| **Body aesthetic** | | | |
| 95. Pimple | X | | |
| 96. Pustule | X | | |
| 97. Wart | X | | |

# Notes

1 For dictionary entries on these phrases see Deignan, 1995: 2; Room, 1999: 149, 713; Trumble and Stevenson, 2002, vol. 1: 258.

2 Earlier results from pilot studies of this corpus have been published in Musolff, 2010c, 2012.

3 Translations of this and following examples and the highlighting of relevant metaphorical expressions through italicization by AM, unless otherwise indicated.

4 *Staatskörper* and *Körper des Staates* also seem to be the oldest expressions, being recorded in dictionaries dating back to the seventeenth century (see Musolff, 2010a: 122–8).

5 Apart from its use in example (3), which relates to a series of high-profile political scandals and ensuing politicians' resignations in Germany, the corpus only contains instances of *politischer Körper* that refer to the USA as a *body politic*, including reviews of a book on 'Obama's body politic' (Haltern, 2009). In contrast to the other German variants, *politischer Körper* thus seems to be perceived as a concept primarily connected with US-American political issues.

6 See Musolff, 2007, 2010a: 23–68. Significantly, *Volkskörper* is used up to the mid-1960s in a more neutral sense as a synonym of *Staatskörper*, i.e. designating any kind of nation state without a critical political slant and no special connection to German history. The later sensitization for the historical and political associations of *Volkskörper*, which can be observed in the corpus, seems to have been part of the process of the German public's 'coming to terms' with the Holocaust from the 1960s onwards (see Eitz and Stötzel, 2007; Niven, 2002).

7 For further pertinent passages depicting the *corps politique* see Rousseau, 1990: 82 (Book I, chapter 4: *Du Pacte Social*) and p. 250 (Book III, chapter 11: *De la Mort du Corps Politique*); for interpretations of Rousseau's linkage between society and state see Derathé, 2000; Bertram, 2003; Wraight, 2008.

8 See A. Renaud, 'Squelettiques métaphores politique', in *Libération*, 21/03/1995; G. Agamben, 'La double identité du peuple', in *Libération*, 11/02/1995; B.-L. Lévy, 'Construire l'Europe politique, ou mourir', in *Le Point* 13/09/2012; interview with R. Debray, Denis Podalydès and Olivier Py, in *Le Monde*, 5/3/2011.

9 A US-English and International English sample exists within the wider corpus but is not taken into consideration here. The following remarks are only based on the British English sample.

10 E.g. with reference to the German political party CDU in *The Guardian*, 3 September 1994.

11 See *The Independent on Sunday*, 20 November 2005 and *BBC Newsnight*, 5 October 2009. Johnson seems to be fond of *body politic*-related rhetoric and uses it to ridicule others even more savagely than himself. In 2009, for instance, he attacked the Labour advisor Damian McBride as 'this lately exploded pustule on the posterior of the British body politic' (*The Daily Telegraph*, 13 April 2009).

12 The assumption of 'optimal relevance' is a constitutive principle for linguistic communication in Sperber and Wilson's *Relevance Theory* (1995: 158). It does not stipulate that communicators always achieve optimal relevance but that they intend their addressees to believe that they do, in terms of a trade-off between the maximum

of 'contextual effects' and a minimum of 'processing effort' in understanding utterances (1995: 125). For discussions of the ramifications of relevance theory for cognitive metaphor analysis see Gibbs and Tendahl, 2006, 2011; Sperber and Wilson, 2008; Tendahl, 2009; Tendahl and Gibbs, 2008; Wilson, 2011; Wilson and Carston, 2006.

**13** One of the most likely transmitters of the King's *mystical/political body* concept in Britain are Shakespeare's works, which continue to be an integral part of popular British culture through school, theatre and mass media. Bodily symbolism and analogies of physiological and political entities pervade Shakespeare's historical dramas and tragedies; see Diede, 2008; Jagendorf, 1990; Patterson, 1991; Peltonen, 2009; Spicci, 2007; Tillyard, 1982.

**14** Kövecses (2002: 133–4 and 2005: 208–215) provides detailed analyses of the conceptual metaphor ABSTRACT COMPLEX SYSTEMS-ARE-PHYSICAL OBJECTS as being based on primary (source-) 'internally grounded' knowledge which is mapped into an 'abstract generic mental space' and thus becomes itself available as a target domain for entailments which may seem at first sight literal and abstract but are in fact derived from concrete source domain concepts (such as, for instance, growth of plans/ organisms as source for concepts of system development).

**15** For BODY-based metonymies for person as grounding for metaphors see Boers, 1999; Pauwels and Simon-Vandenbergen, 1995.

**16** See in particular the comparison of English and Chinese metaphors by Yu (1998, 2003, 2008) and the work by Kövecses (2002, 2005).

**17** Cf. e.g. *The Economist*, 5 June 1999: 'Germany is unlikely soon to shed its title as the sick man of Europe. [. . .] Germans must find it more galling since it was coined in the last century by the Russian tsar, Nicholas I, to describe Ottoman Turkey – a once dynamic polity that failed'.

**18** In Rousseau's analogy, the *mind/brain* is the equivalent of the executive power, the *heart* that of the legislative power; see Rousseau, 1990: 256–8 (1994: 121–2).

**19** See *Profil*, 30 September 2011.

**20** His main defence was that he had also cited 'American and Jewish scientists' (see *Frankfurter Rundschau*, 19 May 2012; *Der Standard*, 28 July 2012), which apparently was supposed to absolve him from all charges of racism.

# References

Bertelli, S. (2001), *The King's Body. Sacred Rituals of Power in Medieval and Early Modern Europe*. University Park, PA: Pennsylvania State University Press.

Bertram, C. (2003), *Rousseau and The Social Contract*. London: Routledge.

Boers, F. (1999), 'When a bodily source domain becomes prominent', in R. W. Gibbs and G. Steen (eds), *Metaphor in Cognitive Linguistics*. Amsterdam: Benjamins, pp. 47–56.

Boisnard, P. (2005), 'Le corps politique, un malade à la recherche de sa thérapie'. *Multitudes. Revue politique, artistique, philosophique*, 50. Available at http://multitudes. samizdat.net/Le-corps-politique-un-malade-a-la (accessed 10 February 2013).

Bourdieu, P. (1990), 'Structures, habitus, practices', in P. Bourdieu (ed.), *The Logic of Practice*. Stanford, CA: Stanford University Press, pp. 52–79.

Charbonnel, N. (2010), *Comme un seul home. Corps politique et corps mystique*, 2 vols. Lons Le Saunier: Aréopage.

Croft, W. (2000), *Explaining Language Change: An Evolutionary Approach*. London: Longman.

Croft, W. and Cruse, D. A. (2004), *Cognitive Linguistics*. Cambridge: Cambridge University Press.

Deignan, A. (ed.) (1995), *Collins COBUILD English Guides 7. Metaphors*. London: HarperCollins.

Deignan, A. (2005), *Metaphor and Corpus Linguistics*. Amsterdam/Philadelphia: John Benjamins.

—— (2008), 'Corpus linguistics and metaphor', in R. W. Gibbs (ed.), *The Cambridge Handbook of Metaphor and Thought*. Cambridge: Cambridge University Press, pp. 280–94.

Derathé, R. (2000), *Jean-Jacques Rousseau et la science politique de son temps*. Paris: Vrin.

Diede, M. K. (2008), *Shakespeare's Knowledgeable Body*. Bern, New York: Peter Lang.

Eitz, T. and Stötzel, G. (2007), *Wörterbuch der 'Vergangenheitsbewältigung': Die NS-Vergangenheit im öffentlichen Sprachgebrauch*. Hildesheim: Olms.

Frank, R. M. (2009), 'Shifting identities: metaphors of discourse evolution', in A. Musolff and J. Zinken (eds), *Metaphor and Discourse*. Basingstoke: Palgrave Macmillan, pp. 173–89.

Gibbs, R. W. and Tendahl, M. (2006), 'Cognitive effort and effects in metaphor comprehension: relevance theory and psycholinguistics'. *Mind & Language*, 21(3), 379–403.

—— (2011), 'Coupling of metaphoric cognition and communication: a reply to Deirdre Wilson'. *Intercultural Pragmatics*, 8(4), 601–9.

Gibbs, R. W., Jr. (2005), *Embodiment and Cognitive Science*. Cambridge: Cambridge University Press.

Gontier, N. (2010), 'On constructing a research model for historical cognitive linguistics (HCL): some theoretical considerations', in M. E. Winters, H. Tissari and K. Allan (eds), *Historical Cognitive Linguistics*. Berlin and New York: De Gruyter Mouton, pp. 31–69.

Grady, J. and Johnson, C. (2003), 'Converging evidence for the notions of subscene and primary scene', in R. Dirven and R. Pörings (eds), *Metaphor and Metonymy in Comparison and Contrast*. Berlin: De Gruyter, pp. 533–54.

Hale, D. G. (1971), *The Body Politic. A Political Metaphor in Renaissance English Literature*. The Hague/Paris: Mouton.

Haltern, U. (2009), *Obamas politischer Körper*. Berlin: Berlin University Press.

Horten, O. (2009), *Kantorowicz, Rousseau, Büchner: Die Übertragung des 'body politic' vom König auf das Volk*. Munich: GRIN.

Hughes, G. (1988), *Words in Time: A Social History of the English Vocabulary*. Oxford: Blackwell.

Jagendorf, Z. (1990), 'Coriolanus: body politic and private parts', *Shakespeare Quarterly*, 41(4), 455–69.

Johnson, M. (1987), *The Body in the Mind. The Bodily Basis of Meaning, Imagination, and Reason*. Chicago: University of Chicago Press.

Kantorowicz, E. H. (1997), *The King's Two Bodies: A Study in Mediaeval Political Theology*. Preface by W. C. Jordan. Princeton, NJ: Princeton University Press.

Koschorke, A., Lüdemann, S., Frank, T. and Matala de Mazza, E. (2007), *Der fiktive Staat. Konstruktionen des politischen Körpers in der Geschichte Europas*. Frankfurt am Main: Fischer.

Kövecses, Z. (2002), *Metaphor: A Practical Introduction*. Oxford: Oxford University Press.

—— (2005), *Metaphor in Culture: Universality and Variation*. Cambridge: Cambridge University Press.

Lakoff, G. (1987), *Women, Fire and Dangerous Things: What Categories Reveal about the Mind*. Chicago: University of Chicago Press.

—— (2008), 'The neural theory of metaphor', in R. W. Gibbs (ed.), *The Cambridge Handbook of Metaphor and Thought*, Cambridge: Cambridge University Press, pp. 17–38.

Lakoff, G. and Johnson, M. (1999), *Philosophy in the Flesh: The Embodied Mind and its Challenge to Western Thought*. New York: Basic Books.

Lakoff, G. and Turner, M. (1989), *More than Cool Reason. A Field Guide to Poetic Metaphor*. Chicago and London: University of Chicago Press.

Musolff, A. (2004), *Metaphor and Political Discourse. Analogical Reasoning in Debates about Europe*. Basingstoke: Palgrave Macmillan.

—— (2006), 'Metaphor scenarios in public discourse', *Metaphor and Symbol*, 21(1), 23–38.

—— (2007), 'Which role do metaphors play in racial prejudice? – The function of anti-Semitic imagery in Hitler's Mein Kampf', *Patterns of Prejudice*, 41, 21–44.

—— (2009), 'Metaphor in the History of Ideas and Discourses: How can we interpret a medieval version of the body–state analogy?', in A. Musolff and J. Zinken (eds), *Metaphor and Discourse*. Basingstoke: Palgrave Macmillan, pp. 233–47.

—— (2010a), *Metaphor, Nation and the Holocaust. The Concept of the Body Politic*. London/New York: Routledge.

—— (2010b), 'Metaphor in discourse history', in M. E. Winters, H. Tissari, and A. Allan (eds), *Historical Cognitive Linguistics*. Berlin and New York: De Gruyter Mouton, pp. 70–90.

—— (2012), 'Cultural differences in the understanding of the metaphor of the "Body Politic"', in S. Kleinke, Z. Kövecses, A. Musolff and V. Szelid (eds), *Cognition and Culture. The Role of Metaphor and Metonymy*. Budapest: Eötvös University Press, pp. 145–53.

Nedermann, C. J. (ed.) (1992), *Medieval Political Thought – A Reader: The Quest for the Body Politic*. London/New York: Routledge.

Nedermann, C. J. (2004), 'Body politics: the diversification of organic metaphors in the later Middle Ages', *Pensiero politico medievale*, 2, 59–87.

Niven, W. (2002), *Facing the Nazi Past: United Germany and the Legacy of the Third Reich*. London: Routledge.

Patterson, A. M. (1991), *Fables of Power: Aesopian Writing and Political History*. Durham, NC: Duke University Press.

Pauwels, P. and Simon-Vandenbergen, A.-M. (1995), 'Body parts in linguistic action: underlying schemata and value judgements', in L. Goossens, P. Pauwels, B. Rudzka-Ostyn, A.-M. Simon-Vandenbergen and J. Vanparys (eds), *By Word of Mouth: Metaphor, Metonymy and Linguistic Action in Cognitive Perspective*. Amsterdam: Benjamins, pp. 35–69.

Peltonen, M. (2009), 'Political rhetoric and citizenship in *Coriolanus*', in D. Armitage, C. Condren, A. Fitzmaurice (eds), *Shakespeare and Early Modern Political Thought*. Cambridge: Cambridge University Press, pp. 234–52.

Reisigl, M. and Wodak, R. (2001), *Discourse and Discrimination. Rhetorics of Racism and Antisemitism.* London and New York: Routledge.

Room, A. (ed.) (1999), *Brewer's Dictionary of Phrase and Fable.* London: Cassell.

Rousseau, J.-J. (1990), *Du Contrat Social. Texte et Contextes*, ed. J. Médina, A. Senik, C. Morali, G. Chomienne. Paris: Magnard.

—— (1994), *The Social Contract*, transl. C. Betts. Oxford: Oxford University Press.

—— (2002), *Discours sur l'économie politique*, Texte et Commentaire. Paris: Vrin.

Semino, E. (2008), *Metaphor in Discourse.* Cambridge: Cambridge University Press.

Sperber, D. and Wilson, D. (1995), *Relevance.* Oxford: Blackwell.

—— (2008), 'A deflationary account of metaphors', in R. W. Gibbs (ed.), *The Cambridge Handbook of Metaphor and Thought.* Cambridge/New York: Cambridge University Press, pp. 84–104.

Spicci, M. (2007), 'The body as metaphor: digestive bodies and political surgery in Shakespeare's *Macbeth*', *Medical Humanities*, 33, 67–9.

Tendahl, M. (2009), *A Hybrid Theory of Metaphor: Relevance Theory and Cognitive Linguistics.* Basingstoke: Palgrave Macmillan.

Tendahl, M. and Gibbs, R.W. (2008), 'Complementary perspectives on metaphor: cognitive linguistic and relevance theory', *Journal of Pragmatics*, 40(1), 1823–64.

Tillyard, E. M. W. (1982), *The Elizabethan World Picture.* Harmondsworth: Penguin.

Trumble, W. R. and Stevenson, A. (eds) (2002), *Shorter Oxford English Dictionary* (5th edn). 2 vols. Oxford/New York: Oxford University Press.

Wilson, D. (2011), 'Parallels and differences in the treatment of metaphor in relevance theory and linguistics', *Intercultural Pragmatics*, 8(2), 177–96.

Wilson, D. and Carston, R. (2006), 'Metaphor, relevance and the emergent property' issue', *Mind & Language*, 21, 404–33.

Wodak, R. (2007). 'Critical discourse analysis', in C. Seale, G. Gobo. J. F. Gubrium and D. Silverman (eds), *Qualitative Research Practice.* London: Sage, pp. 185–201.

—— 'The discourse-historical approach', in R. Wodak and M. Meyer (eds), *Methods of Critical Discourse Analysis. Introducing Qualitative Methods.* London: Sage, pp. 63–94.

Wraight, C. D. (2008), *Rousseau's* The Social Contract: *A Reader's Guide.* London: Continuum Books.

Yu, N. (1998), *The Contemporary Theory of Metaphor: A Perspective from Chinese.* Amsterdam/Philadelphia: Benjamins.

—— (2003), 'Metaphor, body and culture: the Chinese understanding of gallbladder and courage', *Metaphor and Symbol*, 18, 13–31.

—— (2008), 'Metaphor from body and culture', in R. W. Gibbs (ed), *The Cambridge Handbook of Metaphor and Thought.* Cambridge: Cambridge University Press, pp. 247–61.

# ARGUMENTATION

# 3

# Argumentation Analysis and the Discourse-Historical Approach

# A Methodological Framework

*Martin Reisigl*
University of Bern

## 1 Introduction

The Discourse-Historical Approach is one of two versions of Critical Discourse Analysis (CDA) with a strong and organized focus on argumentation. The second version is that developed by Isabela Ieţcu-Fairclough and Norman Fairclough (see, e.g., Ieţcu, 2006a, 2006b; Ieţcu-Fairclough, 2007; Fairclough and Fairclough, 2010, 2012, 2013).[1]

The following chapter will only focus on the Discourse-Historical Approach to the critical analysis of argumentation. It will outline basic conceptual and methodological assumptions about the nature of argumentation and the relationship between argumentation analysis and the Discourse-Historical Approach. The main ideas to be presented and explained in the following have been clear for many years, but it is the first time that they are summarized for the English language readership. There is an urgency to explain them in English, because there circulate several misunderstandings in the English-speaking scientific community of critical discourse analysts with respect to the relationship between argumentation analysis and the Discourse-Historical Approach. One of my central goals is to do away with some of these confusions by offering a theoretical and methodological contribution and by responding to major criticisms.

The chapter is divided into six parts. First, I will sketch a short history of the Discourse-Historical approach to argumentation. Then, I will explain my general understanding of the notion of argumentation (loosely following Josef Kopperschmidt, who is – unfortunately – hardly known to English-only readers). Third, some explanatory hints are given with respect to the relationship of argumentation, explanation and narration. The fourth part will briefly outline a methodological framework for the formal-structural, content-related and normative argumentation analysis from the perspective of the Discourse-Historical Approach. Fifth, I will comment on three strands of criticism of the Discourse-Historical Approach and its methods of argumentation analysis, hoping to be able to refute most of these criticisms. Finally, I will draw some conclusions.

## 2  Argumentation analysis and the Discourse-Historical Approach: A brief history

The DHA's interest in argumentation analysis dates back to the second half of the 1980s, when strategies of justification were focused in on the historically oriented studies of post-war discourses about the Austrian involvement in National Socialism and Anti-Semitism (Wodak et al., 1990). At that time, the integration of argumentation analytical categories into the approach was still quite arbitrary. The research team occasionally referred to Habermas, Kienpointner, Kopperschmidt, Perelman, Toulmin and Völzing.

In the study of the discursive construction of national identity (Wodak et al., 1998; Wodak et al., 2009[1999]: 35–42), we extended the analytical focus in order to be able to grasp various groups of argumentation strategies that promote the construction, justification or relativization, reproduction, transformation and destruction of national identification and identity and images of the nation and its past. Already in this study, the concepts of *topos* and *locus* were clearly conceived of as argumentation analytical categories and not as literary motifs or common places, as has been falsely suggested by Igor Žagar (2010: 21). However, at that time, no clear and systematic distinction between sound and fallacious argumentation schemes was made, though a normative alignment of the approach to argumentation was already essential. One important reason for not having offered lots of schematic reconstructions of argumentation in the book is a banal pragmatic one: the book was first published in German by Suhrkamp (in 1998), and this publishing house prefers continuous text without formal analysis and does not like to include too many figures, tables and diagrams in the small paperback format. However, the second edition of the English translation contains an additional chapter that summarizes the development of the discourse on the Austrian nation and identity between 1995 and 2008. This chapter is already based on a clear methodical distinction between sound argumentation schemes and fallacies (Wodak et al., 2009[1999]: 220–31).

The book *Discourse and Discrimination* represents a further development: it makes reference to the ten pragma-dialectical rules for critical discussion in order to be able to distinguish sound from fallacious argumentation (Reisigl and Wodak, 2001: 69–80). It explicitly introduces and defines the concept of *topos*, as it has been elaborated by Manfred Kienpointner (1992, 1996) and Martin Wengeler (1997), whose articles and books are scarcely known by the English-language readership. The definition of *topos* was not exclusively formal, but also field- and content-oriented. This orientation towards the contents of argumentation schemes – although still on a rather abstract level – was particularly due to the work of Martin Wengeler, and partly also inspired by Kindt (1992) and Kienpointner, Kindt (1997).

The reference to the Pragma-Dialectical rules did not mean that the whole model of critical discussion was adopted. There are various points on which I do not follow Pragma-Dialectics (see below, section 6.1). Besides Pragma-Dialectics, the work of Josef Kopperschmidt serves as a basic point of orientation. The integration of Kopperschmidt's work into the argumentation theoretical framework (e.g. Kopperschmidt 1989, 2000) is not acknowledged by English readers, because most of the relevant texts are in German (Reisigl, 2003a, 2004, 2005, 2006, 2007a, 2007b, 2007c). Kopperschmidt developed an abstract argumentation theory that strongly relies on Habermas.

The Discourse-Historical Approach, as I understand it, connects formal, functional and content-related aspects of argumentation in an integrative framework. However, it is particularly interested in the analysis of contents of argumentation schemes. This approach to Critical Discourse Analysis tries to distinguish between sound and fallacious argumentation, where possible. The normative basis for this distinction are – first and foremost – the pragma-dialectical rules of critical discussion.

The Discourse-Historical Approach is the only school of Critical Discourse Analysis that includes argumentation and multi-perspectivity as formal constitutive elements (cf. fn. 1) in the theoretical conception of 'discourse'. According to this approach, macro-topic-relatedness, pluri-perspectivity, and argumentativity are crucial elements of any discourse. That is to say: 'discourse' is considered to be:

(a) a complex of context-dependent semiotic practices that are situated within specific fields of social action (in political contexts: the fields of law making procedure, of the formation of public opinion, attitude and will, of political administration, of political advertising, of political control or protest, etc.);

(b) socially constituted as well as socially constitutive;

(c) related to a macro-topic and to the argumentation about validity claims (truth and normative rightness), which involves social actors with different perspectives (see Reisigl and Wodak, 2009: 89).

In contrast to this understanding of 'discourse', Norman Fairclough's approach to discourse leaves open the question of how the theoretical concept of discourse relates to argumentation: '[. . .] a discourse is a way of signifying a particular domain of social practice from a particular perspective, and a genre may predictably draw upon a particular range of discourses, though a given discourse may be drawn upon in various genres.' (Fairclough, 1995: 14; see also Fairclough, 2010: 96). Here, one perspective correlates to one discourse, whereas argumentation always involves more than one perspective and should thus be an inter-discursive phenomenon. As a theoretical consequence, the analysis of argumentation should always imply the analysis of various discourses. It is not clear for me how Fairclough's approach grasps the interdiscursive nature of argumentation from a methodological point of view, and how it theoretically conceptualizes an argumentation-related dialogic interaction between arguers in terms of discourse analysis and genre theory.

## 3  The notion of 'argumentation': A general characterization

My conception of argumentation follows the theory of Josef Kopperschmidt. According to Kopperschmidt, who further develops Habermas, argumentation is a non-violent linguistic as well as cognitive pattern of problem-solving that manifests itself in a more or less regulated sequence of speech acts which, altogether, form a complex and more or less coherent network of statements or utterances. Argumentation serves the methodical challenging or justification of validity claims such as truth and normative rightness (Kopperschmidt, 2000: 59 f.). Its basic purpose is to persuade – either in the sense of convincing by sound arguments or in the sense of influencing somebody suggestively and manipulatively by fallacies. Whereas the validity claim of truth relates to questions of knowledge, epistemic certainty and theoretical insight, the validity claim of normative rightness relates to practical questions of how to do the right thing, i.e. to questions of practical norms or ethical and moral standards, to questions of what should be done or must not be done or what is recommended or forbidden. A great deal of what Fairclough and Fairclough (2011, 2012) discuss under the labels of 'practical reasoning', 'practical arguments' and 'claim for action' relates to the validity claim of normative rightness.

As Kopperschmidt convincingly argues, argumentation is not an autonomous speech act per se – such as an assertion or a declaration. There are no argumentative or conclusive speech acts as such, as scholars of argumentation theory sometimes assume. Under certain conditions, all types of speech acts can fulfil an argumentative function (Kopperschmidt, 2000: 59). However, the validity claim of truth is prototypically performed by an assertive speech act or takes the form of an assertive speech act at the level of the pragmatic deep structure, whereas the validity claim of normative rightness prototypically assumes the form of a directive speech act at the level of the pragmatic deep structure (where the primary illocutionary act may be paraphrased as: 'Do x!', 'Don't do x!'). Obviously, the literally uttered secondary illocutionary act often deviates from the intended primary illocutionary act. This complicates argumentation analysis. Relying on Habermas' distinction between the four validity claims of truth, normative rightness, truthfulness (honesty, sincerity) and understandability, we can idealize the relationships between types of speech act, their functions and primarily involved validity claims. This is shown in Table 3.1.

**Table 3.1** The relationship between types of speech act, functions and validity claims

| Type of speech act | Function and example | Primarily involved validity claim |
|---|---|---|
| **expressive speech act** | performs the function of expressing feelings:<br>*Thank you very much!* | **truthfulness** with respect to the sincerity of feelings |
| **declarative speech act** (including assertive declarations) | performs the function of making the uttered propositional content become reality by the act of utterance, thus changing reality:<br>*With this I declare this contract invalid.* | **truthfulness** (plus conventional procedure, adequate persons and circumstances, correct and complete performance of the procedure) |
| **assertive speech act** | performs the function of expressing that the speaker or writer makes a claim of truth:<br>*They will move to Bern. (High degree of certainty.)* | **truth** (the person who asserts something commits to knowing the truth); **can question any of the four validity claims** |
| **commissive speech act** | performs the function of expressing the willingness and commitment to fulfil an obligation in the future:<br>*I promise it to you.* | **truthfulness** with respect to the willingness to be committed |
| **interrogative speech act** (vs. Searle, who treats them as directives) | performs the function of expressing that a speaker or writer<br>(a) does not know something,<br>(b) wants to obtain the lacking information from the person who has been asked, and<br>(c) assumes that the asked person knows the answer:<br>*Why did you do that?* | **can question any of the four validity claims** (and simultaneously assumes a claim of **truth** in the sense that the other person should know the answer/truth) |
| **directive speech act** | performs the function to transfer the speaker's or writer's action plan to the addressee who is expected to do what the speaker or writer wants him or her to do (e.g. a request):<br>*Stop it!* | **normative rightness** |

understandability

Note that I do not follow Searle's proposal to consider questions to be a specific sub type of directive speech act, but prefer to assume two distinct types of speech act, since questions clearly differ from directive speech acts. They have another, i.e. more open, 'incomplete' propositional structure (see Wunderlich, 1976: 190 f., 235). There is a second distinctive characteristic of my understanding of the relationship between speech acts and argumentation: in contrast to Pragma-Dialectics (Van Eemeren and Grootendorst, 1984: 37 ff.) as well as Fairclough and Fairclough (e.g. 2012: 13, 18, 23, 95), I do not regard argumentation to be a speech act, macro-speech act or complex speech act, but consider argumentation as an abstract pattern of text formation or discourse formation (see below). There are at least two reasons for this terminological decision: (1) In contrast to 'speech act', the concept of 'macro-speech act' or 'complex speech act' is theoretically underdeveloped. We have a pragmatically rather well-defined typology of speech acts (more or less at sentence level), but no elaborate theory of macro-speech acts or complex speech acts that makes a clear distinction between different types of macro-speech acts or complex speech acts. On the other hand, textlinguistics and discourse analysis offer a rather clear-cut distinction between basic patterns of text formation or discourse formation. They are narration, argumentation, explanation, description and instruction. (2) The indistinct use of the term 'speech act' for units of various order, functions, complexity and size levels conceptual differences that can be explicated by distinct terms. Thus, I prefer to use dissimilar terms for the metalinguistic description of different pragmatic units such as assertion and argumentation.

As already said, argumentation is an abstract pattern of text formation (in German: '*Vertextungsmuster*') or discourse formation (Kopperschmidt, 2000: 94). However, no argumentative text types or genres exist as such. Rather, we are faced with text types or genres (such as discussions, debates, reviews, forensic or judicial pleadings, scientific articles) that contain many elements of argumentation.

Not all elements or components of argumentation become linguistically manifest. Argumentation is frequently enthymemic, i.e. shortened on the linguistic surface structure. Each of its basic functional elements (argument, conclusion rule, claim) can potentially have been omitted and thus have to be completed 'en thymō', i.e. in the mind, by inference. This complicates argumentation analysis and especially the analytical distinction between sound and fallacious argumentation.

# 4 The relationship of argumentation, explanation and narration

As a basic pattern of text or discourse formation, argumentation can be theoretically distinguished from other elementary patterns of text formation such as explanation, narration, description and instruction. However, these patterns sometimes intersect.

As for the relationship between argumentation and explanation: argumentation can be conceived of as the linguistic and cognitive action pattern which follows the aim of justifying or questioning validity claims that have become problematic or have been questioned. In other words: argumentation has the pragmatic purpose of persuasion. Taking up Habermas's distinction between four validity claims, we can state that truth and normative rightness relate to argumentation in various theoretical and practical contexts of social life, whereas comprehensibility primarily relates to explanation – apart from the fact that it is a basic prerequisite and condition for successful communication (as indicated in Table 3.1). Pragma-Dialectics holds a similar view: 'While argumentation is an attempt to convince the listener of the acceptability of a standpoint with respect to a proposition, an explanation is aimed at increasing the listener's understanding of the proposition represented by the statement explained (explanandum)' (Snoeck Henkemans, 2001: 240).

That is to say: explanation can be conceived of as a primarily proposition-related linguistic and cognitive action pattern that aims at making something comprehensible, and consists in making something clear, clarifying something, rendering something more precisely or specifying something. Differently from argumentation, explanation is not produced by a controversial claim: 'In contrast to a justification, the starting claim of an explanation is not contested. The fact that water comes to the boil at 100 degrees Celsius is not questioned. This fact is rather accepted and taken as the starting point for a question of understanding. [. . .] Explanations do not try to justify or defend the starting claim, but to make it comprehensible' (Ecker, 2006: 29; see also Fairclough and Fairclough, 2012: 110).

At least three sub types of explanation can be distinguished: (1) Metalinguistic explanation makes the meanings of notions, words or texts explicit. (2) Instructive explanation aims to teach and enable somebody to use an object or to act in a procedural way – for instance by explaining how a machine apparatus works or is controlled. (3) Causal explanation represents and clarifies causal relationships between causes and effects, means and purposes or intentions/motives and results/consequences. It is this last form of explanation that cannot always neatly be separated from argumentation. This is particularly relevant for scientific contexts, where argumentation and explanation intertwine if (hypothetical) claims about causal relationships (causal explanations) are questioned and have thus to be justified with respect to a theoretical validity claim to truth. In science, the questioning need not always be 'uttered' by a real antagonist. It can also be realized as a self-critical internal interrogation or as a procataleptic anticipation of possible objections of others.

Apart from this sometimes complex relationship between argumentation and explanation, argumentation may also overlap with narration. This can happen in contexts where narrative episodes are told as illustrating examples that back a specific claim (illustrative argumentation scheme).

# 5 Methodology of argumentation analysis

Argumentation analysis can be done from different analytical perspectives. We can distinguish between (a) the functional, formal and content-related analysis of argumentation, (b) the analysis of the macro-, meso- or micro-structure of argumentation, (c) the analysis of the representation (coverage, report, quotation, etc.) of argumentation in contrast to the performing of argumentation, and (d) the analysis of sound in contrast to fallacious argumentation (see Kopperschmidt, 1989; Toulmin, 1969; Kienpointner, 1992, 1996; Wengeler, 1997, 2003). Of course, a combination of these perspectives is often the most prolific way of doing argumentation analysis. In the following sections, I will not focus on (b), i.e. the analysis of the macro-, meso-, and micro-structure of argumentation, though this part of structural analysis is also very important. The respective aspects of analysis relate to the distinction between different stages of argumentation, to questions of single and complex, multiple and compound as well as co-ordinate and subordinate argumentation and to questions of a corpus-based analysis of argumentation.

## 5.1 *Functional analysis of argumentation*

Stephen Toulmin (1969) proposes a functional approach to the analysis of the structure of argumentation that includes six basic elements and steps (a precursor of this functional model is Cicero's five-part concept of *epicheireme*; see Cicero 1998: I, 57–76: 56–123).

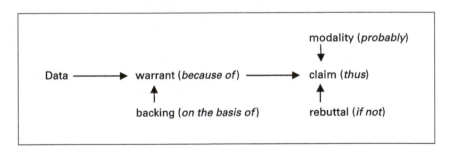

**FIGURE 3.1** *Toulmin's functional approach to argumentation.*

The six central elements are:

**(1)** *claim* (C): the statement/thesis in question, which is argued and has to be justified;

**(2)** *data/grounds* (D): the evidence, facts used to prove the claim;

(3) *warrant/conclusion rule* (CR): the hypothetical argumentation scheme that serves as a bridge between claim and data, that leads from the data to the claim (= topos; see below);

(4) *rebuttal* (R): the statement that indicates the condition or circumstances under which it is not possible to use the bridge/warrant;

(5) *backing* (B): a statement that supports the warrant, that helps to prove that the warrant/conclusion rule is true;

(6) *modality* (M): qualifier that indicates or limits the strength of the claim that is formulated on the basis of the data and the warrant.

Toulmin's functional model of argumentation can be reduced to three basic elements which each argumentation must contain explicitly or implicitly (Kienpointner, 1996: 75).

**FIGURE 3.2** *A simplified functional approach to argumentation.*

According to this simplified mode, the *argument* gives the reason for or against a controversial claim/thesis, the *conclusion rule* guarantees the connection of the argument to the *claim*, and the claim represents the disputed, contested statement that has to be justified or refuted (Kienpointner, 1996: 75).

## 5.2 *Formal analysis of argumentation*

The formal analysis of argumentation relies on the reduced functional model of argumentation which integrates the three basic elements just mentioned: argument – conclusion rule – claim. That is to say: the formal approach to argumentation analyses the structure of argumentation as syllogism. From the three elements, the conclusion rule is seen as the central element, since it connects the argument with the conclusion, the claim.

This conclusion rule is an argumentation scheme also known as *topos* (Greek for 'place') or *locus* (Latin for 'place'). *Topoi* can be described as central parts of argumentation that belong to the premises. They justify the transition from the argument(s) to the conclusion (Kienpointner, 1992: 194). *Topoi* are not always expressed explicitly, but can be made explicit as conditional or causal paraphrases such as 'if x, then y' or 'y, because x' (for more details see Reisigl and Wodak, 2001: 69–80). Focusing on these conclusion rules, Kienpointner (1996: 83–184) distinguishes between nine classes of content-abstract, i.e. formal argumentation schemes (a different typology and discussion of such content-abstract argumentation schemes is to be found in Kienpointner, 1992: 231–416):

**(1)** scheme or topos of definition

**(2)** scheme or topos of the species and the genus

**(3)** scheme or topos of comparison (scheme/topos of similarity, scheme/topos of difference)

**(4)** scheme or topos of the part and the whole

**(5)** causal scheme or causal topos (scheme or topos of cause/consequence and of intention)

**(6)** scheme or topos of contradiction

**(7)** scheme or topos of authority

**(8)** scheme or topos of example

**(9)** scheme or topos of analogy.

Let me illustrate the formal structure of these argumentation schemes or topoi by just giving two examples. The scheme or topos of authority can rely on epistemic authorities that are intoduced to justify a claim of truth or on deontic authorities that are referred to in order to justify a claim of normative rightness. This scheme or topos can formalized as follows:

**CR:**  If authority X says that A is true/that A has to be done, A is true/A has to be done.

**A:**  X says that A is true/that A has to be done.

**C:**  Thus, A is true/A has to be done.

The scheme or topos of similarity, which is a subtype of the scheme or topos of comparison (Kienpointner, 1996: 103–16), gets its persuasive force from a comparison that stresses resemblance. It goes as follows:

**CR:**  If A and B are similar with respect to X, they have to be treated similarly with respect to X.

**A:**  A and B are X similar with respect to X.

**C:**  Thus, A and B have to be treated similarly with respect to X.

The formal structure of all other classes of formal argumentation schemes or topoi mentioned by Kienpointner (1992, 1996), who strongly relies on the new rhetoric of Perelman and Olbrechts-Tyteca (2000 [1958]), can be made explicit similarly.

## 5.3 *Content-related analysis of argumentation*

Some argumentation theoretical approaches (e.g. Wengeler, 1997, 2003 and Reisigl and Wodak, 2001; see also Kienpointner, 1992: 117) regard topoi not just as the abstract, general and formal warrants or conclusion rules. Following the observation that argumentation is always topic-related and field-dependent (i.e. depending on the configuration of social domains, disciplines, theories, etc.), *topoi* are also formalized as recurring content-related conclusion rules that are typical for specific fields of social action, disciplines, theories, etc. The tradition of identifying content-related argumentation schemes or topoi can be traced back to pre-Aristotelian rhetoric (see, e.g. Rubinelli, 2009) and is already strong in ancient Roman rhetoric (Cicero, Quintilianus). As Sara Rubinelli (2009) has stated, this tradition can also be linked to Aristotle, though Aristotle – whose concept of *topos* is far from being unequivocal (see Bornscheuer, 1976: 40 ff.; Kienpointner, 1992: 115, 178 ff.; Knape, 2000: 39 ff., 49 ff.) – tended towards a more formal, content-abstract conception of *topos* and towards an understanding of *topos* both as an abstract argumentation scheme and an instruction or generative principle of how to make or find premises or arguments (see also Žagar, 2009: 62 ff.). In this sense, *topos* is not a static, but a dynamic concept. Among its distinctive features are the inter-individual habitualization, potentiality, intentionality and conventionality (Bornscheuer, 1976: 93 ff.).

Not only ancient, but also modern argumentation theory does not just focus on 'formal topoi', but also on 'material topoi'. Many of the argumentation schemes collected by Walton, Reed and Macagno (2008) can, for instance, also be interpreted as content-related argumentation schemes. In discourse analysis, such content-related topoi tell more about the specific character of discourses (subject positions, controversial claims, justification strategies, ideologies, etc.) than a purely functional or formal analysis.

Reisigl and Wodak (2001) strongly base the content-related argumentation analysis of discrimination in discourses on Wengeler's studies of discourses about migration in Germany and Austria (see Wengeler, 1997, 2003) and on Kienpointner and Kindt's analysis of discussions about asylum in Germany and Austria (see Kienpointner and Kindt, 1997). The argumentation schemes adopted in Reisigl and Wodak (2001) have not been chosen randomly. They have been selected on the basis of the similarity between the research objects that have been analysed: discourses on migration and asylum. In this sense, the principle of 'hypolepsis' has been applied, i.e. the principle to grasp the unknown by systematically connecting it with the known (with the already elaborated analytical tools in existing discourse analytical approaches).

Another catalogue of material topics has to be worked out both on the basis of specific empirical data and the consultation of already-existing catalogues with respect to the discourse on the (Austrian) nation and national identity (see Reisigl, 2007a: 42 ff.). Here again, some of the content-related argumentation schemes or topoi already developed by Wengeler proved to be useful for the analysis (due to the topical proximity and intersection of the discourse on migration and the discourse on national identity). However, also discourse-specific topoi have been identified during the empirical analysis. The same holds true with respect to a third example of argumentation analysis carried out within the framework of the Discourse-Historical Approach: the analysis of right-wing populist rhetoric in Austria. A selection of frequent content-related populistic topoi and the respective fallacies in Austrian political discourses is listed in Table 3.2 (for more details see Reisigl, 2002, 2007c, 2008).

**Table 3.2**   Frequent content-related populistic topoi and fallacies in Austria

| | | |
|---|---|---|
| Topos of people | Argumentum ad populum (ad verecundiam, hasty generalization) | Version 1 (negative version):<br>    If the people refuse a political action or decision, then the action should not be performed/the decision should not be taken.<br>Version 2 (positive version):<br>    If the people favour a specific political action or decision, then the action should be performed/the decision should be taken. |
| Topos of democratic participation | Fallacy of democratic participation | Version 1:<br>    If a specific political decision, action or non-action concerns all citizens/the people, then the citizens/the people should be asked for the opinion.<br>Version 2:<br>    If I or we have the power, the people will participate in political decisions democratically. |
| Topos of anger (of 'the man in the street' /'the ordinary people') | Fallacy of anger | If 'the man in the street'/the 'ordinary people' become(s) angry and displeased, then a political action has (not) to be performed in order to resolve anger and displeasure. |
| Topos of burdening ('the man in the street'/'the ordinary people') | Fallacy of burdening or weighing down | If a person, the 'man in the street', the 'ordinary people', 'the Austrian' is burdened by specific problems, one should act in order to diminish these burdens. |
| Topos of exonerating ('the man in the street'/ the ordinary people') | Fallacy of exonerating | If a person, 'the man in the street'/'the ordinary people' is (over)burdened or overloaded by political measures, one should do something in order to exonerate the person, 'the man in the street'/ 'the ordinary people'. |

| Topos of liberty/of liberating ('the man in the street'/'the ordinary people') | Fallacy of liberty or liberating | Version 1: If you support us (our petition), we guarantee freedom. Version 2: If I or we get the power, we will guarantee the freedom and liberate or save the 'man in the street'/ the 'ordinary people'. |
|---|---|---|
| Topos of repaying the diligent and good workers/nationals | Fallacy of repaying the diligent and good workers/ nationals | If you support/vote for my party/movement/if I or we get the power, then the diligent and good workers/nationals will be repaid. |
| Topos of decency or respectability | Fallacy of decency or respectability | Version 1: If somebody is not decent and respectable, she or he should not be/become a politician. Version 2: If I or we get the power, we will perform a decent and respectable policy and work for the decent and respectable |
| Topos of dirty politics and of the necessity of clearing up and cleansing | Fallacy of dirty politics and of the necessity of clearing up and cleansing | Since politics is a dirty business, one/we must clear up, must have a clean-out, must muck out the stable. |
| Topos of law and order | Fallacy of law and order | If I or we get the power, we will provide for/ guarantee law and order. |

## 5.4 Sound and fallacious argumentation

Discourse analysis that claims to be critical is well-advised to rely on a normative model when doing argumentation analysis. From a normative point of view, we can distinguish between sound and fallacious argumentation, although the distinction is often difficult to make, since it heavily depends on the previous topic-related knowledge of the analysts and on the respective 'field' in which the argumentation is embedded. A central normative basis for the Discourse-Historical Approach is the Pragma-Dialectics with its ten rules for rational dispute and constructive arguing (Van Eemeren and Grootendorst, 1992; Van Eemeren et al., 2009):

(1) *The freedom rule* (freedom of arguing): Parties must not prevent each other from advancing or casting doubt on standpoints.

**(2)** *The burden-of-proof-rule* (obligation to give reasons): Whoever advances a standpoint is obliged to defend it if asked to do so.

**(3)** *The standpoint rule* (correct reference to previous discourse by the antagonist): An attack on a standpoint must relate to the standpoint that has actually been advanced by the protagonist.

**(4)** *The relevance rule* (obligation to 'matter-of-factness'): A standpoint may be only defended by advancing argumentation relating to that standpoint.

**(5)** *The unexpressed premise rule* (correct reference to implicit premises): A person can be held to the premises she or he leaves implicit. Conversely, antagonists must not be attacked on premises which cannot be inferred from their utterances.

**(6)** *The starting point rule* (respect of shared starting points): A standpoint must be regarded as conclusively defended if the defence takes place by means of arguments belonging to the common starting point. A premise must not falsely be taken as a common starting point, and, conversely, a shared premise must not be rejected.

**(7)** *The validity rule* (logical validity): The arguments used in a discourse must be valid or capable of being validated by the explicitization of one or more unexpressed premises.

**(8)** *The argumentation scheme rule* (use of plausible arguments and schemes of argumentation): A standpoint must be regarded as conclusively defended if the defence takes place by means of arguments in which a commonly accepted scheme of argumentation is correctly applied. A standpoint must not be considered to be conclusively defended if the defence has not taken place by means of argumentation schemes which are plausible and correctly applied.

**(9)** *The closure rule* (acceptance of the discussion's results): A failed defence must result in the protagonist withdrawing her or his standpoint, and a successful defence in the antagonist withdrawing her or his doubt about the standpoint.

**(10)** *The usage rule* (clarity of expression and correct interpretation): Formulations must be neither puzzlingly vague nor confusingly ambiguous, and must be interpreted as accurately as possible.

If these rules are violated, we are no longer faced with sound topoi, but with fallacies. With the help of these norms of argumentation, nationalist, 'xenophobic', populist and other manipulative fallacies can be identified within the framework of the Discourse-Historical Approach.

# 6  Reply to some criticisms

In the course of the last few years, the Discourse-Historical Approach has been criticized from at least three perspectives, for its approach to argumentation analysis. The critique has partly been 'internal' and partly 'external'. It has partly been reasonable and partly based on misunderstanding, misreading and non-reading. In the following three sections, some major points of this critique shall be commented on. Due to the lack of space, a more detailed examination and discussion of the various criticisms must follow elsewhere.

## 6.1  Is the combination of Critical Theory and Pragma-Dialectics theoretically consistent and do the ten rules for critical discussion suffice for a normative foundation of critique? (Forchtner and Tominc)

Bernhard Forchtner and Ana Tominc are both advocates of the Discourse-Historical Approach. They nonetheless formulate criticism that is worth dealing with more closely (see Forchtner, 2010, 2011; Forchtner and Tominc, 2012; Forchtner, 2014). The two major points they make are: (1) the theoretical combination of Critical Theory/Habermas and Pragma-Dialectics (relying on Popper) leads to theoretical inconsistency or contradiction. (2) The ten rules for critical discussion are not sufficient as a normative basis for the foundation of the critique. Thus, Habermas's model should be given more importance.

Further to (1): I want to react to the first point with three answers (further comments on the relationship between Pragma-Dialectics and the Discourse-Historical Approach can be found in Ihnen and Richardson, 2011):

(i)   With respect to the ten rules for critical discussion, the connection between Pragma-Dialectics and Critical Rationalism is probably not as close as it may seem to be. There are critics of Pragma-Dialectics who hold the view that Pragma-Dialectics does not (narrowly) follow Popper's and Albert's approaches. Christoph Lumer and Sandro Nannini (2012: 61–8) even assert:

> [. . .] what in pragma-dialectics happens on the level of the dialogue rules is exactly the opposite of what critical rationalism requires. Critical rationalism criticises positive, foundationalist justification and fosters negative criticism of hypotheses, which have to be advanced without justification, whereas pragma-dialectics instead requires positive justification if the opponent asks for it [. . .] So, pragma-dialectical critical discussions absolutely do not model the critical rationalist procedure of conjecture and refutation.

Although I consider Lumer's critique to be overstated and do not share Lumer's neopositivist (foundationalist) perspective and strong concept of objectivity, I take into consideration that 'positive justification' may play a more important role in Pragma-Dialectics than in Critical Rationalism (see, for instance, rule 8, the argumentation scheme rule).

**(ii)** Habermas partly includes Popper's criterion of fallibilism into his own model of truth: 'It cannot [. . .] be excluded that new information and better arguments are put forward' (Habermas, 1992: 278). In this sense, the contrast between Critical Rationalism and Habermas may not be as big as it is suggested by Forchtner and Tominc – even though it is clear that there are other differences in the theories of Habermas and Popper.

**(iii)** The ten rules can be integrated into a normative theory of argumentation without adopting all theoretical assumptions of Pragma-Dialectics. I deviate from Pragma-Dialectics, at least with respect to the following points:

**(1)** As already said, argumentation involves, in my view, not a speech act or a macro-speech act as such, but a pattern of text or discourse formation realized by a related sequence of speech acts.

**(2)** Whereas Pragma-Dialectics considers a fallacy to be a speech act as well ('A fallacy is defined as a speech act which prejudices or frustrates efforts to resolve a difference of opinion'; Van Eemeren et al., 1996: 299), I regard a fallacy prototypically not as a single speech act, but as a sequence of related speech acts (at least at the level of the pragmatic deep structure).

**(3)** The resolution of a difference of opinion between the protagonists and antagonists is not always the main or only purpose of argumentation. In the action field of political advertising, the purpose can also be to gain as many followers as possible, to gain a majority against the opponent(s), etc.

**(4)** On the level of the pragmatic deep structure, the validity claim of normative rightness does, in my view, not correspond to the assertive speech act (as suggested by Pragma-Dialectics), but to a directive speech act (containing deontic modality).

**(5)** Whereas Pragma-Dialecticians assume that specific directive speech acts cannot be part of argumentation ('Directives such as orders and prohibitions are fundamentally banned from a critical discussion'; Van Eemeren et al., 2007: 13), I think that under certain conditions all types of speech acts can be involved in argumentation, including orders and prohibitions that can function as claims (Do x! = You must do x).

**(6)** I assume that a fallacy does not always violate just one rule, but may violate more than one rule simultaneously.

**(7)** Several of the ten rules per definition potentially transcend – or potentially should transcend – the local context of a specific critical discussion (e.g. freedom of arguing, matter-of-factness, logical validity, use of plausible arguments) and can be connected with Habermas's theory. That is to say: the ten rules can be specified in a way as to allow me to – at least partly – build a bridge to Habermas. The consent aimed at by the Pragma-Dialectical rules should take potential 'external criticism' into consideration. It should not just be based on the concept of 'local intersubjectivity', but rely on a potentially context-transcending idea of intersubjectivity – which, however, need not lead to a universalist reading of the idea of intersubjectivity. In order to bring Habermas's model (e.g. his idea of an ideal-speech situation referring to free access, equal rights, absence of coercion, and truthfulness) a bit closer than probably intended by the Pragma-Dialecticians to the ten rules, I propose to supplement the rules with the following additions (the supplements are in italics).

- Rule 1: Parties must not prevent each other from advancing or casting doubt on standpoints. *Parties must be aware that non-present third parties affected by the issue in question may advance and question standpoints as well.*

- Rule 2: Whoever advances a standpoint is obliged to defend it if asked to do so. *Parties must be aware that non-present third parties concerned or affected by the issue in question may ask to defend a standpoint as well.*

- Rules 1, 2 and 4 relate to Habermas's claims for free access, equal rights and absence of coercion.

- Rules 3, 4, 5, 6, 7, 8 and 9 all relate to various aspects of truthfulness/ sincerity, even though the concept of truthfulness may include further aspects that are not yet grasped by the rules. Whoever tries to be truthful, however, will try to avoid the violation of these seven rules.

- Rule 7: The arguments used in a discourse must be valid or capable of being validated by the explicitization of one or more unexpressed premises. It is obvious that the question of logical validity does not just relate to the 'local logic' of arguers involved in a specific discussion, but to commonly established rules of logic, although it is also clear that 'everyday argumentation' and even scientific argumentation is often enthymemic and hardly ever strictly follows the rules of formal logic. However, rule 7 asks that – at least – the explicitation of enthymemic argumentation should not contradict the logic.

- Rule 8: A standpoint must be regarded as conclusively defended if the defence takes place by means of arguments in which *a commonly accepted* scheme of argumentation is correctly applied. A standpoint must not be considered to be conclusively defended if the defence has not taken place by means of argumentation schemes *which are plausible and correctly applied*. Here, the two passages can be interpreted as indicating that rule 8 is rooted in common agreement based on social conventions, habits or routines of arguing that transcend their purely local context. Furthermore, the repertoire of socially accepted, plausible argumentation schemes, for instance, relates to questions of justice: the formal argumentation scheme named 'topos of comparison' is obviously linked to various concepts of justice. An egalitarian concept of justice relies on the topos of similarity (see the example in section 5.2), a differentialist concept of justice ('*suum cuique*', i.e. 'to each his or her own'; 'to each what he or she deserves') relates to the topos of difference and the concept of 'balancing justice' relates to the topos of difference as well as the topos of similarity, prioritizing the latter (in the sense that differences that cannot be removed should – at least – be minimized).

**(8)** Pragma-Dialecticians themselves hint at the context-transcendence of the rules and their application. Van Eemeren, Garssen, Meuffels (2009) have empirically tested the extent to which the ten rules are conventionally valid. They conclude that 'the body of data collected indicates that the norms that ordinary arguers use when judging the reasonableness of discussion contributions correspond to a rather large degree with the pragma-dialectical norms from critical discussion' (Van Eemeren et al., 2009: 224). Thus, the ten rules do not just relate to a local intersubjective consent. In a similar vein, Houtlosser, van Eemeren (2007: 64 f.) say:

> Although we agree with Walton and Krabbe that fallacy judgments are in the end always contextual judgments that depend on the specific circumstances of situated argumentative acting, we do not agree that the norms underlying these judgments are context-dependent. In our view, the norms expressed in the rules for critical discussion are general – who knows even universal – norms for sound argumentation that are not limited to one particular type of argumentative activity – or 'dialogue type.' It is true that argumentative discourse always takes part in a certain context of argumentative activity, but this does not mean that the soundness norms are automatically relative. The context-dependency of judgments of argumentative discourse lies in the way in which the conduct of argumentative discourse is conventionally disciplined in a certain activity type by specific criteria for determining

whether or not a certain type of maneuvering agrees with the relevant norm, which criteria may vary to some extent per argumentative activity type – in a law case, for instance, different criteria apply to making a legitimate appeal to authority, e.g. by referring to a certain law code, than in a political debate. [. . .] Using the rules for critical discussion as a context-*in*dependent standard, we take the peculiarities of the various argumentative activity types into account when we start evaluating whether these rules have been obeyed or violated.

Further to (2): As far as the second point of critique is concerned, I agree that the ten rules for critical discussion do not suffice for the normative underpinning of the critique intended within the framework of the Discourse-Historical Approach and that Habermas's Discourse Ethics and theory of deliberative democracy should be given more weight, although I cannot specify this point in the present context (see Forchtner, 2010, 2011; Forchtner and Tominc, 2012 and Forchtner, 2014, where some possible stronger links between the DHA and Habermas are indicated). However, already in the book *Discourse and Discrimination* (2001: 263 f.) at least two additional sources are mentioned on which to found the critique: (a) basic democratic and ethical principles such as justice and equality and (b) the psychological as well as ethical principle of empathy – in Mead's sense of 'taking the role of the other', especially of victims of social discrimination, and in the sense of the *erweiterte Denkungsart* ('extended way of thinking') as suggested by Kant, Arendt and Benhabib. As I have tried to show under point 7 above, it can be fruitful to integrate more of Habermas's work into the Pragma-Dialectical rules in order to make their (potentially) general normative claims more explicit. Anyway, Forchtner and Tominc rightly ask for a more profound attempt to integrate Habermas's Discourse Ethics into the theoretical framework of the DHA. Such an integration is also desirable for the work of scholars influenced by Habermas and influencing Habermas, e.g. Alexy (1996 [1983]), Miller (2006), etc.

## 6.2 Does the DHA consider topos to be a ready-made topic or literary motive and not an argumentation scheme? (Igor Žagar)

A polemical critique of the DHA's use of the concept of *topos* has been put into words by Igor Žagar (2009, 2010). Here, I cannot fully deal with all the different objections made by Žagar. Thus, I will concentrate on three points which I consider the most central. They are: (1) the proponents of the DHA should be more explicit when reconstructing the argumentation structure of the empirical data. (2) *Topos* has to be understood as a formal and functional concept. (3) The concept of *topos* as it is used in the DHA corresponds to the understanding of *topos* as a recurring motif or theme (purely semantic interpretation of the term).

Further to (1): As for the first point, I agree with Igor Žagar that there should be more explicit and detailed reconstructions in future analyses of argumentation within the theoretical framework of the Discourse-Historical Approach. This requirement comes also to the fore with respect to argumentation didactics (Reisigl, 2004, 2007a). The methodology outlined in section 5 can serve as a basis for such reconstructions – in addition to analytical categories referring to stages and macro- as well as meso-structures of argumentation, which cannot be dealt with in the present context. This methodology should, in my view, be further developed and assume the form of a sectoral argumentation theory specialized for the needs of social and human sciences as well as historical theory. Such a sectoral argumentation theory ought to turn special attention to the analysis of field-specific content-related argumentation schemes (topoi and fallacies). More methodological rigour, empirical anchoring and critical self-reflection will help to avoid the arbitrary coining of content-related categories (see also section 7).

On the other hand, quite a large part of Žagar's critique relating to the first point has to be refuted as a result of misreading, misunderstanding and non-reading. Some misunderstandings are (a) due to the shorter English translation of some texts and requirements of 'brevitas', which seem to be more pervasive in the English publishing world than in the German one, (b) due to the unawareness of basic texts relevant for the Discourse-Historical Approach only published in German (e.g. Wengeler, 1997, 2003; Kopperschmidt, 1989, 2000; Kienpointner, 1992, 1996) and (c) due to inaccurate reading. I will come back to one example of such a misunderstanding, inaccurate reading and non-reading below in my answer to objection 3.

Further to (2): Žagar holds the view that *topos* – as an argumentation-related notion – has to be understood as an abstract formal and functional concept in the tradition of Aristotle and should rather not be seen as a content-related category of analysis. A similar claim is made by Fairclough and Fairclough (2012: 23 f., 246), though they prefer not to work with the concept of topos within their theoretical framework. As I have tried to make clear in section 5, the ambiguous Aristotelian concept of topos is not the only possible point of authoritarian reference for topos analysis. There is also an old tradition of doing content-related topos analysis in the area of argumentation theory (a tradition that can even be linked to Aristotle), and there are various modern proposals of understanding *topos* as a dynamic content-related concept (see, for instance Wengeler, 1997, 2003; see also Kienpointner, 1998: 564–7 and 2013: 302). But even if *topos* is operationalized as a content-related concept in argumentation theory, it is obvious that it simultaneously remains a functional concept, for a topos serves as a conclusion rule (warrant) that connects an argument with a claim. This double quality of *topoi* has never been denied by those who opt for a content-related analysis of argumentation schemes. However, it should also have become clear that *topos* need not be exclusively defined in abstract formal terms (in addition to its functional characterization).

Further to (3): Žagar has argued that the concept of *topos* as it is used in the Discourse-Historical Approach is best understood in terms of a recurring motif or theme, i.e. in terms of semantic interpretation of the term that follows the terminological tradition of literary studies. In order to back his claim, he refers, among other things, to analytical catagories of *locus amoenus* and *locus terribilis* (Žagar, 2010: 21):

[. . .] in *The Discursive Construction of National Identity*, where 49 *topoi* are listed (without any pattern of functioning), we can also find (1999: 38–39) *locus amoenus* (*topos* of idyllic place) and *locus terribilis* (*topos* of terrible place). These two *topoi* have absolutely nothing to do with connecting arguments to conclusions, but are literary *topoi per excellence*, formulated and defined by E. R. Curtius. To clarify this: there is nothing wrong with literary topoi, their purpose just is not connecting possible arguments to possible conclusions.

Here as well as elsewhere, Žagar took the bait. If he had read the book carefully, he would have found the following explanations of the concepts of *locus amoenus* and *locus terribilis* on p. 97 f.:

We do not view the *locus amoenus*, however, as a literary topos in a narrow sense, as one which paints an Arcadian idyllic landscape with green, lush meadows, cool forests, clear brooks, melodious twittering of birds etc., but rather as a 'beautiful landscape' often mentioned in a more general sense to refer to the common national territory or serving to depict a rather abstract ideal political place where human beings live together happily, in affluence, in harmony and without conflicts. The 'island of the lucky', coined by Pope Paul VI in 1971 and soon renamed 'island of the blessed' (Bruckmüller 1996, p. 125), rhetorically points to this idyllic place, the *locus amoenus*. Where it occurs in the political speeches, it frequently not only serves the purpose of mere self-presentation but is part of a comparative scheme by means of which the strategy of emphasis of inter-national difference is realised. We can say that on the whole this strategy, which aims at construction of identity and emphasizes differences between Austria and other states, was rare in the commemorative speeches; if it occurred it was usually in connection with positive achievements such as prosperity, freedom, democracy and social stability. However, the less speakers were interested in perpetuating the status quo and the more they were interested in a radical political change – of course to their own advantage – the less positive were their assessments of the current political situation and the more they tended to present the political achievements they viewed positively as being in danger. Thus they might have warned of a *locus terribilis* or portrayed certain political continuities in a negative light, that is, presented them as ancient and fossilized structures. This held true for the opposition parties (FPÖ, Greens and Liberal Forum) as well as the smaller party of the coalition government, the ÖVP.

(Wodak et al., 2009 [1999]: 97 f.)

I am the author of these lines. I wrote them in order to make it unmistakingly clear that we deliberately re-interpret the concepts of *locus amoenus* and *locus terribilis* in an argumentation theoretical sense and not in the sense of a literary topos. Among other things, the longer German version of the book (Wodak et al., 1998: 227 f.) offers the following example for the argumentation-related *locus amoenus*. It is taken from a speech given by the former Austria Chancellor Franz Vranitzky on 7 May 1995:

> But we really have no reason for becoming immersed in self-doubts. Living standards in Austria are surpassed only by a few countries in international comparison – if measured with respect to political stability, social peace, life expectancy, access to education, and spending power of the population. Today, nobody has doubts about the ability of our Republic to survive. We can look optimistically into the future.

Here, Vranitzky combines the argumentation-related *locus amoenus* with a topos of comparison and, strictly speaking, with the topos of (positive) difference. Such argumentation is typical for positive national self-presentation, especially for politicians who want to promote national identification and – in the specific case – simultaneously to maintain their own political power. The combination of the two topoi can be made explicit as the following conclusion rule:

> Since today's Austria is such a lovely place in comparison to other countries / in comparison to its past, you should be proud to be Austrian / you should be optimistic / you should not become immersed in self-doubts.

Let me stress that all other topos-related concepts dealt with in books such as Reisigl, Wodak (2001) and Wodak, de Cillia, Reisigl, Liebhart (2009 [1999]) have also been intended to be argumentation-related categories and not literary topoi.

In sum, Žagar's first criticism is important and should be taken into consideration, but, all in all, Žagar's polemical attack is not a 'well-argued critique of the use of *topos* in DHA', as has been contended by Fairclough and Fairclough (2012: footnote 3).

### 6.3 Is the DHA a non-analytic and taxonomic approach to argumentation and does it consider argumentation to be a strategy in itself? (Fairclough and Fairclough)

A third critical assessment of the Discourse-Historical Approach to argumentation analysis is made by Isabela and Norman Fairclough. In what follows, just five of their critical remarks shall be focused on: (1) The Discourse-Historical Approach is (primarily) classificatory and taxonomic, and that may lead to a rather static and atomistic view 'without a coherent account of the character of the whole' (Fairclough and Fairclough, 2012: 22, see also 246 f., footnote 5). It focuses on representation rather than action.

(2) The Discourse-Historical Approach regards argumentation as a (discursive) strategy in itself, whereas the approach offered by Isabela and Norman Fairclough conceives of argumentation as a complex speech act, and whereas an argumentation theory grounded in speech act theory does not allow seeing argumentation as a strategy. (3) In the framework offered by Isabela and Norman Fairclough, it is not possible to regard argumentation as an object of the same (strategic) order as reference, predication, perspectivation or intensification. (4) The DHA is not analytic. Its studies do not offer argument reconstruction as a basis for analysis and normative or explanatory critique. Thus, there can be a risk of arbitrary evaluation. (5) The content-related approach to *topos*, 'which identifies a wide range of topoi at a very detailed concrete level' (Fairclough and Fairclough, 2013: 24), obscures the abstract argumentative schemes that lie behind particular arguments and 'can lead to an enormous proliferation of categories of analysis' which may 'prevent a synthetic grasp of the nature of the object of study' (Fairclough and Fairclough, 2012: 25). Due to the lack of space, only short replies to these five points are possible.

Further to (1): The Discourse-Historical Approach is not taxonomic, but typologically oriented. A taxonomy (from Greek '*taxis*', order and Greek '*nómos*', law) is a rather rigid, complete and hierarchical classification on the basis of a close system of discrete categories and divisions as well as sub-divisions, classes as well as sub-classes, levels as well as sub-levels, etc. Usually, it does not allow for the intersection of categories, multiple membership and functional polyphony of discursive means and elements. In contrast, a typology is a less rigid and not at all exhaustive overview and ordering of salient, prototypical or representative categories relating to a specific complex of interrelated types, in our case, of discursive strategies, means or phenomena. The schematic overviews and tables in DHA studies such as Reisigl, Wodak (2001: 38, 46); Reisigl (2002: 182 ff, 185 ff. etc.); Reisigl (2007a: 34 f, 43, 84 etc.); Wodak, de Cillia, Reisigl, Liebhart (2009: 36–42); Reisigl, Wodak (2009: 91, 112) have never been intended as taxonomies, but as typologies, i.e. as weaker and more open orders of categories with potential intersections, and not as closed classes organized according to strict laws (*nómoi*). When analysing discourses (including disciplinary meta-discourses) and discussing relationships between categories, I have never used the term 'taxonomy', but always 'typology', and have repeatedly upheld Wittgenstein's concept of 'family resemblance' as a prolific concept (see e.g. Reisigl 2011: 24; 2013: 72). If readers read texts such as Reisigl (2003b), Reisigl (2007: 151–279) or Reisigl (2008: 106–13), they should – hopefully – not get the impression of an atomistic and static approach that is primarily interested in questions of representation, but develop the picture of a holistically oriented approach to discourse with a strong interest in the analysis of action and practice.

Further to (2): The view that the Discourse-Historical Approach regards argumentation as a strategy per se is a misreading which tends towards building up a fallacy of composition that violates the Pragma-Dialectical rule 7. This fallacy goes: 'Since the DHA proponents talk about strategies of argumentation, they think the whole issue of argumentation just to be a question of strategy.' But to talk about strategies of argumentation does not reasonably lead to the conclusion that argumentation is solely a strategy. It does only mean that argumentation is also a strategic issue. As explained in section 3, argumentation can be seen as a non-violent and conventionalized linguistic as well as cognitive pattern of problem-solving that is realized by a sequence of functionally, formally and thematically interrelated speech acts, and the way of relating these speech acts can be strategically organized, for instance with the help of topoi in the sense of argumentation schemes and instructive rules of how to employ these schemes. Such a strategic interpretation of topoi or loci is – by the way – also assumed by Sara Rubinelli, who repeatedly writes about Aristotelian and Ciceronian topoi in terms of strategies of argumentation (see, for instance, Rubinelli, 2009: 13, 132, 144 ff.). In Fairclough and Fairclough (2012: 23 f.), we do not only find a tendency to regard argumentation as a (complex) speech act (I have already said that I do not follow this proposal, in section 3), but also a tendency to separate strategy from discourse as well as to separate discourse from action:

> However, although strategies have a partly discursive character, we would not treat 'strategy' as a discursive category. 'Strategy' is a category within theories of action, not within theories of discourse. It is action and, in the case of politics, political action, that may be strategic, not discourse in itself. Language is, of course, a form of action, as speech act theory has long recognized, but strategies (we argue) involve goals which are *outside* and *beyond* discourse, i.e. they involve desired *changes in the world*, not in discourse.
>
> (Fairclough and Fairclough, 2012: 24)

This argumentation is, in my view, far from being clear. It should be discussed in detail. Here, I can only raise some questions. If strategies have a partly discursive character, why should they not be treated as a category of discourse theory? (Note that the term 'discourse strategy' is not only employed in the DHA, but also in Interactional Sociolinguistics and in political discourse theory concerned with the analysis of hegemonic power.) If 'strategy' is a category of action and discourse is a form of action, isn't there also common terrain that invites employment of the concept of 'discursive strategies'? If we accept that discourse as well as argumentation do always include a cognitive or mental dimension (and not only a verbal dimension) and that a 'goal' is a desired outcome that is planned by somebody and achieved with the help of some means: then why should a 'goal' be a category *outside* and *beyond* discourse (in view of the fact that such an aspiration is a mental and emotional state and that a 'desired change' should not be confused with the change itself)? In my view, these questions await an answer.

Further to (3): With respect to the relationship between the five groups of discursive strategies distinguished within the theoretical framework of the Discourse-Historical Approach, Fairclough and Fairclough (2012: 23) falsely suggest that the proponents of the DHA take nomination, predication, argumentation, perspectivization and intensification as well as mitigation to be categories of the same order. In fact, we write in various texts that the five groups of discursive strategies are placed at different levels of linguistic organization and complexity (e.g. Reisigl and Wodak, 2001: 44, 2009: 94), that, for instance, predications can already be contained in nominations (Reisigl and Wodak, 2001: 54), that nominations as well as predications enter as relevant elements in argumentations or speech acts that form the network of an argumentation and that intensification as well as mitigation operate upon illocutionary acts (Reisigl and Wodak, 2001: 83 f., 2009: 94). So, here again the approach in question has been represented in a distorted manner.

Further to (4): Fairclough and Fairclough (2013) make the claim that the main difference between their own approach and the DHA is that proponents of the DHA do not reconstruct arguments as a basis for analysis and critique. This is a grave critique. In my view, it can easily be rejected, among many other things, by the reference to texts such as Reisigl (2006: 196–202), Reisigl (2007b: 260–9), Reisigl (2008: 106–18), Reisigl (2013: 82–4). I hold the view that my critique of fallacious argumentation is, at least for the most part, based on inter-subjectively comprehensible normative criteria. However, the successful refutation of this claim of lack of analysis and argument reconstruction relies on the question of what is to be understood as 'argument reconstruction' and 'analysis'. As the previous discussion has shown so far, there is not just one way of doing argument reconstruction and argumentation analysis.

Further to (5): As far as the last point is concerned, I have already made clear that the concept of *topos* need not be exclusively interpreted as an abstract argumentation scheme, but that it is also sensible to specify it at a more concrete level of content, since a content-related approach to argumentation tells a lot about field-dependent 'mentalities', discourse positions and ideological orientations. In contrast to Isabela and Norman Fairclough, I think that the analysis of content-related topoi and fallacies can contribute a great deal to the holistic and 'synthetic grasp of the nature of the object of study' (Fairclough and Fairclough, 2013: 25), indeed even much more than a purely functional and formal analysis that abstracts from the content of a discourse. However, the risk of introducing too many arbitrary analytical categories has to be minimized by the development of a sectoral argumentation theory and methodology specialized for the study of argumentation in human and social sciences as well as historical theory. I will summarize some important points that have to be taken into consideration when building up such a theory and methodology in the last section of my chapter.

# 7 Conclusions

Critical discourse analysts should not content themselves with a purely descriptive analysis of argumentation, because they have critical ambitions and take a critical stand. Thus, they should also integrate a normative dimension into their model. Consequently, CDA has to distinguish between reasonable and fallacious argumentation.

The more adequate and the more differentiated the descriptive tools for argumentation analysis are and the more explicit and the more compelling the normative ground is, on which the critique is based, the more convincing the formulation of critique will be.

An adequate description presupposes that the analytical model offers – at least – a conceptual distinction between the following argumentation-related dimensions:

**(a)** functional categories,

**(b)** formal categories (formal topoi/fallacies),

**(c)** field- and topic-dependent, content-related categories (content-related topoi/fallacies),

**(d)** categories for describing argumentative meso- and macro-structures, e.g.:

- stages of argumentation

- simple/multiple argumentation (how many arguments for a claim?)

- mixed/non-mixed (how many claims?)

- coordinate vs. subordinate argumentation (dependency of arguments?),

**(e)** categories to separate the representation of argumentation by quotation from the performance of argumentation.

The pragma-dialectical rules of rational argumentation are a good normative basis for the evaluation of argumentation within the framework of the Discourse-Historical Approach. However, they are not a sufficient basis. In addition, the reference to democratic norms and ethical principles of justice and equality as well as to the principle of empathy or *erweiterte Denkungsart* (Kant, Arendt) are important normative sources. Establishing a stronger theoretical link to the theories of Jürgen Habermas, Robert Alexy and Max Miller is desirable. It will strengthen the normative basis for the Discourse-Historical Approach.

The content-related analysis of argumentation is especially interesting for Critical Discourse Analysis, particularly for approaches which opt for a topic-related definition of 'discourse' and are interested in the analysis of ideology, subject positions, contested claims and justification strategies, i.e. for the Discourse-Historical Approach, but also the other approaches (cf. the Introduction to this volume).

There is a methodological demand for the development of a sectoral argumentation theory specialized for the requirements of social and human sciences as well as historical theory.

This theory should – among other things – concentrate on comprehensive criteria that allow us to construct plausible, field- and topic-dependent typologies (not taxonomies!) of content-related topoi. The methodological operationalization of content-related topoi could take the subsequent criteria into consideration:

**(a)** Follow the principle of moving back and forth between theory and empirical analysis: starting from existing typologies of content-related topoi, you should check whether your empirical data contains topoi as they have already been formulated theoretically in previous research. If so, you can work with an already-prefabricated content-related topos. If not, you should try to analytically construct new topoi, avoiding being too specific and too arbitrary.

**(b)** Semantic indicators: the frequency of a specific lexical item and discourse topics can be an indicator for a specific content-related topos or fallacy in a discourse (focus on semantic relation of quasi-synonymy), e.g. 'freedom' in neo-liberal and nationalist discourse fragments. However, lexical items employed to label topoi (e.g. 'threat' in 'topos of threat' or 'comparison' in 'topos of comparison') need not appear explicitly on the textual 'surface'. There are also syntactic indicators: the 'topos of justice' can, for instance, be expressed through a syntactic construction such as 'a Roland for an Oliver' or 'tit for tat'.

**(c)** A validity claim of truth or normative rightness should be identifiable next or close to the supposed content-related argumentation pattern. The argumentation analysis may often start with the search for a controversial claim, especially if you are not sure whether the sequence of speech acts you are going to analyse relates to argumentation.

**(d)** Lexical keywords appear in the first or second part of the formulas 'if x, then y' and 'y, because of x'. However, there seem to be specific tendencies of distribution: most of the topoi identified by Wengeler (1997) occur in the first part of 'if x, then y'. Some topoi can be formulated variably (e.g. the topos of advantage: 'If we/you do x, this will lead to the advantage y.' versus 'If x is or were an advantage, x should be strived for.'

**(e)** Tropes (metaphors, synecdoches, metonymies) are possible cognitive and linguistic indicators for content-related topoi and fallacies. Future research should closely (empirically and theoretically) explore the connection between metaphors, metonymies as well as synecdoches and argumentation, particularly with respect to their fallacious potential. Not only metaphors, but also synecdoches and metonymies can express implicit fallacious conclusion rules – synecdoches, for instance, conveying hasty generalizations.

# Note

1   I am deliberately using the adjectives *strong* and *organized* [focus]. There are of course many more strands of CDA having argumentation 'somewhere within their purview', as noted in the Introduction to this volume.

# References

Alexy, R. (1996[1983]), *Theorie der juristischen Argumentation. Die Theorie des rationalen Diskurses als Theorie der juristischen Begründung.* Frankfurt am Main: Suhrkamp.

Bornscheuer, L. (1976), *Topik. Zur Struktur der gesellschaftlichen Einbildungskraft.* Frankfurt am Main: Suhrkamp.

Cicero, M. T. (1998), *De inventione. Über die Auffindung des Stoffes / De optime genere oratorum.* Darmstadt: Wissenschaftliche Buchgesellschaft.

Ecker, M. W. (2006), *Kritisch Argumentieren.* Aschaffenburg: Alibri Verlag.

Fairclough, I. and Fairclough, N. (2012), *Political Discourse Analysis. A Method for Advanced Students.* London: Routledge.

—— (2013), *Political Discourse Analysis: A Method for Advanced Students.* London: Routledge.

Fairclough, N. (1995), *Critical Discourse Analysis. The Critical Study of Language.* London: Longman.

—— (2010), *Critical Discourse Analysis. The Critical Study of Language* (2nd edn). London: Longman.

Fairclough, N. and Fairclough, I., (2010), 'Argumentation analysis in CDA: analyzing practical reasoning in political discourse' in R. De Cillia, H. Gruber, M. Krzyżanowski and F. Menz, (eds), *Diskurs, Politik, Identität. / Discourse, Politics, Identity.* Tübingen: Stauffenburg. pp. 59–70.

Forchtner, B. (2010), 'Jürgen Habermas and the critical study of language'. *CADAAD – Critical Approaches to Discourse Analysis across Disciplines,* 4(1), 18–37.

—— (2011), 'Critique, the discourse-historical approach and the Frankfurt School'. *Critical Discourse Studies,* 8(1), 1–14.

—— (2014), 'Rhetorics of judge-penitence: claiming moral superiority through admissions of past wrongdoing'. *Memory Studies,* 7, in press.

Forchtner, B. and Tominc, A. (2012), 'Critique and argumentation. On the relation between the discourse-historical approach and pragma-dialectics'. *Journal of Language and Politics,* 11(1), 31–50.

Habermas, J. (1992), *Faktizität und Geltung. Beiträge zur Diskurstheorie des Rechts und des demokratischen Rechtsstaats.* Frankfurt am Main: Suhrkamp.

Houtlosser, P. and van Eemeren, F. H. (2007), 'The contextuality of fallacies'. *Informal Logic,* 27(1), 59–67.

Iețcu, I. (2006a), *Discourse Analysis and Argumentation Theory: Analytical Framework and Applications.* Bucharest: Bucharest University Press.

—— (2006b), *Dialogue, Argumentation and Ethical Perspective in the Essays of H.-R. Patapievivi.* Bucharest: Bucharest University Press.

Iețcu-Fairclough, I. (2007), 'Populism and the Romanian "Orange Revolution". A discourse-analytical perspective on the Presidential Election of 2004'. *Studies in Language and Capitalism,* 2, 31–74 (http://www.languageandcapitalism.info/).

Ihnen, C. and Richardson, J. E. (2011), 'On combining pragma-dialectics with critical discourse analysis', in E. T. Feteris, B. Garssen and F. A. Snoeck Henkemans, (eds), *Keeping in Touch with Pragma-Dialectics: In Honor of Frans H. van Eemeren.* Amsterdam: John Benjamins, pp. 231–44.

Kienpointner, M. (1992), *Alltagslogik. Struktur und Funktion von Argumentationsmustern.* Stuttgart-Bad Cannstatt: frommann-holzboog.

—— (1996), *Vernünftig Argumentieren. Regeln und Techniken der Argumentation.* Reinbek bei Hamburg: Rowohlt.

—— (1998), Inventio. In G. Ueding (ed.), *Historisches Wörterbuch der Rhetorik. Volume 4: Hu-K.* Tübingen: Niemeyer, pp. 561–87.

—— (2013), Review of: Isabela Fairclough, Norman Fairclough (2012), *Political Discourse Analysis: A Method for Advanced Students.* London: Routledge 2012. In *Journal of Language and Politics*, 12(2), 295–304.

Kienpointner, M. and Kindt, W. (1997), 'On the problem of bias in political argumentation. An investigation into discussions about political asylum in Germany and Austria'. *Journal of Pragmatics*, 27, 555–85.

Kindt, W. (1992), 'Argumentation und Konfliktaustragung in Äußerungen über den Golfkrieg'. *Zeitschrift für Sprachwissenschaft*, 11, 189–215.

Knape, J. (2000), *Allgemeine Rhetorik.* Stuttgart: Reclam.

Kopperschmidt, J. (1989), *Methodik der Argumentationsanalyse.* Stuttgart: frommann-holzboog.

—— (2000), *Argumentationstheorie zur Einführung.* Hamburg: Junius.

Lumer, C. and Nannini, S. (2012), *Intentionality, Deliberation and Autonomy.* London: Ashgate.

Miller, M. (2006), *Dissens. Zur Theorie diskursiven und systemischen Lernens.* Bielefeld: Transcript.

Perelman, C. and Olbrechts-Tyteca, L. (2000 [1958]), *Traite de l'Argumentation. La Nouvelle Rhetorique* (5th edn). Brussels: Editions de l'Universite de Bruxelles.

Reisigl, M. (2002), 'Dem Volk aufs Maul schauen, nach dem Mund reden und angst und bange machen – Von populistischen Anrufungen, Anbiederungen und Agitationsweisen in der Sprache österreichischer PolitikerInnen', in, W. Eismann, (ed.), *Rechtspopulismus. Österreichische Krankheit oder europäische Normalität?* Vienna: Cernin-Verlag. pp. 149–98.

—— (2003a), *Wie man eine Nation herbeiredet. Eine diskursanalytische Untersuchung zur sprachlichen Konstruktion der österreichischen Nation und österreichischen Identität in politischen Fest- und Gedenkreden.* Vienna: unpublished PhD.

—— (2003b), 'Rede als Vollzugsmeldung an die (deutsche) Geschichte. Hitler auf dem Wiener Heldenplatz', in, J. Kopperschmidt, (ed.), *Hitler der Redner.* Munich: Fink. pp. 383–412.

—— (2004), 'Argumentation und kausalitätsbezogene Explikation in studentischen Arbeiten – Eine Fallstudie', in, S. Göpferich and J. Engberg, (eds), *Qualität fachsprachlicher Kommunikation.* Tübingen: Narr. pp. 151–75.

—— (2005), 'Rechtfertigung', in, G. Ueding (ed.), *Historisches Wörterbuch der Rhetorik (HWRh). Band 7.* Tübingen: Niemeyer. pp. 649–76.

—— (2006), 'Argumentation und kausalitätsbezogene Explikation', in H. Gruber, M. Rheindorf, K. Wetschanow, M. Reisigl, P. Muntigl and C. Czinglar, *Genre, Habitus und wissenschaftliches Schreiben. Eine empirische Untersuchung studentischer Texte.* Münster, Hamburg, Berlin, Vienna, London: LIT Verlag, pp. 175–204.

—— (2007a), *Nationale Rhetorik in Fest- und Gedenkreden. Eine diskursanalytische Studie zum "österreichischen Millennium" in den Jahren 1946 und 1996.* Tübingen: Stauffenburg.

—— (2007b), 'Probleme des Argumentierens in Seminararbeiten – Eine schreibdidaktische Herausforderung', in H. Gruber and U. Doleschal (eds), *Academic Writing in Languages other than English/Wissenschaftliches Schreiben abseits des englischen 'Mainstreams'.* Frankfurt am Main u.a.: Lang Verlag, pp. 253–84.

—— (2007c), 'The dynamics of right-wing populist argumentation in Austria', in F. H. Van Eemeren, J. A. Blair, C. A. Willard and B. Garssen (eds), *Proceedings of the Sixth Conference of the International Society for the Study of Argumentation*, Amsterdam: Sic Sat 2007/International Center for the Study of Argumentation, pp. 1127–34.

—— (2008), 'Analyzing political rhetoric', in R. Wodak and M. Krzyżanowski (eds), *Qualitative Discourse Analysis in the Social Sciences.* London: Palgrave, pp. 96–120.

—— (2011), 'Pragmatics and (critical) discourse analysis – commonalities and differences', in, C. Hart, (ed.), *Critical Discourse Studies in Context and Cognition*. Amsterdam: Benjamins, pp. 7–26.

—— (2013), 'Critical discourse analysis', in R. Bayley, R. Cameron and C. Lucas (eds), *The Oxford Handbook of Sociolinguistics*. Oxford: Oxford University Press, pp. 67–90.

Reisigl, M. and Wodak, R. (2001), *Discourse and Discrimination. Rhetorics of Racism and Antisemitism*. London: Routledge.

—— (2009), 'The discourse-historical approach', in R. Wodak and M. Meyer (eds), *Methods of Critical Discourse Analysis* (2nd rev. edn). London: Thousand Oaks; New Delhi: Sage, pp. 87–121.

Rubinelli, S. (2009), *Ars topica. The Classical Technique of Constructing Arguments from Aristotle to Cicero*. Amsterdam: Springer.

Snoeck Henkemans, F. A. (2001), 'Argumentation, explanation and causality. An exploration of current linguistic approaches to textual relations', in T. Sanders, J. Schilperoord and W. Spooren (eds.) *Text Representation. Linguistic and Psycholinguistic Aspects*. Amsterdam/Philadelphia: Benjamins, pp. 231–46.

Toulmin, S. (1969), *The Uses of Argument*. Cambridge: Cambridge University Press.

Van Eemeren, F. H. and Grotendorst, R. (1984), *Speech Act in Argumentative Discussions. A Theoretical Model for the Analysis of Discussions Directed towards Solving Conflicts of Opinion*. Dordrecht: Floris Publications.

—— (1992), *Argumentation, Communication, and Fallacies. A Pragma-Dialectical Perspective*. Hillsdale/New Jersey: Laurence Erlbaum Associates.

Van Eemeren, F. H., Garssen, B. and Meuffels, B. (2009), *Fallacies and Judgments of Reasonableness. Empirical Research Concerning the Pragma-Dialectical Discussion Rules*. Dordrecht: Springer.

Van Eemeren, F. H., Grootendorst, R. and Snoeck Henkemans, F.A. (1996), *Fundamentals of Argumentation Theory. A Handbook of Historical Backgrounds and Contemporary Developments*. Mahwah, New Jersey: Laurence Erlbaum Associates.

Van Eemeren, F. H., Houtlesser, P. and Snoeck Henkemans, F.A. (2007), *Argumentative Indicators in Discourse. A Pragma-Dialectical Study*. Dordrecht: Springer.

Walton, D., Reed, C. and Macagno, F. (2008), *Argumentation Schemes*. Cambridge: Cambridge University Press.

Wengeler, M. (1997), 'Argumentation im Einwanderungsdiskurs. Ein Vergleich der Zeiträume 1970–1973 und 1980–1983', in, M. Jung, M. Wengeler and K. Böke,(eds), *Die Sprache des Migrationsdiskurses. Das Reden über "Ausländer" in Medien, Politik und Alltag*. Stuttgart: Westdeutscher Verlag, pp. 121–49.

—— (2003), *Topos und Diskurs*. Tübingen: Niemeyer.

Wodak, R., De Cillia, R., Reisigl, M. and Liebhart, K. (2009[1999]), *The Discursive Construction of National Identity*. Edinburgh: Edinburgh University Press.

Wodak, R., De Cillia, R., Reisigl, M., Liebhart, K., Hofstätter, K. and Kargl, M. (1998), *Zur diskursiven Konstruktion nationaler Identität*. Frankfurt am Main: Suhrkamp.

Wodak, R., Pelikan, J., Nowak, P., Gruber, H., De Cillia, R. and Mitten, R. (1990), *'Wir sind alle unschuldige Täter!' Diskurshistorische Studien zum Nachkriegsantisemitismus*. Frankfurt am Main: Suhrkamp.

Wunderlich, D. (1976), *Studien zur Sprechakttheorie*. Frankfurt am Main: Suhrkamp.

Žagar, I. (2009), 'Topoi in critical discourse analysis'. *Šolsko polje*, 5(6) 47–73 (http://www.pei.si/UserFilesUpload/file/digitalna_knjiznica/SP/2009/SP_XX_2009_5-6/SP_XX_2009_5-6.html).

—— (2010), 'Topoi in critical discourse analysis', *Lodz Papers in Pragmatics*, 6(1) 3–27 (http://versita.metapress.com/content/w6745773511l3282/).

# 4

# It Is Easy to Miss Something You Are Not Looking For

# A Pragmatic Account of Covert Communicative Influence for (Critical) Discourse Analysis

*Steve Oswald*

University of Fribourg

## 1 Introduction

The study of discursive influence is possibly the most striking unifying factor in all Critical Discourse Studies (henceforth CDS) research since its inception. Taking on board the Habermasian assumption according to which 'language is [. . .] a medium of domination and social force' and that '[i]t serves to legitimize relations of organized power' (Habermas, 1969: 259), many researchers in the critical paradigm of discourse analysis have devoted scholarly effort to describing and explaining how discourse can become – or, in some cases, simply is – an instrument of ideology, power and domination. In other words, the critical strand of discourse analysis has always explored how language can be used to influence people's minds and behaviours by conveying ideologically loaded contents and persuasive or deceptive messages of various kinds. One of the earliest systematic attempts to tackle this issue by resorting to linguistic theory can be traced to the Critical Linguistics movement, which originated at the University of East Anglia in the 1970s. Through the study of public discourse and of the way particular representations are conveyed by linguistic structures, Tony Trew, Bob Hodge, Gunther Kress and Roger Fowler have paved the way, with *Language and Control* (1979), for what turned out to be an extremely prolific new direction of research at the interface between language and society.

While being typically concerned with the social implications of language use, the critical paradigm in discourse studies has gradually incorporated over the past 20 to 30 years cognitive insights as an additional layer of analysis, mainly through the study of conceptual metaphor and of the cognitive processes at play when humans build representations which lead them to acquire new beliefs or modify them on the basis of communicated information (see e.g. Chilton, 1996, 2004; Hart, 2010; Charteris-Black, 2006a, 2006b; Musolff, 2004, 2006; Van Dijk 2008). The idea behind this cognitive turn was, to quote Chilton, to account for the type of mental constructions 'taking place in the minds of interacting individuals' (Chilton, 2005: 24) when they are processing discourse, and in particular ideologically loaded discourse. In other words, the research question introduced by cognitive approaches to discourse seeks to address the psychological side of discourse processing and to provide an account of why and how such discourse can come to be effective in the first place.

The purpose of this chapter is to contribute to the development of the cognitive turn in CDS by exposing and illustrating some of the advantages of a cognitive pragmatic approach to discourse and its relevance to CDS more generally in answering the above-mentioned question. The focus of the analysis will be the relationship between language and beliefs in communicative settings in which language users are trying to influence their addressee (and also, more largely, an audience). I will start by concentrating my attention on the phenomenon of deception as one particular type of communicative influence and characterize it as the covert exploitation of basic cognitive mechanisms at play behind the (naïve) interpretation of discourse. In doing so, I will be led to construe influence in 'operational' terms, as a type of interpretative constraint bearing on information selection. The primary goal of this chapter is therefore to explain how deception manages to covertly steer the audience's interpretation of a speaker's given message so as to obfuscate the deceptive intent. In the second stage of the theoretical exposition, I will extend the model in an attempt to capture further phenomena of communicative influence, such as persuasion.

In order to introduce some of the main issues related to the study of deception, section 2 will briefly discuss some descriptive problems involved in its definition. Section 3 will develop some arguments to defend a pragmatic take in what regards the *explanation* of deceptive communication; I will spell out a cognitive pragmatic take on deception and highlight how it can be relevant to discourse analytical research. Section 4 will extend the model to argumentation and illustrate it with the analysis of an excerpt of the French presidential debate that took place in May 2012 between Nicolas Sarkozy and François Hollande.

## 2 Defining and analysing deception

Conceptualizing deception is not an easy task.[1] Researchers from traditions and disciplines as varied as philosophy, psychology, linguistics, discourse analysis, sociology and communication science have discussed its properties and tried to identify its necessary and sufficient conditions (see Oswald, 2010, chapters 1 and 2 for a review). In this effort, criteria such as speaker interest, covertness, truth, social inequality (or power relationships) and intention have been put forth to describe the phenomenon.[2] For the purposes of this chapter I will opt for a characterization that takes into account three recurring defining features of deceptive communication across the literature, namely that deception is necessarily covert, intentional, and purposeful.[3] I consequently adopt the following *descriptive* definition of deception:

(a) An utterance is deceptive if it is intentionally used as a means to attain a perlocutionary goal the speaker is covertly pursuing.

This definition echoes that of Puzynina (1992), itself referred to in Galasiński (2000) and Blass (2005) for instance, and highlights the three defining properties just mentioned. I consider it to be a phenomenon of perlocutionary interest because like many researchers I take deception to be a means to attain a goal. This brings to the fore the idea that deception is a type of language *use*, thereby capturing the idea that deceptive speakers do something in particular in communication. We will see shortly that the explanatory contribution of a cognitive pragmatic account of communication precisely rests on an elaboration of this very idea (section 3).

Given that intentions are private (or externally inscrutable, as Papafragou, 2006 puts it) and that any communicative phenomenon construed in terms of intentionality inevitably runs the risk of being tagged as a speaker category and left out of the analysis for that reason, one could consider that the deceptive intention seems to be such that it falls outside the scope of phenomena captured by pragmatic inquiry. To put it bluntly, how could a theory positing that communication is a matter of intention recognition capture a phenomenon whose success precisely rests on the concealment of an intention? There are two ways of going about this puzzle: the first is to consider that deception is not a communicative phenomenon and to conclude that it cannot be approached by pragmatics, as it falls outside of the range of phenomena covered by the discipline. I am reluctant to consider that such is the case, to the extent that deceptive communication is still communication: contents go through in deception, even if they are uncooperative *in a certain respect* (which is, as we will see next, what needs to be precisely characterized), and deceived addressees still do understand something from the speaker's message. The second option enjoins us to distinguish between the types of intentionality involved here: in standard cooperative communication, what a speaker wants to communicate is 'doubly' intentional in the sense that she intends her addressee both (i) to recognize the contents she wants to convey,[4] and (ii) to recognize that she wants to share those contents with him.[5] In deceptive exchanges, the speaker certainly wants to communicate something and indeed makes manifest that she does, but she crucially does not want her addressee to recognize one particular intention, namely that she is pursuing a covert perlocutionary goal. Once we take stock of these two layers of intentionality distinguished according to their communicative status (i.e., whether they are meant to be identified by the hearer as being meant by the speaker or not), we can treat deception as a communicative phenomenon, because regardless of how we look at it, it is part of a communicative exchange – albeit only as a by-product or some sort of add-on. Recognizing that deceptive communication still qualifies as communication will allow us to proceed in its analysis, as we shall see further along.

Reflecting on the intentional nature of deception will however not allow us to inquire about how deception works, but rather about what it is and whether there are ways to detect it. In other words, research along these lines seeks to answer the 'what' questions: what is deception, what are its properties, and can we use our knowledge of those properties to identify deception in someone's discourse? While much can be said on these particular questions, the purpose of this chapter is to tackle a separate set of questions. I will accordingly move on to fleshing out an account meant to address complementary preoccupations, which are more relevant in my view to discourse analysis. I will suggest, as part of an on-going effort to explore another facet of the phenomenon (see Maillat and Oswald, 2009, 2011; Oswald, 2010, 2011; Maillat, 2013), that even if a cognitive pragmatic approach to communication does not take us very far in identifying deception in discourse, it has significant advantages when it comes to answering the 'how' question that should account for the mechanisms responsible for successful deception.

# 3 The pragmatics of deception

## 3.1 *What it means to account for deception from a cognitive pragmatic perspective*

The goal of any (linguistic or discursive) explanatory account of deception is to identify why and how the phenomenon comes about. This ideally takes the shape of a predictive model grounded on identified causal relationships that allow us to understand the phenomenon in its 'natural environment'. What I am advocating to this end is a naturalistic – and to a certain extent mechanistic – perspective. Whereas identifying the necessary and sufficient conditions of communicative deception only takes us so far, trying to account for its success constitutes a perhaps more fruitful direction of research. For this we need to elaborate an operational definition of deception so as to highlight the processes at its core that need accounting for.

From (a) above, we will retain the idea of covertness because it represents a feature of deception that can be exploited and further elaborated in the type of account defended here. When something is hidden from someone, it means that s/he has no access to it. From the perspective of the cognitive processes taking place in the mind of the deceived addressee, this means that some information sets which could have led him to postulate that something about the speaker's discourse was problematic have not been accessed or mobilized. In the case of deception, the information sets that have to remain concealed are presumably those which contain critical information that would lead him to question the message or the speaker's motives and intentions. Consequently, the information sets a deceptive speaker has to conceal are those which could bring to the fore – i.e., get the hearer to represent:

**(i)**   Internal inconsistencies within the message, such as logical or pragmatic contradictions and infelicities.

**(ii)**  Inconsistencies between the message's content and the addressee's values and beliefs, the realization of which might trigger further processing about the reasons these inconsistencies are present.

**(iii)** Critical information the addressee had not previously represented and which he can use to invalidate or question the content of the message.

**(iv)**  Reasons to doubt the speaker's benevolence and/or competence.

In sum, any piece of critical information that puts the addressee in a position to question the speaker's message or her willingness to be cooperative is a potential threat to the success of deception.[6]

Managing to prevent *access* to critical information is thus arguably a significant part of the deceptive process; but in order to increase its chances of being successful, deception also needs to make sure that what the message communicates is accepted by the addressee as reliable, relevant and true information – people are not gullible to the point of believing just anything, and therefore the deceptive message's content itself must remain within the boundaries of what is contextually plausible. It proves quite difficult to precisely characterize the notion of acceptance given that it may denote a range of different things, such as holding something to be true, morally acceptable, convenient, etc. In order to group the different items into one consistent category, I will construe acceptance as the situation in which an individual has included a mental representation in her/his cognitive environment, independently from her/his reasons for doing so; that is, the situation in which the individual holds the representation to be true or probably true (in the terms of Sperber and Wilson, 1995).[7] The parameter at stake here to determine whether such representations will make it to the cognitive environment of language users is the extent to which said representations are believable, and this can be envisaged in terms of the epistemic *strength* of information: the stronger the assumption, the more chances it has of entering the cognitive environment. Critical discourse analysis, through the study of legitimation strategies and argumentation (see e.g. Van Leeuwen and Wodak, 1999; Iețcu-Fairclough, 2007; Richardson, 2004) has already identified a number of such discursive strategies. What can be added from a cognitive perspective is that these are meant to make sure that the target assumptions are perceived to be very likely: in other words, legitimation strategies try to boost the epistemic strength of target assumptions in order to increase their chances of belonging to the addressee's cognitive environment.

Providing an answer to the question of how discursive influence works, from the cognitive perspective adopted here, therefore consists in identifying the parameters that are responsible for the inclusion of an assumption in an individual's cognitive environment. Two such parameters can be identified: on the one hand information accessibility and on the other epistemic strength. If we now link them with the issue of communicative deception and its success, we can elaborate a definition of what deception does, from the perspective of information-processing. Successfully deceived addressees are those (i) who have failed to access critical information or who have deemed it epistemically weak and (ii) who have been led to easily access the content of the message and furthermore who deem it epistemically strong. I can now formulate the following working definition which characterizes what deceptive communication does, in terms of the cognitive phenomena at play during its operation:

(b) Deceptive communication is successful when the addressee has accepted the content of the utterance, which he perceives as epistemically strong, while simultaneously having been prevented from representing critical information that would have allowed him to question said content (provision: such critical information exists and could be accessible to him).

Deceptive discourse is thus a twofold cognitive process: on the one hand it prompts the hearer to easily infer a specific content which he does not realize is problematic, while on the other it drives him away from spotting that that content (including the intention with which it was formulated) and its acceptance by the hearer is instrumental to the satisfaction of one of the speaker's covert perlocutionary goals.

Let me get back, for methodological purposes, to the difference made earlier between accounting for what manipulation is and accounting for how manipulation works. Answering the 'what' question requires the analyst to study deception as an object envisaged from the perspective of the speaker. However, the account is not informative and explanatory enough if we limit ourselves to looking at things from that perspective, mainly because we can never be 100 per cent certain about a speaker's intentions. Alternatively, gaining insights into the way deception works will allow us to apprehend the phenomenon more exhaustively; when it comes to answering the 'how' question, as we try to specify the conditions under which deception is successful, the perspective must be shifted *to that of the hearer*. Deceptive discourse is only effective if its addressees process it in such a way that it goes unnoticed; the answer to the question 'why can deception be effective' is therefore likely to be answered by looking at how information-processing can be constrained to fulfil deceptive goals. The question at stake seeks to elucidate the relationship between language and beliefs; this is typically an object of psychological inquiry and therefore calls for a theoretical framework that is able to combine insights from both linguistics and psychology. In short, we need an information-processing model that will provide criteria to determine under which conditions information becomes more and less salient (salience being understood as a common property of both accessible and strong information), assuming that salience positively affects selection and inclusion in the cognitive environment. Relevance Theory provides such a model.

## 3.2  *Relevance theory*

Initially defined by Charles Morris as the study of 'the relation of signs to interpreters' (Morris, 1938: 6), and very broadly as the discipline dealing with the 'biotic aspects of semiosis, that is, with all the psychological, biological and social phenomena which occur in the functioning of signs' (1938: 108), research in pragmatics has come to explore over the years the different directions of research anticipated by Morris – and more. As a consequence, the field of pragmatics nowadays includes philosophical, psychological, anthropological, sociological and cognitive approaches to language use. The most recent trends in pragmatics are informed by cognitive science and aim to account for the cognitive underpinnings of human communication, both theoretically and, more recently, experimentally (see Noveck and Sperber, 2004).

Relevance Theory (see Sperber and Wilson, 1986, 1995; Wilson and Sperber, 2012; henceforth RT) represents one of the most evolved alternatives within the field, and I will now attempt to show how its account of information-processing mechanisms can provide a valuable framework for the development of an explanatory account of discursive influence.[8] I should also note that although CDA has resorted to pragmatics in the past, notably by borrowing some of its concepts for analytical purposes, no principled account has been elaborated to consistently assess and illustrate how issues of meaning (and their handling by a cognitive pragmatic theory) can be theoretically, methodologically and epistemologically grounded within the Critical Discourse Studies agenda.[9]

As a general theory of human cognition, RT focuses on the cognitive mechanisms at play in communication, with the goal of explaining how it is that people manage to understand each other through the use of verbal stimuli. Within the theory, the process of understanding language is conceived as the main task of a specific mental module, the comprehension module, dedicated exclusively to processing verbal material and delivering representations about the meaning (which is taken to correspond to speaker meaning) of a given utterance. RT models the comprehension process by construing it as an input-processing-output mechanism. Its input is constituted by a minimal representation of the speaker's/writer's utterance that is derived from the linguistic material chosen by the speaker to express it: this representation is the result of syntactic parsing, disambiguation, reference resolution, and concept retrieval processes. It is subsequently combined with implicit and explicit available contextual assumptions. The representation arrived at after this inferential step is the output of the process – the interpretation – and is taken to correspond to speaker meaning. The task of the comprehension module is thus to process the input utterance in order to identify the contextually intended meaning, that is, the most relevant meaning given the circumstances.

Probably the most crucial feature of RT, for our purposes, is that it posits clearly identified constraints on how information is selected in the interpretative process: information selection is driven by considerations of relevance, relevance being technically defined in terms of two extent conditions:

### Extent conditions of relevance:

Extent condition 1: an assumption is relevant in a context to the extent that its contextual effects in this context are large.
Extent condition 2: an assumption is relevant in a context to the extent that the effort required to process it in this context is small.

(Sperber and Wilson, 1995: 125)

The second condition stipulates that the contents that are more likely to be selected as relevant during the comprehension procedure are those which do not require significant effort to be represented (i.e., those which are easily accessible in terms of processing effort) and the first condition identifies as relevant those assumptions which yield significant contextual effects (i.e., those which are useful to the cognitive system because they are deemed reliable and epistemically strong). The assumptions that best satisfy this effort/effect ratio are those that our cognitive system will deem most relevant.[10]

Such an account of meaning is tailored to explain how addressees infer relevant interpretations. The process itself is not assumed to be error-proof, to the extent that the meaning derivation procedure is heuristic, and therefore fallible. Extent conditions of relevance obtain in standard communication, but this does not mean that they guarantee systematic extraction of the intended meaning: misunderstandings do occur, and one of the ways RT accounts for this is by postulating, in those cases, a mismatch between the contextual assumptions intended by the speaker and those that the addressee actually mobilizes. However, the strength of RT is that it provides clearly formulated hypotheses about the parameters which determine the inclusion of any given assumption in the cognitive environment of an addressee, as he processes the speaker's utterance. In what follows I turn to articulating how such a framework can be used to explain why and how deception can work.

## 3.3 Deception and cognitive constraints on relevance

In (b) above, I characterized deception as a double cognitive constraint: it manages to keep critical information under the radar and 'favourable' information salient.[11] As previously mentioned, deception takes advantage of the inherent fallibility of information-processing mechanisms. Specifically, it implements cognitive constraints in order to make sure that certain information sets are processed at the expense of other information sets, the mobilization of which would be required to defeat the attempt to deceive. The cognitive underpinnings of this mechanism have been detailed by Maillat and Oswald (2009, 2011) through their pragmatic model of the Contextual Selection Constraint, in which they frame manipulation as a double constraint characterized along the dimensions of accessibility and epistemic strength. More precisely, deception is a strategy in which critical information is made less accessible and/or epistemically weaker, while 'favourable' information is rendered more accessible and epistemically stronger. The same cognitive operations can therefore constrain the (perceived) relevance of information by maximizing it or by minimizing it alongside epistemic strength and accessibility variation. The advantage of this model is to be found in its simplicity, as it postulates a single principle, that of informational (ir) relevance, to explain how information sets can be backgrounded (sometimes to the extent that they might even fail to be represented at all) or foregrounded. To summarize, deception can under this perspective be construed as a cognitive constraint on informational attention: it works by driving people's attention away from information that would defeat it and by focusing their attention on information that will not. The model thus holds that you may fall prey to deception because it is very easy for you to miss something you are not led to look for.

## 3.4 A cognitive framework for discourse analysis

The cognitive pragmatic account of deception advocated here is not designed to cover all aspects of deceptive communication – it has in fact little if nothing to say about the social and institutional aspects of deception. Instead, it limits its focus to the operational linguistic and pragmatic aspects of information processing involved in successful deception. Its usefulness within CDS is therefore to be found in its ability to assess the relationship between linguistic material (together with its informational context of occurrence) and the inferences that it licenses, alongside its perlocutionary effects. The idea is that the more an addressee will be led to represent critical information, the more deception is likely to be unsuccessful; in parallel and simultaneously, the more an addressee is led to fail to represent critical information, the more deception is likely to be successful. What I want to highlight at this point is that if we turn to (classical and mainstream) CDS, we will find converging accounts, albeit not cognitive accounts, of many discursive strategies that do just that.

As I said, the usefulness of this model of deception for CDS is that it allows us to ground the study of deceptive strategies on an explanatory cognitive model. We can thus reasonably expect this cognitive framework to be able to revisit many of the linguistic and pragmatic strategies that have been identified in the study of deceptive, persuasive and ideologically-loaded communication over the years, thereby opening the field to their cognitive reinterpretations. An established area of research, namely the subfield of argumentation theory which studies fallacies, is already being explored through this new lens: Maillat and Oswald (2009, 2011), Oswald (2011) and Oswald and Hart (2014) provide some general pointers on how fallacies can be approached from a cognitive perspective; Maillat (2013) applies the framework to the *ad populum* fallacy; Oswald and Lewiński (forthcoming) and Lewiński and Oswald (2013) develop an account of the straw man fallacy; Oswald and Hart (2014) explore source-related fallacies; and Oswald (forthcoming) takes a more global perspective to flesh out a cognitive pragmatic account of rhetorical effectiveness. The example that will be discussed in the next section proceeds with this line of study by focusing on a complex instance of fallacious political discourse.

Alongside argumentative fallacies, many other discursive strategies can be cognitively reinterpreted in this vein. In fact, any communicative or discursive strategy meant to draw the audience's attention away from the problematic nature of the message while at the same time foregrounding specific representations would be in principle interpretable within the proposed model. That is, any strategy used to constrain the meaning that an addressee may derive from a speaker's message so as to mislead him into entertaining problematic contents can be envisaged as the result of weakening or strengthening constraints on the relevance of information. Let me mention some of them:

- Early literature in critical linguistics on phenomena such as *passivization* or *nominalization* (see Fowler et al., 1979) can be revisited: to the extent that these 'transformations' achieve obfuscation of critical information, they can be described as weakening strategies. In the case of passivization, one could construe the removal of the agent's responsibility in the semantic structure of the clause as the result of a cognitive constraint meant to diminish the accessibility of the agentive role in the representation of the event. As far as nominalization is concerned, the loss of information resulting from the transformation of a predicate into a noun can also be seen as the result of a strategy meant to decrease the accessibility of said information without losing anything in terms of syntactical appropriateness and semantic interpretability.

- Similarly, abundant literature on the strategies of *positive self-representation* and *negative other representation* (see e.g. Van Dijk, 1994; Wodak and Van Dijk, 2006; KhosraviNik, 2008, 2010) constitutes another area of CDS research amenable to cognitive pragmatic explorations: negative other representation and positive self-representation strategies are successful when they are able to conceal their illegitimacy, i.e., when they are able to be perceived as epistemically strong, while the critical reasons that could undermine them go unnoticed.

● Meaning constituents such as *presuppositions* or *implicatures*, for instance, are also among the set of pragmatic phenomena that have been taken by discourse analysts to fulfil strategic functions in discourse and which can also be cognitively reinterpreted: implicatures may very well make certain contents salient by playing on contextual constraints and presuppositions might lead addressees to take for granted or simply fail to question information that should be questioned (see Saussure, 2012; Polyzou, 2013), which cognitively amounts to managing to decrease the perceived relevance of said information.

● *Metaphor* is another cognitive and discursively exploited phenomenon whose persuasive and even manipulative potential has been discussed at length in cognitive linguistics (see Chilton, 2005; Charteris-Black, 2006a, 2006b; and Hart, 2010 for illustrative studies). Extended metaphors in particular can be argumentatively exploited to confer epistemic strength to specific propositions because they provide ideal discursive structures that can be used for argumentative purposes (Oswald and Rihs, 2014).

Examples of discursive strategies that can be cognitively reinterpreted can be multiplied as long as they are concerned with meaning and representation, illustrating how the model advocated here can enrich existing accounts by grounding them in a psychologically-plausible framework. In what follows I turn to exemplifying the type of analysis that can be performed with this model with a concrete example taken from political discourse. We will see in what respect a construal of influence in terms of cognitive constraints on information processing can prove useful and thereby offer an original contribution to extant accounts of discursive influence.

# 4  Analysing deception and fallacious argumentation

## 4.1  Fallacious ≠ deceptive

Let me here make some cautionary remarks in order to avoid potential misconceptions about the type of phenomena this model is able to capture, which should not be limited to deceptive communication. Even though it is in principle designed to capture deception, the cognitive pragmatic model referred to here and presented in more detail in Maillat and Oswald (2009, 2011), Oswald (2010) and Maillat (2013) is in principle extendable to cover additional phenomena of discursive influence.

I have provided in sections 2 and 3 above two distinct yet complementary definitions of deception: definition (a) is descriptive and defines deception from a phenomenological perspective while definition (b) provides an operational definition of deception which specifies when successful deception occurs in terms of information processing. However, (b) denotes deception only when (a) also obtains. This means that an utterance can be qualified as deceptive only under the condition that (b) specifies how (a) is achieved in a given discourse.

The analytical usefulness of (b) is nevertheless not restricted to cases of deception: when one observes that a given discourse implements the cognitive constraints of (b) without the conditions specified in (a) obtaining, the discourse under observation cannot be deemed deceptive; nevertheless, it does not follow that whatever happens in terms of discourse processing is irrelevant for the analyst interested in discursive influence. Fallacious argumentation may or may not be deceptive: this depends on whether the speaker is pursuing a covert perlocutionary goal – i.e., it depends on the presence of a deceptive intention. In case she is not (for instance, in case she simply makes a reasoning mistake in the argument she formulates), we can still analyse her discourse in terms of the parameters specified in (b). This means that whether argumentative fallacies are deceptive or not in a given context has no incidence on the possibility of performing an analysis informed by the specifications of (b). Weakening and strengthening *effects* in the addressee's processing of information can still occur without deception being present, that is, without the presence of a deceptive *strategy*.

These considerations bear at least two important consequences for (cognitive) discourse analysis, especially if we recall the difference between identifying deception in a given discourse and explaining how it works. First, the study of discursive influence so construed will allow the analyst to explain how an addressee can be persuaded by a given discourse without necessarily needing to settle the thorny question of establishing whether the discourse is deceptive or not.[12] Second, as mentioned above in section 3.4, it allows us to address the complex variety of discursive influence strategies within one single framework. As a consequence, it should not be claimed that fallacies are necessarily deceptive, even if they can be analysed with the same tools that were designed to analyse deceptive communication.

## 4.2 *Analysing an argumentative debate from a cognitive pragmatic perspective*

The data I will be analysing comes from the French presidential debate that took place after the first round of the election, on 2 May 2012, between François Hollande and Nicolas Sarkozy, the remaining two candidates. The particular passage I will be focusing on concerns a discussion about the presidential balance sheet of Sarkozy's first term. As expected in such circumstances, Sarkozy had previously taken credit for many positive outcomes of his action as French President while Hollande accused him of not wanting to acknowledge his failures. Here is the exchange:[13]

**(1)** Hollande:  You are always happy with yourself, which is extraordinary. No matter what happens, you are happy. The French people are not, but you, you are happy. I therefore have to add, since you mention it, regarding growth, that we are . . .

**(2)** Sarkozy:  You are shamelessly lying, and I should accept it?

**(3)** Hollande:  For now, I haven't said anything that would justify this expression.

**(4)** Sarkozy:  It's a lie.

**(5)** Hollande:  What is?

**(6)** Sarkozy:  It's a lie.

**(7)** Hollande:  What is? What is? What is?

**(8)** Sarkozy:  You are lying when you say that I'm always happy with myself and that I do not acknowledge my responsibilities. It's a lie.

**(9)** Hollande:  So you are very unhappy with yourself, I must have made a mistake. I must have committed an error and I am therefore apologizing to you: you are very unhappy with yourself.

**(10)** Sarkozy:  This is not a small joke contest.

**(11)** Hollande:  No, it is no joke. I cannot let you call me a liar here.

## 4.2.1 Argumentative reconstruction

An argumentative analysis of this sequence requires a minimal reconstruction of the argumentative exchange in order to identify its key meaningful argumentative movements; the reconstruction yields the following paraphrase:

Hollande:  You are always happy with yourself.

Sarkozy:  You are shamelessly lying.

Hollande:  I am not lying because I haven't said anything that would justify this expression.

Sarkozy:  You are lying when you say that I'm always happy with myself and that I don't acknowledge my responsibility.

Hollande:  I must have made a mistake; you are very unhappy with yourself.

Sarkozy:  This is not a small joke contest.

Hollande:  I cannot let you call me a liar here.

This sequence can be further broken down into four movements corresponding to what the participants do in terms of argumentative significance. A first movement can be identified as Sarkozy's attack, in (3), of Hollande's standpoint (2) in which he states that Sarkozy is always happy with himself. Immediately after the attack, Hollande attempts to rebut it in (4) with a counterargument ('I haven't said anything that would justify this expression').

The second movement starts in (5), where Sarkozy reformulates the counterargument he just provided in (3). In so doing, he specifies the nature of his objection by introducing a conjunction, thereby making his counterargument a complex one. These two movements are argumentatively interesting in themselves (to the extent that one could see (5) as setting the stage for a straw man fallacy in case we fail to ascertain that Hollande accused, albeit implicitly, Sarkozy of not wanting to take responsibility), but I will focus on the rest of the exchange instead, which is particularly prone to receiving an analysis within the above-mentioned cognitive framework.

The third argumentative movement lies in Hollande's apparent acceptance, in (6), of part of Sarkozy's reformulation in (5); Hollande further specifies his thought by acknowledging that he 'must have made a mistake'. From a strictly literal perspective, Hollande's utterance thus amounts to a resolution of the dispute, since he apparently concedes that his standpoint (2) should be rejected. However, the utterance is ironic, which indicates that Hollande is in fact pursuing his argumentative strategy. He does this by adding that Sarkozy is very unhappy with himself, which amounts to an indirect attack on Sarkozy's credibility: a president who is extremely unhappy with himself cannot come across as a reliable candidate for an additional term, which is why (6) can be said to play an argumentative role in the exchange as well.

In the final movement, Sarkozy, in (7), attempts to counter the attack by calling into question the seriousness of (6), which thereby simultaneously counts as an attempt to undermine Hollande's sincerity by explicitly exposing the joke. Finally, in (8), Hollande only apparently rebuts (7): even though the rebuttal seems to respond to the immediately preceding utterance, it is in fact replying to the charge of lying that was present in (3) and (5).

The sequence is therefore quite complex and can be summarized as follows:

- 1st movement: standpoint by Hollande (2), counterargument by Sarkozy (3), rebuttal of the counterargument by Hollande (4).

- 2nd movement: reformulation of the standpoint and subsequent specification by Sarkozy (5).

- 3rd movement: apparent concession of the counterargument by Hollande (and therefore apparent resolution of the dispute), indirect attack on Sarkozy (6).

- 4th movement: attempt by Sarkozy to counter the indirect attack (7), apparent rebuttal by Hollande of the counterattack and final counterargument (8).

As already mentioned, the remainder of my analysis will focus on the 3rd and 4th movement.

## 4.2.2 Fallacy fest

The analytical significance of Hollande's contribution has to be found in the quality of his argumentative moves. From the perspective of argumentative validity or soundness, (6) displays features of three different well-known fallacies, namely the straw man fallacy, the false dilemma and the *ad hominem* fallacy.

The straw man is a 'fallacy of argumentative discussion in which an arguer misrepresents her adversary's standpoint or arguments in such a way that they become easier to refute, and then attacks the misrepresented position as if it were the one actually defended by the adversary' (Lewiński and Oswald, 2013: 165). In (6), Hollande abusively misrepresents Sarkozy's thoughts by claiming that the latter is very unhappy with himself, which is not straightforwardly equivalent to repeating what Sarkozy had previously said in (5), namely that it is not true that he is always happy with himself. In order to construct this misrepresentation, Hollande furthermore relies on an abusive simplification of an alternative emerging from Sarkozy's negative formulation in (5): in particular, Hollande tries to force mutually exclusive contents in the alternative by implicitly establishing that if one is not always happy with oneself, then one must be very unhappy with oneself. This is typical of the fallacy known as the false dilemma, which consists in reducing an alternative to two mutually exclusive options when in fact a whole range of other options could be relevant. Finally, by virtue of the ironic tone of (6), Hollande can also be said to launch a personal attack on Sarkozy's *ethos*, leading the audience to infer that Sarkozy's unhappiness with his own performance is symptomatic of his unreliability and incompetence as a head of the state.[14] With one single utterance, Hollande's contribution to the argumentative exchange engages three different fallacies. We will now look at the formulation of the utterance and at the pragmatic significance of these three fallacies in order to show how they can act as constraints on information processing geared at driving the audience's attention away from spending time on their fallacious nature.

With (6), Hollande is responding to Sarkozy's complex reformulation of a previous counterargument. By uttering (5), Sarkozy was indeed negating a conjunction, in this case amounting to something like 'it is not true that I am always happy with myself and that I do not acknowledge my responsibilities'. Now, a natural and reasonably expected defence, in line with Hollande's previous defence in (4), would be for him to argue that he is not a liar and that what he said is indeed true. However, in (6), Hollande opts for a concession instead, with the particularity that he concedes only something which resembles the first conjunct of Sarkozy's refutation: Hollande only responds on Sarkozy's degree of satisfaction with respect to his action. So instead of continuing with the same line of argument, Hollande is apparently conceding something Sarkozy allegedly said, as a way of superficially resolving the dispute. From the perspective of argumentative resolution, we could thus at first sight infer that Hollande abandons his initial standpoint. But this apparent resolution serves an additional argumentative purpose, namely setting up the straw man. The negation of 'not being happy' is semantically compatible with many interpretations: depending on the context, it could mean 'being sometimes happy', 'never being happy', 'being in a state where happiness/unhappiness is irrelevant', 'being sometimes unhappy', 'being always unhappy', etc. So when one says that one is not happy with oneself, it does not necessarily mean that one is unhappy with oneself, which is nevertheless the proposition which Hollande attributes to Sarkozy. The misattribution at the core of the straw man therefore relies on a false dilemma, for a complex alternative is reduced abusively to only two mutually exclusive options in (6). Moreover, (6) focuses on the first conjunct of (5) under the scope of the negation while disregarding the second; a reasonable reaction to (5) would need to address the latter as well.

A textbook straw man consists in misrepresenting an opponent's words so as to *refute* them easily. Hollande, somewhat surprisingly, does not do this, as he concedes what he presents as corresponding to Sarkozy's counterargument and subsequently acknowledges his own mistake instead. If we compare the role of (6) and its literal meaning, a first problem arises: (6) functions as an attack, and yet a concession cannot by definition be interpreted as an attack, since it is supposed to grant an opponent's point. As a consequence, since Hollande appears to agree with Sarkozy (if only at face value), his previous obligation to defend himself from the charge of lying (which he contracted in (4)) is no longer perceived as relevant, which means that the dispute about lying seems to be resolved. Of course, this part of the exchange should precisely not be taken at face value, because Hollande is issuing only a 'pretend-concession': on the one hand he concedes a misrepresentation of (5), which is, as we have just seen, based on a false dilemma, and on the other hand the concession is in fact ironic. Furthermore, (6) is used to discredit Sarkozy, which is why it can be counted as an *ad hominem* attack.

Sarkozy recognizes the damaging potential of the irony of (6), and tries, in (7), to counter it by meta linguistically highlighting its inappropriateness in the debate. But, again, Hollande attempts to steer things to his advantage: his serious answer in (8) is actually misdirected. While we would expect it to respond to Sarkozy's immediately preceding charge of trying to be funny (7) – and we have actually no clear indication at first to infer that such will not be the case – in fact it relates to (3) and (5), namely the charge of being a liar, which is off-topic at this point, given Hollande's previous (apparent) concession. Yet, defending oneself from a serious charge such as that of lying may pass for legitimate defence; after all, he was just accused of lying, and he can still go back to that accusation because he has previously admitted a mistake, but not a lie. After having pretended to settle the discussion about lying, he makes it relevant again – technically, indeed, he has not responded to it yet.

### 4.2.3 Rhetoric, weakening and strengthening strategies

The overall rhetorical strategy of Hollande could be described as twofold: on the one hand he produces a 'multi-fallacious' argument which, due to the ironic tone of (6), is also presented as a joke (we will shortly see how this plays out to his advantage); on the other, he manages to divert attention away from a critical evaluation of his fallacious move. This requires him to manage to constrain not only Sarkozy's cognitive processing, but also his audience's (i.e. millions of TV viewers).

Let us first discuss the way Sarkozy's reactions are constrained by Hollande. The ironic attack in (6) leaves Sarkozy with two choices: either he addresses the misrepresentation to show that his opponent is abusively representing his words or he tries to counter the attack because he perceives how damaging it can be for his *ethos* to be the butt of the joke. This is the solution he opts for in (7) and his reaction can thus be seen as fulfilling face-work to restore his own image. Instead of going for a defence, he accuses his opponent of not being serious, hoping to neutralize the threat on his own face: if he manages to discredit Hollande this way, chances are that he will also manage to defuse the threat. Retrospectively, this means that (6) has favoured a face-repair priority, and it is therefore fair to assume that it has strengthened the need for repair (or counter-attack), in cognitive terms, by making this need a priority. But we still need to justify why this is so. *Ad hominem* attacks are typically described as unreasonable owing to the type of reaction they bring about, which constitutes a derailment from the argumentative discussion about the initial standpoint (see Van Eemeren and Grootendorst, 1996; Van Eemeren and Houtlosser, 2008): victims of such attacks usually feel the need to justify themselves and try to restore their image. It is not hard to see how this can become a priority particularly in political communicative contexts such as a presidential debate: the potentially disastrous consequences, in terms of image, generate a trouble that urgently needs to be resolved and thereby legitimizes the expenditure of efforts in view of that goal. We can thus assume that it cognitively translates into the high salience of the trouble perceived, and that it *ipso facto* focuses the cognitive system's attention towards resolving it. Among the options at Sarkozy's disposal, the need to repair or to counter-attack to highlight his opponent's inappropriateness (one should not joke in a presidential debate), is consequently strengthened.

Once Sarkozy counter-attacks by threatening Hollande's *ethos* in (7), Hollande has a more advantageous choice, to the extent that his opponent has accused him of two different things in the exchange: in (3) and (5) he called him a liar, and in (7) he accuses him of not being serious. Of the two charges, Hollande can therefore select the one that he feels will be rhetorically more useful. He opts for defending himself from being a liar, even though that particular accusation seemed (but only seemed) to have been settled in the preceding exchange. By responding to it, however, he can still present himself as a victim of unfair treatment: a response to an accusation of being a liar is potentially more serious and damaging for the author of the accusation than a response to an accusation of trying to be humorous. Hollande is therefore attempting to undermine Sarkozy's image by making his first accusation relevant again. Hollande is therefore controlling what is relevant in the exchange: at first he constrains Sarkozy's choices by pushing him to counter-attack, which then allows him to defend himself with more room for manoeuvre; it just so happens that he, unlike his opponent, has a choice, which allows him to select the accusation that best fits his strategy.

In the debate, Hollande also needs to manage the way TV viewers judge him and his contribution to the exchange. I suggest that the ironic joke embedding the *ad hominem* in (6) has cognitive repercussions for the audience: it keeps the audience busy processing the joke instead of devoting resources to a potential argumentative evaluation that would reveal its fallaciousness and its poor argumentative relevance (from the perspective of argumentative reasonableness).

Irony is typically a phenomenon managed by the comprehension module which solicits cognitive resources to be understood: irony triggers an implicit meaning that cannot be made explicit without losing its effect. What I suggest is that in the example processing the irony takes precedence over the evaluation of the *ad hominem* argument, which is only represented after the irony has been perceived and understood. This means that before the audience can even begin to recognize (6) as an *ad hominem*, a prior cognitive task has to be carried out, namely understanding the ironic nature of Hollande's statement. Now, a specific likely effect of irony is the perception of humour, which involves complex cognitive processing (see Baldwin, 2007; Wild et al., 2003; Ruch, 2001): I suggest that this weakens the chances of critical evaluation of the argument. Once (6) has been understood, in principle the representation that was yielded can be picked up for several other purposes, including critical evaluation, which is what happens in standard and reasonable argumentative settings. However, in this case I claim that the humorous nature of (6) might take over and become more relevant, i.e. more cognitively salient, than its critical evaluation.[15] The attack conflates humorous and argumentative functions (the former being more enjoyable, more accessible and more relevant with respect to the interpretation of irony) and this weakens the chances of the *ad hominem* being defeated, simply because its argumentative nature might no longer appear to be relevant.

Once Hollande has joked around, he goes back to being serious by (illegitimately) reacting to (3) and (5) instead of (7). He takes the opportunity offered by Sarkozy's previous accusation to divert the audience's attention away from the fallacious nature of his own intervention by foregrounding his status as a victim of a false accusation, which, as he implies, is a very serious matter. Again, this is meant to obfuscate the fallacious nature of (6), whose relevance is thereby weakened: the discussion is no longer about being funny or serious, but about having been called a liar. In other words, even if he indulged in the non-seriousness of humour, he is perfectly able to return to a serious conversational attitude by setting the pace and managing to impose the topical contents of the exchange. The perception that he may be legitimated to do so probably results from his timely recalling of the accusations against him. We can consequently take (8) to implement a twofold constraint; on the one hand it increases the relevance of contents related to a serious attack by making them accessible and epistemically significant: after all, Hollande is responding to a serious charge about his honesty, thereby raising expectations for contents which are relevant to that particular goal. A politician who is called a liar in a political debate of such importance is expected to defend her/himself; Hollande knows that his audience expects those contents to be formulated one way or another, and since he has previously conceded only a mistake, he can now take the opportunity to firmly oppose Sarkozy on his charge. On the other hand, but also simultaneously, this allows him to drive the audience's attention away from the evaluation of the ironic personal attack he has previously launched. In other words, he weakens the chances of his audience spotting the fallaciousness of (6), because (8) relates to (3) and (5) – and crucially not to (6). The relevance of his joke, which could prove to be disadvantageous with respect to his credibility as a debater, is thereby weakened as (8) brings to the fore the seriousness of a grave accusation.

# 5  Conclusion

This chapter has tried to give a coherent picture of how research in cognitive pragmatics can contribute to the (critical) study of discourse. It has outlined a cognitive model of deception postulating in a nutshell that deception has some prospects of being successful only when its target is unaware of its operation; this can be achieved by manipulating information focus in the meaning comprehension procedure so as to weaken the likelihood of critical scrutiny on behalf of the deceived addressee. Deception therefore works, in sum, because you are not looking for it.

More specifically, I have characterized the cognitive constraints unfolding in deception as constraints on relevance, amounting to constraints on informational accessibility (related to processing effort) and on the strength of information (relating to cognitive effects). While the model was originally aimed at accounting for deceptive communication, its operational focus allows us to extend it to non-deceptive instances of discursive influence. I have presented and illustrated how it can be used to analyse argumentative discourse so as to gain insights into the reasons that make argumentative fallacies effective. The basic claim behind this discussion is that they work precisely because they manage to lead us away from their critical evaluation.

One of the advantages of the type of approach presented here is its explanatory power: it is grounded on recent developments in cognitive science and consequently affords experimental testing (within experimental pragmatics, for instance, but also within more traditional cognitive psychology, which has been concerned with biases and illusions, see Pohl, 2004). These domains of scientific inquiry can guide our understanding of the mechanisms governing cognitive processing and begin to explain why and how discourse can effectively impact belief formation. Moreover, reliance on such approaches is a step further in addressing and accounting for the complexity of communication. We do not communicate single-purposely and many times our utterances fulfil different goals, be they argumentative, conversational, informative, etc. Acknowledging that behind this complexity lies a corresponding cognitive complexity which we can in fact learn from through cognitive science research may get us closer to a richer and more informed discipline of discourse analysis.

# Notes

1  In the literature on the topic, the term manipulation is often used to refer to what I call here deception (I have used the term myself in the past). I will however privilege the latter here because the term 'manipulation' can be understood in the very basic sense of 'operating/using an object' and thus, if applied to communication, could come to denote the mere act of assembling linguistic or conceptual material in a certain way, which restricts the conceptual scope of the phenomenon I am concerned with in this chapter.

2  See Maillat and Oswald (2009: 350–61) and Galasiński (2000: 17–33) for more extensive discussions of the problems involved in defining the concept of deception.

3  See Oswald (2010: 103–21) for a complete rationale behind this choice.

4  I adopt here the conventional notation in pragmatics where speakers are denoted as females and addressees as males.

5  This is a distinction made by Sperber and Wilson in terms of *communicative* intention and *informative* intention (see Sperber and Wilson, 1995: 29–31).

6  Recent research in cognitive anthropology (see Sperber et al., 2010) postulates that human communication evolved and stabilized in such a way that humans have developed epistemic vigilance filters targeted at assessing source reliability and message consistency. One way of describing how deception operates would therefore be to consider that it manages to overcome these vigilance filters (see Oswald and Hart, 2014; Oswald and Lewiński, forthcoming; Oswald, 2011 for an elaboration of this idea concerning different argumentative fallacies).

7  The cognitive environment of an individual will be defined, following Sperber and Wilson (1995: 38–46) as the set of assumptions that are manifest to her/him (i.e., those which s/he takes to be true or probably true at a given time).

8  I will obviously not be able to summarize here the entire theory and its philosophical and epistemological grounding; for a concise introduction to RT I refer the reader to Wilson and Sperber (2002).

9  Quite a few pointers about how a cognitive pragmatic approach to discourse could look can nevertheless be found in the work of Saussure (see Saussure, 2007a, 2007b, 2012).

10  For an illustration of how the interpretative procedure unfolds, see the example given in Wilson and Sperber (2002: 263).

11  By 'favourable contents', I mean all the contents which do not lead the addressee to be critical about the linguistic material he is processing. These are targeted at creating an impression of coherence and consistency with the discourse they are embedded in.

12  This, of course, can also be part of the analysis as a further question of inquiry, but it does not constitute a necessary step in the explanation of how influence works.

13  The English translation is my own; a transcript of the debate is available on the website of the French newspaper *Libération* at http://www.liberation.fr/politiques/010118726-la-transcription-exhaustive-du-debat, and the video is available at http://youtube/UhLYmyOxlRY (both last accessed on 7 April 2013).

14  The extent to which this is an actual *ad hominem* fallacy is debatable; in order to count as one, the argument would need to be completely made explicit and the

reconstruction would need to show how a premise about one of Sarkozy's psychological traits is used to argue for the falsity of a statement. This is arguably the case here, even more so if we take into account Sarkozy's immediate reaction to try to counter the attack. However, suffice it to say that Hollande's move definitely sets the stage for the *ad hominem*; whether he exploits it as such or not is irrelevant here, because the point of (8) is to elicit a response Hollande will then be able to exploit.

**15** Many *ad hominem* attacks are combined with humour, particularly in political discourse (see e.g. Van Eemeren and Houtlosser's 2008 analysis of an *ad hominem* at the Canadian House of Commons), and this is perhaps not coincidental. Studies of verbal humour have already pointed out (see e.g. Attardo, 1994) that humour can be expressed through contradiction, incongruity and in particular flawed reasoning. See also Oswald (forthcoming) for a discussion of another humorous example involving a formal fallacy and its non-detection, namely affirming the consequent.

# References

Attardo, S. (1994), *Linguistic Theories of Humor*. New York: Mouton de Gruyter.

Baldwin, E. (2007), *Humor Perception: The Contribution of Cognitive Factors*. Psychology Dissertations. Paper 31 Georgia State University.

Blass, R. (2005), 'Manipulation in the speeches and writings of Hitler and the NSDAP from a relevance theoretic point of view', in L. de Saussure and P. Schulz (eds), *Manipulation and Ideologies in the Twentieth Century: Discourse, Language, Mind*. Amsterdam: Benjamins, pp. 169–90.

Charteris-Black, J. (2006a), *Politicians and Rhetoric: The Persuasive Power of Metaphor*. Basingstoke: Palgrave Macmillan.

—— (2006b), 'Britain as a container: immigration metaphors in the 2005 election campaign'. *Discourse & Society*, 17(6), 563–82.

Chilton, P. (1996), *Security Metaphors: Cold War Discourse from Containment to Common House*. New York: Peter Lang.

—— (2004), *Analysing Political Discourse: Theory and Practice*. London: Routledge.

—— (2005), 'Manipulation, memes and metaphors: the case of *Mein Kampf*', in L. de Saussure and P. Schulz (eds), *Manipulation and Ideologies in the Twentieth Century: Discourse, Language, Mind*. Amsterdam: Benjamins, pp. 15–43.

Fowler, R., Hodge, R., Kress, G. and Trew, T. (1979), *Language and Control*. London: Routledge and Kegan Paul.

Galasiński, D. (2000), *The Language of Deception. A Discourse Analytical Study*. London: Sage.

Habermas, J. (1969), *Technik und Wissenschaft als Ideologie*. Frankfurt: Suhrkamp.

Hart, C. (2010), *Critical Discourse Analysis and Cognitive Science: New Perspectives on Immigration Discourse*. Basingstoke: Palgrave.

Iețcu-Fairclough, I. (2007), 'Populism and the Romanian "Orange Revolution": a discourse-analytical perspective on the presidential election of December 2004'. *Studies in Language & Capitalism*, 2, 31–74.

KhosraviNik, M. (2008), 'British newspapers and the representation of refugees, asylum seekers and immigrants between 1996 and 2006'. Centre for Language in Social Life, Lancaster University.

—— (2010), 'The representation of refugees, asylum seekers and immigrants in British newspapers: a critical discourse analysis'. *Journal of Language and Politics*, 9(1), 1–28.

Leeuwen, T. van and Wodak, R. (1999), 'Legitimizing immigration control: a discourse-historical analysis'. *Discourse Studies*, 1(1), 83–118.

Lewiński, M. and Oswald, S. (2013), 'When and how do we deal with straw men? A normative and cognitive pragmatic account'. *Journal of Pragmatics*, 59, Part B, 164–77.

Maillat, D. (2013), 'Constraining context selection: on the pragmatic inevitability of manipulation'. *Journal of Pragmatics*, 59, Part B, 190–9.

Maillat, D. and Oswald, S. (2009), 'Defining manipulative discourse: the pragmatics of cognitive illusions'. *International Review of Pragmatics*, 1(2), 348–70.

—— (2011), 'Constraining context: a pragmatic account of cognitive manipulation', in C. Hart (ed.), *Critical Discourse Studies in Context and Cognition*. Amsterdam: Benjamins, pp. 65–80.

Morris, C. (1938), *Foundations of the Theory of Signs*. Chicago: The University of Chicago Press.

Musolff, A. (2004), *Metaphor and Political Discourse: Analogical Reasoning in Debates about Europe*. Basingstoke: Palgrave.

—— (2006), 'Metaphor scenarios in public discourse'. *Metaphor and Symbol*, 21(1), 23–38.

Noveck, I. and Sperber, D. (2004), *Experimental Pragmatics*. Basingstoke: Palgrave Macmillan.

Oswald, S. (2010), *Pragmatics of Uncooperative and Manipulative Communication*. PhD dissertation, University of Neuchâtel, ms.

—— (2011), 'From interpretation to consent: arguments, beliefs and meaning'. *Discourse Studies*, 13(6), 806–14.

Oswald, S. and Hart, C. (2014), 'Trust based on bias: cognitive constraints on source-related fallacies'. *Virtues of Argumentation: Proceedings of the 10th International Conference of the Ontario Society for the Study of Argumentation*.

Oswald, S. and Rihs, A. (2014), 'Metaphor as argument. Rhetorical and epistemic advantages of extended metaphors'. *Argumentation*, 28(2), 133–59.

Papafragou, A. (2006), 'Epistemic modality and truth conditions'. *Lingua*, 116, 1688–702.

Pohl, R. (2004), *Cognitive Illusions. A Handbook on Fallacies and Biases in Thinking, Judgement and Memory*. Hove and New York: Psychology Press.

Polyzou, A. (2013), *Presupposition, (ideological) knowledge management and gender: a socio-cognitive discourse analytical approach*. Unpublished PhD Thesis, Lancaster University, Lancaster, UK.

Puzynina, J. (1992), *Jezyk w swiecie wartosci [Language in the world of values]*. Warsaw, Poland: Panstwowe Widawnictwo Naukowe.

Richardson, J. E. (2004), *(Mis)Representing Islam: The Racism and Rhetoric of British Broadsheet Newspapers*. Amsterdam: Benjamins.

Ruch, W. (2001), 'The perception of humor', in A. Kaszniak (ed.), *Emotion, Aualia, and Consciousness*. Tokyo, Japan: Word Scientific Publisher, pp. 410–25.

Saussure, L. de (2007a), 'Procedural pragmatics and the study of discourse'. *Pragmatics & Cognition*, 15(1), 139–60.

—— (2007b), 'Pragmatic issues in discourse analysis'. *Critical Approaches to Discourse Analysis across Disciplines*, 1(1), 179–95.

—— (2012), 'Cognitive pragmatics ways into discourse analysis: the case of discursive presuppostions'. *Łód Papers in Pragmatics*, 8(1), 37–59.

Sperber, D. and Wilson, D. (1986), *Relevance, Communication and Cognition.* Oxford: Blackwell.

—— (1995), *Relevance. Communication and Cognition,* (2nd edn), Oxford: Blackwell.

Sperber, D., Clément, F., Heintz, C., Mascaro, O., Mercier, H., Origgi, G. and Wilson, D. (2010), 'Epistemic vigilance'. *Mind & Language*, 25(4), 359–93.

Van Dijk, T. (1994), 'Discourse and inequality'. *Lenguas Modernas*, 21, 19–37.

—— (2008), *Discourse and Context. A Sociocognitive Approach.* Cambridge: Cambridge University Press.

Van Eemeren, F. and Grootendorst, R. (1996), '*Argumentum ad hominem*: a pragma-dialectical case in point', in H. van Hansen and R. Pinto (eds), *Fallacies. Classical and Contemporary Readings*. University Park, PA: The Pennsylvania State University Press, pp. 223–8.

Van Eemeren, F. and Houtlosser, P. (2008), 'Rhetoric in a dialectical framework: fallacies as derailments of strategic manoeuvring', in E. Weigand (ed.), *Dialogue and Rhetoric*. Amsterdam: Benjamins, pp. 133–51.

Wild, B., Rodden, F. A., Grodd, W. and Ruch, W. (2003), 'Neural correlates of laughter and humour'. *Brain*, 126, 2121–38.

Wilson, D. and Sperber, D. (2002), 'Relevance Theory'. *UCL Working Papers in Linguistics*, 14, 249–87. Available at: http://www.ucl.ac.uk/psychlangsci/research/linguistics/publications/wpl/02papers/wilson_sperber

—— (2012), *Meaning and Relevance*. Cambridge: Cambridge University Press.

Wodak, R. and Van Dijk, T. (2006), *Racism at the Top*. Drava: Austrian Ministry of Education, Science and Culture.

## SOCIAL COGNITION

# 5

# Discourse-Cognition-Society

# Current State and Prospects of the Socio-Cognitive Approach to Discourse

*Teun A. van Dijk*

Pompeu Fabra University, Barcelona

## 1 Introduction

The critical study of discourse should be based on a multidisciplinary theory explicitly relating discourse structures with societal structures and thus describe and explain how structures of power and power abuse are discursively enacted and reproduced. The main thesis of a socio-cognitive contribution to this theory is that these relations between discourse and society are cognitively mediated. In this chapter I sketch the current state of this socio-cognitive approach as well as its future prospects, based on our research of the past 30 years (see also Van Dijk, 2008a, 2008b).

Most earlier and contemporary theories in Critical Discourse Studies (CDS), as well as in neighbouring disciplines, such as sociolinguistics and linguistic anthropology, assume a direct link between discourse and society (or culture). It is generally assumed in these disciplines that social variables such as those of social class, power, gender, ethnicity or age directly cause or control language variation and structures of text and talk. The problem is that the nature of these causal or similar direct relationships is not made explicit but taken for granted or reduced to unexplained correlations.

Another fundamental problem is that societal structures and discourse structures are of a very different kind and hence cannot enter in a causal relationship in the first place. A socio-cognitive theory assumes that social structures need to be interpreted and represented cognitively and that such mental representations affect the cognitive processes involved in the production and interpretation of discourse. The same principle holds true for the reverse relationship, namely how discourse is able to affect social structure – namely through the mental representations of language users as social actors.

Similar theoretical limitations characterize contemporary 'interactionist' approaches to talk, for instance in Conversation Analysis (CA) and Discursive Psychology (DP). These approaches directly link the structures of talk with structures of interaction at the micro-order of society. They thereby ignore that also this relationship is cognitively mediated: trivially, language users not only act but also think when they speak.

Denying or ignoring the existence or the relevance of this cognitive dimension of interaction is in many ways a contemporary version of similar arguments defended by behaviourism decades ago, such as the alleged lack of 'observability' or 'sociality' of cognitive representations. Many aspects of conversation, such as the role of implicit or implicated meanings, thus remain without explicit description or explanation. Indeed, even more generally, the very definition of the fundamental notion of 'action' without a cognitive basis is thus reduced to a behaviourist concept of 'observable' conduct. In fact, the same is true for the meaning of text or talk, which also hardly can be theoretically accounted for in terms of observability in the common empiricist sense.

From the point of view of contemporary cognitive science these statements may seem trivial although the detailed theoretical and analytical implications of these assumptions are only partly understood. Even the cognitive psychology of discourse until today has no explicit theory of how social and communicative 'environments' affect text and talk. Hence, one of the tasks of this chapter is to sketch the main tenets of just such a theory as the core of the cognitive interface of the relations between discourse and society.

# 2 Cognition

The cognitive interface of the relations between discourse and society is as complex as the very structures of text and talk, on the one hand, and those of society, on the other hand, and we are here able only to summarize some of its most relevant notions (see also Introduction, this volume; Hart, this volume). Hence, we ignore many details of the properties of Working Memory and various aspects of Episodic and Long Term Memory, cognitive processing as well as their neuropsychological foundations (of many contemporary studies in these areas, see, e.g., Baddeley, 2007; Tulving and Craik, 2000).

Instead, we focus on those aspects of the structure and role of personal and social cognition that directly account for the most fundamental properties of the production and comprehension of discourse (for details, see Graesser et al., 2003).[1]

## 2.1  *Personal vs. social cognition*

A first crucial distinction of the cognitive framework underlying language use and discourse is that between *personal* and *social cognition*. This distinction is vaguely reflected in the division of labour between cognitive and social psychology, although we obviously deal with cognition in both cases.

Personal cognition accounts for the ways individual language users, as members of linguistic, epistemic and social communities, subjectively produce and understand text and talk. Although such an account is framed in terms of the mental and neurological structures and processes of individual language users, it must be based on socially shared representations of individual social actors as members of various social collectivities. At the same time these mental representations and processes are activated, applied and adapted to the properties of ongoing and situated social interaction and communication, through which they are acquired, changed and socially reproduced in the first place. In other words, the personal and the social in discourse processing are inextricably intertwined.

In this chapter we limit our account of personal cognition, and hence the subjective and unique properties of individual text and talk, to a brief summary of the role of different kinds of mental model. On the other hand, the social dimension of the cognitive interface between discourse and society will be described in terms of the structures and the role of knowledge on the one hand, and shared social attitudes and ideologies, on the other hand.

## 2.2  *Situation models*

Many studies in the last three decades of the cognitive psychology of discourse have shown the fundamental role of *mental models* for the production and comprehension of discourse and more generally for interaction and the perception of the environment (Garnham, 1987; Gentner and Stevens, 1983; Johnson-Laird, 1983; Oakhill and Garnham, 1987; Van Dijk and Kintsch, 1983).

Thus, it has generally been assumed that the understanding of discourse involves the ongoing activation, updating or construction of *situation models* that represent the events or the situation the discourse is *about* (Van Dijk and Kintsch, 1983). Since such models are the cognitive correlate of what was traditionally called the 'referential' aspect of language use, such models may also be called *semantic*. They account for what in philosophical terms is called aboutness, that is, the 'intentional' or representational aspect of language use.

Situation models should not be confused with the (intensional) *meaning* of discourse, which is a specific and different level and aspect of discourse processing. Indeed, situation models are independent of language use: our mere experience and observation of, and our participation in, events or situations take place in terms of situation models, whether or not we talk about them. In other words, our ongoing experience and understanding of the events and situations of our environment take place in terms of mental models that segment, interpret and define reality as we 'live' it (Shipley and Zacks, 2008). Although the structures of language use (e.g., sentences and stories) are influenced by the more primitive structures of these mental models, the mental models of our everyday experiences are independent of text or talk. Indeed, in order to survive, primates needed such models to interact with their environment before they could speak in the first place (Plotkin, 2007).

Mental models are assumed to be represented in Episodic Memory, that is, the part of Long Term Memory where we represent our autobiographical experiences or personal 'memories' (Baddeley et al., 2002; Tulving, 1983, 2002). Although as yet no explicit theory of the structures of mental models has been formulated, it is plausible that they consist of hierarchical structures formed by a limited number of fundamental categories that define the basic structure of our experience: a spatio-temporal setting, participants with different identities, roles and relations, aims, and an action or event. Interestingly, these structures also appear in the semantic case structure of the sentences of natural languages (Fillmore, 1968) as well as in stories about such events and situations (De Fina and Georgakopoulou, 2012). Here we encounter the first evidence for the projection of mental structures on structures of language use, text and talk.

Mental models are *multimodal*. They represent the complex, *embodied* experience of events and situations, including visual, auditory, sensorimotor and emotional aspects of an experience (Barsalou, 2008; Zwaan, 2004). As such they are also uniquely personal. Indeed, they not only represent our knowledge of an event, but may also feature our evaluative personal opinion or emotions about an event – which again may be expressed (or not) in many ways in the sentences or stories about such an experience.

In sum, the understanding of text or talk not only involves the construction of its *meaning* (or *intension*) in terms of some semantic representation, but also the construction of its *referents* (or *extension*) in terms of mental models stored in Episodic Memory. Conversely, talking or writing about specific events, as is the case for storytelling or news reports, is based on the personal, subjective, situation models language users construe of such events. Obviously, such situation models may also be (partly) expressed and communicated by other semiotic systems, such as drawings, paintings, dance, gestures or music.

Since we deal with mental models as the interface between discourse and the social or natural environment, we shall see below how discourse structures resemble but also differ from the structures of mental models. One crucial difference is that models are much more complete and only partially expressed in text and talk because of the well-known epistemic and pragmatic fact that recipients only need 'half a word' to reconstruct an intended mental model with help of the inferences based on situationally and socio-culturally shared generic knowledge – to which we turn below. This also explains the obvious consequence that recipient models may be different from intended speaker models. Recipients construe their understanding of discourse, that is, their mental model, not only with the expressed meaning of the discourse as well as socially shared knowledge and ideologies. They also activate strictly personal old models based on earlier discourse or experiences. In other words, this cognitive approach to discourse in terms of mental models also explains the classical distinction between speaker meaning, discourse meaning and recipient meaning.

## 2.3  Context models

So far strangely ignored in the cognitive psychology of discourse processing is the obvious fact that language users not only construe 'semantic' mental models of the events or situations they talk *about*, but also 'pragmatic' mental models of the very ongoing communicative experience or situation *in which* they are currently engaged. These dynamically changing and subjective mental models of the ongoing communicative situation account for what traditionally was called the *context* of language use and discourse, for instance in sociolinguistics (cf. Fetzer, this volume). They also provide the necessary cognitive interface for contemporary interactionist approaches that lack an explicit *theory* of context (for a multidisciplinary theory of context, see Van Dijk, 2008a, 2009; see also Givón, 2005; for a more interactionist approach to context, see Duranti and Goodwin, 1992).

It is at this point where we arrive at the kernel of the cognitive interface between discourse and society. *Context models* represent the aspects of the communicative environment, and hence the social parameters of language use, as they are defined to be *relevant* by and for the participants (for a more abstract approach to relevance, see Sperber and Wilson, 1995).

Mental models of communicative situations – like all mental models – feature at least a spatio-temporal setting, participants in various identities, roles and relationships, an ongoing action and its goals. However, *specific* of context models is that the roles, actions and goals of the participants are communicative and not only more generally interactional.

These parameters of context models provide the basis of *indexicals*, such as *deictic expressions* referring to the time, place, participants and action of the communicative situation, as well as the *appropriate conditions* of speech acts (Searle, 1969). Indeed, the main function of context models is to control the ways language users are able to adapt their ongoing discourse and interaction to the current (and ongoingly changing) communicative situation.

As is the case for semantic situation models, pragmatic context models are *multimodal*, specifically also featuring the very experience of speaking, writing, listening or reading, and also feature evaluative *opinions* and *emotions* (happiness, fear, etc.) associated with the communicative situation (see also Royce and Bowcher, 2007).

As is the case for all mental models, context models are also represented in Episodic Memory. And just like (semantic) situation models, we later may recall and tell a story *about* an earlier communicative event in which we participated, in the same way as we may refer to and speak about properties of the current communicative situation, namely by deictic expressions or other indexicals. In this case the semantics and pragmatics of discourse overlap because situation models and context models overlap.

With the postulation of semantic situation models and pragmatic context models we have defined the theoretical core of the cognitive interface between discourse and society: thus, first of all, language users are able to mentally represent social events and situations and talk *about* them, which is crucial for the survival of the species as well as for interaction in everyday life (Van Dijk, 2014). At the same time their talk is controlled by their subjective context models representing communicative, and hence social, events and situations, in such a way that their talk, and hence their communicative interaction, is *adapted* to the communicative and social environment. In other words, we thus have defined the cognitive basis of the fundamental semantic and pragmatic aspects of language use and discourse through an interface that links the nature, conditions and control of discourse structures to the represented events and situations of the social world, on the one hand, and more specifically with the social aspects of the communicative situation on the other hand.

## 2.4  The knowledge device

One of the crucial parameters of context models is the knowledge language users need to have about the knowledge of the recipients. Virtually all structures of language, from stress and intonation, topic-focus articulation of sentences, word order, foregrounding and backgrounding, evidentials, modalities, local and global discourse coherence and schematic organization, storytelling and argumentation, speech acts and conversational interaction are profoundly and ongoingly influenced by a pragmatic knowledge device (K-device) that defines the *Common Ground* (Clark, 1996) of language users in interaction and communication (for detail, see Van Dijk, 2008a, 2014).

Thus speakers need not express and hence may *presuppose* the information or knowledge they know or believe recipients already have or may easily infer themselves from socially shared knowledge (to which we shall turn below).

Similarly, many structures of discourse should be defined in terms of the relationship between given, known, presupposed or backgrounded information, on the one hand, and new, renewed, unsuspected or foregrounded knowledge, on the other hand (Lambrecht, 1994). Indeed, besides the many other functions of language and discourse, the communicative function is the basis and the core of the other ones, namely the transmission and the acquisition of new knowledge and relating it to old knowledge. Speech acts such as assertions and questions are thus defined by this epistemic aspect of context models.

The knowledge or beliefs of speakers about those of the recipients is a well-known aspect of the classical philosophical, psychological and neurological issue of *Other Minds* (Givón, 2005). Besides their neurological basis in terms of mirror neurons which enable the fundamentally interactive nature of language, mutual knowledge and Common Ground in talk and text based on generally simulating knowledge and intentions of others by analogy to our own, as well as shared experience (models) of the same or previous communicative situations and the shared, socio-cultural knowledge of members of the same linguistic and epistemic communities (among many studies on other minds, shared knowledge and intentions as the basis of human interaction see, e.g., Goldman, 2006; Tomasello, 2008).

The K-device ongoingly manages these different sources of knowledge so as to make sure that all aspects of ongoing text or talk are *epistemically appropriate* in the current communicative situation.

We see that besides the other structures of semantic and pragmatic mental models underlying discourse production and comprehension, and hence all verbal interaction, mutual and shared knowledge and its ongoing management and expression is a fundamental aspect of the cognitive interface of discourse and the social environment. Without such a cognitively (and socially) based epistemic component, many if not most aspects of text and talk cannot be accounted for.

## 2.5  Social cognition I: socio-cultural knowledge

We have seen that and how semantic situation models and pragmatic context models are needed as part of the cognitive interface between discourse structures and the structures of the communicative and social environment in which and about which language users interact and communicate. They specifically define the subjective, personal and ongoing contextual nature of all language use and discourse.

However, language users are not merely individuals but also social actors who are members of linguistic, epistemic and social communities and societal groups, institutions and organizations. As members of linguistic communities, they share a natural language. As members of epistemic communities they share various kinds of socio-cultural knowledge about public events as well as generic structures of the natural and social world. As members of social groups and communities they share norms and values and the attitudes and ideologies based on them.

Indeed, the K-device of context models would not be able to operate without such shared socio-cultural knowledge of the members of epistemic communities, allowing the necessary inferences about the nature of the current communicative situation – such as the general norms and conditions of speech acts, conversations or various discourse genres.

Similarly, such socially shared knowledge is crucial in the very construction of situation models about specific events and situations, namely as instantiations or 'applications' of more generic or abstract knowledge and its inferences. Thus, we only are able to construe a specific personal mental situation model of a story about a bank robbery, if we have and apply more general knowledge about banks, money, thieves and their actions.

Despite the fundamental nature of socially shared knowledge, we as yet barely understand the details of their representation in memory, besides the assumption of its representation in the 'semantic' part of Long Term Memory, as well as its conceptual and prototypical structures, its organization in scripts and other schemas as well as epistemic domains (e.g., plants, animals, human beings, social groups, etc.), and its possibly multimodal foundation in various regions of the brain (among a vast number of studies on the cognitive psychology of knowledge, see, e.g., Anderson, 1980; Barsalou, 2008; Collins and Quillian, 1972; Rosch and Lloyd, 1978; Schank and Abelson, 1977).

Whatever the details of the cognitive and neurological structures of the representation of socio-culturally shared knowledge in our minds/memory and brains, relevant for our discussion is first of all their role in the construction of mental models of communicative and other social situations – and hence as the socially shared basis of all individual text and talk about specific events as well as all interaction in general.

The same mental models are involved in the generation of inferences derived from general knowledge, for instance as a basis of local and global discourse coherence. In other words, mental models on the one hand need general knowledge for their construction, and general knowledge may in turn be produced by the generalization of situation models. Indeed, most of the general knowledge we have about the world beyond our daily experiences, such as about natural catastrophes, wars, social conflicts, countries and famous people, is derived from the generalization and abstraction of mental models of specific instances of public (mostly media) discourse.

Secondly, such general knowledge may be the cognitive basis of discourse genres and structures that express such knowledge directly, as is typically the case for expository and pedagogical genres, as well as the (often) implicit arguments of argumentative discourse and interaction. In the same way as some structures of mental models are correlated with the structure of sentences and discourse, it may be that some structures of expository discourse exhibit underlying generic knowledge structures, as is the case for conceptual categories and relations, as well as the fundamental parameters of reality, such as those of time and causality of events, and the size, weight, form, appearance, actions or functions of landscapes, things, animals and persons.

## 2.6 Social cognition II: attitudes and ideologies

So far, much of the cognitive interface between discourse and society, with the exception of context models, is standard theory of the cognitive psychology of discourse processing. Yet, we have seen that mental models may feature personal opinions of language users, and these are not just based on generic socio-cultural knowledge, but also on evaluative representations shared by the members of social groups: *attitudes*, such as our attitudes about immigration, abortion, homosexual marriage, the free market or wars (Eagly and Chaiken, 1993; Pratkanis et al., 1989).

As forms of socially shared cognition, attitudes are probably also represented in semantic or 'social' memory, in which we store all general, generic and socially shared beliefs that are necessary as a basis to form specific, local and personal mental models and their opinions. As is the case for generic knowledge, at present little is known about the cognitive structures of attitudes, beyond hypotheses about their schematic organization (e.g., as an abstraction of mental models, for instance about immigration), the role of underlying norms and values defining what is good or bad, permitted or prohibited.

Like socio-culturally shared knowledge, *attitudes are essentially social* (Jaspars and Fraser, 1984). They should not be confounded with personal opinions as stored in mental models, as is quite common in traditional attitude research. They are shared by members of social groups, each with their own identity, actions, norms and values, relations to other groups and resources (as the basis of their power and reproduction). Thus, whereas the K-device of context models is the specific interface between the epistemically controlled structures of discourse and the shared social knowledge of communities, attitudes represent the relationship between social groups and their members and the ways members as language users express opinions about social events, situations, people or groups. More generally, such attitudes are at the basis of all social practices of group members, as is the case for ethnic prejudices as a basis for specific forms of discrimination and exclusion in general, as well as for racist text and talk in particular.

Crucial for our theoretical framework is that the relationship between social structure, such as domination relations between groups, as exercised for instance in discriminatory social practices, is mediated by mental representations of such attitudes. It is also in this way that – conversely – discriminatory discourse and other social practices are involved in the daily reproduction of social structures of domination and resistance. Obviously, we need this component as a theoretical basis for all critical studies of discourse. Thus, racism, sexism and other forms of social inequality do not directly influence discourse, nor vice versa does discriminatory discourse influence societal structures of domination. This is only possible *through the cognitive interface of socially shared attitudes and the personal mental models* (in turn influencing personal actions and discourse) based on them.

It is also through such socially shared attitudes that group members are able to *cooperate* in the attainment of personal and social goals, because they allow individual social speakers and actors to infer the opinions and current goals of other group members. Thus, racism and hence white group power is not reproduced by individually bigoted people, but by the joint or separate daily cooperation of (white) group members to exclude, marginalize and problematize members of other ethnic groups in many different everyday situations.

## 2.7 *Ideologies*

Many social attitudes have a broader and more general socio-cognitive basis that allows different attitudes to be formed, acquired and applied, namely by underlying *ideologies*. Thus, there are many different sexist or racist attitudes about different social issues, but they may at a more abstract level be based on underlying sexist or racist ideologies. Such ideologies are the basic cognitive self-schema of a group and its interests, and defined by such general categories as the identities, actions, goals, norms and values, relations with other groups and the (power) resources of a group. In other words, together with socially shared group knowledge, they are the cognitive core of social groupness (Van Dijk, 1998).

Ideologies obviously not only have socio-cognitive properties, but also societal ones, for instance in terms of interest groups, their leaders and institutions, and especially how the ideologies of the groups are shared, reproduced, taught and acquired by their members, for instance by schooling and indoctrination and by specific discourse genres, such as catechisms, party programmes, lectures, hymns, protest songs among many other genres (see Cap and Okulska, 2013).

The theoretical framework sketched so far shows that there is quite a distance between abstract underlying ideologies, on the one hand, and their expression in discourse, on the other hand. Thus, ideologies are more specifically specified in socially shared attitudes about particular 'issues' or group concerns (such as racist ideologies may be applied and specified in the formation of attitudes about immigration or employment quota).

These attitudes are in turn instantiated in the personal opinions of group members in their situation models, and these biased situation models may finally be (partly) expressed in discourse and other social practices as controlled by context models.

This may also mean that underlying ideologically based opinions of group members in a specific context are not expressed at all, e.g., because they are found inappropriate or otherwise counterproductive (against the goals) in the current communicative situation, as represented in the context model of the speaker. More generally the difference between discourse structures and model structures is crucial, and hence cannot be mutually reduced to each other. Thus, we may *explain* many aspects of discourse structures, such as local and global coherence, implicitness, indexicals, speech act conditions, as well as ideological structures, in terms of underlying situation and context models, but do not *reduce* such structures to mental models.

We now have reviewed the major components of the cognitive interface between discourse structures and social structures, by relating personal, subjective semantic and pragmatic models as well as their underlying forms of socio-cultural knowledge, attitudes and ideologies, with represented social events, communicative situations and members of epistemic communities and social interest groups, institutions and organizations. This complex framework also explains how communities, social groups and power relations are reproduced by discourse and other social practices based in turn on underlying personal mental models as well as socially shared forms of cognition.

# 3 Society

The minds of language users are concretely embodied in real persons who besides being unique individuals are members of social groups, institutions and organizations, and who interact and communicate with other members through text and talk. Thus, in the same way as we need a cognitive interface in order to describe and explain many properties of discourse, we also need a societal basis for both cognition and discursive interaction. Above we have summarized the socio-cognitive dimension of this societal basis, namely in terms of socially and culturally shared mental representations (knowledge, attitudes, ideologies, norms, values) of groups and communities. Below, we shall see that part of the social order, at the micro-level, is constituted by social interaction in general, and communicative interaction and discourse in particular. Crucially, though, the societal basis needs further analysis that goes beyond that of discursive social interaction. Accounting for institutional talk, for instance, presupposes a theory of institutions and their roles in society. Shared social knowledge presupposes epistemic communities, whereas ideologies presuppose specific social groups.

## 3.1 *Power*

Specifically relevant for the critical study of discourse is the analysis of power and power abuse. Of the vast number of characteristics of societal structure, which are obviously beyond the scope of a single chapter, we shall therefore briefly summarize some of the properties of power and how they are related to discourse (for detail, see Van Dijk, 2008b).

Although power relations between individuals are also discursively created, expressed and reproduced by discourse, CDS is specifically interested in *social* power relations between groups, organizations or institutions. One of the ways to define such social power is in terms of control. One group has power over another group if it is able to control (specific) actions of (the members of) another group, thereby limiting the freedom of the other group (see, e.g., Lukes, 2004; Stewart, 2001).

Since discourse is a form of action, power may be exercised by controlling discourse, that is,

**(i)**   specific structures of context, such as Setting (Time, Place), Participants (and their Identities, Roles and Relations), Social Acts and their Intentions, as well as Knowledge,

**(ii)**  specific structures of text or talk (genre, topics, lexicon, metaphors, etc.).

In order to be able to exercise such power, groups need a power basis, which may be material or symbolic. Relevant to symbolic power resources is preferential access to public discourse, as is the case for the symbolic elites, such as politicians, journalists and professors. Thus, each social group is not only characterized by its structures, relations to other groups, the characteristics of its members, but also the presence or absence of power resources. More specifically, a group may be defined in terms of the nature of its access to and control of public discourse. Thus, journalists have active access to the construction of news, politicians may have active access to parliamentary debates, and professors to the production of scholarly discourse, whereas most common citizens have only passive access, as recipients to such forms of discourse, or only as participants in the representation of discourse, for instance as news actors or citizens talked about in political or educational discourse.

## 3.2  *Example: The reproduction of racism*

Whereas this offers one dimension of the complex framework that relates discourse and a specific dimension of society, namely social power defined as control, obviously detailed empirical research is required to spell out exactly what social group or institution controls what discourse structures in what communicative situations. Thus, if we want to analyse how racism is reproduced in society as a form of power abuse, or domination, of one (European) group over other (non-European) groups, we obviously need much further analysis of all dimensions. However, even in summary, the Discourse-Cognition-Society triangle finds an excellent illustration in an analysis of racism (for detail, see Van Dijk, 1984, 1987, 1991, 1993, 1998, 2009b).

Racism as a social system of domination has two major dimensions, that of socially shared representations (prejudiced attitudes), and specific social practices of illegitimate treatment (discrimination). Crucial for the reproduction of the system is the reproduction of the social representations on which it is based. This happens through forms of racist text and talk, one of the forms of discriminatory social practice. Although all dominant group members may have access to specific discriminatory practices and discourse in everyday interaction, most influential are the discriminatory public discourses of the symbolic elites in politics, the media, education and scholarship. If these elites control the topics, lexicon, arguments, pictures, metaphors of the discourse about immigrants and minorities, and if discourse structures may affect, as explained, the formation by the recipients of mental models of ethnic events, these models may also be ideologically biased, and when generalized form or confirm the prejudices shared in the dominant group. Finally, specific negative attitudes may be further abstracted from and form underlying racist ideologies that sustain the socio-cognitive basis of the system of racism. Racist ideologies, as is the case for many ideologies, are generally organized by a bipolar schema of Positive Self-Presentation and Negative Other-Presentation (Derogation), a schema that also influences the structure of specific racist attitudes (e.g. on immigration or quotas), and these may finally influence the concrete mental models group members form of specific ethnic events they participate in or read or hear about. Ideologically based polarized racist mental models, depending on context, may be expressed in racist practices such as discourse that is similarly organized between US vs. THEM, at all levels (pictures, topics, lexicon, metaphors and so on).

We see that the analysis of a form of social domination, or power abuse, such as racism, requires analysis of the three fundamental dimensions of Discourse, Cognition and Society. Racism as a system is based on shared social representations (prejudices), which however can only be acquired by specific structures of public discourse influencing the formation of racist mental models. But socially speaking the production of such discourses is controlled by the symbolic elites. Such an analysis is not only relevant at the global level of societal reproduction of racism, but also for the analysis of specific, individual communicative events, at the micro-level.

It hardly needs repeating that this summary of a general theory, intended to introduce and explain the relevance of a socio-cognitive approach in Critical Discourse Studies, is unable to specify the vast amount of details required for the analysis of specific cases. For an analysis of racist news in the press, for instance, one would need previous analysis of the social representations and prejudices of the journalists, the everyday practices of news gathering, who are interviewed or otherwise have access to the journalists, the cognitive processes and the contextual constraints (size, deadline, style, preferred contents, etc.) of newswriting, the many structures of news reports and the ways these are read, stored and recalled by the readers, among many other and more detailed structures. But also in the study of specific cases, we always find a combination of social structures and interaction, discourse structures and underlying cognitive structures such as models, knowledge and ideologies.

# 4. Discourse

## 4.1 Linking discourse with cognition and society

Despite the fundamental role of the analysis of cognitive and social structures for the multidisciplinary explanation of text and talk, the discourse component is of course the specific and central aim of any critical study of discourse. So, in this last section we focus on the relations between discourse structures and their socio-cognitive embedding. A more or less complete account of these relationships would require a multi-volume encyclopaedia, so we can only summarize some fundamental principles. Indeed, especially also for our students, it is crucial to present some guidelines of how to do a *socio-cognitive analysis* of discourse (for other approaches, see e.g., Schiffrin et al., 2013; Titscher et al., 2000; Van Dijk, 2001, 2007; see also the other chapters in this book).

The first principle of a socio-cognitive analysis (henceforth CGA) is that such an analysis goes beyond the classical 'autonomous' theories and methods of discourse and conversation analysis that study the grammatical, semantic, pragmatic, rhetorical, stylistic, narrative, argumentative, interactive or other structures of text and talk. On the one hand, a CGA presupposes the results of these earlier theories and methods, but on the other hand corrects and extends them, because many structures (such as those of coherence or manipulation, among many others) can only be formulated in social and/or cognitive terms.

Secondly, as argued above and unlike the presupposition of most theories in CDS, sociolinguistics or linguistic anthropology, *there are no direct links between social structures and discourse structures*, because all discourse production, comprehension and uses are mediated by the mental representations of the participants. Thus, if in critical studies a link is established between discourse and social power, such an account should be seen as a shortcut, as incomplete or as tacitly presupposing mental structures of members and processes that remain unaccounted for in the analysis.

Discourse structures are essentially different from social structures, such as those of groups, communities, institutions, nation states and their properties and relations. Hence I repeat that the latter can only influence or be influenced by text or talk by a mental interface that links the mental representation of social structures with the mental structures representing discourse. This is not only the case for societal macrostructures and relations, such as those of the system of racism and its reproduction by the mass media, but also at the micro-level of everyday interaction, such a journalists interviewing news actors. Thus, it is true that instances of talk are at the same time social speech acts and forms of social (inter)action and as such the fundamental order of society – that is, phenomena where the discursive and the social coincide. Yet, the structures of talk as social interaction should not only be described in the autonomous terms of, for instance, turn taking, interruptions and sequential organization, but also in terms of the mental representations of the participants. Thus, it is not sufficiently accounted for in Conversation Analysis that *turns do not directly occasion next turns, but the mental production of next turns is occasioned by the interpretation, and hence the mental representation, of previous turns.* In other words, we should account for text and talk at three levels, the level of discourse sequencing, social sequencing at the micro-level, both mediated by sequences of mental representations and processes.

For instance, journalists writing a news report or interviewing a news actor are engaging in many organizational social acts, at various levels, but are able to do so only on the basis of vast amounts of social and political knowledge in general, and specific knowledge of news events as represented in mental models. Such knowledge at the same time influences the structures of the news report or interview in many ways, such as its local and global coherence, overall schematic organization, implications, presuppositions, actor and action descriptions, foregrounding and backgrounding, indexicals, topic-focus articulation, the interactional structures of interviews and many more.

In a broader framework these combined discourse-cognition-action sequences may play a role in the reproduction of racism or the management of an economic crisis, and then again relate global discourse actions (publication) of newspapers, prejudices and ideologies of journalists, and the reproduction of social inequality in society. In other words, the Discourse-Cognition-Society triangle can be analysed at all micro- and macro-levels of description.

Take for instance the use of the metaphor of *waves* routinely used by the mass media and politicians to describe the arrival of a large group of immigrants in the country. Such a metaphor first of all may be described as part of a sequence of negative Other-description in a news report or editorial, and as a form of appraisal, to be accounted for in the semantics of discourse. Secondly, a cognitive analysis describes the metaphor as a way of embodied conceptualization of large groups of foreigners in terms of large amounts of water in which we may drown, and hence as a vital threat. Such a representation is part of a socially shared negative attitude (prejudice) about immigrants, which in turn may be based on a racist ideology. Thirdly, the metaphor used in this way by politicians and newspapers in order to stimulate fear of immigration is socially a way to (re)produce racism and politically to persuade people to vote for candidates of anti-immigration parties. Of course, each of these levels and dimensions of the account of metaphor need much more analytical detail, but it should be clear that adequate critical analysis requires all levels of description. Limiting the analysis of metaphor to a mere semantic-rhetorical figure of speech or as a way of thinking, emphasizing large numbers of people obviously would be an inadequate under-analysis of the data.

## 4.2  A sample CGA-analysis: An editorial

To illustrate these general principles, let us examine in some detail how the structures of discourse are to be related to those of cognition and society. As an example, we use a newspaper editorial, a prominent daily discourse genre which however has received relatively little theoretical attention in discourse and genre studies. Socially, this genre is a routine macro-act of public opinion expression and formation of (the editors of) a newspaper, functioning to influence public opinion on relevant social and political events and issues. Cognitively, editorials express opinions, attitudes and ideologies, and presuppose vast amounts of social and political knowledge, and hence require cognitive analysis in order to describe their production, reception and reproduction in epistemic communities and ideological groups. Discursively, editorials are a genre of persuasive discourse. We may therefore expect a variety of rhetorical and argumentative structures, appraisals, ideological structures, descriptions of social events, actors and situations, epistemic structures, and pragmatic structures of assertions, recommendations, advice for other social actors and institutions, as well as forms of politeness when criticizing powerful actors or institutions. Crucial is that all these discursive, cognitive and social structures, strategies and processes take place, in combination, and at several levels, at the same time.

The text we use for the analysis is an editorial on immigration published on 13 December 2012 in the British tabloid newspaper *The Sun*, well known for its stance against immigration.

1   *The Sun Says*

2   ***Influx impact***

3   IF you think the country is changing before your eyes, you are right. It is.

4   Proof comes in the 2011 Census. It shows a three million rise in the foreign-

5   born population of England and Wales since 2001.

6   And in the Census's most startling statistic, Londoners describing

7   themselves as white British are in the minority at just 45 per cent.

8   Immigration can be a sign of a dynamic society. The South East in particular

9   would grind to a halt without industrious foreign workers.

10   Controlled immigration of talented newcomers is welcome, and the

11   Olympics showcased the friendly and positive side of the new-look Britain.

12   But the sheer scale of the influx, and its pace, raise serious questions.

13  Labour, who recklessly threw open our doors to the world, never asked

14  Britain if it wanted such a level of immigration.

15  Nor did it consider how public services such as housing, hospitals and

16  schools would cope. They can't.

17  And unlimited cheap foreign labour is frustrating the Government's attempts

18  to make work pay better than benefits.

19  A sensible debate on immigration was silenced by Labour's poisonous

20  charge of 'racism' against anyone who dared raise the issue.

21  The upshot is that immigrants suffer as badly as anyone else from

22  overwhelmed public services.

23  If anything, the 2011 Census is behind the times already as new migrants

24  arrive. Nor does it include tens of thousands here illegally.

25  Coming decades will see further changes in our national makeup. But there

26  is no turning the clock back.

27  The challenge now is to ensure future immigration is in line with what the

28  country can cope with.

## 4.2.1 Context analysis

Systematic discourse study not only requires an analysis of discourse structures but also of the structures of context defined as the relevant parameters of the communicative situation as it is construed by participants in their context models. Thus, the journalist writing this editorial is assumed to have a context model defined by the parameters on the left and a selection of discourse properties on the right of Table 5.1.

These context parameters are *relevant* properties of the communicative situation of editorial writing because they systematically control and define the *appropriateness* of the discourse in that situation. That is, an editorial is appropriate if it published in a newspaper, on a particular date, and in a specific city and country, written by a journalist as editorialist, expresses opinions on recent events or situation, and intends to influence public opinion and social or political policy. Within the framework of an SCA this means that discourse structures are not only described as such, but also as being controlled by the cognitive parameters of the context model, knowledge, attitudes and ideologies of the writer, as well as assumptions about those of the

**Table 5.1**   Context parameters and discursive manifestations of the editorial

| Context parameters | Discourse structures |
| --- | --- |
| • The **spatiotemporal** dimension of the communicative event,<br>• Him- or herself as a journalist of the *Sun* and as a British citizen (among other **identities**),<br>• In the **role** of current editorial **writer**, writing for **readers** of the Sun,<br>• Engaged in the speech act of asserting opinions and as producing an **editorial**, defined as a newspaper **genre**, as well as other **social actions**,<br>• With the **aim** of influencing the opinions of the readers and the immigration policies of British politicians,<br>• And expressing **attitudes** and **opinions** and presupposing **knowledge** about recent immigration and the increasing ethnic diversity of the country, among many other forms of socially shared knowledge, as well as underlying social and political ideologies. | • Dateline of the article: December 13, 2012; Location: London; deictic expressions: *the country* (3, 27), *now* (27); *coming decades* (25); present tense;<br>• *The Sun Says*; deictic expressions: *our national makeup* (25); *our doors* (13)<br>• *The Sun Says* (1); deictic expressions: *you* (3)<br>• Opinion expressions: *startling statistic* (6); *raises serious questions* (12), *Labour, who recklessly (. . .)*(13), *Labour's poisonous charge* (19),<br>• *The challenge now is . . .* (27–8)<br>• Knowledge: *The country is changing; statistic; coming decades will see . . .*, etc.<br>• Negative attitude about immigration and about Labour's policies. |

readers. This discourse-cognition analysis is then finally placed in the institutional-organizational framework of the newspaper, its relation to its readers and with other organizations or institutions, such as the government. Note though that such a description is not merely the result of macrosociological description by the analyst, but represented in the very context model of the writer and readers. In other words, the discourse analysis is totally integrated with a cognitive and a social analysis.

## 4.2.2  Text structures

Since a complete analysis of all the relevant discourse structures of the editorial would require many hundreds of pages, we focus on those *variable* structures that are specifically controlled by cognitive and social structures. This means that we ignore obligatory grammatical structures of English that do not vary by cognition and context, as well as those of specific discourse grammar, such as the interpretation of the pronouns and verbs of minimal sentences *It is* (3) or *They can't* (16), following the first sentence of the same lines, and defining a specific compact style of editorial syntax.

### 4.2.2.1 Semantic structures

Given their central role in discourse analysis beyond sentence syntax, and for critical discourse analysis in particular, let us focus on the semantic structures of the editorial.

**Semantic Macrostructure.** The overall coherence of discourse is defined by its semantic macrostructure or discourse topic, dominating the local meanings of the discourse as partly expressed by its constituent sentences. Thus, the whole text is conceptually organized by the macropropositions such as 'Uncontrolled immigration is bad for the country'. Part of that macroproposition is conventionally expressed by the headline as an obligatory category of the conventional schematic structure (its *superstructure*) of the editorial: *Influx impact*. But locally it organizes all the semantic information related to the arrival of (allegedly too) many immigrants: *foreign-born population* (4–5), *three million rise* (4), *white British* (6–7), *immigration can be a sign of a dynamic society* (8), *new immigrants arrive*, etc. Another main topic, controlling various local propositions, is for instance that Labour's immigration policies were reckless, as well as the topic defining the actual recommendation of the editorial, namely that current government policy should limit immigration.

Although semantic macrostructures are assumed to define the notion of the overall discourse topic, they are not always explicitly expressed in the text. Rather, they define the top levels of the mental situation model that represents overall meanings of the author and reader of the discourse. In other words, such discourse structures can only be defined in terms of underlying cognitive structures, such as the hierarchical nature of mental models. At the same time, these macrostructures are also those overall meanings that are best recalled by the readers.

It is at this point where the social and political functions of the editorial and its overall topics also play a role. *The Sun* as an influential tabloid with millions of readers has significant influence on public opinion and government policy. Thus, its overall opinions on immigration are not only locally relevant for the interpretation of this particular editorial, but play a fundamental role in the national debate. Thus, mental models of specific events and the opinions instantiated in them, also influence socially shared mental representations, that is, attitudes and prejudices about immigration and immigrants. In other words, our socio-cognitive analysis-related discourse structures (topics, macrostructures), with top level structures of mental models and their prominence in episodic memory, and these in turn with socially shared attitudes, and the influence on public opinion of citizens and voters, government policies and party politics. The explicitly expressed negative appraisal of Labour in this editorial more specifically relates to the powerful role of the mass media, and especially of a tabloid like the *Sun*, and its relations to the political parties, and hence as part of the power structure in the country.

In brief, discourse topics of editorials are socio-politically relevant, but this relevance is cognitively mediated by the role of topics in memory, and hence in the process of discourse processing, comprehension, and hence for the formation of public opinion, and its consequences for national policies, as the main persuasive function of editorials.

**Local coherence.** Discourse is not only globally coherent, but also locally. This local coherence takes two forms, an intensional (meaning) and an extensional (referential) one. Intensional relations are functional and hold between expressed propositions, such as Generalization, Specification, Example, Explanation and so on.

Thus, in line (1) the brief last sentence *It is*, is a Repetition and Confirmation of what it stated in the conditional clause of the previous sentence. And in the next lines, the proof mentioned in line (4) is followed by a proposition about a three million rise that is a Specification of that proof. In order to be able to establish these relationships, however, author and reader need to activate *conceptual knowledge* of the world, relating Census with quantitative data about the population.

On the other hand, coherence is not only based on meaning relations and conceptual knowledge, but also defined in terms of causal, temporal, part-whole relations between the *facts* denoted by the sentences of the discourse, as they are represented in the mental models of authors and readers. Indeed, in that sense, a discourse is coherent if it has a mental model. Thus, the event of the changing country mentioned in line (1) is related to the *cause* of a three million rise in line (4). Such a postposed causal proposition at the same time functions intensionally as an Explanation. Thus, most of the propositions of this editorial are locally connected by direct or indirect temporal and causal relations in the mental models of the author, such as:

Three million rise of foreign-born population → Country is changing
Whites in London are a minority → Country is changing
Without industrious foreign workers → South East would halt → immigration can be a sign of a dynamic society
(But) Unlimited cheap foreign labour → Frustrates government's attempts to make work pay better than benefits
etc.

Note though that the temporal and causal relations defining mental models are often only implicit in discourse, and require inferences instantiating socio-culturally shared knowledge of the world. In other words, also local discourse coherence is multiply dependent on underlying mental model structures and more general socio-cultural knowledge.

But what are the social and political conditions or functions of this kind of local coherence, beyond the obvious fact that socio-cultural knowledge is defined for epistemic communities? First of all, such local coherence also depends on group attitudes and ideologies. Thus, to describe the fact that white people in London are now a minority in the negative evaluative terms of a 'startling statistic', presupposes an attitude and ideology according to which London or Britain should be white, or that whites should at least be a majority. Most crucial however is the statement that increasing immigration is bad for the country, e.g., because housing, hospitals and schools would not cope. Such causal reasoning, however, presupposes a mental model in which specifically foreigners are a problem, not the fact that there are more people in the country. Indeed, the newspaper would not object to an increase of the autochthonous population and ignores that an increase of foreign workers leads to an increase in revenues to pay for extra schooling, housing and hospitals and hence would mean an increase of personnel and hence have a positive effect on the labour market. In other words, the local coherence of this editorial is premised on a specific mental model of the current situation in the UK, in which foreigners are focused upon as a major cause of social breakdown. Such a model is itself an instantiation of a socially shared negative attitude about immigration, based on a racist or xenophobic ideology.

Finally, in the triangular account of socio-cognitive analysis, these mental models, attitudes and ideologies expressed in an editorial of an influential tabloid have important social conditions and consequences, namely as a contribution to the formation or confirmation of racist attitudes among the population, on the one hand, and politically as an opponent of Labour and as partisan of the Conservative Party and its anti-immigrant policies. Again, discourse meanings and their underlying mental representations are not innocent, but multiply connected to social and political conditions and consequences. Note though that the discourse-society relation is not direct, but mediated by mental models of journalists and readers, and shared social and political attitudes and ideologies, without which text and talk would not make sense in the communicative situation.

**Disclaimers and the denial of racism.** One prominent feature of discourse about immigrants are disclaimers, which express brief positive self-presentation (e.g., I am not a racist. . .) with extensive and dominant negative other-presentation (but. . .). This text is a characteristic example of such a disclaimer. Thus, even *The Sun* in 2012 no longer can openly align itself with the extremist racist position that Britain should be or remain white and without any foreign workers. On the contrary, in lines (8–9) it is conceded that a specific kind of immigrant (industrious and talented ones) may be positive for a 'dynamic' society and a new-look Britain. Thus, the main argument of the editorial is not against immigration or immigrants in general, but against 'the sheer scale of the influx' – threatening that whites may become a minority in their own country or city. This moreover presupposes that most immigrants are not white, and would hardly be consistent with an opposition against immigrants from Romania and Bulgaria that the newspaper and other conservative institutions are opposing.

Disclaimers not only have characteristic semantic structures, but especially important contextual and cognitive implications. First of all, they express specific negative models of recent immigration events, as well as more general negative attitudes against immigrants. However, such opinions and attitudes may be inconsistent with liberal, modern, non-racist or non-xenophobic norms, values and hence the public image of the speaker or author. Hence the contextual relevance of the first pair part of a disclaimer as a form of positive self-presentation, intended to block negative evaluations by the recipients.

The social and political conditions and consequences of disclaimers are obvious, and can be formulated in terms of the social image, prestige, and hence the symbolic capital of speakers, authors and institutions. At the same time, as part of a persuasive discourse, they may diminish negative opinions of the authors and hence a bigger chance their argument will be accepted – which enhances the social and political influence of the newspaper, and hence its power. At the same time, by emphasizing the negative part of the disclaimer, the newspaper enhances ethnic prejudice in society and thus contributes to the reproduction of racism.

That such a concern is quite relevant in the context model of the author becomes obvious in lines (18–19), which we repeat in full:

A sensible debate on immigration was silenced by Labour's poisonous charge of 'racism' against anyone who dared raise the issue.

Indeed, in this editorial as well as in many news and opinion articles in the same newspaper as well as other conservative media, the denial of racism, and the attack on anti-racists is a standard strategy of negative discourse on immigration. In this example, this is done by several other strategic moves of persuasive discourse featuring the typical bipolar structures of ideological discourse, in which positive qualities of in-groups and negative qualities of out-groups are enhanced:

- vagueness ('raising the issue' instead of militating against immigration)
- non-partisan consensus ('anyone who . . .')
- positive self-presentation ('sensible debate', 'dared')
- negative other-presentation, metaphor and hyperbole ('poisonous charge', 'silenced' by Labour)

**Metaphor.** The study of conceptual metaphor has made significant contributions to the critical analysis of discourse because it showed how specific metaphorical expressions are related to embodied ways of thinking. Hence the link between discourse and cognition is an inherent part of the very description of metaphorical text and talk. This is specifically also the case for public discourse about immigration, as we already saw when we discussed the example of the ubiquitous use of the WAVE-metaphor for the arrival of large groups of immigrants. We argued that this metaphor is hardly innocent, because it precisely defined situation models in recipients in which immigration is seen as a threat, as a danger of drowning in immigrants, and hence as propagating fear among the population. It is not surprising that also in this editorial similar metaphors are prominent, as is the case in the topic expressing headline: *influx* (repeated in line 12), as well as in this context negative action of *opening the doors* attributed to Labour. Similar, accusations of racism are conceptualized as *poisonous* (19), and hence also ideologically express negative Other-presentation and as enhancing the threat to a 'healthy' debate.

The social and political implication of such mental models and their generalization in shared attitudes and ideologies hardly need to be spelled out – as the election campaigns of many parties in Europe have shown, with similar threatening metaphors, e.g. *Das Boot ist Voll* (The boat is full) in Germany, made explicit in this editorial by such expressions as 'what the country can cope with' (27–8).

**Other discourse structures.** For brevity's sake we have focused only on some, mostly semantic, discourse structures. The point of this succinct analysis was to show how specific discourse structures have cognitive foundations that are crucial for their description and explanation. We also saw that the combined discourse-cognition structures are themselves related to knowledge, attitudes and ideologies shared by groups, communities and organizations, and that social and political aims, status, influence and power both condition as well as follow from these discursive practices through cognitive mediation.

In our example, thus, we would need to engage in a detailed analysis of the **argumentation** of the newspaper, partly made explicit in our analysis of local coherence and its implicit propositions. The main standpoint is that the UK cannot cope with (massive) immigration, and the arguments are especially sought in the assumed '*overwhelming*' of the public services. For these and other arguments to be cogent, they also need to make explicit many implicit assumptions of mental models and derived from socio-cultural shared knowledge and attitudes. Socially and politically the same argument is relevant because it specially addresses the concerns of the citizens about the quality of the public services, thus confirming the prejudice that foreigners are the main cause of their lacking quality.

Part of the argumentation and typical of negative discourse and media reports on immigration is the **number game** (*three million, 45%*, etc.) of the editorial, sustaining the crucial quantity dimension of the main argument: too many immigrants (or in more formal style: *the scale of the influx*, 12). Again, these are not just meaning or rhetorical hyperboles, but confirm the embodied, threatening nature of the mental model presented by *The Sun*.

Among many other semantic and rhetorical structures, similar arguments may be developed for *Sun*-style **alliterations** (*Influx Impact*), **colloquial style** addressing readers (*if you think . . .*), **hyperboles** and **worst case descriptions** (*startling statistic, unlimited cheap labour*), many forms of positive self-presentation (*dynamic society, newcomers are welcome, friendly and positive side of the new-look Britain*, etc.).

# 5 Conclusion

The study of discourse should be multidisciplinary. Language use, text and talk are at the same time linguistic, cognitive and socio-cultural and political acts. A coherent theory of discourse should make explicit how these acts are related, both at the micro- and the macro-levels of analysis. Especially also for Critical Discourse Studies it is crucial that discourse structures are not directly related to social structures of groups, power and domination. Discourse can only have social and political conditions and consequences if we recognize that discourse is produced by language users as social participants who not only speak and act, but also think, know and feel. This means that in the same way as our analysis of text and talk should be systematic and detailed, also the underlying cognitive analysis should be explicit and sophisticated. Only with this missing link made explicit are we able to understand how discourse is able to function in the reproduction of power abuse and the resistance against it. A brief analysis of especially some of the semantic structures of an editorial in *The Sun* shows how a socio-cognitive analysis relates discourse structures with social structures, via an analysis of cognitive structures, and how such an editorial may contribute to the reproduction of racism in society.

# Note

1 Not only in the cognitive psychology of discourse, but also on the societal and discursive dimensions of this chapter there is a vast literature. Hence, we shall only cite a few relevant books for background reading of this paper, or where specific notions have been borrowed from other authors.

# References

Anderson, J. R. (1980), *Concepts, Propositions, and Schemata: What are the Cognitive Units?* Lincoln: University of Nebraska Press.
Baddeley, A., Conway, M., and Aggleton, J. (eds) (2002), *Episodic Memory. New Directions in Research*. Oxford: Oxford University Press.
Baddeley, A. D. (2007), *Working Memory, Thought, and Action*. Oxford: Oxford University Press.
Barsalou, L. W. (2008), 'Grounded cognition'. *Annual Review of Psychology*, 59, 617–45.
Cap, P., and Okulska, U. (eds) (2013), *Analyzing Genres in Political Communication: Theory and Practice*. Amsterdam: Benjamins.

Clark, H. H. (1996), *Using Language*. Cambridge: Cambridge University Press.

Collins, A. M. and Quillian, M. R. (1972), 'Experiments on semantic memory and language comprehension', in L. W. Gregg (ed.) *Cognition and Learning*. New York: Wiley, pp. 309–51.

De Fina, A. and Georgakopoulou, A. (2012), *Analyzing Narrative. Discourse and Sociolinguistic Perspectives*. Cambridge: Cambridge University Press.

Duranti, A. and Goodwin, C. (eds) (1992), *Rethinking Context: Language as an Interactive Phenomenon*. Cambridge: Cambridge University Press.

Eagly, A. H. and Chaiken, S. (1993), *The Psychology of Attitudes*. Fort Worth: Harcourt Brace Jovanovich.

Fillmore, C. J. (1968), 'The case for case', in E. Bach, and R. T. Harms (eds). *Universals in Linguistic Theory*. New York: Holt, Rinehart and Winston, pp. 1–88.

Garnham, A. (1987), *Mental Models as Representations of Discourse and Text*. New York: E. Horwood Halsted Press.

Gentner, D. and Stevens, A. L. (eds) (1983), *Mental Models*. Hillsdale, NJ: Erlbaum.

Givón, T. (2005), *Context as Other Minds. The Pragmatics of Sociality, Cognition and Communication*. Amsterdam: Benjamins.

Goldman, A. I. (2006), *Simulating Minds. The Philosophy, Psychology, and Neuroscience of Mindreading*. Oxford: Oxford University Press.

Graesser, A. C., Gernsbacher, M. A. and Goldman, S. R. (eds) (2003), *Handbook of Discourse Processes*. Mahwah, N.J: Erlbaum.

Jaspars, J. and Fraser, C. (1984), 'Attitudes and social representations', in R. M. Farr and S. Moscovici (eds.), *Social Representations*. Cambridge: Cambridge University Press, pp. 101–23.

Johnson-Laird, P. N. (1983), *Mental Models. Towards a Cognitive Science of Language, Inference, and Consciousness*. Cambridge, MA.: Harvard University Press.

Lambrecht, K. (1994), *Information Structure and Sentence Form. Topic, Focus, and the Mental Representations of Discourse Referents*. Cambridge: Cambridge University Press.

Lukes, S. (2004), *Power. A Radical View*. Basingstoke: Palgrave Macmillan.

Oakhill, J. and Garnham, A. (1987), 'Interpreting elliptical verb phrases at different times of day: Effects of plausibility and antecedent distance'. *Language and Speech*, 30(2), 145–157.

Plotkin, H. C. (2007), *Necessary Knowledge*. Oxford: Oxford University Press.

Pratkanis, A. R., Breckler, S. J. and Greenwald, A. G. (eds) (1989), *Attitude Structure and Function*. Hillsdale, NJ: Erlbaum.

Rosch, E. and Lloyd, B. B. (eds) (1978), *Cognition and Categorization*. Hillsdale, NJ: Erlbaum.

Royce, T. D. and Bowcher, W. L. (eds) (2007), *New Directions in the Analysis of Multimodal Discourse*. Mahwah, NJ: Erlbaum.

Schank, R. C. and Abelson, R. (1977), *Scripts, Plans, Goals, and Understanding*. Hillsdale, NJ: Lawrence Erlbaum.

Schiffrin, D., Tannen, D. and Hamilton, H. E. (eds) (2013), *The Handbook of Discourse Analysis*, (2nd edn). Malden, Mass.: Blackwell.

Searle, J. (1969). *Speech Acts: An Essay in the Philosophy of Language*. Cambridge: Cambridge University Press.

Shipley, T. F. and Zacks, J. M. (eds) (2008), *Understanding Events. From Perception to Action*. Oxford: Oxford University Press.

Sperber, D. and Wilson, D. (1995), *Relevance: Communication and Cognition*. Cambridge, MA: Blackwell.

Stewart, A. (2001), *Theories of Power and Domination. The Politics of Empowerment in Late Modernity*. Thousand Oaks, CA: Sage.

Titscher, S., Meyer, M., Wodak, R. and Vetter, E. (2000), *Methods of Text and Discourse Analysis*. Thousand Oaks, CA: Sage.

Tomasello, M. (2008), *Origins of Human Communication*. Cambridge, MA: MIT Press.

Tulving, E. (1983), *Elements of Episodic Memory*. Oxford: Clarendon Press.

—— (2002), 'Episodic memory: from mind to brain'. *Annual Review of Psychology*, 53(1), 1–25.

Tulving, E. and Craik, F. I. M. (eds) (2000), *The Oxford Handbook of Memory*. Oxford: Oxford University Press.

Van Dijk, T. A. (1984), *Prejudice in Discourse. An Analysis of Ethnic Prejudice in Cognition and Conversation*. Amsterdam: Benjamins.

—— (1987), *Communicating Racism: Ethnic Prejudice in Thought and Talk*. Newbury Park, CA: Sage.

—— (1991), *Racism and the Press*. London: Routledge.

—— (1993), *Elite Discourse and Racism*. Newbury Park, CA: Sage.

—— (1998), *Ideology: A Multidisciplinary Approach*, London: Sage.

—— (2001), 'Multidisciplinary CDA: a plea for diversity', in Ruth Wodak and Michael Meyer (eds) *Methods of Critical Discourse Analysis*. London: Sage, pp. 95–120.

—— (2008a), *Discourse and Context. A Socio-cognitive Approach*. Cambridge: Cambridge University Press.

—— (2008b), *Discourse and Power*. Basingstoke: Palgrave Macmillan.

—— (2009), *Society and Discourse. How Social Contexts Influence Text and Talk*. Cambridge: Cambridge University Press.

—— (2014), *Discourse and Knowledge*. Cambridge: Cambridge University Press.

Van Dijk, T. A. (ed.) (2007), *Discourse Studies*. 5 vols. Sage Benchmarks in Discourse Studies. London: Sage.

—— (2009b), *Racism and Discourse in Latin America*. Lamham: Lexington Books.

Van Dijk, T. A. and Kintsch, W. (1983), *Strategies of Discourse Comprehension*. New York, Toronto: Academic Press.

Zwaan, R. A. (2004), 'The immersed experiencer: toward an embodied theory of language comprehension'. *Psychology of Learning and Motivation: Advances in Research and Theory*, 44, 35–62.

# 6

# Applying Social Cognition Research to Critical Discourse Studies

# The Case of Collective Identities

*Veronika Koller*

Lancaster University

## 1 Introduction: 'Customer focus'

On 3 May 2007, the BBC Radio 4's flagship news programme *Today* featured an interview, conducted by senior presenter John Humphrys (JH), with Detective Chief Superintendent David Tucker (DT) of the National Association of Chief Police Officers in the UK. They discussed the investigation into the murder of Paul Kelly, who was stabbed to death outside a pub in Bath on New Year's Day that year, and the problem with witnesses holding back information. Several minutes into the interview, the following exchange occurred (see Appendix for the whole extract):

**DT:** what we're trying to do is to use ehm local policing through the neighbourhood policing initiative to bring forward customer focus                    to try and

**JH:**                                        [sharp intake of breath] ooh

**DT:** get more information in to understand crime issues

**JH:** You'll forgive me for saying so but I could hear people wincing when you said customer focus there. It's an odd sort of language to use in this context isn't it that's the language of commerce trying to flog people things

**DT:** I think it's—we need to build those sorts of relationships with ehm with all of the people of the UK—

**JH [raised voice]:**     But we're not customers of the police are we . you're not selling us a service we should all be working together as a community you're—we're not your customers and you're not our . suppliers

What is happening in this vignette? A speaker takes issue with his interlocutor using a noun phrase from business discourse, 'customer focus', in the context of policing. Far from just being a squabble over words, however, the exchange is a snapshot of discursive, social and cognitive change as it is happening. It turns the spotlight on nothing less than fundamental ideological differences and far-reaching questions of collective identity.

Focusing on the latter, this chapter presents an approach to the study of collective identity that applies insights from social cognition research to critical discourse studies. Drawing on social cognition theory, collective identities are understood as socio-cognitive representations of the group self, including its attributes, relational behaviour, goals and values, which are constituted and negotiated by the interactions within a discourse community. Both discourse, as instantiated in textual interaction at the micro-level, as well as the models of collective identity that it communicates are shaped by meso-level contexts of text production, distribution, reception and appropriation, which are in turn linked to the changing socio-political context and its ideologies at the macro-level. In this chapter, I advocate the socio-cognitive analysis of discourse, along with elements from the discourse-historical approach, to enable the researcher to investigate what representations of collective identities are salient in a discourse community at a given historical moment, how changes in those models can be traced in concrete texts and to discuss why these changes are taking place.

To show how collective identities can usefully be analysed in this way, the chapter is structured as follows: in the next section, I will first unpack what we mean by 'critical discourse studies' and then outline discourse-historical and socio-cognitive approaches within it. I will then, in section 3, draw on the literature on social cognition to theorize collective identities as socio-cognitive representations. Section 4 introduces a research paradigm for analysing collective identities in discourse that combines discourse analytical and socio-cognitive categories, distinguishing between the text level and the features and linguistic devices that are relevant there on the one hand, and the level of context and the discourse goals and functions at stake there on the other. The paradigm also elaborates on the socio-cognitive aspects of the macro-level of the social context, the meso-level of the discourse practice context and the micro-level of text. To illustrate this framework, I will in section 5 return to the above radio interview and analyse a longer extract from it to see how it constructs and reflects ongoing changes in the speakers' socio-cognitive representations of collective identities. The chapter will conclude with a summary and briefly outline possible areas of application of the socio-cognitive approach to critical discourse studies.

First then, let us turn to 'critical discourse studies' and two of the approaches that have been advanced in that area.

## 2 Critical discourse studies: Discourse-historical and socio-cognitive approaches

Given that 'critical', 'discourse' and 'studies' all belong to a group of words that are overused but all too often under-defined in the social sciences, it seems worthwhile providing some working definitions. To begin with, 'critical' is used to denote the social and semiotic analysis of text-in-context with the aim of making transparent taken-for-granted assumptions, identifying how relations of power are established, reinforced and subverted by discourse participants, and contributing to the emancipatory efforts of marginalized groups. The emancipatory aim needs applied work, e.g. guidelines and consultancy on language use or communication training, which necessarily involves the recontextualization of research in non-academic discourses.[1] This is captured by Reisigl and Wodak's (2009) notion of prognostic critique. Likewise, they refer to the analysis of the role of discourse in establishing, maintaining or challenging power as socio-diagnostic critique, while text or discourse immanent critique addresses contradictions and dilemmas within texts and discourses themselves. The excerpt reproduced at the beginning of this chapter and analysed in section 5 represents such a dilemma at the textual level.

To proceed, 'discourse' is here defined as language use as social practice that is based on and shapes cognition. Following the distinction between discourse as either an uncountable or a count noun (Fairclough, 2010: 95–6), discourse as an uncountable noun can be pre-modified to indicate the historical or national context and/or the social realm in which the discourse under investigation is enacted, e.g. 'late nineteenth-century Italian political discourse'. Discourses as count nouns can be differentiated by indicating stance and topic as well as locality, producer and channel of distribution,[2] e.g. 'a nationalist discourse on immigration in British newspapers' or 'the environmentalist discourse of the Conservative party'. This way of naming discourses can be abstracted as in Figure 6.1. To repeat a central tenet of critical discourse studies, discourse thus defined does ideological work in that participants draw on linguistic resources to encode combinations of beliefs, values, norms, goals and emotions in order to gain, maintain or challenge power and influence.

Finally, the term 'studies' is a more comprehensive notion than 'analysis', which suggests a certain methodology and can therefore lead to the misunderstanding that one can 'do a CDA' of something. By contrast, 'critical discourse studies' (CDS) allows more leeway for the eclectic approach to methods that is typical of critical text-based analysis. Methods should be chosen for their potential to answer specific research questions and analytical parameters can be at least partly data-driven. It should be stressed, however, that claims in critical discourse studies need to be based on textual evidence, which can only be gained by detailed semiotic, including linguistic, analysis or, where appropriate, by conversation analysis.

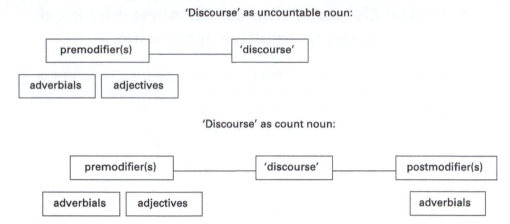

**FIGURE 6.1** *Naming discourses.*

Two of the main strands in CDS are the discourse historical approach (e.g. De Cillia et al., 1999; Reisigl and Wodak, 2009) and the socio-cognitive approach (e.g. Hart, 2011; Koller, 2005; Van Dijk, 2003, 2009, this volume). Both start from a specific social problem or phenomenon that is created, reinforced and challenged through discourse. The socio-cognitive dimension of the phenomenon under investigation is its conceptualization in the form of a socio-cognitive representation (SCR) that is both reflected and reinforced through discourse. What makes a social phenomenon problematic from a critical standpoint is that it involves the unequal distribution of power between discourse participants, leading to marginalization, discrimination and, ultimately, suffering. To see how discourse and cognition contribute to such a problem, researchers focusing on socio-cognitive aspects would analyse texts in their socio-political contexts in order to infer underlying SCRs, such as collective identities, while analysts in the discourse-historical paradigm would link textual analysis back to the context of discourse production, distribution and reception as well as to the wider social and historical context. (It should be noted that discourse-historical studies need not be diachronic; the historical context in question can also be the immediate present. The point is that the linguistic data are contextualized by means of triangulation, i.e. by looking at texts in various genres and by various producers, all of which instantiate the discourse at hand.) Detailed textual analysis is central in both approaches. In discourse-historical work, such an investigation helps to see what linguistic devices are used to realize the discursive goals of producing, preserving, transforming and destroying in- and out-groups.[3] In socio-cognitively oriented research, on the other hand, linguistic analysis reveals what devices are used to express SCRs. From a critical perspective, repeatedly exposing text recipients to certain SCRs transported in texts, under similar conditions of reception, may help to align recipients' cognition with that of the text producer and thereby build an advantage for the latter's in-group. It should be noted, however, that recipients actively co-construct the texts' meaning, adopting or changing the representations they are confronted with according to their own background, which makes the success of any attempt at cognitive alignment uncertain. In summary, the discourse-historical approach is important in the analysis of collective identities as these are always historically contingent, while the socio-cognitive approach is indispensable when collective identity is understood as a socio-cognitive representation. In the next section, I will elaborate on the notion of socio-cognitive representations with regard to collective identities.

## 3 Socio-cognitive representations and collective identities

Extending a concept from social psychology (Moscovici, 2001), socio-cognitive representations (SCRs) can be defined as the coherent cognitive structures that are jointly acquired, held and presupposed by members of a group. As such, they combine beliefs/knowledge, values, norms, goals and emotions, and give rise to attitudes and expectations. In contrast to schemas,[4] SCRs are not individually held mental models but cognitive structures shared by members of a particular group. As such they are 'socially and discursively constructed in the course of . . . communication', establish social identities and relations by being communicated, and are subject to 'continual transformation . . . through the ebb and flow of intergroup relations' (Augoustinos et al., 2006: 258–9). To the extent that SCRs establish relations of power within and between groups, they can be seen as the building blocks of ideology (see Koller, 2014, on the elements, structure, genesis and function of ideologies). Furthermore, the relevance of any particular representation will vary across contexts and situations, depending e.g. on whether fellow group members or external audiences are addressed. Although they can stabilize through repeated activation, SCRs are overall more dynamic and flexible than schemas, not least because they are not necessarily internally consistent but can show contradictory elements that lead to their change over time (Augoustinos et al., 2006: 99). The intertextual negotiation, the possible internal contradictions and the adaptability of SCRs call for at least some discourse-historical elements in the analysis of their textual manifestation.

While socio-cognitive representations can capture any abstract or concrete object, they find a specific form in collective identities. In this context, it is useful to distinguish between individual/collective identity on the one hand and personal/social identity on the other. Individual personal identity captures the representation of the self-as-person independent of social context and is as such part of one's SCR of oneself that is derived from individual experiences, characteristics and capacities. It is worth pointing out, however, that such a 'notion of personal identity is a fiction [as a]ll forms of self-construal must be social' (Augoustinos et al., 2006: 25). At the very least, individual identity represents the self-as-person socially, i.e. in relation to other individuals. More relevant to this chapter are collective identities, which can again be individual, i.e. capturing intra-group relations in the in-group, or social, i.e. part of one's SCR of oneself that is derived from the social groups and categories to which one belongs, together with the value attached to such groups (Augoustinos et al., 2006: 309). The present focus is on such collective social identities, which pertain to inter-group relations between in-group and affiliated or out-groups. The bulk of critical discourse studies has addressed the discursive construction of us vs. them in the form of positively evaluated in-groups and negatively evaluated out-groups. However, this not only disregards the category of affiliated groups, but also overlooks the fact that not all in-group representations are imbued with positive values. Indeed, as Gee (1992: 109) has observed, 'certain social circumstances can lead to an individual . . . disowning "people like us (me)"'. Nor does the discursive construction of an in-group always need a complementary out-group (for examples of both phenomena, see Koller, 2008).

Collective social identities have been theorized as being projected, transformed or constituted in and through discourse. The first of these notions sees discourse as a means by which members of a group convey an image of themselves or the group as a whole and thus assumes a pre-discursive identity. A further development of this theory holds that identity is transformed through projection. According to this line of thought, what is conveyed through discourse is a selective and embellished version of the self, i.e. the ideal rather than the actual self (Markus and Nurius, 1986). The transformative aspect comes in through affiliated and out-groups mirroring their perceptions of the in-group back to itself (cf. Christensen and Askegaard, 2001). Finally, a social constructivist approach to discourse and identity denies any pre-discursive identity, but sees any representation of the self as constituted through projection. In this framework, identity is not unveiled, but produced in the discursive projection which it claims to draw on. In analysing collective identities in discourse, I take a transformative view which also accounts for the notion of identity as a socio-cognitive representation: people engage in social, including discursive, practices and in doing so act on specific SCRs about themselves and others. Some people, by dint of their social roles, are in the position to produce and distribute more or less influential texts that are vehicles for their producers' SCRs. Other people receive these texts and doing so repeatedly under similar conditions of reception is likely to impact on their social practices and indeed SCRs. This impact may be one of the producers' intentions with the text, preferably to align their SCRs with those of the discourse recipients. We can thus theorize a mutually constitutive relationship between discourse and social cognition, where discourse is instantiated in texts that project and transform SCRs, both the discourse producers' and the recipients'. Socio-cognitive representations that a text producer holds about a social group, be it their own or another, thus translate into the textual construction of a collective identity. Hence, a socio-cognitive approach to critical discourse studies is well suited to analysing collective identities and is especially relevant at the interpretation stage of analysis, which addresses the question as to why text producers have selected a range of linguistic devices to construct groups in a particular way. The next section will elaborate on the stages and levels of analysing collective identities in discourse.

## 4  Analysing collective identities in discourse: A research paradigm

A critical analysis of collective identity in discourse will combine discourse analytical procedures with socio-cognitive categories, to describe the linguistic features of texts and explain them with recourse to the discourse practice and social contexts. The discourse analytical procedures involve the content and semiotic analysis of texts at the micro-level as well as the analysis of contexts at the meso- and macro-levels. Discourse features and concrete linguistic devices are relevant at the text level, while the context level involves questions about discourse goals and functions. Moreover, while socio-cognitive categories are relevant at both the text and context levels, they are most pertinent at the explanation stage, which involves context analysis; this is because SCRs cannot simply be read off texts but have to be inferred from the linguistic findings. The three interrelated levels of discourse, and the generic research questions they entail, are represented in Figure 6.2 (see also Fairclough, 2010: 133).

Starting at the micro-level of individual texts, the analysis can be divided into content and semiotic analysis, both of which are descriptive. Content analysis addresses the

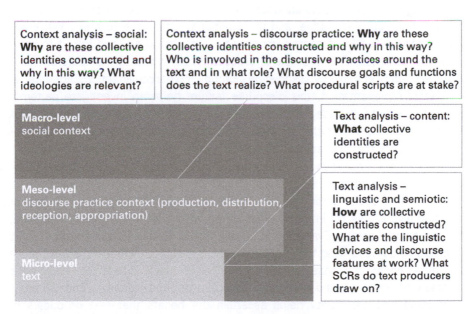

**FIGURE 6.2** *Levels of analysing collective identity in discourse.*

question as to what identities are constructed or not, and encompasses ascertaining presences and absences in the text as well as identifying propositions and possibly argumentation strategies.[5] The semiotic analysis looks at how identities are constructed by investigating discourse features and linguistic and, where relevant, other semiotic devices. In addition, links between and across features can mean that they reinforce, supplement or contradict particular textual constructions of collective identity. This part of the text analysis looks at the discourse features that are used, e.g. modality or turn-taking, and the concrete linguistic and conversational devices that these take, e.g. modal verbs or interruptions. While analysing certain features and devices may be of help when addressing collective identity in discourse, it should be understood that there is no definitive list; while it is advisable to aim for consistency in applying analytical categories across texts, individual instances of language use will show different characteristics depending on what genre they represent, what audience they are aimed at and what discourses they instantiate. Therefore, any list of discourse features and linguistic devices should be handled flexibly enough to incorporate features and devices that are particularly important for the text under investigation, and to disregard those that are not.

Having said that, any analysis of collective identity will centre on the discourse feature of social actor representation (Van Leeuwen, 1996, 2008), which bridges content and linguistic analysis at the text level, asking what groups and individuals are referred to and how, and whether social actors are included or excluded, genericized or specified, activated or passivized beneficially. In socio-cognitive terms, social actor representation communicates particular SCRs of social groups, including beliefs and/or knowledge about them, the attitudes towards and expectations of them that ensue from beliefs and/or knowledge, and the emotions that accrue to them. While social actor representation is of central importance, other features feed into it to provide cumulative evidence. One example is process types, which further differentiate the collective identity at stake by associating a group with particular actions. Together with social actor representation, this discourse feature helps to investigate patterns of transitivity in texts (Halliday and Matthiessen, 2004: 168–259; Thompson, 2004: 88–105). Apart from attitudes and expectations as well as emotions concerning the social actors that the actions are ascribed to, this feature specifically relies on knowledge about processes, i.e. on scripts. Another discourse feature that is likely to be relevant is evaluation, which throws light on the norms and values component of a specific SCR of social actors as well as on the emotions related to it. Analysing evaluation also allows for inferring what stereotypes and ideal types text producers hold about social actors. Evaluation is closely related to modality, through which the text producer conveys what they perceive a social group to be like in the past, present and future, constructs possible developments for them (epistemic modality) and indicates what they see as desirable for the group (deontic modality). Such an analysis of likelihood and desirability helps ascertain the beliefs that text producers hold about a social actor group and the goals that they define for it. As goals are motivated by values – social actors strive to attain what they believe to be good and/or important and hence desirable – the analysis of modality is linked to the norms and values ascertained by analysing evaluation. Two final possible discourse features of interest are intertextuality and interdiscursivity, which show what other texts, genres and discourses are appropriated by text producers. Analysing these features not only ascertains inter-group relations but also reflects on collective identity by showing what features are borrowed to construct an identity. To the extent that intertextuality and interdiscursivity can be used to align or distance the text producer with or from the producers of other texts and discourses, this feature also addresses the norms and values that are part of the text producer's SCRs about their own and other social groups.

Text analysis identifies and describes semiotic features, which are influenced by discourse practice and social context, and can be explained by them. In contrast to descriptive text analysis, context analysis is explanatory, seeking to explain why certain identities are (not) constructed and if they are, why they are constructed in the particular way described in the previous analytical stage. In explaining the results of the text analysis, context analysis takes recourse to social and discourse practice contexts, and their cognitive underpinnings. When looking at the meso-level of the discourse practice context, the analyst focuses on the discursive practices that surround the text, i.e. the roles of, and relationships between, members of a discourse community, asking who is communicating to whom about what, and whether the text is designed for a particular audience, e.g. by drawing on assumed shared knowledge. A further point of interest is under what conditions production, distribution, reception and appropriation of texts take place, including the question as to how restricted access to certain distribution channels is. Analysis of the discourse practice context also looks at discourse goals, i.e. the overall aim that the discourse producer pursues by using language as a social practice, such as out-group denigration or self-enhancement. These goals are realized by particular discourse functions, e.g. politeness or impoliteness. Linking context to text, discourse functions translate into discourse features, which in turn manifest in concrete linguistic (more broadly: semiotic) and conversational devices. In socio-cognitive terms, analysis of the discourse practice context investigates what procedural scripts about producing, distributing, receiving and appropriating texts are enacted.

Discourse practice and the SCRs underlying it not only impact on the micro-level of text, but are in turn also influenced by the macro-level of social context. Thus, socio-cultural and socio-economic conditions give some discourse participants preferred access, or block access, to means of production and distribution on a large scale, while simultaneously endowing them with a certain degree of credibility, or lack thereof. Context analysis also aims to identify what ideologies are relevant, where ideologies can be defined as a network of beliefs that gives rise to expectations, norms and values about events, ideas and people. It thus helps to account for the findings from text analysis by discussing what roles the wider social context and the ideologies at stake in it allocate to social actors as well as by inquiring if the social formation is changing and if so, how and why.

By way of illustrating the framework, I will in the following section return to the radio interview introduced earlier and see what conflicting collective identities are negotiated there.

## 5 Sample analysis: 'Customer focus' revisited

As mentioned at the beginning of this chapter, the text chosen to illustrate the above research paradigm is the closing part of an interview on BBC Radio 4's *Today* programme; a transcript can be found in the Appendix. In the following, I will analyse the text for social actor representation, interdiscursivity and deontic modality as well as other relevant features such as metaphor and negation, and then account for the use of these discourse features by relating them to the text's discourse practice and social contexts.

Starting with social actor representation, this feature is remarkably complex in the data extract and perhaps best captured in the form of a diagram (Figure 6.3, in which solid arrows indicate explicit mentions and broken arrows implicit links).

The social actors represented are first of all the participants in this instance of discourse, in that the interviewer and interviewee refer to themselves, each other and the radio audience. The audience is further constructed as representative of the British public while the interviewee also casts himself as representative of

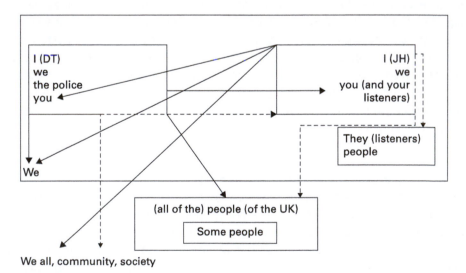

**FIGURE 6.3** *Social actor representation in the interview.*

the police in general. The latter social actor is genericized and referred to in its function, and is also exclusively represented as active, while the general public is also passivized once ('you as supplying us with a service', turn 10). It is over the status of the police as a social actor group that the conflict between the two speakers erupts.

Picking out only two linguistic aspects of social actor representation in the data, we can first note the three uses of 'we'. The most inclusive form, while mentioned by both speakers, is referred to by the interviewee, David Tucker (DT), as 'all of the people of the UK' (turn 7), while the interviewer, John Humphrys (JH), uses the more abstract terms 'community' and 'society' (turns 8 and 10), which can typically be found in political discourse. By contrast, DT recontextualizes lexis that is typical of corporate discourse – which leads to the disagreement between the speakers in the first place – such as 'customer focus'/'customers', 'service', 'consume' (turns 3, 9 and 11) and, more indirectly, 'choosing' (turn 11). DT also incorporates a discourse on emotions and relationships, which originates in the private sphere and is here realized in the words 'relationship(s)' (turns 7, 9 and 11), 'confident' and 'trust' (turn 11). We are thus dealing with a case of multiple interdiscursivity (Koller, 2010) in that corporate discourse is integrated into news discourse via a third discourse, i.e. that on emotions and relationships, which has become characteristic of corporate discourse. The lexis from corporate discourse is taken up by JH in his social actor representation, but coupled with negation to refute the redefinition of the police–public relationship that DT attempts. Thus, we find JH stating that 'we're not customers of the police . . . you're not selling us a service . . . we're not your customers and you're not our suppliers . . . we have no choice' (turns 8 and 10).

This stark contrast between the first and the second person plural brings us to the second aspect of the speakers' social actor representation, namely the fact that JH identifies with some of the groups he mentions whereas DT largely represents his in-group as acting on others. The interviewer constructs himself as representative of the inclusive 'we', both when repeating a deontic proposition ('we have no choice', turn 10) and when changing the social actor from the first to the third person in 'I have to have the policy it's essential for the wellbeing of society' (turn 10).[6] He also relates to the programme's listeners when ascribing his own reaction to the interviewee's use of business terminology to the audience: 'I could hear people wincing when you said customer focus there' (turn 6); this example constructs him as being close to listeners while at the same time seeking to gain credibility from their ascribed reaction. By contrast, DT only uses one instance of evidentiality and person deixis to draw on shared knowledge with the audience, namely when he cites the programme itself (turn 1). He thus establishes a relationship with the audience, as indeed he does through the use of the inclusive 'we' (turns 1 and 3). Otherwise, he enacts the corporate 'we' and represents it as impacting on others, realized most obviously in the transitive process 'we are delivering you a service' (turn 9). The word 'deliver' is repeated by DT later (turn 11), again with an abstract direct object, i.e. the anaphoric 'that' referring back to 'trying to make people confident'. We therefore have a metaphoric expression that is once more reminiscent of corporate discourse,[7] as are some other instantiations of the JOURNEY metaphor in DT's turns, i.e. 'to bring forward' and 'the way forward' (turns 3 and 11). This metaphoric expression combines with continuous aspect when the speaker pursues his discourse goal of informing listeners about how the police address the issue of lacking support from the public: 'what we're trying to do is . . . to bring forward customer focus', 'we are delivering you a service', 'what we're trying to do is deliver that' (turns 3, 9 and 11). Together, the two devices convey a sense of a dynamic organization and thus lend persuasive overtones to the information.

In terms of deontic modality, the interviewee's insistence that 'we need to build those sorts of relationships with . . . all of the people of the UK' (turn 7) redefines the police's relationship with the public, while 'what we're trying to do is deliver that' (turn 11) informs listeners about ongoing efforts. The interviewer on the other hand seeks to resist a redefinition of the relationship between police and public, using the discourse features of negation in connection with social actor representation. For example, he states explicitly that 'we're not customers of the police . . . we should all be working together as a community' (turn 8).

The discourse features employed by both speakers reflect their socio-cognitive representation of the police as a service provider (DT) as opposed to an executive authority (JH). The respective SCRs involve expectations of what the police should be doing, i.e. provide a service vs. work with the community, as well as norms and values which are expressed as goals of the police's actions. Both speakers are adamant in their position, claiming that 'we need to build those sorts of relationships' (turn 7; see also turn 11), i.e. ones like those between customers and service-providers, and countering that 'we should all be working together as a community' (turn 8). Because identities are relational, the competing SCRs of the police entail SCRs for the British public as consumers or beneficiaries of the police's actions, respectively.

Looking at discourse practice, both speakers pursue certain discourse goals in this instance of language use. The police representative starts out (turns 1, 3 and 5) with the discourse goal of informing the public, as represented by the programme's listeners, about what the police are doing to address the problem of unreported crime and to encourage witnesses to contact the police. In doing so, however, his discourse goal gets reframed by the interviewer's intervention and his subsequent metalinguistic comment (turns 4 and 6).[8] For the next few turns, DT defends himself against JH's repeated criticism and in the process shifts his discourse goal to redefining the relation between the police and the public (turns 7, 9 and 10), while still seeking to pursue his original goal of informing listeners about police initiatives (turn 11). Both speakers also use interruptions to background their interlocutor's beliefs and foreground their own, with the interviewer also using paralinguistic cues, interjection and pitch to that end.

The text is produced by speakers who have privileged access to national radio, an otherwise restricted channel of communication. The interview that they co-produce, and the SCRs they communicate through it, therefore have a wide reach, which raises the stakes for their conflict. As the interview is part of a live broadcast, text production coincides with distribution and reception. Recipients could in principle be any member of the British public, although the speakers are of course aware that only a segment of that public will listen to the programme, meaning that they produce text with a specific audience in mind; in the case of the *Today* programme, this is likely to be an educated adult audience, some members of which may well be in positions of professional power. Assumptions about the audience are made explicit both when JH claims that they are 'wincing' (turn 6) at DT's use of business language and when DT expresses his belief that they are interested in, if not supportive of, his SCR of the police as a service provider. Both speakers therefore seek to enlist the audience for their worldview.

The audience is not passive, however, with the programme's website (http://www.bbc.co.uk/programmes/b006qj9z) and more recently its Facebook page (https://www.facebook.com/thetodayprogramme) and hashtag (#r4today) making it interactive. In fact, JH refers to listeners' online reactions right at the end of the interview ('We'll see what they have to say about it', turn 12). On the message board for the *Today* programme of 3 May 2007 (http://www.bbc.co.uk/dna/mbtoday/F5963509?thread=4115942), the editorial team started a discussion by posting the following:

> Should the police treat the public as 'customers', and should the public in turn regard the police in the same way they would a supermarket? On Thursday's programme Detective Chief Superintendent David Tucker of the Association of Chief Police Officers talked of 'bringing forward customer focus' as a way of encouraging information from the public towards understanding crime issues. He went on to say the police 'need to have a relationship that is built on the idea that we are delivering you a service and you consume that service'. Is he right – is this how we should view the police in the modern age?

Before quoting DT verbatim, the editorial team elaborate on his SCR of the police and the public in a somewhat polemical manner by comparing the former to a supermarket.[9] This elaboration is likely to prime discussants to answer the post's final question negatively and thereby continues JH's attempts during the interview to gain the audience's support. Perhaps unsurprisingly then, none of the 90 messages on the board expresses any support for DT's attempt at renegotiating the relationship between police and public. In fact, one poster addresses JH directly and echoes his use of negation:

> As I said in my email to the Today programme . . . Good on you, John, for challenging this ambiguous use of language. Policing is not a packaged product, it's a public

service. We don't buy police protection, it's a duty provided to us as citizens. The fact that we pay for public services in our council tax, etc. does not make us customers.

(message 7)

Over the course of ten days, the discussion came to focus on the quality and conditions of policing in the UK rather than any collective identity for that social actor group, but the earlier postings make metalinguistic comments on DT's use of language, denouncing it as devoid of meaning (which from a discourse analytical point of view it is certainly not), inappropriate in its interdiscursivity and even politically insidious:

This nonsensical language (message 37); How can people take such drivel even remotely seriously? (message 13); this ridiculous gobbledegook (message 15); patronising gobbledygook, spin and psychobabble (message 62)

it seems our Police force have swolled [sic] a mangement [sic] speak hand book (message 4); American bussiness [sic] jargon, clap trap (message 39)

this kind of double-speak (message 6); this sort of Orwellian speak (message 29)

The discourse practice context thus shows that the interviewee's SCR is widely refuted, even though we can only speculate what the message boards posts would look like if the first posting had not primed discussants for a negative response. As it stands, the message board justifies JH in aligning his views with that of his audience.

Apart from negotiating the relationship between each other, and between themselves and the audience, JH and DT also express and thereby reinforce ideal and actual SCRs of themselves, the other speaker and the British public, as represented by the audience. DT expresses his social collective identity as a representative of the police by constructing the latter as a service provider who is dynamic, future-oriented, makes an effort to change, but is separate from and acts on the public. Accordingly, his ideal SCR of the public is as a consumer who is separate from and acted upon by the police. JH, by contrast, sees the public as a beneficiary of the police's actions. To the extent that he identifies with the public, this SCR of the public constitutes his ideal collective self, while his actual SCR of the police is as an executive authority that can be collectively identified with the public.

The above analysis throws a spotlight on an ideological conflict that erupts over an instance of language use. What is at stake are two belief systems about what the police is or should be, and, underlying that, beliefs about the appropriate place of corporate norms in contemporary society. In their encounter, both participants speak as representatives of a social group or institution and see their ideologically informed expectations about each other confounded: that the police officer appropriates features of corporate discourse leads to a strongly evaluative, even emotional reaction, by the interviewer, while for his part, said officer reacts with confusion and surprise to see his views contested (evidenced implicitly in the false start in turn 7 and explicitly in turn 11). While the interviewee aligns himself with a consumer capitalist ideology about the public that regards them as customers first and foremost and sets up a goal for them and the police force to forge a supplier–customer relationship, the interviewer and parts of the audience subscribe to a historically older view of the public as citizens in the first instance, who benefit from, and collaborate with, the police.

This leaves the question as to why the two ideologies clash at this particular historical moment and what social change is indicated by this conflict. What the interview and the reactions to it throw into relief is the aftermath of the political and economic transition from a bureaucratic state with expert authority over citizens to the state as a service provider in partnership with the private sector. This partnership is fraught with tension, however, as the simultaneous privatization of the public sector makes it compete with the private sector. The fact that this competition is skewed by vastly different availability of funds in the respective sectors only makes the tension more palpable. The transition from public to private sector as the provider of essential services such as policing and healthcare, and the concomitant shift from the public-as-citizens to the public-as-consumers, is underscored by the tendency of globalization to disconnect local groups, places and cultures, and replace them with collective identities that are based on consumption.

# 6 Conclusion

In this chapter, I have discussed the notion of collective identities as socio-cognitive representations, developed a research paradigm for analysing such identities in discourse and illustrated that framework by analysing an extract from a radio interview that revolves around an ideological conflict. In the analysis, I have combined discourse analytical tools with socio-cognitive categories, looking at discourse features and linguistic devices at the micro-level of text and explaining the findings by discussing discourse goals and functions at the meso-level of discourse practice as well as political and economic changes at the macro-level of social context. Throughout, I have accounted for what SCRs, scripts and ideologies we can infer the text producers to hold and advocate. Studies such as the present one could be further extended by more triangulation; in the present case it would be worthwhile to go beyond the interview and message board and include, for example, documents on neighbourhood policing initiatives, policy papers and ethnographic studies of local communities.

The analysis has shown that collective identities develop in a non-linear fashion, as can be seen in diachronic studies (e.g. Koller, 2008) but also in synchronic moments of contestation. More broadly, a focus on language shows how collective identities are constructed through text and discourse, and demonstrates how social and economic factors at the macro-level indirectly impact on the selection of linguistic features at the micro-level. A socio-cognitive critical analysis of discourse can therefore enrich related disciplines such as social psychology, social cognition research and social anthropology, especially with a view to social identities, intra- and inter-group relations, stereotypes or ideal types, as well as the organization of social relations in groups based on ethnicity, sexual identity, age, consumption, etc. In all these cases, the comparative study of the discursive construction and cognitive structure of collective identity shows what identities are at stake, how they are communicated and why they are constructed in particular ways.

# Notes

**1** Beyond that, we need studies on the discourse of a wider range of powerful groups. For example, corporate discourse is still under-researched in critical discourse studies, despite corporations' immense power in the absence of democratic legitimization. Patterns of discrimination there differ from those found in political discourse, in that corporate discourse producers typically discriminate on the basis of a person's disposable income and their availability for paid employment. According to this logic, people have value only as potential consumers or employees.

**2** Stance is perhaps the most tenuous aspect of a discourse to identify. It is linked to producer in that particular discourse producers are likely, although not guaranteed, to exhibit particular stances.

**3** While the terms are used metaphorically here, the material impact of discourse means that the strategies can all too soon become literal; as for the destruction of out-groups, this finds its most horrendous example in discourses preparing the ground for genocide.

**4** Cognitive and socio-cognitive terminology includes partially overlapping notions such as 'schemas', 'scripts', 'gestalts', 'idealized cognitive models', 'mental models', to name only a few. For an excellent discussion and differentiation, see Ziem (2008: 22–35).

**5** Subsuming argumentation under content analysis is a moot point and this discourse feature may rather be located halfway between content and semiotic analysis.

**6** Incidentally, 'wellbeing' is another borrowing from political discourse, realizing as it does the BODY POLITIC metaphor (Musolff 2009).

**7** In the British context, 'deliver' is strongly associated with New Labour's public sector policies (Fairclough, 2000: 17–18), which even became known as 'deliverology' (ascribed to Nicholas Macpherson, senior civil servant at the Treasury).

**8** At the same time, JH tries to save DT's face by enacting the discourse function of negative politeness, here realized by the linguistic devices of apologies (turn 6), tag questions (turns 6 and 8) and mitigating adverbs (turn 10). However, given the force of his resistance, this may be no more than a token gesture.

**9** Invoking the scripts related to a supermarket taps into the audience's everyday lived experience. It is therefore not surprising that four discussants take up and elaborate the term, e.g. 'The police serve members of the general public and referring to them as customers is part of a general trend to manage all services as if they were supermarkets' (message 52).

# References

Augoustinos, M., Walker, I. and Donaghue, N. (2006), *Social Cognition: An Integrated Introduction* (2nd edn). London: Sage.

Christensen, L. T. and Askegaard, S. (2001), 'Corporate identity and corporate image revisited: a semiotic perspective'. *European Journal of Marketing*, 35(3–4), 292–315.

De Cillia, R., Reisigl, M. and Wodak, R. (1999), 'The discursive construction of national identities'. *Discourse and Society*, 10(2), 149–73.

Fairclough, N. (2000), *New Labour, New Language?* London: Routledge.

—— (2010), *Critical Discourse Analysis* (2nd edn). London: Longman.

Gee, J. P. (1992), *The Social Mind: Language, Ideology, and Social Practice*. New York: Bergin & Garvey.

Halliday, M. A. K. and Matthiessen, C. M. I. M. (2004), *Introduction to Functional Grammar* (3rd edn). London: Arnold.

Hart, C. (2011), 'Moving beyond metaphor in the cognitive linguistic approach to CDA: construal operations in immigration discourse', in C. Hart (ed.), *Critical Discourse Studies in Context and Cognition*. Amsterdam: Benjamins, pp. 172–92.

Koller, V. (2005), 'Critical discourse analysis and social cognition: evidence from business media discourse'. *Discourse & Society*, 16(2), 199–224.

—— (2008), *Lesbian Discourses: Images of a Community*. New York: Routledge.

—— (2010), 'Lesbian nation: a case of multiple interdiscursivity', in R. de Cillia, H. Gruber, M. Krzyżanowski and F. Menz (eds), *Discourse, Politics, Identity*. Tübingen: Stauffenburg, pp. 369–81.

—— (2014), 'Cognitive linguistics and ideology', in J. R. Taylor and J. Littlemore (eds), *Companion to Cognitive Linguistics*. London: Bloomsbury, pp. 234–52.

Markus, H. R. and Nurius, P. S. (1986), 'Possible selves'. *American Psychologist*, 41, 954–69.

Moscovici, S. (2001), *Social Representations: Explorations in Social Psychology*, ed. G. Duveen. New York: New York University Press.

Musolff, A. (2009), *Metaphor, Nation and the Holocaust: The Concept of the Body Politic*. London: Routledge.

Reisigl, M. and Wodak, R. (2009), 'The discourse-historical approach (DHA)', in R. Wodak and M. Meyer (eds), *Methods of Critical Discourse Analysis* (2nd edn). London: Sage, pp. 87–121.

Thompson, G. (2004), *Introducing Functional Grammar* (2nd edn). London: Arnold.

Van Dijk, T.A. (2003), 'The discourse-knowledge interface', in G. Weiss and R. Wodak (eds), *Critical Discourse Analysis: Theory and Interdisciplinarity*. Basingstoke: Palgrave Macmillan, pp. 85–109.

—— (2009), 'Critical discourse studies: a socio-cognitive approach', in R. Wodak and M. Meyer (eds), *Methods of Critical Discourse Analysis* (2nd edn). London: Sage, pp. 62–86.

Van Leeuwen, T. (1996), 'The representation of social actors', in C. R. Caldas-Coulthard and M. Coulthard (eds), *Texts and Practices: Readings in Critical Discourse Analysis*. London: Routledge, pp. 32–71.

—— (2008), *Discourse and Practice: New Tools for Critical Analysis*. London: Routledge.
Ziem, A. (2008), *Frames und sprachliches Wissen: Kognitive Aspekte der Semantischen Kompetenz*. Berlin: de Gruyter.

# Appendix

1   DT: This morning I was listening to your programme and we were hearing that 70 per cent of violent crime goes unreported      we know that the British Crime Survey

2   JH:          hm

3   DT: shows us that there is more crime than figures in police statistics . so we know that but what we're trying to do is to use ehm local policing through the neighbourhood policing initiative to bring forward customer focus          to try and get

4   JH:                                             [sharp intake of breath] ooh

5   DT: more information in to understand crime issues

6   JH: You'll forgive me for saying so but I could hear people wincing when you said customer focus there . it's an odd sort of language to use in this context isn't it that's the language of commerce trying to flog people things

7   DT: I think it's—we need to build those sorts of relationships with ehm with all of the people of the UK—

8   JH [raised voice]: But we're not customers of the police are we . you're not selling us a service we should all be working together as a community you're—we're not your customers and you're not our . suppliers

9   DT: But I think that we need to have a relationship that is built upon the idea that we are delivering you a service and you consume that service

10   JH: Yea but we have no choice you see . if I'm a customer of various organisations and I buy their product or not as I choose . I have to have the police it's essential for the wellbeing of society . it's a great misnomer surely to talk about you as supplying us with a service and us being your customers       we've no choice

11   DT:          but       but I think the whole thrust of this conversation is that some people are choosing not to be our customers and I think that that's a major problem . you may not like the terminology and—but that's what it's about . it's trying to make people confident to come forward and what we're trying to do is deliver that by creating very good relationships at local level through neighbourhood policing and then at a more national level we have an initiative to make the skills of our officers available to support local investigations where officers have particular skills around faith language and culture we try and make those skills available to all of our colleagues . and this

is trying to make us more responsive so that we are trying to get this idea of service so that people will trust us more and come forward with information . and I would have thought that you and your listeners would be very interested and would agree with that as a way forward

12   JH: We'll see what they have to say about it Detective Chief Superintendent David Tucker . many thanks for joining us

Key
. short pause of less than one second
(x) longer pause
— (self-)interruption

## CONCEPTUALIZATION

# 7

# Construal Operations in Online Press Reports of Political Protests

*Christopher Hart*

Lancaster University

## 1 Introduction

One of the most successful new 'schools' or 'approaches' in CDS is represented by a body of work applying insights from Cognitive Linguistics (Chilton, 2004; Dirven et al., 2003; Hart, 2010, 2011a; Hart and Lukeš, 2007). This body of work includes but is not limited to Critical Metaphor Analysis (e.g. Charteris-Black, 2004; Koller, 2004; Musolff, 2004). At the theoretical core of this 'Cognitive Linguistic Approach' (CLA) are the notions of *conceptualization* and *construal*. Conceptualization is the dynamic cognitive process involved in meaning-making as discourse unfolds. This process entails language connecting with background knowledge and global cognitive abilities to yield local mental representations. To the extent that the CLA focuses on the relation between discourse and conceptualization, it addresses the cognitive import of (ideologically imbued) linguistic representations (cf. Stubbs, 1997: 106). Construal refers to the different ways in which a given scene, guided by language, can be conceptualized. Alternative 'construal operations' are reliant on different cross-domain cognitive systems and realize different (ideological) discursive strategies. In this chapter, I discuss some of the specific construal operations which, invoked in the audience, are the locus proper of ideological reproduction in discourse. I do so in the context of two contrasting online news texts reporting on the G20 protests in London, 2009.[1] In section 2, I outline a typology of construal operations which may be taken as an (evolving) heuristic for analyses conducted from the perspective of the CLA. In sections 3 through to 5 I discuss different construal operations in turn and show how they contribute to the ideological and (de)legitimating quality of discourse on political protests. Finally, in section 6, I offer some conclusions.

# 2 The Cognitive Linguistic Approach

The incorporation of Cognitive Linguistics in CDS is now a well-established practice. I will not rehearse again here the motivations for, or arguments in favour of, using Cognitive Linguistic methods of analysis in CDS (see Hart, 2011b, in press). Rather, I will outline a framework for the CLA and illustrate its utility through analyses of selected examples. The CLA focuses on the relationship between representations in text and cognition. Its major concern is with the cognitive import of linguistic (lexical and grammatical) constructions presented in texts. In so doing, it responds to a significant issue in CDS which we can label the problem of cognitive equivalence (cf. Stubbs, 1997; O'Halloran, 2003; Widdowson, 2004; Billig, 2008). The issue concerns the extent to which alternative linguistic structures have any (measurable) effects on our cognition of the situation or event being described (see Hart, 2013a, 2013b). This is a significant issue for CDS for if structures in discourse are to play any ideological role in shaping and sustaining social structures, then they must first and foremost function in shaping and sustaining the cognitive structures (ideologies) which at root motivate, support and legitimate social action (Chilton, 2005; Van Dijk, 1993).

In the CLA, cognitive import is approached in terms of the conceptual structures and processes which linguistic constructions invoke in the minds of the audience.[2] These short-term structures are built up in working memory for purposes of local understanding during discourse. They may be subsequently discarded. However, strengthened by repeated patterns of activation as well as other linguistic and contextual factors, they may alternatively come to constitute long-term conceptual structures in the form of frames and conceptual metaphors which provide the cognitive basis of ideologies (Dirven et al., 2003; Hart, 2010; Koller, in press). Cognitive Linguistics is therefore especially useful for CDS in so far as it is able to 'lay bare the structuring of concepts and conceptions' (Dirven et al., 2003: 4) which constitute ideologies. In particular, Cognitive Linguistics addresses 'the structuring within language of such basic conceptual categories as those of space and time, scenes and events, entities and processes, motion and location, and force and causation' (Talmy, 2000: 3). These are, of course, precisely the ideational categories that CDS has traditionally been interested in for the way that they are represented in discourse may carry some ideological weight (Kress and Hodge, 1993; Van Dijk, 1995). According to the CLA, however, this ideological potential of language (to create and sustain patterns of belief and value which serve specific interests) is only realized through the conceptualizations which representations in discourse invoke. The aim of the CLA is then to disclose the particular conceptual parameters along which ideology is enacted.

A major claim of Cognitive Linguistics, and thus the CLA in CDS, is that language serves as a prompt for an array of cognitive processes. These processes are conceptual in nature where language is conceived as a system of conventionalized form-meaning pairings or 'symbolic assemblies' (Langacker, 2008). Crucially, this applies to both lexical and grammatical units. This follows from a view of language in which there is no principled distinction between grammar and lexicon; all linguistic knowledge is conceptual in nature. Words and constructions are therefore equally symbolic. The difference between them is a matter only of degree of abstraction. From this perspective, grammatical constructions are in and of themselves meaningful by virtue of the (highly abstract) images that they invoke.

A further central claim of Cognitive Linguistics is that language is embodied. That is, language emerges out of the kind of experiences we have with our bodies and the physical environment we inhabit (Lakoff and Johnson, 1999). This includes, for example, visuo-spatial, kinetic and proprioceptive experience as well as observations that make up a naïve physics. As a consequence, language is not seen as an autonomous mental faculty cut off from other areas of cognition and the cognitive processes involved in language use are not considered unique to language (Croft and Cruse, 2004). They are, rather, manifestations of more general cognitive processes which are also found to function in other non-linguistic domains of cognition, including perception (2004). The construal operations invoked by language are thus grounded in domain-general cognitive systems which also support analogous perceptual processes (2004). Language, on this account, can direct us to 'see' the situation or event being described in different ways. These alternative construals, as 'ways of seeing', depend on parameters of conceptualization including what we choose to look at, how closely we examine it, which elements we pay most attention to, where we see the scene from, and whether we observe it directly or through some refracting medium (Langacker, 2008: 55). Crucially, for CDS, such construal operations serve, in specific contexts, to realize alternative ideological *discursive strategies* (Reisigl and Wodak, 2001) as the construals they produce encode a particular, legitimating or delegitimating representation of reality.[3] In the CLA, four types of discursive strategy are proposed: *structural configuration, framing, identification* and *positioning*.[4] The various construal operations involved in realizing these strategies are presented, also in relation to the cognitive systems upon which they rely, in Figure 7.1.[5]

Structural configuration is the most basic strategy. In structural configuration, realized through schematization, the speaker imposes on the scene described an abstract image-schematic representation. This skeletal representation provides an holistic structure to the situation or event which captures relations such as topology, sequence and causation. Schematization also defines the participant roles involved in an event. This construal operation is grounded in the same system that supports Gestalt perception – our ability to perceive a complex scene as the sum of its parts. This basic schematic representation is then subject to various forms of 'elaboration' in

| System / Strategy | Gestalt | Comparison | Attention | Perspective |
|---|---|---|---|---|
| Structural Configuration | Schematization | | | |
| Framing | | Categorization | | |
| Framing | | Metaphor | | |
| Identification | | | Figure/Ground | |
| Identification | | | Granularity | |
| Identification | | | Viewing Frame | |
| Positioning | | | | Point of View |
| Positioning | | | | Deixis |

(Construal operations)

**FIGURE 7.1** *Construal operations in the CLA.*

which the skeletal structure is 'fleshed out' to provide further content specifications (Langacker, 2002: 103). Framing strategies are an example of such elaboration. Framing strategies concern the attribution of particular qualities to the entities, actors, actions and processes that make up a situation or event as alternative categories and metaphors, which as a function of the frame-based knowledge they access carry different evaluative connotations or logical entailments, are apprehended in their conceptualization.[6] Framing strategies are grounded in our ability to compare domains of experience. Identification strategies concern the presence and relative salience of social actors in the conceptualization. They are realized in various construal operations which Langacker (2002) groups together under the banner of 'focal adjustments'. These operations are manifestations of more general attentional abilities. Ultimately, however, identification strategies can be accounted for by shifts in point of view and are thus ancillary to positioning strategies (Hart, 2014). Positioning strategies, then, pertain to the manipulation of (metaphorical) space and the relative 'coordinates' of actors and events within the conceptualization. They are realized in the vantage point from which the scene is construed and the location, orientation and distance of other discourse elements relative to this 'ground' (or 'deictic centre (cf. Chilton, 2004; Cap, 2013)). Positioning is not restricted to the domain of literal space but occurs also in spatialized conceptualizations of time and modality (Chilton, 2004; Cap, 2013). In what follows, I discuss each of these construal operations in turn and demonstrate, in the context of contrasting online newspaper reports of the 2009 London G20 protests, how they may function ideologically in contributing to the realization of alternative discursive strategies.[7]

# 3 Structural configuration

Structural configuration is a strategy by means of which speakers impose on the scene described a particular image-schematic representation. Image schemas are abstract, holistic knowledge structures derived from repeated patterns in early, pre-linguistic experience (Johnson, 1987; Mandler, 2004). They are naïve theories about the way the world works (Johnson, 1987; Mandler, 2004). One ubiquitously instantiated image schema is the ACTION-CHAIN schema (or 'billiard ball' model) in which there is a transfer of energy from an AGENT to a PATIENT (sometimes via an INSTRUMENT) resulting in a change in state to the PATIENT. Image schemas later come to form the meaningful basis of many lexical and grammatical units. The ACTION CHAIN schema, for example, underpins the prototypical transitive clause which describes a physical interaction between two or sometimes three participants (Langacker, 1991: 238). Here, the AGENT, encoded as Subject, is the *source* of the energy flow whilst the PATIENT, encoded as (direct) Object, is the energy *sink*. If present, the INSTRUMENT, encoded as indirect Object in a prepositional phrase, constitutes an energy *transmitter*. In discourse, such image schemas get called up by their lexical and grammatical counterparts to constitute our understanding of the basic internal topological and relational structure of the entity, event or situation under conception. Consider (1) which invokes the full ACTION CHAIN schema modelled in Figure 7.2.

(1) At one point, [a black-clad man in the crowd AGENT] [struck ACTIONᴬ] [an officer PATIENT] with [a long pole INSTRUMENT]

(*Telegraph*, 1 April 2009)

In (1), the interaction between the protester and the police officer is construed as unidirectional based on an *asymmetrical* ACTION schema in which the transfer of energy flows from the protester (AGENT) to the police officer (PATIENT) via an INSTRUMENT, a long pole. The protester as the energy source is the initiator of the interaction and therefore

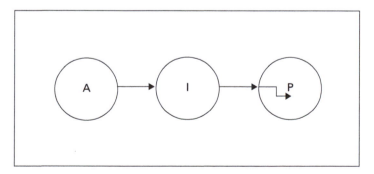

**FIGURE 7.2** *Asymmetrical* ACTION *schema (including* INSTRUMENT*).*

bears sole responsibility for the violent encounter. Crucially, however, from a critical perspective, language has the facility to recruit alternative image schemas to conceptualize the same (kind of) situation and thus impose upon it alternative, ideologically vested, construals. By way of contrast, then, consider (2) in which the encounter between police and protesters is construed as bidirectional based on a *reciprocal* ACTION schema.

**(2)**  By about 8pm, [running battles ~ACTIONR~] between [riot police ~AGENT~] and [demonstrators ~AGENT~] were taking place across London Bridge.

(Guardian, 1 April 2009)

The schema invoked to conceptualize the scene in (2) – modelled in Figure 7.3 – involves a mutual transfer of energy. No one participant can thus be assigned the status of AGENT with the other cast in the role of PATIENT (there is no INSTRUMENT in this example). Rather, both participants are agentive in the process and responsibility for the violent event is therefore equally apportioned.

Examples (1) and (2) represent alternative structural configuration strategies. In (1) the event is configured in a way which conforms to the classic ideological square (van Dijk 1998) with the 'in-group' – the police from the perspective of the *Telegraph* – represented sympathetically as victims of violence and the 'out-group' – the protesters – represented punitively as perpetrators of violence. The same one-sidedness is not seen in (2) which pays more heed to the role of the police in the violence that ensued.

In the two G20 articles, both papers actually prefer asymmetrical rather than reciprocal ACTION schemas. However, there is a systematic difference in terms of who gets cast in which role within these schemas.[8] In the *Telegraph*, it is primarily the protesters who are cast in the role of AGENT as in (1). In the *Guardian*, by contrast, the police are more often cast in the role of AGENT as in (3). This contrast further represents alternative strategies in structural configuration in which different degrees of attention are given to the part played by the police in the violence that unfolded.

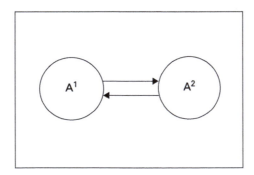

**FIGURE 7.3** Reciprocal ACTION *chain.*

**(3)**   . . . [at least 10 protesters sitting down in the street close to the Bank of England <sub>PATIENT</sub>] were left with bloody head wounds after [being charged <sub>ACTION</sub>ᴬ] by [officers with batons <sub>AGENT</sub>] at around 4.30pm.

(Guardian, 1 April 2009)

Although the *Guardian*, in examples like (3), clearly does recognize the contributory role of the police in the violence that occurred, it nevertheless employs several strategies which serve to mitigate the police action. One such strategy is schematizing an event which in reality would almost certainly have involved some form of physical interaction between an AGENT and a PATIENT as a purely MOTION event. This alternative structural configuration strategy is instantiated in (4). The schema invoked is not an ACTION schema but represents instead an alternative domain of familiar experience in which one entity (a TRAJECTOR) is seen to move along a path defined relative to a LANDMARK. The particular MOTION schema invoked by (4) is modelled in Figure 7.4.[9] In this schema, the police are represented as following a path of motion which finds them located inside the protesters' camp. The vector in the image schema thus represents a trajectory rather than a transfer of energy with the terminus of the vector a location rather than another human participant. The schematization therefore glosses over any physical effect of the event which may have been felt by the protesters. Neither does it point to any impact on the LANDMARK.

**(4)**   Then, at around 7pm, [the police <sub>TRAJECTOR</sub>] [moved in <sub>MOTION</sub>] on [the climate camp <sub>LANDMARK</sub>]

(Guardian, 1 April 2009)

Similarly (5) encodes a MOTION event but in this instance, with the protesters as the entity whose location is at issue, the impact of the force of the motion is recognized. Whilst (4), then, designates a purely MOTION event without reference to any resistance from or effect on the landmark, (5) designates a violent form of motion which results in damage to the LANDMARK. The schema invoked by (5) is modelled in Figure 7.5. The stepped arrow represents the resultant impact of the event on the LANDMARK.

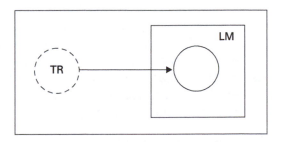

**FIGURE 7.4** *MOTION INTO LANDMARK schema.*

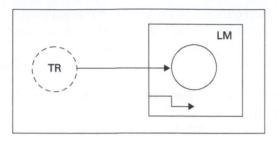

**FIGURE 7.5** *MOTION WITH IMPACT ON LANDMARK schema.*

**(5)**  [A small number of demonstrators _TRAJECTOR_] [forced their way into _MOTION_[IOL]] [the building on Threadneedle Street _LANDMARK_] near the Bank of England after smashing windows . . .

(*Telegraph*, 1 April 2009)

The euphemistic sense of 'move in' in (4) is close to being metaphorical. In the CLA, metaphor is a well-known conceptual device for concealing or accentuating certain aspects of reality and thereby dampening or heightening affect (e.g. Charteris-Black, 2004; Chilton, 2004). We turn to metaphor as a framing device in the next section.

# 4 Framing

Frames for cognitive linguists are areas of *culture-specific* experience encoded in long-term semantic memory (Fillmore, 1982). They stand as the conceptual background against which particular concepts are understood. Crucially, from a critical perspective, when any one element of a frame is introduced in discourse, the remainder of that frame becomes automatically activated (1982: 111). In framing strategies, speakers are therefore able to make conceptually salient particular areas of knowledge (whilst simultaneously suppressing others). The specific knowledge areas accessed, in turn, give rise to patterns of inference and evaluation.

Framing strategies are grounded in a general ability to compare domains of experience. The most basic framing device is categorization. The act of categorization involves comparison in so far as the entity, event or situation in question is judged as belonging to the same class of prior experiences to which a particular linguistic expression has been previously applied (Croft and Cruse, 2004: 54). The ideological function of categorization can be seen most clearly in the categorization of social actors (Van Leeuwen, 1996). The most obvious instance of ideological difference in the G20 data comes in the headlines of the two newspapers:

**(6)**  Rioters loot RBS as demonstrations turn violent

(*Telegraph*, 1 April 2009)

**(7)** G20 protests: riot police clash with <u>demonstrators</u>

*(Guardian*, 1 April 2009)

Although both examples represent instances of functionalization in van Leeuwen's model, there is a clear difference in framing between them. In (6) the categorization accesses a RIOT frame which contains entries to do with violence and vandalism. The categorization is consequently more likely to invite condemnation. The categorization in (7), by contrast, accesses a DEMONSTRATION frame containing entries for marching and chanting, etc. Categorizing the actors involved as *rioters* versus *demonstrators* thus connotes opportunistic criminality rather than an organized display of political discontent.

The ideological function of metaphor as a framing device is now well-recognized (Lakoff, 2001, 2003; Chilton and Lakoff, 1995; Chilton, 1996; Santa Ana, 2002; Koller, 2004; Musolff, 2004). Metaphorization involves comparing experience, via a mapping, in two distinct domains (Lakoff and Johnson, 1980, 1999). Typically, a more abstract social domain (the *target domain*) is compared to a more familiar domain of experience (the *source domain*) encoded in image schemas and/or cognitive frames in order to provide structure and facilitate reasoning procedures within the target. Ideology comes in to play as the choice of source domain mediates and shapes our understanding of the target situation making way for certain 'logical' deductions as *entailments* of the metaphor (1980, 1999). Metaphor permeates 'everyday' discourse as much as political discourse and the same or similar metaphors may be as much a feature of natural language, where they are relatively innocuous, as they are of institutionalized Discourses, where they may or may not take on particular ideological qualities. From a critical perspective, the metaphors we should be primarily concerned with are those which are specific to the Discourse in question, which function in specific ways in political contexts, or which represent context-specific variants of metaphors that naturally make up the conceptual system.

Two well-documented conceptual metaphors are ANGER IS HOT LIQUID INSIDE A CONTAINER (Kövecses, 2002) and ARGUMENT IS WAR (Lakoff and Johnson, 1980). The dominant metaphors employed in the two G20 texts seem to be specific variants of these. Ideologically, however, there is a difference as to which is used by each newspaper. The dominant metaphor in the *Telegraph* can be expressed as VIOLENCE IS HOT LIQUID INSIDE A CONTAINER. This conceptual metaphor is instantiated in the following examples:

**(8)** . . . a largely peaceful demonstration <u>spilled over</u> into bloody violence in the centre of London.

*(Telegraph*, 1 April 2009)

**(9)** Clashes later <u>erupted</u> at Mansion House Street and Queen Victoria Street near the Bank.

*(Telegraph*, 1 April 2009)

The image invoked is of a potentially dangerous liquid previously contained 'boiling up' and escaping from the container. In (9) this is realized specifically in the image of a volcano erupting. Such a conceptualization is likely to invite an emotive response and, further, suggests the need to control the liquid. In the target domain this equates to the controversial police tactic known, presumably by no coincidence, as 'kettling'.[10] The particular metaphorical construal invoked by (8) and (9) thus seems to rationalize and sanction the police handling of events.

The dominant metaphor in the *Guardian*, by contrast, can be expressed as VIOLENCE IS WAR and is instantiated in the following examples:

**(10)** The G20 protests in central London turned violent today ahead of tomorrow's summit, with a <u>band of demonstrators</u> close to the Bank of England <u>storming</u> a Royal Bank of Scotland branch, and baton-wielding police <u>charging</u> a sit-down protest by students.

(*Guardian*, 1 April 2009)

**(11)** Much of the protesting, from an estimated 4,000 people in the financial centre of the capital, was peaceful, but some bloody <u>skirmishes</u> broke out . . .

(*Guardian*, 1 April 2009)

**(12)** By about 8pm, running <u>battles</u> between riot police and demonstrators were taking place across London Bridge

(*Guardian*, 1 April 2009)

The vocabulary highlighted belongs, with lesser or greater degrees of conventionality and semantic looseness, to the domain of WAR. According to Semino, war metaphors in political discourse 'tend to dramatize the opposition between different participants . . . who are constructed as enemies' (2008: 100). Crucially, however, such militarizing metaphors seem to suggest some degree of purpose and precision on the part of the protesters as well as the police. It may even be argued that the use of *storm* in particular (in contrast, say, to *invade*) appraises the protesters' actions as being born of noble intent.[11] Ideologically, then, the VIOLENCE IS WAR metaphor found in the *Guardian* is more sympathetic to the protesters' cause than the naturalizing metaphor VIOLENCE IS HOT LIQUID IN A CONTAINER found in the *Telegraph*.

# 5 Positioning (and identification)

The final strategy-type we will discuss in this chapter is positioning and its interrelation with identification. Positioning strategies rely on a more general capacity to adopt a (simulated) perspective. Specifically, positioning strategies relate to where we situate ourselves and where other entities are located relative to this 'coordinate' (cf. Chilton, 2004; Cap, 2013). They are effected through conceptual shifts in point of view and deixis. Positioning strategies can pertain to positions in space but also metaphorical 'positions' in time as well as in epistemic and axiological 'space' (Chilton, 2004; Cap, 2013). We can also distinguish between *semantic* positioning, where a simulated point of view forms part of the conventionalized meaning of a given linguistic expression, and *pragmatic* positioning, where point of view corresponds with the conceptualizer's actual situatedness or what they take as their broader, deictically-specified spatial, temporal, epistemic and axiological 'ground'. In this chapter we focus very narrowly on spatial point of view as encoded in the conventionalized semantic values for particular grammatical constructions (for further discussion see Hart, 2014; for a more pragmatic account see Cap, this volume). Here, positioning strategies can be seen to co-occur in a mutually dependent way with structural configuration strategies where many, if not all, grammatical constructions include as part of their conventionalized meaning an image-schematic representation and a particular point of view from which the scene described is 'seen' (Langacker, 2008: 75). This simulated position is part of the conceptualization that a given construction conventionally invokes and thus forms part of the meaning of that construction.

The most familiar modality in which we necessarily adopt a particular perspective is vision. The argument from Cognitive Linguistics, recall, is that the conceptual processes involved in language are manifestations of more general processes which find parallel expression in other cognitive domains, including vision. There are thus obvious links between the meaning-making processes we describe in linguistic approaches to CDS and the visuo-spatial variables described in multimodal media and discourse studies (e.g. Kress and Van Leeuwen, 2006). In this section, I therefore adopt the vocabulary of film studies to account for certain positioning phenomena in language. The reader should recognize, however, that this is not just by way of analogy but is motivated by the fact that the kind of visuo-spatial experience captured in a grammar of visual design constitutes precisely the kind of embodied experience which language builds upon in the first place. Several point of view operations could be discussed here. However, we restrict ourselves to two particularly productive ones: panning and zoom.

## 5.1 Panning

The point of view operation of panning underpins several grammatical distinctions, including the distinction between asymmetrical and reciprocal ACTION schemas as well as distinctions in information sequence and voice within them. Let us take first the distinction between reciprocal and asymmetrical transactive constructions. Asymmetrical constructions seem in some sense to be one-sided; that is, they seem to ask the conceptualizer to 'take sides'. Reciprocal constructions, by contrast, are more neutral and ask the conceptualizer to recognize the active role of both participants in the process. I argue that this is due, on top of basic differences in schematization, to the alternative points of view that these constructions encode.

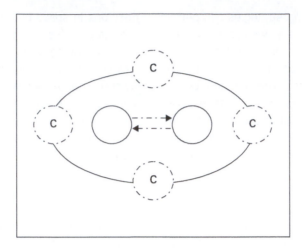

**FIGURE 7.6** *Panning.*

The distinction between reciprocal and asymmetrical transactive constructions represents a point of view shift best characterized as *panning* where the 'camera' swings around the scene on a horizontal axis to present a view from alternative anchorage points. This is modelled in Figure 7.6 where the broken vectors represent potential directions of energy transfer which may be instantiated in particular conceptualizations. The broken circles (C) represent potential (cardinal) points of view from which the scene can be construed. This idealized cognitive model is instantiated in different ways in specific conceptualizations as modelled in Figure 7.7.

In reciprocal constructions the point of view encoded is one in which the simulated position of the conceptualizer is such that their orientation (measured as an imagined vector following their sagittal axis) runs perpendicular to the vectors representing the transfer of energy between participants. Two positions are available in this mode, as modelled in Figure 7.7 (a) and (b). In the construals invoked by reciprocal constructions, then, the conceptualizer is literally occupying the middle ground between both participants. The metaphorical sense in which this construction asks the conceptualizer to adopt a more neutral stance, I suggest, is a product of this spatial perspective. In asymmetrical constructions, the point of view encoded is from a position such that the conceptualizer's orientation is in-line with the vector representing the transfer of energy from one participant to another. Again, two positions are available with the conceptualizer located either at the tail end or the head end of the vector as in Figure 7.7 (c) and (d). In asymmetrical constructions, then, the conceptualizer is literally positioned on the side of one participant in opposition to the other and the metaphorical sense in which asymmetrical constructions seem to ask the conceptualizer to 'see' things from 'one side' in confrontation with the other, is again a function of this spatial positioning strategy.

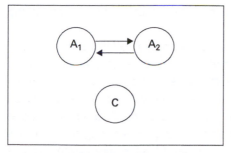

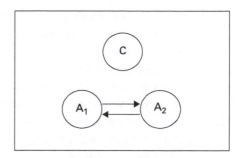

(a) Reciprocal ACTION schema
$A_1$ = First, $A_2$ = Second

(b) Reciprocal ACTION schema
$A_2$ = First, $A_1$ = Second

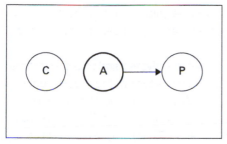

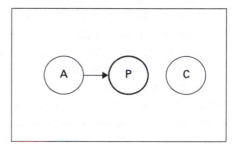

(c) Asymmetrical ACTION schema
Active voice

(d) Asymmetrical ACTION schema
Passive voice

**FIGURE 7.7** *Spatial points of view.*

The question then is what determines the point of view in reciprocal constructions as being that in Figure 7.7 (a) or 7.7 (b) and similarly what determines the point of view in asymmetrical constructions as being that in 7.7 (c) or (d). The answer, I suggest, is information structure and voice respectively. Let us take reciprocal constructions first.

Consider the contrast between (13) and (14).

**(13)** [Riot police$_{AGENT}$[1]] [clash with$_{ACTION}$[R]] [demonstrators $_{AGENT}$[2]].

(*Guardian*, 1 April 2009)

**(14)** [Protesters$_{AGENT}$[2]] [clashed with$_{ACTION}$[R]] [police$_{AGENT}$[1]] around the Bank of England.

(*Telegraph*, 1 April 2009)

Based on the presumption that the necessarily sequential organisation of the clause going from left to right (in English) reflects iconically the spatial organisation encoded in the meanings of the alternative grammatical forms (Perniss et al., 2010), and assuming a structural configuration strategy in which the police are assigned as participant $A_1$ and protesters as $A_2$, we may say that the construction in (13) invokes a conceptualization as modelled in 7.7 (a) with the police located to the left of the conceptualizer and the protesters to the right.[12]

Conversely, the construction in (14) invokes a conceptualization as modelled in 7.7 (b) with the protesters positioned to the left of the conceptualizer and the police to the right. Now, ideologically, reciprocal constructions, although relatively neutral compared to asymmetrical constructions, are not entirely value-free. As McManus (2003) states, 'right and left have their symbolic associations and always it is right that is good and left that is bad'. Whilst we might stop short of such a strong claim there is certainly linguistic evidence that spatial left is generally associated with positive valence whilst spatial right is associated with negative valence. This is reflected, for example, in the polysemy of the word 'right' as well as in idiomatic expressions like 'right-hand man' versus 'two left feet'. Thus, (13) may be said to invite a more negative appraisal of the police's part in the interaction whilst (14) may be said to invite a more negative appraisal of the protesters' part.

In asymmetrical constructions, only one participant is activated and thus the transfer of energy is unidirectional from an AGENT to a PATIENT. Asymmetrical constructions require a voice choice between active and passive. Whether the point of view is that presented as in Figure 7.7 (c) or (d) is a function of this voice choice. The active voice encodes a view from the perspective of the AGENT as in 7.7 (c). The passive voice, by contrast, encodes a view from the perspective of the PATIENT as in 7.7 (d). It is here that positioning can be seen to interact with identification. In the active voice, the AGENT is in the foreground of the conceptualizer's attention. That is, they are the FIGURE whilst the PATIENT is the GROUND (Talmy, 2000).[13] In the passive voice, this is reversed and the PATIENT is the FIGURE and the AGENT the GROUND.[14] This is represented in Figure 7.7 by the bold outline. Consider the difference between (15) and (16).

(15) [Riot police wielding batons _AGENT_] [managed to force [the crowds _PATIENT_] back _FORCE_].
(*Telegraph*, 1 April 2009)

(16) [Officers standing on the steps at the front of the Bank of England _PATIENT_] [were pelted _ACTION_A_] [with fruit _INSTR_] [as [protesters _AGENT_] scrambled beneath them _CIRC_].
(*Telegraph*, 1 April 2009)

Whilst (16) can be characterized as encoding a view as in 7.7 (d) (15) may be said to encode a view as in Figure 7.7 (c). Based on this analysis, we may need to reinterpret the ideological function of the active/passive distinction. In orthodox interpretations, the active voice is said to highlight the role of the AGENT in the process whilst the passive voice is analysed as distancing the AGENT and thereby detracting attention from relations of causality (Kress and Hodge, 1993). Ideologically, the active voice is thus said to be used to draw attention to negative behaviours of the out-group whilst the passive voice is used to direct attention away from negative behaviours of the in-group. Observations of voice function, however, are often made in relation to isolated examples (cf. Widdowson, 2004).

On the analysis presented here, the role of voice is to position the conceptualizer with respect to participants in the event in contrasting ways. In the active voice, the conceptualizer sees the scene from the perspective of the AGENT in a position of conflict with the PATIENT. In the passive voice, the conceptualizer sees the scene from the perspective of the PATIENT in a position of antagonism with the AGENT. On this analysis, the active voice does indeed highlight the role of the AGENT by locating them in the conceptual foreground but places the conceptualizer literally and metaphorically on their side. We should therefore expect to find positively construed behaviours of the in-group expressed most frequently in the active voice as in (15) where the event is positively construed as a FORCE event pertaining to the location of the PATIENT rather than being construed as an ACTION event (see Hart, 2013b).[15] Similarly, whilst the passive voice does initially distance the AGENT, it locates the conceptualizer on the side of the PATIENT and, thus, in the dynamic conceptualization invoked, the energy transfer from the antagonistic AGENT (sometimes via an INSTRUMENT) is construed as directed not only at the PATIENT but toward the conceptualizer too. Active versus passive constructions, then, seem to include as part of their meaning a deictic dimension. The ideological function of the passive voice can therefore be characterized as something more akin to a spatial proximization strategy (Cap, 2006, 2013, this volume). If correct, we should expect to find negatively construed behaviours of the out-group directed at the in-group most frequently expressed in the passive voice as in (16).[16] Such a pattern of distribution, which we seem to find in the *Telegraph*, would conform to the classic ideological strategy of positive-Self versus negative-Other representation.[17] The interpretation presented here would therefore be greatly strengthened by a comprehensive and detailed corpus-based analysis of voice alternates across different newspapers to see whether their distribution fits with expectations given what we already know about the ideological orientations of different news institutions.

## 5.2  Zoom

The final construal operation we will discuss is *zoom*. This point of view shift takes place on the distal rather than the horizontal (or anchorage) plane. It underpins a number of grammatical constructions relating to the expression of causality. Zoom concerns the distance of the camera from the scene depicted. The greater the zoom, the less of the scene is able to be captured. The camera must then focus on particular parts of the scene. Conversely, a wide-angle lens with negative zoom is able to capture much more. Language similarly has the facility for conceptualizations which zoom in or out on the scene described resulting in a more or less restricted viewing frame. This is modelled in Figure 7.8.[18] Figure 7.8 (a) represents the idealized cognitive model for zoom with three potential points of view: long shot, medium shot and close-up. Figure 7.8 (b)–(d) represent the specific viewing frames which result from instantiations of these points of view. The viewing frame is that portion of evoked conceptual content currently in focus. The most obvious means by which language zones in on particular facets of the reference situation is through explicit mention of that portion (Talmy, 2000: 258). Here, again, positioning and identification can be seen to interact. Indeed, one of the ideological functions of zoom is to conceptually background causation including in the form of social actors. In discourse on political protests, this is often seen in relation to the causes of injuries. Consider (3) reproduced below as (17) in contrast to (18):

**(17)** . . . [at least 10 protesters sitting down in the street close to the Bank of England $_{PATIENT}$] were [left with bloody head wounds $_{RESULT}$] [after [being charged $_{ACTION}$$^A$] by [officers with batons $_{AGENT}$] at around 4.30pm $_{CIRC}$].

(*Guardian*, 1 April 2009)

**(18)** One man, [bleeding from the head $_{RESULT}$], was repeatedly seen to apparently goad officers.

(*Telegraph*, 1 April 2009)

A medial shot is represented by (17). The viewing frame covers the full action chain invoked. The resultant of the interaction, injuries, is expressed as part of a verb phrase in the main clause and the cause of these injuries is fully spelled out in the circumstantial clause. This is modelled in Figure 7.8 (b). In (18), by contrast, only the resultant of the interaction is expressed. There is no reference at all as to how the injuries might have been sustained. An extreme close-up with the viewing frame covering only the final element in the action chain is represented by (18). This is modelled in Figure 7.8 (c). The action chain is still invoked since we know that injuries are the result of some form of interaction and the AGENT therefore remains within the *scope of attention* (Langacker 2008). However, located beyond the purview of the current viewing frame they are unspecified. Close-up versus medial shots, then, serve to exclude or include issues of causation. Ideologically, we find the cause of injuries to protesters included within the viewing frame in (17) but excluded in (18). In other words, (17) presents a point of view from which police violence is not seen.

If one function of zoom is to crop the viewing frame in order to conceal aspects of causation, another is to expand the viewing frame in order to include within it some mitigating causal circumstance. In this case, the point of view is that of a long shot. Consider (19) and (20):

**(19)** [Hundreds of protesters cheered as office equipment including a printer was carried out of the building $_{CAUSE}$] . . . before [riot police wielding batons $_{AGENT}$] [managed to force [the crowds $_{PATIENT}$] back $_{FORCE}$].

(*Telegraph*, 1 April 2009)

**(20)** [Police $_{AGENT}$] [used [truncheons and batons $_{INSTR}$] to beat back $_{ACTION}$$^A$] [the protesters $_{PATIENT}$] [each time they surged forward $_{CAUSE}$]

(*Guardian*, 1 April 2009)

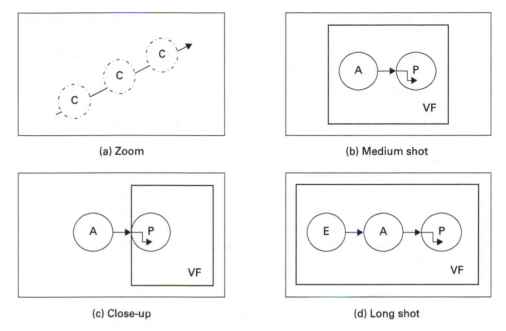

**FIGURE 7.8** *Zoom and viewing frames.*

Any event is not in reality temporally and causally discrete but is, rather, part of an ongoing sequence of causal interactions. In extending the viewing frame, as in both (19) and (20), the conceptualization takes in some preceding event which is recognized as a directly causal or at least mitigating factor in relation to the main event. This is modelled in Figure 7.8 (d).[19] Ideologically, then, we find in both the *Telegraph* and the *Guardian* examples of events in which the police are agents construed in this way but no similar examples vis-à-vis events in which protesters are agents. This serves to present police actions as provoked, retaliatory or restorative. They are no longer the source of the energy transfer. By contrast, protester actions, in not being seen from this distal point of view, are construed as unprovoked instances of gratuitous violence.[20]

# 6 Conclusion

In this chapter, I have outlined a Cognitive Linguistic Approach to CDS highlighting a number of strategies and construal operations responsible for the enactment of ideology in discourse. I have done so in the context of online press reports of political protests and the London G20 protest in particular. The main aim of this approach is to address the conceptual import of linguistic representation and to disclose the ideological qualities of those conceptualizations invoked in discourse by linguistic expressions. Several claims have been made about the nature of conceptual counterparts to specific linguistic constructions/alternations. Some of these claims remain more speculative than others at this stage. However, I hope to have presented an account which is at least internally coherent and psychologically plausible. The Cognitive Linguistic Approach is inherently interdisciplinary, relying on insights from linguistics, discourse studies and cognitive psychology. The last section on positioning suggests the need for further interdisciplinarity through a greater degree of collaboration between linguistic and multimodal approaches to discourse studies and perhaps also the need to reverse the direction of influence that we currently find between them. Empirically, I have pointed to a number of ideological differences in the conceptualizations invoked by the *Telegraph* and the *Guardian* to construe the violence that occurred at the G20 protests. The most striking observation here is that the *Telegraph* virtually ignores any possibility of police violence whilst the *Guardian* is more balanced adhering neither to a discourse of police violence but nor to one of police innocence.

# Notes

1  The data is intended as purely illustrative with only qualitative analysis being presented. The contribution of the chapter is to outline the CLA as a particular framework for CDS. This is not to say, however, that this framework cannot be combined with Corpus Linguistic techniques to harvest further quantitative insights in a larger-scale empirical investigation. Neither is it to say that the framework is restricted in its utility to investigations of discourse on political protests (cf. Hart, 2011b, 2011c).

2  This is in contrast to van Dijk's socio-cognitive approach in which the mental models which guide discourse production are theorized in propositional terms (Van Dijk, 1997, 1998, 2010).

3  Following Reisigl and Wodak (2001), discursive strategy is defined as a more or less intentional/institutionalized plan of discourse practices whose deployment ultimately achieves some social action effect. They are interpreted here as involving both a linguistic and a conceptual dimension as they are performed through particular locutions but bring about perlocutionary effects only through the conceptualizations that those locutions evoke.

4  The typology of discursive strategies presented in the CLA is not intended to compete with the one detailed in the discourse-historical approach (DHA). The two schools are concerned with different levels of meaning. Broadly, the strategies identified in the CLA operate at a lower level compared to those outlined in the DHA. They may thus be thought of as contributing to or supporting in different ways the higher-level strategies defined in the DHA.

5  This typology supersedes the one presented in previous work (Hart, 2011c, 2013a, 2013b).

6  It should be noted that these strategies should not be taken as discrete and incapable of intersection. Rather, they are often co-extant in discourse, may be mutually dependent, and sometimes merge into one and other. Hence, the term *typology* is favoured over *taxonomy* (see Reisigl, this volume). To give an example, in categorizing a

scene, the speaker necessarily imposes on it a particular image-schematic representation. At the same time, in imposing a particular internal structure the speaker defines the scene as belonging to a higher-level category. The distinction between them can be seen, however, where the same basic schema is elaborated in different ways. For example, the American HOUSE frame and the Russian DOM frame both instantiate a CONTAINER schema but, when applied metaphorically in international relations discourse to structure the concept of NATION, invoke subtly different construals as a function of the culture-specific encyclopaedic knowledge bases that they encode (Chilton, 1996).

**7** Around 35,000 people attended the initial G20 protests in London on 28 March 2009 with 5,000 people involved in the 'G20 Meltdown' protest outside the Bank of England on 1st April. A Royal Bank of Scotland branch was also broken into and a 'climate camp' set up outside the European Climate Exchange on Bishopsgate. The protests, which were targeting a range of policy issues pertaining to capitalism and climate change, witnessed outbreaks of violence and police use of a controversial crowd control technique known as 'kettling'. One bystander, Ian Tomlinson, died after being beaten by Metropolitan Police Officer Simon Harwood. The data presented below is taken from online reports published in *Guardian* and *Telegraph*. These papers take alternative political stances and appeal to different audiences with the papers and their readers likely to hold more liberal versus more conservative values respectively. Both papers focus on the violence that occurred at the protest. However, some subtle differences in conceptualization can be seen which reflect, reinforce or contribute to constructing alternative Discourses of civil disorder. The data is available at: http://www.telegraph.co.uk/finance/g20-summit/5089870/G20-protests-Rioters-loot-RBS-as-demonstrations-turn-violent.html and http://www.guardian.co.uk/world/2009/apr/01/g20-summit-protests. Accessed 26.4.2013.

**8** See Hart (2013a) for a basic quantitative analysis of the distribution of different schemas in this data.

**9** This schema also provides the meaning of the lexical item *enter* (Langacker, 2008: 32–3).

**10** Kettling involves complete enclosure of protestors by police cordon for given periods of time, often without access to toilets or water, etc., followed by partial cordoning allowing protesters to leave the scene only by specific designated routes.

**11** Evidence in support of the positive prosody of *storm* comes from its use in relation to the police in the *Daily Mail* two days following the protests: 'Riot police *storm* G20 protesters' squats . . .' (*Daily Mail*, 3 April 2009).

**12** The assignment of participants as $A_1$ and $A_2$ is arbitrary. If we assign them the other way around then (13) would invoke a point of view as in Figure 7.7(b) rather than Figure 7.7(a) and (14) would invoke a point of view as in Figure 7.7(a) rather than Figure 7.7(b). The point, however, is that there would still be a point of view shift which results in a reversed left/right alignment relative to the conceptualizer.

**13** Positioning can also be seen to interact with identification in other point of view operations. For example, a bird's-eye view, as encoded in certain types of metonymy and multiplex-to-uniplex construals, results in a loss of granularity (see Hart, 2014). Similarly, the kind of dynamic attention involved in expressions of fictive motion is analogous to a tracking shot.

**14** In the agentless passive voice, the AGENT may be within the scope of attention but outside the current viewing frame (see Hart, 2014 for further discussion).

**15** The use of *managed to* also suggests a positive evaluation of a valiant restorative effort.

**16** Although the main clause in (16) is an agentless passive construction, the AGENT of the action is strongly implied in the circumstantial clause.

**17** In line with this macro-strategy, ostensibly negative behaviours of the in-group are either not mentioned or reconstrued in legitimating terms, for instance, schematized as FORCE or MOTION event rather than an ACTION event. At the same time, ostensibly positive behaviours of the out-group are either not mentioned or reconstrued in delegitimating terms.

**18** For purposes of illustration, the INSTRUMENT is left out of these models but it should be recognized that in each case there would be an INSTRUMENT intermediate in the energy transfer between AGENT and PATIENT.

**19** In Figure 7.8(d) the cause event (E) is presented as a single THING but it would, of course, have its own internal structure.

**20** It is worth noting here some important differences between (19) and (20). In (19), the main event is a FORCE event whilst in (20) it is an ACTION event (compare force back with beat back). Thus (20) attributes a greater degree of violence to the police. However, the action is still encoded as a reaction and is therefore mitigated. There is also a difference in information structure. In (19) the CAUSE is expressed first whilst in (20) it is only expressed at the end of the utterance. Thus, (19) keeps the CAUSE conceptually salient throughout whilst in (20) it only comes into focus later.

# References

Billig, M. (2008), 'The language of critical discourse analysis: the case of nominalization'. *Discourse & Society*, 19, 783–800.

Cap, P. (2006), *Legitimization in Political Discourse*. Newcastle: Cambridge Scholars Press.

—— (2013), *Proximisation: The Pragmatics of Symbolic Distance Crossing*. Amsterdam: John Benjamins.

Charteris-Black, J. (2004), *Corpus Approaches to Critical Metaphor Analysis*. Basingstoke: Palgrave Macmillan.

Chilton, P. (1996), *Security Metaphors: Cold War Discourse from Containment to Common House*. New York: Peter Lang.

—— (2004), *Analysing Political Discourse: Theory and Practice*. London: Routledge.

—— (2005), 'Missing links in mainstream CDA: modules, blends and the critical instinct', in R. Wodak and P. Chilton (eds), *A New Research Agenda in Critical Discourse Analysis: Theory and Interdisciplinarity*. Amsterdam: John Benjamins, pp. 19–52.

Chilton, P. and Lakoff, G. (1995), 'Foreign police by metaphor', in C. Schäffner and A. I. Wenden (eds), *Language and Peace*. Aldershot: Ashgate, pp. 37–60.

Croft, W. and Cruse, D. A. (2004), *Cognitive Linguistics*. Cambridge: Cambridge University Press.

Dirven, R., Frank, R. and Putz, M. (eds) (2003), *Cognitive Models in Language and Thought: Ideology, Metaphors and Meanings*. Berlin: Mouton de Gruyter.

Fillmore, C. (1982), 'Frame semantics', in Linguistics Society of Korea (eds), *Linguistics in the Morning Calm*. Seoul: Hanshin Publishing Co., pp. 111–37.

Hart, C. (2010), *Critical Discourse Analysis and Cognitive Science: New Perspectives on Immigration Discourse*. Basingstoke: Palgrave.

—— (ed.) (2011a), *Critical Discourse Studies in Context and Cognition*. Amsterdam: John Benjamins.

—— (2011b), 'Moving beyond metaphor in the cognitive linguistic approach to CDA: construal operations in immigration discourse', in C. Hart (ed.), *Critical Discourse Studies in Context and Cognition*. Amsterdam: John Benjamins, pp. 171–92.

—— (2011c), 'Force-interactive patterns in immigration discourse: a cognitive linguistic approach to CDA'. *Discourse & Society*, 22(3), 269–86.

—— (2013a), 'Event-construal in press reports of violence in political protests: a cognitive linguistic approach to CDA'. *Journal of Language and Politics*, 12(3), 400–23.

—— (2013b), 'Constructing contexts through grammar: cognitive models and conceptualisation in British Newspaper reports of political protests' in J. Flowerdew (ed.), *Discourse in Context*. London: Continuum, pp. 159–84.

—— (in press), 'Cognitive linguistics and critical discourse analysis', in E. Dabrowska and D. Divjak (eds), *Handbook of Cognitive Linguistics*. Berlin: Mouton De Gruyter.

—— (2014), *Discourse, Grammar and Ideology: Functional and Cognitive Perspectives*: London: Bloomsbury.

Hart, C. and D. Lukeš (eds) (2007), *Cognitive Linguistics in Critical Discourse Analysis: Application and Theory*. Newcastle: Cambridge Scholars Publishing.

Johnson, M. (1987), *The Body in the Mind: The Bodily Basis of Meaning, Imagination, and Reason*. Chicago: University of Chicago Press.

Koller, V. (2004), *Metaphor and Gender in Business Media Discourse: A Critical Cognitive Study*. Basingstoke: Palgrave Macmillan.

—— (2014), 'Cognitive linguistics and ideology', in J. R. Taylor and J. Littlemore (eds), *Companion to Cognitive Linguistics*. London: Bloomsbury, pp. 234–52.

Kövecses, Z. (2002), *Metaphor and Emotion: Language, Culture, and Body in Human Feeling*. Cambridge: Cambridge University Press.

Kress, G. and Hodge, R. (1993), *Language as Ideology* (2nd edn). London: Routledge and Kegan Paul.

Kress, G. and van Leeuwen, T. (2006), *Reading Images: The Grammar of Visual Design* (2nd edn). London: Routledge.

Lakoff, G. (2001), 'Metaphor and war: the metaphor system used to justify the war in the gulf'. *Journal of Urban and Cultural Studies*, 2, 59–72.

—— (2003), Metaphor and war again. Available at http://www.alternet.org. Accessed 16 July 2014.

Lakoff, G. and Johnson, M. (1980), *Metaphors We Live By* Chicago: University of Chicago Press.

Lakoff, G. and Johnson, M. (1999), *Philosophy in the Flesh: The Embodied Mind and its Challenge to Western Thought*. New York: Basic Books.

Langacker, R. (1991), *Foundations of Cognitive Grammar, Vol. II: Descriptive Application* Stanford: Stanford University Press.

—— (2002), *Concept, Image, and Symbol: The Cognitive Basis of Grammar* (2nd edn). Berlin: Mouton de Gruyter.

—— (2008), *Cognitive Grammar: A Basic Introduction*. Oxford: Oxford University Press.

Mandler, J. (2004), *The Foundations of Mind: Origins of Conceptual Thought*. Oxford: Oxford University Press.

McManus, C. (2003), *Right Hand, Left Hand: The Origins of Asymmetry in Brains, Bodies, Atoms and Cultures*. London: Weidenfeld & Nicolson.

Musolff, A. (2004), *Metaphor and Political Discourse: Analogical Reasoning in Debates about Europe*. Basingstoke: Palgrave Macmillan.

O'Halloran, K. (2003), *Critical Discourse Analysis and Language Cognition*. Edinburgh: Edinburgh University Press.

Perniss, P., Thompson, R. and Vigliocco, G. (2010), 'Iconicity as a general property of language: evidence from spoken and signed languages'. *Frontiers in Psychology*, 1, 227.

Reisigl, M. and Wodak, R. (2001), *Discourse and Discrimination: Rhetorics of Racism and Anti-Semitism*. London: Routledge.

Santa Ana, O. (2002), *Brown Tide Rising: Metaphors of Latinos in Contemporary American Public Discourse*. Austin: University of Texas Press.

Semino, E. (2008), *Metaphor in Discourse*. Cambridge: Cambridge University Press.

Stubbs, M. (1997), 'Whorf's children: critical comments on critical discourse analysis (CDA)', in A. Ryan and A. Wray (eds), *Evolving Models of Language*. Clevedon: British Association for Applied Linguistics, pp. 100–16.

Talmy, L. (2000), *Toward a Cognitive Semantics*. Cambridge, MA: MIT Press.

Van Dijk, T. A. (1993), 'Principles of critical discourse analysis'. *Discourse & Society*, 4(2), 243–89.

—— (1995), 'Discourse analysis as ideology analysis', in C. Schäffner and A. I. Wenden (eds), *Language and Peace*. Ashgate: Aldershot, pp. 17–36.

—— (1997), 'Cognitive context models and discourse', in M. Stamenow (ed.), *Language Structure, Discourse and the Access to Consciousness*. Amsterdam: John Benjamins, pp. 189–226.

—— (1998), *Ideology: A Multidisciplinary Approach*. London: Sage.

—— (2010), *Discourse and Context: A Socio-Cognitive Approach*. Cambridge: Cambridge University Press.

Van Leeuwen, T. (1996), 'The representation of social actors', in C.R. Caldas-Coulthard and M. Coulthard (eds), *Texts and Practices: Readings in Critical Discourse Analysis*. London: Routledge, pp. 32–70.

Widdowson, H. (2004), *Text, Context, Pretext: Critical Issues in Discourse Analysis*. Oxford: Blackwell.

# 8

# Expanding CDS Methodology by Cognitive-Pragmatic Tools

# Proximization Theory and Public Space Discourses

*Piotr Cap*

University of Łódź

## 1 Introduction

Critical Discourse Studies (CDS) counts, without exaggeration, among the most vigorously developing research enterprises located at the intersection of contemporary linguistics and social sciences.[1] Colonizing, day in and day out, new discourse domains, from the top-most level of (mediatized) state politics to the bottom-most level of (individual) discourses of social concern such as health or environment, CDS is committed to a necessarily broad spectrum and a large number of different, often interdisciplinary and converging, methodologies (cf. Introduction, this volume). The goal of this paper is to contribute one such methodological tool, *proximization theory* (Cap, 2006, 2008, 2010, 2013), a recent cognitive-pragmatic development designed to account for strategic regularities underlying forced construals in political/public discourse.

Originally meant to deal with legitimization issues in state political discourse (especially interventionist discourse, cf. Cap, 2006), proximization seems now well applicable in the vast area of public discourses, including such heterogeneous domains as preventive medicine, cyber-threat or policies to contain climate change. Of course, as will be demonstrated, the implementation of proximization to account for these discourses entails certain changes to the initial assumptions and design of the theory. In that sense, the secondary goal of the paper is to use the CDS empirical scope and data to upgrade proximization theory.

The paper is structured as follows. In Section 2 I give a necessarily compact overview of proximization as a concept and a theory. In Section 3 I provide a sample illustration of the descriptive and explanatory power of proximization in its 'cradle' domain of state political discourse. In Section 4, I extend the original scope of proximization theory to cover several public space discourses which CDS practitioners have recently developed much interest in: health (cf. Koteyko, this volume; Knapton and Rundblad, this volume), environment (cf. Stibbe, this volume; Bevitori, this volume) and modern technology. Section 5 is a summary statement on what the analyses of these discourses promise in the way of further implementation of proximization in critical studies and, conversely, what modifications of proximization theory must be put in place to process greater and more varied amounts of CDS data.

## 2 Proximization: The concept and the theory

In its most general and practical sense, proximization is a discursive strategy of presenting physically and temporally distant events and states of affairs (including 'distant' adversarial ideologies) as increasingly and negatively consequential to the speaker and her addressee. Projecting the distant entities as gradually encroaching upon the speaker-addressee territory (both physical and ideological), the speaker may attempt a variety of goals, but the principal goal is usually *legitimization of actions and policies* the speaker proposes to neutralize the growing impact of the negative, 'foreign', 'alien', 'antagonistic', entities.

Proximization is a relatively new concept in linguistics. The verbal forms 'proximize', 'proximizing' (i.e. bringing [conceptually] closer), are first found in Chilton (2004), while the nominal term 'proximization' was originally proposed by Cap (2006), who also first used it to mark an *organized, strategic deployment of cognitive-pragmatic construals in discourse*. Ever since, proximization has developed into a cognitive-linguistic, pragmatic, as well as a critical discourse analytic concept accounting for the symbolic construal of relations between entities within the Discourse Space (DS) (cf. Chilton, 2005) – most notably, the symbolic shifts whereby the peripheral elements of the DS are construed as the central ones, members of the 'deictic center' (Chilton, 2005; Cap, 2006) of the Space. The explanatory power of proximization has been utilized within a number of different theoretical frameworks and thematic domains. Chilton (2005, 2010) relates to it in his cognitive-linguistic Discourse Space Theory (DST); Cap (2006, 2008, 2010) makes it a theoretical premise for several case studies of the Iraq war rhetoric; in a similar vein, Hart (2010) incorporates it (as a coercive strategy) in his multidisciplinary approach to metaphoric construals of the speaker-external threat.

Proximization has been shown to operate within diverse discourse domains, though most commonly in *state political discourses*: crisis construction and war rhetoric (Chovanec, 2010; Okulska and Cap, 2010), the (anti-)immigration discourse (Hart, 2010), political party representation (Cienki et al., 2010; Kaal, 2012), and construction of national memory (Filardo Llamas, 2010, 2013). There have also been studies of proximization in works at the intersection of political genres. In the most comprehensive one, Dunmire (2011) investigates proximization patterns in a US foreign policy document (the 2002 National Security Strategy articulating the '[G. W.] Bush Doctrine') and how they were followed in speeches enacting the Doctrine (see also Dunmire, this volume).

All these theoretical and empirical threads have been recently reviewed and revisited in Cap (2013), a monograph proposing an integrated *proximization theory*. The theory follows the original concept of proximization, which is defined as a forced construal operation meant to evoke closeness of the external threat, to solicit legitimization of preventive measures. The threat comes from the DS peripheral entities, referred to as ODCs ('outside-deictic-centre'), which are conceptualized to be crossing the Space to invade the IDC ('inside-deictic-centre') entities, that is the speaker and her addressee. The threat possesses a spatio-temporal as well as ideological nature, which sanctions the division of proximization in three aspects. 'Spatial proximization' is a forced construal of the DS peripheral entities encroaching *physically* upon the DS central entities (speaker, addressee). 'Temporal proximization' is a forced construal of the envisaged conflict as not only imminent, but also momentous, historic and thus needing immediate response and unique preventive measures. Spatial and temporal proximization involve strong fear appeals and typically use analogies to conflate the growing threat with an actual disastrous occurrence in the past, to endorse the current scenario. Finally, 'axiological proximization' is a construal of a gathering ideological clash between the 'home values' of the DS central entities (IDCs) and the alien and antagonistic (ODC) values. Importantly, the ODC values are construed to reveal potential to materialize (that is, prompt a physical impact) within the IDC, the speaker's and the addressee's, home territory.

Proximization theory and its Spatial-Temporal-Axiological (STA) analytic model assume that all the three aspects or strategies of proximization contribute to the *continual narrowing of the symbolic distance* between the entities/values in the Discourse Space and their negative impact on the speaker and her addressee. As such, goes proximization theory, the strategies of proximization constitute prime legitimization devices in political interventionist discourse; the discourse addressees will only legitimize pre-emptive actions against the 'gathering threat' if they perceive the threat as personally consequential. The last tenet of proximization theory in Cap (2013) is that although any application of proximization principally subsumes all of its strategies, spatial, temporal and axiological, the degree of their representation in discourse is continually motivated by their effectiveness in the evolving context. Extralinguistic contextual developments may thus cause the speaker to limit the use of one strategy and compensate it by an increased use of another, in the interest of the continuity of legitimization.

# 3  A study of proximization in (state) political discourse

As has been mentioned, the main application of proximization theory has been so far to (state) political discourse soliciting legitimization of interventionist preventive measures against the external threat (cf. Dunmire, this volume). In this section I provide a necessarily brief example of such an application, discussing instances of the US discourse of the war-on-terror. Specifically, I outline how and what proximization strategies were used to legitimize going to war in Iraq (March 2003), and what adjustments in the use of the strategies were made later (from approximately November 2003), as a result of contextual changes.

## 3.1  Initiating legitimization through proximization

Below I look at parts of G. W. Bush's speech at the American Enterprise Institute (AEI), which was delivered on 26 February 2003.[2] The speech took place only three weeks before the first US and coalition troops entered Iraq on 19 March; as such, it has been considered (e.g. Silberstein, 2004) a manifesto of the Iraq war. The goal of the speech was to list direct reasons for the intervention, while also locating it in the global context of the war-on-terror declared by Bush on the night of the 9/11 attacks. The realization of this goal involved a strategic deployment of various lexico-grammatical choices reflecting different proximization strategies.

Providing his rationale for war, Bush had to confront the kind of public reluctance faced by many of his White House predecessors: how to legitimize the US involvement in military action in a far-away place, among a far-away people, of whom the American people knew little (Bacevich, 2010). The AEI speech is remarkable in its consistent continuity of attempts to overcome this reluctance. It amply applies spatio-temporal and axiological proximization strategies, which are performed in diligently designed pragmatic patterns drawing from more general conceptual premises for legitimization:

(1) We are facing a crucial period in the history of our nation, and of the civilized world. [. . .] On a September morning, threats that had gathered for years, in secret and far away, led to murder in our country on a massive scale. As a result, we must look at security in a new way, because our country is a battlefield in the first war of the 21st century. [. . .] We learned a lesson: the dangers of our time must be confronted actively and forcefully, before we see them again in our skies and our cities. And we will not allow the flames of hatred and violence in the affairs of men. [. . .] The world has a clear interest in the spread of democratic values, because stable and free nations do not breed the ideologies of murder. [. . .] Saddam Hussein and his weapons of mass destruction are a direct threat to our people and to all free people. [. . .] My job is to protect the American people. When it comes to our

security and freedom, we really don't need anybody's permission. [. . .] We've tried diplomacy for 12 years. It hasn't worked. Saddam Hussein hasn't disarmed, he's armed. Today the goal is to remove the Iraqi regime and to rid Iraq of weapons of mass destruction. [. . .] The liberation of millions is the fulfillment of America's founding promise. The objectives we've set in this war are worthy of America, worthy of all the acts of heroism and generosity that have come before.

In a nutshell, the AEI speech states that there are WMD[3] in Iraq and that, given historical context and experience, ideological characteristics of the adversary as opposed to American values and national legacy, and Bush's obligations as ruling US president, there is a case for legitimate military intervention. This complex picture involves historical flashbacks, as well as descriptions of the current situation, which both engage proximization strategies. These strategies operate at two interrelated levels, which can be described as 'diachronic' and 'synchronic'. At the diachronic level, Bush evokes ideological representations of the remote past, which are 'proximized' to underline the continuity and steadfastness of purpose, thus linking with and sanctioning current actions as acts of faithfulness to long-accepted principles and values. An example is the final part in (1), 'The liberation is [. . .] promise. The objectives [. . .] have come before'. It launches a temporal analogy 'axis' which links a past reference point (the founding of America) with the present point, creating a common conceptual space for both the proximized historical 'acts of heroism' and the current and/or prospective acts construed as their natural 'follow-ups'. This kind of legitimization, performed by mostly temporal and axiological proximization (the originally past values become the 'here and now' premises for action),[4] draws, in many ways, upon the socio-psychological predispositions of the US addressee (Dunmire, 2011). On the pragmatic-lexical plane, the job of establishing the link and thus winning credibility is performed by assertoric sequences, which fall within the addressee's 'latitude of acceptance' (Jowett and O'Donnell, 1992).[5] The assertions there reveal different degrees of acceptability, from being indisputably acceptable ('My job is [. . .]'; 'The liberation of millions [. . .]'), to being acceptable due to credibility developed progressively within a 'fact-belief series' ('We've tried diplomacy for 12 years [FACT] [. . .] he's armed [BELIEF]'), but none of them is inconsistent with the key predispositions of the addressee.

At the 'synchronic' level, much denser with the relevant lexical and pragmatic material, historical flashbacks are not completely abandoned, but they involve proximization of *near* history and the main legitimization premise is not (continuing) ideological commitments, but the *direct physical threats* looming over the country ('a battlefield', in Bush's words). As the threats require a swift and strong pre-emptive response, the 'default' proximization strategy operating at the synchronic level is spatial proximization, often featuring a temporal element. Its task is to raise fears of imminence of the threat, which might be 'external' apparently, but could indeed materialize within the US borders anytime. The lexico-grammatical carriers of the spatial proximization include such items and phrases as 'secret and far away', 'all free people', 'stable and free nations', 'Saddam Hussein and his weapons of mass destruction', etc., which force dichotomous, 'good against evil' representations of the IDCs (America, Western [free, democratic] world) and the ODCs (Saddam Hussein, Iraqi regime, terrorists), located at a relative distance from each other. This geographical and geopolitical distance is symbolically construed as shrinking, as, on the one hand, the ODC entities cross the DS towards its centre and, on the other, the centre (IDC) entities declare a reaction. The ODC shift is enacted by forced inference and metaphorization. The inference involves an analogy to 9/11 ('On a September morning [. . .]), whereby the event stage is construed as facing another physical impact, whose ('current') consequences are scrupulously described ('before we see them [flames] again in our skies and our cities'). As can be noticed, this fear appeal is much strengthened by the FIRE metaphor, which contributes the imminence and the speed of the external impact (Hart, 2010). The IDC 'shift' (towards the ODCs) is much less symbolic; it involves an explicit declaration of a pre-emptive move to neutralize the threat ('must be confronted actively and forcefully before . . .', 'we will not allow the flames . . .', 'When it comes to our security and freedom, we really don't need anybody's permission').

While all spatial proximization in the text draws upon the presumed WMD presence in Iraq – and its potential availability to terrorists for acts far more destructive than the 9/11 attacks – Bush does not disregard the possibility of having to resort to an alternative rationale for war in the future. Consequently, the speech contains 'supporting' ideological premises, however tied to the principal premise. An example is: 'The world has a clear interest in the spread of democratic values, because stable and free nations do not breed the ideologies of murder', which counts as an instance of axiological proximization. This ideological argument is not synonymous with Bush's proximization of remote history we have seen before, as its current line subsumes acts of the adversary rather than his/America's own acts. As such it involves a more 'typical' axiological proximization, where the initially ideological conflict turns, over time, into a physical clash. Notably, in its ideological-physical duality it forces a spectrum of speculations over whether the current threat is 'still' ideological or 'already' physical. Since any result of these speculations can be effectively cancelled in a prospective discourse, the example quoted ('The world . . .') shows how proximization can interface, at the pragmalinguistic level, with the mechanism of implicature (Grice, 1975, etc.).

### 3.2 Maintaining legitimization through adjustments in proximization strategies

Political legitimization pursued in temporally extensive contexts – such as the timeframe of the Iraq war – often involves redefinition of the initial legitimization premises and coercion patterns and proximization is well suited to enact these redefinitions in discourse – which in turn promises a vast applicability of proximization as a theory. The legitimization obtained in the AEI speech and how the unfolding geopolitical context has put it to test is a case in point, providing a lucid illustration for these claims. Recall that although Bush has made the 'WMD factor' the central premise for the Iraq war, he has left half-open an 'emergency door' to be able to reach for an alternative rationale. Come November 2003 (a mere eight months into the Iraq war), and Bush's pro-war rhetoric adopts (or rather has to adopt) such an emergency alternative rationale, as it becomes evident (to all political players worldwide) that there have never been weapons of mass destruction in Iraq, at least not in the ready-to-use product sense. The change of Bush's stance is a swift change from strong fear appeals (enacted, before, by spatial proximization of the 'direct/emerging threat'), to a more subtle ideological argument for legitimization, involving predominantly axiological proximization. The following quote from G. W. Bush's Whitehall Palace address of 19 November is a good illustration:

(2) By advancing freedom in the greater Middle East, we help end a cycle of dictatorship and radicalism that brings millions of people to misery and brings danger to our own people. By struggling for justice in Iraq, Burma, in Sudan, and in Zimbabwe, we give hope to suffering people and improve the chances for stability and progress. Had we failed to act, the dictator's programs for weapons of mass destruction would continue to this day. Had we failed to act, Iraq's torture chambers would still be filled with victims, terrified and innocent. [. . .] For all who love freedom and peace, the world without Saddam Hussein's regime is a better and safer place.

The now dominant axiological proximization involves a dense concentration of ideological and value-oriented lexical items (e.g. 'freedom', 'justice', 'stability', 'progress', 'peace' vs. 'dictatorship', 'radicalism') as well as of items/phrases indicating the human dimension of the conflict ('misery', 'suffering people', 'terrified victims' vs. 'the world' [being] 'a better and safer place'). All of these lexico-grammatical forms serve to build, as in the case of the AEI address, dichotomous representations of the DS 'home' and 'peripheral/adversarial' entities (IDCs vs. ODCs), and the representation of impact upon the DS 'home' entities. In contrast to the AEI speech, however, all the entities (both IDCs and ODCs) are construed in abstract, rather than physical, 'tangible' terms, as respective lexical items are not explicitly but only inferentially attributed to concrete parties/groups. For example, compare phrases such as 'all free people', 'stable and free nations', [terrorist] 'flames of hatred', etc., in the AEI address, with the single-word abstract items of general reference such as 'dictatorship' and 'radicalism', in the Whitehall speech. Apparently, proximization in the Whitehall speech is essentially a proximization of antagonistic values, and not so much of physical entities as embodiments of these values. The consequences for maintaining a legitimization stance which began with the AEI address are enormous. First, there is no longer a commitment to a material threat posed by a physical entity. Second, the relief of this commitment does not completely disqualify the original WMD premise, as the antagonistic 'peripheral' values retain a capacity to materialize within the DS center (viz. '. . . a cycle of *dictatorship and radicalism* that brings millions of people to misery and *brings danger to our own people*', reiterating 'The world has a clear interest in the spread of democratic values, because *stable and free nations do not breed the ideologies of murder*' from the AEI speech). Third, as the nature of ideological principles is such that they are (considered) global or broadly shared, the socio-ideological argument helps extend the spectrum of the US (military) engagement ('Burma', 'Sudan', 'Zimbabwe'), which in turn forces the construal of failure to detect WMD in Iraq as merely an unlucky incident amongst other (successful) operations, and not as something that could potentially ruin US credibility. (Though the very switch to the ideological stance and axiological proximization seem to betray Bush's belief that much of the credibility did get damaged and there is a pressing need to restore it.) Add to these general factors the power of legitimization ploys in specific pragmalinguistic constructs ('programs for weapons of mass destruction',[6] the enumeration of the 'new' foreign fields of engagement [viz. 'Burma', etc., above], the always effective appeals for solidarity in compassion [viz. 'terrified victims' in 'torture chambers']) and there are reasons to conclude that the autumn 2003 change to essentially axiological discourse (subsuming axiological proximization) has helped a lot towards saving credibility and thus maintaining legitimization of not only the Iraq war, but the later anti-terrorist campaigns as well. The flexible interplay and the discursive switches between spatial and axiological proximization (both aided by temporal projections) in the early stages of the US anti-terrorist policy rhetoric have indeed made a major contribution.

# 4 Proximization in public space discourses

This section elaborates on the postulate salient in the title of the paper, that the descriptive power of proximization theory goes beyond state political discourse (such as the US anti-terrorist rhetoric) and can be successfully used to account for a broader range of legitimization discourses in the space of public communication explored by critical scholars. There seem to be good prospects as many of these discourses demonstrate analogies with regard to function (soliciting approval for preventive measures) as well as the conceptual/cognitive arrangement (involving dichotomous representations of 'home/good' [IDC] vs. 'foreign/alien/bad' [ODC] entities). At the same time, there are disanalogies, including, as will be shown, some different characterizations of the IDC and ODC camps in different discourses. In what follows I discuss both the analogies and the disanalogies, on the example of three legitimization discourses which appear to attract an increasingly greater attention within the CDS community: health, environment and modern technology.

## 4.1  Health: Proximization in cancer prevention discourse

The main reason why it seems worthwhile to apply proximization to the analysis of cancer discourse is that much of this discourse involves metaphoric construals of an *enemy* entity (cancer) posing an *imminent threat of impact* on the *home* entity (patient). In response, the patient and her healthcare team wage a 'war on cancer', which is often a *preventive* kind of war. Although, as will be argued, the construals underlying the war on cancer metaphor are not entirely synonymous with the proximization construals in state interventionist discourse, there is apparently enough similarity to consider the discourse of cancer prevention a possible empirical field for the application of proximization theory.

The war metaphor has been the prevailing metaphor used to describe and 'combat' cancer since at least 1971, when US President Richard M. Nixon declared a federal 'war on cancer' with the National Cancer Act. Following this legislation, as well as Sontag's (1978) seminal book *Illness as Metaphor*, medical discourse, both in and outside the US, has quickly implemented the concept, adding the war on cancer metaphor to an already rich inventory of metaphors involving 'wars' on other negative social phenomena, such as drugs, poverty and illiteracy.

Van Rijn-van Tongeren (1997) claims the concepts of war and cancer reveal a perfect metaphoric correspondence: there is an enemy (the cancer), a commander (the physician), a combatant (the patient), allies (the medical team), as well as formidable weaponry (chemical, biological, and nuclear weapons, at the disposal of the medical team). Another analogy, she argues, is that both concepts connote 'an unmistakable seriousness of purpose' (1997: 46). Based on these observations, she describes the 'war on cancer' in terms of the following conceptual scenario:

(3) Cancer is an *aggressive enemy* that *invades* the body. In response, the body *launches an offensive* and *defends* itself, *fighting* back with its *army of killer T-cells*. However, this is not enough and doctors are needed to *target, attack* and try to *defeat, destroy, kill* or *wipe out* the cancer cells with their *arsenal* of *lethal weapons*. However, cancer cells may become *resistant* and more specialised treatments are required, such as *magic bullets* or *stealth viruses*.

(Van Rijn-van Tongeren [1997], emphasis original)

The consecutive stages of the scenario are widely represented in discourse. Van Rijn-van Tongeren (1997) gives, among many others, the following examples (emphasis original). Van Rijn-van Tongeren's data come, in general, from various publications, including scholarly monographs, textbooks and articles (viz. examples [5–7]), but also bulletins and newspaper articles aimed at the broader public (example [4]).

(4) The next trial involves several hundred patients, helping microwaves become another *cancer-fighting tool*.

(5) This molecule called Sumo, is then *attacked* by an enzyme called RNF4, a process that also *destroys* the cancer-causing proteins.

(6) A second gene, called LMTK2 is a promising *target* for new drugs to treat the disease.

(7) This activates only those antibodies surrounding cancer, which then attract the immune system's *army of killer T-cells*, to *destroy* the tumor.

Van Rijn-van Tongeren's scenario, as well as the examples, ring some familiar notes. As in the proximization arrangement of political interventionist discourse, there is an 'alien' entity ready to invade (or actually invading) the 'home' entity, i.e., here, the body of the patient. The 'alien' entity is construed as evil and actively operating ('aggressive enemy'), thus the impact probability is high. The 'home' entity has the capacity to deliver a counter-strike, which is defensive/neutralizing, as much as offensive/preventive in character ('the body *launches an offensive* and *defends* itself, *fighting* back with its *army of killer T-cells'*). This is, however, where the analogies seem to end. The 'alien' entity cannot be described as a truly 'external' entity (ODC), since cancer cells develop inside of the patient's body. Furthermore, the body is not, technically, the only 'home' entity (IDC) that counters the alien entity, since its '*army of T-cells*' gets support (medical treatment) from another party (the physician), which the latter has not been 'invaded'. These and other differences call for a more extensive, textual look at the cancer prevention discourse, to distinguish the areas which can be described in terms of the STA model, from those which might not be describable quite as easily, unless the model is revised to deal with a broader spectrum of data. The following is a text that appeared in the spring 2011 edition of the Newsletter of the British Association of Cancer Research (BACR). Its argument, structure, and lexis all seem quite representative of the contemporary discourse of cancer prevention and treatment, both specialized and popular (cf. Semino, 2008):

(8) Some say we can contain melanoma with standard chemotherapy measures. The evidence we have says we must strike it with a full force in its earliest stages. We will continue to conduct screening programmes to spot the deadly disease before it has spread throughout the body. We must be able to wipe out all the infected cells in one strike, otherwise it takes a moment before they continue to replicate and migrate around the body. We now aim to develop a new treatment that targets the infected cells with precision, effectively destroying the engine at the heart of the disease, and doing minimal harm to healthy cells. We will inject specially-designed antibodies coated in a light-sensitive shell. The coating prevents the antibodies from causing a massive immune reaction throughout the body. Once the 'cloaked' antibodies have been injected, we will shine the new strong ultraviolet light on the engine and the infected cells.

The analysis of this text in terms of proximization theory and the STA model must involve, same as the analysis of the US anti-terrorist discourse in Section 3, at least three, interrelated levels: the conceptual level of organization of the Discourse Space (DS), the level of lexis responsible for the enactment of strategic changes to the DS principal organization, and the coercion level, where the text is considered an example of legitimization discourse which aims to win support for specific actions performed by the speaker. At the DS conceptual level, we must be able to determine the presence of the IDC ('home', 'central') entity and the ODC ('alien', 'external', 'peripheral') entity, the existence of a conceptual shift whereby the ODC entity impacts the IDC entity, and a preventive or reactive posture of the IDC entity. Looking at (8), this arrangement indeed holds in general, though there are some deviations. The IDC status can be assigned, most directly, to the patient's body, which is invaded by cancer cells, which thus emerge as the ODC entity. This basic proximization construal follows the standard metaphoric conceptualization of the body as a container (Lakoff and Johnson, 1980). But the container metaphor is only partly of relevance here since the patient's body is not a typical IDC, in the sense of where the impact it undergoes comes from. In that sense, the cancer cells, responsible for the impact, are not a typical ODC, either. As has been pointed out, cancer cells develop, technically, *inside* of the patient's body. At the same time, *causes* of cancer are put down to internal (e.g. genetic), as well as external (e.g. civilizational), factors. The picture gets even more complex if we consider the aspect of agency. While the body has an internal defence mechanism, fighting the cancer cells involves mostly external resources, i.e. measures applied by the physician. Thus, in terms of neutralization of the ODC impact, the physician becomes an IDC entity as well, and even more so considering he remains under the cancer *threat* himself. What we arrive at, then, is a rather broad concept of the IDC entity, involving the patient and, by the attribution of agency and the recognition of common threat, the physician, as well as a vaguely construed concept of the ODC party, involving the infected cells in the patient, but also a whole array of cancer-provoking factors, 'located' externally. Looking at (8), it appears that the only (though crucial!) part of the default proximization arrangement that cancer discourse does not alter in any way is the construal of the very impact. Indeed, it seems that all of its characteristics, like speed, imminence and deadliness, are there in the text, which in that sense resembles the two texts of state political discourse in Section 3.

This last observation explains why there are fewer analytic problems at the level of lexis. In proximization discourse, lexical markers of the ODC *impact* generally count among the most plentiful, within all the linguistic material categorized (Cap, 2013). As a result, the abundance of such markers in (8) makes its phrases resemble many of the discourse items and sequences we have seen above in the war on terror rhetoric.[7] The ODC impact speed is coded explicitly in phrases such as '*spread throughout* the body', 'it takes *a moment*', 'replicate and migrate around', and can also be inferred from 'we must strike it with a full force *in its earliest stages*', 'we must be able to wipe out all the infected cells *in one strike*' and '*the engine* at the heart of the disease'. The imminence is construed in, for instance, 'before it has spread throughout' and 'in its earliest stages', presuppositions of the ODC's inevitably fast growth. The effects of the impact are explicitly marked by the 'deadly disease' phrase.

At the coercion-legitimization level, the STA model recognizes in (8) an attempt to solicit legitimization of a non-standard course of treatment, sanctioned by the momentousness of the decision-making context ('We *now* aim'), as well as by the clear evidence the speaker possesses ('The evidence we have says') which speaks in favour of the treatment. Since the legitimization is sought by the physician acting, in a way, 'on behalf of' the patient, and not by the patient herself, we again face the problem of who, under the current design of the STA model, belongs to the deictic centre and who, thus, is acting (or is supposed to act) in response to the ODC threat. The recurrence of this issue at the coercion-legitimization level of analysis of cancer discourse delineates a possible avenue for the modification of selected structural elements of proximization theory (as in Cap, 2013), to make it able to process data beyond the state-political interventionist discourse. Apparently, what we need first is revision of the size and range of the Discourse Space and its deictic centre in proximization operations.

## 4.2 *Environment: Proximization in climate change discourse*

As will become clear, the same conclusion holds for the application of proximization to the discourse of climate change. Climate change is a relatively new domain of discourse studies, investigated amply within the CDS paradigm (e.g. Boykoff, 2008; Berglez and Olausson, 2010; Krzyżanowski, 2009). Thus far, studies in climate change have revealed a unilateral focus: most of them concentrate on climate change as a form of *transnational crisis*. There are, however, two different ways in which this broad conception is approached in actual analysis. These result – probably – from two rather contradictory views that emerge from the media and the related discourses. On the one hand (cf. Krzyżanowski, 2009), there exists a tendency to frame climate change as a general issue of interest and critical importance to entire societies and all social groups. Within that trend, climate change is described mainly as a threat to the entire humanity which thus must be dealt with by entire societies or the global populace as a whole. On the other hand, the somewhat contradictory approach (cf. Boykoff, 2008) sees climate change as a problem which cannot be handled by entire societies but by selected individuals who, due to their knowledge and expertise, are able to cope with different facets of climate change.

Where does proximization, as an analytic device, belong then? It seems, tentatively, that the former, 'global' view invites proximization better than the 'particularized' view. It would be quite unrealistic to approach data subsuming the latter view hoping to establish any uniform conception of the discourse deictic centre and its agents in the first place. We have seen already from the analysis of cancer discourse how difficult that might be. In the current case, assuming climate change is dealt with by a number of different (locationally, politically, rhetorically, perhaps ideologically) *individual expert voices* in the vast and heterogeneous area of the world social space, an attempt to ascribe any stable and homogeneous discursive strategies or practices to these actors would probably fail. On the contrary, if we take the global *institutionalized* discourse of climate change, a discourse that evens out the individual legitimization-rhetorical and other differences and conceptually consolidates the deictic centre (concretizing, at the same time, the deictic periphery), chances emerge that proximization, as a concept that always benefits from clarity of the in-out distinction, may indeed be applicable. To determine that applicability, I will discuss excerpts from the speech 'Emerging Security Risks' by the NATO Secretary General Anders Fogh Rasmussen. The speech was given in London, on 1 October 2009:

(9) I want to devote a little more time today discussing the security aspects of climate change, because I think the time has come for a change in our approach.

First, I think we now know enough to start moving from analysis to action. Because the trend lines from climate change are clear enough, and grim enough, that we need to begin taking active steps to deal with this global threat.

We know that there will be more extreme weather events – catastrophic storms and flooding. If anyone doubts the security implications of that, look at what happened in New Orleans in 2006.

We know sea levels will rise. Two thirds of the world's population lives near coastlines. Critical infrastructure like ports, power plants and factories are all there. If people have to move they will do so in large numbers, always into where someone else lives, and sometimes across borders.

We know there will be more droughts. According to evidence, by 2025 about 40 per cent of the world's population will be living in countries experiencing water shortages. Again, populations will have to move. And again, the security aspects could be devastating.

If you think I'm using dramatic language, let me draw your attention to one of the worst conflicts in the world, in Darfur. One of the main causes was a long drought. Both herders and farmers lost land, including to the desert. What happened? The nomads moved South, in search of grazing land – right to where the farmers are. Of course, a lot of other factors have contributed to what has happened – political decisions, religious differences and ethnic tensions. But climate change in Sudan has been a major contributor to this tragedy. And it will put pressure on peace in other areas as well. When it comes to climate change, the threat knows no borders.

There are more examples, but to my mind, the bottom line is clear. We may not yet know the precise effects, the exact costs or the definite dates of how climate change will affect security. But we already know enough to start taking action. This is my first point: either we start to pay now, or we will pay much more later.

You get the point. Climate change is different than any other threat we face today. The science is not yet perfect. The effects are just starting to be visible, and it's difficult to pin down what will actually change because of climate change. The timelines are not clear either. But that only makes the threat bigger. Sailors never thought the mythical North-West Passage would ever open. But it is opening. Anything's possible.

The security challenges being discussed today are big, and they are growing. They might also seem overwhelming. But I firmly believe that a lot can be done – to address the root causes, to minimize their impact, and to manage the effects when they hit.

But for the topic, Rasmussen's speech could easily count in the discourse of the early stages of the Iraq war. Rasmussen's construal of climate change is in terms of a global threat whose outlines are 'clear enough' and consequences 'devastating'; thus, an immediate (re)action is necessary ('either we start to pay [costs of the climate change] now, or we will pay much more later'). Similar to Bush's rhetoric, the threat 'knows no borders' and a delay in response 'makes the threat bigger'. Analogy is used, like in the anti-terrorist discourse, to a past event (the war in Darfur), to endorse credibility of future visions. The visions involve construals of future events as personally consequential, thus strengthening the fear appeals ('Two thirds of the world's population lives near coastlines [. . .] If people have to move they will do so in large numbers, always into where someone else lives [. . .]'). Another familiar strategy is the construal of the moment of impact as virtually unpredictable ('the timelines are not clear'). Construing the climate change threat as continual and extending infinitely into the future, Rasmussen centralizes 'the now' and the near future as the most appropriate timeframe in which to act preventively.

Again, a number of Rasmussen's phrases subsume items belonging to the standard arsenal of lexico-grammatical choices recognized by proximization theory (cf. Section 3 as well as the formal categories of proximization items proposed in Cap, 2013). Note, first and foremost, the frequent use of 'threat' (a spatial proximization item), the use of 'catastrophic', 'tragedy' (spatial proximization), the ample presence of verbs in the progressive ('growing') indicating the closeness of the threat (spatial and temporal proximization), the use of a modal auxiliary ('could') construing conditions raising impact probability (temporal proximization), or the application of the present perfect ('the time has come') construing change from the 'safe past' to the 'threatening future' (temporal proximization). The frequent repetitions of the 'will' phrases in the speech ('We know that there will be more extreme weather events') deserve a separate comment. Resembling the war on terror items enacting foresight and, in general, political competence of the speaker (Dunmire, 2011; Cap, 2013) they have an even stronger appeal in Rasmussen's speech – by adding to its evidential groundwork (Bednarek, 2006). In places, then, Rasmussen's climate change discourse forces construals of threat in a yet more direct and appealing fashion than – cf. Section 3 – the Iraq war discourse of the Bush government.

Rasmussen's success in proximizing the climate change threat is not hindered by its global character. The globality of the threat does not result in vagueness or weakening of the ODC's (i.e. the climate change) agentive capacity. Conversely, listing specific consequences such as storms, floodings, droughts, and linking them to specific places, regions or countries (New Orleans, Darfur, Sudan), concretizes the ODC in terms of its proven capacity to strike whichever part of the IDC's (i.e. the world) territory. This is obviously, as in any kind of state interventionist discourse (Keyes, 2005; Kaplan and Kristol, 2003), the most effective pre requisite to solicit prompt legitimization of preventive measures. The latter are, somewhat surprisingly, missing from the speech but we can assume (which later developments seem to prove) that the goal of Rasmussen's address is, first and foremost, to alert public attention to the gravity of the issue so the follow-up goals, involving specific actions, could be enacted as a matter of course. The spatial and temporal proximization strategies used in the speech make a significant contribution and, given the recurrence of some of the forms (for instance all the lexical as well as grammatical forms construing the threat as growing with time), one can say their application has been a strategic choice.

A methodological-theoretical note is in order here. As can be seen from the analysis of Rasmussen's address and its analogies to the discourse of the war on terror, the STA proximization model can be applied in CDS both *critically* and *descriptively*, or, to put it better, as an integrated critical-descriptive analytic device. This is because of the nature of the data investigated. In the vast space of public communication, different discourses reveal different kinds and degrees of manipulation with regard to forced construals. Sometimes (as in the examples from Bush) a virtual threat is construed in real terms, but elsewhere (as in the environmental discourse analysed above) the threat is real from the beginning and the only act of manipulation is to discursively amplify its size and impact. Thus, the proximization model can provide a handle on persuasion and legitimization in CDS in general, regardless of the normative background. Whether the analyst 'agrees' with the text (as would be expected in the case of Rasmussen's address) or 'disagrees' with it, wishing to uncover the manipulation in an act of socio-political critique (as can be seen from most of the analyses of Bush's pro-war rhetoric), she still engages in the same critical-descriptive procedure. The only difference is how much of the analyst's data is, at the end of the day, highlighted 'critically' and how much remains merely identified, 'described', with little critical social mission behind. The STA-based analyses of different discourses in the public communication space are bound to vary significantly in that regard.

## 4.3  Modern technology: Proximization of cyber-threat

According to Sandwell (2006), the discourse of cyber-terror is a direct consequence of 9/11; cyber-threats are construed within the 'general context of uncertainty and common anxiety' following the WTC and the Pentagon terrorist attacks. The most extreme manifestations of cyber-fear, says Sandwell, are articulated around the '[post-9/11] boundary dissolving threats, intrusive alterities, and existential ambivalences created by the erosion of binary distinctions and hierarchies that are assumed to be constitutive principles of everyday life' (2006: 40). As such, the discourse of cyber-terror is not merely a US discourse, it is a world discourse. Its principal practitioners are the world media, and the press in particular, which, on Sandwell's view, perpetuate the threat by creating mixed representations of 'the offline and the online world, the real or physical and the virtual or imagined' (2006: 40).

Neither Sandwell (2006) nor other scholars (e.g. Graham, 2004) go on to speculate on the motives that might underlie such fear-inducing representations. This is unfortunate since establishing the motives is of clear relevance to the analysis of the discourse of cyber-terror as, potentially, a legitimization discourse. There are two hypotheses that emerge. On the first, the media discourse of cyber-terror has a strong political purpose: it aims to alert the people, the government and the state's security structures to the seriousness of the issue, thus exerting pressure on the state to implement or strengthen defence measures. Such a discourse can be considered a legitimization discourse since the measures become pre-legitimized by discourse construals reflecting a true intent to influence the state's policies. On the other hypothesis, the press representations of cyber-terror have no real political purpose and only pretend to have it; the motives are purely commercial and the central aim is to increase readership.

There are clearly not enough data to determine which of the two hypotheses (if any) is correct. Thus, the proximization analysis that follows cannot possibly address the coercion-legitimization level. In other words it cannot tell, from the macro functional perspective, *why* the proximization strategies, *as a whole*, have been used. Notwithstanding that, it is definitely thought-provoking to identify so many of the particular forms operating over relatively small text instants. The two examples below are excerpts from a book by Dan Verton, a respected IT journalist working with the influential *Computerworld* magazine.[8] In the book (2003), he recaps the thoughts presented in the 2002 issues of *Computerworld*:

(10) This is the emerging face of the new terrorism. It is a thinking man's game that applies the violent tactics of the old world to the realities and vulnerabilities of the new high-tech world. Gone are the days when the only victims are those who are unfortunate enough to be standing within striking distance of the blast. Terrorism is now about smart, well-planned indirect targeting of the electronic sinews of the whole nations. Terrorists are growing in their evil capacity to turn our greatest technologies against us. Imagine, one day, overloaded digital networks, resulting in the collapse of finance and e-commerce networks, collapsed power grids and non-functioning telephone networks. Imagine, another day, the collapse, within seconds, of air traffic control systems, resulting in multiple airplane crashes; or of any other control systems, resulting in widespread car and train crashes, and nuclear

meltdowns. Meanwhile, the perpetrators of the war remain undetected behind their distant, encrypted terminals, free to bring the world's mightiest nations to their knees with a few keystrokes in total impunity.

(Verton, 2003: 55)

(11) Armed with nothing but a laptop and a high speed Internet connection, a computer geek could release a fast spreading computer virus that in a matter of minutes gives him control of thousands, perhaps millions, of personal computers and servers throughout the world. This drone army launches a silent and sustained attack on computers that are crucial for sending around the billions of packets of data that keep e-mail, the Web and other, more basic necessities of modern life humming. At first the attack seems to be an inconvenience – e-mail traffic grinds to a halt, Web browsing is impossible. But then the problems spread to services only tangentially related to the Internet: your automated-teller machine freezes up, your emergency call fails to get routed to police stations and ambulance services, airport- and train-reservation systems come down. After a few hours, the slowdown starts to affect critical systems: the computers that help run power grids, air-traffic control and telephone networks.

(Verton, 2003: 87)

Similar to the discourse of climate change, (10) and (11) construe a broad spectrum of the IDC entities: there is seemingly no entity in the world, whether a nation or an individual that is *not* under threat. Forcing the construal involves a number of lexico-grammatical ploys, such as, in text (10), abundant pluralization of the affected entities (e.g. 'victims', 'nations', 'networks', 'systems', etc.) or, in (11), depicting the cyber-threat in personally consequential terms ('*your* automated-teller machine freezes up, *your* emergency call fails to get routed to police stations and ambulance services'). Unlike in the discourse of climate change – but similar to cancer discourse – we face a problem with demarcating the ODC entities. Unless we take Verton's 'cyber-terrorists' to count among 'terrorists' in the ideological, geopolitical and locational sense of alterity we have recognized so far, we have to admit the cyber-terrorists make, as if, isolated 'ODC cells' among the IDC entities. Because of the short history of the cyber-threat discourse and, as has been mentioned, the shortage of data, especially reference data, the dilemma is apparently unresolvable. Thus, again, the part of the current conceptual scenario that remains most in line with the 'default' proximization scenario is the act of proximization as such, the symbolic shift of the threat entity in the direction of the IDC entities. Though neither (10) nor (11) construes a clear picture of the *source* of the threat, they include a large number of lexico-grammatical forms construing its speed, imminence, as well as devastating effects.

Most of these forms echo the language choices and strategies from the war on terror discourse exemplified in Section 3, and, to the clear benefit of proximization as a theory, from the two discourses that we have approached earlier in the current section. The cyber-threat is construed as having redefined, once and for all, the 'old world' security arrangement ([10]: 'Gone are the days when [. . .]'). The 'new world' arrangement is far more 'vulnerable': not only do the 'old' ideologies of 'evil' and 'violence' continue to exist, but the ones exercising them have now acquired new formidable ('high-tech') tools. As a result, the current threat is 'growing', its 'blast' can reach entire 'nations', and the impact is unpredictable, it can come 'one day' or 'another'. Both (10) and (11) construe the impact as ultra-fast ([10]: 'within seconds'; [11]: 'fast spreading', 'in a matter of minutes') and massively destructive ([10]: 'airplane crashes', 'nuclear meltdowns'; [11]: 'affect critical systems'). Virtually all of these forms seem readily categorizable in terms of 'spatial', 'temporal' and 'axiological' items as proposed in Cap (2013; recall also a necessarily compact overview in Section 2). For instance, the 'fast spreading' phrase works towards spatio-temporal proximization, the 'blast' towards spatial proximization, and 'one day' enacts indefiniteness and thus uncertainty about the future, in line with the strategy of temporal proximization. In contrast to the discourse of climate change, as well as cancer discourse, we find also a few phrases forcing axiological construals ('evil capacity', 'violent tactics'). Intriguingly, (11) features a discourse sequence similar to Bush's argument establishing a threatening connection in 'a cycle of dictatorship and radicalism' that eventually 'brings danger to our own people' (recall Section 3.2). The sequence in (11), spanned by 'At first the attack seems to be an inconvenience' and 'After a few hours, the slowdown starts to affect critical systems', proximizes the threat along quite similar, 'apparently minor/abstract -toward- genuinely major/physical' progress line, except that in the current construal the starting point ('At first [. . .]') involves no ideological element such as 'dictatorship' or 'radicalism'.

# 5 Outlook: Proximization in CDS

The landscape of discourses where proximization and proximization theory can help CDS in its descriptive commitments and practices seems enormous, far more extensive than the three discourses analysed (pre-analysed, in fact) above. The domains addressed in CDS in the last 25 years have been at least the following: racism, xenophobia and national identity (Reisigl and Wodak, 2001; Van Dijk, 1987; Wodak, 1996, 1999), gender identity and inequality (Koller, 2008; Litosseliti and Sunderland, 2002; Morrish and Sauntson, 2007), media discourse (Bell, 1991; Bell and Garrett, 1998; Fairclough, 1995; Fowler, 1991; Montgomery, 2007; Richardson, 2007) and discourses of national vs. international politics (Chilton, 2004; Wilson, 1990).[9] This list, by no means exhaustive, gives a sense of the spectrum of discourses where proximization seems applicable. Why does it? Since the central commitments of CDS include exploring the many ways in which ideologies and identities are reflected, enacted, re-enacted, negotiated, modified, reproduced, etc., in discourse, any 'doing' of CDS must involve, first of all, studying the original positioning of the different ideologies and identities, and, in most cases, studying also the 'target positioning', that is the *change* the analyst claims is taking place through the speaker's *use* of discourse. Thus, doing CDS means, eventually, handling issues of the conceptual arrangement of the Discourse Space (DS), and most notably, the crucial issue of the DS *symbolic re-arrangement*. As such, any CDS practice may need the apparatus of proximization to account for both the original and the target setup of the DS. The most relevant seem those of the CDS domains whose discourses force the distinction between the different ideologies and/or identities in a particularly clear-cut and appealing manner, to construe opposition between 'better' and 'worse' ideologies/identities. This is evidently the case with the discourses of xenophobia, racism, nationalism or social exclusion, all of which presuppose in-group vs. out-group distinction, arguing for the 'growing' threat from the out-group. It is also the case with many national discourses, where similar opposition is construed between 'central-national' and 'peripheral-international' interests – the ongoing debate over the future of the eurozone is a case in point.

What CDS landscape can offer in the way of domains, it cannot yet offer in the way of its own analytic tools (see the critique in e.g. Chilton, 2010), which makes proximization even more applicable. The STA model is hoped to offer one such tool. Reversely, the STA model should itself benefit from inclusion in the CDS focus, as more extensive applications of the model should productively influence its cognitive-pragmatic framework, 'data-driving' the possible new or modified components. This paper has indicated that one of the most direct challenges to proximization theory resulting from further applications of the STA model is *proposing a DS conception universal enough* to handle different ranges of the deictic centre and the deictic periphery, in particular discourses. The three discourses in Section 4 have made it evident enough, and the challenge will only continue to grow as more discourses are investigated. To respond to it, proximization theory will need further input from Cognitive Linguistics, but, apparently, there are issues CL itself needs to answer first, to offer such an input. As Dirven et al. (2007) point out, in the past 30 years CL's treatment of discourse has hardly moved from the description to the interpretation stage, i.e. the *practice* of discourse has not been critically analysed. Fauconnier and Turner (2002) stress the focus of CL on the formal issues of conceptual representation, grammatical organization and general meaning construction, but at the same time admit to CL's lack of focus on discourse social functions associated with particular instances of that general construction and organization. How do these limitations affect representation of the Discourse Space and its rearrangement following proximization? It seems that, as of today, proximization theory (and its interface with CDS) must remain happy with the CL's mere *recognition* of the core ability of discourse to force structured conceptualizations, with various levels of organization reflecting alternate ways in which the same situation, event or phenomenon can be construed (Verhagen, 2007). Such a capacity has been endorsed in this paper: we have been able to define the 'prototypically-central' and 'prototypically-peripheral' entities of the DS in a state-political interventionist discourse, as well as indicate the existence of entities (in the three public space discourses) revealing different kinds/degrees of deviation from such a prototypical characterization. But we may be unable to prescribe, as yet, a stable DS composition for many other discourses where proximization, as a discourse symbolic operation, could be identified. The reason lies within CL as the 'cognitive part' of the theoretical groundwork of proximization theory. Apparently, CL is not yet geared to describe 'the structured conceptualizations with various levels of organization' in terms of the levels, direct/indirect, subordinate/superordinate, of *social functions*. The sooner it develops this capacity, the more quickly will proximization theory be able to assist CDS in its analytic agenda.

# Notes

1   See a comprehensive, four-volume overview by Wodak (2012).
2   The parts are quoted according to the chronology of the speech.
3   Weapons of mass destruction.
4   This is a secondary variant of axiological proximization. As will be shown, axiological proximization mostly involves the adversary (ODC); antagonistic values are 'dormant' triggers for a possible ODC impact.
5   Jowett and O'Donnell (1992) posit that the best credibility and thus legitimization effects can be expected if the speaker produces her message in line with the psychological, social, political, cultural, etc., predispositions of the addressee. However, since a full compliance is almost never possible, it is essential that a novel message is at least tentatively or partly acceptable; then, its acceptability and the speaker's credibility tend to increase over time.
6   The nominal phrase '[Iraq's] programs for WMD' is essentially an implicature able to legitimize, in response to contextual needs, any of the following inferences: 'Iraq possesses WMD', 'Iraq is developing WMD', 'Iraq intends to develop WMD', 'Iraq intended to develop WMD', and more. The phrase was among G. W. Bush's rhetorical favourites in later stages of the Iraq war, when the original premises for war were called into question.
7   Let alone intriguing metaphoric correspondences. Apart from the analogies listed by Van Rijn-van Tongeren (1997), note that (8) may force construal of the screening programmes as intelligence, the infected *cells* as terrorist *cells*, the new treatment as air strikes *on* the terrorist cells, and the healthy cells as civilian population ('We now aim to [. . .], doing minimal harm to healthy cells').
8   www.computerworld.com
9   Plus of course the domains addressed in Section 4.

# References

Bacevich, A. (2010), *Washington Rules: America's Path to Permanent War*. New York, NY: Metropolitan Books.

Bednarek, M. (2006), 'Epistemological positioning and evidentiality in English news discourse: a text-driven approach'. *Text & Talk*, 26, 635–60.

Bell, A. (1991), *The Language of News Media*. Oxford: Blackwell.

Bell, A. and Garrett, P. (eds) (1998), *Approaches to Media Discourse*. Oxford: Blackwell.

Berglez, P. and Olausson, U. (2010), 'The 'climate threat' as ideology: interrelations between citizen and media discourses'. Paper presented at the conference Communicating Climate Change II – Global Goes Regional. University of Hamburg.

Boykoff, M. (2008), 'The cultural politics of climate change discourse in UK tabloids'. *Political Geography*, 27, 549–69.

Cap, P. (2006), *Legitimization in Political Discourse: A Cross-disciplinary Perspective on the Modern US War Rhetoric*. Newcastle: Cambridge Scholars Press.

—— (2008), 'Towards the proximization model of the analysis of legitimization in political discourse'. *Journal of Pragmatics*, 40, 17–41.

—— (2010), 'Axiological aspects of proximization'. *Journal of Pragmatics*, 42, 392–407.

—— (2013), *Proximization: The Pragmatics of Symbolic Distance Crossing*. Amsterdam: John Benjamins.

Chilton, P. (2004), *Analysing Political Discourse: Theory and Practice*. London: Routledge.

—— (2005), 'Discourse space theory: geometry, brain and shifting viewpoints'. *Annual Review of Cognitive Linguistics*, 3, 78–116.

—— (2010), 'From mind to grammar: coordinate systems, prepositions, constructions', in V. Evans and P. Chilton (eds), *Language, Cognition and Space: The State of the Art and New Directions*, London: Equinox, pp. 640–71.

Chovanec, J. (2010), 'Legitimation through differentiation: discursive construction of Jacques *Le Worm* Chirac as an opponent to military action', in U. Okulska and P. Cap (eds), *Perspectives in Politics and Discourse*. Amsterdam: John Benjamins, pp. 61–82.

Cienki, A., Kaal, B. and Maks, I. (2010), 'Mapping world view in political texts using discourse space theory: metaphor as an analytical tool'. Paper presented at RaAM 8 conference, Vrije Universiteit Amsterdam.

Dirven, R., Polzenhagen, F. and Wolf, H.-G. (2007), 'Cognitive linguistics, ideology and critical discourse analysis', in D. Geeraerts and H. Cuyckens (eds), *The Oxford Handbook of Cognitive Linguistics*. Oxford: Oxford University Press, pp. 1222–40.

Dunmire, P. (2011), *Projecting the Future through Political Discourse: The Case of the Bush Doctrine*. Amsterdam: John Benjamins.

Fairclough, N. (1995), *Media Discourse*. London: Edward Arnold.

Fauconnier, G. and Turner, M. (2002), *The Way We Think: Conceptual Blending and the Mind's Hidden Complexities*. New York, NY: Basic Books.

Filardo Llamas, L. (2010), 'Discourse worlds in Northern Ireland: the legitimisation of the 1998 Agreement', in K. Hayward and C. O'Donnell (eds), *Political Discourse and Conflict Resolution. Debating Peace in Northern Ireland*. London: Routledge, pp. 62–76.

—— (2013), '"Committed to the Ideals of 1916". The language of paramilitary groups: the case of the Irish Republican Army'. *Critical Discourse Studies*, 10(1), 1–17.

Fowler, R. (1991), *Language in the News: Discourse and Ideology in the Press*. London: Routledge.

Graham, S. (2004), 'War in the "Weirdly pervious world": infrastructure, demodernisation, and geopolitics'. Paper presented at the conference on Urban Vulnerability and Network Failure. University of Salford, UK.

Grice, P. (1975), 'Logic and conversation', in P. Cole and J. L. Morgan (eds), *Syntax and Semantics 3: Speech Acts*, New York, NY: Academic Press, pp. 41–58.

Hart, C. (2010), *Critical Discourse Analysis and Cognitive Science: New Perspectives on Immigration Discourse*. Basingstoke: Palgrave Macmillan.

Jowett, G. S. and O'Donnell, V. (1992), *Propaganda and Persuasion*. Newbury Park, CA: Sage.

Kaal, B. (2012), 'Worldviews: spatial ground for political reasoning in dutch election manifestos'. *CADAAD*, 6(1), 1–22.

Kaplan, L. and Kristol, W. (2003), *The War over Iraq: Saddam's Tyranny and America's Mission*. San Francisco, CA: Encounter Books.

Keyes, C. (2005), 'Defining just preemption'. Available at: http://www.usafa.af.mil/jscope/JSCOPE05/Keyes05.html (accessed 15 June 2010).

Koller, V. (2008), *Lesbian Discourses: Images of A Community*. London: Routledge.

Krzyżanowski, M. (2009), 'Europe in crisis: discourses on crisis-events in the European press 1956–2006'. *Journalism Studies*, 10, 18–35.

Lakoff, G. and Johnson, M. (1980), *Metaphors We Live By*. Chicago, IL: University of Chicago Press.

Litosseliti, L. and Sunderland, J. (eds) (2002), *Gender Identity and Discourse Analysis*. Amsterdam: John Benjamins.

Montgomery, M. (2007), *The Discourse of Broadcast News: A Linguistic Approach*. London: Routledge.

Morrish, E. and Sauntson, H. (2007), *New Perspectives on Language and Sexual Identity*. Basingstoke: Palgrave Macmillan.

Okulska, U. and Cap, P. (eds) (2010), *Perspectives in Politics and Discourse*. Amsterdam: John Benjamins.

Reisigl M. and Wodak, R. (2001), *Discourse and Discrimination: Rhetorics of Racism and Anti-Semitism*. London: Routledge.

Richardson, J. (2007), *Analysing Newspapers: An Approach from Critical Discourse Analysis*. Basingstoke: Palgrave Macmillan.

Sandwell, B. (2006), 'Monsters in cyberspace: cyberphobia and cultural panic in the information age'. *Information, Communication & Society*, 9, 39–61.

Semino, E. (2008), *Metaphor in Discourse*. Cambridge: Cambridge University Press.

Silberstein, S. (2004), *War of Words*. London: Routledge.

Sontag, S. (1978), *Illness as Metaphor*. New York, NY: Farrar, Straus and Giroux.

Van Dijk, T. (1987), *Communicating Racism: Ethnic Prejudice in Thought and Talk*. London: Sage.

Van Rijn-van Tongeren, G. (1997), *Metaphors in Medical Texts*. Amsterdam: Rodopi.

Verhagen, A. (2007), 'Construal and perspectivization', in D. Geeraerts and H. Cuyckens (eds), *The Oxford Handbook of Cognitive Linguistics*. Oxford: Oxford University Press, pp. 48–81.

Verton, D. (2003), *Black Ice: The Invisible Threat of Cyberterrorism*. New York, NY: McGraw Hill.

Wilson, J. (1990), *Politically Speaking: The Pragmatic Analysis of Political Language*. Oxford: Blackwell.

Wodak, R. (1996), *Disorders of Discourse*. London: Longman.

—— (1999), *The Discursive Construction of National Identity*. Edinburgh: Edinburgh University Press.

Wodak, R. (ed.) (2012), *Critical Discourse Analysis* (4 vols). London: Sage.

# 9

# 'Bad Wigs and Screaming Mimis'

# Using Corpus-Assisted Techniques to Carry Out Critical Discourse Analysis of the Representation of Trans People in the British Press

*Paul Baker*

Lancaster University

## 1 Introduction

On 21 December 2012, Richard Littlejohn, a columnist for the British middle-market conservative newspaper The *Daily Mail*, wrote an opinion piece about a school-teacher called Lucy Meadows who had transitioned from male to female. Littlejohn strongly disapproved of the teacher's decision to remain at the same school, asking 'has anyone stopped for a moment to think of the devastating effect all this is having on those who really matter? Children as young as seven aren't equipped to compute this kind of information'. He went on to write 'he is putting his own selfish needs ahead of the well-being of the children he has taught for the past few years.'

Three months later Lucy Meadows committed suicide. She was posthumously reported as being harassed by members of the press[1] and at the end of her inquest the coroner told the reporters present 'And to the press, I say shame, shame on all of you'.[2] Online petitions at change.org and sumofus.org called for Littlejohn's resignation although at the time of writing Littlejohn had not resigned. This story serves as a stark illustration of the real-world consequences of what can happen when the media take an interest in trans people, and also highlights what some people have perceived as a general transphobic stance in the British press. Around the same time, another opinion column by Julie Burchill in the online version of *The Observer* (a liberal broadsheet Sunday newspaper) entitled 'Transsexuals should cut it out', referred to 'the very vociferous transsexual lobby' and used other pejorative phrases like 'a bunch of bed-wetters in bad wigs' and 'screaming mimis' (13 January 2013). Hundreds of readers used the Comments section to criticize Burchill and within hours an editorial decision was made to remove the article from the website. Subsequently, 800 complaints were made about the article to the Press Complaints Commission (PCC). At the time of writing, the British press is largely self-regulated by the PCC, a voluntary organization made up of representatives from publishers.[3] The PCC has an Editors' Code of Practice with 16 sections. Section 12i states that: 'The press must avoid prejudicial or pejorative reference to an individual's race, colour, religion, gender, sexual orientation or to any physical or mental illness or disability.' However, section 1iii states that: 'The Press, while free to be partisan, must distinguish clearly between comment, conjecture and fact.' This perhaps helps to explain why opinion columnists are able to avoid censure by the PCC, and indeed, in March 2013, Burchill's article was found not to have breached the PCC's Code of Practice. In the case of Lucy Meadows, the PCC made the *Daily Mail* remove photographs and the Littlejohn column from its website but Littlejohn was not required to apologize or resign.

Burchill's article provoked a debate about representation of trans people and freedom of speech, with some commentators, such as Jane Fae in the *Independent*, writing that 'the trans community . . . is now a stand-in for various minorities . . . and a useful whipping girl for the national press . . . trans stories are only of interest when trans folk star as villains'.[4] A submission to the Leveson Inquiry[5] by the group Trans Media Watch argued that the British press had created and sustained 'a climate of ridicule and humiliation' as well as 'singling out individual transgender people and their families for sustained personal intrusion' (2011: 10).


## 2 Corpus approaches to critical discourse analysis

While Littlejohn and Burchill's articles clearly caused offence, I wondered whether these criticisms about the representation of trans people in the press held true *generally*. It is possible to 'cherry-pick' a few cases (see Mautner, 2007: 54), perhaps focusing on the worst representations, but in the interests of fairness and full coverage, there is wisdom in exploring a much larger set of data in order to obtain a better idea of the overall trend. For such an endeavour, techniques associated with corpus linguistics are advocated as a useful way of aiding critical discourse analysis (see Baker et al., 2008).

Corpus linguistics is a method of analysis which involves collecting large amounts of language data in computerized format, and then using computer programs which can sort, count and perform statistical tests on that data in order to quickly and accurately identify patterns that would be difficult for the human eye to spot alone (Hunston, 2002). A corpus is simply a collection of electronically encoded texts, which are sometimes annotated with additional information either at the text level (e.g. information about the sex of the author or the genre of the text is encoded) or at the linguistic level (e.g. individual words can be annotated according to their grammatical or semantic categories). Texts are collected so that they can be as representative as possible of the language variety under examination. Reference corpora, which aim to represent a particular language (usually at a particular point in time) can stretch to millions or billions of words, with thousands of text samples from many genres of speech, writing and computer-mediated communication. Specialized corpora are often smaller and aim to more fully represent all of the language produced from a certain restricted text type (such as all the published fiction of a single author or all newspaper articles about a certain topic published in a five-year period in one country).

Since becoming popular in the 1990s Corpus Linguistics was initially strongly associated with language description, grammar, lexicography and language teaching. In 1995 Hardt-Mautner published one of the first papers advocating the connection of critical discourse analysis and corpus linguistics, arguing that concordance programs allow exhaustive description of key lexical items, raise new questions, allow qualitative investigation of quantitative results and give the analyst a much firmer grip on their data (1995: 23–4). Since the mid-2000s, corpus approaches have been increasingly used either alongside existing critical discourse analysis approaches as a form of triangulation or combined with CDA to form a new 'hybrid' form of analysis. For example, Baker et al. (2008) describe a nine-stage model of Corpus-Assisted Critical Discourse Analysis which combines CDA with corpus linguistics, and involves moving recursively between different levels of analysis, using frequency and concordancing information to derive and test new hypotheses. A related approach has been taken by Partington (2003) called Corpus Assisted Discourse Analysis (CADS), although the two approaches differ in that CADS aims to conduct research from a more ideologically objective stance, whereas Baker et al.'s model is influenced by Reisgl and Wodak's Discourse-Historical Approach (DHA) and allows research to be conducted from an explicit 'position' if researchers so desire, along with advocating examination of corpus texts within their social and historical context while considering conditions of reception and production, intertextuality and interdiscursivity.

I have argued that corpus approaches to discourse analysis help to reduce researcher bias in that human analysts will not always be able to accurately predict the frequencies of words or co-occurrences of words (known as collocates) in a corpus and so computer software will direct us to frequently-occurring phenomena which might otherwise have been overlooked (Baker, 2006: 10–14). As Fairclough (1989: 54) notes in his discussion of the media: 'A single text on its own is quite insignificant: the effects of media power are cumulative, working through the repetition of particular ways of handling causality and agency, particular ways of positioning the reader, and so forth'. It is this incremental or cumulative effect of discourse which corpus approaches are especially able to pinpoint, by showing that words or phrases occur in particular contexts, repeatedly, priming text recipients so that certain representations or ways of looking at the world are not only automatically triggered but gradually appear to be common-sense ways of thinking (see Stubbs, 1996: 195; Hoey, 2005).

Additionally, if the corpora used for analysis are large enough, they are more likely to offer a fuller range of discourse positions around a particular subject, in comparison to a single text or smaller sample of texts. As well as revealing commonly accessed discourses, a large corpus might also contain resistant or minority discourses, which may only be cited once or twice. Identifying such discourses is generally not as easy as recognizing the more frequent ones, but at least researchers have a better chance of finding them if they exist in the texts under analysis.

For the purposes of this chapter, I aim to carry out such a corpus-assisted study in order to examine the representation of trans people in the British press. Due to space limitations, this cannot be an exhaustive study, but it is instead intended to illustrate some of the techniques and tools used by corpus linguists, and how they can be effectively used in critical discourse analysis. In the following sections, after describing how I built a corpus (or body of texts), I go on to detail the way that corpus methods were employed to focus in on a small number of words for close examination, and what such an examination reveals about the representation of trans people in UK newspapers.

## 3 Building the corpus

The online searchable database Nexis UK was used in order to collect a small corpus of articles about trans people. Only national UK newspapers were considered as in Britain such newspapers have the widest readerships and the most influence. The newspapers collected were the *Express*, *The Guardian*, *The Independent*, the *Daily Mail*, the *Mirror*, *The Observer*, the *Sunday People*, *The Star*, *The Sun*, *The Telegraph* and *The Times* (see Baker et al. 2013: 4–17 for an overview of the British press). Where available, the Sunday versions of these newspapers were also collected. It should be noted that Nexis treats *The Guardian* (a daily newspaper) and *The Observer* (a Sunday newspaper) separately although the two newspapers are both owned by The Guardian Media Group and are viewed as sister newspapers. They are treated separately here too. The *Sunday People* is published only on Sundays so did not contribute much data to the corpus.

Nexis UK returns articles that contain words specified by users, as well as allowing searches to be limited to certain time periods and newspapers. Five hundred articles at a time can be saved to a user's computer. Although archiving goes back to the late 1990s, as this was intended to be a small, illustrative study I decided to look for data across the period of a single year – 2012. In order to develop a search term I used a mixture of introspection, trial and error (e.g. reading articles produced by an initial search term in order to identify terms I had not thought of), and consulting various guidelines on appropriate language to refer to trans people (described in more detail below). I wanted to include a set of terms ranging from those considered to be sensitive or appropriate to those seen as pejorative. The search terms eventually produced were:

transsexual OR transgender OR trans OR transgendered OR trannie OR tranny OR mtf OR ftm OR cross-dresser OR transvestite OR intersex OR intersexed OR sex change OR shemale OR genderbender

Nexis also returns articles containing the plural forms of search terms which was useful in obtaining fuller coverage. However, less helpfully, Nexis sometimes produces duplicates of articles although it enables users to check an option to reduce the probability of this happening. Even with this option turned on, the search produced duplicates, due to Irish or Scottish versions of newspapers appearing in the database. Additionally, some newspapers issued multiple editions of newspapers on the same day, also producing duplicates. A further problem involved the search term *trans* which returned a large number of irrelevant stories (e.g. about trans fats). Fortunately, Nexis allows users to specify terms which act as excluders e.g. if a word appears then the article should *not* be collected. Therefore, an additional set of terms were used to reduce the appearance of duplicates or irrelevant articles, based on reading the unwanted articles and identifying terms that would remove them. This included excluding terms like *transfat* and *trans-border*, as well as phrasing which indicated duplicate articles such as 'Edition 1; Scotland' or 'Ulster Edition'.

Table 9.1 shows the total number of articles collected for each newspaper. In total there were 902 articles in the corpus, consisting of 661,189 words. The three newspapers which had the highest number of articles all skew to the right politically, to different degrees: *The Times, The Telegraph* and *The Sun.*

As a way of gaining an idea about what others have said about the search terms, I referred outside the corpus to three sets of guidelines on appropriate language use. These are guidelines written by groups whose goal is support of and better representation for trans people: GLAAD (Gay & Lesbian Alliance against Defamation), the Beaumont Society and the Gender Identity Research and Education Society (GIRE). These guidelines were not used here as a blueprint for the 'correct' ways to use terminology; the guidelines did not always agree with each other and I also found reports of people criticizing them. Clearly, the writers of the guidelines cannot represent the views of every trans person in the world, but they are still useful to consider as they raise points about the choices that people make when using language to refer to trans people, helping interpretations of language use in the newspaper corpus.

As a preliminary stage in the analysis it was decided to employ the free-to-use corpus analysis software AntConc (Anthony, 2013) to investigate the frequencies of different search terms across each newspaper. This was used in order to narrow the

**Table 9.1**   Number of articles for each newspaper

| Newspaper | Total articles |
|---|---|
| Express | 50 |
| Guardian | 121 |
| Independent | 62 |
| Mail | 78 |
| Mirror | 44 |
| Observer | 44 |
| People | 7 |
| Star | 94 |
| Sun | 131 |
| Telegraph | 123 |
| Times | 148 |
| Total | 902 |

focus of the analysis to a smaller number of words which would provide the best overall coverage. After that, these words were subjected to a more detailed qualitative analysis in order to identify similar patterns of representation.

## 4  Finding a focus

Table 9.2 shows the overall frequencies of terminology used in the corpus for each newspaper (ordered according to overall frequency in the corpus). An asterisk at the end of a word acts as a wildcard, so *transgender** refers to *transgender, transgenders, transgendered*, etc. Due to the fact that some newspapers contain a great deal more text than others, it is misleading to note that *The Guardian* and *The Times* use the term *transgender** the most, as these broadsheet newspapers simply contain a lot of text, particularly compared to the less verbose tabloid newspapers. It is more relevant to make a comparison within a newspaper, asking which term a particular newspaper favours. Therefore, for each newspaper, the most frequently used term is in a shaded cell.

For some newspapers, the frequencies are too low to draw much of a conclusion, other than the terms simply do not appear to be used very much. Seven of the newspapers have *transgender** as the most frequent term, and the guidelines I consulted tend to view *transgender* as one of the most, if not the most, appropriate

**Table 9.2** Frequencies of terminology for each newspaper

| Term | Exp | Guard | Ind | Mail | Mirror | Obs | People | Star | Sun | Tel | Tim | Total |
|---|---|---|---|---|---|---|---|---|---|---|---|---|
| transgender* | 18 | 79 | 29 | 70 | 17 | 7 | 0 | 20 | 32 | 55 | 78 | 405 |
| transsexual* | 19 | 60 | 21 | 34 | 8 | 33 | 1 | 17 | 47 | 37 | 43 | 320 |
| transvestite* | 21 | 36 | 21 | 26 | 13 | 15 | 1 | 30 | 36 | 39 | 39 | 277 |
| sex change* | 6 | 8 | 5 | 26 | 8 | 2 | 2 | 24 | 25 | 19 | 16 | 141 |
| cross(-)dress* | 7 | 14 | 2 | 13 | 12 | 12 | 1 | 18 | 23 | 22 | 7 | 131 |
| trans | 4 | 22 | 2 | 13 | 2 | 0 | 0 | 3 | 5 | 14 | 8 | 73 |
| tranny(s)\|trannie(s) | 1 | 4 | 2 | 2 | 4 | 0 | 0 | 15 | 6 | 2 | 17 | 53 |
| intersex* | 1 | 4 | 5 | 1 | 0 | 3 | 0 | 0 | 4 | 3 | 4 | 25 |
| shemale* | 0 | 1 | 0 | 0 | 0 | 0 | 0 | 0 | 0 | 0 | 2 | 3 |
| ftm | 0 | 0 | 0 | 0 | 0 | 0 | 0 | 0 | 1 | 0 | 0 | 1 |
| genderbender* | 0 | 0 | 0 | 0 | 0 | 0 | 0 | 0 | 0 | 1 | 0 | 1 |
| mtf | 0 | 0 | 0 | 0 | 0 | 0 | 0 | 0 | 0 | 0 | 0 | 0 |
| Total | 77 | 228 | 87 | 185 | 64 | 72 | 5 | 127 | 179 | 192 | 214 | 1430 |

term to use. It is perhaps then notable that *The Observer* and *The Sun* appear to prefer *transsexual\** over *transgender\** while *The Star* and the *Express* have more references to *transvestite\**. This gives a first indication that certain newspapers may not normally use the most sensitive linguistic choices when referring to trans people.

It is also notable that *shemale, ftm, genderbender* and *mtf* are very rare across the whole corpus. An analysis of their use in context indicates that when they are used it is to generally to cite them as being abusive terms, indicating that on the measure of naming strategies, the newspapers generally adhere to a base level of sensitivity. However, while Table 9.2 tells us about preferred terminology, it does not reveal very much about representation. As a second step it is useful to take a broad-brush view by examining collocates of the terms, as shown in Table 9.3. A collocate is a word which occurs near or next to another word more often than would be expected if words just appeared in a random order. Examining collocates can help us to get an idea about the way that a word is most typically used, although care must be taken that we do not over-interpret collocational information.

There are a wide range of ways of calculating collocation (see McEnery et al., 2006: 210–20 for an overview) and a number of choices relating to cut-off points need to be made about what will actually count as a collocate for the purposes of a single piece of research. For example, we must decide on the span or number of words either side of the search term, as well as whether we stipulate a minimum overall frequency for two words to co-occur, and if so, what that minimum frequency should be. Sometimes the limitations of the corpus tool available to us will restrict our choices, while time and space considerations may mean we use settings that give us more or fewer collocates to examine. For the purposes of this research, to find collocates I used the Mutual Information (MI) technique, stipulating that collocates needed to have a MI score of 3 or above, as suggested by Hunston (2002: 71) as being evidence for collocation. Additionally, words had to occur together at least five times, and I used a fairly tight span of three words either side of the search term. As Table 9.3 suggests, the more frequent a word, generally the more collocates it will elicit.

Due to space limitations I was not able to examine every term in detail, so I decided to focus on three, using a number of criteria which were partly based on information obtained from Tables 9.2 and 9.3. I wanted to take into account at least half of the overall references to these words in the corpus, so it was decided to focus on the first two terms: *transgender\** and *transsexual\** which were most frequent and together encompassed 50.8 per cent of references to the search terms. Both of these words also had the most collocates, although they had quite different collocates so I felt that it would be interesting to explore some of them in more detail. Additionally, the guidelines I had examined had tended to view *transgender* as an appropriate term (although one set of guidelines gave a couple of exceptions to that, described below). On the other hand, one of the guidelines was less enthusiastic about *transsexual\**, so comparing two terms (one largely accepted by groups representing trans people, the other seen as more problematic) felt like a good strategy for obtaining an overall idea

**Table 9.3** Collocates of search terms

| Term | Freq. | Collocates |
|---|---|---|
| transgender* | 405 | bisexual, contestants, intersex, students, lesbian, communities, issues, gay, community, people, equality, person, support, group, help, or, woman, men, women, young, children, many, being, and, were, who, are, other, first, as, rights, for, about, says, has |
| transsexual* | 320 | assassin, hitman, pre, op, soldier, dancers, youngest, female, character, wants, lesbian, male, hit, film, who, called, or, also, man, gay, even, a, as, has, their, rights, people, by, can, about, said, and, an, from, have, was, when, had, for |
| transvestite* | 277 | ego, alter, dancers, plays, playing, dress, gay, male, who, a, as, or, also, like, were, not, says, was, with, he, and, on, for, in, an, about |
| sex change* | 141 | operation, operations, having, had |
| cross(-)dress* | 131 | like, who, but, as, a |
| trans | 73 | play, people, said, t, are, for |
| tranny(s)\|trannie(s) | 53 | a, and, in, the |
| intersex* | 25 | transgender, are, he, and |

about representation. As a third term I chose *tranny/trannie* as this term had been singled out by one of the guidelines as definitely pejorative, and I was drawn to the fact that the broadsheet newspaper *The Times* (unexpectedly) had the highest number of references to this term. In the sections below, I focus on more detailed qualitative analyses of these three terms.

## 4.1 *Transgender (community)*

The first term to be examined was *transgender*\*. The guidelines examined generally stated that *transgender* is an appropriate over-arching term for a range of different types of people. The GIRE guidelines note that 'transgenderism has had different meanings over time'.[6] The GLAAD guidelines state that *transgender* is appropriate as an adjective, e.g. 'X is transgender' or 'a transgender man'. They also state that *transgender* should not be used as a noun and the term *transgendered* should not be used either. Noun uses of terms like *transgender, black* and *gay* can be seen as problematic as they discursively essentialize and reduce a person to a single defining characteristic.

It was decided to first examine the frequencies of these different usages in the corpus. This was done via scrutinizing a concordance of the term *transgender*\*. A concordance is simply a table showing every citation of a search term in a corpus, within a few words of context either side. Concordances can be sorted alphabetically (e.g. one word to the left of the search word) in order to make patterns easier to identify, and they can be expanded so entire texts can be read.

The term *transgender** is almost always used in the corpus as an adjective with only one out of 405 cases occurring as an essentializing noun, although it refers to a non-human context:

> Comprehensive research has shown that even tiny concentrations of chemicals in such things as detergents, packaging, medications and even personal care products such as shampoo, as well as powerful drugs such as steroids and oral contraceptives, can combine to form cocktails of chemicals that can turn male fish into impotent *transgenders*.
>
> (*The Times*, 24 February 2012)

A larger number of instances of *transgendered* (34) appear in the corpus, spread across all of the newspapers apart from the *Express* and *The People*. None of these cases are referred to in the articles as being problematic, and some citations appear to be used in a way which could be interpreted as well-meaning e.g.:

> Start by contacting the Beaumont Society, who help transgendered people and their families.
>
> (*The Sun*, 17 March 2012)

A notable aspect of *transgender** is that it contains a semantic prosody (Louw, 1993) for support indicated by the collocates *communities, community, issues, equality, support, group, help* and *rights* in Table 9.3. None of these words collocate with any of the other search terms (apart from *rights* which also collocates with *transsexual**). As noted above, care must be taken not to over-interpret such collocates. Words like *help* and *support* may mostly relate to transgender people helping others or they may relate to transgender people being the recipients of help, or they may be used to mean something else. There is the possibility, for example, they may be used critically or sarcastically in individual articles. Thus, concordances of these collocational pairs need to be carefully read.

In eight out of nine cases the collocate *help* referred to transgender people as receiving help, while six out of seven cases of *support* referred to support groups for transgender people or them being offered support. On the surface, these collocates appear to be suggestive of positive representations – it is good to help people. However, the lack of cases which show *transgender** people as helping and supporting others (or themselves), perhaps indicates a somewhat limiting, if again well-meaning representation.

It was decided to examine *community* and *communities* in more detail as this was the only case where both the singular and plural forms of a word appeared as collocates, and was felt to be particularly salient. Additionally, in an earlier study I had examined the term *Muslim community* (Baker et al., 2013), and noted that some journalists used it in a critical way, so I felt it would be interesting to see if this was also the case for *transgender community*. A search of *transgender\* communit\** produced 34 concordance lines across eight newspapers (the *Mirror*, *the Observer* and the *People* did not use the term). Reading through the concordance lines, I began to group usages which referred to similar topics or suggested similar stances.

First, it was noted that 14 (41 per cent) of the references included the transgender community alongside other communities, usually gay, lesbian and/or bisexual:

> 'I don't consider civil partnerships less equal to marriage. There are other problems facing the gay, lesbian and transgender community.'
>
> (*The Sun*, 7 April 2012)

The popularity of this practice of joining together a range of identity groups who are viewed as having minority or diverse sexualities and/or genders, is sometimes signified by the acronym *LGBT*. One interpretation of this practice is that it indicates inclusivity – rather than merely focusing on equality-based issues around, say, gay men. However, it could also be argued that the appearance of the 'T' at the end of a list could be suggestive of a hierarchy, or could be seen as paying lip-service to inclusivity (this practice is not confined to the press). All of the 14 cases in the corpus place the transgender community at the end of the list. While this term is generally used uncritically, one journalist uses it in a sarcastic way:

> Good morning, ladies and gentlemen, not forgetting members of the Gay, Lesbian, Bisexual and Transgender community. This is Captain Cameron speaking, but you can call me Dave.
>
> (Richard Littlejohn, 16 March 2012)

In this article, Richard Littlejohn imagines that the British Prime Minister, David Cameron, has ordered his own plane but would have to share it with his coalition partners, the Liberal Democrats. In incongruously singling out LGBT people, one interpretation is that Littlejohn wants to imply that they receive special mention or consideration by the Coalition Government. Later in the article, the flight announcer says that the terms 'husband', 'wife', 'mother' and 'father' have been banned and that honeymooning same-sex couples will receive unlimited complimentary champagne. This article, in addition to the one about Lucy Meadows which inspired this research, suggests that Littlejohn has a particular problem with trans people as well as other groups.

However, Littlejohn is not a lone voice in the media. The theme of banned words also appears in four concordance lines about Brighton council apparently trying to ban titles, e.g.:

A CITY is proposing to ban titles such as Mr, Mrs, Miss and Ms in case they offend the transgender community.

(*Daily Mail*, 26 October 2012)

The phrase 'offend the transgender community' contributes towards a construction of this community in terms of its propensity for offence. An alternative wording such as 'A city is proposing a ban on titles in order to show sensitivity towards the transgender community' would not have placed the focus on offence. It is often useful to look beyond the concordance to gain an impression of the overall stance of the article, particularly in terms of who is quoted as part of the perspectivization of an article (Reisgl and Wodak, 2001: 81). For example, the *Daily Mail* article also quotes the Conservative Party who describe the proposal as 'ludicrous'. Similarly, an article on the same story in *The Telegraph* (26 October 2012) quotes a Conservative councillor as saying that the proposal is 'political correctness gone too far'. Both articles therefore appear to serve the function of painting the council as wrongheaded and the transgender community as offended over trivialities. However, an article in *The Guardian* (26 October 2012) suggests that the above newspapers had misinterpreted the story, noting that Brighton council had not banned titles but that tick boxes in forms which ask people to choose a gender e.g. *Mr, Mrs* or *Miss* would not be used. The use of verbs like *ban* and *offend* therefore suggest that some newspapers have exaggerated the story.

A similar use of *transgender community* relates to Oxford University allowing male students to wear skirts in exams. The article reports from the LGBT student union officer:

She said there was an active transgender community 'in Oxford, and every member she had spoken to had found sub-fusc, under the old regulations, to be stressful'.

(*Mail on Sunday*, 29 June 2012)

This article also provides quotes from an unnamed student who describes the change as 'unnecessary', as well as seeking the opinion of an alumni student, the former Conservative MP Anne Widdicombe, who is quoted as saying it will save 'a silly row' and noting 'If men want to prance around in skirts, that is entirely up to them'. While Widdicombe is not against the decision, her use of lexis like *silly* and *prance* could be interpreted as dismissive and patronizing towards trans people.

Even in left-leaning newspapers, there are understated indications that the transgender community needs to be negotiated. For example, the actress Chloë Sevigny is reported as playing a 'transgender hitman' in a new British drama, and she is quoted as saying:

'I was afraid of the pressure from the gay community or the transgender community and how they would feel, and wanting to be respectful.'

(*The Guardian*, 19 May 2012)

One reading of the above statement is that the actress wants to be respectful. However, the suggestion that she is afraid of pressure from the transgender community contributes towards a perception of the transgender community as having the ability to cause pressure (which is something to be afraid of).

Another subtle indication of this discourse is in the following article which begins:

> Here's a trenchant headline for you: 'Transgender community celebrates "great diversity of gender identity" in new book.'
>
> (Damian Thompson, *Daily Telegraph*, 28 July 2012)

It is notable that it is the headline rather than the transgender community which is described as *trenchant*, although it is possible to interpret the word as still being associated with that community. To gain a better idea about the meanings and associations of the word *trenchant*, I explored its usage in the 100 million word British National Corpus (BNC) which contains general English. The BNC had 63 cases of *trenchant*, of which 14 have *critic(s), criticism(s)* or *critique* in the L1 (one place to the left) position. Other L1 words include *opposition, dislike, dismissal* and *attack*. I would suggest then, that *trenchant* contains a semantic prosody for strong criticism and the use of this word in the *Telegraph* article helps to contribute towards a more subtle representation of the transgender community as being critical of things. A related representation is found in *The Guardian* via the use of *assertive*.

> The householder who answers grins nervously at Nargis, who is a 'hijra' – a member of Pakistan's increasingly assertive transgender community.
>
> (*The Guardian*, 9 June 2012)

These references to different transgender communities as having the capacity for offence, causing pressure, being assertive or implicitly trenchant indicates that the press collectively view such a community as a force to be reckoned with, although individual journalists place a different political slant on this. This representation of the transgender community is not unique. I found an almost identical construction when looking at the term *Muslim community* (Baker et al., 2013), while sections of the British press view gay rights groups as politically militant (Baker, 2005), and Jaworksa and Krishnamurthy (2012: 404) have noted that the terms *feminism* and *feminist(s)* collocate with *radical, militant* and *raging*. Within conservative discourse it is therefore a common legitimation strategy, to paint a minority or oppressed group as (too) easily offended, over-reacting with anger and thus in receipt of undeserving special treatment, often classed as 'political correctness gone too far'. It is also notable that the more negative references to the *transgender community* do not specifically refer to people by name, making it more difficult to attribute actual offence (or denial of offence) to anybody. Let us move on to another term to see if it contains similar patterns of representation around it.

## 4.2 Transsexual*

There were 320 occurrences of *transsexual** in the corpus, the second most frequent search term after *transgender**. Joanna Darrell, writing for The Beaumont Society, notes that 'Some people consider this term derogatory because the word 'sexual' is part of the term',[7] although the GLAAD guidelines do not note the word as being problematic. Table 9.3 shows that apart from *rights*, there were no collocates which seemed to directly relate transsexuals to equality or support. Instead, the collocates *pre* and *op* (occurring together 26 times) referred to pre op transsexuals (who had not had surgery). The term *post-op transsexual* only occurred once in the corpus. In some parts of the corpus there appears to be particular fascination with the sexual organs of transsexual people, particularly people who retain sexual organs they were born with, while living as a member of the opposite sex:

> I'm confronted by a transsexual with a huge penis. "Someone sent me a photo of a tranny", he says, sheepishly. Wow! I say. Is that genuine?
>
> (*The Guardian*, 21 April 2012)

> I realise that this is the acid test of a successful transsexual, but even when Mia showed us her penis in the shower (credits for prosthetics artist and prosthetics supervisor were well earned), it was a hard one to swallow, if you'll pardon the inescapable metaphor.
>
> (*The Observer*, 27 May 2012)

The first example above is notable for the rewording of *tranny* as *transsexual*. The journalist distances himself from *tranny* but still prints it when quoting the interviewee, as well as using the verb *confronted* to describe the photograph, which implies that the person in the picture is intimidating (perhaps linking through to the earlier discourse around transgendered community as quick to take offence). This small excerpt also discursively exoticizes and 'others' trans people as a shared object of fascination for the interviewee, interviewer and presumably the audience. The second example uses a pun about oral sex: 'hard one to swallow' again, in focusing on the genitalia of *transsexual** people, and positioning them discursively as part of a joke.

As with *transgender**, the collocates *gay* and *lesbian* (seven and five times each as collocates) indicated the presence of *transsexual(s)* as occurring at the end of a list of other identity groups. The collocates *assassin* (12) and *hitman* (5) refer to the story mentioned above about the actress Chloë Sevigny playing a transsexual hitman in a television drama. Additionally, *character* (5) refers to either the hitman or a transsexual character in the soap opera Coronation Street. The collocate *soldier* (7) refers to a reality television programme called Mother Truckers which looks at the lives of female lorry drivers and includes 'Vikki, a former soldier and transsexual who wants to be treated as one of the girls – or boys' (*The Times*, 9 February 2012). Another collocate *dancers* (8), refers to a story about opposition to a proposed lap dancing club in a town (note how the word 'even' positions transsexual dancers as particularly problematic):

He has now provoked fresh debate by putting up a notice in the proposed club advertising for male, female, homosexual, transvestite and even transsexual dancers.
(*Daily Telegraph*, 2 July 2012)

Perhaps what is notable about these collocates is that they represent transsexual* people as either being fictional characters and/or appearing in contexts that are designed to entertain members of the public. This appears to be different to transgender* which tends to be used on 'real' or non-entertaining people. Transsexual people thus appear to be represented as more exotic or unreal compared to transgendered people.

An important distinction with *transsexual** is that it can be used as either a noun or an adjective as shown in the following two examples:

It's estimated between 5 and 10 million women worldwide have had the surgery, many for cosmetic reasons, and a significant proportion for reconstruction following a mastectomy, or *for transsexual people* transitioning from male to female.
(*The Guardian*, 12 January 2012)

The Met now has four *transsexuals* – who have had ops – and eight hermaphrodites, born a mix of male and female.
(*The Sun*, 4 June 2012)

As with *transgender*, it could be argued that using *transsexual** as an adjective is a more sensitive strategy in that it implies that trans status is one aspect of a person's identity, whereas the noun usage reduces a person to that single trait.

I examined the 313 cases of *transsexual(s)* in the corpus and noted where they were nouns or verbs. Table 9.4 shows the frequencies across each newspaper. Collectively, well over half of the cases of *transsexual(s)* in the British press occur as essentializing nouns, and this figure is particularly high for two right-leaning tabloids, *The Star* and *The Sun*. However, it is perhaps surprising to see the left-leaning *The Guardian* as also having a relatively high proportion of such cases (2 in 3).

One way of analysing representation is to consider the verb processes which occur around the term *transsexual(s)*, either describing people as engaging in or having actions done to them. Concordance analyses were carried out of the term and verb processes are summarized in Table 9.5, which identifies processes that position transsexual people as either the agent (actor) or patient (acted upon). Similar processes have been grouped together.

Table 9.5 shows the term *transsexual(s)* as involved with a range of different types of activities, some of which can be linked together. For example, the representation of this group of people as victims, either of prejudice or of physical violence, perhaps

**Table 9.4**    Noun vs. adjective uses of *transsexual(s)*

| Newspaper | Noun | Adjective | Total | Preference for noun |
|-----------|------|-----------|-------|---------------------|
| Star | 15 | 2 | 17 | 88% |
| Sun | 33 | 14 | 47 | 70% |
| Guardian | 37 | 18 | 55 | 67% |
| Times | 28 | 15 | 43 | 65% |
| Express | 12 | 7 | 19 | 63% |
| Independent | 11 | 10 | 21 | 52% |
| Telegraph | 19 | 18 | 37 | 51% |
| Observer | 16 | 17 | 33 | 48% |
| Mail | 13 | 19 | 32 | 41% |
| Mirror | 3 | 5 | 8 | 38% |
| People | 0 | 1 | 1 | 0% |
| Total | 187 | 126 | 313 | 60% |

**Table 9.5**    Verb processes positioning transsexual people as agent or patient

| Construction | As agent | As patient |
|--------------|----------|------------|
| As victim | told tales of rejection and sexual mortification, led a hard life, born and grow up alone, can't find work, claims male lorry drivers bully her | killed, persecuted, stir up hatred against, targeted, raped, found by the side of the road |
| As aggressor/ criminal | abducts his long-lost rent-boy son, works as a contract killer, used someone else's name, working for an underground gang boss, harassing her neighbour | imprisoned, arrested, jailed, having her 19th allegation of rape investigated, accused of killing, ordered to do community service, had her punishment reduced |
| Receiving help | get psychotherapy | treated for problems, offered understanding and support |
| (Struggle for) equality | held equality placards, reveals her struggle for acceptance, wants to be accepted, wants to be one of the girls, fight for official acceptance, won a campaign to enter a beauty contest, suing health bosses, gaining recognition as a protected group | allowed to choose their sex |

| Gaining acceptance and positive appraisal | won Eurovision | celebrated, welcomed, praised in parliament, honoured, openly accepted in Thailand, voted as a winner |
|---|---|---|
| Having surgery or other procedures | preparing for a sex change, transitioning from male to female, had ops, saving up for an operation, awaiting an operation, paid £60,000 to achieve the perfect look, forked out a fortune on hair transplants, undergo genital surgery | features have been surgically altered, raise funds for a sex change |
| Having relationships | has a fling, dated, running off with a priest | had an affair with, met online, met on holiday |
| Labelled or grouped | | labelled, pictured by people, counting the number of |
| Angry | upset, offend, complaining | |
| Commanding attention | likes to be centre of attention, erupt in bizarre scenes, sparked controversy, command headlines, confronted | |
| In work | ran a club, pay taxes, took up lorry-driving, waves a hairdryer | |
| Is a parent | discovers she is a father, gave birth | |

helps to explain the presence of other categories for receiving help, struggling for equality and gaining acceptance and approval. It is perhaps notable that in the 'struggle for equality' category, most of the verb processes position the term *transsexual(s)* as the agent, e.g. they are the ones who are struggling for equality, others are not trying to do this on their behalf. However, in terms of gaining acceptance and approval, this is mainly something which others bestow on them. Perhaps this is not surprising: transsexual people are not represented as having to accept themselves, but the overarching narrative indicates that their acceptance and equal rights are something that others can grant them, rather than them being able to take such matters for granted. It is perhaps also unsurprising to see a number of processes related to having surgery, although critically we might question whether the focus on undergoing surgery (noting also the collocate *pre-op*) detracts from other aspects of the lives of transsexual people and indicates what some people may view as intrusive curiosity about whether or not surgery has or will take place.

Alongside representations of transsexual people as victims, it is perhaps more surprising to see them represented as aggressors or criminals. Three such cases are shown below.

The pre-op transsexual, who was jailed for sex offences, wears his hair in pigtails and must be called 'Miss' by staff, who can be disciplined if they refuse.

(*Mirror*, 11 November 2012)

A TRANSSEXUAL who was ordered to do community service in a graveyard after harassing her neighbour has had her punishment reduced after complaining that the lawnmower she had to push was too heavy.

(*Daily Telegraph*, 24 May 2012)

A TRANSSEXUAL is having her NINETEENTH allegation of rape investigated by police. The woman, in her 30s, has so far cost taxpayers £200,000 over the past ten years. But Scotland Yard is refusing to say if any of her complaints have resulted in conviction.

(*The Sun*, 15 April 2012)

These three stories all represent individual transsexual people negatively. The first two refer to crimes committed by transsexual people, while the third one strongly implies that the transsexual person is wasting police time and taxpayers' money by making repeated false accusations of rape. It might be asked whether the fact that the accuser is 'a transsexual' is relevant to that story, although it should be noted that the Press Complaints Commission Code of Practice section 12ii cites that 'Details of an individual's race, colour, religion, sexual orientation, physical or mental illness or disability must be avoided unless genuinely relevant to the story'. This list does not explicitly include gender. All of the stories also refer back to a representation mentioned earlier, that of trans people as either complaining and/or being given special treatment that they do not deserve.

Two other categories in Table 9.5 were encountered in the earlier analysis of *transgender**: Angry and Receiving Help, and concordance analyses reveal that the verb processes associated with them contribute to previously mentioned representations relating to transgender people as needing special treatment in case they are offended and transgender people being the recipients of help and support. Two categories that have not been encountered before are 'Commanding Attention' and 'Having Relationships'. The first one represents transsexual people as either drawing attention to themselves or attracting it in other ways.

It is thought to be only the fourth case of its kind in the world, and comes four years after American transsexual Thomas Beatie, 38, sparked controversy by announcing his pregnancy.

(*Mail on Sunday*, 19 February 2012)

. . . transsexual Luke who 'likes to be the centre of attention' . . .

(*The Sun*, 12 June 2012)

It's odd that a transsexual punk can still command headlines, when Grace appears to inhabit a world more relaxed about the matter than almost any I can think of.

(*The Guardian*, 23 July 2012)

The 'Having relationships' category is interesting because the verb processes here do not seem to imply long-term or stable relationships: *has a fling, dated, running off with a priest, had an affair with, met online, met on holiday.* Instead they imply impermanence while a couple of cases suggest extra-marital relationships. Verb processes such as *married, settled down with* or *entered into a relationship* do not tend to appear in the immediate vicinity of *transsexual\**.

## 4.3 *Tranny*

The final search term I want to explore in more detail is a more informal term: *tranny* (sometimes spelt as *trannie* – from this point I mainly use *tranny* to refer to both). In the British press this term is usual meant as a shortened version of *transvestite*, although sometimes can refer to *transsexual* or *transgender*.

This term is sometimes considered pejorative: the Gay & Lesbian Alliance against Defamation (GLAAD) write:

What words are offensive to transgender people? These words should not be used: 'transvestite,' 'she-male,' 'he-she,' 'it,' 'trannie,' 'tranny,' and 'shim.' These words are dehumanizing, and using them to refer to any person is similar to using an anti-gay epithet

http://www.glaad.org/transgender

GLAAD's stance on *tranny* has been criticized by a number of high-profile people, including the actress Susan Sarandon[8] (reported in the *New York Daily News*, 9 November 2010) and the female impersonator RuPaul (reported in the *Dallas Voice*, 28 June 2009).[9] It is possible that some people could use the term in a reclaimed way or associate it with positive traits. With those points in mind, how is *tranny* used in the British national press?

With just 53 occurrences in the corpus and only four collocates which were all high frequency grammatical words (*a, and, in, the*), a different technique needed to be used in order to identify patterns of representation around *tranny*. This was achieved by reading concordance lines and grouping those which appeared to be contributing towards similar sorts of representations (shown below). None of the groups of concordance lines were particularly frequent, but with such a small amount of data, this would perhaps be expected.

The first pattern related to a representation of *tranny* negatively, either by implying or stating that looking like a tranny is bad and associated with poor style or theatricality.

I hate that tranny look, and the programme painted Liverpool in such a bitchy, bad light.

(*Sunday Times*, 2 December 2012)

The cast was fine, particularly Eileen Atkins, as ever reminding us what a tranny panto turn Maggie Smith has become.

(*Sunday Times*, 16 September 2012, A. A. Gill)

By the way, every pair of shoes you've bought in the past year is hideous. Great, clumpy, round-toed platform things – ghastly. They look like a tranny centaur night out.

(*Sunday Times*, 16 September 2012, A. A. Gill)

Some of the articles referred to a female pop star called Jessie J who identified as bisexual during a radio interview in 2011[10]:

To combat this, next series they're going to keep Jessie J in a centrifuge machine like an inarticulate tranny kaleidoscope.

(*The Sun*, 21 December 2012)

Jessie J was described as wanting to dispel rumours or change her style:

POP princess Jessie J wants to change her trademark style because she looks like a tranny.

(*Daily Star*, 30 May 2012)

Being ages in the toilet isn't going to help Jessie dispel rumours she's a tranny.

(*The Sun*, 29 June 2012)

As well as a potential conflation of the pop star's bisexual identity with a trans identity (a kind of double 'othering'), these articles imply that 'trannys' are generally seen as unsuccessful at 'passing' as a member of the opposite sex, and that to look like a tranny is therefore bad. However, one article was more positive about this apparent style of clothing, describing it as 'chic' and 'bang on trend'.

TRANNY CHIC – Chiffon shirts, high-waisted jeans – Chloë Sevigny's preop transsexual wardrobe in Hit and Miss is bang on trend

(*Sunday Times*, 10 June 2012)

A second set of articles related to the previously discovered representation of trans people as being given unnecessary special treatment, sometimes linked to them as prone to take offence:

Fake trannies are 'offensive'. STUDENTS have been told not to cross-dress for fun on nights out.

(*Daily Star*, 23 February 2012)

Kids, 4 labelled trannies. BARMY watchdogs have praised school bosses who label children as young as four 'transgender'.

(*Daily Star*, 20 June 2012)

Watchdog slaps ban on bookie tranny ad.

(*Daily Star*, 24 February 2012)

A third set (comprising just two cases), positions trannies as part of somewhat outlandish social groups, and implies that they are the object of entertainment for a viewing audience. The use of 'freaks' in the first example below is notable for its association with circus entertainment.

Priceless footage depicts the wide-eyed, gurning night owls, 'tranny freaks' and trustafarians who gravitate to Shangri-La.

(*The Guardian*, 9 June 2012)

A series by Katy Grannan, of portraits taken on the streets of San Francisco, is absorbing – Grannan's stark light and sharp focus picks out every flaw in the sagging bodies of her old bikers, thinning trannies and over-dressed eccentrics.You want to know their stories.

(*The Times*, 5 May 2012)

Two other cases associate trannies with celebrity 'sex romps' as part of a tabloid discourse found only in the *Daily Star*.

X FACTOR hit a new low when wannabes went on a sex-crazed rampage. Rylan Clark romped with a tranny on a dancefloor, then ran naked through streets.

(*Daily Star*, 16 October 2012)

FURIOUS Chantelle Houghton last night claimed ex Alex Reid had tranny romps and a sex dungeon.

(*Daily Star*, 31 October 2012)

As described above, a pattern was found where the term *transsexual** was associated with transient or extra-marital relationships, and the references to 'romps' with trannies seems to contribute to this overall representation.

Being a tranny or being interested in them is also viewed as a source of fear and worry, particularly within the context of *The Sun*'s Dear Deidre advice column:

Tranny fear – Dear Deidre I HAVE a girlfriend who I love very much but I'm fascinated by pornography involving transsexuals.

(*The Sun*, 8 November 2012)

SHOULD I ADMIT I'M TRANNY?; Dear Deidre

(*The Sun*, 16 July 2012)

Additionally, two *Daily Mirror* articles refer to biological aspects in order to make jokes:

It's difficult to win a BAFTA for a one-off performance but Bean is so convincing as a tranny you'd swear he had both off.

(*Daily Mirror*, 14 August 2012)

Hills laid Accused writer Jimmy McGovern's £100 bet at 12–1 for a Bean Bafta but, after watching the rough cut – that's tonight's episode, not McGovern's barnet – wanted to quickly slash those odds to evens. That was a surprise – in full tranny clobber a quick slash ain't easy.

(*Daily Mirror*, 14 August 2012)

In the first example, a word play joke is made by linking the 'one-off performance' of an actor who played a tranny, with the somewhat reductive term 'both off' (most likely referring to the actor's testicles). In the second article, there is word play around the word *slash*, first used to mean cutting (the odds), but then as a British slang term for urination.

Three more potentially positive representations of trannies were also found in the corpus. One was in *The Times* by the television reviewer, A. A. Gill (whose consistent use of *tranny* as noted in some of the above articles was the reason for the relatively high frequency of this word in *The Times*).

Behind the pearls and eyelashes, Perry is a cultured and clever trannie, possibly one of the most cultured and clever transvestites this country has ever produced. On camera, he is able to organise complex and abstract thoughts, and explain them with an unpatrician clarity, without art snobbery.

(*The Sunday Times*, 10 June 2012)

While this article could be interpreted as associating the artist and television presenter Grayson Perry with positive traits (*cultured, clever*), there are other structures in the sentence which are perhaps less positive. For example, Gill prefaces his praise of Grayson with the phrase 'beneath the pearls and eyelashes' which implies that Grayson's appearance does not indicate that he would be cultured and clever. Grayson is thus constructed as the exceptional case, rather than being typical. Added to that is the fact that groups like GLAAD consider *trannie* to be pejorative in itself, as well as

Gill's use of terms like *tranny panto* and *tranny centaur night out* in other articles cited above, which also imply that he uses the term mockingly.

A couple of other articles are more straightforwardly positive:

I heard about a fun run involving a record-breaking number of trannies flying the flag for floral frocks, big wigs and preventing prostate cancer.

(*The Sunday Times*, 22 July 2012)

But, on Canal Street, Bean learnt the many motivations for transvestism. 'I met some trannies who were doing it for a laugh and some because they were seriously considering transexual surgery. There were others whose wives and girlfriends enjoyed it and even went shopping for clothes with them. Tracie's story is not supposed to be atypical. There is no typical story.'

(*The Times*, 11 August 2012)

The first article describes trannies as raising money for charity while the second implies that trannies are diverse: 'there is no typical story', and notes that some wives and girlfriends view trannies positively. However, these more positive representations are clearly in the minority, amid a range of more negative ones.

# 5 Conclusion

The analytical techniques I used did not uncover articles that matched Julie Burchill's article in terms of being so strongly derogatory towards trans people as a group, nor did they find any which made an explicitly judgemental attack on a single named trans person, as Richard Littlejohn's article did. These two articles appear to represent an extreme position on a continuum of press disapproval. However, the analysis did find a great deal of evidence to support the view that trans people are regularly represented in reasonably large sections of the press as receiving special treatment lest they be offended, as victims or villains, as involved in transient relationships or sex scandals, as the object of jokes about their appearance or sexual organs and as attention-seeking freakish objects. There were a scattering of more positive representations but they were not as easy to locate and tended to appear as isolated cases, rather than occurring repeatedly as trends. Therefore, the claims about trans people being a 'whipping girl' for the British press, cited by Jane Fae in the introduction to this chapter, appear to be borne out by the analysis. The lack of reference to trans people in the PCC Code appears to have resulted in a particularly negative set of representations overall.

As this chapter was meant to be illustrative of corpus techniques rather than comprising a full analysis, it cannot fully do justice to the question of whether the British press are institutionally transphobic. Future research would involve a more detailed examination of the other search terms and their collocates, as well as considering other linguistic ways of representing trans people, for example, by looking at pronoun choice, the use of distancing quotes around certain terms or legitimation strategies, topoi and argumentative fallacies that repeatedly occur in the texts. Analysis of photographs used alongside articles would also add a visual dimension to complement the corpus analysis.

Despite the partial analysis shown here, I hope that this chapter has demonstrated some of the advantages of using corpus techniques from a critical discourse analysis perspective. For CDA, I would advocate that corpus analysis works best when combined with a range of approaches which consider context in various ways. This often involves interrogation of the linguistic context around particular words in a text via concordance lines or reading full articles, but it should also involve consideration of the social practices around texts – in this case, examination of the PCC Code of Practice and other guidelines written by trans-friendly organizations. Corpus approaches thus offer a good balance between quantitative and qualitative analyses, although it should be remembered that while corpus analysis involves computers doing much of the spade-work of analysis, it remains up to humans to interpret, explain and evaluate the patterns that are presented.

# Notes

1 http://www.guardian.co.uk/society/2013/mar/22/lucy-meadows-press-harassment Accessed 16th July 2014

2 http://www.guardian.co.uk/uk/2013/may/28/lucy-meadows-coroner-press-shame Accessed 16th July 2014

3 Due to the ineffectiveness of the PCC in responding to complaints about journalists hacking the telephone voicemails of high profile people, in December 2011 it was announced that it would be disbanded, although in early 2013 this had not yet taken place.

4 http://www.independent.co.uk/voices/comment/burchills-attack-follows-the-same-pattern--trans-stories-are-only-of-interest-if-we-star-as-villains-8449812.html Accessed 16th July 2014

5 The Leveson Inquiry was a judicial public enquiry into the ethics, culture and practice of the British press as a result of a telephone hacking scandal.

6 http://www.gires.org.uk/assets/Schools/TransphobicBullying.pdf Accessed 16th July 2014

7 http://www.beaumontsociety.org.uk/Help%20&%20advice/Beaumont%20Training/Transgender%20diversity%20training%209%20-%20transphobia.pdf Accessed 16th July 2014

8 http://www.nydailynews.com/entertainment/gossip/word-susan-sarandon-doesn-problem-glee-ful-tranny-article-1.453038 Accessed 16th July 2014

9 http://www.dallasvoice.com/rupaul-approves-tranny-1018688.html Accessed 16th July 2014

10 http://www.mtv.co.uk/news/jessie-j/259667-jessie-j-bisexual-dates-girls-and-boys Accessed 16th July 2014

# References

Anthony, L. (2013), AntConc (Version 3.2.4w) [Computer Software]. Tokyo, Japan: Waseda University. Available at http://www.antlab.sci.waseda.ac.jp/

Baker, P. (2005), *Public Discourses of Gay Men*. London: Routledge.

—— (2006), *Using Corpora in Discourse Analysis*. London: Continuum.

Baker, P, Gabrielatos, G. and McEnery, T. (2013), *Discourse Analysis and Media Bias: The Representation of Islam in the British Press*. Cambridge: Cambridge University Press.

Baker, P., Gabrielatos, C., KhosraviNik, M., Krzyzanowski, M., McEnery, T and Wodak, R. (2008), 'A useful methodological synergy? Combining critical discourse analysis and corpus linguistics to examine discourses of refugees and asylum seekers in the UK press'. *Discourse and Society*, 19(3), 273–306.

Fairclough, N. (1989), *Language and Power*. Harlow: Longman.

Hardt-Mautner, G. (1995), *Only Connect. Critical Discourse Analysis and Corpus Linguistics*. UCREL Technical paper 5. Lancaster University.

Hoey, M. (2005), *Lexical Priming. A New Theory of Words and Language*. London: Routledge.

Hunston, S. (2002), *Corpora in Applied Linguistics*. Cambridge: Cambridge University Press.

Jaworksa, S. and Krishnamurthy, R. (2012), 'On the F word: a corpus based analysis of the media representation of feminism in British and German press discourse'. *Discourse and Society*, 23(4), 401–31.

Louw, B. (1993), 'Irony in the text or insincerity in the writer? – The diagnostic potential of semantic prosodies', in M. Baker, G. Francis and E. Tognini-Bonelli (eds), *Text and Technology: In Honour of John Sinclair*. Amsterdam and Philadelphia: John Benjamins, pp. 157–76.

Mautner, G. (2007), 'Mining large corpora for social information: the case of *elderly*'. *Language in Society*, 36, 51–72.

McEnery, T., Xiao, R. and Tono, Y. (2006), *Corpus-Based Language Studies: An Advanced Resource Book*. London: Routledge.

Partington, A. (2003), *The Linguistics of Political Argument*. London: Routledge.

Reisigl, M. and Wodak, R. (2001), *Discourse and Discrimination: Rhetorics of Racism and Antisemitism*. London: Routledge.

Stubbs, M. (1996), *Text and Corpus Analysis*. London: Blackwell.

Trans Media Watch (2011), *The British Press and the Transgender Community. Submission to The Leveson Inquiry into the culture, practice and ethics of the press*. London: BM TMW.

# 10

## Digital Argument Deconstruction

## An Ethical Software-Assisted Critical Discourse Analysis for Highlighting Where Arguments Fall Apart

*Kieran O'Halloran*

King's College London

## 1 Introduction

### *1.1 Orientation*

I highlight and model a recent practical form of critical discourse analysis (CDA) that I have developed and which is aimed at undergraduates. I refer to it as *digital argument deconstruction*. This approach helps to establish critical purchase on arguments in the public sphere that attack the standpoint of a relatively powerless Other, particularly when readers might not know this standpoint so well. The strategy enables the analyst to see where an argument might be distorting the standpoint of the relatively powerless other that it criticizes. It draws on corpus linguistic method – the analysis of collections of electronic texts – as well as recent affordances of the World Wide Web.

Crucially, this practical form of CDA involves the analyst evaluating the argument from the perspective of a relatively powerless Other. Adopting a 'surrogate subjectivity', the analyst ascertains whether or not an argument distorts the standpoint of the relatively powerless which it criticizes. In turn, the analyst explores whether or not this results in the cohesive structure of the argument – how the text of the argument ties together through its vocabulary and grammar – falling apart or 'deconstructing'. An argument's credibility and capacity to persuade are, amongst a number of things, dependent on effective cohesion. Showing where an argument's cohesion deconstructs because of such distortion thus diminishes its credibility. In other words, digital argument deconstruction highlights a penalty for an argument should an author distort the Other's standpoint. In contrast to other forms of practical CDA, digital argument deconstruction has a pronounced *ethical* emphasis though the ethical and the political can be related as I show.

In the last few years, one technological innovation of the World Wide Web has been the appending of electronic discussion forums to online texts. The facility allows readers to post responses to a text and to debate issues raised in it. Discussion forums are particularly salient in online newspapers, and especially following argumentative texts such as editorials and opinion pieces. Digital argument deconstruction sees a discussion forum of online comments as a conveniently useful supplement to the preceding argument. The strategy uses corpus linguistic method to extract useful information from this digital supplementation. This information helps highlight where the argument may have distorted the standpoint of the relatively powerless it criticizes which, in turn, leads to its cohesion falling apart from the perspective of the relatively powerless Other. In essence, looking at the argument through the lens of the digital supplement can facilitate a critical reading of it. As this approach to critical reading of arguments uses corpus linguistic method and digital social media, and is deconstructive in ethos, this is why I call it digital argument deconstruction.

## 1.2 *Organization*

In the next section, I explain in detail how digital argument deconstruction works as well as a technique of corpus linguistic analysis which it employs. A theoretical stimulus for this practical approach is an idea from the French philosopher, Jacques Derrida. In Section 3, I highlight how a discussion forum can be viewed as a supplement to the preceding argument in a sense akin to Derrida's conception of the supplement. Looked at in this way, the discussion forum can be shown to destabilize the structure of the argument. Section 4 includes the argument I examine to illustrate digital argument deconstruction. This argument criticizes the so-called 'new atheism' associated with intellectuals such as Richard Dawkins and Daniel Dennett. Section 4 also includes corpus linguistic analysis of the discussion forum which supplements this argument. On this basis, in Section 5 I demonstrate how critical purchase on the argument is facilitated. Finally, in Section 6, I reflect on the deconstructive analysis and flag the benefits of the approach. I also draw out the ethical dimension to digital argument deconstruction, and indicate how this relates to the political.

# 2 Digital argument deconstruction

## 2.1 Otherness, the World Wide Web and CDA

CDA investigates how language use may be affirming and indeed reproducing the perspectives, values and ways of talking of the relatively powerful, which may not be in the interests of the relatively powerless.[1] Crucial to CDA is a focus on the relationship between language, power and ideology. CDA consists of an interdisciplinary set of approaches which attempt to describe, interpret and explain this relationship. In CDA, 'critical' is usually taken to mean studying and taking issue with how dominance and inequality are reproduced through language use:

> . . . CDA research combines what perhaps somewhat pompously used to be called 'solidarity with the oppressed' with an attitude of opposition and dissent against those who abuse text and talk in order to establish, confirm or legitimate their abuse of power. Unlike much other scholarship, CDA does not deny but explicitly defines and defends its own socio-political position. That is CDA is biased – and proud of it.
>
> Van Dijk (2001: 96)

The aim of CDA is *political* – to ameliorate discourse which contributes to the reproduction of social inequality (Fairclough, 1989: 1; Chouliaraki and Fairclough, 1999: 32–33). Critique of text in CDA is ultimately guided by the analyst's political subjectivity with opposes socio-political inequality.

With the advent of the World Wide Web, and particularly where user-generated content is possible, in my opinion there is much potential for doing something different: *using digital tools to ascertain the key foci/concerns of a relatively powerless Other, and in a convenient and rigorous manner*. Digital argument deconstruction taps into this newer opportunity for practical critical engagement with argument, indeed to *drive* such engagement without the traditional usage of descriptive metalanguages such as systemic functional grammar in pedagogically-oriented CDA.[2] Critique of argument in digital argument deconstruction is powered from the perspective of the relatively powerless Other. It means, in effect, that the analyst takes on a non-pre-formed *surrogate subjectivity*. As I elaborate in section 6, the surrogate subjectivity is an ethical subjectivity.

## 2.2 The dialectical dimension of argumentation

I have not yet said what I mean by 'argument'. Here is a definition by the argumentation theorist, Douglas Walton, which I follow. To say something is a successful 'argument' for Walton (2006: 1):

[. . .] means that it gives good reason, or several reasons, to support or criticize a claim [. . .] there are always two sides to an argument, and thus the argument takes the form of a dialogue [. . .]. The basic purpose of offering an argument is to give a reason (or more than one) to support a claim that is subject to doubt, and thereby remove that doubt.

Walton's definition above recognises both the logical dimension to argument (the giving of reasons) and the dialectical dimension to argument. Dialectic refers to the dialogical exchange structure in a debate as well as the rules which govern how participants respond to one another. Dialectic is fairly obvious in a formal face-to-face debate – whether real or virtual. In written argument, dialectic is reflected in how the arguer is in critical dialogue with an opposing standpoint, anticipating its objections.

In contemporary argumentation studies, a prominent dialectical approach is *pragma-dialectics* (Van Eemeren and Grootendorst, 2004). On this model, participants employ argumentation to test the acceptability of each other's standpoints. This is done by adhering to rules which govern the argumentation. If any of these rules is flouted, the argumentation is regarded as unreasonable. Pragma-dialectics is then a normative perspective on argumentation. One of its norms is that participants must not distort the other party's position – what is known as the *standpoint rule*:

> Attacks on standpoints may not bear on a standpoint that has not actually been put forward by the other party.
>
> Van Eemeren and Grootendorst (2004: 191)

If an arguer flouts this rule then their argument is fallacious. It is what is commonly known as a 'straw man fallacy' – i.e., the arguer has erected a distorted representation of their opponent to then easily knock it down.[3]

## 2.3  *Digital argument deconstruction, dialectic and cohesive structure*

Digital argument deconstruction accords with the standpoint rule of pragma-dialectics. Meaningful and rational debate cannot be achieved if arguers do not represent each other's standpoints accurately. It is, usually, for this reason that straw man arguments are rejected. But, since digital argument deconstruction is a form of critical discourse analysis, it sees misrepresentation of the standpoint of the relatively powerless as helping to sustain the existing status quo. If the audience of the written argument is not very familiar with its topic, they may be unaware of the 'other side' of the argument. They might be swayed by its criticism of the opposition's standpoint when, in fact, it is a straw man. Or, if they are not swayed by the argument, at least they are not in a position to appreciate its distortion.

The initial move in digital argument deconstruction develops the reader's knowledge so that they can see how the 'other side' describes itself, how the relatively powerless which is criticized normally represents its standpoint. (Henceforth, 'SotC' refers to 'Standpoint of the Criticized'). In turn, this would allow the reader to ascertain whether or not the argument that they have selected is responding to accurate SotC representations. A basic assumption of this strategy is that if it can be proved that the argument has distorted how the relatively powerless criticized usually represents its standpoint, this may lead to deconstruction of the argument's cohesive structure. This is particularly the case if the argument's author has not indicated convincingly why they have avoided this usage. Generating knowledge of accurate SotC representations, in digital argument deconstruction, is aided by recent digital conditions.

## 2.4 Using a discussion forum to effect comparison with a preceding argument

The innovation, in recent years, of discussion forums which succeed on-line arguments is a convenient source for a new and potentially useful form of comparison – particularly useful for a reader who does not know SotC so well: seeing the degree to which the arguer responds to representations of SotC found in the forum. The greater the volume of posts, the greater the chance that the forum will contain contributions which are knowledgeable about SotC, and thus describe it accurately, because i) posters empathize with SotC; ii) posters are knowledgeable about SotC even if they disagree with it. In turn, should the preceding argument not respond to accurate SotC representations, the greater the chance the analyst is alerted to this via the comparison.[4]

What if the analyst finds that the argument does not frame the position it criticizes using SotC representations which are predominantly used in the forum? After such a conveniently illuminated discrepancy, it would then be worth going to the trouble to do the following: checking with another source to see whether or not the SotC representations mostly used in the forum are accurate.

## 2.5 Keyword mining

The comparison between argument and discussion forum is facilitated by use of corpus linguistic text mining software. Corpus linguistics is the branch of linguistics concerned with analysis of collections of electronic texts ('corpora').[5] The digital argument deconstruction of this chapter uses a text mining technique developed in corpus linguistics. This is called *keyword* analysis. A keyword is a word which occurs '[. . .] with unusual frequency in a given text [. . .] by comparison with a reference corpus' (Scott, 1997: 236). A *reference corpus* is a large electronic collection of texts from the same language which has been sampled across a variety of genres. Because of this, a reference corpus is seen as a representative snapshot of a language, a norm of language use.

Keywords are established through statistical measures such as log likelihood (see Dunning, 1993). Importantly, the log likelihood value, as a statistical measure, reduces arbitrariness in what is selected as salient. I must emphasize that keyword analysis should not only be quantitative – keywords would also need to be qualitatively explored in the texts of a discussion forum to understand their usage.[6]

## 2.6  Why is keyword analysis of a discussion forum useful?

Keyword analysis of the discussion forum following an online argument can help establish concepts which are habitually used in the SotC. Focusing on the highest keywords returns the critical mass of concepts in the forum, making it likely we avoid capturing interpersonal aspects of communication, which are not relevant to digital argument deconstruction, e.g., abuse, silliness. If the analyst finds that keywords in the discussion forum are absent from or marginal in the argument, then they could be 'on to something' – it may be that the argument does not discuss SotC accurately. From such a conveniently ascertained discrepancy, it would now be worth going to the effort to seek confirmation that the keyword analysis does indeed reflect normal SotC representations. To be clear, this strategy does not naively assume there will be a homogenous set of opinions on a topic. It does, however, make the reasonable assumption that there will be conceptual norms for how the criticized represents its standpoint whether people agree or disagree with that standpoint.

In order to stimulate how I use keywords in a discussion forum supplement for purposes of digital argument deconstruction (see Section 5), I appropriate the way in which the philosopher Jacques Derrida conceives of the supplement.

# 3  Using online comments in a discussion forum as a digital supplement

## 3.1  Derrida's supplement

We normally think of the word 'supplement' as meaning something extra, an add-on. And when things are added to, they usually get bigger. For Derrida, this understanding of the supplement is only half right. This is because a supplement adds only to replace a lack of something and so is weirdly both an addition and not an addition. While a supplement may only seem like an add-on and thus *outside* that which is supplemented, in fact it is simultaneously *inside* that which it is added to. Derrida writes that every supplement:

. . . harbors within itself two significations whose cohabitation is as strange as it is necessary [. . .] [The supplement] adds only to replace. It intervenes or insinuates itself *in-the-place-of*.

(Derrida, 1976: 144–5)

For Derrida, then, the 'logic of supplementation' is an undecideable inside-outside relation (Derrida, 1976: 215). As illustration, consider a vitamin supplement. On the one hand, it adds extra vitamins to the diet from outside; the vitamins are in surplus of the normal diet. (After all, we do not put a vitamin tablet onto our dinner plate and eat it with our meat and two veg.) As a result, the diet increases from 'normal diet' to 'normal diet + vitamin supplement'. On the other hand, from inside the diet the supplement can be seen as replacing vitamins which are lacking. (Why would we take a vitamin supplement unless we thought we were suffering a vitamin deficiency?) From this other perspective, the vitamin supplement does not increase the diet because it fills a gap within it in addressing a deficiency.

## 3.2 *Discussion forums as supplements*

In line with the logic of supplementation, an online discussion forum appended to an argument is, potentially, an inside/outside supplement to the argument if it can alert the reader to deficiencies within its representation of SotC. In such an event, the discussion forum then would not only lie outside the original argument as an add-on, an extra. Let's say that an analyst does find keywords which are present in a discussion forum supplement but absent/marginal from the argument. Assuming the analyst can corroborate that these keywords are really used by the criticized to characterize its standpoint, then they have a non-arbitrary basis for intervening in the argument. They can use these keywords to 'add to replace' what can be perspectivized, on the logic of supplementation, as lacking in SotC representation, intervening to replace an absence *inside* the argument with keywords *outside* the argument.

This replacement of deficiency may or may not have an adverse effect on the stability of an argument's cohesion. The analyst needs to show any adverse effects on cohesion by mapping possible effects of this intervention. Since an argument's capacity to persuade is dependent, in part, on effective cohesion, should the cohesive structure of the text of the argument be disturbed by this intervention, then its credibility diminishes. *And, if this happens, one can say that the argument's cohesive structure is unstable relative to how the relatively powerless criticized normally represents its standpoint.* Furthermore, digital argument deconstruction does not assume that deficiency of accurate SotC representation is deliberate. While it may be that omission or distortion of SotC suits the author's rhetorical line, these absences may be due to the author's ignorance of how the SotC prototypically represents itself.

A coda: to reiterate from the introduction, my use of Derrida's notion of the supplement is an appropriation. Though Derrida is synonymous with a 'strategy' of critical reading called 'Deconstruction', I am *not* doing Derridean Deconstruction. While I appropriate the idea of the supplement as being simultaneously inside and outside that which is supplemented, this does not mean that I concur with Derrida's vision in which word meaning is ultimately undecideable because it is being continually supplemented by other meanings (Derrida, 1976). That said, while I reject Derrida's philosophy of language, I subscribe to his ethical outlook (see Section 6).

# 4 'New atheism' and normal conceptual usage for its standpoint

## 4.1 Atheism as relatively powerless

I demonstrate a digital deconstructive analysis of an argument in an online version of a newspaper. The argument appeared in the UK based newspaper *The Guardian*, on 30 December 2007.[7]

The argument I focus on is entitled 'The New Atheism'. Its author, Brendan O'Neill, uses this expression to capture the ethos of a number of books published in 2006 and 2007 which set out atheistic positions: Dawkins (2006), Dennett (2006), Harris (2006) and Hitchens (2007). I see atheism as relatively powerless as compared with organized religion. From a UK context, this may, at first glance, seem a somewhat odd claim. For example, it is not as if atheists are barred from high office – the current Deputy Prime Minister, Nick Clegg, is openly atheist. However, the existence of an established church – 'The Church of England' – means there is systemic privilege for Christianity in the UK. For example, the Church of England (C of E) is granted privileged access to the UK Parliament. The 26 most senior C of E Bishops are automatically granted membership to the upper chamber of Parliament (The House of Lords) – where they have the right to speak and vote on all legislation. It is also worth noting that 34 per cent of state-funded schools in England, 14 per cent in Scotland, 15 per cent in Wales and 94 per cent in Northern Ireland are designated with a religious character. Except for in Scotland, these schools are allowed to discriminate against students in their admission policies, favouring those of the faith over those of other faiths and of no faith, or even favouring those of other faiths over those of no faith. In December 2013 the Fair Admissions Campaign flagged this issue and established that 16 per cent of state-funded places in England and Wales, or 1.2 million, are subject to such admissions policies.[8]

An argument criticizing 'new atheism' in a UK newspaper is, thus, taking place against this background. However, the online version of *The Guardian* has a global readership. In April 2013, for instance, there were 81 million online visits; only a third of these were from the UK.[9] It is straightforward to show that systemic privileging of religion is marked in many parts of the world, including liberal nations such as the USA. Indeed, the death penalty for atheism or blasphemy is possible in 13 countries.[10] Misrepresentation of atheism in a popular global communication platform, whether the atheism is 'old' or 'new', has the potential to contribute to the sustaining of a planetary status quo which systemically privileges religion.

## 4.2 The argument: 'The New Atheism'

O'Neill's argument totals 926 words and consists of 10 paragraphs and 42 sentences. It is laid out below in accordance with its original paragraph structure (indicated with capital letters); I have numbered all the sentences. (Underlining below signals hyperlinks in the original article.) Though it is a relatively long piece of data, the reader will see that it is important to include the entire argument. This is because there is instability across its cohesive structure, as I will show.

1. [headline] The New Atheism

2. [sub-headline] There is more humanity in the 'superhuman' delusions of the devout than there is in the realism of the hectoring atheists

[A]
3. 'New atheism' was the surprise political hit of 2007.
4. God-bashing books by <u>Hitchens</u>, <u>Dawkins</u> and other thinkers who come out in a rash when they hear the word 'religion' flew out of the bookshops.
5. Philip Pullman's anti-divine <u>Golden Compass</u> hit the big screen.
6. Everywhere, God was exposed as a fraud and God botherers were given an intellectual lashing.

[B]
7. I am as atheistic as it gets.
8. But I will not be signing up to this shrill hectoring of the religious.
9. The new atheists have given atheism a bad name.
10. History's greatest atheists, or the 'old atheists' as we are now forced to call them, were humanistic and progressive, critical of religion because it expressed man's sense of higher moral purpose in a deeply flawed fashion.
11. The new atheists are screechy and intolerant; they see religion merely as an expression of mass ignorance and delusion.
12. Their aim seems to be, not only to bring God crashing back down to earth, but also to downgrade mankind itself.

[C]
13. There's something bitterly ironic in the fact that the new atheists pose as the successors to Darwin.
14. Darwin himself had little interest in baiting the devout.

15. In the early 1880s, he was asked by the radical atheist <u>Edward Aveling</u> to endorse a new book on evolutionary theory.

16. Darwin, caring little for Aveling's 'anti-religious militancy', refused. He <u>wrote</u> to Aveling: 'It appears to me . . . that direct arguments against Christianity and theism produce hardly any effect on the public; and freedom of thought is best promoted by the gradual illumination of men's minds which follows from the advance of science. It has, therefore, been always my object to avoid writing on religion . . .'

[D]

17. Marx, too, believed that direct assaults on religion were pointless.

18. He <u>argued</u> that religion existed as spiritual compensation for social alienation, and believed that once the true nature of religion as a comfort blanket in an alienated society had been revealed, it would become clear that religion is merely a secondary phenomenon dependent for its existence on socioeconomic circumstances.

19. Radical critics should focus their intellectual ire on the degraded society that sustains religion rather than on attacking religion itself: 'The criticism of heaven turns into the criticism of earth, the criticism of religion into the criticism of law, and the criticism of theology into the criticism of politics.'

[E]

20. Old atheists sought to 'illuminate men's minds', through advancing science or deepening our understanding of capitalist society.

21. New atheists take exactly the opposite approach.

22. They expend all of their energy on attacking the institution of religion and its ridiculous adherents.

[F]

23. Consider their bizarre and fevered obsession with religious symbols, such as crucifixes worn around the neck, or statements of religious belief by public figures like Tony Blair or <u>Nick Clegg</u>: their distaste for anything that looks or sounds vaguely religious exposes the shallow anti-intellectualism of their new atheism.

24. Their opposition to religion is not driven by a profound or radical vision, as was Darwin's and Marx's, but rather by a dinner-party disdain and moral revulsion for the stupidity of the religious.

25. Where old atheism was driven by a passionate belief in progress, new atheism springs from today's crisis of secularism.

26. It is because new atheists have lost their own belief in progress and Enlightenment that they turn harshly against those who still cling to visions of a better society or 'kingdom'.

**[G]**

27. The inhumanity of the new atheism is best illustrated by its move from the world of social critique into the realm of sociobiology.

28. Some new atheists believe humans must be <u>genetically predisposed</u> to believing in a higher being.

29. Marx and others saw religion as the product of socioeconomic circumstances, and thus believed that religion would wither away as humanity proceeded along the path of progress.

30. New atheists see religious belief as a kind of animalistic instinct, driven by DNA.

31. Where Marx viewed people's turn towards religion as an understandable response to the harsh reality of alienation in capitalist society, new atheists see it as the product of mankind's twisted genetic makeup.

**[H]**

32. So what is their solution?

33. Mass genetic therapy?

34. Compulsory injections of the correct DNA – you know, the kind possessed by intelligent and well-bred people who can see through religious delusion?

35. The new atheists' abandonment of a social outlook leads them to adopt some very grim, anti-human views.

**[I]**

36. The key difference between the old and new atheism is in their views of mankind.

37. For atheists like <u>Marx,</u> religion expressed, in a backward and limited form, human aspirations to greatness: 'Man . . . looked for a superhuman being in the fantastic reality of heaven and found nothing there but the reflection of himself.'

38. He continued: 'The criticism of religion ends with the teaching that man is the highest being for man, hence with the categorical imperative to overthrow all relations in which man is a debased, enslaved, forsaken, despicable being . . .'

39. Today, Hitchens says of religion's destructive impact: 'What else was to be expected of something that was produced by the close cousins of chimpanzees?'

40. For Marx, religion had to be abolished because it made man despicable; for new atheists religion exists precisely because man is despicable, little more than a monkey.

**[J]**

41. New atheists will continue to ridicule the religious in 2008.

42. But there is more humanity in the 'superhuman' delusions of the devout – in their yearning for a sense of purpose and greatness – than there is in the monkeyman realism of the hectoring atheists.

Using the text mining software, WMatrix, I generated a frequency list of words repeated at least twice in the argument (see Appendix 1). The most frequent lexical word is 'religion' (21 instances). Knowledge of repeated words is needed because i) it facilitates the tracing of the argument's cohesive structure and ii) I compare unusually common concepts in the discussion forum supplement with their frequency in the argument. I could have used a number of different text mining tools to generate word frequencies. I employ WMatrix (Rayson, 2009) because I also use it to generate keywords from the online forum appended to O'Neill's argument (see below). This will help illuminate if O'Neill responds to how 'new atheism' usually describes its standpoint.

## 4.3  Discussion forum supplement

### 4.3.1  Keywords

The planetary reach of the online version of *The Guardian – www.theguardian.com –* is useful for my purposes since, for global phenomena such as 'new atheism', the responses in a discussion forum are likely to be less nationally parochial than they may otherwise be. In the discussion forum appended to the argument, there are 365 individual posts. The word count for the combined posts is 69,252.[11]

I generate keywords with WMatrix from a corpus of these discussion forum posts.[12] In order to make my examination manageable, I use the keyword cloud function of WMatrix which shows only the 100 highest keywords (Figure 10.1). In WMatrix, a log likelihood value of ≥7 (p <0.01)[13] confers keyness on a word. The larger the log likelihood value, the greater the salience of the keyword. See also Appendix 2 for log likelihood values for these keywords as well as their frequencies.

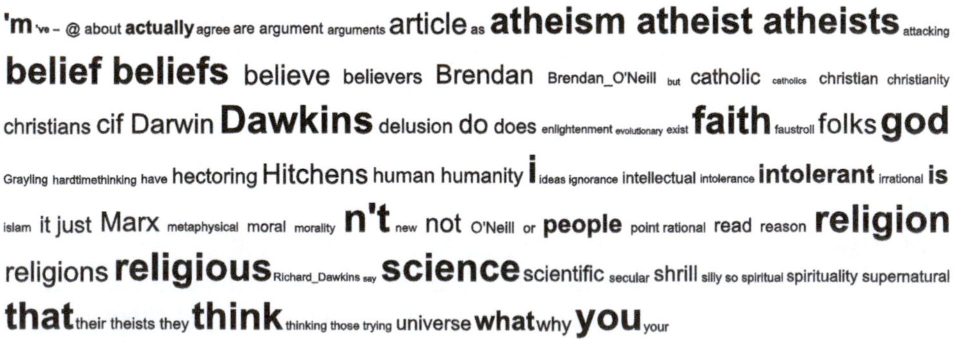

**FIGURE 10.1** *Keyword cloud showing the 100 highest keywords in the discussion forum; keywords with higher log likelihood values are in larger font size.*

## 4.3.2 Keywords 'faith' and 'belief'

Figure 10.1 shows that 'faith' is a significant keyword in the forum. However, it is absent from the argument. Overwhelmingly, O'Neill represents 'new atheism' as being critical of the general category *religion* [4, 11, 22, 24, 31, 39, 40]. As I flagged earlier, 'religion' is the most frequently used lexical word (21 instances).

The semantically close 'belief' is also a significant keyword in the forum as are its cognates, 'beliefs', 'believe' and 'believers' (see Figure 10.1). However, 'religious belief' only occurs twice in the argument [23, 30]. I should stress that quantitative comparison is not enough. It is important to understand qualitatively how these keywords are used in the forum. When I inspected the forum qualitatively, I found that 'faith' and 'belief' are used mostly in a way equivalent to religious belief. Generally speaking, whether or not posters are agreeing or disagreeing with 'new atheism', are religious or non-religious (as far as one can tell in some cases), predominantly they ascribe to it the following: *either* the view that faith/belief in a supernatural power is irrational in the absence of scientific evidence *or* that scientific evidence is irrelevant to faith/belief in a supernatural power. Here are some examples of posters who agree with 'new atheism' (keywords bolded):

> **Post 102** In context, this "**new atheism**" is entirely understandable [. . .] 9/11/01 was a **faith** based initiative [. . .]. We [the US] have a sustained undermining of **science**, both in teaching—as creation mythology/"intelligent design theory" is pushed in schools—and in research—as there is tremendous opposition to stem-cell research based on profound misunderstanding [. . .].

> **Post 150 Richard Dawkins** pointing out the difference between evidence-based **argument** and **belief** systems based on **faith** does not strike me as being **hectoring** or **shrill** [. . .].

## 4.3.3 Qualitative corroboration

A significant value of the relatively new technology of online discussion forum supplementation is that we do not have to travel very far from the argument to get, potentially, an insightful 'outside' angle on it. Text mining of the discussion forum supplement enables a convenient, relatively speedy and possibly illuminating *quantitative* perspective on how an argument represents SotC. However, we cannot automatically assume that keyword evidence for SotC representation, from even a large forum, is *qualitatively* correct about SotC – particularly where the identity of posters may be unclear. Should a quantitative conceptual disjuncture be (conveniently) found between the argument and discussion forum, the following would then be worth the effort: exploring whether or not it can be qualitatively confirmed that the discussion forum does indeed reflect how the relatively powerless criticized normally represents its standpoint.

Out of a number of potential sources that I found, in the end I chose the following by Taylor (2010) – a definition of 'new atheism' from *The Internet Encyclopedia of Philosophy* (IEP), 'a peer-reviewed academic resource'.[14] Let me quote part of the opening summary, which gives a good idea of the central foci of 'new atheism':

'[. . .] New Atheists tend to share a general set of assumptions and viewpoints [. . .]. The framework has a metaphysical component, an epistemological component, and an ethical component. Regarding the *metaphysical component*, the New Atheist authors share the central belief that there is no supernatural or divine reality of any kind. The *epistemological component* is their common claim that **religious belief** is irrational. The *moral component* is the assumption that there is a universal and objective secular moral standard [. . .]. [I]t is used to conclude that religion is bad in various ways [. . .].

The New Atheists make substantial use of the natural sciences in both their criticisms of **theistic belief** and in their proposed explanations of its origin and evolution [. . .]. They believe empirical science is the only (or at least the best) basis for genuine knowledge of the world, and they insist that a **belief** can be epistemically justified only if it is based on adequate evidence. Their conclusion is that science fails to show that there is a God and even supports the claim that such a being probably does not exist. What science will show about **religious belief**, they claim, is that this **belief** can be explained as a product of biological evolution. Moreover, they think that it is possible to live a satisfying non-religious life on the basis of secular morals and scientific discoveries.'

[my bold]

As reflected in the first two components (metaphysical and epistemological), and also in the importance placed on science, the critical thrust of 'new atheism' is that *religious belief* is irrational given the absence of scientific evidence for the existence of a supernatural being.[15]

I have solid qualitative corroboration that the discussion forum keywords '(religious) belief'/'faith' are part of normal conceptual usage by 'new atheists'. In other words, O'Neill does not respond to how 'new atheism' normally describes its standpoint when he characterizes it via the more general category of 'religion'. In Section 5, I replace the deficiency of normal representation of 'new atheism' in O'Neill's argument, and then explore the effects on its cohesive structure. In doing this, in effect I adopt a surrogate subjectivity – the discursive position of a 'new atheist'.

# 5  Digital deconstructive analysis of the 'new atheism' argument

## 5.1  Deconstruction of cohesive structure in paragraph [B]

### 5.1.1  'Old atheism' as critical of the institution of religion

O'Neill structures the entire argument through a binary opposition: 'old atheism' = POSITIVE and 'new atheism' = NEGATIVE. When O'Neill refers to the 'old atheists' – Darwin and Marx – he brings in quotations which show that the emphasis of their antipathy is to the *institution of religion*. This can be seen in the quotation from Darwin that O'Neill brings into [16] where Christianity is mentioned. Immediately afterwards in [17], O'Neill says that Marx believed that 'direct assaults on religion were pointless' [17], and so we understand 'religion' here to mean a religion such as Christianity. Antipathy to the institution of religion is also evident in [10] and [19] where religious values are alluded to, and in [38] and [40] respectively where O'Neill refers to Marx's wish to 'overthrow' the social relations of religion and that religion be 'abolished'.[16] Reflecting its critique of the institution of religion (or perhaps what O'Neill chooses to emphasize), when he characterizes 'old atheism' O'Neill always uses the category 'religion' rather than 'religious belief' [10, 16, 17, 18, 19, 24, 29, 31, 37, 38, 40].

In contrast, as we have seen, the standpoint of 'new atheism' is that *religious belief* is irrational given the absence of scientific evidence for the existence of a supernatural being. In other words, 'new atheists'' primary target is not the institution of religion, but the delusion of religious believers. It is this tension which, as I show, leads to instability in the cohesive structure of O'Neill's argument.

### 5.1.2  Cohesion between sentences 10 and 11

The binary opposition, 'old atheism' = POSITIVE and 'new atheism' = NEGATIVE, first appears in paragraph [B]. This paragraph is a summary of the argument:

**[B]**
7.  I am as atheistic as it gets.
8.  But I will not be signing up to this shrill hectoring of the religious.
9.  The new atheists have given atheism a bad name.

**[NEW ATHEISM = _NEGATIVE_]**

10.  History's greatest atheists, or the 'old atheists' as we are now forced to call them, were humanistic and progressive, critical of religion because it expressed man's sense of higher moral purpose in a deeply flawed fashion.

**[OLD ATHEISM = _POSITIVE_]**

11. The new atheists are screechy and intolerant; they see religion merely as an expression of mass ignorance and delusion.

12. Their [new atheists] aim seems to be, not only to bring God crashing back down to earth, but also to downgrade mankind itself.

**[NEW ATHEISM = _NEGATIVE_]**

In sentence [11], O'Neill represents 'new atheism' as viewing 'religion merely as an expression of mass ignorance and delusion'. Given the results detailed in Section 4.3, this representation of the SotC can be said to be deficient. Let me now explore the effects on cohesive structure by addressing this deficiency. I replace 'religion' with 'religious belief' in sentence [11] (I could have used 'faith' instead), crossing out 'religion':

11. The new atheists are screechy and intolerant; they see ~~religion~~ **religious belief** merely as an expression of mass ignorance and delusion.

Sentences [8, 9, 11 and 12] refer to 'new atheism'; 'old atheism' is first mentioned in [10]. Sentences [10] and [11, 12] originally link through the same general category, 'religion'. But, following my intervention, there is no longer linkage between [10] and [11] via the common category of 'religion'. This has adverse effects on the binary opposition structure in paragraph [B] of 'old atheism' = POSITIVE / 'new atheism' = NEGATIVE – it deconstructs as shown in Figure 10.2.

Put another way, the intervention highlights that the original cohesive structure of [B] is unstable relative to normal standpoint representation by 'new atheists'. Note that I did not also alter 'religion' in sentence [10] because O'Neill is describing '_old atheism_' there rather than 'new atheism'.

**[OLD ATHEISM = POSITIVE]**

[B]

10. History's greatest atheists, or the 'old atheists' as we are now forced to call them, were humanistic and progressive, critical of **religion** because it expressed man's sense of higher moral purpose in a deeply flawed fashion.

_DECONSTRUCTION OF BINARY OPPOSITION_                    _COHESION DISRUPTS_

11. The new atheists are screechy and intolerant; they see ~~religion~~ **religious belief** merely as an expression of mass ignorance and delusion.

12. Their [new atheists] aim seems to be, not only to bring God crashing back down to earth, but also to downgrade mankind itself.

**[NEW ATHEISM = _NEGATIVE_]**

**FIGURE 10.2** _Deconstruction 1._

### 5.1.3 Inside-outside interventions via a surrogate subjectivity

By replacing 'religion' with 'religious belief', it might look as if I have intervened in the argument from the outside only – the outside being the supplements of the discussion forum, see Taylor (2010). And, if you intervene from the outside in a text, it is not surprising if its cohesive structure falls apart! Construing what I did only as an outside intervention is misleading, however. This is because the category of 'religious belief' is, from a 'new atheist' perspective, the key category *inside* 'religion'. It is just that O'Neill's use of the general category of 'religion' obscures this. I needed to go *outside* the argument to appreciate this properly. So, while from one viewpoint I changed, from the outside, 'religion' into 'religious belief', from another viewpoint, I did the following: by adopting a surrogate subjectivity, taking on the perspective of a 'new atheist', I threw into relief the category of 'religious belief' which is semantically subsumed within 'religion', i.e., digging out from *inside* 'religion' the more specific category which is key to the 'new atheist' perspective. On the logic of supplementation in relation to a surrogate subjectivity, I thus conducted an 'inside-outside intervention'. The deconstructions which follow are also inside-outside interventions.

### 5.1.4 Collocation of TOLERANCE and (religious) belief

There is a further adverse effect on the argument from this deconstruction. Now that the second clause of [11] has become a reasonable reflection of how 'new atheism' normally describes its standpoint, a tension is revealed between 'religious belief' and 'intolerant' in this sentence. Intuitively, it is difficult to see how one can be intolerant of something that cannot be seen – in this case, the *mental states* of religious believers. Corpus linguistic evidence supports this intuition. Table 10.1 shows common collocation[17] of the lemma[18] TOLERANCE with 'religion(s)', 'religious' and 'religious belief' using a 1.5 billion word corpus of English, the UKWaC corpus accessed via the software Sketchengine.[19] The collocations are calculated within four places to the left of the *node word* and four places to the right of it.[20] The node word is the word being investigated for its collocational behaviour – in the above example, 'TOLERANCE'. The strength of collocation was calculated using the t-score function of Sketchengine. T-score is a measure of the strength of collocation which is commonly used in corpus linguistics. T-scores over 2 are 'normally taken to be significant' (Hunston, 2002: 72); t-scores over 10 are very significant (Hunston, 2001: 16).

Table 10.1 indicates that while it is habitual for forms of the lemma TOLERANCE to collocate with 'religion(s)' and 'religious', there is little evidence of forms of the lemma TOLERANCE collocating with the category, 'religious belief(s)'. In turn, accurately representing the standpoint of 'new atheism' in sentence [11] by replacing 'religion' with 'religious belief' introduces a collocational oddity which supports the intuition of real world oddity, i.e., intolerance of the *mental state* of religious belief. For another reason, then, the cohesive stability of paragraph [B] is dependent on exclusion of 'religious belief' in its representation of 'new atheism's' standpoint.

**Table 10.1**   Frequency and t-score values for collocation in the 1.5 billion word corpus, UKWaC, of 'religion(s)', 'religious', 'religious belief(s)' with the lemma TOLERANCE for an *n* ± 4 word span; values are for both lower-case and initial capital letter instances of TOLERANCE

| Collocation values for frequency and t-score | | | | | | |
| --- | --- | --- | --- | --- | --- | --- |
| | Religion(s) | | Religious | | Religious belief(s) | |
| | freq. | t-score | freq. | t-score | freq. | t-score |
| intolerance | 40 | 6.3 | 267 | 16.3 | 5 | 2.2 |
| intolerant | 35 | 5.9 | 18 | 4.2 | | |
| tolerance | 106 | 10.2 | 386 | 19.6 | 8 | 2.8 |
| tolerant | 76 | 8.7 | 46 | 6.7 | 4 | 1.9 |
| toleration | 21 | 4.6 | 234 | 15.3 | | |
| Intolerance | 4 | 2.0 | 17 | 4.1 | | |
| Tolerance | 27 | 5.2 | 69 | 8.3 | | |
| tolerated | 31 | 5.5 | 14 | 3.6 | | |
| tolerate | 20 | 4.4 | 14 | 3.6 | | |
| tolerating | 6 | 2.4 | 3 | 1.7 | | |
| Toleration | 4 | 2.0 | 18 | 4.2 | | |

## 5.1.5  Explaining how God metaphors can be seen to exclude 'religious belief'

'God' occurs four times in the argument [4, 6, 12]. Interestingly, all these occurrences are in the first two paragraphs (see bold below) where they are used in descriptions of 'new atheism':

**[A]**
3.   'New atheism' was the surprise political hit of 2007.
4.   **God**-bashing books by Hitchens, Dawkins and other thinkers who come out in a rash when they hear the word 'religion' flew out of the bookshops.
5.   Philip Pullman's anti-divine Golden Compass hit the big screen.
6.   Everywhere, **God** was exposed as a fraud and **God** botherers were given an intellectual lashing.

**[B]**
[. . .]
12.   Their aim seems to be, not only to bring **God** crashing back down to earth, but also to downgrade mankind itself.

Three usages of 'God' involve metaphor ('bashing' [4]; 'fraud' [6]; 'crashing' [12]); 'God botherers' [4] is a slang expression. Since the argument is in a newspaper, the use of metaphor/slang here would seem to have an interpersonal function to help attract the reader into the argument by use of colourful imagery/informality.

'God' is a keyword in the discussion forum. Very common expressions in the forum which contain this keyword also use two other keywords, 'belief' or 'believe' – such as in 'belief in God' or 'believe in God'. Out of 439 instances of 'belief/ve' in the forum, a quarter (113 instances) are realized in these expressions as well as in related ones such as 'belief in the supernatural'. This is largely in relation to the 'new atheist' perspective, corroborated in Section 4.3.3, that there is no rational/scientific evidence for 'belief in God'. Despite the interpersonal function of the 'God metaphors' in paragraphs [A] and [B], on the logic of supplementation we can nevertheless perspectivize the argument as atypically lacking, in its discussion of the standpoint of 'new atheism', the collocations *belief/faith* and *God/supernatural being*. In other words, use of these metaphors enables a circumvention or exclusion of such collocation whether this is premeditated or not.

On the basis of this evidence-based comparison, we can make the following judgement: use of metaphor which enables omission of 'belief/ve in God' also contributes to the impression of stability in the binary opposition structure, in paragraph [B], of 'old atheism' = POSITIVE and 'new atheism' = NEGATIVE. By this I mean that if O'Neill had expressed himself using 'belief/ve in God' instead of the God metaphors, this would have had repercussions for the stability of the binary opposition. This is because, as we saw, the cohesive felicity of the binary opposition is dependent on repeated use of the general category 'religion' in sentences [10 and 11] and *not* also use of the specific category of '(religious) belief'. For example, this alternative version of the first part of sentence [12]:

'Their [new atheists] aim seems to be, not only to bring belief in God to an end . . .'

could be seen to conflict with the cohesion in [B] achieved by repetition of 'religion' in sentences [10 and 11].

## 5.2  Deconstruction of cohesive structure elsewhere in the argument

### 5.2.1  Sub-binary opposition structure across the argument

Knowledge of normal conceptual usage for 'new atheism' does not just adversely affect, in [B], O'Neill's binary opposition structure of 'old atheism' = POSITIVE versus 'new atheism' = NEGATIVE. There is deconstruction of cohesive structure in other parts of the argument. In order to show this, I need firstly to provide more detail on the global structure of the argument.

The binary opposition structure of 'old atheism' = POSITIVE and 'new atheism' = NEGATIVE is, in fact, a *supra*-binary opposition structure which subsumes two *sub*-binary oppositions:

- sub-binary opposition 1: 'old atheism' is + DEEP / – HECTORING / + PROGRESSIVE *versus* 'new atheism' is – DEEP / + HECTORING / – PROGRESSIVE;

- sub-binary opposition 2: 'old atheism' is associated with HIGH VIEW OF HUMANKIND of the RELIGIOUS *versus* LOW VIEW OF HUMANKIND of 'new atheism'.

I refer the reader to Appendix 3 where the argument is annotated for these sub-binary oppositions. But, as brief illustration, below are some examples of annotated text from Appendix 3. Sub-binary opposition 1 can be seen, for instance, in [20–22]:

### OLD ATHEISM: + DEEP / – HECTORING / + PROGRESSIVE = *POSITIVE*

20. Old atheists sought to 'illuminate men's minds', through advancing science or deepening our understanding of capitalist society.
21. New atheists take exactly the opposite approach.
22. They expend all of their energy on attacking the institution of religion and its ridiculous adherents.

### NEW ATHEISM: – DEEP / + HECTORING / – PROGRESSIVE = *NEGATIVE*

In sub-binary opposition 2, the 'low view of mankind' ascribed to 'new atheists' derives, for O'Neill, from their sociobiological views:

### NEW ATHEISM: LOW VIEW OF HUMANKIND = *NEGATIVE*

27. The inhumanity of the new atheism is best illustrated by its move from the world of social critique into the realm of sociobiology.

This alleged socio-biological view is that religious belief derives from instinct (paragraph [G]). Another and related reason that O'Neill gives for 'new atheists' having a low view of mankind is the opinion he attributes to Christopher Hitchens: since religion was created by early homo sapiens (sentence [39]), it is not something to value. In contrast, O'Neill argues that 'old atheists' espouse a high view of mankind since they share the aspiration of the religious for a sense of purpose and greatness (sentence [42]). Sub-binary opposition 2 is evident in this extract:

### OLD ATHEISM is associated with HIGH VIEW OF HUMANKIND of the RELIGIOUS = *POSITIVE*

37. For atheists like <u>Marx,</u> religion expressed, in a backward and limited form, human aspirations to greatness . . .

[. . .]

**40.** . . . for new atheists religion exists precisely because man is despicable, little more than a monkey.

**NEW ATHEISM: LOW VIEW OF HUMANKIND = _NEGATIVE_**

## 5.2.2 Deconstruction of sub-binary opposition structures in paragraph [B]

Let me now return to paragraph [B], the first substantive paragraph of the argument. On first read, the detail of the binary structuring of [B] – that it contains sub-binary oppositions 1 and 2 – is not completely clear. It is only on consuming the entire argument that we understand, for example, why O'Neill thinks that 'new atheists' 'downgrade mankind' [12]. As I demonstrated in Section 5.1, there is cohesive disruption between sentences [10] and [11; 12] which leads to deconstruction in the _supra_-binary opposition of 'old atheism' = POSITIVE and 'new atheism' = NEGATIVE. However, with knowledge of the _sub_-binary opposition structure in the argument, deconstruction of the supra-binary in paragraph [B] necessarily means the _sub_-binary oppositions 1 and 2 in this paragraph also deconstruct, as shown in Figure 10.3.

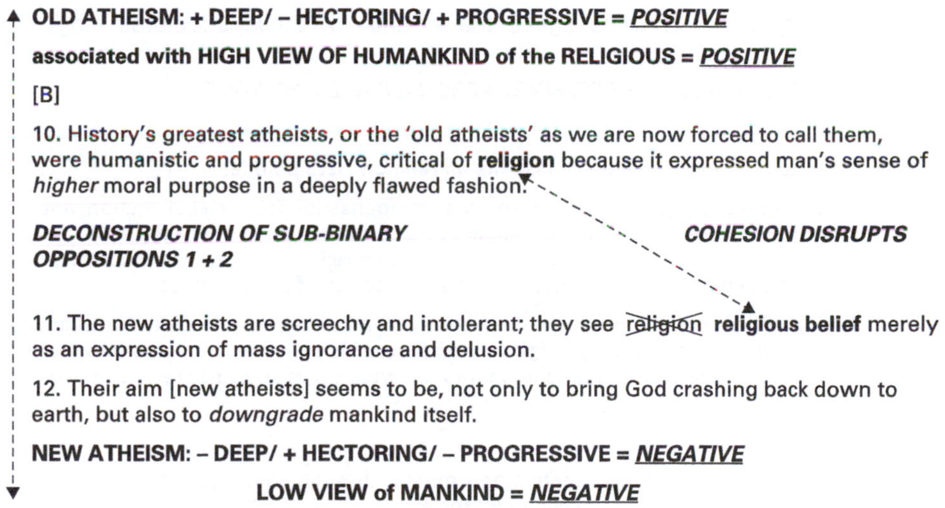

▲ **OLD ATHEISM: + DEEP/ – HECTORING/ + PROGRESSIVE = _POSITIVE_**

**associated with HIGH VIEW OF HUMANKIND of the RELIGIOUS = _POSITIVE_**

**[B]**

10. History's greatest atheists, or the 'old atheists' as we are now forced to call them, were humanistic and progressive, critical of **religion** because it expressed man's sense of _higher_ moral purpose in a deeply flawed fashion.

_DECONSTRUCTION OF SUB-BINARY_                    _COHESION DISRUPTS_
_OPPOSITIONS 1 + 2_

11. The new atheists are screechy and intolerant; they see ~~religion~~ **religious belief** merely as an expression of mass ignorance and delusion.

12. Their aim [new atheists] seems to be, not only to bring God crashing back down to earth, but also to _downgrade_ mankind itself.

**NEW ATHEISM: – DEEP/ + HECTORING/ – PROGRESSIVE = _NEGATIVE_**

▼                    **LOW VIEW of MANKIND = _NEGATIVE_**

**FIGURE 10.3** _Deconstruction 1 elaborated upon._

## 5.2.3 Deconstruction of sub-binary opposition structure elsewhere in the argument

It might have been possible to brush aside the deconstruction in paragraph [B] as a local weakness for the argument's cohesive structure. However, once we account for sub-binary oppositions 1 and 2 across the argument we realize that: i) much, if not most, of the argument is tied together by these sub-oppositions; ii) paragraph [B] is a *summary* of an argument which is based on sub-oppositions 1 and 2. As a result, the deconstruction of sub-binary oppositions in [B] is likely to be replicated elsewhere in the argument, which is indeed the case. Take the link between paragraphs [D] and [E], for example. This is structured using sub-binary opposition 1. Like paragraph [B], cohesion relies on the common lexical tie of 'religion'. This is between sentence [22] (paragraph [E]) – where 'new atheism' is mentioned – and sentences in paragraph [D] – where 'religion' is mentioned seven times in relation to 'old atheism'. (See Figure 10.4. Sentence [20] is a summary of paragraph [D].)

Once we replace, in sentence [22], the deficiency of accurate representation of new atheism's standpoint, there is no longer a common lexical link of 'religion' facilitating cohesive contrast between 'old atheism' and 'new atheism'. In turn, there is deconstruction of sub-binary opposition 1 here.

As another example, consider paragraph [G] where O'Neill attributes to 'new atheism' the socio-biological view that humans are genetically conditioned to believe in a higher being. (This attribution is not quite right. Rather, 'new atheists' hold that 'religious belief . . . can be explained as a product of biological evolution'. See the quotation from Taylor (2010) in Section 4.3.3.) O'Neill sets up the argument in sentences [27 and 28]. Having done this, he employs both sub-binary opposition 1 and (half of) sub-binary opposition 2. Once again, the efficacy of these structures hinges on

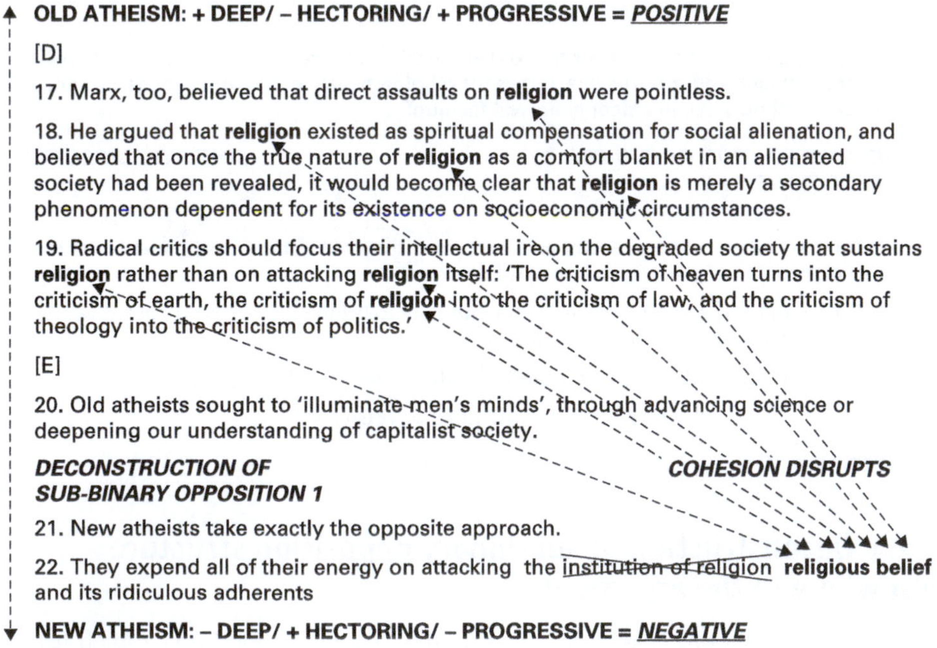

**OLD ATHEISM: + DEEP/ – HECTORING/ + PROGRESSIVE = *POSITIVE***

[D]

17. Marx, too, believed that direct assaults on **religion** were pointless.

18. He argued that **religion** existed as spiritual compensation for social alienation, and believed that once the true nature of **religion** as a comfort blanket in an alienated society had been revealed, it would become clear that **religion** is merely a secondary phenomenon dependent for its existence on socioeconomic circumstances.

19. Radical critics should focus their intellectual ire on the degraded society that sustains **religion** rather than on attacking **religion** itself: 'The criticism of heaven turns into the criticism of earth, the criticism of **religion** into the criticism of law, and the criticism of theology into the criticism of politics.'

[E]

20. Old atheists sought to 'illuminate men's minds', through advancing science or deepening our understanding of capitalist society.

***DECONSTRUCTION OF***                                    ***COHESION DISRUPTS***
***SUB-BINARY OPPOSITION 1***

21. New atheists take exactly the opposite approach.

22. They expend all of their energy on attacking the ~~institution of religion~~ **religious belief** and its ridiculous adherents

**NEW ATHEISM: – DEEP/ + HECTORING/ – PROGRESSIVE = *NEGATIVE***

**FIGURE 10.4** *Deconstruction 2.*

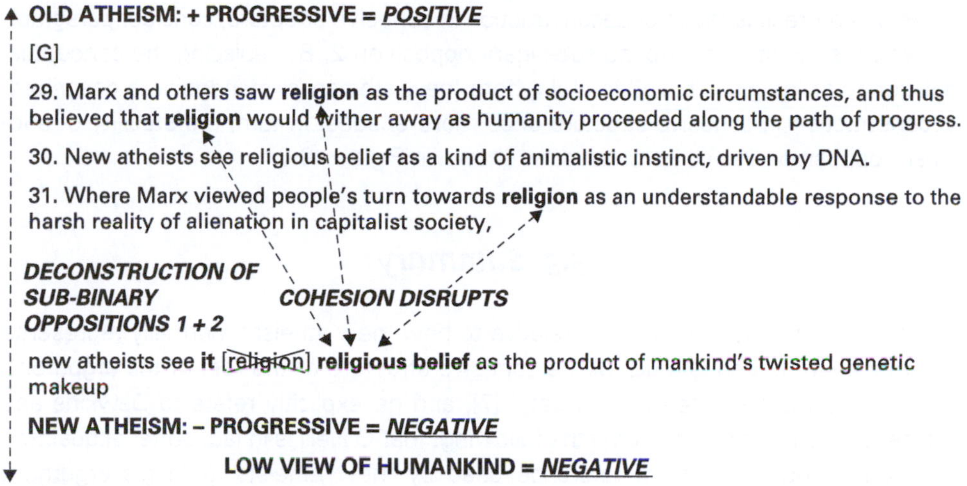

**▲ OLD ATHEISM: + PROGRESSIVE = _POSITIVE_**

[G]

29. Marx and others saw **religion** as the product of socioeconomic circumstances, and thus believed that **religion** would wither away as humanity proceeded along the path of progress.

30. New atheists see religious belief as a kind of animalistic instinct, driven by DNA.

31. Where Marx viewed people's turn towards **religion** as an understandable response to the harsh reality of alienation in capitalist society,

**_DECONSTRUCTION OF_**
**_SUB-BINARY_**            **_COHESION DISRUPTS_**
**_OPPOSITIONS 1 + 2_**

new atheists see **it** [religion] **religious belief** as the product of mankind's twisted genetic makeup

**NEW ATHEISM: – PROGRESSIVE = _NEGATIVE_**

**LOW VIEW OF HUMANKIND = _NEGATIVE_**

**FIGURE 10.5** *Deconstruction 3.*

common cohesion of the word 'religion'. This cohesion takes place both within sentence [31] as well as between sentence [31] and sentence [29]. And, once we replace the deficiency of how new atheism normally represents its standpoint – this time in sentence [31] – cohesion disrupts. In turn, the sub-binary oppositions 1 and 2 here deconstruct, as shown in Figure 10.5.

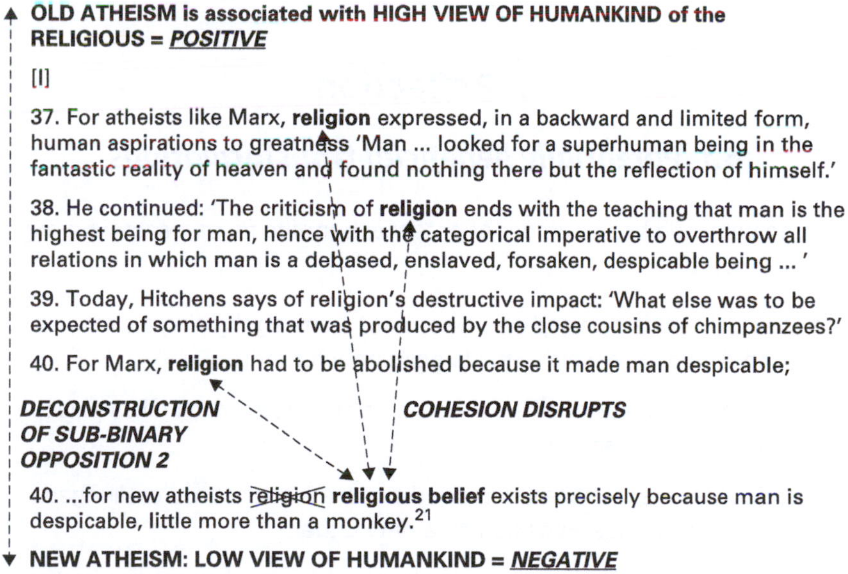

**▲ OLD ATHEISM is associated with HIGH VIEW OF HUMANKIND of the RELIGIOUS = _POSITIVE_**

[I]

37. For atheists like Marx, **religion** expressed, in a backward and limited form, human aspirations to greatness 'Man ... looked for a superhuman being in the fantastic reality of heaven and found nothing there but the reflection of himself.'

38. He continued: 'The criticism of **religion** ends with the teaching that man is the highest being for man, hence with the categorical imperative to overthrow all relations in which man is a debased, enslaved, forsaken, despicable being ... '

39. Today, Hitchens says of religion's destructive impact: 'What else was to be expected of something that was produced by the close cousins of chimpanzees?'

40. For Marx, **religion** had to be abolished because it made man despicable;

**_DECONSTRUCTION_**
**_OF SUB-BINARY_**            **_COHESION DISRUPTS_**
**_OPPOSITION 2_**

40. ...for new atheists religion **religious belief** exists precisely because man is despicable, little more than a monkey.[21]

**▼ NEW ATHEISM: LOW VIEW OF HUMANKIND = _NEGATIVE_**

**FIGURE 10.6** *Deconstruction 4.*

As one more illustration of deconstruction in cohesive structure, consider paragraph [I], which is constructed around sub-binary opposition 2. By replacing the conceptual deficiency of 'religious belief' in [40] where 'new atheism's' standpoint is described, deconstruction in cohesive structure once more ensues. In turn, the stability of sub-binary opposition 2 is compromised, as shown in Figure 10.6.

## 5.3 *Summary*

Not only is paragraph [B] unstable relative to how 'new atheism' normally represents its standpoint, but so is much of the cohesive structure of the rest of the argument. Given O'Neill is 'as atheistic as it gets' [7], and he explicitly refers to Dawkins and Hitchens, could not one presume the following: that O'Neill is in fact better acquainted with the standard terms of reference used by 'new atheists' than his argument suggests? This leads me to go further than previously and speculate that O'Neill's use of 21 instances of 'religion', no instances of 'faith', and only 2 instances of 'religious belief' is not accidental but reflects a deliberate exclusion/marginalization strategy. That is, by using the too general/vague category of 'religion', O'Neill is able to occlude the more specific, and more relevant, categories of 'religious belief' and/or 'faith'. It would not serve O'Neill's argument to mention too often the more specific categories 'religious belief' and/or 'faith' in relation to what he is criticizing. Since these elements of religion are the most vulnerable to criticism from atheists – i.e., including O'Neill himself – I am led to suppose that it would be better for him to exclude or marginalize these concepts in the argument in order to avoid contradicting himself.

# 6 Reflection

## 6.1 *Potentially beneficial transformations*

The approach outlined has a number of potential benefits for students who might use it in an assignment:

- intellectual satisfaction and empowerment from highlighting a straw man argument on a topic which was (largely) new for them;

- expanded awareness of different domains of debate which takes place in a critically focused manner;

- consciousness is refreshed/expanded since the analyst has challenged themselves to decide a position on a new Other;

- the analyst's rhetorical sensitivity is sharpened, e.g., they are in a better position to see where categories in an argument are insufficiently specific from the perspective of the Other and, in turn, where they block appreciation (whether intended or not) of the standpoint of the Other;

- insight through transformation – often a pleasurable experience; the analyst is able to see where their initial reading was naïve/shallow relative to the standpoint of a relatively powerless Other;

- the analyst's unpredictable interruption of Self via 'digital hospitality' to an Other leads to an unpredictable surrogate deconstructive reading; in turn, this avoids routine performance of critical Self;

- the analyst now has some quantitative facts about what is important to a relatively powerless Other. This is useful for contributing, in an informed way, to future debate relating to the Other.

## 6.2 Digital hospitality and ethical responsiveness to a relatively powerless Other

I mentioned, earlier in this chapter, that digital argument deconstruction is an ethical form of practical CDA and that this approach aligns with Derrida's ethical outlook. Let me elaborate. In the philosophical outlook of Jacques Derrida, showing hospitality to the Other, allowing Self to be interrupted by the Other's viewpoint because of potentially beneficial transformations, is to act ethically.[22] My showing in effect 'digital hospitality' to a relative powerless Other is not only an ethical move in this tradition – especially given the transformations I have indicated above – but has a different emphasis from other practical CDA. To view an argument from the position of the relatively powerless which it criticizes, the analyst adopts a surrogate and thus ethical subjectivity in Derridean terms. By definition, this ethical subjectivity is not pre-figured. This is different, thus, from traditional CDA where the analyst criticizes a text from a pre-formed political subjectivity. Nevertheless, ethical subjectivity and political subjectivity are potentially relatable with this method (see Section 6.3).

The reader may perhaps be thinking 'why might someone want to go to the trouble to explore the possibility of cohesive deconstructions in an argument which result from its straw man status? If they find out that the argument is a straw man, why not just leave it as that?' To explore potential deconstruction of cohesion in an argument is to deepen ethical responsiveness to the relatively powerless Other, not just trying on their shoes, but walking about in them in the argument. In other words, a deeper ethical responsiveness to the relatively powerless Other goes beyond appreciating that an argument which criticizes it is dialectically fallacious. It also tries to empathize with the kind of rhetorical problems the relatively powerless Other is likely to detect in the argument as a result of it not addressing the Other's standpoint.

## 6.3  What might happen after a digital argument deconstruction?

### 6.3.1  Ethical responsiveness does not lead to political commitment

The analyst may have started from fairly open digital hospitality. They used the resources of the Web to expand their horizons and find out about the standpoint of a previously unknown relatively powerless Other. But, having highlighted instabilities in the cohesion of an argument relative to a rigorously founded surrogate (ethical) subjectivity, it is time for the analyst to assert critical independence. And this might mean the following: while dialectically the analyst derived satisfaction from revealing a straw man argument, and ethically was happy to show hospitality to a new Other and have their Self unpredictably interrupted and horizons expanded, all the same they do not wish to align with the Other's desire for political change. They may have good reasons. Just because texts are produced by a relatively powerless Other, this does not make their reasoning sound. Despite welcoming the guest into their home, and bending over backwards to see their point of view, in the end the analyst may come to the conclusion that it is time for their guest to leave. I should say, though, that their hospitality was not in vain since the benefits flagged in Section 6.1 still apply. It is important to stress too that not every relatively powerless or marginal Other will be worth empathizing with in the first place (e.g. racist organizations, terrorists, theocratic religious groups).

### 6.3.2  Ethical responsiveness leads to political commitment

But what if the analyst has no reason to reject the Other's standpoint? The injunction of this method to show digital hospitality to a relatively powerless Other means direct engagement with an argument from the Other's viewpoint is fostered. And, because Self has been interrupted in a focused manner, there is the prospect of another transformation – the analyst potentially chooses a new political commitment. Merely 'finding out about' a relatively powerless Other is, I would argue, less likely to lead to this transformation. In other words, political commitment to an Other is more likely to ensue when we make the effort to 'get under their skin'. An ethical responsiveness to the Other can, thus, be a basis for alignment with the Other's desire for political change.

### 6.3.3  Ethically enriching an existing political orientation/commitment

Instead of starting from fairly open digital hospitality, the analyst might begin more narrowly. They choose an argument because it criticizes a relatively powerless Other which they *already* align with politically, but have a weaker ethical responsiveness to.

As illustration, it is quite possible for someone to be already politically committed to the removal of C of E bishops from the UK House of Lords, but not ethically responsive (in the sense of showing hospitality) to the standpoint of 'new atheism'. In other words, they look at the issue mainly from their own pre-figured political viewpoint. Using the method outlined above, the politically oriented analyst can enable/enrich ethical responsiveness.

## 6.4 Issues around the choice of argument

Probably a common choice determiner of an argument for training this approach on will be the analyst's political orientation. But, if an analyst already has a political *and* ethical responsiveness to the relatively powerless Other criticized in the argument, then they are probably not showing hospitality if they proceed to a deconstructive analysis. In such an event, there would be little point in exploring possible cohesive faults in the argument – Self is not being interrupted. It would be a little like having a dinner party for one's twin sister who lives next door – the familiarity might be comforting, but the experience may not be so extending for the host.

Why not choose a relatively powerful Other to show ethical responsiveness to rather than a relatively powerless Other? After all, it is not as if relatively powerless authors cannot create straw man arguments against the relatively powerful. Just because you are relatively powerless, this does not absolve you of the dialectical responsibility to avoid straw man arguments. Corpus linguistic method is ethically-neutral. The corpus-based approach of this chapter could, thus, be used to deconstruct straw man arguments written by the relatively powerless that criticize the relatively powerful.

This is not something that interests me, however. This is because, as the reader will know, I am not only oriented to the dialectical. I have yoked corpus linguistic method to Derridean hospitality ethics also. The actual standpoint of the relatively powerless is less likely to be known or understood than that of the relatively powerful who is associated with the status quo. To be ethical is to be digitally hospitable by reducing the invisibility of the Other. It is to go to the trouble to allow Self to be interrupted, walking around the text of the argument in the shoes of the relatively powerless for the purposes of exciting an unpredictable and by proxy critical engagement with the argument. It is to appreciate how the relatively powerful might distort the standpoint of the relatively powerless, which intentionally or not helps to maintain dominance.

## 6.5 Other possible deconstructions of O'Neill's argument

Because the procedure for locating salient concepts in the forum is corpus-based and statistically informed, it reduces arbitrariness in making judgements of conceptual deficiency and where to intervene in the argument. However, notice I say 'reduces'. Inevitably, I have to make some arbitrary choices, e.g. of the number of keywords to examine so as to make my use of the supplement manageable. (That said, I always select statistically significant words.) I should say also that I have not necessarily exhausted deconstruction of cohesive structure relative to how 'new atheism' normally describes its standpoint. Further exploration of the argument on the basis of the same keywords may reveal more deconstruction in cohesive structure. And, investigating more keywords could lead to further revelation of instabilities in the argument. It is possible too that others using the same technique of analysis may notice further rifts in the argument's cohesive structure. This might involve cohesive structure which includes repeated words in Appendix 1 which I did not trace. This aside, I do consider that I have revealed major faultlines in cohesion which have adverse repercussions for the argument's credibility.

From a scholarly perspective, one might say the more comprehensive a deconstruction of an argument the better. This means, as I have tried to do, providing a sufficiently detailed annotation of an argument's macro structure (see Appendix 3). A scholarly approach would also seek to provide *explanation* of where metaphor might help to create cohesive stability through exclusion of collocation normally used by the criticized to express its standpoint (see Section 5.1.5). From another angle, such comprehensiveness and explanation may not be deemed so necessary by a relatively time-poor reader who has a less scholarly orientation. This could be to see whether or not there is one devastating deconstruction in the argument which they can then communicate in a short post to an online discussion forum underneath that argument. Should this kind of deconstruction be evident, then this reader may well experience deconstructive satisfaction. The argument is sufficiently problematized, relative to their time-poor state and specific goals – there is no need to explore the possibility of further deconstruction. In sum, the degree of comprehensiveness of a digital deconstructive analysis will ultimately depend on expectations of rigour in a particular setting.

The technique of digital argument deconstruction may not work on every argument. But this could be for the following positive reason – the argument actually responds to how the relatively powerless it criticizes normally represents its standpoint. The converse is that this analytical technique could act as an argument filter. Why bother to engage with an argument's reasoning if its cohesive structure deconstructs relative to accurate SotC representations?

## 6.6  *More thoughts on digital supplements*

### 6.6.1  Alternative digital supplements for keyword analysis

Other relevant digital supplements could be taken or aggregated from the World Wide Web and keywords generated from them for purposes of digital argument deconstruction. For example, a Google search led me to http://www.richard dawkinsfoundation.org/fourhorsementranscript, a transcript of Dawkins et al. (2007). This is a text of 20,536 words known as 'Four Horsemen'. It is a colloquy of the 'new atheists', Richard Dawkins, Daniel Dennett, Sam Harris and Christopher Hitchens. This source is thus highly relevant qualitatively. Keyword (quantitative) analysis of the transcript using WMatrix corroborates keywords in *The Guardian* discussion forum, e.g., 'faith' is a highly significant keyword (47; LL=263.9), and is indeed the highest noun keyword.[23] See Appendix 4 for a concordance of the 47 instances of 'faith' from this transcript. The reader will see these instances of 'faith' mostly have the sense of 'religious belief'.

Because it is a colloquy of 'new atheists', coming from the 'apocalyptic horsemen's mouths', it is a better electronic supplement to use for argument deconstruction than the discussion forum. However, because I knew enough already about 'new atheism', Dawkins, etc., I was able to locate and judge the relevance of this source fairly easily. A novitiate may not be able to do this so readily. For those new to the topic of an argument, the discussion forum appended to it is a particularly convenient place to start exploring possible deconstruction in the cohesive structure of the argument. This is due to its proximity and the fact that many readers of an argument in a quality newspaper who are motivated to post a comment are likely to be knowledgeable about the topic.

## 6.6.2 Avoiding digital supplements?

A general objection might go as follows: if we have to follow up keyword analysis by looking for qualitative evidence, why bother with quantitative investigation of a digital supplement in the first place? Why not go straight to an encyclopedia entry, or other relevant source, to find out accurate SotC representations?

A significant value of the quantitative (keyword) analysis of an electronic supplement, in tandem with quantitative (word frequency) analysis of the preceding argument, is that it can readily alert the reader to potentially relevant conceptual absences or infrequencies in the argument. A qualitative contrast may not throw this into relief so easily. Another advantage of the quantitative contrastive analysis is that, if a conceptual juncture is revealed between argument and supplement, this usefully provides the reader with a *focused rationale* for facilitating potential problematizing of the argument. Avoiding keyword analysis of a relevant supplement and going straight to the encyclopedia entry would mean the reader's focus is more diffuse. They may be less sure of what to look for in the encyclopedia entry, or other relevant qualitative source, in order to facilitate potential problematizing of the argument. Put another way, the growth of a surrogate subjectivity is a direct reflex of the useful capacity of corpus analysis to help access in a concentrated manner a common standpoint(s) across multiple texts. Lastly, relying on the encyclopedia entry means relying on qualitative evidence only. The age we live in is awash with digitized data. It is a passé methodology, to my mind, which ignores the potential for generating useful quantitative evidence from data taken or aggregated from the Web. See also O'Halloran (2012, 2013a, 2013b, forthcoming) for related work in digital argument deconstruction where instabilities in cohesive structure of arguments are not only illuminated via keyword analysis, but via collocation analysis of mega-corpora consisting of over one billion words.

# 7  Conclusion

I have offered an alternative corpus-based practical CDA, whose focus is the revealing of straw man arguments made against a relatively powerless Other. It thus has a dialectical focus. Crucially, however, it also has an ethical emphasis – in Derridean terms – hence 'dialethical'.[24] The approach could also be seen to provide an ethical bearing for the standpoint rule of pragma-dialectics. Digital conditions, and corpus linguistic technique, facilitate the generation of a surrogate subjectivity. Ethical responsiveness to the Other can be deepened by revealing potential instability of cohesion in an argument relative to the surrogate subjectivity.

I have demonstrated how looking at an argument through the lens of a digital supplement can facilitate a critical reading of that argument relative to the standpoint of the relatively powerless; I am thus advocating a form of critical analysis of an argument which is preceded by aggregation of digital public sphere data. Despite the ethical emphasis, I hope it is clear that with this method the ethical and the political are relatable in principle. Developing an ethical responsiveness to a relatively powerless Other with this approach could lead to a political commitment as I have suggested. Since it is driven by use of digital tools and corpora, the approach is 'metalinguistic-lite'. There is then no need to use systemic functional grammar, for example, in the alternative pedagogical CDA I have outlined. And, given corpus software is not so difficult to learn, all this makes the method not only practicable, but also accessible to non-linguists.[25]

# Appendix 1

# Frequencies of all repeated words in 'the new atheism' text

| | | | | |
|---|---|---|---|---|
| 53 the | 5 be | 3 humanity | 2 delusion | 2 moral |
| 46 of | 5 it | 3 It | 2 delusions | 2 out |
| 22 to | 5 New | 3 its | 2 direct | 2 people |
| 21 and | 5 society | 3 little | 2 DNA | 2 product |
| 21 religion | 4 an | 3 mankind | 2 earth | 2 public |
| 19 a | 4 anti | 3 more | 2 expressed | 2 purpose |
| 19 in | 4 because | 3 not | 2 For | 2 radical |
| 17 atheists | 4 being | 3 old | 2 genetic | 2 rather |
| 15 as | 4 belief | 3 progress | 2 given | 2 realism |
| 14 is | 4 Darwin | 3 social | 2 greatness | 2 reality |
| 14 s | 4 God | 3 superhuman | 2 have | 2 science |
| 13 new | 4 into | 3 they | 2 heaven | 2 sense |
| 12 that | 4 see | 3 were | 2 higher | 2 socioeconomic |
| 11 by | 4 than | 3 who | 2 himself | 2 something |
| 9 for | 4 there | 3 with | 2 hit | 2 Their |
| 9 religious | 3 Aveling | 2 against | 2 Hitchens | 2 them |
| 9 their | 3 believed | 2 alienation | 2 human | 2 There |
| 8 on | 3 but | 2 all | 2 I | 2 through |
| 8 The | 3 despicable | 2 are | 2 intellectual | 2 turn |
| 7 atheism | 3 devout | 2 attacking | 2 itself | 2 views |
| 7 criticism | 3 driven | 2 been | 2 kind | 2 Where |
| 7 or | 3 from | 2 best | 2 like | 2 which |
| 7 was | 3 had | 2 But | 2 men | 2 will |
| 6 man | 3 He | 2 capitalist | 2 merely | 2 would |
| 6 Marx | 3 hectoring | 2 circumstances | 2 minds | |

# Appendix 2

# The 100 highest keywords, including frequency ('Freq') and log likelihood values ('LL'), in the discussion forum

| Keyword | Freq | LL | Keyword | Freq | LL |
|---|---|---|---|---|---|
| religion | 336 | 1665.17 | Hitchens | 40 | 220.09 |
| atheists | 227 | 1249.02 | Marx | 44 | 210.46 |
| religious | 264 | 1127.97 | people | 239 | 207.66 |
| god | 200 | 1100.46 | Darwin | 37 | 203.58 |
| atheism | 141 | 764.05 | not | 569 | 197.82 |
| atheist | 117 | 632.37 | intolerant | 36 | 189.02 |
| **belief** | 141 | 604.86 | cif | 34 | 187.08 |
| i | 1093 | 545.37 | folks | 34 | 187.08 |
| that | 1232 | 525.72 | does | 146 | 185.47 |
| Dawkins | 90 | 495.21 | delusion | 32 | 167.24 |
| n't | 445 | 463.60 | **believers** | 34 | 166.65 |
| you | 707 | 384.81 | christians | 44 | 165.24 |
| science | 84 | 363.00 | humanity | 31 | 161.80 |
| **faith** | 86 | 339.49 | hectoring | 29 | 159.57 |
| **beliefs** | 77 | 337.06 | universe | 34 | 150.52 |
| think | 188 | 316.27 | it | 884 | 146.14 |
| do | 365 | 310.95 | read | 71 | 146.01 |
| is | 1195 | 304.30 | just | 187 | 145.03 |
| what | 327 | 249.59 | catholic | 45 | 142.57 |
| Brendan | 47 | 249.02 | scientific | 41 | 136.10 |
| article | 77 | 246.86 | why | 117 | 130.57 |
| **believe** | 114 | 232.50 | shrill | 25 | 129.21 |
| 'm | 142 | 222.99 | human | 57 | 125.86 |
| religions | 44 | 220.18 | actually | 61 | 122.95 |

| | | | | | |
|---|---|---|---|---|---|
| moral | 40 | 122.48 | silly | 26 | 78.35 |
| about | 230 | 120.18 | 've | 75 | 76.02 |
| argument | 42 | 117.73 | have | 432 | 75.98 |
| O'Neill | 21 | 115.55 | islam | 19 | 75.18 |
| supernatural | 27 | 114.91 | rational | 19 | 75.18 |
| christian | 45 | 113.10 | secular | 19 | 75.18 |
| are | 561 | 110.79 | thinking | 44 | 72.89 |
| @ | 20 | 110.05 | morality | 18 | 72.84 |
| reason | 63 | 107.19 | – | 13 | 71.53 |
| intellectual | 29 | 105.08 | Richard_Dawkins | 13 | 71.53 |
| theists | 19 | 104.54 | hardtimethinking | 13 | 71.53 |
| Brendan_O'Neill | 18 | 99.04 | enlightenment | 17 | 70.62 |
| spirituality | 18 | 99.04 | ignorance | 19 | 70.57 |
| their | 323 | 98.59 | irrational | 15 | 70.48 |
| they | 425 | 96.08 | ideas | 42 | 70.15 |
| as | 562 | 94.48 | exist | 30 | 68.31 |
| or | 387 | 94.46 | so | 201 | 67.76 |
| Grayling | 17 | 93.54 | new | 180 | 66.73 |
| those | 154 | 90.70 | intolerance | 15 | 66.71 |
| agree | 38 | 88.74 | attacking | 19 | 66.57 |
| metaphysical | 16 | 88.04 | faustroll | 12 | 66.03 |
| your | 200 | 85.10 | trying | 47 | 65.78 |
| christianity | 26 | 82.71 | evolutionary | 14 | 65.24 |
| spiritual | 26 | 82.71 | but | 453 | 64.65 |
| arguments | 32 | 82.43 | say | 91 | 64.01 |
| point | 61 | 80.24 | catholics | 16 | 63.05 |

# Appendix 3

# 'The new atheism' argument annotated for sub-binary oppositions 1 and 2

**1**   [headline] The New Atheism

**2**   [sub-headline] There is more humanity in the 'superhuman' delusions of the devout

**[HIGH VIEW OF HUMANKIND of the RELIGIOUS = *POSITIVE*]**

than there is in the realism of the hectoring atheists

**[NEW ATHEISM: + HECTORING = *NEGATIVE*]**

**[A]**

**3**   [Introductory paragraph] 'New atheism' was the surprise political hit of 2007.

**4**   God-bashing books by Hitchens, Dawkins and other thinkers who come out in a rash when they hear the word 'religion' flew out of the bookshops.

**5**   Philip Pullman's anti-divine Golden Compass hit the big screen.

**6**   Everywhere, God was exposed as a fraud and God botherers were given an intellectual lashing.

**[B]**

**7**   I am as atheistic as it gets.

**8**   But I will not be signing up to this shrill hectoring of the religious.

**[NEW ATHEISM: + HECTORING = *NEGATIVE*]**

**9**   The new atheists have given atheism a bad name.

**10**   History's greatest atheists, or the "old atheists" as we are now forced to call them, were humanistic and progressive, critical of religion because it expressed man's sense of *higher* moral purpose in a deeply flawed fashion.

**[OLD ATHEISM: + DEEP / – HECTORING / + PROGRESSIVE = *POSITIVE*]**
**[OLD ATHEISM associated with HIGH VIEW OF HUMANKIND of the RELIGIOUS = *POSITIVE*]**

**11**   The new atheists are screechy and intolerant; they see religion merely as an expression of mass ignorance and delusion.

**12**   Their aim seems to be, not only to bring God crashing back down to earth, but also to *downgrade* mankind itself.

**[NEW ATHEISM: – DEEP / + HECTORING / – PROGRESSIVE = *NEGATIVE*]**
**[NEW ATHEISM: LOW VIEW of MANKIND = *NEGATIVE*]**

**[C]**

13  There's something bitterly ironic in the fact that the new atheists pose as the successors to Darwin.

14  Darwin himself had little interest in baiting the devout.

**[OLD ATHEISM: – HECTORING = *POSITIVE*].**

15  In the early 1880s, he was asked by the radical atheist Edward Aveling to endorse a new book on evolutionary theory.

16  Darwin, caring little for Aveling's 'anti-religious militancy', refused. He wrote to Aveling: 'It appears to me . . . that direct arguments against Christianity and theism produce hardly any effect on the public; and freedom of thought is best promoted by the gradual illumination of men's minds which follows from the advance of science. It has, therefore, been always my object to avoid writing on religion . . .'.

**[D]**

17  Marx, too, believed that direct assaults on religion were pointless.

**[OLD ATHEISM: – HECTORING = *POSITIVE*].**

18  He argued that religion existed as spiritual compensation for social alienation, and believed that once the true nature of religion as a comfort blanket in an alienated society had been revealed, it would become clear that religion is merely a secondary phenomenon dependent for its existence on socioeconomic circumstances.

19  Radical critics should focus their intellectual ire on the degraded society that sustains religion rather than on attacking religion itself: 'The criticism of heaven turns into the criticism of earth, the criticism of religion into the criticism of law, and the criticism of theology into the criticism of politics.'

**[E]**

20  Old atheists sought to 'illuminate men's minds', through advancing science or deepening our understanding of capitalist society.

**[OLD ATHEISM: + DEEP / – HECTORING / + PROGRESSIVE = *POSITIVE*].**

21  New atheists take exactly the opposite approach.

22  They expend all of their energy on attacking the institution of religion and its ridiculous adherents.

**[NEW ATHEISM: – DEEP / + HECTORING / – PROGRESSIVE = *NEGATIVE*]**

**[F]**

23  Consider their bizarre and fevered obsession with religious symbols, such as crucifixes worn around the neck, or statements of religious belief by public

figures like Tony Blair or Nick Clegg: their distaste for anything that looks or sounds vaguely religious exposes the shallow anti-intellectualism of their new atheism.

**[NEW ATHEISM: – DEEP = _NEGATIVE_]**

24  Their opposition to religion is not driven by a profound or radical vision, as was Darwin's and Marx's,

**[OLD ATHEISM: + DEEP / + PROGRESSIVE = _POSITIVE_]**

but rather by a dinner-party disdain and moral revulsion for the stupidity of the religious.

**[NEW ATHEISM: – DEEP = _NEGATIVE_]**

25  Where old atheism was driven by a passionate belief in progress,

**[OLD ATHEISM: + PROGRESSIVE = _POSITIVE_]**

new atheism springs from today's crisis of secularism.

26  It is because new atheists have lost their own belief in progress and Enlightenment

**[NEW ATHEISM: – PROGRESSIVE = _NEGATIVE_]**

that they turn harshly against those who still cling to visions of a better society or 'kingdom'.

**[NEW ATHEISM: + HECTORING of the religious for HIGH VIEW OF HUMANKIND = _NEGATIVE_]**


**[G]**

27  The inhumanity of the new atheism is best illustrated by its move from the world of social critique into the realm of sociobiology.

**[NEW ATHEISM: LOW VIEW OF HUMANKIND = _NEGATIVE_]**

28  Some new atheists believe humans must be genetically predisposed to believing in a higher being.

29  Marx and others saw religion as the product of socioeconomic circumstances, and thus believed that religion would wither away as humanity proceeded along the path of progress.

**[OLD ATHEISM: + PROGRESSIVE = _POSITIVE_]**

30  New atheists see religious belief as a kind of animalistic instinct, driven by DNA.

31  Where Marx viewed people's turn towards religion as an understandable response to the harsh reality of alienation in capitalist society, new atheists see it as the product of mankind's twisted genetic makeup.

**[NEW ATHEISM: LOW VIEW OF HUMANKIND / – PROGRESSIVE = _NEGATIVE_]**

**[H]**

32 So what is their solution?

33 Mass genetic therapy?

34 Compulsory injections of the correct DNA – you know, the kind possessed by intelligent and well-bred people who can see through religious delusion?

35 The new atheists' abandonment of a social outlook

**[NEW ATHEISM: – PROGRESSIVE = _NEGATIVE_]**

leads them to adopt some very grim, anti-human views.

**[NEW ATHEISM: LOW VIEW OF HUMANKIND = _NEGATIVE_]**

**[I]**

36 The key difference between the old and new atheism is in their views of mankind.

37 For atheists like Marx, religion expressed, in a backward and limited form, human aspirations to greatness. 'Man . . . looked for a superhuman being in the fantastic reality of heaven and found nothing there but the reflection of himself.'

**[OLD ATHEISM associated with HIGH VIEW OF HUMANKIND of the RELIGIOUS = _POSITIVE_]**

38 He continued: 'The criticism of religion ends with the teaching that man is the highest being for man hence with the categorical imperative to overthrow all relations in which man is a debased, enslaved, forsaken, despicable being . . .'

**[OLD ATHEISM associated with HIGH VIEW OF HUMANKIND of the RELIGIOUS = _POSITIVE_]**

39 Today, Hitchens says of religion's destructive impact: 'What else was to be expected of something that was produced by the close cousins of chimpanzees?'

40 For Marx, religion had to be abolished because it made man despicable; for new atheists religion exists precisely because man is despicable, little more than a monkey.

**[NEW ATHEISM: LOW VIEW OF HUMANKIND = _NEGATIVE_]**

**[J]**

41 New atheists will continue to ridicule the religious in 2008.

**[NEW ATHEISM: + HECTORING = _NEGATIVE_]**

42 But there is more humanity in the 'superhuman' delusions of the devout – in their yearning for a sense of purpose and greatness

[HIGH VIEW OF HUMANKIND OF THE RELIGIOUS = *POSITIVE*]

than there is in the monkeyman realism of the hectoring atheists.
[NEW ATHEISM = LOW VIEW OF HUMANKIND / – DEEP / + HECTORING /
– PROGRESSIVE = *NEGATIVE*].

# Appendix 4

## Concordance for 'faith' in The Four Horsemen transcript

it's almost an ontological commitment of atheism to say that all faith claims are in some sense equivalent. You know, the media says a move that they don't accept when done in the name of another faith. [DD] Exactly. [CH] But now, in which case, could I ask you to say that you look forward to a world where no one had any faith in the supernatural? [RD] I want to answer this. Whether it's expect to, or wish to, see that. [SH] What do you mean by 'faith'? [CH] Well I don't think it's possible, because it replicates significant phrase to me: "There's a reason that it's called faith!" He said it very decisively, almost aggressively, that there's almost aggressively, that there's a reason that it's called faith. And that was, to him, the absolute knockdown clincher. You can but an argument that suggests that what we're up to, criticising faith, is a bad thing. [RD] Oh, that's much easier. [SH] That we

Well I don't think it's possible, because it replicates so fast, faith. As often as it's cut down, or superseded, or discredited, it have a question for the three of you. Is there any argument for faith, any challenge to your atheism that has given you pause, that

The only argument that I find at all attractive, and this is for faith you asked as well as for theism, is what I would, I suppose I'd all I got from this report was that this was the first time his faith had ever really been explicitly challenged. And so it's true to Western Europe, is largely the result of the fact that we honour faith so much in our discourse that the community has not become as What do you mean 'something like faith'? [DD] Yeah, and how like faith? [CH] Something like the belief that there must be more than we unintelligently there, I think. What do you mean 'something like faith'? [DD] Yeah, and how like faith? [CH] Something like the belief I'd actually in a sense welcome the persistence of something like faith. I feel I've put it better now than I did at the beginning.

What does moderation consist of? It consists of having lost faith in all of these propositions, or half of them because of the do with the fear of extinction, or annihilation [SH] So you mean faith in supernatural paradigms? [CH] Yes, the wish. Wish thinking. . . . [DD] I could give you several discoveries which would shake my faith right to the ground. [SH] No, no! Let me just broaden the that we could share. [SH] Dan Dennett believes that, that's not faith. [DD] Yeah, sure. [SH] I mean, we know there's more than we we reasonably think we can accomplish? And then this article of faith that I think circulates, unfortunately, among people of our precisely that they'll say that they're in a permanent crisis of faith. There is indeed a prayer, "Lord I believe, help thou my that. The less you believe it, the more your demonstration of faith. [SH] The more you prove it's true. [CH] Yes, and the struggle, evidence is especially noble". I mean, this is the doctrine of faith. This is the parable of Doubting Thomas. And so you start with

(continued)

# Appendix 4   Continued

cast of mind in, I think, a very long end note in 'The End of Faith', where I say, "any text can be read." Well, with the eyes of where I say, "any text can be read." Well, with the eyes of faith you can make magical (?prescience/impressions) out of any text. the people I know who call themselves believers, or people of faith, do that all the time. I wouldn't say it was schizophrenia, be nothing to be faithful about. [SH] Right, that's the point of faith. [CHI] If everyone has seen the resurrection, and if we all knew and moderates tend to argue that this is somehow a triumph of faith, that faith is somehow self-enlightening, whereas it's been hurt feelings card, and reminds you how wonderful taking it on faith is. I mean, there aren't any new tricks, these tricks have I think it may be easier than we're supposing to shake peoples' faith. There's been a moratorium on this for a long time. We're just beginning of a new wave of explicit attempts to shake peoples' faith. And it's bearing fruit, and the obstacles it seems to me are false. And for that reason, because they're forced by preferring faith to reason, latently at least, equally dangerous. [RD] Equally knockdown clincher. You can't argue with it because it's faith and he said it proudly and defiantly rather than in any sort of And he said I accept all your rational arguments, however it's faith. And then he said this very significant phrase to me: "There's religious person feels the same criticism of other people's faith that we do, as atheists. I mean, they reject the pseudo of others, and they see the confidence tricks in other people's faith, and they see it rather readily. You know, every Christian tend to argue that this is somehow a triumph of faith, that faith is somehow self-enlightening, whereas it's been enlightened you can't put it forward. We're not going to let you play the faith card. Now if you want to defend what your holy book says, in for me. Say what you think that move is. [DD] Somebody plays the faith card. [CHI] Yes. [DD] They say look, I am a Christian and we internal to their faith or the contradiction between their faith and what we've come to know to be true about the universe, and of what they knew to be true and what they were told by their faith that I think we have to just highlight the fact that it's I'm constantly getting e-mail from people who have lost their faith and in effect been argued out of it. And the straw that broke Dan Barker's making a collection of clergymen who've lost their faith but don't dare say so, because it's their only living. It's the for people to be shown the contradictions, internal to their faith or the contradiction between their faith and what we've come to real objective is. Do we, in fact, wish to see a world without faith? I think I would have to say that I don't. I don't either Because that is harder for me to imagine, than a world without faith, I must say. [SH] Well, you brought up the bell curve – I mean, the curriculum of becoming a scientist and never have your faith explicitly challenged, because it's taboo to do so, and now we

# Notes

1 For a recent compendium of CDA work, see Wodak (2013).

2 See, for example, Fowler et al. (1979); Kress and Hodge (1979); Kress (1985); Fairclough (2001); Bloor and Bloor (2007).

3 In another contemporary approach to argumentation, 'Informal Logic', *dialectical obligations* are a feature (e.g. Johnson (2003)).

4 If the social media platform attracts intelligent readers, all to the good.

5 See, for example, Baker (2009), Flowerdew (2011), Hunston (2002), McCarthy and O'Keeffe (2010), McEnery and Hardie (2011), Sinclair (2004), Stubbs (1996; 2001).

6 Undertaking qualitative analysis of keyword usage will also help ensure that keywords are part of genuine posts rather than, say, spam.

7 *The Guardian* is regarded as a digital innovator, such as in relation to the continuously developing space it affords for readers to comment and discuss argumentative journalism http://www.abc.net.au/news/2013-01-16/guardian-launching-australian-online-edition/4466636 [Accessed February 2014].

8 http://freethoughtreport.com/wp-content/uploads/2013/07/FOTReport2013.pdf [Accessed February 2014].

9 http://www.guardian.co.uk/help/insideguardian/2013/may/24/theguardian-global-domain [Accessed February 2014].

10 http://freethoughtreport.com/wp-content/uploads/2013/07/FOTReport2013.pdf [Accessed February 2014].

11 The whole argument and the discussion forum appended to it can be found at: http://www.guardian.co.uk/commentisfree/2007/dec/30/thenewatheism. At the time of publication of O'Neill's argument, *The Guardian* had a policy of closing a forum after three days.

12 WMatrix has online access to one reference corpus – the British National Corpus (BNC) Sampler. This consists of around one million words each of the BNC Sampler spoken corpus and the BNC Sampler written corpus (the whole of the BNC consists of ten million words of spoken and ninety million words of written English). On the rule of thumb that 'we should at least try to obtain reference corpora which reflect some aspect of the smaller corpus or text sample we are studying' (Baker, 2006: 43), I chose to compare the argument with the BNC Sampler written corpus. Information can be obtained on the composition of the BNC Sampler written corpus at http://ucrel.lancs.ac.uk/bnc2sampler/sampler.htm. Programs other than WMatrix are available for generating keywords (e.g. AntConc, Wordsmith Tools). But, they require the user to be able to get their hands on a reference corpus – something which may not be readily available.

13 In reporting statistical significance, $p < 0.01$ indicates a 1 in 100 likelihood that the result could occur purely by chance.

14 http://www.iep.utm.edu/n-atheis/#H1 [Accessed February 2014].

15 The prominence that criticism of 'religious belief' is given in 'new atheism' is also reflected in four of the eight section headings in Taylor (2010): 'Faith and Reason', 'Arguments For and Against God's Existence', 'Evolution and Religious Belief', 'Alleged Divine Revelations'. (The other section headings are 'The Moral Evaluation of Religion', 'Secular Morality', 'Secular Fulfilment', 'Criticism of the New Atheists'.)

**16** See Marx's Critique of Hegel's 'Philosophy of Right', p. 131. http://marxists.org/archive/marx/works/download/Marx_Critique_of_Hegels_Philosophy_of_Right.pdf [Accessed February 2014].

**17** The term 'collocation' describes a regular co-occurrence of words, over a designated word span, in texts of a corpus.

**18** The lemma of a word consists of all its grammatical instances. Lemmas are indicated conventionally by capitals. The noun lemma COLLAPSE includes the noun singular form 'collapse' and the noun plural form 'collapses'. The verb lemma COLLAPSE includes the verb forms 'collapse', 'collapses', 'collapsed', 'collapsing'. A broad conception of the lemma COLLAPSE would include its noun and verb forms.

**19** The UK Web as Corpus (UKWaC) was built in 2007. From information on the Sketch Engine website (http://www.sketchengine.co.uk/), it consists of 1,318,047,961 words and 1,565,274,190 tokens [website accessed February 2014 ]. UKWaC derives from World Wide Web sites with a UK internet domain name, and contains a wide variety of topics and registers. Since the aim was to build a corpus of British English, only UK Internet domains were included (see Ferraresi et al. 2008).

**20** The word span for this collocation investigation is conventionally represented as $n \pm 4$ where $n$ is the node word. $n \pm 4$ is the standard span for searching for collocation in corpus linguistics (Jones and Sinclair, 1974).

**21** Given O'Neill's hyperbole, Dawkins et al. are still unlikely to endorse the proposition ascribed to 'new atheism', in the second clause of sentence 40, even if it does now contain 'religious belief'. And, in any case, chimpanzees are apes not monkeys.

**22** See Derrida (1999a, 1999b, 2000) as well as Levinas (1969), an important influence for Derrida's ethics.

**23** In a different source – a three minute video – Richard Dawkins summarizes a central argument of 'The God Delusion', the argument which links the epistemological to the moral component http://www.amazon.com/The-God-Delusion-Richard-Dawkins/dp/0618918248/ref=sr_1_1?ie=UTF8&qid=1330788377&sr=8-1 [Accessed February 2014]. The following extract provides further corroboration of the keyword analysis of the discussion forum:

> 'The great majority of people on this planet do believe that there is some kind of a supreme being [. . .] historically it's always been very important to people their belief in some sort of a supreme being [. . .] I give in the book the argument [. . .] that there is no supernatural supreme being and that belief in such a being can under some circumstances be rather a bad thing' [my bold].

**24** See O'Halloran (forthcoming) where the ethical foundation for digital argument deconstruction also includes the thinking of Gilles Deleuze and Félix Guattari.

**25** My own experience of teaching digital text analysis and systemic functional grammar is that students take much less time to assimilate the former than the latter.

# References

Baker, P. (2006), *Using Corpora in Discourse Analysis*. London: Continuum.
Baker, P. (ed.) (2009), *Contemporary Corpus Linguistics*. London: Continuum.

Bloor, M. and Bloor, T. (2007), *The Practice of Critical Discourse Analysis*. London: Hodder Arnold.

Chouliaraki, L. and Fairclough, N. (1999), *Discourse in Late Modernity: Rethinking Critical Discourse Analysis*. Edinburgh University Press, Edinburgh.

Dawkins, R. (2006), *The God Delusion*. London: Black Swann.

Dawkins, R., Dennett, D., Harris, S. and Hitchens, C. (2007), *Four Horsemen, Discussions with Richard Dawkins, Episode 1 (transcript)*. Available at: http://www.richarddawkinsfoundation.org/fourhorsementranscript (accessed February 2014).

Dennett, D. (2006), *Breaking the Spell*. London: Penguin.

Derrida, J. (1976 [1967]), *Of Grammatology*, trans. G. C. Spivak. Baltimore: Johns Hopkins University Press.

—— (1999a), *Adieu*, trans. P.-A. Brault and M. Nass. Stanford: Stanford University Press.

—— (1999b), 'Hospitality, justice and responsibility: a dialogue with Jacques Derrida' in R. Kearney and M. Dooley (eds), *Questioning Ethics*. London: Routledge, pp.65–83.

—— (2000), *Of Hospitality*, trans. R. Bowlby. Stanford: Standford University Press.

Dunning, T. (1993), 'Accurate methods for the statistics of surprise and coincidence'. *Computational Linguistics*, 19(1), 61–74.

Fairclough, N. (1989), *Language and Power*. London: Longman.

—— (2001), *Language and Power* (2nd edn). London: Longman.

Ferraresi, A., Zanchetta, E., Baroni, M. and Bernardini, S. (2008), 'Introducing and evaluating UKWaC', in S. Evert, A. Kilgarriff and S. Sharoff (eds), *Proceedings of the 4th Web as Corpus Workshop, Marrakech, 1 June: Can we beat Google?*, 47–54. Available at: http://www.lrec-conf.org/proceedings/lrec2008/workshops/W19_Proceedings.pdf (accessed February 2014).

Flowerdew, L. (2011), 'Corpus-based discourse analysis', in J. P. Gee and M. Handford (eds), *Routledge Handbook of Discourse Analysis*. London: Routledge, pp. 174–87.

Fowler, R., Hodge, B., Kress, G. and Trew, T. (1979), *Language and Control*. London: Routledge and Kegan Paul.

Harris, S. (2006), *The End of Faith*. New York: Free Press.

Hitchens, C. (2007), *God is not Great*. New York: Atlantic Books.

Hunston, S. (2001), 'Colligation, lexis, pattern, and text', in M. Scott and G. Thompson (eds), *Patterns of Text: In Honour of Michael Hoey*. Amsterdam: John Benjamins, pp. 13–33.

—— (2002) *Corpora in Applied Linguistics*. Cambridge: Cambridge University Press.

Johnson, R. H. (2003), 'The dialectical tier revisited', in Frans H. van Eemeren, J. Anthony Blair (eds), *Anyone Who has a View: Theoretical Contributions to the Study of Argumentation*. Charles A. Willard, and A. Francisca Snoeck. Henkemans. Dorcrecht: Kluwer Academic Publishers, pp. 41–54.

Jones, S. and J. Sinclair (1974), 'English lexical collocations'. *Cahiers de Lexicologie*, 24. pp. 15–61.

Kress, G. (1985), *Linguistic Processes in Sociocultural Practice*. Oxford: Oxford University Press.

Kress, G. and Hodge, R. (1979), *Language as Ideology*. London: Routledge and Kegan Paul.

Levinas, E. (1969 [1961]), *Totality and Infinity: An essay on Exteriority*, trans. A. Lingis. Pittsburgh, PA: Duquesne University Press.

McCarthy and O'Keeffe (eds) (2010), *The Routledge Handbook of Corpus Linguistics*. Abingdon: Routledge.

McEnery, T. and Hardie, A. (2011), *Corpus Linguistics: Method, Theory and Practice*. Cambridge: Cambridge University Press.

O'Halloran, K. A. (2012), 'Electronic deconstruction: revealing tensions in the cohesive structure of persuasion texts'. *International Journal of Corpus Linguistics*, 17(1), 91–124.

—— (2013a), 'Deleuze, Guattari and the use of web-based corpora for facilitating critical analysis of public sphere arguments'. *Discourse, Context and Media*, 2(1), 40–51.

—— (2013b), 'A corpus-based deconstructive strategy for critically engaging with arguments'. *Argument and Computation*, 4(2), 128–50.

—— (forthcoming), *Deconstructing Arguments in the Digital Age*. Abingdon, UK: Routledge.

Rayson, P. (2009), Wmatrix: a web-based corpus processing environment. Computing Department, Lancaster University. Available at: http://ucrel.lancs.ac.uk/wmatrix (accessed February 2014)

Scott, M. (1997), 'PC analysis of key words – and key key words'. *System*, 25(2), 233–45.

Sinclair, J. (2004), *Trust the Text: Language, Corpus and Discourse*. Abingdon: Routledge.

Stubbs, M. (1996), *Text and Corpus Analysis: Computer Assisted Studies of Language and Institutions*. Oxford: Blackwell.

—— (2001), *Words and Phrases: Corpus Studies of Lexical Semantics*. Oxford: Blackwell.

Taylor, J. E. (2010), 'The new atheists', in *Internet Encyclopedia of Philosophy*. Available at: http://www.iep.utm.edu/n-atheis/ (Accessed February 2014).

Van Dijk, T. (2001), 'Multidisciplinary diversity', in Wodak, R. and Meyer, M. (eds), *Methods of Critical Discourse Analysis*. London: Sage, pp. 95–120.

Van Eemeren, F. and Grootendorst, R. (2004), *A Systematic Theory of Argumentation: The Pragma-Dialectical Approach*. Cambridge: Cambridge University Press.

Walton, D. (2006), *Fundamentals of Critical Argumentation*. Cambridge, UK: Cambridge University Press.

Wodak, R. (ed.) (2013), *Critical Discourse Analysis* (4 vols). London: Sage.

**SOUND AND VISION**

# 11

# Critical Discourse Analysis and Multimodality

*Theo van Leeuwen*
University of Technology, Sydney and
University of Southern Denmark

## 1 Introduction: multimodality

The term multimodality refers to the integrated use of different semiotic resources (e.g. language, image, sound and music) in texts and communicative events. It therefore indexes a phenomenon, rather than a method, or, as Kress has formulated it (2010: 54), it 'names a field of work and a domain to be theorized' – although it could be argued that the 'mode' in 'multimodality' makes it sound more semiotic than rival terms such as 'intermediality' (Elleström, 2010) and 'multisensoriality' (Classen, 1993). The theoretical and methodological underpinnings of multimodality have for the most part come from linguistics. Once linguists had moved from studying isolated sentences to studying texts, they soon realized that communication is multimodal, that spoken language as it is actually used cannot be adequately understood without taking non-verbal communication into account, and that many forms of contemporary written language cannot be adequately understood unless we look, not just at language, but also at images, layout, typography and colour. So in the 1960s American linguists (and anthropologists) began to extend linguistic paradigms to the study of non-verbal communication (e.g. Birdwhistell, 1973; Pittenger et al., 1960) and French structuralist semioticians began to apply linguistic methods to the study of news and advertising photographs (e.g. Barthes, 1977) and many other modes and media, including films, music, comic strips and graphic design. More recently the work of Halliday (1978,

1985) has inspired 'grammars' of semiotic modes such as visual images (O'Toole, 1994; Kress and Van Leeuwen, 1996), sound and music (Van Leeuwen, 1999), and body action (Martinec, 2000, 2004), to name just a few, and accounts of the way in which different semiotic modes, for instance text and image, are integrated into multimodal texts (e.g. Royce, 1998; Martinec and Salway, 2005; Van Leeuwen, 2005). By now, multimodality has its own bi-annual conference, a range of edited books (e.g. Ventola et al., 2004; Norris, 2004; Royce and Bowcher, 2007; Jewitt, 2009; O'Halloran and Smith, 2011; Dreyfus et al., 2011; Djonov and Zhao, 2013) and all the other trappings of a fully-fledged discipline.

Theoretically, multimodal studies are, as Djonov and Zhao (2013) explain, informed by three distinct traditions: social semiotics (e.g. Kress and Hodge, 1988; Van Leeuwen, 2005); interaction analysis (e.g. Norris, 2004); and cognitive theory (e.g. Forceville and Urios-Aparisi, 2009). The social semiotic approach is based on the Hallidayan idea (Halliday, 1978) that semiotic resources develop in response to social and cultural needs and that semiotic practices cannot be understood without taking into account both their broader, 'macro' social and cultural context and their narrower, 'micro' situational context, and often works with Halliday's 'metafunctional' theory, in which discourse co-deploys resources for making ideational, interpersonal and textual meaning, and therefore should be analysed at each of these levels. Interaction analysis stems from the tradition of American micro-analysis of social situations, and more specifically from the work of Scollon (e.g. 2001). Norris (2004), for instance, studies how micro interactions, in all their multimodal complexity, weave together into interactional practices with their attendant participant identities. This then forms an empirical basis for theoretical reflections on issues such as agency, identity and habitus. Forceville has influentially applied Lakoff and Johnson's (1980) cognitive metaphor theory to multimodal communication, especially in commercial advertising, and also pointed at the potential of his approach for critical discourse analysis (Forceville, 2013).

## 2 Multimodality and critical discourse analysis

The work of multimodal discourse analysts is not necessarily critical in the sense of critical discourse analysis, that is, focused foremost on the role of discourse, be it multimodal or otherwise, in maintaining and legitimating inequality, injustice and oppression in society (cf. Richardson and Colombo, this volume). Educational applications often celebrate the multimodal texts and communicative events they investigate, for instance in studies of the development of multimodal literacy in young children (e.g. Kress, 1997), of multimodal learning resources, including textbooks, toys, CD-Roms and the internet (e.g. Jewitt, 2006), and of multimodal classroom interaction. Such work sees multimodality as a key towards better learning and stresses that the learning potential of different modes needs to be better understood by teachers, and that multimodal literacy needs to be more fully integrated into the curriculum in ways that can be inspired by studying the spontaneous learning of very young children, or by studying other forms of informal learning, such as playing with toys or computer games. In the same vein, multimodal analysis is applied to improving communication and learning in museums, tourist communication, health and workplace communication, organizational communication and so on.

Nevertheless, there has always been a critical strand within multimodal discourse analysis. This was to a large extent due to the example set by Gunther Kress and Bob Hodge (Kress and Hodge, 1978, 1988). Their first book, *Language and Ideology* (1978) had been a forerunner of critical discourse analysis. Influenced by Whorf and Halliday as well as Marx, they had shown how grammatical systems allow reality to be interpreted in different ways, and how grammatical constructions can realize ideological meanings. In their second joint book, *Social Semiotics* (1988), they extended this to other modes of communication, showing, for instance, how the grammatical system of modality can be applied to visual images, where it may use different signifiers, but nevertheless does the same kind of communicative work it does in language, namely creating 'social definitions of the real'. They showed, not only how the grammar of modality was deployed in the press to lessen the credibility of left-wing politicians in the Thatcher era, but also how it was used in comic strips to make readers identify with the 'good' characters, and distance themselves from the 'bad' characters (Kress and Hodge, 1988: 121ff). Though published a few years before Kress and Van Leeuwen would introduce the term 'multimodality' (which previously had had a restricted use in the psychology of perception), *Social Semiotics* opened up the field, presenting a comprehensive theoretical framework for the social semiotic analysis of multimodal texts, comparing and contrasting it with the main traditions in semiotics (Saussure and Peirce), and applying it to a wide range of multimodal examples from art and literature as well as popular culture.

This work was further developed in Kress and Van Leeuwen's *Reading Images: The Grammar of Visual Design* (1996), which presented visual grammatical systems using Hallidayan system networks and which provided detailed methods of analysis with clear formal criteria, which have subsequently been applied in a range of contexts, many of them not related to critical discourse analysis. On the other hand, many of Kress and Van Leeuwen's examples demonstrated the potential of their methods for critical discourse analysis. One of their key examples was taken from an Australian social studies textbook for primary school children titled *Our Society and Others* (Figure 11.1).

The book's chapter on Aboriginal Australians included a section on their material culture, and this section included a page on which two nineteenth-century engravings were shown side by side – on the left a picture of Aboriginal artefacts, formally arranged, and shown against a white background (a stone axe, a bark basket and a wooden sword); on the right a moonlit scene of two British settlers stalking up towards a group of Aborigines seated around a fire, their guns ready. Kress and Van Leeuwen used these pictures on the one hand as examples of specific visual grammar structures. The picture of the Aboriginal artefacts was an example of a 'classificational' image, an

The British used guns

< Stone axe, bark basket and wooden sword

**FIGURE 11.1** *The British Used Guns (Oakley, 1985).*

image in which a number of different objects or people are arranged symmetrically and given the same size, the same orientation to the horizontal and vertical axis, and so on, so as to signify that, somehow, they belong to the same category, even though that category is not always verbally labelled. The picture on the right was an example of a 'narrative' image, in which the two main 'volumes' of the picture, the two most visually salient entities (the 'British' and the Aboriginal people round the fire) are linked by a 'vector', an oblique line (here formed by the guns and the stance of the settlers' bodies) running from the one to the other and signifying an action ('aiming a gun at') in which one 'volume' (the one from which the vector emanates, i.e. the settlers) is the Actor, the entity that does the action, and the other the Goal, the entity that is affected by the action (here the Aboriginal people). But Kress and Van Leeuwen also pointed out that such structures construct particular versions of the realities they depict. It would have been possible to have a 'classificational' picture of antique British guns, and a 'narrative' picture of Aboriginal people attacking the colonists, for instance. After all, in the early nineteenth century, when these engravings were made, Aboriginal people often attacked the settlers who invaded their land. Moreover, the captions offered different constructions of the same events. The caption of the 'narrative' picture, for instance, read 'The British used guns', thus eliminating the affected party, the Aboriginal people. Finally, the left-right structure realized a 'Given-New' relation in which the picture of the 'primitive' Aboriginal tools is the Given, and the picture of the gun-using colonists the New, the element treated as not yet known to the readers and therefore containing the key message. Such observations, based on explicit and replicable methods of analysis, can lead to critical analyses – the chapter in the school book, for instance, showed the colonization of Australia and the subjection of its Aboriginal inhabitants as the inevitable outcome of British technological superiority.

But Kress and Van Leeuwen did not explicitly describe their methods as a form of critical analysis. They just revealed an interest in multimodal critical discourse analysis through their choice of examples, and through their often brief interpretations of these examples. Today multimodal critical analysis still remains relatively marginal and tentative within the field of multimodality, and at times little more than an afterthought – Bednarek (2013: 52), for instance, distances herself somewhat from CDA by calling her approach 'critical with a small c' and balancing it with a 'positive perspective'. In a recent international conference on multimodality only 12 of the 123 papers had an explicitly critical aim, going by the abstracts (Fifth International Conference on Multimodality, 2010). Still, the idea of 'critical multimodal discourse analysis' is beginning to get a foothold, especially with the publication of an edited volume on *Critical Multimodal Studies of Popular Culture* in the Routledge Studies in Multimodality book series (Djonov and Zhao, 2013). Many of the chapters of this book, too, engage with critical discourse analysis only tentatively, as in the above-mentioned chapter by Bednarek, or in the chapter by Tan (2013), who describes in considerable detail the development of business news, but in the end sits on the fence as to how its increased conversationality is to be evaluated, or as in the chapter by Zhang and O'Halloran (2013), which provides an excellent description of the new genre of 'scifotainment' and briefly criticizes it as oversimplifying science, but does not really demonstrate this oversimplification, and leaves it as 'an open question' which needs more work (Zhang and O'Halloran, 2013: 174). On the other hand, the title of the book and its inclusion in the Routledge book series on multimodality firmly puts critical multimodal studies on the map, the introduction clearly states the common heritage of multimodality studies and critical discourse analysis and the critical purpose of critical discourse analysis (and critical literacy studies), the book emphasizes the importance of critically analysing popular culture (a point to which I will return), and many of the chapters begin to model what critical multimodal studies can be like. The chapter by Gorfinkel (2013) for instance, shows how popular Chinese television shows reconstruct Macau as part of China, and how, in these shows, mixed race Macanians are at once excluded from true Chinese identity and included in the context of a discourse of China's relation with the West. The chapter by Thomas focuses on critical literacy and clearly demonstrates the critical power of student-created multimodal narratives. And the chapters by the editors themselves are fine examples of multimodal critical discourse analysis. Zhao (2013) critically analyses an 'alternative' women's magazine, and comes to the conclusion that it differs from traditional women's magazines only in style, creating emotion-sharing language to position its readers just as much as consumers as traditional magazines, and mixing culture and consumption, interviews and product promotion, just as happens today in so many other media. Djonov and Van

Leeuwen (2013) criticize both the genre of the bullet-pointed list, and the way the Australian Labour party recontextualized the federal treasurer's Budget into a bullet-pointed list which depoliticized the speech and presented the proposed surplus as an achievement of profit rather than as the result of potentially controversial spending cuts, all this in the form of a 'report card' with 'checklist' style bullet points.

However, one cannot help concluding that multimodal critical discourse analysis needs to be more explicit about what the term 'critical' means, and about what distinguishes critical discourse analysis from discourse analysis. Discourse analysis is by nature descriptive, and description is an often underestimated, or even maligned, fine art. Any form of critical discourse analysis must go beyond description and also evaluate what it has described, and it must be explicit about the values on which this evaluation is based, and about the critic's commitment to these values. Critical *discourse* analysis therefore needs to balance description and critique, basing critique explicitly on descriptive analysis, as well as on explicit accounts of the values at stake. These values may be political or aesthetic, but they are ultimately always moral, and moral values are not 'subjective'. They are socially shared values, to whose reflections in critical cultural and social theory critical discourse analysts should be attentive.

Another important point here is the unhelpful term 'positive criticism', which implies that 'non-positive' forms of critique are negative and hostile. However, a critical discourse analysis which determines beforehand whether it is negative or positive cannot be critical in any meaningful sense. Critical evaluation must be made on the basis of evidence, keep an open mind as to whether the ultimate judgement is to be negative, positive, or a bit of both, and be willing, in principle, to be negative. Negative critique may make a positive contribution by identifying problems that need tackling. Not everybody will like this. Critique can be dangerous. But without it, and without fostering critical ability in education, we will become a society of ants.

A further point is the danger, in critical multimodal discourse analysis, of methodological excess. A genre analysis, for instance, is not a critical analysis unless the genre in question and its workings in society are critically evaluated, as recently formulated by Molek-Kozakowska (2013: 324) in relation to late-night satirical TV talk shows:

> A critical genre analysis [. . .] aims at interrogating [. . .] generic conventions. [. . .] As generic conventions are potentially power-invested, it is crucial to move beyond genre description and interpretation [. . .] to the stage of explanation of social consequences of the rise, popularity, proliferation, or cross-fertilization of certain genres. In accordance with the overall philosophy of CDA/CDS [Van Dijk, 1993, 2011], the strategic potential of discourses should be demystified and not just documented or expounded.

The best critical discourse analysts do not identify themselves and their work foremost in terms of some methodology, be it systemic-functional linguistic, conversation analysis or some other method. They identify themselves with the critical goal of their work, and engage with social-critical and cultural-critical and political-critical ideas as well as with methods that can anchor critique in methodical description.

# 3 The importance of multimodality for critical discourse analysis

The tendency amongst critical discourse analysts has been to analyse speeches by politicians, parliamentary debates and media reports, editorials and TV interviews. However, critical discourse analysts have also analysed school textbooks, advertisements, the books of management gurus, transcripts of doctor-patient and workplace meeting interactions, and much more. In all such fields communication has become much more multimodal. Yet much work in critical discourse analysis remains firmly mono-modal, looking only at written and spoken language. A scan of the issues of *Language and Politics* and *Critical Discourse Studies*, at the time of writing, revealed that on average only 1 in 17 articles critically analysed multimodal discourse. Only a handful of critical discourse analysts argue strongly for the inclusion of multimodality, for instance Chouliaraki in her work on the televisual representation of suffering (2006), or Fairclough (2000: 4) in his work on the language of New Labour, where he stresses the importance of non-verbal communication in political discourse, though admitting that he finds it 'elusive' and 'difficult to describe in print' (2000: 97):

> Communicative style is a matter of language in the broadest sense – certainly verbal language (words), but also all other aspects of the complex bodily performance that constitutes political style (gestures, facial expressions, dress and hairstyle, and so forth). A successful leader's communicative style is not simply what makes him or her attractive to voters, it conveys certain values which can powerfully enhance the political 'message'.

Ruth Wodak, too, has moved to the critical study of multimodal popular culture, for instance in her work on the television series *The West Wing* (2009), which, she says, blurs the boundaries between politics and popular culture, and between fiction and reality, and creates a 'virtual world of politics which seems transparent and where complexity is reduced into understandable elements and units with real human beings who experience similar emotions "like everybody else"' (Wodak, 2009: 186). Ultimately, she forcefully argues, this can have serious political consequences, as

> . . . the comparison of the world in *The West Wing* with political realities leads to even more disappointment with one's own and the politicians' perceived helplessness when confronting current global problems, such as climate change, wars, economic depressions, and so forth. Helplessness, fear, danger and insecurity

lead to anger, the search for scapegoats, the potential for mobilization through new simple promises and explanations, and the wish for new charismatic leaders.

In a similar way, she has analysed key multimodal aspects of a comic strip distributed to 500,000 people during the 2010 election campaign of the right-wing Austrian Freedom Party (Wodak and Forchtner, 2014), a comic which uses the historical siege of Vienna by the Turks to frame current immigration issues. But most CDA method textbooks do not include multimodal methods – Machin and Mayr (2012) are an exception here.

The study of multimodal texts is not only of importance for critical discourse analysis because so many contemporary texts are multimodal. It is also important in relation to CDA's key aim – studying the maintenance and legitimation of inequality, injustice and oppression, and this for two reasons. The first, as already noted in relation to Ruth Wodak's work on *The West Wing*, is the importance of popular culture and entertainment media in contemporary politics. Media scholars knew this well before it was picked up by critical discourse analysts. In their 1983 book *Televising Terrorism*, Schlesinger et al. compared non-fictional (news, current affairs, documentary) and fictional (television series and serials with SAS teams as the heroes) representations of terrorism, at the time especially of the IRA bombing campaigns, and concluded that fictional series such as *The Professionals* on the one hand draw significantly on journalism but on the other hand provided a 'reactionary populist version of the official perspective' which 'allowed very little space for alternative or oppositional viewpoints' (1983: 87). This perspective is all the more effective because of the audience's affective identification with the heroes, and because the audience's engagement with the development of the drama demands full engagement with the logic of the story and suspension of disbelief, i.e. of a critical attitude. Successful stories cast a spell on the audience. Most of all, there is the argument that 'it is just entertainment', 'it is only a story', which for many people makes the critic a spoilsport or overly 'politically correct'. For this reason critical discourse analysts must not only ground their analysis in well-founded and replicable methods, but also understand how stories do their work, and how crucial that work is in the contemporary representation and legitimation of injustice and violence.

The second reason is that discourses which legitimate injustice and violence, such as racist, colonialist and sexist discourses, persist much longer in visual communication than in its verbal equivalents. The anti-semitic representations in Figure 11.2 date from the late nineteenth century (even then such pictures were found in satirical magazines, just as, later, they were found in Nazi entertainment films). As Figure 11.3 shows, they persist in today's entertainment media, as in the figure of 'Watto', the mean-tempered, greedy second-hand shop owner with a gravelly, Hebrew-sounding accent from *Star Wars – The Phantom Menace*.

Similarly in still popular comic strips such as *Tin Tin*, nineteenth-century orientalist stereotypes continue unabated, to become part of the mental furniture of the next

Plate 5. Üstökös, 6 May 1868, p.139
Borsszem Jankó, 1 June 1873, p. 6.

**FIGURE 11.2** *'The Jew' as merciless, mercenary and sly in late nineteenth-century Hungarian satirical magazines.*

**FIGURE 11.3** *Watto, the mean-tempered, greedy second-hand shop owner in* Star Wars – The Phantom Menace (1999).

**FIGURE 11.4** *Frame from* The Blue Lotus *(1946).*

generation (Figure 11.4). And 'golliwog' dolls are still around, still cherished by many as an innocent childhood tradition.

The power of such representations lies precisely in the fact that their ideological meanings can be so easily denied by arguments such as that 'it is only a story' or 'only a toy', or that words are 'precise' while images are 'polysemous'. For this reason critical discourse analysts should now prioritize popular texts over 'serious' or 'highbrow' texts, and images over verbal text:

> Visually communicated racism can be much more easily denied, much more easily dismissed as 'in the eye of the beholder' than verbal racism [. . .] it is for this reason that a consideration of images should have pride of place in any inquiry into racist discourse. If images seem to just show 'what is', we need to show that that may not always be quite so. If images seem to just allude to things and never 'say them explicitly', we need to make these allusions explicit.
>
> (Van Leeuwen, 2000: 335)

## 4 Examples of critical multimodal discourse analysis

I will end by discussing some examples of critical analysis of multimodal discourse.

Peled-Elhanan (2012) is a book-length study of the representation of Israelis and Palestinians in Israeli school books which pays particular attention to the layout of the books. The 'framing' of illustrations, for example, can become a metaphor for the segregation of the people represented in those illustrations: different population groups, such as Palestinians, Jewish-Ethiopians and Bedouins, are never shown together in one and the same picture, but always separate, 'framed in special windows' which 'mark things off but also decide what is included' (2012: 144). In the same way representatives of some population groups may be given a central or otherwise highly salient position in the layout, while others are represented in small, marginalized pictures. As Peled-Elhanan concludes (2012: 164):

> Layout is a powerful means not only for perpetuating official narratives but also for creating alternative interpretations and weaving the writer's own perceptions into the official educational discourse.

Just as critical discourse analysts discovered that ideology is not only expressed through relatively clear contrasts such as that between 'freedom fighter' and 'terrorist', but also through the subtle differences between different grammatical structures, so multimodal critical discourse analysts are discovering that racism is not only conveyed through racist stereotypes, but also through the at first sight merely formal structures of layout.

Machin (2004) analysed how, in the internet image bank Getty Creative Images, photographic images can be searched for the concepts they express, rather than for the people, places and events they record and document. The visual expression of concepts by means of staged photographs has of course long existed in advertising but today, Machin shows, it also extends to the editorial content of newspapers and magazines, where we traditionally expect 'records of reality'. The images in the Getty Creative Images image bank leave space for words and have restricted colour palettes to facilitate their use in page layout, and they are generic rather than specific, using a range of decontextualizing devices and a restricted vocabulary of attributes to indicate the identity of people and places (hard hat + rolled up blueprint = 'architect'; laptop = 'office'; non-descript skyscraper = 'city', etc.). They are therefore deliberately designed to be used in multiple contexts, and sold over and over. And the concepts they seek to illustrate, labelled for ease of searching, focus on the positive values of contemporary corporate discourse – freedom, creativity, innovation, determination, concentration, spirituality, well-being and so on – and voided of all political content: pictures of 'freedom' mostly show people jumping for joy, or in an open-topped car on a virtually empty road, just as in the advertisements – with just a few images of the Statue of Liberty and the American flag thrown in, with or without warplanes overhead. His work shows the importance of analysing not only texts but also the online systems we use to make texts. Getty Images advertises itself as creating 'a visual language for the globe'. As critical discourse analysts we must ask: What can be said in that language? And: What cannot be said in that language? And why?

Van Leeuwen (2008) developed a framework for analysing how the identity of 'social actors' can be signified verbally, visually – and with the Playmobil range of toy figurines and accessories. Social actors can, for instance, be represented as individuals or as 'types', and individually or collectively, and they can be functionalized (categorized by what they *do*, e.g. their profession or some kind of activity), or classified – categorized by what they are deemed to *be* (e.g. by gender, class, ethnicity or nationality). His analysis demonstrates that many identity categories can be expressed verbally as well as visually. But not every category can be expressed in every mode, and the ways in which the same categories are expressed in different modes adds further meanings and values. The minimalistic characters of Playmobil offer a range of such categories, Van Leeuwen shows, a microcosm of the social world. But even this system constructs reality in specific ways. The 'ethnic family' box, for instance, contains a father, a mother and three children, all with brown skin and identical hair colour, and with a mother who wears her hair in a bun. The 'family' (no further qualification) comes in a box with a father, a mother and two children, all pink-skinned and with different hair colours, hence with a modicum of individuality. And here the mother has long blond hair, signifying youthful feminine attractiveness. A message is built into the 'system' – 'ethnic families' have more children, less individuality and women who grow old earlier.

# 5 Conclusion

The term 'critical analysis of multimodal discourse' suggests a solid merger between critical discourse analysis and multimodality. Although some critical discourse analysts focus on multimodal texts and some multimodal analysts do take a critical stance, and although some important steps in the right direction have been taken, it cannot be said that such a merger has as yet fully taken place, despite the increasingly important role of multimodal discourse in many social and political contexts, especially since the emergence of the internet.

What can we therefore say, by way of conclusion?

Firstly, the discipline of multimodality has produced reliable methods for the critical analysis of multimodal discourse, even though it has itself as yet only tentatively been concerned with critical discourse analysis and has, for the most part, focused on the design of effective communication in education, museums, hospitals and clinics, and so on. Critical discourse analysis is duty bound to plead for caution here. Contemporary corporate discourse is replete with positive self-affirmation, relentless optimism and unquestioned belief in progress, and this kind of discourse increasingly infects other fields as well. This can be engaging, but it can also mask or silence other realities that are much less positive.

Meanwhile critical discourse analysis itself needs to pay more attention to the multimodality of contemporary communication, because the discourses that need critical scrutiny are now overwhelmingly multimodal and mediated by digital systems that take multimodality entirely for granted. This includes the systems we use for semiotic production and consumption, such as PowerPoint, Photoshop, Adobe After Effects, and so on, and the systems we use for social interaction, whether in the workplace, where so many interactions that used to be face to face are now online, following non-negotiable, intransigent protocols, and in personal life, where communication with friends and family becomes structured by systems like Facebook. To give just one example, on an app produced by Sesame Street ('Elmo's ABC'), a red frog acts as teacher and storyteller. Though designed for children, the app also has a button for parents, who can 'add objects', including their own voice, and 'monitor' their child's progress to see what the child did with the app, how many words s/he could correctly match with pictures, how many upper case and how many lower case letters s/he could identify, etc. Instead of being able to unlock the world of stories, or the world of literacy, parents are now constructed, by this relatively simple digital tool, as facilitators, providing the child with digital technology, as monitors, keeping an eye on their child's progress, and as being able to inject just a little bit of themselves into a structure for learning which is entirely designed by a global edutainment corporation. Meaningful critique of such devices barely exists, with media reviews mostly focusing on functionality. In my view, the modus operandi of such technologies, praised everywhere as the next great advance in education, and playing an increasingly important role in our daily lives generally, should become the next frontier of critical discourse analysis.

# References

Barthes, R. (1977), *Image-Music-Text*. London: Fontana.

Bednarek, M. (2013), 'The television title sequence: a visual analysis of *The Flight of the Conchords*', in E. Djonov and S. Zhao (eds), *Critical Multimodal Studies of Popular Discourse*. London, Routledge, pp. 36–54.

Birdwhistell, R. (1973), *Kinesics in Context*. Harmondsworth: Penguin.

Chouliaraki, L. (2006), *The Spectatorship of Suffering*. London: Sage.

Classen, C. (1993), *Worlds of Sense: Exploring the Senses in History and Across Cultures*. London: Routledge.

Djonov, E. and Van Leeuwen, T. (2013), 'Bullet points, new writing, and the marketization of public discourse: a critical multimodal perspective', in E. Djonov and S. Zhao, (eds), *Critical Multimodal Studies of Popular Discourse*. London, Routledge.

Djonov, E. and Zhao, S. (eds) (2013), *Critical Multimodal Studies of Popular Culture*. London: Routledge.

Dreyfus, S., Hood, S. and Stenglin, M. (eds) (2011), *Semiotic Margins – Meanings in Multimodalities*. London: Continuum.

Elleström, L. (2010), *Media Borders, Multimodality and Intermediality*. London, Palgrave Macmillan.

Fairclough, N. (2000), *New Labour, New Language?* London: Routledge.

Fifth International Conference on Multimodality (2010), *Program and Abstracts*, University of Technology, Sydney.

Forceville, C. (2013), 'The strategic use of the visual mode in advertising metaphors', in
    E. Djonov and S. Zhao (eds), *Critical Multimodal Studies of Popular Discourse*. London:
    Routledge, pp. 55–70.
Forceville, C. and Urios-Aparisi, A. (eds) (2009), *Multimodal Metaphor*. Berlin: Mouton de
    Gruyter.
Gorfinkel, L. (2013), 'Multimodal constructions of the nation: how China's music-
    entertainment television has incorporated Macau into the national fold', in
    E. Djonov and S. Zhao (eds), *Critical Multimodal Studies of Popular Discourse*. London:
    Routledge, pp. 93–108.
Halliday, M. A. K. (1978), *Language as Social Semiotic*. London: Arnold.
—— (1985), *Introduction to Functional Grammar*. London: Arnold.
Jewitt, C. (2006), *Technology, Literacy and Learning – A Multimodal Approach*. London:
    Routledge.
—— (ed.) (2009), *The Routledge Handbook of Multimodal Analysis*. London: Routledge.
Kress, G. (1997), *Before Writing: Rethinking the Paths to Literacy*. London: Routledge.
—— (2010), *Multimodality: A Social-semiotic Approach to Contemporary Communication*.
    London: Routledge.
Kress, G. and Hodge, R. (1978), *Language as Ideology*. London: Routledge.
—— (1988), *Social Semiotics*. Cambridge: Polity.
Kress, G and Van Leeuwen, T. (1996), *Reading Images: The Grammar of Visual Design*.
    London: Routledge.
Lakoff, G. and Johnson, M. (1980), *Metaphors We Live By*. Chicago: University of Chicago
    Press.
Machin, D. (2004), 'Building the world's visual language: the increasing global importance
    of image banks'. *Visual Communication*, 3(2), 316–36.
Machin, D. and Mayr, A. (2012), *How to Do Critical Discourse Analysis*. London: Sage.
Martinec, R. (2000), 'Types of processes in action'. *Semiotica*, 130(3/4), 243–68.
—— (2004), 'Gestures that co-occur with speech as a systematic resource: the realization
    of experiential meanings in indexes'. *Social Semiotics*, 14(2), 193–213.
Martinec, R. and Salway, A. (2005), 'A system for image-text relations in new (and old)
    media'. *Visual Communication*, 4(3), 337–72.
Molek-Kozakowska, K. (2013), 'The late night TV talk show as a strategic genre', in
    P. Cap and U. Okulska (eds) *Analyzing Genres in Political Communication – Theory
    and Practice*. Amsterdam: John Benjamins, pp.321–44.
Norris, S. (2004), *Analyzing Multimodal Interaction – A Methodological Framework*.
    London: Routledge.
Oakley, M. (1985), *Our Society and Others*. Sydney: McGraw-Hill.
O'Halloran, K. and Smith, B. A. (eds) (2011), *Multimodal Studies – Exploring Issues and
    Domains*. London: Routledge.
O'Toole, M. (1994), *The Language of Displayed Art*. London: Leicester University Press.
Peled-Elhanan, N. (2012), *Palestine in Israeli School Books – Ideology and Propaganda in
    Education*. London: I. B. Tauris.
Pittenger, R .E., Hockett, C. F. and Danehy, J. J. (1960), *The First Five Minutes*. Ithaca, NY:
    P. Martineau.
Royce, T. (1998), 'Synergy on the page: exploring intersemiotic complementarity in
    page-based multimodal text'. *JASFL Occasional Papers*, 1(1), 25–50.
Royce, T. and Bowcher, W. L. (2007), *New Directions in the Analysis of Multimodal
    Discourse*. Mahwah, NJ: Lawrence Erlbaum Associates.
Schlesinger, P., Murdock, G. and Elliott, P. (1983), *Televising Terrorism*. London: Comedia.

Scollon, R. (2001), *Mediated Discourse: The Nexus of Practice*. London: Routledge.

Tan, S. (2013), 'Representations of the institutional "self" in web-based business news discourse', in E. Djonov and S. Zhao (eds), *Critical Multimodal Studies of Popular Discourse*. London: Routledge, pp. 125–42.

Thomas, A. (2013), 'Intermodal complementarity and social critical literacy in children's multimodal texts', in E. Djonov and S. Zhao (eds), *Critical Multimodal Studies of Popular Culture*. London: Routledge, pp. 55–70.

Van Leeuwen, T. (1999), *Speech, Music, Sound*. London: Palgrave.

—— (2000), 'Visual racism', in M. Reisigl and R. Wodak (eds), *The Semiotics of Racism – Approaches in Critical Discourse Analysis*. Vienna: Passagen Verlag, pp. 351–62.

—— (2005), *Introducing Social Semiotics*. London: Routledge.

—— (2008), *Discourse and Practice – New Tools for Critical Discourse Analysis*. New York: Oxford University Press.

Ventola, E., Charles, C. and Kaltenbacher, M. (2004), *Perspectives on Multimodality*. Amsterdam: John Benjamins.

Wodak, R. (2009), *The Discourse of Politics in Action – Politics as Usual*. London: Palgrave Macmillan.

Wodak, R. and Forchtner, B. (2014), 'Embattled Vienna 1683–2010: rightwing populism, collective memory and the fictionalisation of politics'. *Visual Communication*, 13(2), 231–55.

Zhang, Y. and O'Halloran, K. L. (2013) 'From popularization to marketization: a study of online science news', in E. Djonov and S. Zhao (eds), *Critical Multimodal Studies of Popular Culture*. London: Roultedge, pp. 44–54.

Zhao, S. (2013), 'Selling the "indie taste": a social semiotic analysis', in E. Djonov and S. Zhao (eds), *Critical Multimodal Studies of Popular Discourse*. London: Routledge, pp. 143–59.

# 12

# Sound and Discourse

# A Multimodal Approach to War Film Music

*David Machin*

Örebro University

## 1 Introduction

Critical Discourse Analysis has a tradition of revealing the details of the way that discourses of war are communicated in political speeches and news texts in ways that may not be so apparent to the casual reader or listener (Van Dijk, 2008; Lazar and Lazar, 2004; Graham et al., 2004). Systematic analyses of linguistic and grammatical choices allow scholars to reveal how the horror that is war, its effects on societies, bodies and civilians and its precise political and economic basis are suppressed. Rather wars are legitimized and naturalized as inevitable and reasonable solutions: challenging an evil enemy, humanitarianism, soldiers as heroes, a moral good, and a clear common collective interest. In Multimodal Critical Discourse Analysis too (Machin and Van Leeuwen, 2005; Machin, 2007; Machin and Van Leeuwen, 2009) scholars have begun to analyse how discourses of war can be realized in photographs, computer games, toys, monuments and entertainment television, revealing, for example, that discourses have changed to foreground the role of Special Forces, peace-keeping and advanced weaponry. In this chapter I explore the way that music and sound can also be used to realize different discourses of war. I show that attention to the underlying system of available semiotic choices in sound, and how these are used in specific cases, allows us to think about the ideas, attitudes, identities and actions signified in music.

I use two film examples about the same set of events and participants to show how music can communicate different discourses of war. The first is the film *A Bridge Too Far* (1977) and the second a miniseries *Band of Brothers* (2001). Both represent the events surrounding the invasion of mainland Europe in World War II. A detailed analysis of sound allows us to make more precise observations about how meanings are being made, taking us beyond using broader adjectives to describe what we hear such as 'aggressive' or 'thoughtful'. Analysis reveals changing discourses of war and soldiery from one of the consensual mass national army to the emphasis of the experience of the service of the individual, a change that has been more widely observed in analyses of war reporting. Analysis also allows us to reflect on the way that 'soldiery as service' itself is foregrounded as the predominant representation of war, backgrounding the effects of war and of the acts of soldiery. As such music too plays an important part in focusing public attention and in naturalizing war.

## 2  A critical discursive approach to music and sound

A social semiotic approach is interested in the way that communicators use semiotic resources to achieve particular goals, to communicate specific ideas, attitudes, values and identities. It explores, on the one hand, the resources available to communicators – in other words the repertoire of sign/meaning potentials upon which they can draw in order to communicate – and, on the other hand, how these are used in specific cases, in particular combinations, to communicate particular meanings (Van Leeuwen, 2005). So, in the case of the music analysed in this paper, rather than being satisfied with adjectives such as 'aggressive' or 'thoughtful', the aim is to describe the details of the features of the music that might communicate such things. We consider how the music utilizes pitch, pitch direction and pitch range, notation, sound qualities and rhythm, in order to communicate its meanings. This social semiotic approach draws in the first place on the linguistic work of Halliday (1978), Hodge and Kress (1988) and Van Leeuwen (2005) and Kress (2010). This has been applied specifically to sound by Van Leeuwen (1999) and to popular music by Machin (2010). Here, in the tradition of CDA, I am concerned with the different discourses communicated by these semiotic choices and whose interests they serve.

To draw out the underlying meaning potentials available to musicians this analysis draws on the work of a number of scholars. The ideas that comprise this work will be explained as we move through the paper. But a number of scholars provide key ideas. Firstly, through a systematic study of classical music the musicologist Cooke (1959) began to create an inventory of meaning potentials for pitch, melody, notation and rhythms. This work was not done from within the tradition of social semiotics but very much represents its spirit as it sought to create a sense of the underlying system of available resources for musicians and composers. Cooke's inventories are drawn upon extensively.

Secondly, I fuse Cooke's work with ideas from Tagg (1982, 1984, 2012). He was interested in how we have historically come to make cultural associations between particular musical patterns and sounds with emotions, attitudes, settings and events, which is why composers can therefore rely on certain combinations of notes as being heard by listeners as 'aggressive' or 'thoughtful'. Tagg (1984) discusses the emergence of sounds and music as communicative acts in hunting and gathering type societies in terms of the way they could be used to express the attitudes and ideas associated with certain activities such as initiation rites, marriage ceremonies, harvests and the hunt. A hunt would use sounds and rhythms that suggested sudden movements and speed of coordination along with waiting and observing. The same sounds and movements would not be suitable for a marriage ceremony or to send a child to sleep (1984: 8).

Together these two authors bring a sense of thinking about the repertoire of semiotic resources available in sound to make meaning and the way that these can be used to both reflect on and create understandings of different kinds of social processes and social roles – what ideas, attitudes, identities and sequences of activity comprise these. This is precisely the aim in this paper, assuming, in the tradition of CDA, that communication and discourses are always deeply ideological and will serve specific individual or group interests.

Two other theorists provide us with a set of ideas that point to the way that sounds come to have meaning for us. Van Leeuwen (1999) in his groundbreaking work on sound and the cognitive psychologist Arnhiem (1969) point to two overlapping ways that sounds can come to have meaning:

- *Provenance*: Sounds and sound qualities can have meaning through cultural accumulation of associations. For example, to a Northern European listener pan pipes suggest 'nature' or simple, ancient cultures especially those from Latin America. The sitar is used to represent Indian culture or perhaps esoteric thought or mysticism in general. Also as Tagg (1982) points out we have become trained to hear certain musical notes and note combinations as communicating specific types of landscape, persons and ideas due to repetition over time.

- *Experiential meaning potential*: Sounds can also have meaning from associations of things in the real world. Arnheim (1969) argued that communication is steeped in 'experiential associations' (117). So, we might clap our hands together to suggest a conflict of interest between two people. There is no actual clapping or physical collision going on in the interaction, but communication works by drawing on our experiential association of these to understand something of the way that people may not agree. In the same way, the sound associated with crashing objects could be thought to suggest discord as opposed to a gentle drifting sound that might mean something more temperate or agreeable.

## 3 The study of film music

There exists a strong body of work on film music from within the field of film studies. This provides a set of highly useful points regarding what film music can be used to accomplish (Manvell and Huntley, 1957; Chion, 2009; Gorbman, 1987; Kassabian, 2001). These studies point to a number of communicative uses of music in film. Music can contribute to action, for example, by providing pace or indicating danger. It can be used to indicate emotions and provide insights into the inner world of actors, to suggest fear, or joy, etc. It can be used to indicate kinds of characters, such as innocent or evil. It can be used to represent settings, either geographical or moments in history – mostly in the forms of clichés. Gorbman (1987) points out that Strauss's waltzes are able to connote Vienna, and accordions Paris (83). It can also be used to create continuity and links between scenes. However, much of this work is oriented to the role of film music rather than attempting a more systematic analysis of sound as communication. Only a handful of authors (Chion, 2009 and Donnelly, 2005) have focused in slightly more detail on sound qualities and signification.

One more detailed study of film music comes from the field of semiotics in the work of Tagg (1982). He discussed the 'Music Mood' collections that were made available for the use in theatre in the 1930s and later silent movies. These collections drew on the classical music of the eighteenth and nineteenth centuries, which had started to use music as a narrative device to represent characters, place and moods. The musical collections would be categorized under 'action', 'comedy', 'danger', 'nature', 'space', etc. We still hear the basic themes and ideas from these pieces today in contemporary film, television, adverts and news. Tagg described some of the basic features of some of these musical categories, such as the sweeping strings that were used to represent large open landscapes.

Overall, from the literature on film music we get an overall sense of its important role in creating ideas about kinds of actions, characters and settings. In this paper a more detailed analysis shows what exactly is being communicated by music by looking at not just *what* music does, but at *how* it does it.

## 4 Analysis of the music

In the analysis that follows I look at a number of different meaning potentials in music and sound: pitch, pitch direction, pitch range, note meaning, sound qualities, articulation and rhythm. Each is dealt with in turn, gradually building up a complete picture of how these meanings combine together. In each case I first describe the meaning potentials and then apply these to each of the film musics in turn. I look at two motifs from *A Bridge Too Far (ABTF)* and one from *Band of Brothers (BOB)*. In both cases the motifs appear in opening sequences and throughout the footage. So we see soldiers mustering or moving out, etc., and hear the motifs.

## 4.1 The meaning of pitch

Pitch relates to how high or low a sound is: a scream would be a high note, thunder a low note. Its meaning potential relates to levels of energy, optimism and weight. The meaning of pitch is rich in metaphorical associations. Cooke (1959: 102) shows that in the history of classical music and opera high pitch has been associated with high levels of energy and brightness and low pitch with its opposite; in other words low levels of energy, contained, immobile and static. We could think of this metaphorically as being like someone speaking in a low deep voice as compared to raising their voice in excitement. Higher pitch can also extend to mean agitation and lower pitch can mean low drooping despair. In Western culture we have the association of up meaning 'feeling good' and down meaning 'feeling bad'. Cooke adds that pitches beyond the range of the human voice can, in the cases of higher tones, give a sense of the ethereal, lightness, transcendence. We can think about the way that solo instruments such as electric guitars or saxophones will play at a high pitch as an expression of emotion. Vocalists with deeper voices such as Tom Waits suggest immobility and lack of energy while those such as Michael Jackson are bright with high energy. Musical arrangements can include both lower pitches in the background with a high-pitched melody on top. An example of this is the theme music used for television news bulletins. Heavier bass notes and drums suggest gravity and importance, while higher pitched horns suggest truth and the energy of news. We can summarize the meaning potentials for pitch as in Table 12.1.

We can apply these to the motifs from *ABTF* and *BOB*. In *ABTF* in the first motif of the music the first time it is heard it is played on the flute. So we find a very high pitch to begin with. This represents the way the flute or fife was played in order to be heard in traditional marching music.

Here we get a sense of lightness and ease. The motif is then repeated with a range of brass and woodwind instruments. But these remain at a medium to higher pitch with bass instruments being used to place more staccato notes underneath to provide rhythm. In this sense the music of war is certainly not dark and depressing but remains at a level of energy and optimism, yet underneath lies a sense of weight and gravity.

The *BOB* melody is slightly different. Again we find both lower and higher pitches. But we find much higher pitches overall in this piece of music. The horns and the choir

**Table 12.1** Meaning potentials of pitch

| Pitch | Positive meaning | Negative meaning |
|-------|------------------|------------------|
| High | Bright/energetic/happy | Lightweight/trivial/flighty |
| Low | Important/solid | Clumsy/depressed/danger |

at times hit and sustain quite high notes. There is a sense of ecstatic high notes and almost otherworldliness here. Bass notes add gravity. War in *ABTF* is light and energetic, whereas in *BOB* it is high emotion and otherworldly.

## 4.2 The meaning of pitch movement

In music, pitch rarely stays at one level, but is characterized by movement up and down. A melody line will usually rise and fall in pitch, or it would be very boring. The direction of this movement can also have meaning potential. Cooke's (1959) work on classical music suggests that ascending melodies are associated with outward expressions of emotions whilst descending melodies are associated with incoming emotion or consolation. This is due to the association of higher pitches with higher levels of energy and brightness and lower pitches with associations of low levels of energy as we saw above. The movement from one to the other expresses a shift in either direction: a movement from a high pitch to a low pitch can communicate a sense of falling of energy or of bleakness; the opposite, a gradual slide from low to high pitch, can give a sense of a picking up of spirits or of an outburst of energy. This will depend on the articulation of the pitch change. A very rapid increase in pitch can mean a burst in energy. Punk music (eg. 'Anarchy in the UK' by the Sex Pistols) often used relatively even melodies which didn't change much in pitch to suggest containment and had the occasional burst of energy. A more gradual increase can suggest something building. National anthems often use stepped increases in pitch to suggest the steady feel of brightness and energy associated with the national spirit. This will be interspersed with some use of lower pitch to also suggest the solemnity and importance of the national project. The lamentful songs of singer-songwriters often descend in melody to give a sense of regret and moodiness. We can summarize these potentials as in Table 12.2.

Before beginning to look at pitch movement in the two pieces of music, I provide graphs which will be of use throughout the rest of analysis to help visualize the melodies. On the graphs the numbers along the bottom, on the horizontal axis, represent the notes that are played in order going from left to right. So above '1' is the first note played and above '2' the second note played and so on. The numbers on the

**Table 12.2**  Meaning potentials of direction of pitch movement

| Pitch direction | Meaning potential |
| --- | --- |
| Ascending melody | Building of mood/outward expression/increase in energy |
| No pitch movement | Emotional stasis/containment/reserved |
| Descending melody | Drooping of emotions/inward contemplation/decrease in energy |

vertical axis represent the values of the note. As they get higher up this axis the higher in pitch they are. So we can look at the way that melodies move up or down in pitch. In Figure 12.1 we look at the first motif for *ABTF*.

This is played the first time through on the flute alone and then on other brass and woodwind instruments. The first two peaks are played in a steady set of steps going up and then steadily back down and the third peak played more as a flurry. The first peaks do not suggest bursts of energy but a measured increase of spirits and something slightly uplifting. At the end it goes up slightly more which suggests a gradual picking up of spirits. Given that this is a marching type song it must feel slightly uplifting, but certainly must not use aggressive bursts of energy or long phrases that would be inappropriate for a longer steady march.

The second motif is slightly different. This can be seen in Figure 12.2.

The pitch movement here is different. Overall there is a gradual movement downwards. Each phrase moves downwards but begins and ends with an increase in pitch. This combination allows a sense of optimistic outbursts of energy – these are quite fast outbursts – that move in a direction of increased gravity and importance.

Figure 12.3 illustrates the first two phrases of the *BOB* motif. It begins with a phrase that involves only ascending movement. This is a highly positive building of energy. The second phrase descends and brings a sense of levelling out, although this descent is only to mid point and ascends again at the end to remain positive and to maintain the sense of higher pitch and optimism.

The third phrase in the motif (see Figure 12.4) is marked in the way that it ascends with only a slight dip rounding off at the end. There is also here a sense of stepped building of emotion as can be seen in the way notes are repeated.

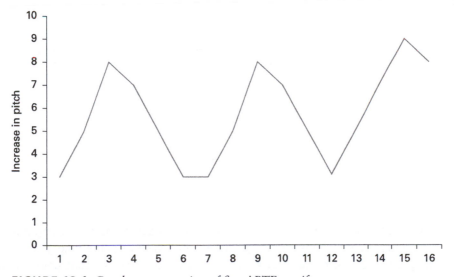

**FIGURE 12.1** *Graph representation of first* ABTF *motif.*

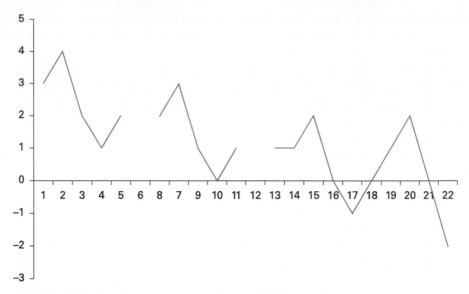

**FIGURE 12.2** *Graph representation of second* ABTF *motif.*

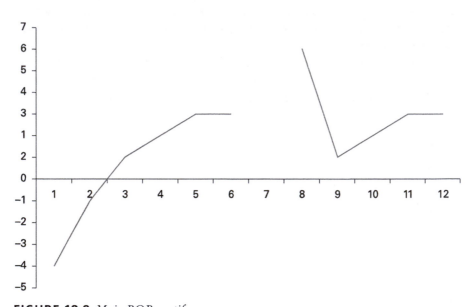

**FIGURE 12.3** *Main BOB motif.*

The difference between the two is that the *ABTF* uses steps of building positive energy and then bursts of energy that gradually move towards something graver. *BOB* uses long phrases that move in one upwards direction. This is about upwards and increasing optimism and emotional energy.

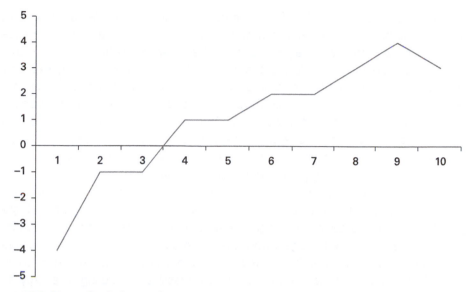

**FIGURE 12.4** *Third phrase of* BOB *motif.*

## 4.3 *The meaning of pitch range*

As well as whether pitch increases or decreases there is important meaning potential in the range of these changes – a large pitch range communicates a sense of letting more energy out whereas a small pitch range means holding more energy in. Linguists have shown that larger pitch ranges in speech are heard as more emotionally expressive whereas more restricted pitch ranges are heard as more contained, reserved or closed. Brazil et al. (1980) note that pitch range in speech is akin to excitement, surprise or anger. A newsreader will speak using a restricted pitch range to suggest a neutral stance and little emotional involvement. We could imagine the difference were they to use a large pitch range. In music soul singers will use a large pitch range to communicate the expression of emotions. In contrast smaller pitch ranges can be associated with holding in or even modesty which often characterizes the melodies of singer-songwriters. The meaning potential of pitch range can be summarized as in Table 12.3.

**Table 12.3**   Meaning potential of pitch range

| Pitch range | Meaning potential | Effect |
|---|---|---|
| High | Emotionally expansive | Emotionally open/subjective |
| Low | Emotionally contained | Repressed/contained/objective |

The graphs can help us to identify the degrees of pitch range. We can look at the number of notes on the vertical axis involved in each phrase or in a motif. In the case of the *ABTF* first motif we find a pitch range of five notes for the first two peaks and a range of six notes if we include the end section. This is fairly emotionally expansive although the fact that it always returns to its starting point allows it to feel more measured. In the second motif of *ABTF* we find the two first phrases move in a shorter more contained pitch range of three notes. This is more emotionally contained. The final phrase covers four notes. Overall we may have a sequence that descends creating a sense of gravity, but each in itself is contained. Rather there is a sense of moving gradually towards something grave rather than an emotional fall.

In the *BOB* music we find something very different. The first phrase ascends directly seven notes. The first note of the next phrase is then a further three notes higher again. This is a range of ten notes and gives a sense of incredible emotional outpouring. The third phrase then begins again from the same starting point as the first phrase and then ascends eight notes. This music, unlike the relative contained nature of that of *ABTF*, is highly emotionally expansive. It is a massive outpouring of energy and emotion.

What we are beginning to develop a sense of here is the more contained gravity and more rapid bursts of energy in *ABTF* and the longer lingering surges in emotion of *BOB*. I will begin to unpick the meaning of these once we have dealt with notation and as we move onto sound qualities.

## 4.4 *Phrasing and articulation in melodies*

Another important aspect of the voicing of the lyrics and melodies is the phrasing. We have already touched on this throughout in more general terms, but here we make a few more specific comments. Bell and Van Leeuwen (1993) have noted that shorter phrases are associated linguistically with sincerity, certainty, weight and therefore with authority. In contrast longer, lingering articulation suggests the opposite. We might therefore expect to hear folk singers using short bursts in their lyrics, to communicate sincerity. The opposite case, where singers produce longer lingering statements, suggests rather slow burning internal emotion as in the case of many jazz or soul singers.

There are different kinds of shorter abrupt articulation to be found in music generally. Traditionally in opera masculine characters have been represented through harsher staccato notes as might be associated with military music which conveys liveliness and certainty, whereas women are represented through longer legato articulation which is more emotionally lingering (McClary, 1991). The masculine staccato notes would be played on brass instruments and with percussion and the feminine, more lingering, legato notes played on strings. However, it is important to note that the meaning potential of staccato notes will be highly dependent on the sound quality of

**Table 12.4** Meaning potentials of note articulation

| Articulation of notes | Meaning potential |
|---|---|
| Shorter dotted notes | Abrupt, lively, hurried, certain, objective/clumsy if played in deep pitched brass or woodwind |
| Longer lingering notes | Emotionally lingering, subjective |

the instrument. We can imagine the difference were sharp fast notes to be played on a deep-sounding euphonium, or low on the range of a bassoon, as opposed to a trumpet. Notes on these deeper instruments played in this way can sound more 'bouncy' as opposed to 'cutting'. These will be more associated with comedy, or awkward characters as the low, bouncy notes suggest lack of mobility, lack of agility or precision.(See Table 12.4.)

For *ABTF* the first motif uses some slightly longer notes but most are dotted bringing a sense of liveliness and certainty. Clearly it would not be suitable for a marching song to have too many longer lingering emotional notes. The second motif follows suit but the weight increases as a range of brass and woodwind provide the melody. Both these are typical of military marching music. In the case of *BOB* we find no shorter dotted notes. It is made entirely of very long lingering notes. We do hear horns played but this is more in the fashion of church music.

## 4.5 *The meaning of musical notes*

Melodies that have the same pitch levels and the same pitch ranges can have very different meanings if these potentials are realized through different choices in actual notes. What we look at next is the meaning potential of each note in the scale. People often know about these different notes as 'do re me fa so la ti do'. Each of these has its own meaning potential which can be realized depending how it is combined with other notes and depending on other things such as pitch which we have dealt with and sound qualities that we come on to shortly.

On a piano there are sequences of eight notes that repeat up the keyboard starting from the 'root note' note 1. Note 8 is in fact the start of the next eight notes and is the same as note 1 (so there are therefore in fact only seven different notes). These are called a 'scale', what we know as 'do re me fa so la ti do'. As can be seen here 'do' is at the start and the end of the sequence. Each note will have a different kind of effect for the listener. Cooke (1959) set out to describe exactly what these meanings were by documenting how they have been used in classical and opera music. I start with notes 1, 3 and 5 which are the 'basic' notes.

Note 1 is the main defining note of the scale. When it is heard it anchors the melody to the scale firmly and roundly. It brings a sense of grounding whenever heard. A melody that used only note 1 would sound very boring and emotionally restricted in terms of pitch range but would sound nevertheless very grounded.

Note 5 is also a common note to find in music. It is similar in sound to note 1 and therefore is also good for grounding the melody. Melodies that use lots of notes 1 and 5, will sound very stable and grounded and basic and will provide a solid connection to the musical accompaniment. Also important in grounding a melody is note 3. These structures using notes 1, 3 and 5, have become the basis of western music.

Note 3 is important for other reasons. It is a happy, joyful note. Or it can be lowered by half a note to create a sadder feel to a melody. This is what is meant by a 'minor' scale. Many people are roughly aware that there are 'major', or happy melodies, and 'minor', or sad melodies. If a melody has the standard 3 then it is a major melody and it tends to sound happy and joyful; if it has the lowered 3 it sounds sad although depending on combination with other semiotic choices the minor 3 can suggest a chilling beauty.

Notes like 1, 3 and 5 allow the music to feel 'easy' or 'rounded'. In contrast, jazz will use many notes that do not create this solid connection in order to create tension. In contrast the music of boy bands, for example, might at no point deviate from notes 1 and 3, such is the importance of creating an 'easy' sound.

Note 2 is associated with transition, the sense that movement is about to happen, or the promise of something to follow. A lengthened note 2 can suggest limbo or entrapment. This is because of its position between the strongly related notes 1 and 3. The listener has a sense that it should settle to the 1 or the 3 giving it an unresolved sound.

Note 4 is used to give a sense of building or moving forwards and can also be used to create sense of space or possibility. Cooke (1959) explains that moving directly from note 1 up to note 4 can give quite an aggressive sense of building or urging on. Moving from note 1 to 4 via note 3 can create a sense of something very positive about to happen.

Note 6 has a similar value as note 3 and can be used to create a sense of brightness to the melody. But there is an important difference: in the fashion of note 2 it brings a sense of needing to be resolved. Again it sits alongside more powerful notes like note 5. Therefore note 6 represents not being in a state of happiness that is accepted but rather a state of flux, or being in a pleasurable context. Typically this can bring a sound of pleasurable longing, or longing for pleasure. This can be used in classical music to communicate nostalgia. When note 6 moves to a more grounding note this can bring a sense of pleasurable longing.

Note 7 is associated with longing and is often used in love songs. It can sound wistful and a little lamentful.

The meaning potentials of these notes can be summarized as in Table 12.5.

**Table 12.5** Meaning potentials of notes

| Note | Meaning potential |
|---|---|
| 1 | Anchoring note |
| 2 | Something unfinished or about to happen |
| 3 | A state of happy or sad/chilling note |
| 4 | Building, moving forwards or creating space |
| 5 | Anchoring note |
| 6 | Pleasurable longing, nostalgia |
| 7 | Wistful or painful |

The first motif of *ABTF* starts on note 3 in all of the phrases. So all phrases start on happy notes. Since this is higher than the 'root' note it brings a 'lifted' feel to the whole tune. It then goes up through note 5 to note 1 an octave higher. These are the very notes that are used for well anchored, simple music. It is therefore a positive, grounded, building of energy. It has a light feel due to the starting note and also due to the high pitch of the flute. In each case the phrase ascends and then it descends back to note 3 going through note 7 and then note 5. Again these are all simple and grounded notes although note 7 brings a slight wistful feel. In the third phrase, which is played much more quickly, we also find simple, grounding notes along with note 7 but also the addition of note 2 giving a sense of something about to happen.

The second *ABTF* motif also starts on the happy note 3. It then moves straight to note 4 to suggest journey and progress. What is notable in this motif is that note 2 is used five times giving a strong sense of something that will be resolved, unfinished business. We also find note 7 used to create wistfulness. War here is happy with a slight wistfulness, characteristic of marching music where men head off to war. But there is a massive sense of something about to be resolved.

In the case of *BOB* the melody opens from a deep, happy, note 3 well below note 1. It then leaps up with its huge surge of emotion first to note 6 suggesting a longing or nostalgia and then grounding with note 1 indicating this is not a complex issue. It then continues upwards using note 2, a sense of something to be resolved and resting on the happy note 3. This is simple, grounded yet happy and nostalgic at a very high and expressive emotional pitch. It then leaps even higher to note 6, again this note brings a sense of nostalgia and pleasurable longing, but this time at a very high pitch, almost at a point of otherworldliness. It then descends to ground back at note 1 before again going through note 2, something about to happen, ending on the happy note 3.

The third phrase follows a similar pattern but hits some of the notes 1 and 2 twice for emphasis as it gradually builds in emotion and energy. It then goes to note 4 to suggest building and again ends on the happy note 3.

Both *ABTF* and *BOB* use happy notes and grounding notes. Neither of these melodies suggests trouble or complexity, or even pain, as could be the case as regards warfare. *ABTF* with its shorter happy bursts suggests simplicity, relative emotional containment with a slight wistful feel – men leaving home for battle in the name of those they leave behind. There is a feeling of being part of something important that is about to be resolved. *BOB* with its huge positive emotional outpourings is also simple and happy with a slight sense of building and something about to happen. But both more extreme lower and higher pitches point to extreme levels of emotion.

What we are beginning to see emerge is the way war is represented in these two films is in some ways the same and in other ways very different through sound. War is happy and positive in both. War could easily be represented through more painful and ungrounded notes to suggest its horrors, loss and lack of control, one where the concept of the soldier and industrial killing is to be despised. At both points in time, therefore, sound represents the actions of soldiers positively. But in the 1970s music points to more measured kinds of emotion and the gravity of the importance of the events. There is also confidence, certainty and closure in the phrasing and articulation. In the twenty-first century there is a shift to the almost emotionally blinding wonderful nature of what was done. This is less about certainty than feeling and emotion with longer, gentle phrasing.

## 4.6  Sound qualities

In the following section we move onto the sound qualities used by the instrumentation and voices. Here we draw on and adapt Van Leeuwen's (1999) observations on voice quality and Machin's (2010) observations on sound quality in popular music. Here we list five sound qualities.

## 4.6.1 Tension

This describes the extent to which the voices speak or sing with an open or closed throat. When we become tense in everyday situations our throats tend to close up. When we are relaxed our throat is open and sounds can resonate. Punk singers often use tight, tense vocalization whereas a female jazz singer like Julie London will use open throat and lingering notes. We can also apply this idea of tension versus openness to the instrument sounds. For a keyboard we can ask whether the keys are struck in a tense way that controls the way the notes resonate not allowing them to ring out or the opposite where they are allowed to ring out. In both these pieces of music we hear relatively little tension. Rather there is a sense of ease and openness. War and soldiery in this case are not tense nor anxious but easy and flowing.

## 4.6.2 Breathiness

This communicates the degree of intimacy suggested by a voice or instrument. To bring out the meaning potential here, we can think of the contexts in which we hear people's breath which can occur when they are out of breath and panting, because of some physical or emotional exertion or strain. It can also be in moments of intimacy and sensuality. When we hear a person's breath when they speak, this may even be a moment of confidentiality as they whisper in our ear, or share their thoughts with us when they are experiencing emotional strain or euphoria. For instruments we may hear the full, delicate texture of the note, the breath on a wind instrument or vibration of strings or these may be much less vivid.

The ideas of Murray Schafer (1977) are also useful in drawing out the way sounds are vividly clear or more indistinct. He makes the distinction between two kinds of soundscape: the lo fi and the hi fi. A lo fi soundscape is typical of our modern cities. There is such a jumble of sounds that we do not really hear any of them distinctly. A car moves along the street but the noise it makes merges with that made by all the others. We may see a person shout but not really hear them. So in this soundscape individual sounds and their origins are obscured. Rock music can also be thought of as lo fi as sounds merge. We can often not hear the sounds of fingers on the frets of guitars or the full texture of a keyboard note. A hi fi soundscape is very different. This is like being in a forest where you hear a branch snap somewhere nearby and a rustle of leaves further away. Sounds here are not competing. There is no overbearing background hum. Some folk music can be thought of as hi fi where the touch of fingers on fretboards and texture of the singer's voice can be clearly heard. This can be used to connote a pre-industrial setting.

In the *BOB* music we hear breathy choral voices. We can also hear different voices, all fairly distinctly. They do not merge into the background and become indistinct. There is a level of intimacy indicated by the texture of the voices and instruments, and, in Murray Schafer's terms, something pre-industrial and pre-modern. *ABTF* starts with a flute sound heard over drums suggesting simplicity of the war of independence soldier wistfully leaving loved ones to brightly go off to fight in their name. The flute is then quickly surrounded by other instruments more in the fashion of Murray Schafer's lo fi soundscape. One interpretation of these differences is that in the case of *BOB* we have something softer and more personalized emotions being expressed that are somehow timeless. In the case of *ABTF* we have something more modern, after the earlier connotations of the pre-modern and something that is about merging with a collective rather than the individual and intimacy.

## 4.6.3 Loud/soft

Louder sounds can mean weight and importance. Such sounds literally take up physical and social space – they can be used to suggest power, status, threat or danger, although they can also be overbearing and unsubtle. Softness, in contrast, can suggest intimacy and confidentiality, although softness can also mean weakness. In rock music the loud, shouting vocals, according to Tagg (1984), represent the individual being heard over the wider society.

In the *ABTF* music the first motif begins softly and gently although we find a powerful drum beat. The music then becomes quite loud and raucous, the celebration of a large number of soldiers moving happily into battle. The *BOB* music has a soft feel given the choral nature. It never becomes loud and invasive, although there is a sense of power that grows throughout with horns and bass drums. While there is a sense of breathiness and hi fi, it is certainly not meek and reserved.

### 4.6.4 Distortion/degrees of raspiness

Sounds can be rough and gravelly or very smooth. Raspiness can mean contamination of the actual tone, worn or dirty. It can also bring a sense of aggression as in growling or suggest something machine-like as in a roaring engine. In the electronic synthesizer music of the 1980s, raspy synthesizers were used to connote mechanization and dehumanization. We hear some of these meanings in rock music with distorted guitars which can suggest excitement as opposed to the well-oiled warm soft sounds of an acoustic guitar on a folk song. Distortion can also mean pure emotion and authenticity where there is no pretence at purity but to reveal the world in all its gritty lack of order and wear and tear. In the *BOB* music we hear much smoothness. There is no sense of wornness here, nor dirt, nor grittiness. This is despite the fact that the visuals show the men in dirt and grit often with dirty worn out clothes for realism. The music in contrast represented something timeless, clean and pristine. The *ABTF* music begins with the smoothness of the flute, simple and untainted, but then shifts to brass instruments that bring slightly more raspiness. Some more contemporary war film music has also used highly distorted electric guitar as in *Black Hawk Down* (2001) to suggest aggression, power and strong gritty emotion.

### 4.6.5 Reverb

Doyle (2006) suggests a number of meanings for echo. Since they are normally experienced in large empty spaces such as churches or rocky mountain valleys, echoes can suggest something on a large epic scale or something sacred. National anthems are often recorded with reverb to bring this sense of scale and sacredness. But also, given the way that reverb can mean epic spaces, it can also be used to communicate isolation. The *BOB* music uses reverb for the choral voices. There is clearly a sense of the epic here and the magnitude of what has been done. This could also be interpreted in the sense of the vast sacred spaces of the cathedral.

These observations on sound qualities allow us to expand on our understanding of our two sets of film music. Both are relaxed with no tension. War has an ease about it. For *ABTF* the first motive is lighter, softer and smoother while the second is slightly grittier and certainly louder and more lo fi as many instruments merge. This lack of

**Table 12.6** Summary of meaning potentials for sound qualities

| Sound quality | Meaning potential |
| --- | --- |
| Breathiness | Intimacy |
| Loud/soft | Taking up social space |
| Raspy/smooth | Grittiness/energy vs. naturalistic and sensual |
| Reverb | Sacred or isolation |

tension and element of power and raspy authenticity adds to the happy notes and the sense of something about to happen – the force of which the soldiers then comprise. The lo fi soundscape brings a sense of the collective, anonymized action.

For *BOB* we find that the high surges in pitch and emotional outpourings are expressed through intimate, soft horns and soft, breathy choral arrangements where voices sing in unison but are not absorbed by the whole. This more contemporary representation of events moves away from the collective, merry army moving towards a destiny, to one where there is room for the individual, where there is an intimate sharing of beautiful other-worldly actions and emotions. Scholars analysing media reports of war have suggested that there has been a move away from broader justifications for war and away from the representation of armies, to the representation of the experience of 'service' for the individual soldiers. Public support is fostered not through accounts of motives but through alignment with 'our boys'.

## 4.7 The meaning of rhythm

Cooper and Meyer (1960) note that rhythm is hard to identify and describe since it is often the product of the interaction of many sounds. Rhythm is not the same as 'beat' as is often assumed to be the case. A rising and falling melody can on its own bring a sense of rhythm. As discussed earlier, Tagg (1984) argues that music associated with a hunt, for example, will include quick and sudden musical movements, perhaps punctuated with periods of waiting. A lullaby, in contrast, would utilize a gentle and regular rhythm. We accept that rhythm is hard to pin down but here draw on Cooke's (1959) sense of it inferring some kind of movement and structuring of movement in time to activate a set of associations.

For Cooke (1959) rhythms are associated with different kinds of bodily movement. They can be even (in pop music) or uneven (as may be the case in jazz). Uneven rhythms can communicate a sense of difficulty, or if the unevenness is repeated a sense of being prevented from moving forwards or remaining in one particular place. Unevenness can also suggest creativity as movement changes, reacting and refusing to conform.

Rhythms can be fast or slow which can suggest energy or relaxation or sluggishness. Rhythms can suggest lightness or weight due to light or heavy bass drum beats respectively. They can suggest stasis through constant beat tones (such as a single bass drum pulse) or forwards motion through alternating tones (such as between a snare and bass drum), hesitation (as in reggae) or progress. They can also suggest a side to side swaying motion (as in swing) as opposed to a forward action like that found in some pop ballads or more relentless and forceful forward motion in military marches. In swing music therefore we can say that there is emotion that is to be dwelt upon rather than a suggestion of momentum. Van Leeuwen (1999) has also drawn attention to the difference between binary rhythms which suggest walking or running, and triple time that we find in waltzes which suggest something more akin to skipping. Also important here is the lack of metronomic time in music. This too has important meaning potential and can suggest something ancient, timeless or spiritual as summarized in Table 12.7.

In the case of *ABTF* we find lightness as the melodies skip along and horns play on down beats, often notes 1 and 5 or 7 to help create movement – that 'oompha' feel. The drums also provide a rolling forwards march motion and certainly no hesitation. These are even rhythms suggesting conformity and ease. We could image a rhythm created by a scared frontline soldier that included hesitation, difficulty and unevenness of loudness.

For *BOB* we hear no overt 'beat' and metronomic time is not strongly present. There is here a sense of the sacred, the spiritual and the timeless. The piece is in fact organized as a piece of music in 6/8 time. Unlike the beat of the march this brings a sense of beats organized in the counts of three. It brings more of lighter skip and side-to-side feel as opposed to a direct forwards motion. Jazz musicians will often use this kind of rhythm for interpretations of popular songs to give them more of a feeling of space and poetry. This feel can also remove any sense of clumsiness.

In summary semiotic choices have been used in the music of these two films to represent war and soldiery. In *ABTF* these are emotionally open, happy with moderate bursts of energy. This is about the large army about to enthusiastically participate

**Table 12.7**    Meaning potentials for rhythms

| Rhythmic quality | Meaning potential |
| --- | --- |
| Even/uneven | Conformity vs. creativity; ease vs. difficulty |
| Fast/slow | Hurry vs. leisurely; energy vs. its lack of; rush vs. patience |
| Lightness/heaviness | Mobility or clumsiness; important vs. unimportant; strength vs. weakness |
| Stasis/motion | Restriction vs. freedom; marking ground vs. progress; hesitation vs. certainty |
| No metronomic time | Sacredness, timeless, spiritual |

collectively in a major event. Repeated patterns and beats move forward with energy. *BOB* is also happy and positive. But there are no bursts of energy nor forward motion. High pitches are high energy and almost ethereal. It is emotionally expansive giving a feeling remembering something beautiful, an event that is almost spiritual. There is a shift away from the event, to the glorious experience of soldiery as service.

# 5 Conclusion

Why does CDA analyse discourses of war and how can the analysis of music and sound play an important part in this? CDA has been interested in the way that wars are legitimized and normalized and in the way that the actual political and economic reasons for war are suppressed by politicians and in news texts. These tend to conceal the actual nature of warfare and its political nature and foreground other aspects, such as the heroism of 'our boys'. I do not wish to suggest that what was accomplished by the defeat of the Nazis in World War II was not necessary, only that certain discourses of the nature and role of soldiery continue to be disseminated. In 1924 Ernst Friedrich published a book called *Krieg dem Kriege* (War against War). It contained photos of grotesquely disfigured young men injured in World War I – a war that killed and maimed many millions of young, mainly working class, men, often through disease. He combined these with images of young, proud, nationalistic soldiers before going off to war and young children dressed in military fashion during times of militaristic fervour, often with sarcastic comments about brave sacrifice and national pride. His aim was to place the actual nature of warfare into the public view. The novels of front-line soldiers too (Remarque, 1987; Sajer, 2001) tell of the heart-breaking humiliations and unspeakable horrors inflicted routinely on civilians in war zones. Yet what is foregrounded in many films and in war commemoration are the soldiers themselves and the act of service. What if at all times the horrors and effects were foregrounded, the results of acts of soldiery?

The music analysed in this paper, whether pointing to nationalist armies or individual feeling, is part of this foregrounding of soldiery and backgrounding the other aspects of war. When a British or American person reads about the actions of 'their boys' in Afghanistan or Iraq, we can consider the way that film music, operating as part of an ensemble of multimodal communication (Norris, 2004) with images and language from other media, plays a part in allowing this kind of focus to seem reasonable, to allow the routine suppression of information on the experiences of the civilians, the horrifically mutilated enemy that is left behind once they move on, once a new set of oil and resources becomes the political focus. Tagg (1984) was interested in the way that music could tutor and prepare us for participation in social events, to understand the nature of the identities and roles that they require. Music could represent war and soldiery entirely as regretful, as awful, as an abuse of life and a failure of civilized action. But in these two pieces of popular film it does not.

# References

Arnheim, R. (1969), *Visual Thinking*. Berkeley, CA: University of California Press.

Bell, P. and Van Leeuwen, T. (1993), *The Media Interview*. Kensington: University of New South Wales Press.

Brazil, D., Coulthard, M. and Johns, C. (1980), *Discourse Intonation and Language Teaching*. London: Longman Higher Education.

Chion, M. (2009), *Film a Sound Art*. New York, NY: Columbia University Press.

Cooke, D. (1959), *Language of Music*. Oxford: Clarendon Paperbacks.

Cooper, G. and Meyer, L. B. (1960), *The Rhythmic Structure of Music*. Chicago: University of Chicago Press.

Donnelly, K. (2005), *The Spectre of Sound: Music in Film and Television*. London: British Film Institute.

Doyle, P. (2006), *Echo and Reverb*. Wesley: University Press of New England.

Gorbman, C. (1987), *Unheard Melodies: Narrative Film Music*. London: British Film Institute.

Graham, P., Keenan, T. and Dowd A. M. (2004), 'A call to arms at the end of history: a discourse–historical analysis of George W. Bush's declaration of war on terror'. *Discourse & Society*, 15(2–3), 199–221.

Halliday, M. A. K. (1978), *Language as Social Semiotic: The Social Interpretation of Language and Meaning*. London: Arnold.

Hodge, R. and Kress, G. (1988), *Social Semiotics*. Cambridge: Polity Press.

Kassabian, A. (2001), *Hearing Film: Tracking Identification in Contemporary Hollywood Film Music*. New York and London: Routledge.

Kress, G. (2010), *Multimodality*. London: Routledge.

Lazar, A. and Lazar, M. M. (2004), 'The discourse of the New World Order: "outcasting" the double face of threat'. *Discourse & Society*, 15(2–3), 223–42.

Machin, D. (2007), 'Visual discourses of war: a multimodal analysis of the Iraq occupation', in A. Hodges and C. Nilep (eds), *Discourse, War and Terrorism*. Amsterdam: John Benjamins, pp. 123–42.

—— (2010), *Analysing Popular Music: Image, Sound, Text*. London: Sage.

Machin, D. and Van Leeuwen T. (2005), 'Computer games as political discourse: the case of Black Hawk Down'. *Journal of Language and Politics*, 4(1).

—— (2009), 'Toys as discourse: children's war toys and the war on terror'. *Critical Discourse Studies*, 6(1), 51–64.

Manvell, R. and Huntley, J. (eds) (1957), *The Technique of Film Music*. London: Focal Press.

McClary, S. (1991), *Feminine Endings: Music, Gender and Sexuality*. Minneapolis: University of Minnesota Press.

Norris, S. (2004), *Analyzing Multimodal Interaction: A Methodological Framework*. London: Routledge.

Remarque, E. M. (1987), *All Quiet on the Western Front*. London: Ballantine Books.

Sajer, G. (2001), *The Forgotten Soldier*. Dulles, VA: Potomac Books.

Schafer, R. (1977), *The Tuning of the World*. New York: Knopf.

Tagg, P. (1982), 'Nature as a musical mood category.' Nordens working paper series. Available at: http://www.tagg.org/articles/xpdfs/nature.pdf (accessed 29 July 2014).

—— (1984), 'Understanding musical time sense,' in Tvarspel – Festskrift for Jan Ling (50 a°r). Gothenburg: Skriften fran Musikvetenskapliga Institutionen. Available at: http://www.tagg.org/articles/xpdfs/timesens.pdf (accessed 29 July 2014).

—— (2012), *Music's Meanings: A modern Musicology for Non-Musos*. New York: Mass Media's Scholars.

Van Dijk, T. A. (2008), *Discourse and Power*. Basingstoke: Palgrave Macmillan.

Van Leeuwen, T. (1999), *Speech, Music, Sound*. London: Macmillan.

—— (2005), *Introducing Social Semiotics*. London: Routledge.

# PART TWO

# Domains of Discourse

# 13

# 'American Ways of Organizing the World'[1]

# Designing the Global Future through US National Security Policy

*Patricia L. Dunmire*

Kent State University

## 1 Overview

Christopher Layne (2006) explains that, since the end of World War II national security strategists, in their quest for 'absolute security', have operated according to the principle of 'strategic internationalism: the belief that to be secure, the United States must exert the full panoply of its power – military, economic, and ideological – on the international system in order to shape its external environment' (119, 7). This principle has undergirded the discourse and practice of the national security strategies of Democratic and Republican administrations throughout the post-Cold War period. Brent Scowcroft, National Security Advisor to George H. W. Bush, for instance, declared that the ending of the Cold War presented the US with a unique 'opportunity to mould an international system' that would be compatible with US interests and values (Scowcroft, 1993). Insisting that the nation's security strategy 'take a longer view', the Obama administration has declared that 'We must . . . work to better shape the outcomes that are most fundamental to our people in the twenty-first century' (United States National Security Council, 2010: 7). As these statements suggest, national security policy represents a crucial mechanism for and site of *global future design* and, thereby, participates in what August Comte identified as the key function of political discourse and practice: the 'determination of the future' (as quoted in Loye, 1978: 123).[2]

This chapter examines the specific ways in which US national security discourse has articulated and legitimated designs of the future of global society during the post-Cold War era (see also Cap, this volume). Taking a discourse-historical approach (Fairclough and Wodak, 1997; Reisigl, this volume), I examine how these designs index a conception of US security policy that predates the post-Cold War era. Such an approach requires moving 'away from the micro-level analysis of the text . . . to higher levels influencing, conditioning, and occasioning texts' and examining 'the text as part of a textual tradition, as a social, cultural, historical phenomenon' (Blommaert, 2005: 125). Moreover, locating a particular discourse historically is what gives critical studies of discourse its 'critical punch' by demonstrating that 'what looks new is not new at all, but the outcome of a particular process that is systemic, not accidental' (Blommaert, 2005: 37). Accordingly, I examine post-Cold War national security documents as 'repositories of historical precedent' (Blommaert, 2005: 127) that serve to re-articulate and sustain a deeply-rooted tradition of US security policy, that of the 'Open Door' (Williams, 1959).

# 2 Analytic framework

I focus my analysis of post-Cold War national security strategy, as manifested in the national security strategy documents of each post-Cold War administration,[3] at the level of strategy rather than the tactics by which that strategy is implemented. As Bacevich (2002: 33) explains, partisan differences concerning foreign policy should not be confused with 'genuine policy differences'. In fact, consensus over foreign policy fundamentals is 'so deep-seated that its . . . premises are asserted rather than demonstrated' (Bacevich, 2002: 33). Thus, these fundamentals constitute the 'doxa' of national security, its unanimous, unquestioned precepts (Bourdieu, 1977: 168). I do not consider the partisan differences in tactics that may exist between presidential administrations or treat each administration's policy as discrete. To do so would 'undervalue the evidence of continuity between administrations and, indeed, between historical eras' (Bacevich, 2002: 72). Rather, I examine the underlying strategy shared by each post-Cold War administration in terms of how it articulates and perpetuates the nation's longer term 'grand strategy.'[4] In so doing, I follow Wallerstein's (2004: 18) prescription that social science research be historical by 'looking at phenomena over longer periods as well as over larger spaces'. Specifically, I situate post-Cold War national security strategy within its appropriate historical context and consider the functions that strategy serves vis-à-vis the modern 'world system' (Wallerstein, 2004).

This approach is in keeping with Thibault's (1991: 124) 'critical intertextual analysis' which seeks to disrupt a given community's 'disjunction of discursive formations' by identifying the intertextual connections that link seemingly disparate texts and historical moments (Lemke, 1995: 98). I examine post-Cold War national security strategy as comprising *thematic formations* – 'recurrent patterns of semantic meaning' – that tie individual strategies together while also indexing their historical conditions of production (Lemke, 1995: 91). Such an approach is important if critical discourse analysts are to resist efforts by politicians and policy makers to 'synchronize' their texts and actions to the 'here-and-now', thereby '[masking] the densely layered history of the discourse' (Blommaert, 2005: 130–31). Such manoeuvring serves as a 'tactic of power' which simplifies complex historical developments and obscures the 'deep layers' of a given system in favour of a reductive, surface-level understanding of that system (Blommaert, 2005: 130, 135, 136).[5]

The following analysis resists this tactic by demonstrating that national security strategies that profess to be new, and that may even look new, are, in fact, the product of enduring, systemic processes. I historicize post-Cold War national security strategy by identifying how it indexes an *archive* which enables the production and meaning of national security strategy. As Foucault (1972: 30) explains, the concept of archive addresses the questions, 'according to what rules has a particular statement been made, and, consequently according to what rules could other similar statements be made?' and 'how it is that one particular statement appeared rather than another?'. The answer to these questions resides in the archive which 'lays down' the 'enunciative possibilities and impossibilities' which account for 'the things said'; it embodies the 'rules of a practice that enable statements to both survive and to undergo regular modification' (145–6).

The archive that provides the enunciative possibilities for post-Cold War security policy is that of the Open Door approach (OD), which has characterized the US approach to foreign policy since the late nineteenth century (Williams, 1959; Layne, 2006). Following Foucault (1972: 147), I understand this archive to represent a 'privileged region: at once close to us, and different from our present existence'; as representing the 'border of time that surrounds our presence, which overhangs it'. In what follows, I summarize the key concepts and themes of the OD, including its articulation as 'Modernization Theory' (Gilman, 2003). I then examine how post-Cold War security strategy indexes key thematic formations comprising the OD archive: the 'Frontier Thesis' of externalizing opportunities and challenges and dangers; the configuration of the modern world system into 'integrated' and 'non-integrated' zones; and, the 'virtuous circle' of economic and political liberalization and democratic peace. Using these thematic formations as 'interpretative leads' (Blommaert, 2005: 11), I examine the ways post-Cold War security strategy discourse 'reaches back to and somehow incorporates or resonates with the already said' as manifested in the Open Door archive (Bauman, 2005: 145). Ultimately, I seek to disjoin each post-Cold War administration's security policy from the immediate context of its production and situate it within the broader historical space in which it circulates and from which it gains meaning.

# 3 Shaping the global future through 'openness' and 'modernization'

Since the end of the Cold War US national security policy has been grounded in 'an expansive conception' of the nation's international role and its political, economic and security interests (Layne, 2006: 2). This conception is rooted in the grand strategy of 'extraregional hegemony' which was crafted during World War II and which guided the nation's diplomatic and military approach to the Cold War (Layne, 2006: 3). The motivation for this strategy, Layne contends, lies in what William Appleman Williams identified as a deliberate programme begun in 1900 to create an 'open door' world, the 'grand design' of which would establish 'the American Way' as 'the global status quo' (Williams, 1959: 8, 52).[6] This goal required creating an international system comprising states that would adhere to US liberal values and institutions and that would be open to US economic infiltration (Layne, 2006: 2). The OD approach was intended to 'win victories without war'; would 'cast the economy and politics of poorer, weaker, underdeveloped countries in a pro-American model'; was 'extremely hard-headed and practical'; and, in the end, was 'certain to produce foreign policy crises' (Williams, 1959: 57).

The particular iteration of the OD approach that held sway during the Cold War was the economic development programme of Modernization Theory (MT). Modernization Theory, which was advocated by both social scientists and foreign policy experts during the 1950s and 1960s, represents the 'most explicit and consistent blue print ever created by Americans for shaping foreign societies' (Gilman, 2003: 5). Modernization theorists sought to 'define the global pattern of change, explain its sources, and shape the world's future' in the image of the West, generally, and the US, specifically (Latham, 2000: 45–6). This unidirectional process of development would ultimately culminate in a progressive 'secular, materialist utopia' similar to that achieved by the 'post-ideological' US of the 1950s and early 1960s (Gilman, 2003: 14). Assuming that history was on the side of US capitalist democracy, modernization theorists asserted that 'the whole world was destined to converge with modernity as limned by the contemporary US' (Gilman, 2003: 4, 5, 14). For their part, policy makers needed to understand that the US '*should* be a universal model for the world' and that they 'had a duty' to promote America's 'liberal social values, capitalist economic organization, and democratic political structures' throughout global society (Gilman, 2003: 4; emphasis in the original; Latham, 2000: 6). Doing so was sure to accelerate the 'natural process through which "traditional" societies could move toward enlightened "modernity" most clearly represented by America itself' (Latham, 2000: 6). Such a programme, moreover, would fulfil 'a compelling national interest' of the US: promoting 'a world environment in which we ourselves can live freely, secure from the menace of hostile states and free from the distraction of chaotic ones' (Millikan and Rostow, 1957: 7). In sum, the security of the United States required the modernization of 'emerging nations' (Latham, 2000: 209).

# 4  Analysis

## 4.1  Frontier thesis: externalizing 'opportunities' and 'difficulties'

The two key components of the OD are economic and political openness: an open international economic system based in free trade and the free flow of capital across national boundaries and the global spread of democracy and liberalism (Layne, 2006: 30). Such an approach is grounded in the logic of the 'frontier thesis': the belief that, throughout its history, the nation's domestic well-being – its economic and political liberty – has depended upon 'sustained, ever increasing overseas economic expansion' throughout a world of nations ideologically sympathetic to the US (Williams, 1959: 15; Layne, 2006: 32).[7] Within this view, the frontier represents a 'gate of escape' from domestic pressures and responsibilities (Turner, 1893). Such expansion was deemed by Woodrow Wilson to be a 'natural and wholesome impulse' and the key to national power (as quoted in Williams, 1959: 71). Regarding the nation's search for 'new frontiers' and, thus, 'new power', the President mused 'who shall say where it will end?' (Wilson, 1902).

An important consequence of this logic is the 'externalization' of the nation's 'opportunities' and 'difficulties' beyond the nation's physical frontiers (Williams, 1959: 42, 45). As Max Millikan and Walter Rostow (1957: 5, emphasis added), two prominent modernization theorists,[8] explained in the early years of the Cold War 'the world is becoming both more interdependent and more fluid than it has been at any other time in history, a condition which presents us with *a great danger and a great opportunity*'. In the early years of the republic, it was the expansion of the nation's physical territory that 'extended the area of freedom' (Williams, 1959: 60). Since then, extending 'freedom' has meant the expansion of US values, interests, and institutions beyond the nation's borders.

The thematic formation of opportunity and challenge/danger features prominently in each administration's conception of national security, as can be seen in Table 13.1. This theme serves to characterize each administration's security environment as dualistic, thereby orienting security principles, goals and strategies to addressing this dualism. Of concern here is the specific ways this dualism indexes the frontier thesis.

### 4.1.1  Externalizing opportunities

This section examines how post-Cold War opportunities are externalized by focusing on statements that frame the opportunities, identify them as to type, specify their beneficiaries and identify their source. Statements representing each of these categories are provided in Table 13.2.

**Table 13.1**   Opportunities and challenges

| | |
|---|---|
| **G. H. W. Bush** | Shaping a security strategy for a new era will require an understanding of the extraordinary trends at work today – an accurate sense of the **opportunities** that history has put forth before us and a sober appreciation of the **dangers** that remain (USNSC, 1991: 1). |
| | It is a new era that holds great **opportunities** – but also great **dangers** (USNSC, 1993: preface). |
| **Clinton** | Never has American leadership been more essential – to navigate the shoals of the world's new **dangers** and to capitalize on its **opportunities** (USNSC, 1995: i). |
| | The security environment in which we live is dynamic and uncertain, replete with a host of **threats and challenges** that have the potential to grow more deadly, but also offering unprecedented **opportunities** to avert those threats and advance our interests (USNSC, 1998: 1). |
| **G. W. Bush** | Transform America's national security institutions to meet the **challenges and opportunities** of the 21st Century (USNSC, 2002: vii). |
| | Engage the **opportunities** and confront the **challenges** of globalization (USNSC, 2006: iii). |
| **Obama** | Even in a world of enormous **challenges**, no threat is bigger than the American people's capacity to meet it, and no **opportunity** exceeds our reach (USNSC, 2010: 52). |

The opportunity framing statements outline the nation's security strategy principles, goals and priorities and circumscribes the more specific articulations of the nation's policies. They index the frontier thesis by presenting an expansive jurisdiction for US national security policy which encompasses events, behaviours and states of affair within the global community as a whole and within particular nations and regions. The George W. Bush administration (USNSC, 2002: preface), for example, conceptualizes the 'historic opportunity' facing the US as an opportunity to 'defend . . . and preserve the peace' and to 'extend the benefits of freedom across the globe'. 'The peace', however, does not concern the security condition of US territory and citizens. Rather, it references a particular conception of the global order that adheres to 'a single, sustainable model for national success: freedom, democracy, and free enterprise' and that is grounded in a system of values that are 'right and true for every person in every society' (USNSC, 2002: preface).

The general thrust of these framing statements – their representation of the jurisdiction, posture and interests of national security policy – is further specified

**Table 13.2** Opportunity statements

|  | Framing | Beneficiary | Source |
|---|---|---|---|
| **G. H. W. Bush** | Our strategy for this new era recognizes the opportunities and challenges before us: encouraging the constructive evolution of the Soviet Union; supporting the independence and vitality of the new Eastern European democracies; championing the principles of political and economic freedom as the surest guarantors of human progress and happiness, as well as global peace (USNSC, 1991: 36). | The demise of the . . . Soviet Communism leaves America and its allies with an unprecedented opportunity to preserve with greater ease a security environment within which our democratic ideals can prosper (USNSC, 1993: 13). | Ideals, capital, goods and services now move around the world with increasing speed, expanding economic opportunity (USNSC, 1993: 9). |
| **Clinton** | The forces of integration offer us an unprecedented opportunity to build new bonds among individuals and nations, to tap the world's vast human potential in support of shared aspirations, and to create a brighter future for our children (USNSC, 1998: iii). | Increasing both the US market share and the size of the African market will bring tangible benefits to US workers and increase prosperity and economic opportunity in Africa (USNSC, 1998: 56). | Many nations around the world have embraced America's core values of representative governance, free market economies and respect for fundamental human rights and the rule of law, creating new opportunities to promote peace, prosperity and greater cooperation among nations (USNSC, 1998: 1). |
| **G. W. Bush** | As we defend the peace, we will also take advantage of an historic opportunity to preserve the peace . . . the US will use this moment of opportunity to extend the benefits of freedom across the globe (USNSC, 2002: ii). | Including all the world's poor in an expanding circle of development – and opportunity – is a moral imperative and one of the top priorities of US international policy (USNSC, 2002: 21). | Trade and open markets will empower citizens in developing countries to improve their lives, while reducing the opportunities for corruption that afflict state-controlled economies (USNSC, 2006: 28). |

*(Continued)*

**Table 13.2**   Continued

|  | Framing | Beneficiary | Source |
|---|---|---|---|
| **Obama** | This will allow America to leverage our engagement abroad on behalf of a world in which individuals enjoy more freedom and opportunity, and nations have incentives to act responsibly, while facing consequences when they do not (USNSC, 2010: 2). | America's national security depends on these vibrant alliances, and we must engage them as active partners in addressing global and regional security priorities and harnessing new opportunities to advance common interests (USNSC, 2010: 11). | Each of these steps will sustain America's ability to lead a world where economic power and individual opportunity are more diffuse (USNSC, 2010: 2). |

through statements characterizing the types of opportunities, their beneficiaries, and the sources from which they arise.

The types of opportunities post-Cold War security strategy is designed to realize fall within four general categories:

- *security:* lasting safety, stability, averting threats

- *economic:* increase prosperity for individuals and nations through jobs and economic development; expand and grow US business, investment, enterprise, exports and access to markets; enlarge community of market economies

- *international integration:* improve and develop international cooperation, international partnerships and common interests; build new bonds among nations

- *ideological:* advance, protect and expand ideals of peace, freedom, democracy, human rights and standards of living.

These opportunities reside in various regions and nations across the globe (e.g., 'from Latin America to Asia to the Pacific', in the 'greater Middle East'). It is important to note, however, that these opportunities are externalized not only in terms of their location but also in terms of the people they benefit and who has access to them. Of course, various constituencies within the US are deemed to be the primary beneficiaries, including: individuals, business, workers, American enterprise, farmers, the American people and American influence. However, as can be seen in Table 13.2, each administration also presents a range of global constituencies it contends will benefit from these opportunities: Africa, all the world's poor and international alliances and partners.

Most of the opportunity statements in Table 13.2 take the form of 'opportunities to' or 'opportunities for', thereby rendering opportunity as an activity to be engaged in or an objective to be achieved. The statement by George W. Bush concerning including the world's poor in a 'circle of opportunity', however, renders opportunity as an abstraction that has meaning and value in and of itself. Similar articulations are made by the other administrations. President Obama, for example, argues for 'An international order advanced by US leadership that promotes peace, security, and opportunity . . .' (USNSC, 2010: 7). Consequently, opportunity represents a value akin to freedom and justice; indeed, the first Bush administration contends that 'opportunity' represents a value that 'defines us as a nation' (USNSC, 1993: preface). Accordingly, opportunity is not only something that resides beyond the nation's borders; it is something the US is obliged to promote beyond those borders.

This expansive posture of US national security to include 'everyone' within its charge is reinforced through characterizations of the sources from which these opportunities derive. Particular regional environments, the nature of US relations with other countries and specific policy initiatives are credited with spawning opportunity. The ultimate source, however, is the configuration of the global order as an open and dynamic economic environment based in free market and democratic principles. This order is led by the US and is based on 'the world's embrace' of core American values: peace, democracy and free market economies. The international order that the US seeks to 'shape', 'advance' and 'protect' is an order that provides an outlet for an expanding US economy, a key tenet of the OD approach (Williams, 1959). It is also an order, however, whose benefits reside and extend beyond US territory. The ultimate goal of national security policy, then, is to seize the opportunity that, in the words of the first Bush administration, 'history has put before us': to provide the principles and strategies that will maintain, shape and advance this post-Cold War global order (USNSC, 1991: 1).

## 4.1.2 Externalizing challenges and dangers

Just as opportunities are externalized, so too are the challenges and dangers outlined in the post-Cold War national security documents. The post-Cold War era comprises political, social, security, military, economic, moral, environmental, technological and arms control challenges and dangers. While each administration has its own way of framing these challenges and dangers, as can be seen in Table 13.3, points of convergence across administrations do emerge.

Unlike the 'clear and present' challenges and dangers of the Cold War era (USNSC, 1995: 33), both the George H. W. Bush and Clinton administrations contend that the 'complex array of new and old security challenges' of the post-Cold War era "are more complex, ambiguous, and diffuse than ever before" (USNSC, 1995: 1; USNSC, 1993: 1). The complexity, diffuseness, and broad scope of these challenges render them not merely as challenges facing the US but as having a bearing on the global community.

**Table 13.3**   Challenge and danger framing statements

| | |
|---|---|
| **G. H. W. Bush** | We need to consider how the US and its allies can best respond to a new agenda of political challenges – such as the troubled evolution of the Soviet Union or the volatile Middle East – in the framework of the moral and political values we share (USNSC, 1991: 2). |
| **Clinton** | Our nation's challenge . . . is to sustain [the role as the world's foremost force for peace, prosperity, and the universal values of democracy and freedom] by harnessing the forces of global integration for the benefit of our own people and people around the world (USNSC, 1998: iii). |
| **G. W. Bush** | Throughout history, freedom has been threatened by war and terror; it has been challenged by the clashing of wills of powerful states and evil designs of terrorists (USNSC, 2002: iii). |
| **Obama** | Just as America helped to determine the course of the 20th Century, we must now build the sources of American strength and influence, and shape the international environment capable of overcoming the challenges of the 21st Century (USNSC, 2010: 1). |

They are globally shared and thus must be addressed within a system of shared political and moral values. Moreover, it's not so much the US that's challenged and endangered; it's freedom – an abstract, amorphous value and political concept that abides no territorial boundaries. In fact, 'a simple truth of this new world', the Clinton administration insists, is that 'an idea that comes under many names – democracy, liberty, civility, pluralism' – is vulnerable to 'attack' by its 'enemies' (USNSC, 1995: 1; 1998: iii). Similarly, the George W. Bush administration insists that it is freedom the US is obliged to defend against its 'determined enemies' (USNSC, 2006: transmittal).

Key to understanding the nature of the post-Cold War challenges and dangers and their rhetorical function is understanding the extent to which the spectre of isolationism, a foreign policy approach antithetical to the frontier thesis, haunts post-Cold War national security policy. Given the dominant Cold War conception of the Soviet threat – that the Soviet Union had an expansionist agenda and posed an existential threat to the US – the ending of the Cold War on terms favourable to the US should have resulted in the US military coming home from Europe and East Asia and in an easing of the nation's role in global affairs (Layne, 2006: 13; Bacevich, 2002: 71). In sum, the US came out of the Cold War with its political and economic systems and values apparently vindicated and its unrivalled position as the world's pre-eminent superpower seemingly secure.

And yet, each administration since the end of the Cold War has viewed the possibility of a retreat from the world stage as impeding the nation's ability to defend its values and interests (Bacevich, 2002: 114). Referring to isolationist tendencies in the US during the 1920s, George Bush, Sr. insisted that such a posture 'had near disastrous consequences then' and a similar posture 'would be even more dangerous now' (USNSC, 1991: 2). For the Clinton administration, US global leadership during World War II and its aftermath and during the Cold War represented the necessary rejection of isolationism and exemplified the approach the US should take in the post-Cold War era (USNSC, 1995: 2). In the words of George W. Bush's administration, the nation must choose between the 'path of fear,' which leads to 'isolationism and protectionism', and the 'path of confidence', which leads to 'leadership . . . and the pursuit of . . . open trade' (USNSC, 2006: transmittal). Not only would American national security suffer 'destructive consequences' if the US were to 'walk away' from 'the emerging challenges and shortcomings of the international system'; the Obama administration insists that 'global security' would suffer as well (USNSC, 2010: 3). Within this context, the articulation and externalization of challenges and dangers in the post-Cold War era serves to legitimate and, thus maintain, an expansive, extra-territorial conception of what constitutes US national security and the strategy needed to ensure that security.

The object of these challenges and dangers – the persons, institutions, nations or actions that these challenges are oriented toward – is wide ranging. Not surprising, various dimensions of the US are identified as being challenged by a host of actors and phenomena: the nation's security, its citizens, workforce, exports, companies, security commitments, cyber networks, intelligence community and borders, as well as the nation's ability to sustain its hemispheric agenda in the face of post-Cold War challenges. US national security, however, must also be concerned with challenges that impact peoples and institutions beyond US borders. It must attend to challenges to: the world's nations, global peace and stability, the international community, international stability, the world, the worldwide community, an international environment and global society.

Challenges and dangers can stem from actions or states of affair within a particular nation or region, the behaviours of a particular actor, the implications and impact of various phenomena or a plan or objective the US seeks to pursue. Table 13.4 provides a breakdown of these sources.

Not surprisingly, the dangers of the post-Cold War era (indicated in bold) come from sources beyond US borders: terrorists and extremists, rogue states, locally dominant powers, the launching of WMD by an aggressor, just to name a few. Similarly, many of the post-Cold War challenges are also born abroad: in China, Africa, the former Soviet republics and from peace operations, the resurgence of democracy in Central and South America and global financial markets. Of particular interest here, however, is the category of action/goals, which comprises statements outlining US participation in global affairs, namely its efforts to promote and consolidate democratic values, protect and broaden open markets, sustain the US's leadership role, promote global prosperity and safeguard the global commons. Through these statements, the US is identified as a source of many post-Cold War challenges but not of any of its dangers. That is, many regions of the world are characterized as the source of aggression, destabilizing

**Table 13.4**    Sources of post-Cold War challenges and dangers

| | |
|---|---|
| **Nations, regions, actors** | China; the Soviet Union; former Soviet republics; former communist countries; Africa; the Gulf region; the Middle East; East Asia; Korea; **terrorists and extremists; rogue states; terrorists with WMD; weak states; Afghanistan; tyrants; dictators; enemies; violent extremists pursuing WMD; proliferation of WMD; a handful of states flouting international norms; locally dominant powers with modern weapons and ambitions**; |
| **phenomena** | upheaval and human migration; easing of tensions with Soviet Union; illegal drugs; terrorism; proliferation of advanced weapons, weapons of mass destruction; the crisis in the Gulf and its aftermath; change and transition to a more open and competitive trading system; crime and drugs; a dramatically evolving world economy; political and economic transformation in Europe and potentially in the Soviet Union; the resurgence of democracy in Central and South America; transnational environmental issues; resource issues; Haitian democracy; subversiveness, lawlessness and insurgency; the evolving security environment; peace operations; global financial markets; weak democracies; unemployment; East Asian financial crisis; political and economic liberty; national reform; clashing of wills, evil designs; matching government efforts; shared health and environmental threats; national security implications of globalization; globalization; **isolationism; US-Soviet relations; nuclear, biological, chemical and conflict; transfers of destabilizing arms and dual use technology; corruption and rule of law issues; drug use; the crossroads of radicalism and technology; terror, violence and chaos; HIV/AIDS, TB and malaria; inadequate safeguarding of nuclear materials; unresolved threats; violent extremism; trends beyond our shores; intermediate range missile deployments; global war; threats of sudden regional conflict; launching a WMD by an aggressor; spread of militarily useful technology, WMD and missiles; globalization** |
| **action/goals** | promoting, consolidating democratic values; promoting market principles; protecting against transnational threats; meeting urgent human needs; ensuring successful transition of former Soviet republics; protecting and broadening open markets; building a peace; reduce government budget deficits, increase savings and investment; renewal at home; aiding former communist countries; enlarging community of market democracies; sustaining US leadership role; monitoring ballistic missile programmes; instilling respect for the rule of law; stabilizing current financial system; institutionalizing Haiti's development; engaging autocratic regimes; following a complex and elusive target; creating a viable, credible Palestinian state; promoting global prosperity; safeguarding the global commons; confronting the Soviet Union |

behaviour and phenomena, conflict, corruption and chaos. The US, by contrast, is rendered as the source of political, military and humanitarian plans and actions that can temper these areas of danger by integrating them into the political and economic systems and values that govern the stable and peaceful areas of the world. And it is through this conception of dangers and challenges that post-Cold War national security strategy indexes another important dimension of the OD archive: the configuration of the world system.

## 4.2 Zones and circles: the configuration of the modern 'world system'

### 4.2.1 Expanding zones of peace, shrinking zones of turmoil

In explaining his support for the US war against Iraq, Thomas Barnett (2003), the Assistant for Strategic Futures for the second Bush administration, identifies the security paradigm shaping our age: 'disconnectedness defines danger'.[9] This disconnect concerns the status of nations and regions which have not been integrated into the 'rule set of democracy, transparency, and free trade' governing the globalized world system. The 'functioning core' of the world system comprises nations and regions that are fully integrated into the global system and that can boast stable governments, increasing standards of living and 'more deaths by suicide than murder'. The 'nonintegrated gap', by contrast, is 'plagued by politically repressive regimes, widespread poverty and disease, routine mass murder, and . . . chronic conflict'. The goal of US security policy, Barnett insists, must be to shrink the gap. This configuration of 'the real world order' was anticipated by what Singer and Wildvansky (1993: 3) termed 'zones of peace, wealth, and democracy' and 'zones of turmoil, war, and development.' Briefly, the zones of peace hold 'most of the power in the world' and comprise modern, future-oriented states that subscribe to 'democracy, market economies, and ethical and social values' (Singer and Wildvansky, 1993: 3, 11). The zones of turmoil comprise traditional, past-oriented nations that are riddled with violence and turbulence and that have difficulty developing politically and economically (Singer and Wildvansky, 1993: 6–7).

As I will demonstrate below, both the integrated/nonintegrated and zones configurations of the geopolitical environment figure prominently within post-Cold War national security strategy. And it is this thematic formation of a bifurcated world system, as well as the policy of shrinking one zone and expanding the other through a process of global integration, that indexes post-Cold War strategy to the OD archive, particularly its articulation as Modernization Theory.

Modernization theorists conceived of the world system as comprising the major powers of the 'Free World' and the communist countries competing over the future of the 'underdeveloped areas' recently set loose by post-World War II decolonization

(Gilman, 2003). Their ultimate goal was to counter the influence of Soviet and Chinese communists in the developing world by making those societies 'more like "us" – and less like the Russians or the Chinese' (Gilman, 2003: 3). Their efforts assumed a fundamental dichotomy between industrialized nations and underdeveloped nations. While industrialized nations were *Western, modern, integrated, free, prosperous, politically healthy and mature, oriented toward the future, stable* and *peaceful*, the underdeveloped areas were *non-Western, traditional, isolated, economically stagnant, politically immature, oriented toward the past, unstable* and *violent* (Millikan and Rostow, 1957).

Modernization theorists were convinced that by expanding democracy and free market capitalism to the underdeveloped areas, the US could create a global environment in which its interests and values were less likely to be threatened. Of course, security policy must protect the country against the 'danger of overt military aggression . . . inherent in the present capabilities and possible future intentions of . . . the Communist bloc countries' (Millikan and Rostow, 1957: 2). The 'fundamental task of American military and foreign policy', however, must be promoting 'the evolution of a world in which threats to our security and, more broadly, to *our way of life* are less likely to arise' (Millikan and Rostow, 1957: 130, 3; emphasis added). The key thematic formations underlying the modernizationists' approach to the OD policy are: an open world system as necessary for US security and prosperity; a dichotomized conception of the world; and the US as leader of and model for the modern world system. As Table 13.5 shows, each administration's security strategy indexes and rearticulates these themes in the post-Cold War era.

The dichotomized depiction of the global community embedded within the OD and MT archive manifests in post-Cold War security strategy through a rhetoric of core/gap and zones of peace/zones of turmoil. Table 13.6 provides a summary of all the terms used by each administration to characterize what are referred to as the integrated and non-integrated nations and regions of the world. As the statements in Table 13.5 show, each post-Cold War administration, like the modernization theorists before them, has viewed the expansion of democracy and free markets and the integration of local, national economies into an open global economic system as the surest way to protect the nation and its fundamental values and to provide for its economic well-being.

The commitment to this expansionist and integrationist approach stems from the post-Cold War administrations' conviction, which they shared with the modernizationists, that uniting US interest and its values would enable US national security policy to serve the needs and interests of the global community. According to Millikan and Rostow (1957: 134–5), if the US is to 'defend and perpetuate the quality of our society as well as to maintain its physical security . . . American statesmancraft' must 'formulate courses of action which . . . harmonize abiding American interests and abiding American ideals'. Such an approach, they insisted, would enable the US to build a 'stable' and 'better' world (ix, 7).

**Table 13.5** Zone statements

| | Dichotomy | Open world for US security | US as leader, model |
|---|---|---|---|
| **G. H. W. Bush** | As we provide American leadership to extend the 'zone of peace' and enhance the forces of integration . . . we must also provide . . . leadership to inhibit forces of fragmentation that threaten order, peace, and stability (USNSC, 1993: 6). | It is in our national interest to help the democratic community of nations continue to grow while ensuring stability (USNSC, 1993: 6). | We must lead because we cannot otherwise hope to achieve a more democratic and peaceful future in a world still rife with turmoil and conflict (USNSC, 1993: 2). |
| **Clinton** | A common purpose – to secure and strengthen the gains of democracy and free markets while turning back their enemies (USNSC, 1998: iii). | All of America's strategic interests are served by enlarging the community of democratic and free market nations (USNSC, 1995: 22). | Our nation's . . . responsibility is to sustain its [leadership] role by harnessing the forces of integration for the benefit of our own people and people around the world (USNSC, 1998: iii). |
| **G. W. Bush** | Expand the circle of development by opening societies and building an infrastructure of democracy (USNSC, 2002: viii). | America's national interests and moral values drive us . . . to assist the world's . . . least developed nations and help integrate them into the global economy (USNSC, 2006: 32). | The US seeks to extend freedom across the globe by leading an international effort to end tyranny and promote effective democracy (USNSC, 2006: 3). |
| **Obama** | • A handful of states endanger regional and global security by flouting international norms (USNSC, 2010: 8).<br>• Without such an international order, the forces of instability and disorder will undermine global stability (USNSC, 2010: 40). | To promote peace and prosperity for all Americans, we will need to lead the international community to expand the inclusive growth of the integrated, global economy (USNSC, 2010: 31). | Our support for the aspirations of the oppressed abroad, who know they can turn to America for leadership based on justice and hope (USNSC, 2010: 10). |

**Table 13.6**   Zone descriptions

| | Integrated core | Non-integrated gap |
|---|---|---|
| G. H. W. Bush | peaceful; stable; cooperative; commonality/ sharedness; independent and integrated; prosperous; democratic; market economies; free; rule of law; human rights; communal; progressive | turmoil; destructive forces; threatening; radicalism; dislocations and dangers; turbulence; upheavals; troubled; volatile; need; security problems; isolated; statist: unstable; crisis-prone; forces of fragmentation; conflict: looking for guidance, needing help; authoritarian; forces of fragmentation that threaten order, peace and stability; ethnic and aggressive nationalistic tensions; explosive; division |
| Clinton | dignity and hope; promise; open; free; secure; forces of democracy | troubling uncertainties; clear threats; wrenching; repressive; violent extremism, militant nationalism and ethnic religious strife; enemies of democracy and free markets; outlaw states and ethnic conflict; repressive; defiant forces of nationalism |
| G. W. Bush | civilized; united; hope; tolerance; opportunity; common interests; principles; liberty; confidence; honour citizens' dignity; empowerment; expansive | terrorists; radicalism; poverty; corruption; poverty, disease, tyrants; failing states; catastrophic technologies; the embittered few; fear; suffering; those who are unwilling or unready to help themselves; disease, war and desperate poverty; rogue states; reject basic human values and hates the US and all it stands for; despair; fear; violate human rights; brutalize citizens; enslavement; narrow; those states that fear freedom |
| Obama | successful; vast diversity; resilience; engaged; shared interests; protect universal rights | failing states; flout international norms; polarization; disorder |

What the modernizationists termed the 'art' of harmonizing ideals and interest has been touted throughout the post-Cold War period. The first Bush administration explained that the application of US power through national security policy must be answerable to 'our own interests and our own conscience – to our ideals and history' (USNSC, 1991: 3). The Clinton administration likewise insisted that grounding security strategy in 'both America's interests and our values', would enable the nation to exercise its global leadership 'in a manner that reflects our best national values and protects the security of this great and good nation' (USNSC, 1995: iii, 33). For George W. Bush's administration, national security policy is based in 'a distinctly American internationalism that reflects the union of our values and our national interests' which, ultimately, will enable the US to 'help make the world not just safer but better' (USNSC, 2002: 1). Similarly, the Obama administration insists that the US 'rejects the false choice between the narrow pursuit of our interests and an endless campaign to impose our values' (USNSC, 2010: 5).

The union of value and interest represents the lodestone of US security strategy and, ultimately, serves to legitimate its OD approach. That is, in pursuing its national security interests, the US acts in accord with values that are not tethered to the history and culture of the US and its Western allies but that represent universal hopes and aspirations. Indeed, the US 'need not be inhibited in supporting values that have proven universal' or in promulgating 'standards we would like all nations . . . to observe, standards which aren't merely Western, but universal' (USNSC, 1991: 13; USNSC, 1998: 54). Rather, it should actively promote the 'single, sustainable model for national success: freedom, democracy, and free enterprise' as this model is rooted in 'basic rights upon which our Nation was founded, and which peoples of every race and region have made their own' (USNSC, 2002: i; USNSC, 2010: 6).

## 4.2.2 The 'virtuous circle' of an Open Door world

In an Open Door world, economic and ideological openness and expansion are taken to be the inevitable 'natural order of things' and to be causally related to international peace and stability (Layne, 2006: 124; Williams, 1959: 26). Such a world operates according to what policy makers call the 'virtuous circle': a 'complex set of linkages' which marries US economic prosperity and the security of its core values to economic, political and ideological openness abroad (Layne, 2006: 194). Through the virtuous circle, 'cooperative economic interaction' replaces 'antagonistic political competition' (Bacevich, 2002: 100). Millikan and Rostow (1957: 39, 130) proposed that Cold War military and foreign policy focus on creating and maintaining 'a world environment . . . within which our form of society can continue to develop in conformity with the humanitarian principles which are its foundation'. This global environment would comprise a 'new international partnership program for world economic growth' which, in turn, would 'maximize the pace of economic growth in the Free World' (Millikan and Rostow, 1957: 55, 109). In short, the US has 'a major and persistent stake in a world environment predominantly made up of open societies' (Millikan and Rostow, 1957: 132).

The nation's stake in such a world has indeed persisted. At its most general level, the thematic formation of the virtuous circle has found expression in each post-Cold War administration's articulation of national security, as the statements in Table 13.7 illustrate.

Throughout the post-Cold War era, national security policy has assumed that, because 'economic and security interests are inextricably linked', the goal of sustaining

**Table 13.7**   Virtuous circle

| G. W. H. Bush | . . . security is indivisible. The safety, freedom and well-being of one people cannot be separated from the safety, freedom and well-being of all (USNSC, 1991: 35). |
|---|---|
| Clinton | The more that democracy and political and economic liberalization take hold . . ., particularly in countries of geostrategic importance . . ., the safer our nation is likely to be and the more our people are likely to prosper (USNSC, 1995: 2). |
| G. W. Bush | A strong world economy enhances our national security by advancing prosperity and freedom in the rest of the world (USNSC, 2002: 17). |
| Obama | [American global leadership] must underpin an international economic system that is critical to both our prosperity and to the peace and security of the world . . . To promote prosperity for all Americans, we will need the international community to expand the inclusive growth of the integrated, global economy (USNSC, 2010: 29, 31). |

and enhancing both 'national security and national prosperity' are 'mutually supportive' (USNSC, 1998: 27; USNSC, 1993: 9). The virtuous circle, then, by linking US security to a particular configuration of the global environment, has also created linkages between national security, global economic development, democracy and peace. During the Cold War these linkages were expressed through MT's approach to economic development. Enabled by the democratic welfare state, the economic development of the 'underdeveloped areas' would, Millikan and Rostow (1957: 39) maintained, ultimately lead to the 'political, cultural, and social improvement' of those areas. They further insisted that economic development programmes would increase the standard of living of underdeveloped nations, a 'necessary condition for the development of stable and peaceful societies . . . *moving in a democratic direction*' (25, 63; emphasis added). Such societies, in the long run, would not 'menace' the US or its allies because they would be guided by the set of 'goals, aspirations, and values' they held in common with the US (Millikan and Rostow, 1957: 1).

In the post-Cold War era, a neo-liberal capitalist economic system has replaced the liberal welfare state as the supposed means for achieving the political and ideological goals espoused by MT (Gilman, 2003: 271; Wallerstein, 2004: 86). However, each administration has adhered to the conception of the virtuous circle that underlies OD policy: economic development is tied to economic openness which is tied to both political and economic freedom. Politically open societies, inevitably, will choose a democratic system of governance, which, when established worldwide, will create a global, democratic peace. This system is self-perpetuating as the stability created by global peace underwrites the free market economic system that provides for economic and political freedom; thus, stability represents the 'paramount value' of the global environment (Bacevich, 2002: 58).[10] Instability, conversely, is viewed as a fundamental threat to the OD as it, in the words of Defense Secretary William Cohen (1999: emphasis added), 'destroys lives *and markets*'. Indeed, as the first Bush administration declared, in the post-Cold War era 'the enemy we face . . . is instability itself' (USNSC, 1991: 26).

Post-Cold War security strategy subscribing to this virtuous circle was inaugurated by the first Bush administration's insistence that the nation must 'continue to support an international economic system as open and inclusive as possible' because it represents 'the best way to strengthen economic global development, political stability, and the growth of free societies' (USNSC, 1991: 2). Free, democratic societies, in turn, support both 'human rights and economic and social progress' (USNSC, 1991: 5). In the end, by helping to 'reduce social and political tensions', global economic growth will bring to fruition the administration's 'overriding goal: real peace . . . an enduring democratic peace based on shared values' (USNSC, 1993: 3, ii). If post-Cold War strategy was implemented correctly, the administration averred, historians would 'look back on the end of the 20th century as the beginning of an "Age of Democratic Peace"' (USNSC, 1993: ii).

In the pursuit of the nation's 'cherished goal' of a 'more secure world where democracy and free markets know no borders,' (USNSC, 1995: iii) the Clinton administration presented three mutually supporting national security goals: 'sustain our security with military forces'; 'bolster America's economic revitalization'; 'promote democracy abroad' (USNSC, 1995: i). Pursuing these goals will help the 'community of democratic nations' to continue growing, thereby 'enhancing the prospects for political stability, peaceful conflict resolution and greater dignity and hope for the peoples of the world' (USNSC, 1995: i). The premise underlying this strategy is that 'the forces necessary for a healthy global economy are also those that deepen democratic liberties' (USNSC, 1998: iv).

Insistent that the 'survival of liberty at home increasingly depends upon the success of liberty abroad' (USNSC, 2006: 3), George W. Bush's administration outlined a programme for creating a global community of 'democratic, well-governed states' (USNSC, 2006: 1). The US must 'ignite a new era of economic growth through free markets and free trade', growth which will come through greater global economic integration which 'spreads wealth across the globe' (USNSC, 2006: 1, 27). In this scheme, economic freedom is a 'moral imperative' that is 'fundamental to human nature and foundational to free societies' (USNSC, 2006: 27). Moreover, 'freedom is indivisible': 'as people gain control over their economic lives, they will insist on more control over their . . . political lives' (USNSC, 2006: 4). Key to this 'new era of economic growth' are 'stable and open financial markets' which enable the type of economic development that 'reinforces diplomacy and defense' (USNSC, 2006: 29, 33).

During its first term, the Obama administration, like its predecessors, insisted that the US act on behalf of an international economic system that is 'critical' to not only the nation's prosperity but also to 'the peace and security of the world' (USNSC, 2010: 29). Such a system allows for the 'free flow of information, people, goods, and services' that has 'advanced peace among nations' (USNSC, 2010: 28). This system, then, must remain open to the US 'trade and investment' that 'spurs global development, and contributes to a stable and peaceful political and economic environment' (USNSC, 2010: 9). In short, the Obama administration insists that the US must help 'shape an international order that promotes a just peace' (USNSC, 2010: 5).

# 5 Discussion

The legitimacy – indeed, the righteousness – of post-Cold War national security strategy derives from the unwavering contention that its ultimate goal is to create and extend the zone of 'democratic peace' which will provide for the prosperity and security of the global community. Rooted in Kant's enlightenment conception of 'perpetual peace' (Kant, 1991),[11] democratic peace theory holds that democracies typically do not wage war against each other and, thus, that democracy is an inherently peaceful form of governance.[12] As such, the more democracy expands globally, the better are the chances for a stable and peaceful global environment.[13] Conceived of as a means for expanding the 'zone of democratic peace', post-Cold War national security policy, consequently, offers the means for shaping an 'international order' that is 'an end in its own right', a 'just' order that 'advances mutual interests, protects the rights of all, and holds accountable those who fail to meet their responsibilities' (USNSC, 2010: 20, 49). It's important to note, however, that although war between democracies may be rare, democratic nations have not shied away from waging war, or 'operations other than war' (Fullenkamp, 1994: 8), against nations that subscribe to other forms of governance. This has clearly been the case for the US which, during the post-Cold War period, has focused the military's 'away games' primarily on the regions of the 'non-integrated gap' because, presumably, they represent a 'strategic threat environment' to the US and its allies (Barnett, 2003). Indeed, since the end of the Cold War, US military action has been concentrated primarily in the non-integrated gap (Barnett, 2003). This geopolitical situation can be boiled down into 'a simple security rule set: a country's potential to warrant a US military response is inversely related to its global connectivity' (Barnett, 2003).

Rather than offering a transparent articulation of US policy, the rhetoric of 'extending the zone of democratic peace' should be understood as masking the motives and goals that underlie US global shaping activities. That is, it should be understood as designed to shape the world system so as to maintain a particular balance of power and a particular division of global economic production. Specifically, the altruistic and magnanimous rhetoric of the OD – that in serving interests and values embraced by the US and western societies, it serves all – is directly challenged by Wallerstein's

(2004 p. 12) conception of the modern world system. According to World Systems Theory (WST), 'free trade' should not be understood as 'trade between equals'. Rather, it involves the transfer of wealth and resources from politically and economically weak regions – the 'periphery' – to regions that are politically and economically strong – the 'core'. Within this conception, Wallerstein (2004: 12) explains, the terms of trade are set so that economic value and profit flow from the weaker periphery to the core. Because of their economic, political and military power, strong states are able to pressure their weaker counterparts to open their frontiers to flows of production that benefit firms within the core (55). These flows, however, are non-reciprocal as the core states do not open their frontiers to firms within the periphery (55). As such, underdevelopment is to be understood not as an 'original state' that only free market capitalism can remedy; it is the very 'consequence of historical capitalism' (12). Moreover, despite the insistence by OD advocates that an open economic system is inextricably tied to a democratic system of governance,[14] the world economy, in fact, is not 'bounded by a unified political structure' (23). Rather it is unified by an international division of labour defined by the core-periphery dynamic (23). Within this configuration, then, modern capitalist democracies do not serve as the 'single, sustainable model' by which others can achieve an increased standard of living and a liberal political system (16). They represent, instead, the mechanism by which some regions and peoples of the world serve the needs and interests of others.

# 6 Concluding remarks

As the archive governing US national security policy, the Open Door approach and its 'dogma of openness' maps out 'the principle upon which the world should be organized, the basis for a broad consensus on foreign policy, and a rationale for mustering and employing American power' (Bacevich, 2002: 26). A key consequence of this dogma is a 'deterritorialized' conception of national security which focuses on securing the nation's values, organizing ideology, and political and economic institutions (Layne, 2006: 119). Within the OD approach, protecting the 'national interest' requires securing US global power and maintaining the 'pattern of order' upon which that power depends (Layne, 2006: 119). The 'primary goal' of national security in such a world, then, is to 'maintain control of the future' (Saperstein, 1997: 50). As the self-appointed 'vanguard of history', the US exercises this control by 'transforming the global order' in such a way as to maintain US global dominance (Bacevich, 2002: 215). Within this configuration of the world system, the post-Cold War rhetoric of 'global democratic peace' clearly helps perpetuate the myth that US security strategy is motivated by an altruistic concern for global society. What is less clear – indeed, what is highly suspect – is how well this rhetoric characterizes the actual role the US has been playing within the post-Cold War global environment.

# Notes

1 Quoted from Gilman (2003: 4).

2 Dunmire (2011) provides an extended discussion of the relationship between political discourse and representations of the future.

3 My data set comprises two national security documents each from both Bush administrations and the Clinton administration. As of the time of writing of this chapter, the Obama administration has only released one national security strategy document. Each document is referenced in the body of this chapter as 'USNSC', the abbreviation for 'United States National Security Council', which is how each document is listed in the bibliography. USNSC 1991 and 1993 are the first Bush administration's documents; USNSC 1995 and 1998 are the Clinton administration's documents; USNSC 2002 and 2006 are the second Bush administration's documents; USNSC 2010 is the Obama administration's document.

4 Layne (2006: 13) defines grand strategy as involving a state's decisions about the threats to its security and how those threats should be managed and addressed. In its 'essence' grand strategy 'is about determining the state's vital interests – those important enough to fight over – and its role in the world' (13).

5 Although not the focus of my analysis, such synchronizing can be seen in each of the post-Cold War national security strategy documents as each administration makes an explicit argument for why the experiential reality of the context in which they were operating – e.g., the immediate aftermath of the Cold War, the terrorist attacks of 9/11 – demands a 'novel', 'unprecedented' approach to national security. See Bacevich (2002) for an analysis of these arguments.

6 Williams (1959: 52) argues that the Open Door policy defined US foreign policy from 1900 to 1958. He traces the first reference to the phrase 'open door' to President McKinley's call in 1898 for the 'enlargement of trade' in the Orient (49). The first of the Open Door Notes appeared in 1899 and outlined the policy as conceived by 'the interplay between private and public leaders' (50). The concept of the open door became official US foreign policy strategy during Theodore Roosevelt's presidency and called for internal reforms to be made by countries the US sought to engage with and deemed the monitoring of such reforms to be the right and the obligation of the US (64).

7 Williams (1959: 22) traces this view to James Madison and explains that Madison conceived of it as his 'guide to policy and action'.

8 Max Millikan and Walter Rostow worked together at the Center for International Studies (CIS) at MIT, which applied MT to 'the concrete problems of development in the 1950s' (Gilman, 2004: 156). The Center, which Millikan headed, grew off MIT's anti-communist propaganda programme 'Project Troy'. Its aim was to 'apply social science to problems bearing on the peace and development of the world community' and to 'throw light on the American role in promoting economic, social, and political change abroad' (as quoted in Gilman, 2004: 159). The work at CIS was based on the premise that policy makers should adopt a 'scientific perspective' on how to 'influence the evolution of the underdeveloped areas' (Rostow, as quoted in Gilman, 2004: 160). The Center published *A Proposal* in 1957, which outlined Rostow and Millikan's recommendations for how US leaders could achieve this evolution and is the source of my analysis of contemporary articulations of MT. For an extended critique of the 'new Mandarins' behind MT, see Chomsky (1967).

9  Barnett served in this position under Vice-Admiral Arthur Cebrowski who was appointed by Secretary of Defense Rumsfeld to head the 'Office of Force Transformation' within the Department of Defense (Lawson, 2011: 570, 572). Barnett and Cebrowski worked together to promote their conception of how the world system operated and of the military strategy that would be most effective vis-à-vis that system (Lawson, 2011: 572). Their views were well received throughout the security community in the aftermath of 9/11, including the Department of Defense (Lawson, 2011: 572).

10  See Mann (1997) for a critique of the valorization of stability within US national security policy.

11  Kant's theory of perpetual peace posited that states subscribing to a republican form of government were less likely to wage war because they could only do so with the consent of the governed. Since citizens were the ones who made the actual sacrifices during war – they did the fighting, provided the financing and assumed the debts incurred during wartime – they 'will have greater hesitation in embarking on so dangerous an enterprise' (1991: 100). Kant's 1795 essay 'perpetual peace' was preceded by James Madison's 'universal peace', portions of which correspond to some of the articles underlying Kant's systematic programme (Madison, 1792).

12  For divergent arguments concerning the claim that democratic nations 'never or rarely' go to war with each other see: Doyle (1983a, 1983b); Kinsella (2004); Layne (1994, 2006); Russert (1993a, 2005); Singer and Wildavsky (1993); Small and Singer (1976).

13  The conception of democratic peace and its implications for global security has recently been endorsed by the Nobel Committee through its awarding of the Nobel Peace Prize to the European Union. In explaining its decision, the Committee notes that the EU has 'for over six decades contributed to the advancement of peace and reconciliation, democracy, and human rights in Europe'. See www.nobelprize.org/nobel_prizes/peace/laureates/2012/press.html for a full account of the Committee's comments. Accessed 13th October 2012

14  For a critique of this argument from within the foreign policy establishment, see Sharma (2012: 6).

# References

Bacevich, A. (2002), *American Empire: The Realities and Consequences of US Diplomacy*. Cambridge, MA: Harvard University Press.

Barnett, T. (2003), 'The Pentagon's new map'. *Esquire*, 139, (3).

Bauman, R. (2005), 'Commentary: indirect indexicality, identity, performance: dialogic observations'. *Journal of Linguistic Anthropology*, 15(1), 145–50.

Blommaert, J. (2005), *Discourse: A Critical Introduction*. Cambridge: Cambridge University Press.

Bourdieu, P. (1977), *Outline of a Theory of Practice*. Cambridge: Cambridge University Press.

Chomsky, N. (1967), *American Power and the New Mandarins*. New York: Pantheon.

Cohen, W. S. (1999), February 18, Remarks delivered to Microsoft Corporation. Available at: www.defense.gov/speeches/speech.aspx?speechid=347 (accessed 18 June 2012).

Doyle M. W. (1983a), 'Kant, liberal legacies, and foreign affairs'. *Philosophy and Public Affairs*, 12(3), 205–35.

—— (1983b), 'Kant, liberal legacies, and foreign affairs: part 2'. *Philosophy and Public Affairs*, 12(4), 323–53.

Dunmire, P. (2011), *Projecting the Future through Political Discourse: The Case of the Bush Doctrine*. Amsterdam: John Benjamins.

Fairclough, N. and Wodak, R. (1997), 'Critical discourse analysis', in T. Van Dijk (ed.), *Discourse as Social Interaction*. London: Sage, pp. 258–84.

Foucault, M. (1972), *Archaeology of Knowledge*. London: Routledge.

Fullenkamp, B. (1994), 'Forward presence and the search for peacetime influence'. Newport, RI: Naval War College. Available at: http://www.dtic.mil/cgi-bin/GetTRDoc?Location=U2&doc=GetTRDoc.pdf&AD=ADA283405 (accessed 15 February 2011).

Gilman, N. (2003), *Mandarins of the Future: Modernization Theory in Cold War America*. Baltimore: Johns Hopkins.

Kant, I. (1991), 'Perpetual peace', in H. S. Reiss (ed.), *Kant: Political Writings*. Cambridge: Cambridge University Press, pp. 93–130.

Kinsella, D. (2004), 'No rest for the democratic peace'. *American Political Science Review*, 99(3), 453–7.

Latham, M. E. (2000), *Modernization as Ideology: American Social Science and 'Nation Building' in the Kennedy Era*. Chapel Hill, NC: University of North Carolina Press.

Lawson, S. (2011), 'Surfing on the edge of chaos: nonlinear science and the emergence of a doctrine of preventive war in the US'. *Social Studies of Science*, 41(4), 563–84.

Layne, C. (1994), 'Kant or cant: the myth of the democratic peace'. *International Security*, 19(2), 5–49.

—— (2006), *The Peace of illusions: American Grand Strategy from 1940 to the Present*. Ithaca: Cornell University Press.

Lemke, J. (1995), 'Intertextuality and text semantics', in P. H. Fries and M. Gregory (eds), *Discourse in Society: Systemic Functional Perspectives*. Norwood, NJ: Ablex, pp. 85–114.

Loye, D. (1978), *The Knowable Future: A Psychology of Forecasting and Prophecy*. New York: John Wiley and Sons.

Madison, J. (1792), 'Universal peace'. *The National Gazette*, 2 February. Available at: http://oll.libertyfund.org/?option=com_staticxtandstaticfile=show.php%3Ftitle=1941andItemid=27#a_07 (accessed 10 February, 2011).

Mann, S. (1997), 'The reaction to chaos', in D. S. Alberts and T. J. Czerwinski (eds), *Complexity, Global Politics, and National Security*. Washington, DC: The National Defense University, pp. 62–8.

Millikan, M. F. and Rostow, W. (1957), *A Proposal: Key to an Effective Foreign Policy*. New York: Harper & Brothers.

Russert, B. (1993a), *Grasping the Democratic Peace: Principles for a Post-Cold War World*. Princeton: Princeton University Press.

—— (2005), 'Bushwacking the democratic peace'. *International Studies Perspectives*, 6, 395–408.

Saperstein, A. (1997), 'Complexity, chaos, and national security policy: metaphors or tools?', in D. S. Alberts and T. J. Czerwinski (eds), *Complexity, Global Politics, and National Security*. Washington, DC: The National Defense University, pp. 44–61.

Scowcroft, B. (July 2 1993), 'Who can harness history? Only the US'. Available at: www.nytimes.com/1993/07/02/opinion/who-can-harness-history-only-the-us.html (accessed 27 October 2012).

Sharma, R. (2012), 'Broken BRICs: Why the rest stopped rising'. *Foreign Affairs*, 91(6), 2–7.

Singer, M. and Wildvansky, A. (1993), *The Real World Order: Zones of Peace/Zones of Turmoil*. Chatham, NJ: Chatham House.

Small, M. and Singer, D. J. (1976), 'The war-proneness of democratic regimes, 1816–1965'. *The Jerusalem Journal of International Relations*, 1(4), 50–69.

Thibault, P. (1991), *Social Semiotics as Praxis*. Minneapolis: University of Minnesota Press.

Turner, F. J. (1893), 'The significance of the frontier in American history'. Paper read at the meeting of the American Historical Association in Chicago, 12 July 1893. Available at: xroads.virginia.edu/~hyper/turner/chapter1.html (accessed 3 December 2012).

United States National Security Council (1991), *National Security Strategy of the United States*. Available at: www.fas.org/man/docs/918015-nss.htm (accessed 3 December 2012).

—— (1993), *National Security Strategy of the United States*. Available at: www.drworley. org/NSPcommon/National%20Security%20Strategy/NSS%20official/NSS-1993-Bush. pdf (accessed 3 December 2012).

—— (1995), *A National Security Strategy of Engagement and Enlargement*. Available at: www.fas.org/spp/military/docops/national/1996stra.htm (accessed 3 December 2013).

—— (1998), *A National Security Strategy for a New Century*. Available at: www.clinton3. nara.gov/WH/EOP/NSC/Strategy/ (accessed 3 December 2012).

—— (2002), *The National Security Strategy of the United States of America*. Available at: www.whitehouse.gov/nsc/nss.html (accessed 3 December 2012).

—— (2006), *The National Security Strategy of the United States of America*. Available at: www.comw.org/qdr/fulltext/nss2006.pdf (accessed 3 December 2012).

—— (2010), *National Security Strategy*. Available at: www.whitehouse.gov/sites/default/ files/rss_viewer/national_security_strategy.pdf (accessed 3 December 2012).

Wallerstein, I. (2004), *World-Systems Analysis: An Introduction*. Durham, NC: Duke University Press.

Williams, W. A. (1959), *The Tragedy of American Diplomacy*. New York: W.W. Norton.

Wilson, W. (1902), 'The ideals of America'. *The Atlantic Monthly*, 2 December.

# 14

# 'Yes, We Can'

# The Social Life of a Political Slogan

*Adam Hodges*
Carnegie Mellon University

## 1 Introduction

**A** central feature of American electoral politics is the campaign slogan. Short, catchy slogans do important political work by reminding the public about the candidate's campaign message. Even in situations where detailed rehearsals of an overarching campaign narrative are not possible, slogans index that narrative and reinforce its message in the minds of voters. Much like an advertising jingle, a campaign slogan is only as effective as its reach. If it diffuses widely and enters into widespread social circulation, the message with which it is associated can also spread. If not, the slogan may be at best an in-group rallying cry among a small number of local supporters. With this in mind, it is important to understand how a political slogan gains traction in public discourse. Namely, what factors impact the circulation of a political slogan? And what is the semiotic process by which a slogan does political work? This chapter suggests some answers to these questions by focusing on the case of the 'yes, we can' slogan associated with the 2008 American presidential campaign of Barack Obama.

The study is situated within the domain of Political Discourse Analysis (PDA). Although Critical Discourse Studies (CDS) broadly recognizes a political dimension to language use – whether it be, for example, gender inequality (e.g. Lazar, 2005), racism (e.g. Van Dijk, 1987, 1991), media representations (e.g. Fairclough, 1995) or the ideological underpinnings of discourse (e.g. Hart, 2011) – PDA places a specific focus on the language of politicians or activities associated with governance (e.g. Fairclough, 2000; Cap, 2002; Cap, this volume; Chilton, 2004; Charteris-Black, 2005; Wodak, 2009; inter alia). As evidenced by the wide array of topics and approaches found in the current volume, CDS scholars (including those involved in PDA) draw from a range of disciplinary perspectives and approaches. Indeed, the forging of interdisciplinary perspectives is vital to the study of language as 'a form of "social practice"' (Fairclough and Wodak, 1997: 258). Moreover, greater understandings of both language and society – and language and politics – benefit from the integration of linguistic analysis with social theory. This chapter therefore starts with the Bakhtinian inspired notion of intertextuality – a concept widely applied within CDS in general (Fairclough 1992; inter alia) and PDA in particular (e.g. Dunmire, 2009, 2011; Hodges, 2008, 2011; Oddo, forthcoming) – and attempts to merge this interest in intertextuality with insights from sociological research on the diffusion of innovations (Rogers, 2003). In doing so, I draw from Enfield's (2008) use of these ideas in work on linguistic change and illustrate how these ideas are relevant to the domain of politics. The aim is to outline the conditions that allow a political slogan to effectively propagate through society in the service of political aims. I begin by providing an overview of the social life of the 'yes, we can' slogan during the 2008 election season. I then illuminate the mechanisms that allow for its diffusion in public discourse, and discuss the process by which the slogan accomplishes political work.

## 2 The social life of a political slogan

On the evening of 8 January 2008, Senator Barack Obama delivered a speech to supporters in New Hampshire after that day's primary election. Although that day he finished behind his main rival for the Democratic nomination, Senator Hillary Clinton, Obama gave an impassioned speech out of which a new slogan arose that would accompany the campaign to its end in November. The speech taps into a spirit of American optimism and emphasizes a determination to keep working for political change. After naming several points of desired change, Obama culminates the speech with a note of optimism and a call for perseverance amidst difficult odds, as seen in excerpt 1.

(1) *Obama's speech in New Hampshire on 8 January 2008*[1]
We know the battle ahead will be long. But always remember that no matter what obstacles stand in our way, nothing can stand in the way of the power of millions of voices calling for change.

   We have been told we cannot do this by a chorus of cynics. And they will only grow louder and more dissonant in the weeks and months to come.

   We've been asked to pause for a reality check. We've been warned against offering the people of this nation false hope. But in the unlikely story that is America, there has never been anything false about hope. (*Applause*)

   For when we have faced down impossible odds, when we've been told we're not ready, or that we shouldn't try, or that we can't, generations of Americans have responded with a simple creed that sums up the spirit of a people: Yes, we can. (*Applause*)

Yes, we can. (*Crowd chants*, 'Yes we can')

Yes, we can.

It was a creed written into the founding documents that declared the destiny of a nation: Yes, we can. (*Cheers*)

It was whispered by slaves and abolitionists as they blazed a trail towards freedom through the darkest of nights: Yes, we can. (*Cheers*)

It was sung by immigrants as they struck out from distant shores and pioneers who pushed westward against an unforgiving wilderness: Yes, we can. (*Crowd responds in unison*, 'Yes we can')

It was the call of workers who organized, women who reached for the ballot, a president who chose the moon as our new frontier, and a king who took us to the mountaintop and pointed the way to the promised land: Yes, we can, to justice and equality. (*Applause; crowd chants*, 'Yes we can')

Yes, we can, to opportunity and prosperity.

Yes, we can heal this nation.

Yes, we can repair this world.

Yes, we can.

And so, tomorrow, as we take the campaign south and west, as we learn that the struggles of the textile workers in Spartanburg are not so different than the plight of the dishwasher in Las Vegas, that the hopes of the little girl who goes to the crumbling school in Dillon are the same as the dreams of the boy who learns on the streets of L.A., we will remember that there is something happening in America, that we are not as divided as our politics suggest, that we are one people, we are one nation. (*Applause*)

And, together, we will begin the next great chapter in the American story, with three words that will ring from coast to coast, from sea to shining sea: Yes, we can. (*Applause; crowd chants in unison with Obama* 'We can')

As seen in excerpt 1, the crowd of supporters responds to his initial utterance of 'yes, we can' with applause and begins chanting the three words. As the speech continues, Obama sets up the phrase as a refrain that punctuates a series of examples used to exemplify the words' connection to past American struggles: 'It was a creed written into the founding documents', 'It was whispered by slaves and abolitionists', 'It was sung by immigrants', 'It was the call of workers'. Each example ends with the words, 'Yes, we can'. The rhetorical parallelism imbues the delivery with a rhythmic quality that echoes the call and response of a preacher and congregation. He then fronts the refrain to sum up the call for change represented by his candidacy in several short lines: 'Yes, we can, to opportunity and prosperity', 'Yes, we can heal this nation', 'Yes, we can repair this world'. The speech ends with a final return to those three words, as the crowd joins in the final 'we can' and erupts into applause.

Of course, the slogan itself is not unique to Obama or his campaign. True to the Bakhtinian perspective on language, the slogan has an intertextual history that reaches back into American history. In his speech, Obama even plays upon this history when he places the spirit of the words into the nation's 'founding documents', as well as the mouths of 'slaves and abolitionists', 'immigrants' and 'workers'. The final allusion to workers shifts from a typical sentiment represented by the words in the first examples to the use of the very phrase itself in struggles for workers' rights. Most notably heard in Spanish beginning in the 1970s as 'sí, se puede', the phrase became a rallying cry of the labour movement led by César Chávez, co-founder along with Dolores Huerta of the United Farm Workers. Thus, not only does the English version of the slogan have direct connections to Chávez and the farm workers, but so does the spirit of progressive struggle characterized in Obama's call for political change.

Just as any text has an intertextual history, it also connects to 'subsequent links in the chain of speech communion' (Bakhtin, 1986: 94). Once introduced in the New Hampshire speech on 8 January, the phrase 'Yes, we can' became a rallying cry for Obama supporters in much the way it had for the United Farm Workers in a previous generation. Although Obama does not reiterate the full rendition of the January 8 speech at subsequent campaign rallies, the slogan nevertheless features as a powerful rhetorical element at those rallies. On 26 January, Obama won the South Carolina primary. On 5 February, he won the majority of states voting on 'Super Tuesday,' and on 12 February he swept the 'Potomac primaries'. In each of his speeches on the evening of these nominating contests, the 'yes, we can' phrase appears and serves as a reminder of the campaign's themes of hope and change, as illustrated in excerpt 2.

(2) *Obama's speech in South Carolina on 26 January 2008*[2]
When I hear the cynical talk that blacks and whites and Latinos can't join together and work together, I'm reminded of the Latino brothers and sisters I organized with and stood with and fought with side by side for jobs and justice on the streets of Chicago. So don't tell us change can't happen. (*Cheers, applause*)

When I hear that we'll never overcome the racial divide in our politics, I think about that Republican woman who used to work for Strom Thurmond, who's now devoted to educating inner-city children, and who went out into the streets of South Carolina and knocked on doors for this campaign. Don't tell me we can't change. (*Cheers, applause*)

Yes, we can. Yes, we can change.

(*Chants of*, 'Yes, we can! Yes, we can!')

Yes, we can.

(*Continued chants of*, 'Yes, we can!')

Yes, we can heal this nation. Yes, we can seize our future. And as we leave this great state with a new wind at our backs, and we take this journey across this great country, a country we love, with the message we've carried from the plains of Iowa to the hills of New Hampshire, from the Nevada desert to the South Carolina coast, the same message we had when we were up and when we were down, that out of many we are one, that while we breathe we will hope, and where we are met with cynicism and doubt and fear and those who tell us that we can't, we will respond with that timeless creed that sums up the spirit of the American people in three simple words: Yes, we can.

Thank you, South Carolina. I love you. (*Cheers, applause*)

The early adoption of the phrase by political supporters at Obama's speeches in New Hampshire and elsewhere represents an important step in the diffusion of this political slogan. With the reiteration of the slogan in those speeches by Obama plus the reverberations of the slogan among chanting supporters, the sound bite spread into the 'circular circulation' (Bourdieu, 1996: 22) of the news cycle. It played on television and radio broadcasts and featured in newspaper articles recounting Obama's campaign rallies. The slogan's association with Obama was further cemented by the release of a music video on 2 February 2008 that turned the slogan into a four-and-a-half minute song entitled 'Yes, We Can'.

The song was produced by the musician will.i.am, lead singer of the Black Eyed Peas, and the video was directed by Jesse Dylan, the son of Bob Dylan. The song's lyrics consist of verbatim quotations from Obama's New Hampshire speech (see again excerpt 1). Words from the speech are set to music as various celebrities alternately sing and speak the words, interwoven with Obama's oratory. The musical refrain of the song is the same as the rhetorical refrain of the speech, only turned into a moving musical score: 'Yes, we can. Yes, we can.' As Mackay (2013) discusses in her multimodal analysis of the song, the background harmony works to bring out the musicality of Obama's oration. The video itself is shot in black and white, moving from one celebrity to another as they sing or speak, juxtaposing the celebrity images with clips of Obama delivering his speech. In all, nearly 40 musicians, actors and athletes took part in the shooting of the video, including celebrities such as John Legend, Herbie Hancock, Scarlett Johansson, Kareem Abdul-Jabbar, Nick Cannon and Common, among others (Kaufman, 2008). Within a few days of its release on the Internet, the video received more than a million views on YouTube; and by the end of 2008 it 'was viewed on YouTube and other video-sharing Web sites more than 20 million times' (Elliott, 2008). Images 14.1 and 14.2 depict screenshots from the video.[3]

The popularity of the 'yes, we can' slogan as it quickly diffused through American society is illustrated by the results of a Google Trends search. Google Trends is a tool provided by the search engine company Google. The search tool provides insight into the popularity of search items. Plugging the search term 'yes we can' into the search engine shows a spike in interest in the term in February 2008, as illustrated in the screenshot in Figure 14.3. The phrase dips throughout the summer and regains popularity around the time of the presidential election in November. A small resurgence also can be seen around the time of Obama's inauguration as president in January 2009. As noted by Hill (2005) and Hodges (2011), technology such as this can be used

**FIGURE 14.1** *A screenshot of the video on YouTube as musician will.i.am sings, 'Yes, We Can'.*

**FIGURE 14.2** *Celebrities such as Scarlett Johansson feature in the video in juxtaposition with clips of Obama speaking.*

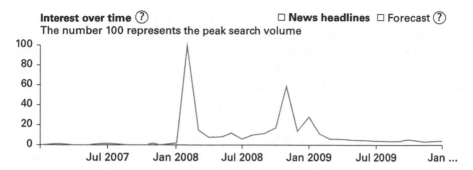

**FIGURE 14.3** *A screenshot from the GoogleTrends timeline shows peak interest in the slogan in February 2008 with subsequent spikes in November 2008 and January 2009.*

to provide a snapshot of the social life of key phrases, mapping where those phrases enter into social circulation and evolve in their usage over time. Figure 14.3 provides a visualization of the slogan's life cycle during the 2008 presidential elections.

## 3 The diffusion of a political slogan

Illuminating the process by which the 'yes, we can' slogan entered into widespread circulation in American society affords discourse analysts an opportunity for better understanding of the way popular sound bites propagate through public discourse in the service of political goals. Fundamental to the circulation of political slogans are the intertextual connections that link the usage of a slogan in a single context to usages across multiple, overlapping contexts where the slogan lives 'its socially charged life' (Bakhtin, 1981: 293). Many political discourse analysts have adopted an intertextual approach (Dunmire, 2009, 2011; Hodges, 2008, 2011; Oddo, forthcoming; inter alia). Complementary to these approaches is Enfield's (2008) work on understanding the circulation of linguistic variants. In his discussion, Enfield (2008) illustrates the usefulness of sociological research on the diffusion of innovations (Rogers, 2003) and anthropological research on the evolution of cultures (Boyd and Richerson, 2005). Although Enfield (2008) applies these ideas to model linguistic change at the level of the (socio)linguistic variable, the ideas can also enrich intertextual approaches to the study of language at the level of discourse – in this case, political slogans.

As a type of cultural variant, a political slogan is subject to a complex set of mechanisms responsible for its diffusion through society. Enfield (2008) discusses several types of *transmission biases* that act as 'conduits or filters for the success or failure of a cultural variant' (Enfield, 2008: 298). One type of bias – the *content bias* – is defined by the properties of variants themselves. Is there anything intrinsic about a particular political slogan that leads to its appeal and hence adoption? Certainly, politicians attempt to package words in a manner that makes future recontextualizations highly likely. Political slogans are designed to be witty, catchy, and most importantly, highly quotable. Intratextual repetition in discourse contributes to these ends, whether through alliteration (e.g. Julius Cesar's 'veni, vidi, vici' or Spiro Agnew's 'nattering nabobs of negativism'), parallelism (e.g. Tony Blair's 'tough on crime, tough on the causes of crime') and/or the rule of three (e.g. John Kerry's 'wrong war, wrong place, wrong time'), among other rhetorical and poetic devices that make slogans easy to remember and fun to repeat. Ultimately, a pithy sound bite provides a campaign with 'a greater chance of having their perspective played over and over again in subsequent media coverage' (Hodges, 2011: 87). In addition, the catchiness of a slogan plays upon social actors' 'compulsion to repeat' (Butler, 1990: 145), which allows the message to spread through public discourse. Thus, 'strategies of entextualization' (Wilce, 2005), which attempt to shape the way words are later recontextualized and understood, often draw upon the poetic dimension of language (Jakobson, 1960) that make slogans easily repeatable. The 'yes, we can' slogan adheres to these principles to give it a certain amount of intrinsic appeal. Namely, the rhetorical devices of parallelism and the rule of three, along with the simplicity of the phrase consisting of three single-syllable words, provides for a rhythmic delivery.

Another type of bias – the *context bias* – is defined by the relations between the variants and the contexts in which they are used. 'Any kind of meaningful structure, be it a word, an artefact, a type of social relation or whatever, will presuppose some kind of contextual frame into which it properly fits, and without which it will not function appropriately' (Enfield, 2008: 299). Where a car presupposes a system of roads or a telephone presupposes a system of telephone lines, a political slogan presupposes a political system with election campaigns designed to persuade voters through rhetorical appeals. More specifically, though, the context bias applies to another type of system fit between the micro-level use of language (i.e. the political slogan) and the macro-level campaign discourse of which it is a part. If there is little connection between a slogan and the larger message of the campaign, the slogan amounts to little more than fanciful words. If, however, the slogan resonates with the larger campaign narrative that is being forwarded, the slogan can function to its fullest extent as a small (but potent) part of a larger whole. The 'yes, we can' slogan provides such a bridge to the overarching narrative of the Obama campaign, which emphasizes an inspirational message of political change brought about by grassroots action. The three-word slogan strongly resonates with that larger narrative and finds a good fit within its discursive system.

Perhaps the most salient biases impacting the diffusion of slogans deal with the ways people factor into the equation, whether through properties of social actors themselves, the relations among social actors or the relations between social actors and the cultural variants. As discussed by diffusion of innovation researchers, people vary in their readiness to adopt and reproduce an innovative behaviour. So there is a *threshold bias* relating to these personality differences, which incline people toward roles ranging from innovators to early adopters and on through later adopters and finally 'laggards', or the last to adopt a new behaviour (Rogers, 2003). Certainly, the earliest adopters of a novel political slogan include the candidate's supporters present at the speeches where the slogan is introduced. The spread of the slogan beyond the immediate environment then relies upon a social network. Here, a *sociometric bias* comes into play where the degrees of connectedness among individuals impact the further spread of the slogan. In the case of a major political campaign, the media form a substantial social network in their own right. As already noted, the intertextual connections between campaign speeches and media reportage provide for a certain amount of social circulation as sound bites enter into the news cycle. Yet beyond the news cycle, for a political slogan to truly catch on in public discourse requires a critical mass of adopters who embrace and continue to repeat the coinage. This requires propagation through an intertextual speech chain.

Agha (2003) defines a speech chain as 'a historical series of speech events linked together by the permutation of individuals across speech-act roles' (247). In the case of the slogan examined here, the candidate utters the slogan in campaign speeches where supporters hear the words. Those hearers then take on the role of speakers as they reiterate the slogan at the campaign rallies where it is in turn heard and recorded by journalists covering the events. Continuing on in the speech chain, journalists recontextualize the slogan within their reportage. In turn, additional supporters hear/read the slogan and provide additional momentum for its propagation when they join in the speech chain. This simplified model of the intertextual connections involved in the propagation of a political slogan underscores the role individuals play in providing the slogan with a social life of its own through repetition in public discourse. The more frequently a slogan is repeated, the more likely others will hear it, adopt it and further its propagation to additional individuals. In this way, a *frequency bias* forms another important mechanism by which a slogan diffuses through the body politic. Yet, most notably, the capacity for a slogan to propagate (and to be repeated frequently) is dependent upon the properties of individuals involved in the speech chain.

Particular individuals hold more sway than others as they model the slogan. The 'publicly perceived properties' of individuals therefore lead to a *model bias* where 'an individual who acts as a carrier of the innovation will affect others' willingness or desire to reproduce it' (268). In her exploration of language and political economy, Irvine (1989) puts forth the notion of a *chain of authentication*. In effect, this is a type of speech chain where the value of a material commodity is authenticated. For example, to effectively evaluate the worth of a gold ring, an expert that possesses the requisite training and credentials – say, a trained jeweller – is needed. This expert vouches for the value of the ring (certifying it is real gold, that it contains a certain purity, etc.) and passes this endorsement on to others (e.g. a buyer) who then in turn pass that information on (e.g. to friends who admire the ring) through a speech chain where the value is reaffirmed. Notably, in this type of speech chain, the expert – who is publicly perceived as possessing certain credentials – plays a substantial role in imbuing the commodity with value and providing the impetus for that value as its ratification continues within the speech chain. Likewise, the publicly perceived properties of early adopters of a political slogan can influence its spread among later adopters. The production of the will.i.am music video provides an important case in point. Armed with a substantial amount of prestige and charisma, as well as social connections, the nearly 40 celebrities involved in the video added a substantial amount of weight to the diffusion of the 'yes, we can' slogan in American society. Further, the ability to put the video on the Internet and attract viewers added substantial frequency to the play the slogan received in public discourse. Moreover, celebrity endorsements are often effective not only because such figures possess social prestige and forms of symbolic power (Bourdieu, 1991) that help them authenticate a message or imbue it with social value, but also because people admire them or socially identify with them. 'This in turn is related to a *conformity bias* by which, all things being equal, people will tend to adopt the same practices as those with whom they socially identify' (Enfield, 2008: 298).

The rapid diffusion of the 'yes, we can' slogan through American society in early 2008 resulted from its capacity to surmount these various types of transmission biases. It worked poetically. It represented a good fit within the overall discursive system of the campaign narrative about hope and grassroots change. It benefited from the social prestige, charisma and authority of early adopters that frequently and creatively repeated the slogan. As such, it not only entered into the news cycle, but it penetrated into pop culture where those modelling the new slogan (a who's who list of famous musicians, actors and athletes in the music video) compelled many to repeat, 'Yes, we can!' One surmises that the far reach of the slogan beyond the confines of the political arena may have even inspired normally non-political individuals to support the cause – the true mark of a successful political slogan.

## 4 The political work of a slogan

Political slogans are created to serve political aims. Chief among those aims is to disseminate and reinforce a campaign message to as wide an audience as possible. Space limits what can be placed on a bumper sticker or campaign poster, and time limits what can be said in a television advertisement or a sound bite on the evening news..However, a pithy slogan can overcome those limitations by standing in for the larger message. Where the full rehearsal of a detailed campaign narrative is not possible, a memorable and highly quotable slogan can act as an economical reminder of that narrative.

Central to a slogan's ability to do this political work is the semiotic process of indexicality whereby an association is established between a slogan (qua signifier) and the larger campaign message (qua signified). In campaign speeches, the larger message of the Obama campaign is elaborated in a narrative about the impossible odds faced by generations of Americans, from the founding fathers to slaves and abolitionists to immigrants and workers (see again excerpt 1). The narrative recounts (often through allusions) the struggles for civil rights, for racial justice and for economic justice that Americans have faced but overcome (see again excerpt 2). Amidst cynicism and doubt and fear, however, Americans involved in those struggles possessed a spirit of optimism and hope that allowed them to prevail. That spirit, the narrative emphasizes, is the same spirit that will allow the current generation to prevail in bringing positive change to the nation through Obama's election. Where even a short synopsis of the narrative, as provided here, becomes too cumbersome, a three-word slogan can convey the message in a succinct and memorable manner.

In effect, the three words, 'yes, we can', become indexically anchored to the Obama campaign's larger message about hope and change. This continuity between the two is achieved through the juxtaposition of the slogan and narrative within the contexts of the candidate's speeches. With that association established, as the slogan travels forward into subsequent contexts it points backward toward the prior contexts in which that narrative was told, thereby reinforcing the indexical ties between slogan and narrative. Intertextuality and indexicality work in tandem to reinforce the ties, a point well recognized in the Bakhtinian perspective on language. As Bauman (2005) notes, 'Bakhtin's abiding concern was with dimensions and dynamics of speech indexicality – ways that the now-said reaches back to and somehow incorporates or resonates with the already-said and reaches ahead to, anticipates, and somehow incorporates the to-be-said' (145). In Silverstein's (2003, inter alia) terms, as 'any socially conventional indexical' sign (e.g. political slogan in this case) leaves a prior context and enters into a new context, it is 'dialectically balanced between' what he calls *indexical presupposition* and *indexical entailment* (195). That is, a sign carries with it 'what is already established between interacting sign-users' (i.e. presupposed indexicality); but the sign also takes on new layers of meaning in the new contexts (i.e. creative or entailed indexicality). For a political slogan to continually renew its association with the larger campaign narrative, it therefore needs to be recontextualized in a manner that maintains fidelity to that narrative.

The process of recontextualization – that is, inserting prior text into new contexts – inevitably reshapes the meanings associated with the text. Yet the amount of transformation can vary along a continuum with varying degrees of fidelity to how the text appeared in previous contexts. Recontextualization can introduce imperceptible differences, subtle shifts in meaning or radical transformations (as with parody). In the terms of Briggs and Bauman (1992), the *intertextual gap* between the re-presentation of a text and its previously established model can be minimized or maximized. In examining the diffusion of innovations, researchers talk of 'reinventions'. As Rogers (2003) emphasizes, 'An innovation is not necessarily invariant during the process of its diffusion. And adopting an innovation is not necessarily a passive role of just implementing a standard template of the new idea. Many adopters want to participate actively in customizing an innovation to fit their unique situation' (Rogers, 2003: 17). This summarizes well the process of recontextualization. As language users appropriate previously uttered words, their own aims and purposes for doing so variously intersect and collide with the previous meanings attributed to those words.

Also of interest from a Bakhtinian (1986) perspective is the role genre plays in framing forms of political communication (Cap, 2012; Cap and Okulska, 2013). The 'recurrent forms' or 'recurrent actions' (Johnstone, 2008: 181) that lead one to assign types of discourse to particular genres are only 'relatively stable' (Bakhtin, 1986: 64). As Bakhtin (1986) emphasizes, they reflect 'all the changes taking place in social life' (65). Through migration (Lemke, 1985), mixing and hybridization, genres 'are thus open to innovation, manipulation, and change' (Briggs and Bauman, 1992: 143; see also, Hanks, 1987: 671, 677). As Cap and Okulska (2013) suggest in their discussion of political genres – and as further illustrated by Mackay (2013) in her examination of the way the 'yes, we can' slogan migrates from the genre of political speech to the genre of political ad set to music – substantial transformation of an intertextual series (here, the phrase 'yes, we can') occurs simply through the shifting generic frameworks in which the migrating text is embedded and received as it is recontextualized in new settings.

As Bakhtin (1986) emphasizes, we continually 'assimilate, rework, and re-accentuate' (89) what has come before us, thus opening up the possibility for various degrees of transformations of circulating texts. As Obama supporters take up the slogan in chants at campaign appearances, they recontextualize the slogan 'seriously, claiming and appropriating it without relativizing it' (Kristeva, 1980: 73). The association with the campaign narrative is reinforced; and, most importantly, it provides impetus to the forward movement of the speech chain as journalists draw from the sound bite in further recontextualizations that recount the use of the slogan by supporters. One such example is found in excerpt 3, the beginning of an article that appeared in the *Los Angeles Times* the day after the New Hampshire primary.

*(3) Article in the* Los Angeles Times *the day after the 2008 New Hampshire primary*[4]
OBAMA HAS NEW RALLYING CRY
His supporters are disappointed by second-place finish, but they're fired up by latest slogan: 'Yes, we can.'

January 9, 2008 | Maria L. La Ganga | Times Staff Writer

NASHUA, N.H. – Sen. Barack Obama got a new campaign slogan Tuesday night when he lost the New Hampshire primary here in an upset that surprised his staunch supporters but left them no less ready for a fight.

'Yes, we can!'

He unveiled it after a long and painful night at Nashua High School South, where 1,500 supporters watched the election results roll slowly in, a night that sobered the men and women who believed that Iowa's victory could take an easy sprint east.

'It was whispered by slaves and abolitionists, as they blazed the trail toward freedom,' Obama said. 'Yes, we can! By immigrants who traveled to a new land, workers who organized, women who reached for the vote,' Obama continued, building to a rousing finish tinged with church cadences. 'Yes, we can!'

And come this morning, when he takes his campaign south and west, Obama vowed, 'we will begin the next great chapter in the American story with three words that will ring from coast to coast, from sea to shining sea.

'Yes, we can!'

They took up the chant here at what was expected to be a celebration but ended up an edgy night. [. . .]

In the article, the journalist recontextualizes the slogan with a high degree of faithfulness to its previous use within the context of Obama's speech. Supporting quotations from the speech help spell out pieces of the larger narrative that the slogan indexes. In addition, four repetitions of the slogan are included within those quotations. The use of reported speech to bring prior text into a new setting can be carried out with 'varying degrees of reinterpretation' (Bakhtin, 1986: 91), underscoring the 'dynamic interrelationship' (Voloshinov, 1973: 119) between the reported and reporting contexts. Yet in reportage such as the type illustrated in excerpt 3, the prior text is actively reconstructed within the confines of the newspaper article in a manner that minimizes the intertextual gap and further reinforces the association between the slogan and the campaign narrative. This helps advance the political work being done by the slogan, and pass the slogan on to others 'in the chain of speech communion' (Bakhtin, 1986: 94).

The music video produced by will.i.am represents a more creative recontextualization than that found in standard media reportage. In the case of the music video, the transformations of the text become more obvious as the slogan is placed into a musical key and the political genre is thereby altered (Cap and Okulska, 2013). Yet the indexical association between the slogan and narrative of hope and change remains. In fact, the generic shift into a musical score even amplifies the emotional appeal of the rhetoric as it turns the music of oratory into the music of song – complete with aesthetically appealing images (see Mackay's 2013 multimodal analysis for a more detailed discussion in this vein; cf. also Van Leeuwen, this volume). Remaining faithful to the overarching message, the music video creatively recontextualizes the slogan in a manner that provides further impetus for its diffusion through public discourse. In the wake of the video's release, media reportage featured stories about the 'Yes, We Can' song; and, most importantly, the slogan/narrative of the Obama campaign – further reinforcing the link.

However, as earlier noted, recontextualization can also be done in a manner that attempts to reshape prior text in line with competing aims. This is clearly illustrated in the case of political slogans where opposing candidates attempt to co-opt one another's message and control the discourse surrounding the campaign. Therefore, once a slogan has gained substantial traction within the political arena, others may attempt to play upon it towards their own political aims. This can be seen as supporters of Senator Hillary Clinton, Obama's main rival in the Democratic nominating process, provided their own creative reinvention of the 'yes, we can' slogan, as described in an article in the *New York Times* the day after Clinton won the primaries in Ohio and Texas.

*(4) Article in the New York Times after the 2008 primaries in Ohio and Texas*[5]
CLINTON SAYS HER CAMPAIGN HAS 'TURNED A CORNER'
By Adam Nagourney
Published: March 5, 2008
Mrs. Clinton took the stage in Columbus before a sea of waving white-and-blue 'Hillary' signs and immediately portrayed her victory in Ohio as an indication of her electability in a general election. And she reprised a line of criticism against Mr. Obama that appeared to have gained her some traction in this contest.

'Americans don't need more promises,' she said. 'They've heard plenty of speeches. They deserve solutions, and they deserve them now.'

As she spoke, the crowd responded with chants of 'Yes, she will!' – apparently an orchestrated response to Mr. Obama's trademark 'Yes, we can!'

Turning one of Mr. Obama's themes against him, she said, 'Together, we will turn promises into action, words into solutions and hope into reality.'

In contradistinction to the emotional appeal of the inspirational 'yes, we can' message of the Obama campaign, Clinton attempts to shift Obama's focus on 'hope' to her own focus on 'reality'. As Clinton plays upon the theme of hope and change, reshaping those elements of the Obama campaign to fit her own political aims, her supporters in the audience provide their own subtle shift to the 'yes, we can' slogan, chanting, 'Yes, she will!' The reformulation of the slogan among chanting supporters draws upon the widespread popularity of the 'yes, we can' phrase while at the same time reinventing the phrase in line with support for Clinton's campaign. This variation on a theme approach can be an effective strategy in that it starts with a well-established phrase that carries previously established social value. That social value benefits the re-inventors of the phrase as they customize it to their own situation, attempting to shift the debate.

As evidenced from these examples, political slogans carry with them the residue of prior contexts. Even the 'yes, we can' slogan that became Obama's so-called trademark carried with it the residue from the earlier contexts in which the Spanish version of the phrase ('sí, se puede') was used by César Chávez to rally labour around the United Farm Workers' push for workers' rights. The Obama campaign built upon those sediments of prior meaning and re-invented the slogan into an effective index of its own campaign narrative. By indexing that narrative in contexts where it cannot be told in detail (e.g. campaign posters, bumper stickers, news reportage), the slogan reaffirms the overarching political message.

# 5 Conclusion

It has become a truism in the field of marketing that even the most innovative products or services do not sell themselves. At the least, information about those products or services must reach potential customers. And to achieve the greatest impact among the target audience, the information must be packaged in a manner that allows it to reach a large number of people in a persuasive manner. Political campaigns are no different (at least as practised in contemporary American politics), in that a campaign's success is predicated upon the ability to persuasively spread its message far and wide. Political slogans (like advertising slogans) aid that objective. This chapter has illuminated some of the factors that allow for the effective diffusion of a political slogan through the body politic.

Crucially, a political slogan, such as the 'yes, we can' mantra of the 2008 Obama campaign, gains its power through the intertextual connections that give it a social life beyond a bounded speech event. Even the most artful slogan cannot spontaneously do political work without first entering into some kind of speech chain that allows it to diffuse across multiple contexts. Poetic prerequisites do constitute one filter among a complex set of transmission biases that impact a slogan's success, but ultimately the propagation of the slogan relies upon the discursive actions of people involved in sustaining or impeding its momentum in public discourse. This raises the issue of the role power plays in the relations among people in the diffusion of a political slogan.

As emphasized in Bourdieu's (1991, inter alia) conception of power as capital, there are forms of capital that extend beyond the traditional focus on economic capital. Cultural capital (in the form of educational credentials), social capital (in the form of social networks) and symbolic capital (in the form of non-material forms of honour and prestige) are all power resources that contribute to the differential reach and influence exerted by some individuals over others. In Irvine's (1989) notion of a chain of authentication, an expert (in possession of substantial cultural capital) plays a central role in the valuation of a commodity. Likewise, in a speech chain that forwards a political slogan, the forms of capital possessed by the 'permutation of individuals across speech-act roles' (Agha, 2003: 247) can impact the social value placed upon the slogan. Within a speech chain, certain voices (such as the celebrities in will.i.am's video) may have more impact than others based upon the forms of capital they possess.

Nevertheless, the success or failure of a political slogan relies upon more than just authoritative pronouncements made by individuals with sufficient capital to wield the Homerian skeptron, to use Bourdieu's (1991: 109) imagery. It requires a network of individuals to propagate the slogan through a web of interactions. In this way, the discursive power involved in the spread of a political slogan is, in line with the perspective put forth by Foucault (1980), diffused across the social body (across each campaign supporter, across each journalist that reports on the slogan's use, across each citizen that reiterates the phrase in daily conversations). It 'circulates' in 'a net-like organization' (Foucault, 1980: 98) so that individuals are not merely beholden to power, but also exercise power as they interact with one another. Power is therefore productive and not merely repressive. In Foucault's words, 'individuals are the vehicles of power' (Foucault, 1980: 98). They are 'the elements of its articulation' (Foucault, 1980: 98). And the articulation of power – that is, the exercise of power – is entwined with language use as individuals come together in everyday interactions to invent and re-invent discursive innovations such as political slogans. Although the conceptions of power put forth by Bourdieu and Foucault are sometimes seen as competing rather than complementary, I suggest that the two need to be considered in tandem to fully account for the effective circulation of political slogans in public discourse.

In sum, the success of a political slogan in spreading a campaign's message lies in the strength of the intertextual web into which it enters. Thus, insight into the power of a political slogan requires examining the web of connections that comprises its social life. This chapter has attempted to do just that while showing that an intertextual approach to discourse analysis can also benefit from complementary perspectives on how innovations diffuse through society.

# Notes

1  This is my own transcription based on the transcript provided by the *New York Times* and modified with additional detail while watching the video of the speech online. The full transcript from the *New York Times* is available at http://www.nytimes.com/2008/01/08/us/politics/08text-obama.html?_r=0&pagewanted=all. The video of the speech on YouTube is available at http://www.youtube.com/watch?v=Fe751kMBwms Accessed 1st October 2012

2  The full transcript of this speech from the New York Times is available at http://www.nytimes.com/2008/01/26/us/politics/26text-obama.html?_r=3&pagewanted=all& Accessed 1st October 2012

3  The video on YouTube is available at http://www.youtube.com/watch?v=jjXyqcx-mYY Accessed 1st October 2012

4  The full *Los Angeles Times* article is available at http://articles.latimes.com/2008/jan/09/nation/na-obama9 Accessed 1st October 2012

5  The full *New York Times* article is available at http://www.nytimes.com/2008/03/05/us/politics/05cnd-primary.html?pagewanted=all&_r=0 Accessed 1st October 2012

# References

Agha, A. (2003), 'The social life of cultural value'. *Language and Communication*, 23, 231–73.

Bakhtin, M. (1981), *The Dialogic Imagination: Four Essays*. M. Holquist (ed.) and C. Emerson and M. Holquist (trans.), Austin, TX: University of Texas Press.

—— (1986), *Speech Genres and Other Late Essays*. V. W. McGee (trans.), C. Emerson and M. Holquist (eds), Austin, TX: University of Texas Press.

Bauman, R. (2005), 'Commentary: indirect indexicality, identity, performance: dialogic observations'. *Journal of Linguistic Anthropology*, 15(1), 145–50.

Bourdieu, P. (1991), *Language and Symbolic Power*. G. Raymond and M. Adamson (trans.), J. B. Thompson (ed.). Cambridge, MA: Harvard University Press.

—— (1996), *Sur la Télévision*. Paris: Liber – Raisons d'Agir.

Boyd, R. and P. J. Richerson. (2005), *The Origin and Evolution of Cultures.* New York: Oxford University Press.

Briggs, C. and Bauman, R. (1992), 'Genre, intertextuality, and social power'. *Journal of Linguistic Anthropology,* 2(2), 131–72.

Butler, J. (1990), *Gender Trouble.* New York: Routledge.

Cap, P. (2002), *Explorations in Political Discourse. Methodological and Critical Perspectives.* Frankfurt am Main: Peter Lang.

—— (2012), 'On genre problems in (political) discourse'. *Topics in Linguistics,* 8, 11–16.

Cap, P. and U. Okulska (eds) (2013), *Analyzing Genres in Political Communication: Theory and Practice.* Amsterdam: John Benjamins.

Charteris-Black, J. (2005), *Politicians and Rhetoric: The Persuasive Power of Metaphor.* Basingstoke: Palgrave.

Chilton, P. (2004), *Analysing Political Discourse.* London: Routledge.

Dunmire, P. (2009), '"9/11 changed everything": an intertextual analysis of the Bush doctrine'. *Discourse & Society,* 20(2), 195–222.

—— (2011), *Projecting the Future through Discourse: The Case of the Bush Doctrine.* Amsterdam: John Benjamins.

Elliott, S. (2008), 'A year the new eclipsed commercial breaks'. *New York Times,* 29 December, Late Edition, Section B, Column O.

Enfield, N. J. (2008), 'Transmission biases in linguistic epidemiology'. *Journal of Language Contact* THEMA, pp. 297–310.

Fairclough, N. (1992), 'Discourse and text: linguistic and intertextual analysis within discourse analysis'. *Discourse & Society,* 3(2), 193–217.

—— (1995), *Media Discourse.* London: Edward Arnold.

—— (2000), *New Labour, New Language.* London: Routledge.

Fairclough, N. and Wodak, R. (1997), 'Critical discourse analysis', in T. Van Dijk (ed.), *Discourse as Social Interaction. Discourse Studies: A Multidisciplinary Introduction* (vol. 2). London: Sage, pp. 258–84.

Foucault, M. (1980), *Power/Knowledge: Selected Interviews and Writings.* New York: Pantheon Books.

Hanks, W. F. (1987), 'Discourse genres in a theory of practice'. *American Ethnologist,* 14(4), 668–92.

Hart, C. (ed.) (2011), *Critical Discourse Studies in Context and Cognition.* Amsterdam: John Benjamins.

Hill, J. (2005), 'Intertextuality as source and evidence for indirect indexical meanings'. *Journal of Linguistic Anthropology,* 15(1), 113–24.

Hodges, A. (2008), 'The politics of recontextualization: discursive competition over claims of Iranian involvement in Iraq'. *Discourse & Society,* 19, 479–501.

—— (2011), *The 'War on Terror' Narrative: Discourse and Intertextuality in the Construction and Contestation of Sociopolitical Reality.* New York: Oxford University Press.

Irvine, J. (1989), 'When talk isn't cheap'. *American Ethnologist,* 16(2), 248–67.

Jakobson, R. (1960), 'Closing statement: linguistics and poetics', in T. Sebeok (ed.), *Style in Language.* Cambridge, MA: MIT Press, pp. 360–77.

Johnstone, B. (2008), *Discourse Analysis* (2nd edn). Malden, MA: Blackwell Publishing.

Kaufman, G. (2008), 'Will.I.Am gathers Common, Nick Cannon, Scarlett Johansson for Barack Obama video', 4 February, *MTV.* Available at: http://www.mtv.com/news/articles/1580884/william-yes-we-can-obama-video.html (accessed 1 October 2012).

Kristeva, J. (1980), *Desire in Language: A Semiotic Approach to Literature and Art*, T. Gora, A. Jardine and L. S. Roudiez (trans.), L. S. Roudiez (ed.). New York: Columbia University Press.

Lazar, M. M. (ed.) (2005), *Feminist Critical Discourse Analysis: Gender, Power and Ideology in Discourse*. London: Palgrave.

Lemke, J. L. (1985), 'Ideology, intertextuality, and the notion of register', in J. D. Benson and W. S. Greaves (eds), *Systemic Perspectives on Discourse*. Norwood, NJ: Ablex Publishing Company, 1: 275–94.

Mackay, R. (2013), 'Multimodal legitimation: looking at and listening to Obama's ads', in P. Cap and U. Okulska (eds), *Analyzing Genres in Political Communication: Theory and Practice*. Amsterdam: John Benjamins, pp. 345–78.

Oddo, J. (2013), 'Precontextualization and the rhetoric of futurity: foretelling Colin Powell's UN Address on NBC News'. *Discourse & Communication*, 7, 25–53.

Rogers, E. (2003), *Diffusion of Innovations* (5th edn). New York: Free Press.

Silverstein, M. (2003), 'Indexical order and the dialectics of sociolinguistic life'. *Language and Communication*, 23, 193–29.

Van Dijk, T. (1987), *Communicating Racism. Ethnic Prejudice in Thought and Talk*. Newbury Park, CA: Sage.

—— (1991), *Racism and the Press*. London: Routledge.

Voloshinov, V. N. (1973), *Marxism and the Philosophy of Language*, L. Matejka and I. R. Titunik (trans.). New York: Seminar Press.

Wilce, J. (2005), 'Narrative transformations: emotion, language and globalization', in C. Casey and R. Edgerton (eds), *Companion to Psychological Anthropology*. Malden, MA: Blackwell, pp. 20–44.

Wodak, R. (2009), *The Discourse of Politics in Action: Politics as Usual*. Basingstoke: Palgrave.

MEDIA DISCOURSE
# 15

# Media Discourse in Context

*Anita Fetzer*
University of Augsburg

## 1 Introduction

This chapter examines the contextual constraints and requirements of media discourse from macro- and micro-oriented perspectives (cf. Introduction, this volume), and their connectedness. It analyses media discourse as public discourse, institutional discourse and professional discourse, considering in particular the multilayered nature of: (1) its participation framework as regards production, reception and audience design, and the construction of agency, identity and newsworthiness, (2) its modes of transmission and multi-modality (cf. Van Leeuwen, this volume; Machin, this volume), including the private-public interface (cf. Mautner, this volume), and (3) the relationship between mass media and social media.

### 1.1 *Media discourse*

Media discourse is intrinsically connected with the advent of printing, access to education and media literacy, and more recently with the electronic transmission and multiplication of data. Without the invention of the printing press in the middle of the fifteenth century, without the steady increase in education, and without regional and social mobility, media discourse could not have flourished the way it did, and without more technologically versatile means and an ever increasing access to those technological devices, e.g. the internet, digitalization and the electronic transmission of data, there would have been no mass-media discourse as we know it today and no computer-mediated communication and instant access to the latest news and news stories. While early forms of media discourse, such as pamphlets, newspapers, magazines and journals, relied heavily on the printed word, more recent forms of media discourse feed on multimodality and interactiveness, including spoken and visual discourses, and a vast amount of background information.

In early editions of newspapers, news was not on the front page. Rather, it was buried in the middle of the newspaper while the front pages carried classified advertisements, and multiple headlines frequently told too much of the story (Smith and Bell, 2008). The latest technological changes, in particular the internet and internet-based radio programmes, television programmes and online editions of newspapers have contributed to the rapid changes in the shape of news discourse, especially through the launching of online editions, viz. clickable headlines, quotes and background information, pictures and videos, keywords and blogs displaying the latest news as well as comment sites and discussion forums, which provide readers with the opportunity to voice their opinions and post follow-up comments on the latest news. The dynamization of mass-media and of their role in making the news through news programmes on TV stations or news sections in online editions of newspapers have had a tremendous impact on the design of news, and on the design of the underlying hypertext configurations. Public and commercial television as well as radio sites carry print, photographs and additional video footage. The increasing degree of interactiveness and the huge amount of background information available on the websites of those organizations assigns ordinary recipients the status of some kind of co-producer and co-designer of media discourse, posting, exchanging and negotiating comments and follow-ups on news stories contributing to yet more current information, which may serve as background information for succeeding media discourse.

Understanding media discourse and mediated communication requires both the understanding of the communicative practices employed and of the language used, and the understanding of the technical affordances. Put differently, the design of digitalized media discourse is interdependent on genre with respect to discursive practice and language use, and on medium factors anchored to technological constraints and requirements, such as (1) synchronicity, viz. simultaneous or delayed communication, (2) granularity, viz. message-based or genre-based contribution, (3) persistence, viz. all the media discourses are stored in a publicly accessible archive, or only selected media discourses are stored, (4) length, viz. institutional and/or medium-specific constraints regulating the number of characters, e.g. a tweet can have a maximum of 140 characters, (5) channels, (6) identity, viz. institutional identity or nickname, (7) audience, viz. open-access or restricted access and (8) format, viz. chronologically ordered media discourse or media discourses listed in reverse order.

Media discourse is a multifaceted concept, which has been influenced, if not shaped by society, and vice versa. During its history it has adapted to the contextual constraints and requirements of changes in technology, e.g., printing and publishing, or multi-modality and interactiveness, which have had their impact on communicative practices and social interaction on the micro domain, and the construction of mediated social reality on the macro domain. Media discourse may refer to discourse produced by the media, transmitted through media and consumed by some kind of mass audience; it may also include discourse performed in the media, as is the case with a large number of radio and television programmes in the fields of entertainment and in public affairs media, e.g., news, documentaries, magazine programmes dealing with politics, social affairs, science and so forth. Media discourse may also refer to discourse about the media, viz. to a kind of meta-discourse, in and through which relations amongst media and society, production, reception and representation, and (critical) media literacy and (critical) media education may be objects of talk.

Media discourse is constrained by the contextual requirement of society and institution with regard to media-specific policies and regulations, such as code of practice, (political) neutrality and data protection, and it is constrained by medium-specific requirements, for instance channel, length and semiotic representation. Adopting Fairclough's conceptualization of discourse, the term 'media discourse' subsumes the following two main senses:

One is predominant in language studies: discourse as social action and interaction, people interacting together in real social situations. The other is predominant in post-structuralist social theory (e.g. in the work of Foucault): a discourse as a social construction of reality, a form of knowledge. My use of 'discourse' subsumes both of these, and indeed sets out to bring them together. The first sense is most closely associated with the interpersonal function of language, and with the concept of genre [. . .]. The second sense is most closely associated with the ideational function of language, and with discourses.

(Fairclough, 1995: 18)

In the following section, the complexity and multi-layeredness of media discourse (see Introduction, this volume, for discussion of multi-layeredness of *discourse* in general) is investigated with respect to its status as public discourse, institutional discourse and professional discourse. Section 3 examines its multi-layeredness considering in particular participation, section 4 addresses the impact of social media on mass media, and section 5 provides an outlook.

## 2 Media discourse: Public, institutional and professional

Media discourse is, by definition, transmitted through some kind of medium, and is, for this reason, shaped by the constraints and requirements of the medium, and at the same time the transmission through the medium allows for overcoming limitations anchored to space and time. Mediated discourse thus enables the participants to overcome distance in communication: they can exchange information with distant, non-present others, and they can connect with each other and share some mediated space and time. The inherent detachment between production and reception does not only shape the encoding and decoding of information but also the negotiation of meaning processes, which are also detached from the face-to-face contexts. The recipients of a media discourse are detached from its context of production and the producers of media discourse are detached from its context of reception. Even though the degree of detachment is gradable, it is still present in digital interactive media.

The communication through a medium has an influence on the production and reception of the information exchanged. For instance, in printed newspapers or magazines, articles can contain only a certain number of printed letters or pictures, radio programmes can code their information in the auditory channel only, and television programmes can use auditory and visual channels. While the producers and recipients of media discourse in the printed media do not share space and time, the producers and recipients of radio talk and TV talk may share time, but not space. Media discourse in the traditional media may be classified as asynchronous communication, in spite of the media having become more and more interactive. The advent of digital media has reduced the degree of asynchrony, and the producers and recipients may now share virtual time and virtual space.

Media discourse is social action which is performed publicly. For this reason, media discourse counts as public discourse and as institutional discourse; it may also count as professional discourse.

## 2.1 Media discourse as public discourse

Media discourse has been defined as transmitted through some kind of medium. The process of mediation allows the mediated discourse to be made public by going on-record via printed outlets, audio outlets, audio-visual outlets or visual outlets, for instance. The process of going on-record is gradual and can be constrained by restricted access to the media. Mass-media discourse and its constituent parts, e.g., setting, discourse identity, discourse topic and discourse style, are, however, public by definition.

Mass media has had a tremendous impact on social interaction in the micro and macro domains of life, and vice versa. They have influenced discourse as social action and interaction on the interpersonal domain, for instance the formation of new lexemes and the levelling of accents, as is reflected in urban dialects, and they have had a massive influence on the social construction of reality, especially on mediated social realities as is reflected in their presentation and positioning of social agents as mediated, if not mediatized or typed individuals regarding their discursive practices, attitudes, beliefs, opinions, lifestyles and identity constructions, or in the presentation and positioning of leading politicians and political parties in election campaigns. Nowadays virtually all parts of life are affected by media discourse. From a macro perspective, the social dissemination of mass-media discourse and its constitutive parts may count as an act of legitimatization: 'Politics and government are now substantially mediated, and most public reflection, debate and contestation over globalization, Europeanization and other processes of change take place within the mass media, which have become the primary space in the public spheres' (Fairclough, 2006: 97).

The connectedness between mass-media discourse, the presentation of social reality (and its constitutive parts) and non-mediated social reality (and its constitutive parts) is of a dialectical nature with some kind of interdependence. This is primarily due to the affordances of the new media with recipients contributing more and more to the ongoing discourse, blurring the boundaries between private and public spheres of life. In our contemporary societies, mass media plays a very important role in the social construction of agency, and of non-agency, which will be elaborated on in section 3.4. The medium provides resources for linguistic and visual representation, and it is the producers who employ them strategically to construct time and space, proximity and distance, and identity and ideology, for instance.

Mass-media discourse is a global element in the dissemination of information, in the formation of news and the negotiation of the status of news, offering various interpretations and reinterpretations, which result from the portrayal of different reactions evoking yet again more preferred frames of interpretation. Messages can never be neutral because they are mediated, and it is the mediation through visual and verbal codes, which provides a frame of reference, signifying preferred interpretations in accordance with the contextual constraints and requirements of culture.

Mass-media discourse in general and media discourse in particular count as public discourse *par excellence* even though their consumption may take place in the private spheres of life. Because of its status as public discourse, media discourse is accessible to a general public, including other media, which may follow-up on programmes, events or people and their contributions, commenting upon them and recontextualizing them, thus constructing intertextuality (Fetzer and Weizman, 2006; Montgomery, 2007; Scannell, 1998). And it is those intertextual references to 'on-the-record' utterances, events, people or programmes which are at the heart of media discourse. This also holds for discourse transmitted by the so-called new (or digital) media, that is computer-mediated discourse on the internet or World Wide Web, with email, chat, blogging, bulletin board system, social networking sites, instant messaging, text messaging and twitter as modes of communication.

## 2.2 *Media discourse as institutional discourse*

Media discourse as mediated discourse and mass-media discourse are a constitutive part of modern society, and they are constrained by the institutional requirements of society. This means that the media are accountable for their social actions as regards content and presentation: they are accountable for the truth and validity of the content as a whole and for the truth and validity of its parts, they are accountable for the social actions, and for the social actions of their personnel, in particular the media presenters, and they are accountable for the appropriateness of discursive practices and discursive styles, especially those of their producers and presenters. The accountability of the media holds – to varying degrees – for the mass media and its constitutive parts, and for computer-mediated discourse and its constitutive parts. The latter need to be in accordance with the requirements of a provider and their national laws, and the former need to be in accordance with broadcasting standards, which may regulate broadcast news as well as other public affairs programmes. Both are further constrained by national and international law. Thus, media discourse and its constitutive parts, viz. setting, participation, in particular production and reception, discourse identity, discourse topic and discourse style are accountable and need to account for their discursive action, if queried.

Media discourse employs discourse genres and their constitutive parts in a strategic manner to construct particular social realities, and participants in media discourse may construct their identities employing all available semiotic resources in a strategic manner. The use of language and other semiotic codes is seen as social practice, and language use is always anchored to genre, which represents a 'universal formative element of human communication' (Luckmann, 1995: 177) operating 'on a level *between* the socially constructed and transmitted codes of "natural" languages and the reciprocal adjustment of perspectives' (1995). In Levinson's terms, activity type (or genre) is 'a fuzzy category whose focal members are goal-defined, socially constituted, bounded, events with *constraints* on participants, setting and so on, but above all on the kinds of allowable contributions' (Levinson, 1979: 368). Closely connected with the cognitive concept of fuzzy category are inferential schemata, which guide participants in their production and interpretation of communicative meaning.

Genre plays a prominent role in communication in general and in media communication in particular, furnishing the producers and recipients with some kind of blueprints for the strategic use of semiotic codes, in particular language:

> Given the focal position of the mass media in contemporary social systems, there can be little argument about their relevance to the study of sociocultural change. What will be less obvious to most social scientists, and more contentious, is that the analysis of the *language* of the mass media can make a substantive contribution to such research.
>
> (Fairclough, 1995: 3)

Mass-media discourse, media discourse and computer-mediated discourse are institutional discourse and public discourse, and to varying degrees also professional discourse.

## 2.3  *Media discourse as professional discourse*

The production of media discourse feeds on the strategic use of semiotic codes, especially on the strategic use of the linguistic code, and on its relationship with other visual and auditory codes. The former is also referred to as (socio)linguistic variation: 'sociolinguistic variation [. . .] is portrayed as rationally tied – via demonstrable means-ends reasoning links – to the kinds of things people are trying to do when they speak, and cross-cultural parallels are viewed as attributable to the existence of similar rational processes underlying human interaction' (Brown, 1995: 154). In any presentation of a media event, the producer, or a team of producers, need to make decisions about how to present social reality, which events, statements, displays of emotions and their relationships to include, how to position the relevant discourse identities, and which identities and relationships to set up for those involved in the programme, such as, e.g. reporters, audiences, third parties, experts and non-experts, and which stories to tell and who is to tell them. More specifically, they need to make decisions about who and what to include in the linguistic presentation and who and what to exclude from it, and who and what to foreground and who and what to background. Moreover, they need to decide what kind of semiotic code to use, whether the semiotic codes are to be congruous, or whether some kind of incongruity is to be constructed. As regards the linguistic code, they need to decide what kind of language to use, viz. whether the social agents should speak a more formal code of language, viz. public language, whether they should speak a more informal code, viz. private language, whether they should speak some regional or social dialect or ethnolect, or whether they should be portrayed as hybrid constructs employing instances of private and public language. Of course, these decisions are related to the type of mass media, to the intended audience, discourse genre and discourse expectations, and to the presupposed common ground. While those decision-making processes about the strategic use of semiotic codes are part of any ordinary communication, it has turned into a more and more professional endeavour in media communication, including computer-mediated communication, not only with respect to professional and technical support, but also with respect to the questions of who scripts the lines and who speaks on whose behalf. The strategic selection of the semiotic codes has become apparent in the mediatization of politics, in particular in political 'branding' (Fairclough, 2006: 101), which is also found in other domains of society such as sports, entertainment or sitcoms.

The continual rise of professionalization is also reflected in the negotiation of meaning and the negotiation of validity within the media frame and outside of that frame. This is due to the steady increase of interactive formats which allow for more professional framing of media discourse. Social agents draw upon orders of discourse in producing media texts, and they make decisions of how to employ the semiotic repertoire and forms to construct their preferred mediated social reality, feeding on discourse genre and style to construct their mediated social reality, as is shown by Fairclough (1995: 39):

These differences in channel and technology have significant wider implications in terms of the meaning potential of the different media. For instance, print is in an important sense less personal than radio and television. Radio begins to allow individuality and personality to be foregrounded through transmitting individual qualities of voice. Television takes the process much further by making people visually available, and not in the frozen modality of newspaper photographs, but in movement and action. It is a technology which harmonizes with our contemporary culture's focus on individualism and its orientation towards personality.

(Fairclough, 1995: 38–9)

Verbally and visually communicated information uses different channels and has different affordances. While the former is more open to on-going changes as regards language production, e.g. nonce meaning or hybrid constructions and mixing of styles, the latter seems to be more persistent. This is because the encoding and decoding of visual texts underlie more traditional and conventional procedures than those of verbal texts. Put differently, the production and reception of verbal texts seem to adapt more rapidly to changing socio-cultural changes, as van Leeuwen (2000) has shown for visually communicated racism.

Changing journalistic practices go hand in hand with changing affordances and emerging differences in between visual texts and verbal texts. Le (2012) argues that there is not only a difference with respect to ideological persistence but also with the framing of events. The advent of hypertext, which consists of nodes and hyperlinks with the multimodal nodes presenting information through verbal, visual and aural resources, may unite those conflicting channels of communication, or it may dis-unite them. That is, the high innovative potential of a verbal text may either be supported by the visual channel, which may share that degree of innovation, or it may be queried, if not reduced by a visual text with more traditional stereotypes.

Media discourse comprises a diversity of discourses and genres employing different modes of communication, different semiotic codes, and visual, audio and audio-visual channels. The more traditional classification of media discourse into visual printed media discourse on the one hand, and audio discourse and audio-visual media discourse on the other, has been refined by an ongoing process of digitalization, transforming the classical unidirectional production and reception format into a more interactive, process-oriented framework, in which the producers of media discourse invite members of the audience to participate locally in the production of media discourse. The multifaceted nature of media discourse is reflected in multi-layered interactional frames, in a multi-layered participation framework and in the multi-valence of the communicative contributions employed by the producers of media discourse and of their intended and unintended perlocutionary effects on a heterogeneous group of recipients. Communicating felicitously in and through the media is thus a complex endeavour which needs to consider the corresponding frames of interaction and the complexity of common ground.

# 3 Participation

Traditional models of communication comprise a sender, a receiver, some information (or thought) which is encoded in a message and then sent through some channel to be decoded by the receiver, as has been illustrated in cognitive semantics with the prevailing metaphorical configuration of the conduit metaphor (Reddy, 1979). The classic participation framework consists of a sender, which is traditionally referred to as speaker or producer, and a receiver, which is called addressee, hearer or recipient. The sender codes some information in the form of a message and sends this message to a hearer who decodes the message and retrieves the information encoded by the sender. The underlying assumption of that model is that the information encoded in the message is identical to the information decoded.

The classic model has undergone a number of relevant changes not only for the dyadic communication between sender and receiver in mundane everyday communication and institutional communication but also for mass communication and one of its most important representatives: media discourse. In a process- and product-based conceptualization of communication, participants produce not just utterances at random but they produce utterances in accordance with the contextual constraints and requirements of a larger, more stable frame of reference, a discourse genre, which has been referred to as communicative genre (Luckmann, 1995) or activity type (Levinson, 1979), and they direct the utterances at a particular set of addressees.

Communication in general and mass communication in particular have been reconceptualized as a dynamic, multi-layered endeavour with multiple interactional frames, multiple interactional roles and a context-dependent participation framework. This is especially true for media discourse, which is not only produced for a particular media event but is also produced within that event, which is embedded in further layers of media discourse. Any media discourse is a part within a larger chain of media discourses, in which that media discourse may become recycled and recontextualized in the form of soundbites, quotations, summaries or represented discourse (Fairclough, 1995; Lauerbach and Fetzer, 2007).

Changes within the social practices of a speech community manifest themselves in changing contextual constraints and requirements anchored to these larger frames of reference. To account for them, a dynamic framework is required, accommodating a top-down perspective considering the media discourse as a whole, and a bottom-up perspective considering media discourses, viz. genres and their constitutive parts. The former is informed by socio-cultural context in general, and the latter considers discourse identity, discursive style, turn taking and context, as well as local-level language use, as is reflected in communicative strategies and other semiotic practices.

## 3.1 *Production format*

Goffman (1981) argues that participation is not a simple either/or affair in which one party speaks, while the other party listens. There are varying degrees of participation: speakers may take up different footings in relation to their own remarks, which may be variously described as animator, author and principal. Thus, whereas the *animator* is the person who actually utters the words, viz. the sounding box, the *author* is seen as the 'author of the words that are heard, i.e. someone who has selected the sentiments that are being expressed and the words in which they are encoded' (Goffman, 1981: 144). The *principal* is 'someone whose position is established by the words spoken, someone whose beliefs have been told, someone who is committed to what the words say' (Goffman, 1981: 144). The *figure* is a figure on stage or in some movie, which performs a scripted part in some play.

In the process of communication, speakers can adopt a footing which displays either greater or lesser involvement, depending on what it is they seek to achieve. Speakers can show identification and solidarity with particular groups and communities stressing their role as *author, animator* and *principal*. Conversely, speakers can also distance themselves from what they are saying through various shifts in footing, thereby deflecting responsibility as *author* and/or *principal* of their remarks. For example, in a political interview, an interviewer may seek to establish a politician's own individual viewpoint by asking 'what do you personally think about a particular issue'. If the politician's response is just to state party policy say along the lines of '*we* have always taken the position that . . .', his or her response is that of only *principal* and *animator*, and the politician's position on *authorship* remains unclear. In spite of the fact that authorship and agency cannot be equated, the acknowledgment of authorship tends to entail the acknowledgment of responsibility and hence also of agency. So, should a politician acknowledge authorship of the policy, then he or she also acknowledges responsibility, as has been shown by Bull and Fetzer (2006).

Goffman's concept of footing and his production and reception formats can be adapted to the contextual constraints and requirements of media discourse and its multi-layered configuration. Here, the production format is even more complex as there may be multiple authorship by ghost- and scriptwriters, and multi-layered identities by the use of nicknames, for instance. In media discourse, the production format is usually represented by media personnel, who may recycle and recontextualize media discourses in further media productions, and the reception format is usually represented by ordinary people. The more recently introduced more interactive communicative formats have blurred these boundaries, as is elaborated on below.

## 3.2 *Reception format*

In communication, the status of interlocutors as speakers and addressees is far more complex, as has been shown for the production format. The multi-layered status of participation also holds for the reception format. Accordingly, Goffman (1981) distinguishes between ratified participants, viz. addressed participants, and non-ratified participants, viz. non-addressed overhearers and eavesdroppers. Ratified participants sub-classify further into *addressee*, that is the informational destination, *hearer*, viz. a ratified participant who is not the primary informational destination, and *direct target*, viz. the goal of the informational destination, and *indirect target*, viz. neither the direct goal nor the direct informational destination. Furthermore, there is the reception role of *audience*, who hear in a special way as they are removed from the scene of the first-frame, mediated interaction. Because of that, the audience can watch and analyse the participants closely, but can only participate directly in the communication through the use of backchannel response in a second-frame interaction, which usually takes place in their homes.

Goffman's participation roles have been refined by Levinson (1988), who refines the production and reception formats along the lines of the basic categories as *source*, viz. the informational origin of message, *target*, viz. the informational destination of message, *speaker*, viz. an utterer, and *participant*, viz. a party with a ratified channel-link to other parties. Derived from the basic categories are *producers*, viz. sources or speakers, *recipients*, viz. addressees or target, *author*, viz. source and speaker, *relayer*, viz. a speaker who is not the source, *goal*, viz. an addressee who is the target, and *intermediary*, viz. an addressee who is not the target. The boundaries between production and reception roles have become fuzzy more recently. This is due to the introduction of more interactive formats, which allow audience participation, viz. either direct audience participation in the studio, or indirect audience participation, viz. members of the audience phoning-in, or sending emails, text messages or tweets. In the former scenario, the audience is promoted to first-frame participants, while in the latter scenario, it has the status of mediated first-frame participants.

The most consequential feature of media discourse is that it is addressed to an absent mass audience and not to a group of co-present participants. The fact that media discourse is produced for such an audience influences both its content and its form. In the case of dialogic interaction being broadcast, the audience may be directly addressed by the journalists and, in some cases, also by their studio guests. As a rule, however, the media audience are in the position of a ratified overhearer (Goffman, 1981), as for instance when journalists and politicians talk to each other in order to display their discourse to the audience. This has consequences for the way in which such discourse is constructed, as has been demonstrated for the news interview by analysts working within the framework of conversation analysis. In refraining from giving feedback to their interviewees, interviewers indicate that the interviewees' answers are not addressed to them but to the audience (Clayman and Hertitage, 2002: 120ff.).

Another consequence of media discourse being addressed to an absent mass audience concerns the construction of meaning by the first-frame participants. Both in ordinary and in mediated face-to-face dialogues, participants may initiate repair sequences. In contrast to everyday discourse, however, there are constraints on the negotiation of meaning in mediated discourse. First, the length of a repair sequence is constrained by the programme's strict time schedule, and second, the audience cannot directly intervene in this process between the first-frame participants by asking clarification questions. They may, however, participate in a mediated manner if there is audience participation, or through other types of mediated discourse, for instance letters to the editor, phone-ins, email, chat or through meta-discourse with other members of the audience. However, such attempts at the negotiation of meaning are always delayed or after the event. The consequences for the first-frame participants are that they have to take particular care in recipient-designing their discourse for an audience that cannot intervene with comprehension questions, as has been pointed out by Fairclough: 'Media reception research has suggested that texts do not have unitary meanings, but are quite variously interpreted by different audiences and audience members, and may be quite various in their effects' (Fairclough, 1995: 16). This holds equally for monologues addressed to the audience. The orientation to a heterogeneous mass audience whose members may have different stores of background knowledge leads to formal features of the discourse such as the explanation of possibly unfamiliar referential terms, or the explication of inferences and jokes.

There is a connection between the features of recipient design of media discourse, its public character, and the rights and obligations of its participants:

> ... the design features [. . .] indicate that it is meant for reception by absent audiences. And this, in turn, establishes the intrinsically public nature of broadcast talk. Talk-in-public, especially political talk, is 'on the record' and this has consequences on what can and cannot be said and for ways of saying and not saying.
>
> (Scannell, 1998: 260)

So, in being produced for a mass audience, mediated discourse is necessarily public discourse. The public and mediated status of its participants and of the activity engaged in is one of the decisive factors, which differentiate their rights and obligations from those of the participants of communicative events in other social domains. Thus interviewees are in a different position from, for instance, suspects being questioned by the police:

> American citizens have a constitutionally protected right to remain silent in the face of police questioning, so that silence cannot be treated as incriminating in courts of law. But public figures have no such protection in the court of public opinion constituted by the news interview.
>
> (Clayman and Heritage, 2002: 241)

This is why, if, e.g., interviewees do not wish to answer a question, they are faced with a dilemma. Answering the question will lead to undesirable consequences as will not answering the question by being evasive or by simply being silent. In media discourse, silence as a response to a question is loaded with additional generalized and particularized inferential meaning: public figures are considered to not fulfil their obligation of informing the public in an appropriate manner.

## 3.3 Audience design

The absent mass audience, who media personnel, such as journalists, politicians and other participant groups of first-frame participants, orient to, is counterfactually conceptualized as an over-arching category for a more or less culturally homogeneous entity. But there is a tension here between the media publicly broadcasting to a mass of addressees who receive this discourse as individuals or small groups mainly in their private environment. Practices of audience address and occasional informal style show the media's orientation to this fact. Also, audiences are differentiated as to sub-cultural milieus, and first-frame participants may intend to address specific segments of the audience in particular, such as members of a political party in the context of a political interview or speech, the electorate in the context of a political interview or debate, and sometimes a nation, or a nation and its allies, in the context of a president's speech:

> In mass communication, a broadcaster's individual style is routinely subordinated to a shared station style whose character can only be explained in terms of its target audience. When we look at ordinary conversation, we can also see the important effect that an audience has on a speaker's style, although the impact is less obvious than for broadcasters. In particular, we know that mass communicators are under considerable pressure to win the approval of their audience in order to maintain their audience size or market share.
>
> (Bell, 1997: 243)

Style shifts of individual speakers are seen as responses to the speaker's audience construing interpersonal alignment or disalignment. Audience design applies to all codes and levels of a language repertoire, monolingual and multilingual. Speakers design their style primarily for and in response to their audience, and they show a fine-grained ability to design their style for a range of different addressees, and to a lesser degree for other audience members (Bell, 1997: 243–8).

Audience design is reflected in the mixing of styles, viz. a more formal public style and a more informal private style, as has also been pointed out by Fairclough (1995), who takes the argument further and connects the mixing of styles with the tension between information and entertainment on the one hand, and the tension between private and public on the other, resulting in public affairs media becoming more and more conversationalized:

> These properties of temporal and spatial setting mean that a communicative event in the mass media can actually be seen as a *chain* of communicative events. [. . .] Notice that such a chain connects the public domain to the private domain; programmes are produced in the public domain using predominantly public domain source materials (e.g. political events), but they are consumed in the private domain, mainly at home and within the family.
>
> (Fairclough, 1995: 37)

Through the introduction of more interactive communication formats in media discourse, the distinction between private domains of life and public domains of life has become increasingly blurred: private agents perform the media role of a private person in public discourse thus adding yet another layer to its inherent multi-layeredness. In a similar vein, the formerly private domain anchored reception role in consuming media discourse has been transported to the public sphere of life, as is reflected in the more and more popular phenomenon of public viewing of mediated sports events or in the opportunity to post comments and negotiate their communicative status on twitter or discussion forums regarding general election coverage, thus construing some virtual community sharing that particular communal space.

In his analysis of radio talk, Gaik (1992: 273) points out that media discourse allows the audience 'to experience possible worlds'. This is because talk is enacted before the audience, employing a ritualized structure, especially openings and closings. Moreover, the audience may encounter reporting and reported voices, identities and social relations, and may thus encounter a diversity of mediated worlds: '[a] phenomenology of media language would have as its task the job of investigating the connections between media, language and the world' (Scannell, 1998: 263).

## 3.4  Transitivity: Agents and non-agents

The representation of social agents in media discourse is another key issue in the analysis of a phenomenology of media language: people can be presented as active agents, viz. as intentional agents who perform actions in a deliberate manner and therefore are in control of their actions. And they can be represented as passive agents, viz. as powerless agents on whom actions are performed thus not being in control of what they do. An important grammatical device anchored to the domain of clause is to represent active agents as 'doers' in their congruent realization as grammatical subject, logical subject and psychological subject and to represent non-active agents ('non-doers') as the semantic role of patient (Halliday, 1994). For instance, in the clause 'the prime minister has announced drastic cuts', 'the prime minister (PM)' agrees with the predicate 'has announced' and is therefore the grammatical subject, the PM is an intentional agent and therefore logical subject, and the PM is realized in the initial position of the clause and therefore the psychological subject. The clause 'drastic cuts have been announced' contains the grammatical subject 'drastic cuts', which is also the psychological subject but not the logical subject of the clause. Here, the intentional agent, who announced the cuts, is not represented overtly and needs to be inferred from the context.

In discourse, agents may not be represented at all and thus may be excluded from the discourse altogether. This may be achieved by the use of nominalizations and other types of grammatical metaphor (Halliday, 1994). Exclusion of agents may be done consistently, that is a social agent is not mentioned throughout the discourse, and there may be temporary suppression or backgrounding. Other relevant means of representation are genericization, for instance 'politicians have lost touch with reality', and specification, e.g. the Prime Minister, association, which is usually realized in parataxis, as in 'politicians, bureaucrats, and ecologists', and dissociation, which singles out one group of an associated unit, e.g. 'ecologists', thus implying that only ecologists are in favour of an issue but not politicians and bureaucrats. Furthermore, there is indetermination, viz. social actors are represented as anonymous individuals, e.g. as 'people', and differentiation, viz. their identity is made explicit, e.g. 'Mr. Smith, leader of the community centre'. Generally, there tends to be a close connection between the social roles that agents are given and their grammatical roles in discourse (Van Leeuwen, 1996).

## 4 Mass media and social media

Most recently, the evolution of the internet has brought about new forms of communication and opened up new arenas for discourse in general and for political discourse in particular, e.g. social networks (Kushin and Kitchener, 2009), online discussion forums, twitter or blogs (cf. Atifi and Marcoccia, 2012, for an overview of the different types of computer-mediated political discourse). This is especially true for the ordinary viewer's voice in mass media as representatives of the audience, as is the case with members of the audience taking over the role of interviewer at some stage in the discourse, or with viewers' comments read out by moderators during some TV or radio programme. The audience, generically speaking, is also invited to enter into a communication with the media and its representatives by phoning, sending emails or posting comments on particular websites. Moreover, almost all relevant mass media organizations are members of social network sites, and they explicitly make their membership known and invite other participants to join them there.

Public domain anchored mass media have thus entered the private domains of society. This not only holds for interactive programmes with explicit audience participation but also for how the news is presented in the media. Analysing the studio as social space, Fitzgerald and McKay (2012) describe the still largely desk-bound activities of the news anchors, but point out that the news studio and presentation style has begun to borrow artefacts, especially domestic furniture, as regards softer colours and other non-verbal signs, as well as language styles, in particular stories, that resemble the domestic sphere in layout and discourse. This tendency goes hand in hand with the more informal interaction in the news studio with direct interactions with external reporters, and with explicit references to news coverage on the channel's website:

> This pragmatic approach to news presentation as part of a strategy to hold on to market share incorporates not only the increased use of informal or vernacular language, but more pictures, shorter stories, giving more emphasis to the personal and experiential, especially by providing more opportunities for audience involvement.
>
> (Fitzgerald and McKay, 2012: 2)

The orientation of mass media towards the private spheres of life is also manifest in the topics covered in the different media outlets. While the so-called yellow press and entertainment programmes on radio and TV have always reported on public figures' private domains of life, the quality press and so-called quality programmes on TV and radio have not focused on those issues. More recently, however, politicians have introduced more and more personal stories thus presenting a more multifaceted and complex self in the media, which is referred to as sensationalism:

> The sensationalism and personalization of the popular press have long been subject of discussion and complaint on a national basis, particularly in advanced capitalist democracies. What has happened over the last fifteen years is that a combination of political, cultural, and technological changes have triggered a set of ripples which have spread across national as well as media boundaries to cause a range of debates about how processes which were once confined to the lower end of the market are now perceived to have infected the whole market.
>
> (Conboy, 2006: 208)

Changing affordances of the mass media have resulted in changing contextual constraints and requirements for felicitous communication in the media, accommodating private domain anchored forms of communication, such as blog and chat, and Facebook and twitter, which in turn underlie changing contextual constraints and requirements. Against this background, social media, which had been a private domain anchored context, has been transformed to a more public, mass media oriented outlet. This is particularly true for microblogs, which occurred with the traditional weblog. Originally, a blog is a personal journal published on the World Wide Web, which consists of discrete entries (or posts). They are displayed in a chronological order so that the most recent post occurs in the initial position. More recently, blogs containing breaking news are found on the website of online newspapers, TV stations and other institutional organizations.

Another private domain anchored digital service has been adapted to the contextual constraints and requirements of social media and, most recently, of mass media. Texting or short-message service has been used primarily on a one-to-one basis even though it allows for multiple recipients through a forwarding device. The original short-message text has focused on private domains of life composed with the help of medium-specific abbreviations, acronyms, contractions, clippings, initialisms and emoticons, as well as a particularized way of unconventional spelling. The length of the text messages also tends to be connected with the communicative actions performed by them. Departing from the short-message text sent to a private-domain anchored recipient, and exploiting its contextual constraints and requirement to the composition and length of possible contributions, the newly developed micro blogging system and social network of twitter has unique properties, communicative perspectives and constraints. Its messages are limited to 140 characters per message, and its topics tend to be of public relevance, or come with the presumption of being of relevance to either the general public or to some followers:

> Microblogging is text messaging and a little more. It can be as effortless as sending a text message from your cell phone to a select group of friends. Anyone can microblog as often as they like, and can promptly read posts from other mind-like bloggers. Microblogging includes the ability to send messages, audio, video and even attached files; it empowers users to make friends; get directions; give and receive advice; review books, restaurants, and movies; obtain up-to-the-minute news; identify, research, and purchase products and services; update customers; inform clients; send calendar and event notices and news; and more.
>
> (Safko and Brake, 2011: 257)

Media discourse in context covers traditional print versions of newspapers, journals and magazines as well as pamphlets and other printed forms of mass communication. It also covers digital discourse produced for a mass audience. The advent of the internet and the ever increasing access to that medium of communication has facilitated the transformation of formerly private domain anchored forms of communication to social media, and it has been re-shaping traditional mass media adopting social media strategies of communication.

# 5 Outlook

Media discourse has been defined as public discourse, institutional discourse and professional discourse. The analysis of the forms and functions of media discourse and media discourses across different periods of time and across different contexts has shown that society as a whole as well as parts of society may influence, if not shape, media discourse and media discourses, and that media discourses may influence, if not shape, parts of society as well as society as a whole.

In its advent, media discourse was printed media discourse produced by few and accessible to few. Printed leaflets, newspapers and magazines expanded as regards their production and as regards their reception, moving towards mass media discourse. Not only the participation framework changed, but also the modalities: mass media discourse started off as mono-modal discourse and moved towards multimodality, and it started off as a primarily unidirectional process of communication and moved towards multi-directionality and interactiveness. Media discourse has become more heterogeneous, more multi-layered and more polyvalent. More recent developments indicate that mass media is interfacing with social media, and that social media is interfacing with mass media, blurring the boundaries between public and private spheres of life.

A contrastive analysis of media discourse as regards its production and reception may shed more light on the increasingly complex and interwoven phenomenon, considering genre and language use, as well as production and reception. While a contrastive perspective may refine our knowledge about contextual constraints and requirements, cultural imprints and inter-cultural communication, considering culture-preferential and culture-specific configurations and practices in different media settings, such as TV, newspaper or CMC, and culture-preferential and culture-specific forms of language use (cf. Fetzer and Lauerbach, 2007; Hauser and Luginbühl, 2012), a reception-anchored perspective would further our understanding of the effects of mass media communication going beyond the traditional encoding-decoding model. In appropriation research, it is not only the recipient who plays a major role in the interpretation of media discourse but also her/his co-recipients (cf. Ayaß and Gerhardt, 2012), considering the impact of the recipients' background knowledge, their appropriation and negotiation of discursive meaning by connecting, disconnecting and interweaving mediated meaning, while at the same time constructing or deconstructing newsworthiness.

The analysis of media discourse requires an interdisciplinary frame of reference comprising media studies and their research on the contextual constraints and requirements for the production, reception and appropriation of media discourse, and for the forms and functions of public and commercial media. Media discourse analysis also needs to consider research in the fields of sociology and social psychology, linguistics, socio-linguistics and critical linguistics, and anthropology and cultural studies.

# References

Atifi, H. and Marcoccia, M. (2012), 'Follow-ups in online political discussions', in A. Fetzer, E. Weizman and E. Reber (eds), *Proceedings of the ESF Strategic Workshop on*

*Follow-ups across Discourse Domains: A Cross-Cultural Exploration of Their Forms and Functions, Würzburg (Germany), 31 May–2 June,* Würzburg: Universität Würzburg. Available at: http://opus.bibliothek.uni-wuerzburg.de/volltexte/2012/7165/. URN: urn:nbn:de:bvb:20-opus-71656, pp. 22–34 (accessed 1 August 2013).

Ayaß, R. and Gerhardt, C. (eds) (2012), *The Appropriation of Media in Everyday Life.* Amsterdam: John Benjamins.

Bell, A. (1997), 'Language style as audience design', in N. Coupland and A. Jaworski (eds), *Sociolinguistics: A Reader and Coursebook.* Basingstoke: Palgrave, pp. 240–50.

Brown, P. (1995), 'Politeness strategies and the attribution of intentions: the case of Tzeltal irony', in E. Goody (ed.), *Social Intelligence and Interaction.* Cambridge: Cambridge University Press, pp. 153–74.

Bull, P. and Fetzer, A. (2006), 'Who are *we* and who are *you?* The strategic use of forms of address in political interviews'. *Text and Talk,* 26(1), 1–35.

Clayman, S. and Heritage, J. (2002), *The News Interview.* Cambridge: Cambridge University Press.

Conboy, M. (2006), *Tabloid Britain: Constructing a Community Through Language.* Abingdon, Oxon: Routledge.

Fairclough, N. (1995), *Media Discourse.* London: Arnold.

—— (2006), *Language and Globalization.* Routledge: Abingdon.

Fetzer, A. and Lauerbach, G. (eds) (2007), *Political Discourse in the Media: Cross-Cultural Perspectives.* Amsterdam: John Benjamins.

Fetzer, A. and Weizman, E. (2006), 'Political discourse as mediated and public discourse'. *Journal of Pragmatics,* 38(2), 143–53.

Fitzgerald, R. and McKay, S. (2012), 'Just like home: remediation of the social in contemporary news broadcasting'. *Discourse, Context & Media,* 1, 1–8.

Gaik, F. (1992), 'Radio talk-show therapy and the pragmatics of possible worlds', in A. Duranti and C. Goodwin (eds), *Rethinking Context: Language as an Interactive Phenomenon.* Cambridge: Cambridge University Press, pp. 271–90.

Goffman, E. (1981), *Forms of Talk.* Oxford: Blackwell.

Halliday, M. A. K. (1994), *Introduction to Functional Grammar.* London: Arnold.

Hauser, S. and Luginbühl, M. (eds) (2012), *Contrastive Media Analysis.* Amsterdam: John Benjamins.

Kushin, M. and K. Kitchener (2009), 'Getting political on social network sites: exploring online political discourse on Facebook'. *First Monday* [Online], 14(11), 18 October.

Lauerbach, G. and Fetzer, A. (2007), 'Introduction', in A. Fetzer and G. Lauerbach (eds), *Political Discourse in the Media: Cross-Cultural Perspectives.* Amsterdam: John Benjamins, pp. 3–30.

Le, E. (2012), 'Gateway to the news: headlines on *Le Monde's* home page and front page'. *Discourse, Context & Media,* 1, 32–44.

Levinson, S. C. (1979), 'Activity types and language', *Linguistics,* 17, 365–99.

—— (1988), 'Putting linguistics on a proper footing: explorations in Goffman's concepts of participation', in P. Drew and A. Wooton (eds), *Erving Goffman. Exploring the Interaction Order.* Cambridge: Cambridge University Press, pp. 161–27.

Luckmann, T. (1995), 'Interaction planning and intersubjective adjustment of perspectives by communicative genres', in E. Goody (ed.), *Social Intelligence and Interaction.* Cambridge: Cambridge University Press, pp. 175–88.

Montgomery, M. (2007), *The Discourse of Broadcast News.* Abingdon: Routledge.

Reddy, M. (1979), 'The conduit metaphor', in A. Ortony (ed.), *Metaphor and Thought.* Cambridge: Cambridge University Press, pp. 284–324.

Safko, L. and D. K. Brake (eds) (2011), *The Social Media Bible*. New Jersey: John Wiley & Sons.

Scannell, P. (1998), 'Media-language-world', in A. Bell and P. Garrett (eds), *Approaches to Media Discourse*. Oxford: Blackwell, pp. 252–67.

Smith, P. and Bell, A. (2008), 'English in mass communications: news discourse and the language of journalism', in H. Momma and M. Matto (eds), *A Companion to the History of the English Language*. Oxford: Wiley-Blackwell, pp. 334–44.

Van Leeuwen, T. (1996), 'The representation of social actors', in C. Caldas-Coulthard and M. Coulthard (eds), *Texts and Practices*. London: Routledge, pp. 32–70.

—— (2000), 'Visual racism', in M. Reisigl and R. Wodak (eds), *The Semiotics of Racism: Approaches in Critical Discourse Analysis*. Vienna: Passagen Verlag, pp. 363–91.

# 16

# Media Discourse and De/Coloniality

# A Post-Foundational Approach

*Felicitas Macgilchrist*
Georg Eckert Institute
Braunschweig

## 1 Introduction

Critical discourse analysis of media is a broad enterprise with its roots in the seminal analyses of the 1970s and 1980s. In this chapter, I outline three relatively new developments, and point to directions in which media discourse analysis is now beginning to move (Section 2). To illustrate these new directions in a concrete analysis, the chapter explores media accounts of Africa (Section 3), and explores the potential of drawing on post-foundational thinking to analyse media discourse (Section 4).

## 2 'The media' and critical discourse analysis

'The media' have provided a core set of material to analyse discourse since critical linguists began to question the neutral role of linguistics and argue that linguistics had a salient role to play in social critique (e.g. Kress and Trew, 1978). The media were central to arguments that critical discourse analysis cannot focus only on texts but must embed textual analysis within analysis of the contexts of production and reception (e.g. Fairclough, 1989, 1995). Media discourse has also been used to support the recent argument that 'critical' discourse analysis (CDA) is one-sided in its top-down analysis of dominant discourse, and must be accompanied, if not replaced, by 'positive' discourse analysis (PDA) (e.g. Martin, 2004).

This central role of media in discourse analysis points to three new directions in which media discourse analysis is now turning. First, what is understood by 'media'? To date, the vast majority of discourse analysis which refers to 'media' actually analyses journalism. Journalism is, of course, a particularly prominent medium in the daily lives of discourse analysts. There are, however, a host of other media which could be the focus of critical discourse analysis (e.g. Stephens, 1992; Benwell, 2005).

Second, how are we to analyse the contexts of production and reception? The majority of discourse analyses still primarily analyse textual products, although this is often augmented by accounts of the production contexts and considerations of how the texts may be used. If we are to take seriously the call for discourse analysis to be embedded in its discursive contexts, however, it seems necessary to go into the field and observe media practices, or at the very least, interview practitioners and/or media users (see NewsTalk&Text Research Group, 2011). In this sense, discourse analysis is analysis of 'text plus'; always analysing text, and also always analysing more than text.

Third, what does it mean to do 'critical' or 'positive' discourse analysis? Despite differences among various approaches to critical discourse analysis, overall they share the presupposition that there is some sort of relation between structure on the one hand and language use on the other (see Weiss and Wodak, 2008: 19ff.), i.e. they presuppose that there is something which 'mediat[es] between the social and the linguistic' (2008). If, however, discourse analysis is about 'bringing a variety of theories into dialogue, especially social theories on the one hand and linguistic theories on the other' (Chouliaraki and Fairclough, 1999: 16ff.), then this presupposition need not be the only useful theoretical frame.[1] A post-foundational approach (see Section 1.3), which posits among other things that the linguistic *is* the social, enables instead a discourse analysis which aims to highlight ambivalences, tensions and contradictions in discourse rather than to demonstrate how discourse appears to be coherently dominant or consistently alternative.

This explicitly ambivalent discourse analysis (ADA!) in turn supports the aim of (critical) discourse analysis to contribute to social change. The thinking behind this is that if we repeatedly demonstrate how 'dominant' discourse is entrenched and stable, our analyses are themselves part of enacting and reproducing this discourse. By pointing to ambivalence and the accompanying gaps and instabilities, analysis can potentially widen the gap, contribute to destabilizing a given discourse, and encourage the development of new discourse.

Drawing on these three new directions, this chapter: (i) explores educational media, i.e. materials explicitly designed for use in educational settings; (ii) includes ethnographic observations from the production process; and (iii) draws on a post-foundational approach to discourse.

## 2.1  *Educational media*

Commercial educational media offer a particularly rich source of mediated discourse, since many educational media producers explicitly describe their role as balancing the demands of commercial media publishing – with its profit-orientation, tight deadlines and strict space constraints – against the more utopian goal of producing materials which will captivate and inspire students (Macgilchrist, 2011a). A sizable market is at stake: although they only publish for the German-speaking market, the three top German educational publishers are among the top 50 global book publishers (*Publishers Weekly*, 2013). At the same time, these media aimed at younger users play a role in shaping what counts as acceptable, desirable ways of being.[2]

## 2.2  *Production practices*

In the ethnographic discourse analysis which underlies this chapter, I followed the production of educational media such as textbooks and other school-based learning materials at a leading German publishing house from 2009 to 2011.[3] I observed teams of authors and editors engaged in lively and controversial discussions about what should be included in the minimal space available in textbooks for secondary level History and Politics/Social Studies in Germany. Two aspects of how textbooks are produced in Germany are particularly relevant to discourse analysis. First, very rarely are books newly designed. Instead, old series are regularly revised and updated. Second, any given publication was the result of numerous redrafts and changes by a broad set of individuals (authors, co-authors, editors, layouters, designers, etc). Thus, iteration, selection and reduction – which are intrinsic to any discursive practice – become explicit as the core practices in developing a publication for the market. Also, this means that educational media is highly unlikely to incorporate radical views. In this sense, the instabilities or transformations in this media discourse make it particularly fruitful for identifying hegemonic formations and discursive shifts in contemporary society.

At this stage, some may ask what distinguishes a *media discourse analysis* from other media analysis or media ethnographies. I see three particularities. First, as I understand it, media discourse analysis stresses the situatedness of knowledge and assumes that knowledge is intricately interwoven with power, i.e. it has an understanding of power as productive of knowledges, subjects, desires, societies, etc. Second, media discourse analysis is not interested in what media texts *mean*, but in the conditions of possibility which enable texts to make sense (to be 'sayable') in a particular discursive formation, i.e. adopting what Foucault (1972) called an *archaeological approach*, since analysts can only analyse the traces (in language and other practices) of these conditions of possibility. Third, media discourse analysis is not primarily interested in what *people* do, but in the *practices* which indicate the socio-historically specific conditions of possibility. In today's media institutions in

Germany, for instance, the recruitment practices (of e.g. editors, authors, layouters) which I observed value a kind of knowledge and expertise which means that media makers are quite likely to be individuals who are marked by, or rather unmarked by, fairly privileged social positions in their current geopolitical locations in (Western) Germany (i.e. living largely white, middle class, able-bodied, heterosexual, West German, etc. lives). It is not individual practitioners who are responsible for the media texts but the hegemonic formation in which they write (Foucault 1984).

## 2.3 *Post-foundational theory*

'Hegemonic formation' need not, however, refer to a coherent episteme for a given period. From Laclau and Mouffe, I take the observation that different 'hegemonic projects' (i.e. not yet hegemonic) are vying to become hegemonic in any socio-historic configuration (Laclau and Mouffe, 1985; see Torfing, 2002). As I suggested above, the significant purchase of a post-foundational (or post-structuralist) critical discourse analysis is, for me, that this theoretical perspective actively encourages the analyst to see fissures and dissonances in the discourse rather than (only or primarily) coherences and domination (see also Billig et al., 1988). Although Fairclough himself has regularly advocated analysing instabilities and paradoxes (e.g. 1995: 33; 2001: 245), the majority of critical discourse analysis has focused on identifying stabilities in dominant discourse. Brookes (1995), for instance, in her analysis of news coverage of Africa, finds a racist discourse which is 'both highly uniform and completely naturalized' (1995: 488). She concludes that this 'entrenched stability holds little possibility for challenge or transformation' (1995: 488).

I suspect one reason Fairclough's call to also explore the instabilities of discourse has not been taken up is the underlying critical realist ontology. Since this assumes a dualism between the natural and social worlds, it assumes that material objects exist as singularites outwith the practices which enact them (see e.g. Laclau and Bhaskar, 2007). For discourse analysis, this has been specified in the understanding of a dialectic relationship between 'discourse' as 'the semiotic moment' and 'other moments in social practices' (Chouliaraki and Fairclough, 1999: 126). Individuals' relationships to discourse are mediated through their position in social structures such as gender, race and class.[4] A post-foundational ontology, on the other hand, questions the a priori division between the natural and the social (see especially Butler, 1990; Latour, 1993; Haraway, 1997). As with any other 'foundations' such as God, rationality or objectivity, nature is made into a foundation in a particular (hegemonic) configuration. This argument is not, it should be noted, an *anti*-foundational idealism in which all foundations have been removed (see Chouliaraki and Fairclough, 1999: 120), but a *post*-foundationalism which argues that any foundation, any grounding, is contingent, partial and political (Laclau, 1990: 34f; Marchart, 2007; Macgilchrist, 2011a). Practices enact/perform materiality. There must be a grounding or we would live in a psychotic universe, but this grounding must be accomplished.

As a result of this, post-foundational writers see antagonism – or disagreement, dissent, negativity, disharmony, non-coherence or conflict – as constitutive of the social (see e.g. Laclau and Mouffe, 1985; Rancière, 1999; Butler et al., 2000; Nancy, 2010). In turn, (critical) discourse analysts in this vein aim to tease out the discursive traces of the constitutive antagonism. The empirical question is: where are the cracks in current configurations of power, exclusion or injustice? In this way, discourse analysis identifies current/potential social change. The political/practical question is: how can analysis or action help make these cracks wider? Thus, White (2001), for instance, unlike Brookes (1995) cited above, foregrounds the *in*stability of racist discourse in order to highlight challenges and transformations always already underway.

# 3 Africa and media discourse

'Merkel Flies on Economic Safari' (Welt Kompakt, 2011). 'Africa is a Country (@AfricasaCountry) New twitter account for the media blog that's not about famine, Bono, or Barack Obama' (Africa is a Country, 2013). These recent media texts indicate the still prevalent articulation of 'Africa' with wildlife and poverty. Although the German Chancellor was visiting economic leaders in large cities, her trip is described as a safari. The twitter account distances itself from what it describes as the dominant discourse about Africa. A quite different impression of contemporary politics, economics or media is given by sites such as Pambazouka News (http://www. pambazuka.org/en/), Global Voices (http://globalvoicesonline.org/) or blogAfrica (http:// blogafrica.allafrica.com/).

That 'Africa' is an entity constituted through political, academic and other discourse is now widely accepted (Mudimbe, 1988). Mbembe suggests that 'discourse on Africa is almost always deployed in the framework (or on the fringes) of a meta-text about the *animal*' (2001: 1, original emphasis). Previous critical discourse analysis has highlighted the racism of news reports on Africa (e.g. Brookes, 1995). Textbooks have been criticized for their representation of Africa (e.g. Poenicke, 2003; Kerber, 2005; Marmer et al., 2010). Three salient issues arise from this critique:

1 Colonial residue: Colonial vocabulary is employed, reproducing power hierarchies and suggesting Africa is a primitive place.

2 Eurocentrism: A Eurocentred perspective is adopted in which European issues are placed in the forefront and black people are presented as passive recipients of white actions. White voices are heard; black people rarely speak in the texts.

3 Mono-epistemicism: Texts assume that only one way of being and knowing is valuable (i.e. modernity, development, progress): Africa is compared to this European/Western/North-Atlantic norm and found wanting.

Each of these issues others Africa in some way. They thus potentially reproduce racist views of global hierarchies, and could (i) lead to discriminatory practices in the everyday life of young people, and (ii) disempower young people of African descent, by making it impossible for them to find role models or positive associations with Africa or African history in media discourse (see Marmer et al., 2010). They also make it difficult for young people to deconstruct colonial thinking, and to construct nuanced understandings of Africa or of epistemic diversity.

As I was observing textbook production, one particular section in a textbook for secondary level Years 9 and 10 History (ages 15–16) struck me as a 'rich point' in the ethnographic fieldwork, i.e. a surprising or exciting observation which did not fit with general expectations (Agar, 1996). In the chapter on imperialism and colonialism, the production team was explicitly and vocally attempting to avoid this othering discourse. Their task was to update (rewrite) an older textbook for the current market. The authors expressed dismay at the way Africa was described in previous textbooks. They agreed that they wanted to show that Africa was not a *tabula rasa* before colonialism, but that highly developed towns had been founded, centres of science and learning were flourishing, and complex global economic relations were well in place. It was important to 'revalue Africa' ('*eine Aufwertung Afrikas*'), i.e. to improve the image of Africa, and they described a need to show students that Africa is 'not so different' ('*nicht so fremd*') (audio-recorded participant observation: GB_20090809_03_1:18:00). The following analysis illustrates how this was enacted.

The analysis is structured along the three critical issues noted above: (3.1) colonial/ decolonized text, (3.2) Eurocentred/decentred perspective, (3.3) development/tradition. The previous book in the series (*History 9/10* as a pseudonym) was published in 2006. The new book to be sold in place of the previous book (thus also *History 9/10*) was published in 2010.

## 3.1 *Decolonizing the text?*

One clear shift in the discourse on Africa in this textbook is the distancing from colonial lexicalizations, as Table 16.1 shows (in translation, emphasis added; for the original German text, see Appendix).[5]

The first pair of extracts illustrates how scare quotes (see Fowler, 1991) flag a distance from the colonial vocabulary of 'explorers'. In 2006 the words 'adventurers', 'explorers' and 'conquistadors' are used as simple descriptive terms, whereas in the new book in 2010, quotations marks indicate that this word is 'someone else's' language: This is what 'the Europeans' said, not what we (the book's authors) say.

In the second pair, the definite article in 2006 implies that 'the white spaces' are a known entity: there are blank spaces on the world map, i.e. there was nothing in Africa, or Africa was not known, before the European states appeared there. The book

**Table 16.1** Distancing from colonial discourse

| History 9/10 (2006) | History 9/10 (2010) |
|---|---|
| The European states' politics of conquering foreign territory goes back as far as the sixteenth century, when Spanish and Portuguese sailors and *adventurers* founded colonial empires, especially in South America. These *explorers* and *conquistadors* . . . | Christian missionaries and – *as the Europeans said* – *'explorers' came* [to Africa]. |
| The race for *the last white spaces on the world map* was, however, also motivated by domestic politics. | Africa, *which contrary to the European view of the time most certainly also included highly developed civilizations*, only became an object of the European powers' colonial desires at a late stage. |
| Task: What *reasons* are given for the imperial politics [in the source texts]? | Task: Compare the *rationalizations* for imperial politics, as they are presented [in the source texts]. |

does not inform readers about any people, places or other history in Africa before colonialism. In 2010, explicit distance is again taken to 'the European view of the time', and the text explicitly mentions 'highly developed civilizations' in the region before the colonial powers arrived.

The third extract from 2006, by asking for 'reasons' ('*begründet*') for the imperial politics, presupposes that there are reasons for colonial politics. In 2010, the use of 'rationalizations' ('*Rechtfertigungen*'; also 'excuses'/'justifications') foregrounds the active work necessary to make imperial politics (seem) legitimate, and could be read as presupposing that this politics was not legitimate.

In 2006 the text creates an antagonism between Europe and Africa. In Europe there are adventurers, explorers and reasons for imperial politics. In Africa there are white spaces. In 2010, this antagonistic relation is dissolved, and a new political frontier is realized which locates Africa and today's Europe (of the authors and the readers) on one side and the Europe of the colonizers on the other side of the frontier. This is done by drawing two antagonistic chains of equivalence, i.e. chains which link various elements into a relation of equivalence (see Laclau and Mouffe, 1985: 127ff.). One chain links the signifiers 'Africa', 'highly developed civilizations' and 'came' (relevant since someone 'goes' *there*, or 'comes' *here*, implying Africa is proximal for the readers). A second chain links 'the Europeans' with the past tense 'said' (i.e. those Europeans then), 'the European view of the time' and 'rationalizations'. The latter (negatively loaded) chain is presented as distanced from today's readers.

Overall, each of these 2010 extracts fulfils in some way the authors' stated intentions of changing contemporary discourse about Africa, of presenting students with an Africa which does not seem as very dissimilar to their own lives in contemporary Germany as previous educational media have implied. They enact a different African history from that previously made available in educational media for schools. At the same time, words such as 'chief' ('*Häuptling*') do still appear. In reproducing advertising images from the colonial period, showing e.g. black men carrying white men, colonial relations are visually reproduced, even if the aim is to critically assess these relations. These non-coherent words show how the 'new' discourse from the most recent revision is layered on top of – and visible alongside – the 'old' discourse from the previous books which are being revised and updated. Section 3 will return to explore some further tensions within the authors' stated intentions.

## 3.2 *Decentring Europe?*

Who acts during this period of history in Africa, and who is the passive recipient of others' actions? One criticism of textbooks is that they tell the story entirely from a European perspective. Selecting imperialism as the focus is already clearly Eurocentred. However, the author team criticized that the gaze always goes from Germany to the rest of the world; it also needs to go in the other direction (GB_20090809_01:18:00). And indeed, a shift is visible between 2006 and 2010 in whose perspective is prioritized in *History 9/10*.

A classic discourse analytical tool, transitivity, demonstrates this shift. I draw on transitivity analysis here as a way of capturing the impression of experience as 'a flow of events, or "goings-on"', i.e. as 'a process unfolding through time' and 'participants being directly involved in this process in some way' (Halliday and Matthiessen, 2004: 170). In this analysis, the primary question is which participants are positioned as central in the process of colonialism: the colonizers or the colonized?

A clear shift in focus is visible for the section on German South-West Africa from 2006 to 2010. In 2006, 33 clauses had colonized or colonizer participants: 11 of the 33 are filled by black participants (e.g. 'the Herero', 'the survivors', 'the tribes', 'government and parliament'), 22 are filled by white participants (e.g. 'German Reich', 'Bismarck', 'settlers', 'European colonial masters'). In 2010, 35 clauses had colonized or colonizer participants: 22 of the 35 are filled by black signifiers (e.g. 'Nama and Herero', 'Witbooi', 'Maharero', 'numerous peoples'), and 13 by white signifiers (e.g. 'German Reich', 'German troops', 'settlers', 'the Germans'). The balance has entirely reversed. Where only one third of the text was centred on black actors in 2006, two thirds is in 2010. This shift is not, however, as clear for other sections on colonialism/imperialism.

A second analytical concept, voice, also highlights shifts in which perspective is centred. Whose voice is heard, and what do they speak about? Table 16.2 indicates changes between 2006 and 2010.

**Table 16.2** The voices of colonial history

| History 9/10 (2006) | History 9/10 (2010) |
| --- | --- |
| On Algeria: 'The French historian G. Hanotaux, Foreign Minister from 1894 to 1898, gives the following reasons for the imperial policies:' | On Algeria: 'In a parliamentary debate on 14 May 1840, the French marshal Thomas Bugeaud remarked that:' |
| On Algeria: '[. . .] The text originated after the defeat of the Kabyle rebellion in 1871:' | On Algeria: 'The Algerian Ferhat Abbas wrote:' |
| On German South-West Africa: 'General Lothar von Trotha, the Commander-in-chief of the protection force in German South-West Africa, on 2 October 1904:' | On German South-West Africa: 'The Herero chief Daniel Kariko said about his experiences with German colonizers around 1900:' |
| On German South-West Africa: 'Otto von Bismarck explained in the Reichstag on 16 June 1884 upon acquiring German South-West Africa:' | On German South-West Africa: 'On 23 February 1904, Theodor Leutwein, governor of the colony, wrote to the colonial administration:' |
| On German South-West Africa: 'A surviving Herero:' | |

Table 16.2 lists the descriptions introducing the source texts in the 2006 and 2010 textbooks. Both books have sections on colonial history in Algeria and German South-West Africa (now Namibia). In 2006, three Europeans – a French historian, German general and German politician – are named. Two local source texts are included, but one backgrounds the source ('the text originated'), and the other remains unnamed, 'a surviving Herero'. In 2010, all four source texts are introduced by named individuals: Bugeaud, Abbas, Kariko and Leutwein.

The table also hints at the issues each person speaks about. Where in 2006, people of colour only speak after they have been defeated (in the Kabyle rebellion and after the massacre of the Herero), 2010 includes more complex statements. Abbas speaks about how to potentially improve the future relationship between France and Algeria. Kariko speaks about the injustices the Herero suffered at the hands of German merchants supported by German police.

Overall, the source texts in 2006 position the European colonizers as the central actors in history. The black population is articulated with defeat and positioned as the unnamed objects of European actions. In 2010, a higher priority is given to black perspectives on colonization. One (named) Algerian – although we are given no information about his status or profession – gives a strong opinion on current political issues.[6] This shifts the balance of power away from a simplistic perpetrator–victim scheme, towards a more complex picture which foregrounds not only the strong power imbalances and injustices, but also important and vocal black leaders and political commentators. At the same time, the overall decision on whose voice will be heard is made in the (Western) European publishing house, with a predominantly white staff.

## 3.3 Picturing modernity?

The primary author of the chapter on imperialism was, as noted above, very explicit in expressing a desire to change the representations of Africa. The most surprising element in this section on German South-West Africa is, he says, 'the modernity of the Nama and Herero. That is a really new insight' (GB_20091106_02_1:52:20). He draws on recent historical research to argue that their textbook is part of a dramatic shift in perceptions of the Nama and Herero. The research 'is really in transition about this' ('unheimich in Fluss an der Stelle'), he says. And: 'It can't be removed, the modernity of these peoples'. An early manuscript included the following (emphasis added).

> Hendrik Witbooi, baptized as a Christian and *the literate leader* of the Nama, criticized African land sales to white settlers and made the initiative, under the weight of the German advance, to end the old enmity between Herero and Nama. [. . .]
> (*Der christlich getaufte, des Lesens und Schreibens kundige Führer der Nama, Hendrik Witbooi, kritisierte afrikanische Landverkäufe an weiße Siedler und ergriff unter dem Eindruck des deutschen Vordringens die Initiative zur Beendigung der alten Feindschaft zwischen Herero und Nama. [. . .]*)

> The Herero developed into a *relatively modern and powerful* cattle raising society and slowly won control, also in military matters, over the northern part of Namibia.
> (*Die Herero entwickelten sich dadurch zu einer für damalige Verhältnisse modernen und machtvollen Viehhaltergesellschaft und gewannen allmählich, auch militärisch, die Oberhand im nördlichen Teil Namibias.*)

Unfortunately for the author, the manuscript is far too long to fit in the book. The text he has written would fill three pages in the textbook, but only two pages are available. Also, the manuscript is what editors and authors refer to as a 'desert of lead' ('*Bleiwüßte*'). It leaves no space for images, diagrams, historical source texts or tasks for the students, without which a contemporary (multimodal) textbook is unthinkable.

After much discussion and debate on how to maintain an emphasis on the modernity of the local population of the time, the team decides to resemiotize the written word as an annotated map (see Figure 16.1).

The annotated map of Africa creates a multimodal chain of equivalence among specific places on the continent and various elements signifying modernity, development or similarity to Europe. The top right illustration of Mombasa, in particular, is very similar in style to similar illustrations of European cities in the Middle Ages.

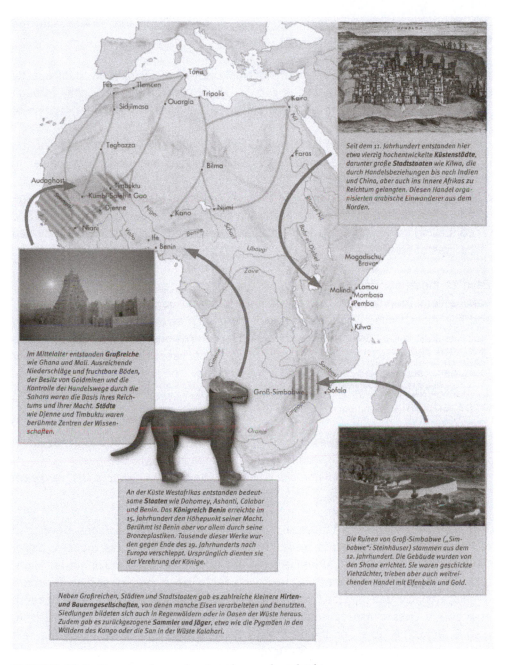

Seit dem 11. Jahrhundert entstanden hier etwa vierzig hochentwickelte **Küstenstädte**, darunter große **Stadtstaaten** wie Kilwa, die durch Handelsbeziehungen bis nach Indien und China, aber auch ins Innere Afrikas zu Reichtum gelangten. Diesen Handel organisierten arabische Einwanderer aus dem Norden.

Im Mittelalter entstanden **Großreiche** wie Ghana und Mali. Ausreichende Niederschläge und fruchtbare Böden, der Besitz von Goldminen und die Kontrolle der Handelswege durch die Sahara waren die Basis ihres Reichtums und ihrer Macht. **Städte** wie Djenne und Timbuktu waren berühmte Zentren der Wissenschaften.

An der Küste Westafrikas entstanden bedeutsame **Staaten** wie Dahomey, Ashanti, Calabar und Benin. Das **Königreich Benin** erreichte im 15. Jahrhundert den Höhepunkt seiner Macht. Berühmt ist Benin aber vor allem durch seine Bronzeplastiken. Tausende dieser Werke wurden gegen Ende des 19. Jahrhunderts nach Europa verschleppt. Ursprünglich dienten sie der Verehrung der Könige.

Die Ruinen von Groß-Simbabwe („Simbabwe": Steinhäuser) stammen aus dem 12. Jahrhundert. Die Gebäude wurden von den Shona errichtet. Sie waren geschickte Viehzüchter, trieben aber auch weitreichenden Handel mit Elfenbein und Gold.

Neben Großreichen, Städten und Stadtstaaten gab es zahlreiche kleinere **Hirten- und Bauerngesellschaften**, von denen manche Eisen verarbeiteten und benutzten. Siedlungen bildeten sich auch in Regenwäldern oder in Oasen der Wüste heraus. Zudem gab es zurückgezogene **Sammler und Jäger**, etwa wie die Pygmäen in den Wäldern des Kongo oder die San in der Wüste Kalahari.

**FIGURE 16.1** *Mapping the modernity of pre-colonial Africa.*

The style also recalls the towns in the popular game Carcassonne. Alongside the illustrations, the textboxes include the following:

> After the eleventh century about 40 highly developed [highly civilized] coastal towns arose including city states such as Kilwa which became wealthy through trade relations which reached China and India but also into the inner regions of Africa. [. . .]
>
> Important cities such as Dahomey, Ashanti, Calabar and Benin developed on the West African coast. The kingdom of Benin reached the peak of its power in the fifteenth century. [. . .]
>
> In the middle ages, vast empires such as Ghana and Mali arose. Their wealth and power was based on having sufficient rain and fertile soil, owning gold mines, and controlling trade routes. Towns such as Djenné and Timbuktu were renowned centres of scholarship.

Each of these extracts describes highly developed aspects of life in Africa before colonization. They describe developed/civilized towns, powerful cities and empires, and specific activities which imply development such as owning gold mines, trading globally, controlling trade routes, and developing centres of scholarship. Specific cities or powers are named, Kilwa, Benin, Mali, Timbuktu, etc., some of which may be familiar to student readers from today's world news or maps.

In addition, one of the tasks refers to the map (Figure 16.1 above; referred to as 54.1 in the textbook):

> Working with a partner, give your impressions of Africa before 1500 (54.1, Review). Compare them with your knowledge about Europe in the Middle Ages.
> (*Bennent in Partnerarbeit Eindrücke von Afrika vor 1500 (54.1, Rückblick). Vergleicht sie mit eurem Wissen über Europa im Mittelalter.*)

This task explicitly inverts the usual traditional/modern, developed/under-developed dichotomy which is created in many media texts about Europe (as modern, highly developed and civilized) and Africa (as backward, under-developed and primitive). Here, it is Ghana, Djenné, Ashanti, etc. which students are invited to see as far more developed or civilized than the Europe of the Middle Ages which they have learnt about in previous classes and educational media (feudalism, peasantry, poverty, famine, plague, etc.). The 'other', on the other side of the antagonistic divide which this text creates, is the Europe of the Middle Ages.

In summary, these images, descriptions and task invite readers to see pre-colonial Africa as a highly developed, civilized ('*hochentwickelt*') place. In an attempt to revalue Africa, similarities with Europe are depicted and an explicit (antagonistic) comparison with Europe is set up in which Africa is positioned as more developed/modern/pleasant. Section 4 now turns to these notions of development and modernity in more detail.

# 4  Modernity, coloniality and media discourse

The materials I have analysed here can be interpreted in various, conflicting ways. By focusing on the selection on colonialism as one of the few topics in which Africa is mentioned at all, they could easily support an argument that educational media accounts of Africa reproduce an entrenched dominant racist discourse reproducing 'Africans' as the colonial objects of European subjects. By focusing on the dramatic changes which have taken place since the overtly racist textbook accounts of Africa and colonialism in the nineteenth and twentieth centuries (see Macgilchrist and Müller, 2012), a positive discourse analysis of progressive social change could be presented.

I (now) find that both of these approaches overlook the complexity and messiness of (media) discourse, and thus the complexity and the messiness of the social (see Law, 2004; Marcus, 1998). It is tempting to present neat and orderly findings. And it is a challenge to present 'messy' or unresolved issues in a readable text. In this section I draw on postcolonial and decolonial thinking to reflect on the analysis above, focusing on a postcolonial horizon of intelligibility (4.1), the challenges of representing and remembering colonialism (4.2), and the possibility of embracing decoloniality (4.3).

## 4.1  Postcolonial horizon of intelligibility

The analysis above has described three shifts between the 2006 book and the revised 2010 book: (i) the lexis was largely decolonized, (ii) the perspective changed, with local perspectives and black individuals playing a much more prominent role, and (iii) pre-colonial Africa was revalued as a place with a rich history. Each of these shifts recalls debates in postcolonial studies (see e.g. Spivak, 1988; Bhabha, 1994). It seems clear that these aspects of a postcolonial perspective have become part of the horizon of intelligibility in this example of contemporary media-making practices. That this is still a relatively novel horizon is shown by the way one author strongly argues for the need to change the way Africa has been presented in previous educational media. It is not simply self-evident that these changes must be made. However, no one else in the team argues with him (and they certainly argue about other representational issues); they all seem to agree that change is necessary. At the same time, the shift is accompanied – or fissured – by several challenges.

## 4.2  Challenges of remembering colonialism

One challenge is that the new book does not completely remove all residues of past colonial relations. Advertising visuals depict e.g. black slaves carrying white masters. The occasional use of lexis such as 'chief' primitivizes the black political leaders of the time. For some observers, the central problem is that African countries or histories are only included within chapters on imperialism and colonialism and thus must inevitably be presented as the colonial object. Africa should be included in entirely different contexts, e.g. examples of technological innovation originating in Africa such as the mobile payment system m-pesa in Kenya and Tanzania; extracts about ALIF, a feminist hip hop band in Senegal; or biographies of Europeans of African descent such as poet and activist May Ayim (see Opitz et al., 1991).[7]

At the same time, a second challenge is whether more, not less, attention should be paid to the responsibility of the colonizers for the atrocities committed in Africa during colonialism. The author team agonizes over how to present the cruelty of the time (GB_20091106_02_1:06:00).

These two challenges are on the level of representation: how should colonialism as a specific historical project be remembered? A third challenge shifts level and refers to the contemporary hegemonic formation which enables representation in the first place. It asks how media discourse engages with what is now being called coloniality. And: is this media discourse opening up or closing down decolonial horizons?

Coloniality is here understood as a hegemonic epistemic frame, enacted today, that produces and legitimizes differences and hierarchies between subjects, knowledges and societies.[8] While its roots lie in the historical project of colonialism since the fifteenth century, I refer here to coloniality as the logic which (precariously) orders global hierarchies today; not only between the global South and the global North but also for the South in the North and the North in the South. For decolonial thinkers the discourse of modernity is intricately tied up with the logic of coloniality (Mignolo, 2007); 'there is no modernity without coloniality, with the latter being constitutive of the former' (Escobar, 2007: 185). Thinking about the coloniality of power means thinking about the ways in which modernity/coloniality, as the living legacy of colonialism, is infused throughout modern societies across the globe as forms of knowledge, social ordering and discriminatory practices (Quijano, 2010).[9]

Coloniality is diffused throughout – and thus reproduced by – contemporary media discourse which operates from sites of epistemic privilege, and plays a role in defining the world in terms of modernity, modernization and development. The analysis above suggests, for instance, how a universal modernity is posited to which all self-evidently aspire. This modernity is flagged by words such as developed and civilization, by activities such as controlling trade routes and creating centres of scholarship, and by visuals such as the city state of Kilwa. The successful revaluing of Africa seems to rest on the presupposition that since around the globe, we all aspire to be highly developed, and pre-colonial Africa was clearly highly developed, Africa is not so very different from Europe. Similarly, the task asking students to compare Africa and Europe in the Middle Ages invites them to see Africa more positively, because it is more developed than Europe. The text interrupts the usual hierarchy of development in which Europe is more developed and Africa less, but it still evaluates *in terms of* development.

In this sense, by avoiding the widely critiqued practice of 'othering', the text engages in 'saming' (see Schor, 1995). The 'same' standards of modernity (science, global trade, powerful civilized cities) which evaluate Europe positively are used to judge pre-colonial Africa a success. The text thus (subtly, non-intentionally) enacts a hegemonic formation in which one local history (European modernity) becomes the universal standard to evaluate ways of knowing and being. This closes down the possibility of engaging with other epistemic frames and of 'thinking with distinct knowledges, beings, logics, cosmovisions, and forms of living' (Walsh, 2010: 3; see Walsh, 2009).

Related to thinking about decoloniality is the challenge of academic writing about these issues. In writing this chapter, I have struggled with various ways of describing the people involved. I use the terms 'black', 'people of colour', 'colonized', 'local', 'white', 'Western' and 'European'. Each comes with its own positioned political baggage (see Arndt and Ofuatey-Alazard, 2011). Perhaps we should not be analysing and writing in ways which demand such broadstroke categorization of individuals, places, groups or histories. Since such categorization itself reproduces 'Africa' as bounded and clearly defined, is it not part of coloniality itself? Or is it simply a practical shorthand? Or perhaps part of the messy and irresolvable ambivalence of contemporary social science?

## 4.3 *Embracing decoloniality*

Decolonial thinking, emerging primarily from scholars in Latin America, aims to make a 'decisive intervention into the very discursivity of the modern sciences in order to craft another space for the production of knowledge – an other way of thinking, *un paradigma otro*, the very possibility of talking about "worlds and knowledges otherwise"' (Escobar, 2007: 179). It suggests 'that an other thought, an other knowledge (and another world, in the spirit of Porto Alegre's World Social Forum), are indeed possible' (2007: 179). A decolonial perspective encourages (educational) media to engage with (i) how the micropractices and relations of power produce mono-epistemic privilege, and (ii) how epistemic diversity can be enacted, i.e. how to foreground and value diverse forms of knowledge, diverse ways of being and living.

The question for media discourse analysis working from this perspective is to explore how these 'knowledges otherwise' are enacted in concrete instances. In the extracts analysed here a major step has been taken to revalue Africa. It is possible that the materials achieve their goal of enabling students to approach the continent with a knowledge of its rich history, and without the logic of inferiorization which is often visible in educational materials – and media discourse more generally – about Africa.

However, the materials are ambivalent – as indeed ambivalences can inevitably be identified in media discourse, if it is analysed from a perspective foregrounding contradictions and fissures. At the same time as engaging with novel ways of representing Africa and colonialism, the textbook does not engage with the coloniality of power or of knowledge. Nor does it embrace epistemic diversity. As I suggested at the outset, it is unlikely that corporate media will be part of dislocating the hegemonic formation within which it is produced. For this reason, discourse analysis of corporate media is perfectly placed not only to identify discursive change and social transformation, but also to point to (provisionally, precariously) hegemonic formations.

# 5 Concluding thoughts

This chapter has analysed media discourse on Africa from a post-foundational perspective. By adopting a chronological approach, it has observed a shift in these contemporary educational media towards a postcolonial discourse about Africa. At the same time, it has pointed to the ways in which the materials – despite authors' explicit intentions – re-enact a hegemonic formation (coloniality) in which European standards of modernity/development are imagined as universal norms. For decolonial thinkers such as Mignolo, Walsh and Escobar, the crucial next step is to explore epistemic diversity and facilitate the decolonization of power, knowledge and being. Not only media discourse but also media discourse analysis should move beyond a Eurocentred perspective, and not remain, as this analysis has, focused on texts originating within Europe. For Law (1994: 6), one way to avoid the 'monster' of modernity is to embrace non-coherence and heterogeneity; to avoid presenting stories which are too orderly and organized. Perhaps a trace of this can be seen in the non-coherence among the various extracts and thus the ambivalence of the pages on colonialism in Africa. A good deal of work, however, is done during the production of educational media to present an orderly and coherent story. The questions of whether – and if so, how – non-coherence is picked up by users of these texts, and whether/how users engage in decolonizing strategies, need, of course, to be postponed to a future study.

# Acknowledgements

I would like to extend my heartfelt thanks to the authors, editors and other media makers who have welcomed me to their meetings, and taken the time to talk to me about their work and about my reflections on their work. I also thank Lars Müller for many conversations about Africa, histories and irresolvable categorization practices.

# Appendix

**Table 16.3**  Distancing from colonial discourse (German)

| History 9/10 (2006) | History 9/10 (2010) |
| --- | --- |
| Die Eroberungspolitik der europäischen Staaten nach Übersee reicht bis in das 16. Jahrhundert zurück, als spanische und portugiesische Seeleute und Abenteurer Kolonialreiche vor allem in Südamerika errichteten. Diesen Entdeckern und Konquistadoren ging es darum,. . . | Christliche Missionare und – wie die Europäer sagten – "Entdeckungsreisende" kamen [nach Afrika]. |
| Der Wettlauf um die letzten weißen Flecken auf der Weltkarte war aber auch innenpolitisch motiviert. | Afrika, das entgegen damaliger europäischer Ansicht sehr wohl auch Hochkulturen kannte, wurde erst spät zum Objekt kolonialer Begierden der europäischen Mächte. |
| Arbeitsauftrag: Wie wird [in den Quellen] die imperialistische Politik begründet? | Arbeitsauftrag: Vergleiche die Rechtfertigungen imperialistischer Politik, wie sie [in den Quellen] vorgetragen werden. |

**Table 16.4**  The voices of colonial history (German)

| History 9/10 (2006) | History 9/10 (2010) |
| --- | --- |
| On Algeria: "Der französische Historiker G. Hanotaux, Außenminister von 1894 bis 1898, begründet die imperialistische Politik Frankreichs folgendermaßen:" | On Algeria: "In einer Parlamentsdebatte äußerte der französische Marschall Thomas Bugeaud am 14. Mai 1840:" |
| On Algeria: "[. . .] Der Text entstand nach der Niederschlagung des Aufstands der Kabylen 1871:" | On Algeria: "Der Algerier Ferhat Abbas schrieb:" |
| On German South-West Africa: "General Lothar von Trotha, der Oberkommandierende der Schutztruppe in Deutsch-Südwestafrika, am 2. Oktober 1904:" | On German South-West Africa: "Der Herero-Häuptling Daniel Kariko sagte übr seine Erfahrungen mit deutschen Kolonisten um 1900:" |
| On German South-West Africa: "Otto von Bismarck erklärte anlässlich der Erwerbung von Deutsch-Südwestafrika am 16. Juni 1884 im Reichstag:" | On German South-West Africa: "Theodor Leutwein, Governeur der Kolonie, schrieb am 23. Februar 1904 an das Kolonialamt:" |
| On German South-West Africa: "Ein überlebender Herero:" | |

# Notes

1  At the same time, Weiss and Wodak draw on Luhmann to argue that 'symbolic practices do not take place within social systems. Instead, they reproduce the latter simply by taking place; the systems reproduced in this way then retroact on the conditions of action. This means that engaging in an action equals system reproduction, or in our concrete case, text production equals system reproduction.' (2003: 10; original emphasis). This I agree with, as with their assertion that 'from an ontological perspective microcontext equals macrocontext' (2003). However, Weiss and Wodak then argue that the only way to make sense of this reasoning is by adopting Giddens' structuration approach. I would suggest that post-foundational thinking offers a different way of making sense of this ontological perspective which enables, as I note above, a novel and fruitful empirical perspective on the contingency and partiality of discourse.

2  Observations about media production tell us nothing yet about the use of these media. A follow-up project is currently underway which follows the textbook analysed here into the classroom, again adopting an ethnographic approach.

3  Ethnography fits well with the premises outlined in Section 1.3, but is not necessary for a post-foundational approach to discourse analysis.

4  Post-foundational discourse theory does not ignore categories such as gender, race or class. Although *in principle* discourse is fluid, some discourse (gender, race, class, etc.) has become sedimented; i.e. these categories have come to seem permanent and objective. Thus the subject positions created by the discourses indeed act as constraints on individual action in the here and now (cf. Butler, 1990; Laclau, 1990: 34f; Phillips and Jørgensen, 2002: 55ff).

5  Due to my promise to the publishing house to anonymize the materials as far as possible in publications, I do not cite the published text. Should any readers be interested in seeing the materials in full, I am happy to send further details or page scans upon request.

6  Abbas could have been described as a political activist, political leader, or the future president of the provisional Algerian nationalist government-in-exile before independence.

7  I thank Joshua Kwesi Aikins for information about the m-pesa. Projects on Black Europe are ongoing at the Pedagogical Centre in Aachen (PÄZ) and the Center of Study and Investigation for Global Dialogues (Diàleg Global). Resources on African British histories are available for instance at http://lookhowfar.eventbrite.com or http://narm2013.eventbrite.com.

8  I am using 'hegemony' in a slightly different sense to the way decolonial thinkers such as Mignolo or Escobar use it. Drawing on Laclau and Mouffe, hegemony is for me a more precarious, provisional formation, which must constantly be iteratively reproduced, and can thus be fissured and dislocated.

9  While theories of 'multiple modernities' critique the notion of one homogeneous modernity, arguing that societies are not all on the path to one singular (Western) modernity, they still distinguish between traditional and modern societies, retain the core assumptions of development and progress, and reify the notion of distinct 'cultures' (e.g. Eisenstadt, 2000; Delanty, 2009). More interesting is Dath and Kirchner's (2012) argument in favour of an explicitly social progress (i.e. towards more social justice).

# References

Africa is a Country (2013), 'Africa is a country'. Available at: https://twitter.com/AfricasaCountry (accessed 1 March 2013).

Agar, M. (1996), *Professional Stranger: An Informal Introduction To Ethnography*. New York: Academic Press.

Arndt, S. and Ofuatey-Alazard N. (eds) (2011), *Wie Rassismus aus Wörtern Spricht: (K) Erben des Kolonialismus im Wissensarchiv Deutsche Sprache. Ein Kritisches Nachschlagewerk*. Münster: Unrast.

Benwell, B. (2005), '"Lucky this is anonymous." Ethnographies of reception in men's magazines: a "textual culture" approach'. *Discourse and Society*, 16(2), 147–72.

Bhabha, H. (1994), *The Location of Culture*. London: Routledge.

Billig, M., Condor, S.,Edwards, D., Gane, M., Middleton, D. and Radley, A. (1988), *Ideological Dilemmas: A Social Psychology of Everyday Thinking*. London: Sage.

Brookes, H. J. (1995), '"Suit, Tie and a Touch of Juju" – the ideological construction of Africa: a critical discourse analysis of news on Africa in the British press'. *Discourse & Society*, 6(4), 461–92.

Butler, J. (1990), *Gender Trouble: Feminism and the Subversion of Identity*. London: Routledge.

Butler, J., Laclau, E. and Žižek, S. (2000), *Contingency, Hegemony, Universality*. London: Verso.

Chouliaraki, L. and Fairclough, N. (1999), *Discourse in Late Modernity: Rethinking Critical Discourse Analysis*. Edinburgh: Edinburgh University Press.

Dath, D. and Kirchner, B. (2012), *Der Implex: Sozialer Fortschritt: Geschichte und Idee*. Berlin: Suhrkamp.

Delanty, G. (2009), *The Cosmopolitan Imagination: The Renewal of Critical Social Theory*. Cambridge: Cambridge University Press.

Eisenstadt, S. N. (2000), 'Multiple modernities'. *Daedalus*, 129(1), 1–29.

Escobar, A. (2007), 'Worlds and knowledges otherwise'. *Cultural Studies*, 21(2), 179–210.

Fairclough, N. (1989), *Language and Power*. London: Longman.

—— (1995), *Media Discourse*. London: Edward Arnold.

—— (2001), 'The discourse analysis of New Labour: critical discourse analysis', in M. Wetherell, S. Taylor and S. J. Yates (eds), *Discourse as Data*. London: Sage, pp. 229–66.

Foucault, M. (1972), *The Archaeology of Knowledge*. London: Routledge.

—— (1984), 'What is an author?', in P. Rabinow (ed.), *The Foucault Reader*. London: Penguin, pp. 101–20.

Fowler, R. (1991), *Language in the News: Discourse and Ideology in the Press*. London: Routledge and Kegan Paul.

Halliday, M. and Matthiessen, C. (2004), *An Introduction to Functional Grammar*. London: Hodder Education.

Haraway, D. (1997), *Modest_Witness@second_Millenium. FemaleMan_Meets-OncoMouse*. New York: Routledge.

Kerber, A. (2005), 'Kolonialgeschichtein deutschen Schulbüchern: Kritisch oder kritikwürdig? (Colonial history in German textbooks: critical or criticizable?)', in H. Lutz and K. Gawarecki (eds), *Kolonialismus und Erinnerungskultur (Colonialism and Cultural Memory)*. Münster: Waxmann, pp. 81–93.

Kress, G. and Trew, A. (1978), 'Ideological transformation of discourse; or how the *Sunday Times* got *its* message across'. *Journal of Pragmatics* 2, 311–29.

Laclau, E. (1990), *New Reflections on the Revolution of our Time*. London: Verso.

Laclau, E. and Bhaskar, R. (2007), 'Discourse theory vs. critical realism'. *Journal of Critical Realism*, 1(2), 9–14.

Laclau, E. and Mouffe C. (1985), *Hegemony and Socialist Strategy: Towards a Radical Politics*. London: Verso.

Latour, B. (1993), *We Have Never Been Modern*. Cambridge: Harvard University Press.

Law, J. (1994), *Organizing Modernity*. Oxford: Blackwell.

—— (2004), *After Method: Mess in Social Science Research*. London: Routledge.

Macgilchrist, F. (2011a), *Journalism and the Political: Discursive Tensions in News Coverage of Russia*. Amsterdam/Philadelphia: John Benjamins.

—— (2011b), 'Schulbuchverlage als Organisationen der Diskursproduktion: Eine ethnographische Perspektive'. *Zeitschrift für Soziologie der Erziehung und Sozialisation*, 31(3), 248–63.

Macgilchrist, F. and Müller L. (2012), 'Kolonialismus und Modernisierung: Das diskursive Ringen um Afrika bei der Schulbuchentwicklung', in M. Aßner, J. Breidbach, A.-A. Mohammed, D. Schommer and K. Voss (eds), *AfrikaBilder im Wandel?* Frankfurt am Main: Peter Lang, pp. 195–208.

Marchart, O. (2007), *Post-Foundational Political Thought: Political Difference in Nancy, Lefort, Badiou and Laclau*. Edinburgh: Edinburgh University Press.

Marcus, G. E. (1998), *Ethnography Through Thick and Thin*. Princeton, NJ: Princeton University Press.

Marmer, E., Marmer, D., Hitomi L. and Sow. P. (2010), 'Racism and the image of Africa in German schools and textbooks'. *The International Journal of Diversity in Organisations, Communities and Nations*, 10, 1–12.

Martin, J. (2004), 'Positive discourse analysis: solidarity and change'. *Revista Canaria de Estudios Ingleses*, 49, 179–200.

Mbembe, A. (2001), *On the Postcolony*. Berkeley and Los Angeles: University of California Press.

Mignolo, W. D. (2007), 'Delinking: the rhetoric of modernity, the logic of coloniality and the grammar of de-coloniality'. *Cultural Studies*, 21(2–3), 449–514.

Mudimbe, V. Y. (1988), *The Invention of Africa: Gnosis, Philosophy, and the Order of Knowledge*. Bloomington and Indianapolis: Indiana University Press.

Nancy, J.-L. (2010), *The Truth of Democracy*. New York: Fordham University Press.

NewsTalk&Text Research Group (2011), 'Towards a Linguistics of News Production'. *Journal of Pragmatics*, 43(7), 1843–52.

Opitz, M., Oguntoye K. and Schultz, D. (eds) (1991), *Showing Our Colors: Afro-German Women Speak Out*. Amherst. MA: University of Massachusetts Press.

Phillips, L. and Jørgensen M. W. (2002), *Discourse Analysis as Theory and Method*. London: Sage.

Poenicke, A. (2003), *Afrika Realistisch Darstellen: Diskussionen und Alternativen zur Gängigen Praxis – Schwerpunkt Schulbücher*. Sankt Augustin: Konrad-Adenauer-Stiftung.

*Publishers Weekly* (2013), 'The world's 60 largest book publishers'. *Publishers Weekly*, 19 July. Available at: http://www.publishersweekly.com/pw/by-topic/industry-news/financial-reporting/article/58211-the-global-60-the-world-s-largest-book-publishers-2013.html (accessed 1 June 2014).

Quijano, A. (2010), 'Coloniality and modernity/rationality', in W. D. Mignolo and A. Escobar (eds), *Globalization and the Decolonial Option*. London: Routledge, pp. 22–32.

Rancière, J. (1999), *Disagreement: Politics and Philosophy*. Minneapolis: University of Minnesota Press.

Schor, N. (1995), 'This essentialism which is not one: coming to grips with Irigaray', in N. Schor (ed), *Bad Objects*. Durham and London: Duke University Press, pp. 44–60.

Spivak, G. C. (1988), 'Can the subaltern speak?', in C. Nelson and L. Grossberg (eds), *Marxism and the Interpretation of Culture*. Urbana: University of Illinois Press, pp. 271–313.

Stephens, J. (1992), *Language and Ideology in Children's Fiction*. London: Longman.

Torfing, J. (2002), 'Discourse analysis and the post-structuralism of Laclau and Mouffe'. Available at: www.essex.ac.uk/ECPR/publications/eps/onlineissues/autumn2002/research/torfing.htm (accessed 31 March 2006).

Walsh, C. (2009), *Interculturalidad, Estado, Sociedad. Luchas (De)Coloniales de Nuestra Epoca (Interculturalism, State, Society. (De)colonial Struggles of Our Times)*. Quito: Universidad Andina Simón Bolivar-Ediciones Abya-Yala.

—— (2010), 'De-coloniality: decolonial thinking and doing in the andes: a conversation by Walter Mignolo with Catherine Walsh'. *Reartikulacija* #10.

Weiss, G. and R. Wodak, (eds) (2003), *Critical Discourse Analysis: Theory and Interdisciplinarity*. Basingstoke: Palgrave Macmillan.

—— (2008), *Critical Discourse Analysis: Theory and Interdisciplinarity*. Basingstoke: Palgrave Macmillan.

Welt Kompakt (2011), 'Merkel fliegt auf Wirtschafts-Safari'. *Die Welt Kompakt*, 12 July, 7.

White, E. F. (2001), 'Africa on my mind: gender, counter discourse, and African-American nationalism', in D. M. Juschka (ed.), *Feminism in the Study of Religion: A Reader*. London: Continuum, pp. 474–97.

# 17

# Discourse and Communication in the European Union

## A Multi-Focus Perspective of Critical Discourse Studies

*Michał Krzyżanowski*

Örebro University

## 1 Introduction

Discourses of international institutions and organizations were not among the core topics of the 'early' critical discourse analysis. The latter was mainly preoccupied with 'explorations of lexico-grammatical meaning in written and mass-mediated texts' (Blommaert, 2001: 5). It also avoided the more *in situ* explorations of discourses other than those of media or politics and rarely focused on discursive practices of such complex social spaces as national or international organizations.

However, contrary to those earlier tendencies, throughout the early 2000s CDA started to develop into a broader field of research – now often defined as Critical Discourse Studies or CDS (cf. Van Dijk, 2007; Wodak, 2009; cf. also Graham, 2002; Richardson et al., 2013). The latter, while still drawing on some of the CDA's original ideas (e.g. on the interplay of language/discourse and ideology, as well as of their constitutive force in social relations), clearly reaches beyond the traditional 'schools' or 'trends' of the movement (for overview and recent developments, cf. Krzyżanowski, 2010a, 2011a). At the same time, CDS has begun to gradually bridge onto new areas and types of analysis. This started to include complex organizational settings. It also entailed application of analyses which, moving beyond the previous text-only approaches, increasingly involved observation of the processes of 'sites of production and reception of discourse' (Van Dijk, 1991) and their logic in the contexts where social and political agency was often limited and/or concealed.

One of such areas which quite unexpectedly became a major topic in recent work in CDS is the research on discourses in/of the European Union (EU). Developing gradually since the late 1990s, work on the EU discursive and communicative practices has not only become a very prominent field of study within CDS as such but has also turned into one of its key areas of contribution to the wider social-scientific scholarship on the changing politics and institutions of contemporary Europe. This was surely enabled by the fact that, even while still in development, CDS work on the EU discourse has clearly reached beyond the solely linguistic or discourse-analytic inspirations and drew extensively on the input from fields as diverse as those of media and communication studies, anthropology of organizations, anthropology of the EU institutions, political science or political sociology. By the same token, CDS contribution to research on the EU discourses has also solidified a very prominent position of the CDS' Discourse-Historical Approach (cf. Krzyżanowski, 2010a; Reisigl and Wodak, 2009; Wodak, 2001, 2009; Wodak and Krzyżanowski, 2008; Reisigl, this volume), which has recently become one of the trademark areas of CDS, widely acclaimed for its extensive contribution to qualitatively oriented social and political studies (cf. Musolff, this volume; Forchtner, this volume).

The present chapter highlights the development of CDS' interest in Europe's supranational institutional discourse. The latter is viewed here as ranging from communication patterns in the European Union to the ways in which Europe/EU are constructed in contemporary European national milieus. The chapter starts with a brief section explaining why the EU and its institutions are interesting and challenging objects of study for CDS as well as providing a brief contextual account on the key developments in the EU of the 1990s and 2000s. Next, the chapter points to the ontology of interest in the EU within CDS by highlighting the inspirations from within and beyond the broadly understood discourse-analysis. Finally, looking at diversity of EU discursive practices in focus of CDS, and, more specifically, the DHA, the chapter moves to the presentation of key research foci explored so far. It does so by looking at diverse studies which might be grouped according to the different studied discursive practices. Hence, on the one hand, the chapter points to the key foci 'inside' the EU institutions and presents diverse DHA studies performing various discursive ethnographies of Europe's evolving institutional contexts. On the other hand, the chapter looks at the 'outside' discourses of the EU including its 'output' communication modes such as policy and political discourses. Still within the outside perspective, the chapter also highlights CDS' contribution to the extensive body of scholarship on the coverage of the EU and its politics in the European media. The chapter looks at the key CDS works on different topics while it also highlights the development of the CDS approach to the study of EU institutions over the years. It does so while, inasmuch as possible, pointing to some key theoretical and analytical concepts which proved to be central in the explorations of discourse of and about the EU from a CDS perspective.

## 2 European Union and its institutions as objects of study

The European Union is anything but a straightforward and a simple object of study. Today, the EU is a conglomerate of 28 European states which span over more than 4 million square kilometres and count more than 500 million inhabitants. Unmatched in size by any other international organization, the EU is governed by a set of key institutions. These include: The *Council of the EU* (EC)[1] which is the Union's ultimate decision-making and legislative body with some executive powers; the largest and one of the oldest institutions of the European integration – i.e. *the European Commission* (previously known as, inter alia, the 'Commission of the European Communities' and thus often abbreviated as CEC)[2] – which is the EU public administration and the executive power of the Union that oversees the implementation of the EU policies in different fields; and *The European Parliament* (EP),[3] i.e. the only directly-elected EU institution which is (together with the EC) the Union's key legislative power with ability to confirm or remove from office key EU officials.[4] Although the EP now also possesses policy-initiative abilities, the key driving force in EU-policy making is the CEC, which also oversees the correct implementation (and tackles eventual infringements) of EU law across all of the Union's member states in over 15 policy fields.[5] That process is directed by the Commission's 30 plus policy-departments (known as Directorates-General)[6] which also evolve according to the change in European social and economic conditions and with the Union's political priorities (cf. Kassim, 2008). Whilst the CEC remains central in the EU policy-making and implementation, other bodies – namely the Council and the European Parliament – are involved in the legislative process (cf. Pollak and Slominski, 2006, for details).

What poses a particular challenge when studying the EU, its politics and institutions is the fact that unlike many other and rather 'stable' politico-organizational milieus (including international ones like, e.g., the UN), it is a constantly evolving organism whose complexity progressively increases. The EU is also peculiar allowing for the fact that its main political and organizational principles and goals are often put in question and/or under a process of redefinition (cf. Krzyżanowski and Oberhuber, 2007). While, to be sure, since its inception in the 1950 the European integration project has witnessed several transformative periods – which saw it evolving from the European Coal and Steel to the European Economic Community – it appears that the last two decades are a period when the Union is indeed in an on-going transformation. Since the early 1990s, the European Community – at that time rebranded into European Union – has embarked on a project of becoming the world's first supranational polity. The foundations for the development of a political EU were laid in the 1992 Treaty of

Maastricht (in force 1993) which stipulated that the EU should become a political organism and must move beyond the strictly economic aims known from the earlier times of the ECSC/EC (cf. above). Thus, ever since Maastricht, we see a development of the gradual 'politicisation of the EU' (Wiener, 2004) and the making of EU into a supranational democracy of previously unparalleled proportions.

Upon becoming a political rather than solely economic organization, the EU of the 1990s accelerated the development of its governance system and in particular of the ways in which the policies created at the supranational level could be transposed and implemented at the national and regional levels of Europe's multilevel polity. This meant a further solidification of the Union's so-called *multilevel system of governance* based on 'continuous negotiation among nested governments at several territorial tiers – supranational, national, regional and local' (Hooghe and Marks, 2003: 1; cf. also Jessop, 1995; Bache and Flinders, 2004; Held, 2006). Within the said system, the EU has embarked on development of many new policy fields – which now span agriculture to taxation and customs[7] – yet has also become bound by the constant mediation between the aforementioned different levels of governance as well as between the level-specific institutions of different kinds. In such a context, EU politics and policy-making have become characterized by the process of the so-called '*Europeanization*' (see, for example: Featherstone and Radaelli, 2004; Mény et al., 1996; or Green-Cowles et al., 2001; see also Krzyżanowski, 2008) whereby diverse national policy fields underwent a substantial change in the process of their adjustment to the respective areas of the EU policies.

However, further to the demands of Europeanization and policy-related processes, some more general questions about the so-called *democratic deficit of the EU* (see, inter alia Majone, 2005; Follesdal and Hix, 2006; Pollak, 2007; Eriksen, 2009; Nicolaïdis, 2010) started to appear with the accelerated development of the political EU. Those questions undertook the issue of the ever-more complex relationship between the EU supranational (political) system and the broadly perceived European citizenry. The latter remained visibly distant from supranational politics and ever more often displayed Eurosceptic tendencies (cf. Taggart and Szczerbiak, 2008). Debates about the Union's democratic deficit aimed to show that, as such, the EU system is not socially representative and, acting through the omnipresent intermediary of nation – state level, cannot become such either. It must be mentioned that, while unresolved until today, the questions related to the EU's democratic deficit were at the foundation of many politically driven actions which the EU undertook in the first decade of the 2000s. Of those actions, the most notable is surely the drafting and adoption of the European Constitution (for details, see inter alia Krzyżanowski and Oberhuber, 2007, Krzyżanowski, 2010a) which, however, remained non-binding until some of its elements were incorporated into the 2007 Lisbon Treaty which at present regulates the functioning of the EU system.

While becoming a new political creature and furthering its multilevel governance – all encompassed under the term of 'deepening' of the European integration (cf.

Jachtenfuchs, 2002) – in the course of the 1990s and 2000s the EU also underwent a series of enlargements. The latter, often termed as the process of 'widening' the EU (2002), started in 1995 which saw the, by far, last 'Western' Enlargement of the Union by countries such as Austria, Sweden and Finland. However, while the said enlargement saw the Union's incorporation of the said wealthy Northern and Central-European states, an unprecedented big bang occurred in the year of 2004 when ten countries, several post-communist Central- and Eastern-European, joined the Union. After the enlargement of the EU by Cyprus, Czech Republic, Estonia, Hungary, Latvia, Lithuania, Malta, Poland, Slovakia and Slovenia, the 'eastward' enlargement of the EU was eventually completed in 2007 with the accession of Bulgaria and Romania. In 2013, Croatia joined the EU as the 28th member while, at present, the EU has four further official candidate countries including Macedonia and Montenegro.

Summing up, the many aforementioned developments in the EU have changed the character as well as the size of the European Union as a whole. However, perhaps most importantly, they also brought a profound change to the EU institutions that, especially in the aftermath of the 2004 Enlargement, needed to alter their organizational patterns in areas ranging from multilingual communication (cf. Krzyżanowski, 2010a, 2014) to intra- and especially inter-institutional collaboration (cf. Egberg, 2004, 2005; Krzyżanowski and Oberhuber, 2007; Pollak, 2007). However, at the same time, the EU of 28 member states had to quite radically rethink the ways in which it not only communicated and negotiated agency inside its institutional system but also how it presented its work and policies to the extra-institutional actors such as European citizens, international markets or, last but not least, the EU member states. That meant that, unlike previously, the European Union had to gradually rethink its information and communication policies (cf., inter alia, Kassim, 2004, 2008; Krzyżanowski, 2012; Michailidou, 2008; Meyer, 1999) and to start treating many 'outside' discourses about the EU with increased attention and scrutiny. By the same token, while willing to gain legitimacy for its policies and actions, the EU also started to invent many new channels, genres and patterns of communication (cf. Krzyżanowski, 2013, forthcoming) which would help to present its actions and activities to the ever more Eurosceptic citizens of Europe.

# 3  Approaching the EU from a CDS perspective: key inspirations

The aforementioned new challenges of the growing complexity, of size as well as of the increasing political expectations towards the EU, caused many social and political scientists to ask some rather unprecedented questions with regard to

European politics. Of all those questions which the academia posed since the early 2000s probably the most central are the ones concerning *agency* and *identity*, which, to be sure, have also been asked with regard to many other milieus than just those of the EU (cf. Krzyżanowski, 2010a). However, in the EU context, issues of agency and identity have been approached at a variety of levels ranging from those of the internal 'social' construction of the European institutions (cf. e.g. Christiansen et al., 2001; Risse, 2004) to the more macro-level work on identity of the European project as engrained in the call for a pan-European Public Sphere (cf. inter alia, Triandafyllidou, et al., 2009; Schulz-Forberg and Stråth, 2010). And, although proposed within a huge diversity of theoretical and methodological paradigms, the said approaches also pointed to the level of *discourse* as indeed central in understanding the on-going search for and negotiation of agency and identity in EU's complex intra-, inter- and extra-institutional contexts.

It is also from the perspective of agency and identity that CDS (DHA) scholars developed their interest in the EU research. However, here, contrary to some of the political – scientific studies proposed in the late 1990s and early 2000s (cf. above), of particular importance for CDS work was the inspiration taken from a broader field of research known as *Anthropology of the European Union* (cf. Bellier and Wilson, 2000a; cf. also Krzyżanowski, 2011b). Its input would eventually be central to the variety of critical-analytic ethnographic studies on the dynamics of EU institutional discursive practices (cf. below for overview). Contrary to the then prevalent EU-analytical approaches interested mostly in the macro-level inter-institutional logic (cf., inter alia, Egberg, 2004, 2005; for overview, cf. Wiener and Diez, 2004), the EU-anthropological approach forged an actor-oriented and context-dependent approach to the problems of culture and identity within EU institutions and beyond. It sought to 'clarify how the EU and its various institutions and policies are understood and experienced in a variety of localities' (Bellier and Wilson, 2000b: 3). Among the said localities, the EU institutions played a central role in the EU-anthropological research as the microcosms of Europe and as new and constantly evolving contexts in which not only policies for Europe were produced but also in which the political, cultural, linguistic and otherwise understood diversity of Europe was both reflected and, perhaps even more importantly, discursively negotiated. Guided by such interests, several seminal studies were produced by the EU-anthropologists (cf. Krzyżanowski, 2011b for overview) exploring organizational practices in such EU institutions as the European Parliament (cf. Abélès, 1992, 1993) or the European Commission (cf. Abélès, 2000, 2004; Abélès et al., 1993; Bellier, 2000; Shore, 2000). The main way of analysing the Union's culture and identity from an EU-anthropological perspective – eventually to be followed very extensively in EU-oriented CDS research (cf. below) – were by means of extensive fieldwork-based ethnographic methods. They allowed observing how *institutional and organizational cultures*, concepts also central to CDS studies (cf. Krzyżanowski, 2011b and below), were (re)produced 'on the ground' and how, simultaneously, identities of (more and less) powerful actors were negotiated discursively in different instances of political and institutional communication.

In fact, the inspiration taken originally from the EU-anthropological research generally spawned CDS scholars' interest in ethnography as a multi-perspective approach to organizational and institutional practice. Following not only EU anthropologists but also what would eventually develop into anthropology or organizations (cf. Wright, 2007; Ybema et al., 2009) or political ethnography (Schatz, 2009, Yanow, 2009), CDS scholars started to turn to systematic ethnographic analyses helping to situate the discourse of the EU institutions in various organizational practices and at various levels of hierarchical structures of the EU polity. While doing so, CDS researchers also embraced the new developments in ethnography by arguing that the latter should move beyond its rather limited, original remit (constrained by certain pre-determined 'field' or 'context'). They argued that ethnography should cease 'to be associated with its objects of study (that is, with "who" or "what" is studied) and become a designate of a certain research perspective (thus, related to a certain "how")' (Oberhuber and Krzyżanowski, 2008: 182). In doing so, CDS scholars have aligned themselves with the new turn in ethnographic research developing in the 1990s and 2000s often termed 'reflexive ethnography' (cf. Davies, 1999) or 'critical ethnography' (Brewer, 2000). In line with those trends, ethnography has aimed to be seen as 'not one particular method of data-collection but a style of research that is distinguished by its objectives, which are to understand the social *meanings* and activities of people in a given "field" or setting' (2000: 11; emphasis in the original). Hence, while still consisting of fieldwork and related techniques of context-sensitive explorations (cf. below), ethnography in the CDS perspective evidenced in its work on the EU has become a designate of a complex and ordered, though not necessarily linear, analytical process (see Wodak et al., 2012 for examples). At the same time, ethnography has been seen as a certain way of conducting research practice which allows triangulating between different stages of analytical analysis and between different sets of data (different genres) gathered in different interrelated social, or, in the case of the EU, organizational and institutional contexts (2012).

While the inspiration taken from the multiple, actor-oriented anthropological and ethnographic views on practices in the EU was central to the development of CDS work on (policies and politics of) European integration, it must also be noted that some of the crucial concepts of CDS' research were derived from the more intra-disciplinary studies proposed within linguistics and the broadly understood discourse studies. Here, quite unusually for the CDA/CDS approaches, the major inspiration came from several conversational-analytic (CA) approaches to organizational discourse (cf. Muntigl et al., 2000, for extensive overview). Probably the key ideas came from the CA-works on the so-called '*talk at work*' (cf, especially, Drew and Heritage, 1992) which looked at the dynamics of institutionally and organizationally conditioned workplace interactions. Those studies helped CDS' research to acquire the necessary analytical language indispensable for its interest in how identity and agency are linguistically and discursively shaped in the EU contexts.

However, the CA perspective on micro-level and mostly face-to-face organizational interactions seemed rather limited for the multilevel approaches favoured by CDS and DHA (for earlier version, cf. Wodak, 1996), especially allowing for the latter's commitment to a multilevel micro-macro mediating definition of context (cf. Wodak, 2001; Reisigl and Wodak, 2009). However, the said CA studies have pointed the eventual CDS interest to the key features conditioning dynamics of discourse in the organizational settings. Of these features, Muntigl, Weiss and Wodak (2000: 5) list 'participants' orientations to goals, constraints on contributions, and specific inferential frameworks' as central. They argue that, in the complex EU contexts, the conditioning of discourse takes place similarly to other organizational settings constantly open to negotiations of 'agency' and 'structure' (or, as CA-rooted studies would have it, to 'goals' and 'constraints'; cf. above). By the same token, the fact of pointing to the salience of the 'inferential frameworks' (2000) helps turning interest to the variety of discursive and non-discursive, organizational and extra-organizational resources which are combined and enacted in discourses within as complex a setting as that of the EU. This peculiar 'internal' multiplicity of discourse is also the reason why the early CDS work on the EU has drawn quite extensively from works arguing for a multi-semiotic and multimodal approach to discourse (see, in particular, Kress and Van Leeuwen, 1996; cf. also Streeck, 1996). Recognizing the necessity of combining various forms of semiosis in discourses of organizations, early CDA research on the EU argued that the eventual analyses of (supranational) discursive organizational practices must take full account on the variety of forms and modes of signification which are at the foundation of the multifarious social and political meanings entangled in the EU discourses.

While the aforementioned areas were the major inspiration for CDS's interest in discursive practices in/of/at the EU, it must be mentioned that many further fields of social and political scientific research on the European Union were crucial to CDS studies. Here, one definitely needs to mention the few 'early' works on language of the European Union (cf., inter alia, Born and Schütte, 1995) which constituted some of the first attempts to not only analyse 'output' texts of the European Union but also show and scrutinize the ways in which those texts are produced and (re)produced inside the EU-institutional contexts. In a similar vein, the CDS research on the media and national-political perceptions of the EU (cf. below) was strongly influenced by diverse studies on the so-called European Public Sphere which were developed within media and communication as well as political studies in the late 1990s and early 2000s (cf. inter alia, Eder and Kantner, 2002; Fossum and Schlesinger, 2007; Kielmansegg, 1996; Koopmans and Erbe, 2004; Risse and Van De Steeg, 2003; Statham and Gray, 2005; Trenz and Eder, 2004).

# 4  Discourses of and about the EU: An inside-outside perspective of CDS

## 4.1  The inside perspective: Discursive ethnographies of the EU institutions

Entitled *European Union Discourses on Unemployment* (cf. Muntigl et al., 2000), the first major CDS work on discursive practices of the EU provided an impressive range of studies which, all in all, aimed to scrutinize the EU from the inside by means of discourse-ethnographic research of institutional milieus as diverse as those of the European Parliament or the much more short-term Competitiveness Advisory Group. Among the central findings of the work by Muntigl, Weiss and Wodak were those which showed that, quite similar to other politico-organizational contexts (e.g. at the national level), the EU institutions tend to be based on a very peculiar form of institutional self-reproduction or 'autopoiesis' (Maturana and Varela, 1980; Luhmann, 1995). In line with the latter, especially middle-range parts of the EU institutional system produced very few new social or political meanings. Instead they were focused on the constant reproduction of ideas and views originating from previous actions or coming from interest groups and power loci located 'higher' in the organizational hierarchy. This, as shown by the authors, was very well reflected in the policy and other output texts of the EU which drew on excessive amounts of intertextuality and focused much more on co-referencing other texts and (in most cases, past) organizational actions rather than on performing the discursive action at hand. By the same token, the process pointed to the ways in which such autopoietic and inherently discursive tendency might be central to patterns of power-reproduction in organizational contexts. As shown by Muntigl, Weiss and Wodak, while seemingly harmless, the discursive autopoiesis of the EU institutions serves very well the many powerful interest groups which can thus influence the shape of policy and other ideas and actions. At the same time, though resting on on-going debate and deliberation – or a form of a seemingly open discourse – EU institutional practice is in fact a multilevel process which very often limits the agency of different actors while making place for ideas originating in sites of organizational power.

While the work by Muntigl, Weiss and Wodak is acclaimed for its aforementioned critical 'inside' approach to EU discourse (which, by the way, also extends onto several related studies; cf. e.g. Wodak, 2003, 2004), it is vital that the study has also set foundations for discourse-ethnographic studies of the EU for the years to come. Its main agenda-setting contribution was dual. On the one hand, it developed a set of key methods of ethnographically informed discourse analysis of the EU ranging from those pertaining to fieldwork to different linguistic approaches (e.g. based on systemic-functional linguistics or CDA) and to the co-construction and intertextuality in EU discourse. On the other hand, it introduced some of the salient interpretive concepts which would become central for many subsequent explorations. Of those, the pivotal one was that of *organizational practices* which helped the authors conceptualize the relationships between institutional discourses and the processes of on-going, dynamic self-organization of an institution. As was suggested by Muntigl, Weiss and Wodak:

> Placing the focus of organisations on the organisation of social interaction requires an in-depth understanding of the kinds of practices that enable and constrain this day-to-day organising process. These *organisational (discursive) practices* make use of numerous resources in producing and reproducing the organisation.
>
> (Muntigl, et al., 2000: 5; my emphasis)

Drawing extensively on the research agenda set out by the aforementioned study, a work by Krzyżanowski and Oberhuber (2007) furthered CDS' approach to EU-institutional discourse by looking at, inter alia, the questions of discursive construction of legitimacy and identity of the Union in the early 2000s. Having studied the widely debated 2002–3 European Convention as an example of an EU-institutional body supposed to lay out the common vision for a democratic EU in the new millennium, the authors looked at how EU political and institutional identity was constructed from a diversity of views and opinions which were rarely channelled into a coherent, collective discourse. As the authors argued, the proof of such a lack of common discursive vision for the future EU was clearly visible in the eventual outcome of the European Convention – that is in the highly ambiguous Draft Treaty Establishing a Constitution for Europe (2003). The latter, instead of laying out a clear and comprehensive idea for the reform of the EU institutions, concerned many secondary issues which were not in the spotlight of EU citizens. Also, the discursive 'practices for drawing up this document in the context of the Convention were deeply at odds with the kind of open process of reflexive self-formation that the constitutional reference suggested' (Krzyżanowski and Oberhuber, 2007: 16).

As Krzyżanowski and Oberhuber argued, while the increasing complexity of the EU has made the combination of (critical) discourse analysis and ethnography a necessity when studying long-standing EU institutions (EP or CEC), it became indispensable when researching such short-lived organizational contexts like the European Convention. As evidenced in the said study, the European Convention as well as other short-lived and internally diversified EU institutional organisms had immense tendency for latent channelling of discursively shaped and sustained power structures. These, as was shown, could be reproduced with greater ease allowing for the fact that, while governed by well-experienced European politicians and skilful organizational officials, those bodies consisted to a large extent of inexperienced members who, in their discourse, often accounted for their institutional activity as the process of 'learning' rather than of 'acting' or 'doing'. At the same time, the ethnographic approach taken by the authors also allowed tracing how the much diversified communication patterns in such institutional bodies as the Convention increase mechanisms of control and allow experienced power-players to channel both internal and external institutional discourse in line with their views and political opinions.

Drawing on the insights and experiences from the aforementioned study, the authors (cf. also Oberhuber and Krzyżanowski, 2008) have elaborated further the DHA-based discourse-ethnographic approach to the EU institutions. As the key features of the approach (cf. Krzyżanowski and Oberhuber, 2007: 21–3 for the full original version; cf. Krzyżanowski, 2011b for the most recent account), the authors listed: problem-orientation, openness and eclecticism in choosing and following different problem-specific theories and methodologies, and a strong devotion to fieldwork and ethnography as the key ways of conducting research and triangulating between different types of material. In fact, by following the last claim, the authors also followed the long-term call of the DHA (initiated by Wodak, 2001) to study 'multiple spaces and genres' at different hierarchical levels of the social – or, in this case, organizational – context at hand. In doing so, the authors also followed the DHA's multi-level approach to context (cf. Reisigl and Wodak, 2001, 2009; Wodak, 2001) which allows mediating between intra and inter-textual as well as local and wider socio-historical conditions of discourse.

CDS' unique approach to the 'inside' research on EU discourses was further elaborated in Wodak's (2009) seminal study on *The Discourse of Politics in Action*. Though including both EU-related and other analyses, the volume by Wodak offered a very intriguing analysis of everyday practices of members of the European Parliament (EP). In her study, Wodak argues that European institutions are riddled by a peculiar internal heterogeneity which, just like contemporary politics in general, is constructed at two levels or, more specifically, on two planes. Wodak characterizes those in a Goffmanian fashion by reintroducing the concepts of '*frontstage*' and '*backstage*' to show how these are, indeed, often incompatible and how the almost solely PR-like practices of the political frontstage are often radically different from everyday 'doing' and wheeling-and-dealing of politics on the backstage. As Wodak argues, however, the evidence from diverse contexts including, very prominently, institutions of the EU, shows that both of those planes must be treated as crucial to today's politico-institutional practice. Hence, when analysing the latter, one must take into account the frontstage expressions and backstage constructions of discourses and ideologies.

In her study, Wodak looks at the EU frontstage – backstage interaction while conducting research at the EP. There, the author, developing a very efficient technique of ethnographic shadowing combined with discursive/textual analysis, points to a growing diversity of factors which contribute to the EU-internal heterogeneity of ideas about Europe in general, and to the self-understanding of the aim and purpose of the EU institutions in particular. As Wodak argues, throughout Europe, 'hegemonic visions of *one* European identity and *one* European public sphere are being challenged' (Wodak, 2009: 62, original emphasis) and, accordingly, there exists a growing need – particularly visible at the supranational level of EU institutions (such as the EP) – to:

acknowledge the many national traditions which override transnational policies, [. . .] to include the complexity of languages, frames, national *Weltanschauungen*, national socialisation patterns of MEPs, the national recontextualisation of European policies, issues of ethnicity, religion, and gender, and so forth.

(2009)

As Wodak continues, the growing internal heterogeneity of the EU institutions can be best explored by looking at the discourses and practices of those who make up those institutions, i.e. their members, officials, etc. Wodak argues that, already at the macro-level, the overall supranational discourse of the EU's self-definition is riddled by a set of deep-seated contradictions. However, according to the author, it is particularly at the micro-level of everyday 'backstage' practices and doings of the members of the EU institutions – such as the Members of the EP (or MEPs) – that we can observe a huge diversity of their discursive constructions of identities, identifications and affiliations. As Wodak argues, the diversity of all those aspects points to the fact that, as such, EU institutions will always remain at the cross-section of national interests (of member states) and, mainly institutional, supranational tendencies and aspirations. Thus, the discursive practices of constructing their own identities by members of the EU institutions must also display huge heterogeneity and point to the, indeed, multiple character of the identities of EU politicians/officials.[8]

Returning to the material from fieldworks conducted in the early 2000s, Krzyżanowski (2010a, 2011b) revisited the studies on the organizational cultures of long- and short-term institutional bodies initiated with the works on the 2002–3 European Convention (cf. above). Revising his earlier analyses of ethnography and interviews at the Convention, Krzyżanowski (2010a) refined the DHA approach to context widely applied to the earlier work on discursive ethnographies of the EU. As he claimed, while the usual multi-level definition of context in DHA emphasizes the multi-level character of discourses and functioning of discourses in as complex spaces as those of the EU, the DHA's traditional approach lacks the focus on agency of different actors and their impact in the process of social construction of contexts (cf. Wodak, 1996, for a similar concern expressed in the earlier DHA approaches to ethnography). Hence, arguing for a more actor-oriented and agency-based definition of context, Krzyżanowski (2010a: 78ff) claimed that, when analysing the EU institutions, one must allow for the simultaneous (social) co-construction of discourses and contexts and avoid danger of reifying the frontiers between the discursive and the non-discursive. Heeding this call, the author turned to the recent ideas on 'context' provided by van Dijk (2008: x), who argued that:

Contexts are thus not some kind of objective condition or direct cause, but rather (inter)subjective constructs designed and ongoingly updated in interaction by participants as members of groups and communities. If contexts were objective social conditions and constraints, all people in the same social situation would speak in the same way.

As Krzyżanowski shows, van Dijk's more 'agentic' approach to context combined with the multi-level yet somewhat 'static' definition of context in DHA proves very fruitful in EU explorations. As he claimed, the combination helps reveal the on-going interplay between structural and agency-based conditions which proved to be central in diverse accounts of organizational and institutional practice analysed by CDS over the years. As the author also argued, the agency-focused yet structurally-conditioned perception of context helps recognize the fact that the EU organizational and institutional realities often do not exist beyond what is discursively constructed by the key actors. This, in turn, proves yet again the salience of the question of power and the role of key players in defining the sense and purpose for many organizational and institutional EU realities whose everyday procedures, let alone the overall goals, often seem to be obscure and not vital to the bureaucratic-like everyday interactions.

Krzyżanowski's (2010a) study is also recognized for its analyses of discursive constructions of identity displayed in interviews with members of the European Convention. His analysis underlines the very heterogeneous, multifarious and actor-specific character of discursive constructions of European identities in supranational politico-institutional contexts. As the author shows, the discourse displayed in the analysed interviews encompasses a set of diverse – if not outright contradictory – visions and conceptions of Europe/the EU. As was shown in the study, practically each of the analysed interviewees presented different visions and conceptions on the future of the EU. Those visions were based on a significantly independent constellation of arguments allowing the speakers to construct their European identities within the process of the promulgation of the features of discourse which were both individually conditioned (personal experience, previous involvement in EU politics, etc.) and collectively typical (e.g. institutionally or nationally specific visions, etc.). As Krzyżanowski also showed, the identity discourses of members of the European Convention rested on a very peculiar 'EU-Europe conceptual puzzle' (cf. 2010a) which, stemming from EU external discourses of the late 1990s and 2000s, created a huge ambivalence on the relationship between geographical 'Europe' and institutional 'EU' while fuelling insecurity about their common goals for the future.

Following the more agency-oriented line of thinking about discourse and context in the EU institutions, Krzyżanowski (2011b) approached their internal (institutional, national, linguistic) heterogeneity from the point of view of how various institutional cultures and their continuity are constructed. Working, yet again, on the example of the European Convention, the author introduced the concept of institutional linearities and, by using a discourse-ethnographic analysis, analysed the varied discursive displays of institutional knowledge and agency that are helping produce new and/or reproduce old institutional and organizational cultures. Looking at how, in their discourses, members of the European Convention construct identifications with different institutions and other entities (incl. their countries of origin, regions, etc.), Krzyżanowski pointed to the importance of discursive processes of institutional socialization and experience in building dynamics of institutional identities and allegiances of members of those institutions. He drew extensively on the concept of *institutional immersion* – called, in line with Anthropology of the EU, *engrenage* (cf. Abélès, 2000, 2004) – and showed that the process of socializing individual officials into a set of institutionally specific practices and schemas eventually assures the linearity of those institutions. However, the discursive construction of those linearities is often based on individual/collective imaginaries of Europeanness, rather than on pronounced awareness of institutional past and future. At the same time, the *engrenage* proves to be a display of the inequality which often lies at the foundations of different EU-institutional bodies. There, as the research shows, those coming from powerful supranational elements of the EU (e.g. the EC or the EP) are often far more successful than, e.g., politicians not socialized in the EU whose voices are often silenced in/through a variety of institutional procedures.

The so far final stage of CDS 'inside' research on European Union discourses took place in the tradition of discourse-ethnographic explorations developed since the early 2000s. While, as previously (cf. above), the focus of the most recent research is also on the role of discourse and communication in shaping the supranational EU-institutional spaces, the special interest of the recent works revolves around EU's multilingualism. Drawing on extensive fieldwork and ethnography at the European Parliament and the European Commission conducted in the final years of the first decade of the 2000s, Wodak, Krzyżanowski and Forchtner (2012) have looked at the dynamics of multilingual communication in the EU contexts while taking into account the different dynamics of those practices at different levels of institutional hierarchies. Further to that, they also analysed differences between semi-official communication (at the EP) and internal 'everyday' communication (at the CEC) illustrating how EU institutions practise multilingualism in their professional everyday work in a context-dependent way.

The most recent discourse-ethnographic work on the EU has in fact seen a turn towards, one may say, the more socio-linguistic areas of interest – such as, e.g., the role of code-switching – which, however, have been explored in the usual multi-level context characteristic of CDS' and DHA's EU-related research. In their study analysing observations of mono- and multilingual meetings at the EP and CEC tied with semi-structured interviews of those institutions' key officials, Wodak, Krzyżanowski and Forchtner have revealed that what can be observed in the EU contexts is 'a *continuum of (more or less) multilingual practices* which are highly *context-dependent* and which serve a range of manifest and latent functions' (2012: 180). Thus, contrary to the earlier (and largely non-ethnographic) work on languages in the EU (cf. Wright, 2000; Phillipson, 2003), CDS' researchers have shown that, in fact, the EU-based institutional interactions cannot be approached from the point of view of ideal models of mono- or multilingualism but instead need to be examined with a recognition of inherent multiplicity of communicative functions rooted at the intersection of individual and collective multilingualisms. As the authors have also emphasized (to a large extent in line with the previous discourse-ethnographic research), power must be seen as an omnipresent factor of supranational institutional interactions. As power becomes salient at many levels of multilingual practices as 'access to the floor, choice of language, choice of topic, and regulation of the macro-flow of interactions' (2012), the recognition of its salience (yet again) becomes pivotal in understanding the communication inside the EU.

## 4.2  The outside perspective I: Discourses of EU policies and politics

The presented CDS body of research on the 'inside' discourses of the EU is to some extent matched by a set of analyses of discourses of EU politics (and politicians) as well as of the EU policies. This line of research has been, in fact, a continuation of much earlier DHA studies of national political discourses (cf. Wodak, 1996 for overview; cf. also Reisigl and Wodak, 2001; Wodak, 2001) which, contrary to the discursive ethnographies elaborated on above, were developed by DHA (then CDA) scholars already from the late 1980s. This line of interests continued in research conducted simultaneously or subsequently to that on the EU (cf. e.g. Krzyżanowski and Wodak, 2009; Wodak et al., 2013 and above).

The first and indeed central piece of CDS research on EU political discourse was conducted in the early 2000s with a view to scrutinizing the ways in which EU politicians developed a new, so-called *speculative discourse about the EU*. Contrary to the previous tendencies, that discourse did not concern EU institutional architecture as much as macro-level ideas about the overall identity and key values of the EU system. Focusing on the speculative talks on Europe of German and French politicians, Weiss (2002), Wodak and Weiss (2004) and Wodak (2010) pointed to the substantial discrepancies in respective visions of the future form and construction of Europe of different politicians (cf. Krzyżanowski 2010a and above for related analyses of EU-internal discourse). The authors have argued for the existence of some key dimensions in speculative discourse about Europe which comprised: *the ideational dimension* (focused on identity, cultural aspects as well as history of the EU), *the organizational dimension* (focused on EU institutions and other modes of 'organizing' Europe) as well as *the standardizing dimension* (focused on normative aspects of the European integration and the search for common values and standards) (Weiss, 2002; Wodak and Weiss, 2004).

According to Weiss and Wodak, the aforementioned dimensions serve as key resources for constructing arguments about the future construction of Europe. They also provide a basis for the discursive construction of political legitimacy of the European project, which, at the period of development of the EU-speculative discourse (i.e. in the early 2000s) found itself in a critical period characterized by questions of its democratic deficit (cf. above). However, as the authors showed, the said discursive search for legitimacy of the EU does not take place in a uniform way and often takes shape according to nationally specific characteristics. And so, the different discursive ideas about the future of Europe are often shaped in line with often expectable national-discursive characteristics. While, for example, in French national discourse, '*legitimation through idea*' is the main concept with Europe being 'primarily a civilisational project, a vision to be realised in the future' (Weiss, 2002: 79), the German perspective deployed mainly '*legitimation through procedure*' which, drawing on the aforementioned organizational dimension of discourse, seems to call for a 'legal-institutional rearrangement of the Union and the reordering of competencies' (2002: 80). As aptly shown in the said studies, unlike what is commonly believed, the supranational European politics is riddled by manifold and sometimes indeed contradictory visions of Europe (such as the French and the German ones). Thus, though often considered a supranational (or 'denationalized') polity, the EU must still cope with many historical – political visions which do not come from the supranational level, but are of a very strongly national – historical provenance.

On the other hand, CDS work on EU policy discourse has focused on diverse topics (areas) of EU activity as well as, therein, on different features of EU policy discourse. In their 2011 research, Krzyżanowski and Wodak studied European Union policies on multilingualism and looked at how discursive analyses thereof can reveal the ontology of the EU's interest in promoting and forging linguistic diversity within and beyond the EU institutions. As the authors showed, the discourse of European Union's multilingualism policy reveals several key tendencies – most prominently that of progressive economization of how Europe's languages are portrayed and argued for – which allows relating the multilingualism-related actions to larger politico-ideological projects of the EU. Here, the authors point to the salience of the 2000 EU Lisbon Strategy which, as an overarching framework for the majority of EU policies since the early 2000s, defined overall goals of European integration from the economic and related perspectives.

A particular virtue of the work by Krzyżanowski and Wodak is located in the fact that, in their study, the authors proposed a new integrative framework for discursive policy analysis linking the approaches of, on the one hand, DHA, with, on the other, analytical tools known from the conceptual history or *Begriffsgeschichte* (cf. Koselleck, 1979, 2002; Åkerstrøm-Andersen, 2003; cf. Krzyżanowski, 2010b for details of this integrated approach). Such a methodological combination allows tracing of the recontextualization of different aspects of EU policy and major EU policy-relevant discourses (on economy, democracy and society, cf. below) and analysing how 'semantic fields' of multilingualism and related concepts changed over the period of development of the Union's respective policy. As the authors argue, a focus on key policy concepts (such as, in the case at hand, multilingualism) allows tracing its discursive change over time while also analysing the dynamics of arguments related to the said concepts. In line with such analysis, one can establish that, increasingly related to the issues of 'skills' or to the political buzzwords such as the 'European knowledge-based economy', a discourse-conceptual analysis of the changing meaning of 'multilingualism' allows tracing its increased economization as well as its role as a hostage to a larger European Union's politico-ideological projects.

In his more general study on the complexities of communication in the EU and the European Public Sphere, Krzyżanowski (2012) also provided analysis of the Union's so-called Communication Policy which was developed since c.2005 in view of the criticism of the EU's inability to communicate its constitutional process to the EU citizenry. Looking in particular at the European Commission's Communication Strategy in the second half of the first decade of 2000s, the author pointed to the fact that, unlike other or previous instances of the Union's information or communication policies, discourses of those at hand became more open in terms of views and ideas. For example, they included different statements on the necessity of constructing a *European Public Sphere* – otherwise, or previously, only heard of in academia (cf. 2012 and Triandafyllidou et al., 2009, for overview) – and recognized its importance for the general rise of public and media interest in European integration.

However, as shown in Krzyżanowski's study, 'while surely fostered in recent years by a variety of actions and policies, the external communication between the EU and the European citizens is still far from being a *fait accompli*' (2012: 208). This mainly results from the structural constraints and from the fact that most of the communication actions and strategies of the EU are very short-lived and, indeed, not far-sighted. They all in all never persist long enough for the European public to become accustomed to certain communication channels and modi and thus do not bring any long-term ailment to the democratic deficiencies in European political communication. On the other hand, even if undertaken, many actions governed by the EU communication policies still remain acts of 'information' rather than 'communication' and do not forge a dialogue between EU polity and the European demos.

Finally, while drawing on the classic apparatus of DHA (cf. Krzyżanowski, 2010a for key elements), Krzyżanowski (2013, forthcoming) has analysed the European Union's recent policy discourse on climate change. In his studies, he has shown that the policy discourse on climate change is a novel policy development which rests on on-going recontextualization of global and international policy frameworks (on climate change) as well as the EU-internal policies and implementation strategies. As he also argued, such a new policy development necessitates more than ever an approach to diachronic analysis of policy discourses which would not only allow their change across time but also their interdependence on discourses originating in different (European and extra-European) spaces. While coping with such multiplicity of the Union's policy discourse on climate change, Krzyżanowski has also argued that, as such, the said policy constitutes a new development in the European Union's long-standing discourses of identity. However, contrary to the recent tendencies in those discourses which in the 2000s have mainly been preoccupied with the EU's internal identity in view of the Union's democratic deficit (cf. above), the discourse of EU climate change policy has strongly reinvigorated the 'global' discourse on the EU identity originally incepted in the 1970s in the situation of the then global oil and economic crisis.

What is also an added value of Krzyżanowski's work on EU policy is the focus on the variety of genres which must be scrutinized when analysing discourses as diverse as those related to, e.g., climate change. As the author argues (cf. Krzyżanowski, 2013 for further details) the recent policy genres can be divided into those of 'the policy' itself as well as those pertaining to 'the policy communication'. While the former encompasses regulations and projects of regulations governing actions and introducing EU-wide measures, the latter supports the 'publicization' of policy and policy-relevant actions by explaining them to the public. As the author shows, the discursive analyses of those genres may reveal a development of discrepancy between discourses which they carry. And so, even if nominally concerning one policy area (i.e. climate change) discourses of policy may often show a change in description of political actions whereas, paradoxically, policy-communication genres, supposed to reflect the policy and its dynamics, would often remain unchanged. Hence, one can also observe a development of a peculiar discursive duality between, on the one hand, discursive construction and prescription of action (within policy discourse) and interpretations of its importance and social, political and economic salience of those actions (within policy-communication discourse).

## 4.3  The outside perspective II: EU in/and discourses of European media

The final area of CDS' contribution to the study of EU discourses concerns analyses and representations of the Union in Europe's national media. It mainly includes studies providing synchronic analyses of media coverage of EU matters which looked at dynamics of media discourses in the period of accelerated European integration of the 1990s and 2000s.[9]

Of the central analyses those surely worth mentioning include a work by Oberhuber et al. (2005) who looked at nationally specific dynamics of media representation of the final stage – and the eventual failure – of the European Union's constitutional process. Focusing on the reporting of the events surrounding and including the 2004 EU Intergovernmental Conference (IGC, called by the Union whenever its new governing treaty is to be debated and adopted), the authors looked at the ways in which the overall failure of the IGC was portrayed and interpreted in different European countries. Analysing reporting in media and public spheres of Austria, France, Germany, Italy, Poland, Spain and the UK, the researchers looked at newspaper coverage in the quality press, to discover whether – in line with the earlier studies on EU political discourses (cf. Weiss, 2002; Wodak and Weiss, 2004; Wodak, 2010 and above) – the reporting of the EU's unfortunate 2004 IGC would also be marred by the diversity of nationally specific interpretations and historically oriented as well as future-bound different visions of the purpose of European integration. As the authors claimed, their study also bore special relevance to the understanding of the democratic logic of construction and re-contextualization of Europe-wide perceptions of EU politics. As they contested, 'for the vast majority of consumers of EU politics, their imaginations and conceptions of the EU are influenced by the reporting of the mass media' (Oberhuber et al., 2005: 263). Thus, the EU reporting may have pivotal importance for creating and instilling different conceptions of the EU among its citizens.

As Oberhuber et al. (2005) showed in their study, the perception of the EU which appears from the national media is in the overwhelming majority of cases negative. As the authors argued, the discourse of the media reporting of the IGC was, in most cases, focused on such issues as: isolated national interests and political personals representing those interests, immense diversity and complexity of the European supranational space, European space as a locus of production and reproduction of detached Euro-elites and, last but not least, the distinction between 'Europe-vision versus Europe-reality' (2005: 260; cf. also Krzyżanowski, 2010a and above for similar features of discourses 'inside' the EU). However, while the authors claimed that the aforementioned features could be seen as to a large extent universal for reporting in different countries, they depicted their combinations as often taking place in nationally specific constellations which help construct related, nationally conditioned arguments. Those arguments comprise, on the one hand, national – historical visions of European integration and, on the other hand, day-to-day national – political features such as, in the case of the 2004 IGC, assessment of the contribution of national politicians to the failure of the constitutional process.

The more recent 'synchronic' CDS studies of media reporting on the EU (cf. Krzyżanowski, 2009a, 2010a; Krzyżanowski and Wodak, 2013) have focused largely on the same area of democratic aspects of media and political communication. They were, however, concerned closely with the issue of Europe's multilingualism and, more specifically, the perceptions of multilingual diversity of the European Union's institutions in Europe's national media. The latter were investigated in several European countries (France, Germany, Poland and the UK) within the broader media framing of the European Union's 2004 Enlargement and, therein, within perceptions of languages and multilingualism as key features of the 'widening' Europe.

As shown in the said studies,

> there exists an immense discrepancy between, on the one hand, descriptions of languages/multilingualism as positive (though clearly cultural, folklore-like) elements of the European cultural space and, on the other hand, the rather negative perception of the increased multilingualism of the EU institutions.
>
> (Krzyżanowski, 2010a: 161)

This discrepancy points to the fact that, as such, multilingualism is seen as an element of Europe's culture which, according to the European media, does not include the EU institutions generally perceived in a negative way, i.e. as complex, distant and elitist. Accordingly, multilingualism of the EU institutions is also seen as too burdensome for Europe, especially in terms of its costs. It is also viewed as not really serving transparency or legitimacy of the European space which, as such, is not viewed as a democratic mirror of the linguistically diverse European geographic and cultural space. Thus, similarly to the European internal-political discourses (cf. Krzyżanowski, 2010a and above), the media discourse about Europe's linguistic diversity is also ridden with the increasing construction of a discrepancy between Europe on the one hand, and the EU on the other. The latter, as shown in the media analyses, suffers from its overtly negative representation in the European media which thus largely contribute to misunderstanding of European politics and to the rise of Eurosceptic tendencies among the European public.

# 5  (Very brief) Conclusions

As evidenced in the outline above, Critical Discourse Studies – and in particular its prominent area of the Discourse-Historical Approach – have contributed immensely to the study of discourse and communication in and of the European Union. The particular contribution of CDS to the study of the EU discursive and communicative practices surely resides in the huge multiplicity of its studies and in the fact that, contrary to many other social and political scientific approaches, the CDS' research has remained problem-oriented as well as open to both theoretical and methodological dialogue. By the same token, CDS' work on the EU remains probably the most wide-ranging of all qualitative approaches to the study of how discourse and communication shape and change contemporary politics of European integration. Indeed, like very few other areas of research, CDS' studies of the EU have retained strong focus on qualitative analysis while also striving to foster diachronic and synchronic explorations as well as comparative analyses across different spaces and genres.

The second and, perhaps, the most salient contribution of CDS to the study of the EU communication resides in its ability to provide a 'micro-macro mediation' (Wodak, 2006) and to link the highlighted 'inside' and 'outside' perspectives on the EU discourse. Thus, as has been shown, CDS has not only been able to follow some of the general interests in the EU research but, while doing so, it has been extremely prolific in relating the 'inside' and 'outside' areas while producing new, including integrative, theoretical and methodological approaches. It has also been able to contribute immensely to the ways in which some of the central social-scientific topics of the late modernity – among them those of 'agency' and 'identity' – are explored in the immensely complex and constantly evolving European institutional and political spaces.

# Notes

1  Cf.: http://www.consilium.europa.eu
2  Cf.: http://ec.europa.eu
3  Cf.: http://www.europarl.europa.eu

**4** Further key EU institutions include: *The Court of Justice of the EU* (http://curia.europa. eu), *The European Court of Auditors*, as well as, since 2009, *The European Central Bank* (http://www.ecb.int).

**5** For details, cf. http://ec.europa.eu/policies/index_en.htm

**6** For details, cf. http://ec.europa.eu/about/ds_en.htm

**7** For details and overview of EU policy areas, see: http://ec.europa.eu/about/ds_en.htm

**8** Although not mentioned here mainly due to its non-ethnographic character, Wodak's work also includes analyses of EU-based online discussion fora about, inter alia, the Union's multilingualism (cf. Wodak and Wright, 2006; Wright and Wodak, 2007). Those studies provided an important insight into how some of the early attempts at communicating the EU with its citizens were based on negotiation of identities in online discourses.

**9** Due to limitations of space this study does not present the CDS' contribution to the diachronic analyses of media discourses about Europe, including the EU. For further details, see Krzyżanowski (2009b, 2011c) and Triandafyllidou et al. (2009).

# References

Abélès, M. (1992), *La Vie Quotidienne au Parlement Européen*. Paris: Hachette.
—— (1993), 'Political anthropology of a transnational institution: the European Parliament'. *French Politics and Society*, 11(1), 1–19.
—— (2000), 'Virtual Europe', in I. Bellier and T.M. Wilson (eds), *An Anthropology of the European Union*. Oxford: Berg, pp. 31–53.
—— (2004), *Identity and Borders: An Anthropological Approach to EU Institutions*. (Twenty First Century Papers No. 4). Milwaukee, WI: University of Wisconsin-Milwaukee.
Abélès, M., Bellier, I. and McDonald, M. (1993), *An Anthropological Approach to the European Commission*. Brussels: The European Commission.
Åkerstrøm-Andersen, N. (2003), *Discursive Analytical Strategies. Understanding Foucault, Koselleck, Laclau, Luhmann*. Bristol: The Policy Press.
Bache, I. and Flinders, M. (eds) (2004), *Multi-Level Governance*. Oxford: Oxford University Press.
Bellier, I. (2000), 'A Europeanised elite? An anthropology of European Commission officials'. *Yearbook of European Studies*, 14, 135–56.
Bellier, I. and Wilson, T. M. (eds) (2000a), *An Anthropology of the European Union*. Oxford: Berg.
—— (2000b), 'Building, imagining and experiencing Europe: institutions and identities in the European Union', in I. Bellier and T. M. Wilson (eds) *An Anthropology of the European Union*. Oxford: Berg, pp. 1–27.
Blommaert, J. (2001), 'Investigating narrative inequality: African asylum seekers' stories in Belgium'. *Discourse & Society*, 12(4), 413–49.
Born, J. and Schütte, W. (1995), *Eurotexte: Textarbeit in Einer Institution der EG*. Tübingen: Gunter Narr.
Brewer, J. D. (2000), *Ethnography*. Buckingham: Open University Press.
Christiansen, T., Jørgensen, K. E. and Wiener, A. (eds) (2001), *The Social Construction of Europe*. London: Sage.

Davies, C. A. (1999), *Reflexive Ethnography*. London: Routledge.

Drew, P. and Heritage, J. (eds) (1992), *Talk at Work: Interaction in Institutional Settings*. Cambridge: Cambridge University Press.

Eder, K. and Kantner, C. (2002), 'Transnationale resonanzstrukturen in Europa. Eine kritik der rede vom öffentlichkeitsdefizit', in M. Bach (ed.), *Die Europäisierung Nationaler Gesellschaften*. Wiesbaden: Westdeutscher Verlag, pp. 306–31.

Egberg, M. (2004), 'An organisational approach to European integration: outline of a complementary perspective'. *European Journal of Political Research*, 43, 199–219.

—— (2005), 'EU institutions and the transformation of European-level politics: how to understand profound change (if it occurs)'. *Comparative European Politics*, 3(1), 102–17.

Eriksen, E.-O. (2009), *The Unfinished Democratization of Europe*. Oxford: Oxford University Press.

Featherstone, K. and Radaelli, C. M. (eds) (2004), *The Politics of Europeanization*. Oxford: Oxford University Press.

Follesdal, A. and Hix, S. (2006), 'Why there is a democratic deficit in the EU: a response to Majone and Moravcsik'. *Journal of Common Market Studies,* 44(3), 533–62.

Fossum, J.-E. and Schlesinger, P. (eds) (2007), *The European Union and the Public Sphere. A Communicative Space in the Making?* London: Routledge.

Graham, P. (2002), 'Critical discourse analysis and evaluative meaning; interdisciplinarity as a critical turn', in G. Weiss and R. Wodak (eds), *Critical Discourse Analysis: Theory and Interdisciplinarity*. Basingstoke: Palgrave Macmillan, pp. 130–59.

Green-Cowles, M., Caporaso, J. A, and Risse, T. (eds) (2001), *Transforming Europe: Europeanization and Domestic Change*. Ithaca, NY: Cornell University Press.

Held, D. (2006), *Models of Democracy* (3rd edn). Cambridge: Polity Press.

Hooghe, L. and Marks, G. (2003), *Unraveling the Central State, But How? Types of Multi-Level Governance*. Vienna: Institute for Advanced Studies.

Jachtenfuchs, M. (2002), 'Deepening and widening integration theory'. *Journal of European Public Policy*, 9(4), 650–7.

Jessop, B. (1995), 'The regulation approach, governance and post-Fordism: alternative perspectives on economic and political change?' *Economy and Society*, 24(3), 307–33.

Kassim, H. (2004), 'A historic accomplishment? The Prodi Commission and administrative reform', in D. G. Dimitrakopoulos (ed.), *The Changing European Commission*. Manchester: Manchester University Press, pp. 33–63.

—— (2008), '"Mission impossible", but mission accomplished: the Kinnock reforms and the European Commission'. *Journal of European Public Policy*, 15(5), 648–68.

Kielmansegg, P. (1996), 'Integration und demokratie', in M. Jachtenfuchs and B. Kohler-Koch (eds), *Europäische Integration*. Opladen: Leske und Budrich, pp. 47–71.

Koopmans, R. and Erbe, J. (2004), 'Towards a European public sphere? Vertical and horizontal dimensions of Europeanized political communication'. *Innovation*, 17(2), 97–118.

Koselleck, R. (1979), *Vergangene Zukunft. Zur Semantik Geschichtlicher Zeiten*. Frankfurt am Main: Suhrkamp.

—— (2002), *The Practice of Conceptual History. Timing History, Spacing Concepts*. Palo Alto, CA: Stanford University Press.

Kress, G. and van Leeuwen, T. (1996), *Reading Images: The Grammar of Visual Design*. London: Routledge.

Krzyżanowski, M. (2008), 'On the Europeanization of identity constructions in Polish political discourse after 1989', in A. Galasińska and M. Krzyżanowski (eds), *Discourse and Transformation in Central and Eastern Europe*. Basingstoke: Palgrave Macmillan, pp. 95–113.

—— (2009a), 'Discourses about enlarged and multilingual Europe: perspectives from German and Polish national public spheres', in P. Stevenson and J. Carl (eds), *Language, Discourse and Identity in Central Europe*. Basingstoke: Palgrave Macmillan, pp. 23–47.

—— (2009b), 'Europe in crisis: discourses on crisis-events in the European press 1956–2006'. *Journalism Studies*, 10(1), 18–35.

—— (2010a), *The Discursive Construction of European Identities. A Multilevel Approach to Discourse and Identity in the Transforming European Union*. Frankfurt am Main: Peter Lang.

—— (2010b), 'Discourses and concepts: interfaces and synergies between *Begriffsgeschichte* and the discourse-historical approach in CDA', in R. de Cillia, H. Gruber, M. Krzyżanowski and F. Menz (eds), *Diskurs – Politik – Identität / Discourse – Politics – Identity. Essays for Ruth Wodak*. Tübingen: Stauffenburg Verlag, pp. 125–37.

—— (ed.) (2011a), *Ethnography and Critical Discourse Analysis* (Special Issue of *Critical Discourse Studies* 8:4). London: Routledge.

—— (2011b), 'Political communication, institutional cultures, and linearities of organisational practice: a discourse-ethnographic approach to institutional change in the European Union'. *Critical Discourse Studies*, 8(4), 281–96.

—— (2011c), 'Towards the historical dynamics of the European public sphere? Searching for 'Europe' and 'European issues' in Polish post-war studies of media contents'. *Culture & Education/Kultura i Edukacja*, 6(85), 25–57.

—— (2012), '(Mis)communicating Europe? On deficiencies and challenges in political and institutional communication in the European Union', in B. Kryk-Kastovsky (ed.). *Intercultural (Mis)Communication Past and Present*. Frankfurt am Main: Peter Lang, pp. 185–213.

—— (2013), 'Policy, policy communication and discursive shifts: analyzing EU policy discourses on climate change', in P. Cap and U. Okulska (eds), *Analyzing Genres in Political Communication: Theory and Practice*. Amsterdam: John Benjamins, pp. 101–34.

—— (2014), 'Multilingual communication in Europe's supranational spaces: developments and challenges in European Union institutions', in J. W. Unger, M. Krzyżanowski and R. Wodak (eds), *Multilingual Encounters in Europe's Institutional Spaces*. London: Bloomsbury Academic, pp. 105–24.

—— (forthcoming), 'International leadership re-/constructed? On the ambivalence and heterogeneity of identity discourses in European Union's policy on climate change'. *Journal of Language and Politics*, 14(1).

Krzyżanowski, M. and Oberhuber, F. (2007), *(Un)Doing Europe: Discourses and Practices of Negotiating the EU Constitution*. Brussels: PIE – Peter Lang.

Krzyżanowski, M. and R. Wodak (2009), *The Politics of Exclusion: Debating Migration in Austria*. New Brunswick, NJ: Transaction Publishers.

—— (2013), 'Dynamics of multilingualism in post-enlargement EU institutions: perceptions, conceptions and practices of EU-ropean language diversity', in A-C. Berthoud, F. Grin and G. Lüdi (eds), *Language Dynamics and Management of Diversity*. Amsterdam: John Benjamins.

Luhmann, N. (1995), *Social Systems*. Stanford, CA: Stanford University Press.

Majone, G. (2005), *Dilemmas of European Integration. The Ambiguities and Pitfalls of Integration by Stealth*. Oxford: Oxford University Press

Maturana, H. R. and Varela, F. J. (1980), *Autopoiesis and Cognition: The Realization of the Living*. Dordrecht: Kluver.

Mény, Y., Muller, P. and Quermonne, J.-L. (eds) (1996), *Adjusting to Europe: The Impact of the European Union on National Institutions and Policies*. London: Routledge.

Meyer, C. (1999), 'Political legitimacy and the invisibility of politics: exploring the European Union's communication deficit'. *Journal of Common Market Studies*, 37(4), 617–39.

Michailidou, A. (2008), 'Democracy and new media in the European Union: communication or participation deficit?' *Journal of Contemporary European Research*, 4 (4), 346–68.

Muntigl, P., Weiss, G. and Wodak, R. (2000), *European Discourses on Un/employment. An Interdisciplinary Approach to Employment Policy-Making and Organizational Change*. Amsterdam: John Benjamins.

Nicolaïdis, C. (2010), 'The JCMS Annual Review Lecture – sustainable integration: towards EU 2.0?' *Journal of Common Market Studies*, 48 (Annual Review), 21–54.

Oberhuber, F. and Krzyżanowski, M. (2008), 'Discourse analysis and ethnography'. in R. Wodak and M. Krzyżanowski (eds) *Qualitative Discourse Analysis in the Social Sciences*. Basingstoke: Palgrave Macmillan, pp. 182–203.

Oberhuber, F., Bärenreuter, C., Krzyżanowski, M., Schönbauer H. and Wodak R. (2005), 'Debating the European Constitution: on representations of Europe/EU in the press?' *Journal of Language and Politics*, 4(2), 227–71.

Phillipson, R. (2003), *English-Only Europe?* London: Routledge.

Pollak, J. (2007), *Repräsentation ohne Demokratie. Kollidierende Modi der Repräsentation in der Europäischen Union*. Vienna: Springer.

Pollak, J. and Slominski, P. (2006), *Das Politische System der EU*. Vienna: UTB.

Reisigal, M. and Wodak, R. (2001), *Discourse and Discrimination. Rhetorics of Racism and Anti-Semitism*. London: Routledge.

—— (2009), 'The discourse-historical approach (DHA)'. in R. Wodak and M. Meyer (eds), *Methods of Critical Discourse Analysis* (2nd rev. edn). London: Sage, pp. 87–121.

Richardson, J., Krzyżanowski, M., Machin, D. and Wodak, R. (eds) (2013), *Advances in Critical Discourse Studies*. London: Routledge.

Risse, T. (2004), 'Social constructivism and European integration', in A. Wiener and T. Diez (eds), *European Integration Theory*. Oxford: Oxford University Press, pp. 159–76.

Risse, T. and van de Steeg, M. (2003), *An Emerging European Public Sphere? Empirical Evidence and Theoretical Clarifications*. Paper presented at the Conference on 'Europeanization of Public Spheres: Political Mobilisation, Public Communication and the EU', Wissenschaftszentrum Berlin, 20–22 June.

Schatz, E. (ed.) (2009), *Political Ethnography: What Immersion Contributes to the Study of Power*. Chicago, IL: The University of Chicago Press.

Shore, C. (2000), *Building Europe: The Cultural Politics of European Integration*. London: Routledge.

Statham, P. and Gray, E. (2005), 'The public sphere and debates about Europe in Britain. Internalized and conflict-driven? *Innovation*, 18(1), 61–81.

Streeck, J. (1996), 'How to do things with things: objets trouvés and symbolization'. *Human Studies*, 19, 365–84.

Taggart, P. and Szczerbiak, A. (eds) (2008), *Opposing Europe? The Comparative Party Politics of Euroscepticism* (vols 1 and 2). Oxford: Oxford University Press.

Trenz, H.-J. and Eder, K. (2004), 'The democratising dynamics of the European public sphere: towards a theory of democratic functionalism'. *European Journal of Social Theory*, 7(1), 5–25.

Triandafyllidou, A., Wodak, R. and Krzyżanowski, M. (eds) (2009), *The European Public Sphere and the Media: Europe in Crisis*. Basingstoke: Palgrave Macmillan.

Van Dijk, T.A. (1991), 'The interdisciplinary study of news as discourse', in K. Bruhn-Jensen and N. Jankowski (eds), *Handbook of Qualitative Methods in Mass Communication Research*. London: Routledge, pp. 108–20.

—— (2007), 'Editor's introduction: the study of discourse – an introduction', in T.A. Van Dijk (ed.), *Discourse Studies* (vol. 1). London: Sage, pp. xix–xlii.

—— (2008), *Discourse and Context: A Sociocognitive Approach*. Cambridge: Cambridge University Press.

Weiss, G. (2002), 'Searching for Europe: the problem of legitimisation and representation in recent political speeches on Europe'. *Journal of Language and Politics*, 1(1), 59–83.

Wiener, A. and Diez, T. (eds) (2004), *European Integration Theory*. Oxford: Oxford University Press.

Wodak, R. (1996), *Disorders of Discourse*. London: Longman.

—— (2001), 'The discourse-historical approach', in R. Wodak and M. Meyer (eds), *Methods of Critical Discourse Analysis* (1st edn). London: Sage, pp. 63–95.

—— (2003), 'Multiple identities: the roles of female parliamentarians in the EU Parliament', in J. Holmes and M. Meyerhoff (eds), *The Handbook of Language and Gender*. London: Blackwell, pp. 671–99.

—— (2004), 'National and transnational identities: European and other identities oriented to in interviews with EU officials', in R. Hermann, M. Brewer and T. Risse. *Transnational Identities: Becoming European in the EU*. Lanham, MD: Rowman and Littlefield, pp. 97–129.

—— (2006), 'Mediation between discourse and society: assessing cognitive approaches in CDA'. *Discourse Studies*, 8(1), 179–90.

—— (2009), *The Discourse of Politics in Action*. Basingstoke: Palgrave Macmillan.

—— (2010), '"Communicating Europe": analyzing, interpreting, and understanding multilingualism and the discursive construction of transnational identities', in A. Duszak, J, House and Ł. Kumięga (eds), *Globalization, Discourse, Media: In a Critical Perspective*. Warsaw: Wydawnictwa Uniwerystetu Warszawskiego, pp. 17–60.

Wodak, R. and Krzyżanowski, M. (eds) (2008), *Qualitative Discourse Analysis in the Social Sciences*. Basingstoke: Palgrave Macmillan.

Wodak, R., and G. Weiss (2004), 'Visions, ideologies and utopias in the discursive construction of European identities: organising, representing and legitimising Europe', in M. Pütz, J.A. Neff-van Aertselaer and T. A. van Dijk (eds), *Communicating Ideologies: Language, Discourse and Social Practice*. Frankfurt am Main: Peter Lang, pp. 225–52.

Wodak, R. and Wright, S. (2006), 'The European Union in cyberspace. Multilingual democratic participation in a virtual public sphere?' *Journal of Language and Politics*, 5(2), 251–75.

Wodak, R., Krzyżanowski, M. and Forchtner, B. (2012), 'The interplay of language ideologies and contextual cues in multilingual interactions: language choice and code-switching in European Union institutions'. *Language in Society*, 41(2), 157–86.

Wodak, R., KhosraviNik, M. and Mral, B. (eds) (2013), *Rightwing Populism in Europe: Politics and Discourse*. London: Bloomsbury Academic.

Wright, S. (2000), *Community and Communication: The Role of Language in Nation-State Building and European Integration*. Clevedon: Multilingual Matters.

—— (ed.) (2007), *The Anthropology of Organizations*. London: Routledge.

Wright, S. and Wodak, R. (2007), 'The European Union in cyberspace: democratic participation via online multilingual discussion boards', in B. Danet and S. C. Herring (eds), *The Multilingual Internet. Language, Culture, and Communication Online*. Oxford: Oxford University Press, pp. 385–407.

Yanow, D. (2009), 'Organizational ethnography and methodological angst: myths and challenges in the field'. *Qualitative Organizational Research Methods*, 4(2), 186–99.

Ybema, S., Yanow, D., Wels, H. and Kamsteeg, F. (eds) (2009), *Organizational Ethnography: Studying the Complexities of Everyday Life*. London: Sage.

# 18

# The Discursive Technology of Europeans' Involvement EU *Culture* and Community of Practice

## Elena Magistro
## University of Bologna

## 1 Introduction

As agreed on by critical discourse analysts of all persuasions (see Introduction, this volume, for an overview of different approaches), discourse is a mode of social practice. This view brings together two main senses of discourse:

> One is predominant in language studies: discourse as social action and interaction, people interacting together in real social situations. The other is predominant in post-structuralist social theory [. . .]: a discourse as a social construction of reality, a form of knowledge.
>
> (Fairclough, 1995b: 18)

As for language, Critical Discourse Analysis (CDA) builds on Halliday's systemic-functionalist approach, theorizing that language systems and language use are not disjointed and self-sufficient entities but are deeply interrelated to fulfil a social function. Halliday (1973) explained that 'language is as it is because of its function in the social structure' and claimed that the meanings conveyed through language can provide information on the 'social foundations' of language itself (65). As for social theory, CDA draws inspiration from the theories of Foucault and Bourdieu. Foucault (1977) proposed an innovative conceptualization of power by claiming that power relations in society are sanctioned and shaped by discourse: power is a dynamic entity subject to evolution on the basis of the discursive practices of social actors. In line with this view, Bourdieu (1991) postulated the key notion of 'habitus': according to Bourdieu, it is by habit that a given status quo, representation of the world or social trajectory imposed by the dominant culture is interiorized and perpetuated by the individual within the social community. In this perspective as well, dominant cultures and power relations are not static but dynamic; nonetheless, they are considered difficult to change because the individuals within a community enjoy limited freedom of deviation from the prevailing practices and beliefs.

Against this conceptual background, it emerges how discourse can have the power to affect and control social dynamics and conditions. In the words of Bourdieu this corresponds to:

> a [symbolic] power of constituting the given through utterances, of making people see and believe, of confirming or transforming the vision of the world and, thereby, action on the world and thus the world itself, an almost magical power which enables one to obtain the equivalent of what is attained through force.
>
> (Bourdieu, 1991: 170)

Hence, discourse can be seen as a socially performative tool in that it is able to produce actual change in society, bringing about the re-signification of ideas, practices, power relations or identities.[1] The very interaction between discourse and identity shall be the focus of this chapter.

## 2 Aim of this chapter

This chapter is about discourse produced by the European Union (EU) and how it plays a part in establishing a sense of European collective identification (cf. Koller, this volume).[2] My discussion shall develop following an inductive approach: it departs from empirical data on EU discourse drawn from the main studies available at the time of writing and leads to general considerations on the rhetorical modes of EU communication and on its capacity to influence identity and social change in the EU community. More specifically, I intend to adopt a meta-empirical stance: from the perspective of Critical Discourse Analysis (CDA), I shall report on and systematize what has been empirically observed, up to the present, on EU discourse in diverse forms and contexts.

To begin with, I shall review analytical studies conducted on multimodal discourse[3] (cf. Van Leeuwen, this volume) produced by the EU that provide evidence of an identity-shaping effort or behaviour on the part of the organization. When I say *discourse produced by the EU* I mean discourse produced by EU institutions, agencies and representatives (i.e. EU Commissioners), as well as by officials directly involved in EU institutional activity (i.e. EU civil servants, members of EU panels and committees). I shall exclude discourse that is about the European Union but that originates from non-EU sources (e.g. national media, academic institutes, the general public, etc.). Albeit telling of identity dynamics, non-EU discourse cannot be indicative of the organization's communicative stance and of its own contribution towards consolidating a sense of European belonging.

The empirical studies discussed are authored by scholars not only in the field of linguistics and discourse analysis but also in other disciplines (e.g. anthropology, political science, sociology, critical theory, etc.). This explains why these studies draw from a variety of analytical approaches: from the rhetoric analysis of the *acquis communautaire*[4] to the survey of EU-run virtual fora and information centres, from the semiotic study of visuals appearing in EU publications of various genres to ethnographic observations within EU bodies and institutions – i.e. official and internal speeches, statements, interviews and debates (among or within EU committees, advisory groups, directorates and so forth).

This list is neither exhaustive nor fully representative of the vast array of approaches and disciplines investigating the interface between EU discourse and European identity. Within the constraints of summarizing in a few paragraphs the main empirical research conducted in this area, I had to omit other contributions that are extremely interesting but that deal with EU discourse and/or European identity from a purely theoretical perspective – i.e. without discussing actual examples of EU discourse. In this respect, I must further specify that this chapter does not attempt to contribute to the intriguing debates about the nature of a European identity and about whether a sense of European belonging is truly needed for the smooth progress and democratic legitimization of the EU. A few scholars have questioned, for example, whether the development of a European consciousness is really necessary or even achievable in the EU scenario (see Levrat, 2011; Delanty, 2005; Banchoff and Smith, 1999; Weiler, 1997); others have posited that a European self should be conceptualized not as a stand-alone identity but as an additional dimension of existing national identities (see for example Risse, 2010). The scope of my discussion does not allow me to deal with these interesting issues.

The proposition underlying this chapter is to concentrate on EU discourse that has been found to encourage or enact Europeans' identification with the project of a united Europe. I shall therefore discuss empirical findings showing how EU discourse constructs social meaning that may affect Europeans' perceptions – their perceptions of Europe as well as their self-perceptions in relation to the EU – and that may eventually establish a European dimension in their identity and social sphere. Within the purpose of this book on Critical Discourse Studies (CDS), my aim is therefore to draw attention to the 'opaque relationships of causality and determination' that may exist between the discursive practices of the European Union and the wider 'social and cultural structures' of the EU community and to highlight the social potential of these practices (Fairclough, 1993: 135) – that is, how such practices can ultimately affect EU-community members' (self-)perceptions and identity stance.

## 3 Survey of empirical studies on EU discourse

Numerous discourse-based analyses have revealed that the European Union contributes to establishing some form of European collective identification through a variety of discursive acts and symbolic practices. There are cases – mostly in times of need or crisis – where communication seems to be approached by the EU even 'as an instrument of propaganda' (Valentini and Nesti, 2010: 399). Määttä (2007), for example, analysed the official text of the much debated European Constitution and observed how discourse on European identity was exploited to create an ideology of identity among the population. He claimed that, due to the normative nature of a constitution, the attempt was to make European identity become legally sanctioned and materialize as a generally accepted value (173; see also Krzyżanowski and Oberhuber, 2007; Gerven, 2005). Similar identity-substantiating intents were documented on the discursive representation of the enlargement process. The enlargement has mostly been conceptualized in terms of the temporal and emotional dimension of Europe's common past and shared future, to the point of being described as a 'historical necessity' of 'profound importance' by the members of the European Convention[5] (Krzyżanowski, 2005: 151; see also Krzyżanowski and Oberhuber, 2007). Some scholars also found that narratives of 'family reunion' are often exploited by EU Commissioners for revitalizing sentiments of European reunification (Petersson and Hellström, 2003: 241; see also Laffan, 2004); other scholars reported on the representation of the enlargement within a framework of continental reintegration primarily to overcome the 'unnatural division' of Europe caused by the Cold War (Sjursen, 2008: 8; see also Caliendo and Napolitano, 2008; Sjursen, 2006). Specifically on Europe's wars, Kølvraa (2012) noted that the idea of leaving behind a past of enmities and conflicts to secure an era of peace and social justice across the continent is also a powerful argument often recalled in EU discourse to 'elicit emotional identification around the call of "Never again!"' (13; see also Forchtner and Kølvraa, 2012).

An ideology of unity also seems to be instilled in EU discourse concerning matters of language policy and multilingualism; on these topics, however, what gets across is rather an ideology of *unity in diversity*, where diversity – i.e. linguistic plurality – becomes a quintessential feature of being European and a distinctive element of Europe's 'cultural richness' (Banùs, 2002: 164; see also Wodak, 2010, 2012; Kraus, 2008, 2011; Đurović, 2009). The same **unity-in-diversity narrative** was observed in EU-policy discourse in the field of higher education: it has been mostly read as a way to construct a cultural version of European identity that is inspired by common values and that concretely experiences plurality through a number of EU-sponsored programmes (Johansson, 2007).

EU discourse has been found to convey an ideology of unity also through the **topoi of inclusion and exclusion** (cf. Forchtner, this volume). Kostakopoulou (2001) and Catenaccio (2007), for example, analysed EU legislation on migration and human rights and reported on the discursive construction of an ideology of exclusion of external migrants, represented as beneficiaries of *granted* rights – thereby implying the positioning of Europeans as beneficiaries of *legitimate* rights. Ifversen and Kølvraa (2007), on their part, investigated EU discourse on the formulation of the European Neighbourhood Policy (ENP)[6] and defined the ENP as a real instrument of identity politics: they claimed that the way the ENP was rhetorically formulated and practically exercised promoted 'a particular version of European identity, a specific European subject which is constructed as an actor in the world' differentiating itself from other (non-EU) actors (3; see also Kølvraa, 2012; Kratochvil, 2009). Other studies in the field of foreign and security policy (CFSP) showed the perpetuation of an image of European cohesion vis-à-vis the rest of the world, with frequent references to the role of the Union as an international actor in tackling global challenges in the interest of its own members (Larsen, 2000, 2004; Koechlin, 2003). Considering the wording of the Treaty on European Union, Delgado-Moreira (1997: 2 par. 5) even talked about the construction of a **defence identity** based on a common line of (military) protection for Europeans. Similarly, Wæver (1996) claimed that official EU discourse features the speech act of security – or the discursive act of 'securitization' – stressing the role of the Union in securing Europeans' protection from *alien* threats. The differentiation of the EU from non-EU actors was also detected in other domains of EU policy-making. For example, Wodak (2000a, 2000b) noted the same construction of a European group 'distinct from other "global players" ' in her analysis of EU policy-drafting in the field of employment (74; see also Weiss and Wodak, 2000), while Busch and Krzyżanowski (2007) found references to an exclusive 'EU's inside' in interviews with members of the European Convention working on the EU's constitutional treaty (117). The identity-building potential of discourses of inclusion/exclusion has been further suggested in a number of additional works;[7] in most cases, the idea of being included – whether entailing or making explicit the exclusion of *others* – is considered to be an effective argument to increase identification with the in-group and generate appreciation for its exclusive *club* character.

Another powerful argument used in EU discourse to negotiate a sense of inclusion is EU citizenship. In this respect, Kostakopoulou (2001) reported on the officialization of a European **civic persona** in EU legislation and treaty provisions. On the same line, Fossum (2003) and Panebianco (2004) – considering excerpts of the *acquis communautaire*[8] – discussed the identity implications of the rights granted to Europeans as a result of their membership in the EU. The discourse of the EU Administration[9] was also found to sponsor a European cultural citizenship with the aim of establishing a supranational identity that is based on cohesion and cooperation in all areas of public interest (Delgado-Moreira, 1997). In a scenario like that of the EU, consisting of Member States that maintain their own sovereignty, the concept of public interest may be more easily endorsed if it coincides with national interest: Gerven (2005), for example, noted that EU discourse invites a sense of belonging by recalling desirable civic values of national inspiration – such as democracy – but also by resorting to the safeguarding principles of a constitution for Europe, largely building on the principles of national constitutions.

Most of all, however, civic discourse seems to be exploited to encourage Europeans' practical involvement in EU integration: Europeans are urged to get involved in the organization primarily through the concrete use of EU services and the actual exercise of rights and opportunities granted to them by virtue of their EU-citizen status. Valentini (2010) brought the case of Europe Direct, the Commission's local information centres, and highlighted arguments of civil involvement to engage Europeans in initiatives and debates that enhance a sense of community. Focusing on EU discourse in the virtual sphere, other scholars suggested that Europeans are discursively encouraged to get involved in EU-related (multilingual) debates and to become active contributors to EU decision- and policy-making – like Wodak and Wright (2006) on the EU's Futurum discussion forum and Tomkova (2010) on public e-consultations by the Parliament and the Commission. The EUROPA website[10] has been found to feature similar attempts to construct a European civic community: a few studies showed that Europeans' participation is encouraged, in particular, through visual semiosis and discursive strategies drawing from persuasive/promotional genres that are generally exploited in the private sector (see Polese and D'Avanzo, 2012; Magistro, 2007, 2010; Caliendo and Magistro, 2009; Caliendo, 2009). In this respect, a parallel was suggested between the EU and the service industry, comparing the organization to a provider of practical benefits and useful services to Europeans (Caliendo and Napolitano, 2008). Krzyżanowski (2010) even found references to the EU's instrumental role as problem-solver and facilitator of interstate cooperation in the discourse of the European Convention. All these observations reveal a functional portrayal of the organization leading to a utilitarian conception of European identity, which seems to be prompted among the general public but also to emerge in some groups directly involved in EU building.

Of all these modes of civic involvement, it is mostly the **direct engagement** in EU institutional settings – especially through employment – that secures positive perceptions of the EU and a solid sense of European belonging. Indeed, some surveys conducted among civil servants at the Commission revealed the identity-shaping potential of the EU working environment, where a collective *esprit européen* seems to be claimed by EU officials (Abélès, 2004: 15; see also Shore, 1995). Shore (2000) attributed a significant role in consolidating a European identity mainly to the way the EU's organizational structure is managed. In his analysis of interviews with Commission officials, he observed that the EU working environment brings about EU employees' consumption of a common socio-professional culture[11] that increases loyalty towards EU ideals and identification with the organization – labelled *engrenage* by the scholar (see also Tóth, 2007). At the same time, and in a less idealistic perspective, Shore also found that the EU socio-professional culture produces a type of identification that relies on the image of the EU as an employer (i.e. a multinational company) rather than an international organization, resulting in expressions of 'corporate identity' among the EU workforce (140). In any case, what has often been observed is that EU employees and officials try to reconcile their national membership with their commitment to EU building. In this respect, Lewis (2005) analysed interviews and negotiations among civil servants working at the Committee of Permanent Representatives (COREPER)[12] and observed a socialization culture based on an expanded notion of self that combines national- and supranational-identity values. Similarly, Wodak (2004, 2009) discussed instances of 'doing politics' while exercising a double membership – national and European – in interviews and speeches among members of the same Committee (COREPER), but also among members of the European Parliament and among European Commissioners. The negotiation of European identity in relation to national identities has been observed in additional studies focusing on statements and interviews with officials engaged in the main EU bodies – i.e. the Commission, the Council, the Parliament and the Court of Justice (see Tóth, 2007; Laffan, 2004; Hooghe, 2001).

As a final remark in this review of empirical research on EU discourse, I cannot fail to mention the use of **symbols and cultural imagery** as a drive to consolidate a European consciousness. The attempt to exploit the evocative power of symbols has been reported in quite a number of works. As shown in Shore's (1993, 2000) extensive ethnographic study on EU information and cultural policies, symbolic images and optimistic discourse are widely exploited by the organization to influence Europeans' perception of culture towards an EU *culture*. For example, Shore (2000) but also Hymans (2004, 2006) discussed the identity implications of the European common currency – the euro – and conducted a semiotic analysis of the euro banknotes and coins, drawing attention to their iconic value. Delanty and Jones (2002) and Fornäs (2008) also referred to the 'monetary construction' of European identity and drew attention to the unity-in-diversity narrative in the euro's design, made of bridges and doors (134). Other scholars focused on the common currency along with further relevant symbols disseminated by the EU – such as the EU anthem, the EU flag and the EU passport – emphasizing their capacity as European-identity creators (Panebianco, 2004) and as conveyors of civic and cultural images of community (Bruter, 2005; Abélès, 2000; Gastelaars and De Ruijter, 1998). Aiello (2007), on her part, discussed the attempt to construct a transnational identity through the visual symbolism of the 50th anniversary Logo Competition, sponsored by the European Commission, and showed that the evocative impact of graphic elements contributed to establishing a recognizable EU repertoire. Even the referential use of colours (i.e. yellow and blue, as in the EU flag) has been read as a subliminal symbol of EU affiliation in EU texts of an informative nature meant for circulation among the general public (Magistro, 2007). Balirano (2009) also mentioned the cohesive intent of the EU web domain .*eu*, widely sold across the Union through a captivating logo campaign and a slogan reading '.eu – Your European identity'. The same intent, then, was noted about the launch of the Commission's *EUTube* along with other new-media initiatives supported by the organization (Podkalicka and Shore, 2010). Finally, **cultural projects** like the European Capital of Culture, the European Cultural Month and the European Year of Intercultural Dialogue were also described as highly symbolic events featuring emotionally charged discourse that celebrates Europe's cultural diversity within the framework of a unifying heritage (Berg, 2011; Sassatelli, 2002; Banùs, 2002). Even the numerous mobility programmes sponsored by the EU in the area of higher education – i.e. Erasmus, Socrates and Lingua – were included among the socially aggregating initiatives that enhance community values and mutual cooperation (Johansson, 2007). The list could go on. What is important to notice is that, whatever the image evoked, Euro-symbolism has been claimed to generate a sense of 'European patriotism' drawing from values of solidarity and responsibility, as well as a wide range of valuable opportunities and a cohesive image of continental 'grandeur' (Jacobs and Maier, 1998: 29).

EU communication captured the attention of a large number of academics. Much valuable research has been conducted – and is still ongoing – on EU discourse and its social implications, albeit not necessarily limited to European identity.[13] For the purpose of this contribution, however, I have limited this review to studies dealing specifically with the role of EU discourse in consolidating a sense of European collective belonging. As I explained at the beginning of this chapter, my aim is to anchor this discussion to the actual discursive approach of the organization and depart from there for any theoretical considerations. In the following sections, I shall therefore comment on the snapshot of EU communication emerging from this review and on its rhetorical modes in terms of how they affect Europeans' perceptions and behaviours. I shall also take the opportunity to discuss additional works on EU discourse that, I believe, can be relevant for clarifying its ultimate social potential.

## 4 The technology of Europeans' involvement

The findings outlined in the previous section suggest that the EU discourse surveyed by the literature encourages or even enacts a dual involvement of Europeans with/in the project of a united Europe. I claim that this involvement is dual in that it entails:

- **emotional involvement**, through the development of an EU *culture* based on feelings of collective belonging, cultural membership and continental grandeur (e.g. same glorious past, common future, leading international role, shared liberal values, rich cultural composition, unifying images, etc.);

- **practical involvement**, through active and steady participation in the EU community – whether virtual or actual (e.g. EU employment, contribution to EU blogs and fora, EU-related political debate, use of EU services, participation in EU-sponsored programmes, recognition of Euro-symbols, etc.).

This twofold involvement brings about what can be defined as the **discursive technology of a European dimension**, comprising a **cultural component** and a **participatory component**.

## 4.1 *The cultural component: EU* culture

As regards the **cultural component of the European dimension**, the literature documents that EU discourse often touches the moral and emotional side of Europeans, recalls their historical memory and distinctive cultural legacies and resorts to democratic values and social conditions that are largely cherished. Namely, Europeans are discursively invited to welcome an emotive and principled cultural membership in the EU which is based on shared values, traditions and objectives. This value- and emotion-oriented technology of Europeans' involvement mostly seems to derive from the desire to negotiate a priori Europeans' appreciation and endorsement of the EU project, with the ultimate goal of legitimizing – at least *on paper* – EU authority.

Cap (2008b) explains that discourse is particularly effective in legitimizing institutional authority when it is able to provide reasonable justifications for it and when it conveys that the institution is engaged in the (alleged) 'vital interest of the addressee' (8; see also Cap, this volume). Now, many vital interests seem to emerge from the discourse-based studies considered. For instance, it has been documented how EU communication asserts communal values of 'liberal inspiration' by making frequent references to fundamental notions like freedom, equality, democracy and security (Castano, 2004: 55; see also Walters and Haahr, 2005; Larsen, 2004). It has also been documented that EU discourse conveys images of a restored continental peace and harmony enabling European nations to peacefully cooperate (Bruter, 2005; Laffan, 2004). This explicit commitment towards 'indisputable ideological principles' offers a convincing foundation to the EU's legitimacy framework, as it provides the organization with non-attackable rationales that justify its activity (Cap, 2005: 13). In other words, what seems to be urged by the EU is a 'moral evaluation' on the part of Europeans: since these ideological principles are indisputable and non-attackable, any moral evaluation will make Europeans perceive the EU as a righteous undertaking worthy of being endorsed (Van Leeuwen, 2007: 92). This corresponds to an attempt to seek 'legitimization through idea', where the positive values and principles evoked and safeguarded at the institutional level represent the idea legitimizing the institution's authority (Wodak and Weiss, 2005: 131).

An extremely powerful rationale for legitimization is the argument of Europeans' vital protection from external threats.[14] In Wæver's view (1995), the commitment to citizens' protection on the part of the State can get to the point of producing discursive acts of securitization:

in this usage, security is not of interest as a sign that refers to something more real; the utterance *itself* is the act [. . .] By uttering 'security', a state representative moves a particular development into a specific area, and thereby claims a special right to use whatever means are necessary to block it.

(Wæver, 1995: 55, emphasis in original)

Hence, *securitizing* means dramatizing an issue to the point of portraying it as a priority matter for the hearer's own safety, with the aim of securing the hearer's consent in authorizing the speaker's protective action.[15] Nowadays, the notion of security is conceptualized not only in terms of civil and military defence but more and more 'within a discourse of wealth, prosperity and resources' (Walters and Haahr, 2005: 9). Hence, yet another strategy aimed at securing legitimization and consensus is the 'positive self-presentation' of the EU (Chilton, 2004: 47; see also Cap, 2005). A portrait of the European Union that brings to light, for example, its international visibility, *club*-style inclusion and palpable benefits – as reported in much of the literature discussed – is a portrait that delineates a fulfilling status quo where the organization becomes essential for the population's 'common good' (Abélès, 2000: 42). In particular, palpable benefits directly improving Europeans' condition represent a convincing argument for endorsement: by inviting Europeans to rationalize about tangible benefits and everyday advantages obtained through EU membership, EU action appears not only morally legitimate but also justified 'on a utility principle' (Caliendo and Magistro, 2009: 199; see also Van Leeuwen, 2007; Van Leeuwen and Wodak, 1999).

In light of these and other arguments for legitimization, EU discourse seems to argue not just for the establishment of a European cultural identity but for its **re**-establishment, for the **re**-discovery of a cultural membership that has always existed but has been obfuscated by decades of conflicts and fragmentation. What should be noted, then, is that the organization seems to be pleading this cause for legitimization on various fronts: historical, ideological, cultural, civic and international. Indeed, the arguments put forward in the EU discourse surveyed are reminiscent of Weber's conceptualizations of legitimacy referred to political authority:

- the *traditional conceptualization of authority* acknowledges the continuity of practices and norms of the past, introducing a **historic-cultural** perspective on what is considered the source of legitimacy – just as the EU resorts to arguments of a common historical past and cultural heritage that gave rise to modern civilization;

- the *rational-legal conceptualization of authority* relies on the principle of legality and provides for rational rules of governance and social support, leading the way to a more **civic** understanding of legitimacy – just as the EU advocates for principles such as democracy, equality, social utility and security;

- the *charismatic conceptualization of authority* recognizes the strength and charismatic qualities of the leading entity, outlining a perspective based on prominence and appeal[16] – just as the EU stimulates Europeans' desire for **inclusion** in a reliable, powerful and internationally salient group.

(adapted from Weber, 1958)

## 4.2 The participatory component: EU community of practice

Moving on to the second aspect, the **participatory component of a European dimension**, it must be noted that there is a clear change of perspective relative to the cultural component. While the cultural component seems to negotiate a priori a sense of European belonging, the participatory component negotiates Europeans' identity and consensus a posteriori, by having a sense of belonging constructed *in practice*, once therefore EU activities and services have been fully experienced and appropriated by Europeans. Many scholars have identified an EU public space – or a European sphere[17] – made of action and interaction as a realistic cradle for establishing mainly a common civil identity.[18]

Focusing on interaction, both the organization's and Europeans' voices are considered to be crucial for the construction of a participatory space. Valentini and Nesti's (2010) comprehensive work on the EU's information policy highlighted that efficient institutional communication becomes essential to establish a democratic dialogue with Europeans: it is only through transparent and capillary EU communication that Europeans' response can be made possible. Obviously, Europeans' response to the organizations' input is just as essential, or EU communication would remain a sterile monologue. The voice of the people is widely acknowledged to be a critical factor for *doing Europe* and for securing the democratization of the European Union.[19] In particular, it is Europeans' regular contribution to EU-related debates and to discursive spheres discussing matters in 'common European terms' that is claimed to be a critical drive for the Europeanization of identity (Risse, 2010: 123; see also Delanty, 2005):

> in debating a particular problem as an issue of common European concern, speakers construct a European community of communication, thereby contributing to a collective European identity.
>
> (Risse, 2010: 123)

Shifting the focus from interaction to action, along with democratic communication, collective action is considered as a fertile ground for growing a shared identity: the main idea is that 'activity in the public sphere [. . .] is about constituting society' (Calhoun, 2003: 260; see also Triandafyllidou and Wodak, 2003). Some scholars add that Europeans will likely and spontaneously identify with their institution once the institution is perceived as a 'real entity' affecting their own lives (Castano, 2004: 53):

> the more aspects of daily life impacted by the institution, the more likely that corresponding social identities will develop around that institution and those who are included in its sphere.
>
> (Herrmann and Brewer, 2004: 14–15)

Now, also a participatory status quo – similar to the cultural status quo discussed in Section 4.1 – has important repercussions in terms of legitimization of the EU. I explained that the establishment of an EU *culture* and a sense of emotional involvement inspired by shared values and interests could result in greater consensus and endorsement of EU authority. Well, Europeans' practical **involvement in** the EU is seen as an even more important condition (than **involvement with** the EU) to consolidate the democratic and legitimate base of the Union.[20] This corresponds to what Wodak and Weiss (2005) define as 'legitimization through procedure' (131): the democratic and active participation of Europeans in the affairs and in the making of the organization represents the procedure sanctioning *in practice* the organization's authority.

There would be a lot to say about the disputed issue of EU legitimacy and whether it is directly linked to, or even dependent upon, the exercise of a European identity. I believe it was important to mention the rhetoric of legitimacy in EU discourse uncovered by the literature but I shall not go as far as questioning the validity of this rhetoric's arguments. Hence, in this chapter I shall not engage in a theoretical discussion about the foundations of EU legitimacy, as this aspect has been – and still is – widely debated in more relevant contexts.[21] Instead, what I would like to draw attention to is the significance and efficacy that the participatory component seems to have for consolidating a sense of European collective belonging.

What emerges from the ideas on Europeans' active participation in EU affairs is that the technology of agency of the members of a community becomes a critical step towards the establishment of a community identity. Walters and Haahr (2005) described 'technologies of agency' as means and modes that 'seek to foster the active involvement of the European citizen in the shaping and conduct of government' (76). In this view, technologies of agency mostly correspond to technologies of citizenship, that is strategies aimed to empower the citizen and increase popular consultation (Dean, 2010: 196). I shall embrace a wider reading in this chapter and argue that technologies of agency encompass all means and modes turning a social group into a fully-fledged community of practice.

The label *community of practice* was coined by Lave and Wenger (1991) with specific reference to learning environments, focusing on how 'newcomers' to an enterprise-driven community construct their collective identity by increasingly participating in the community's socio-cultural practices and by embracing values, repertoires and roles that are meaningful to the community (29). Critical discourse analysts Eckert and McConnell-Ginet (1992) elaborated on this notion and claimed that a community of practice is 'an aggregate of people who come together around mutual engagement in an endeavor'; in turn, engagement in the endeavour contributes to generating communal 'ways of doing things, ways of talking, beliefs, values, power relations – in short, practices' that are appropriated by (and distinctive of) the community members (464). Schnurr et al. further synthesized this idea and proposed a list of conditions that characterize a community of practice:

- mutual engagement, including regular interaction

- a joint, negotiated enterprise

- a shared repertoire developed over a period of time (e.g. jargon, activities, routines, etc.)

(adapted from Schnurr et al., 2008: 213–14)

Looking back at the literature surveyed, it becomes apparent how EU discourse has often been found to ultimately encourage the establishment of an EU community of practice through the technology of Europeans' agency. Indeed, the literature highlights how, in various contexts, Europeans have been urged: (i) to gather around activities and services that are salient and beneficial in their own lives; (ii) to accomplish a communal endeavour in securing the community's wellbeing, protection and global influence; and (iii) to embrace symbolic repertoires and practices that are recognizable to and distinctive of the community.

I explained that a community of practice is generally conceived in terms of a collective commitment around things that are important to the community's members and in terms of full participation towards a shared enterprise. This participation, however, is not meant to be limited to the creation of an utilitarian 'community of deeds' (Schmitter, 1996: 150) but assumes an important affective dimension: 'being active' in the practices of the community and, ultimately, 'constructing identities' in relation to the community (Wenger, 1999: 4). Hence, the establishment of a community of practice is about creating spaces, practices and motivations that lead a social group not only to participate in the making of its own community but also to develop identities in relation to the community. This leads to the conclusion that, through the discursive technology of Europeans' agency, Europeans' practical involvement in the EU could be consolidated to the point of making them develop a sense of loyalty and dedication towards the EU community, to the point of endowing the EU community of practice with an enterprise-driven collective identity.

# 5 The rhetoric of appeal and persuasion

The empirical studies described in the literature review documented recurrent references to universally accepted values and to practical benefits that are meant to improve Europeans' condition and well-being. Whether lexical, semantic or semiotic, redundancy is a widely exploited technique of advertising aimed at fixing the name or other features of the product in the buyer's mind and to express 'an index of rank, esteem, intimacy or self-confidence' further attracting the buyer towards a desirable possession (Cook, 2001: 156). More precisely, the frequent evocation of positive principles, concepts or symbols can generally be seen as a technique of 'soft selling': a form of indirect exhortation conveying, by implication, that 'life will be better with the product' (2001: 15). Transferring this idea to the EU scenario, the bottom line would read that Europeans' lives will be better with the EU.

The literature also reported on cases where the European Union is portrayed as an exclusive in-group whose members get protected and enjoy access to special advantages. The following examples are quite self-explanatory:

> EU citizens crossing the external borders are subject only to a minimum check and can use separate lanes dedicated to EU citizens.
>
> (European Commission, 2010)[22]

> Lucky you had a European Insurance Card!
>
> (European Commission, 2012)[23]

This communicative approach is reminiscent of a specific type of advertising: prestige advertising. Leech (1966) defined prestige advertising as the sale-oriented promotion that focuses on the positive representation of a brand and on the 'firm's achievements' (65): it mostly aims to create an elite vision of the brand based on its exclusive features. The findings suggest that there are cases where EU communication appropriates this genre, thus recontextualizing it from the private to the institutional sphere. Namely, the literature refers to instances of EU discourse where the organization is attributed an image of grandness and exclusivity, the appeal of a historic undertaking and the reputation of a charismatic actor that occupies a leading position on the world stage. The following examples are taken from different EU-discourse events:

- an informative booklet intended for the general public:

  > The European Union is built on an institutional system that is the only one of its kind in the world.
  >
  > (European Communities, 2005)

- the words of a member of the European Convention, in charge of drafting the Treaty establishing a Constitution for Europe:

  > Europe [. . .] I see it as a *civilisation* I see it a lot more in philosophical terms than in mechanical design [. . .] but *it is also a piece of art* so let us be proud of *our* artistic talent.
  >
  > (adapted from Krzyżanowski, 2005: 151, emphasis in original)

- a speech given by Romano Prodi at the time when he was President of the European Commission:

  > We have learnt to our cost the madness of war, of racism and the rejection of the other and diversity. Peace, rejection of abuse of power, conflict and war are

the underlying and unifying values of the European project. [. . .] Let us not forget that the Union is a unique political project and the only true political and institutional innovation in the world. And it is this innovatory approach that continues to hold out prospects of security and stability to the Member States [. . .] and which indeed has become a global reference point.

(adapted from Ifversen and Kølvraa, 2007: 26–7)

These and many other similar statements contribute to generating an aura of appealing prestige around the project of a united Europe. Bruter (2005: 28) explains that the reproduction of 'seducing perceptions of Europe' through discourse that is 'cleverly chosen' makes inclusion in the EU community a desirable condition and EU integration a charismatic project, thereby facilitating Europeans' endorsement.

This advertising-like approach – I argue – represents a further aid towards legitimization. Chilton (2004, 2005) postulated that legitimization can be conceptualized in spatial terms: referring specifically to security-related political discourse, he claimed that the immediate protective intervention of the political actor appears justified and even desirable when the actor is able to focus the attention on the imminence and proximity of dangerous events or threatening *aliens*.[24] This postulation has been further expanded by Cap (2005, 2008a, 2008b) into a 'proximization' model complementing Chilton's spatial conceptualization with a temporal and an axiological dimension. Drawing from Cap, my argument is that, through the use of appealing discourse, the EU initiates a process of proximization that is anchored in time and axiology rather than in space: instead of drawing attention to the proximity of non-EU entities – thus legitimizing the need for immediate protection of the in-group, as it is the case in Wæver's securitization – prestige advertising shifts the focus to the value and charm of the EU front, the sheltered and strong *deictic centre* opposed to the *outside-of-the-deictic-centre* periphery (Cap, 2010). Adopting this focus, the image of the organization is upgraded with respect to non-EU entities and convincingly redefined through conceptual trajectories that are axiology- and time-based: on one hand, the just common values of the in-group that need to be safeguarded (axiological) and, on the other hand, the historical implications of EU belonging for momentous action on the continental and world scenes (temporal).

In light of these considerations, what seems to be at stake in the EU discourse surveyed is more than **technology of emotional and practical involvement** of Europeans: it is also **technology of appeal and persuasion**. Europeans are called to play a role that exceeds that of simple agents: from recipients that are merely receptive of the EU, they are urged to become claimants that proactively seek and desire the EU. Put differently, Europeans are encouraged to become not just 'active citizens' but also voracious and 'conscientious consumers' of the EU project (Walters and Haar, 2005: 124). This new role of Europeans as eager consumers introduces a conceptual shift: from the building of the European Union to its sale and consumption, where the organization and its offerings become the public commodity being negotiated and, possibly, sold and used by the population (Magistro, 2007: 53). Through elements of prestige advertising, then, Europeans are encouraged not just to desire the EU but to *aspire* to a full involvement in/with it; namely they are encouraged to become consumers that are not only voracious but also ambitious and bold-thinking. This turns the EU not into *any* commodity but into a luxury commodity that is not available for mass consumption, rather for the enjoyment of a restricted members' *club*. Hence, through the 'marketization' of institutional discourse,[25] social meaning is 're-elaborated' to suit instrumental wants (Fairclough, 1993: 141): for example, to affect citizens' perceptions – and self-perceptions – in the direction of the institution's own idea of community and identity. A European identity, that is.

Now, one could advocate that Europeans may find it difficult to reconcile a European identity with the integrity of their own national identities, no matter how persuasive EU discourse becomes. Without necessarily supporting this argument, numerous scholars have reported on waves of scepticism towards European integration at the national level or have discussed Eurobarometer polls about Europeans' identity perceptions, concluding that identification with the nation appears far more intense than identification with Europe.[26] As a matter of fact, this national *difficulty* seems to be acknowledged even by the organization itself. In a few studies on EU discourse (2007, 2011, 2012), I found that strategies of linguistic politeness were consistently used in various kinds of EU informative materials. My studies revealed that politeness served a dual purpose: on one hand, it helped minimize the threat that portraying an EU-compliant scenario could represent for sceptical national-identity bearers (national-identity saving function); on the other hand, politeness was used to assert cooperation in pursuing shared goals, while acknowledging the primacy of national prerogatives (national-identity boosting function). More precisely, the texts contained several reassuring arguments that avoided invading Europeans' national sphere or forcing them into an only-European dimension; most importantly, they contained arguments that frequently acknowledged the relevance of Europeans' national condition. These attempts clearly emerge in the following examples:

- the first example is taken from a booklet released by the Directorate General for Communication of the European Commission:

  Citizens are entitled to know what the EU is doing, why it is doing it, and how it will affect them. They also have a right to take part in the political process, through an effective two-way dialogue with the EU and its institutions.

  (European Commission, 2006)

- the second text was released as a reference guide on the contents of the Treaty establishing a Constitution for Europe:

  The European Constitution does not replace the national Constitutions of the countries of Europe. It coexists with these Constitutions.

  (European Communities, 2004)

- even the official text of the Constitutional Treaty itself contains similar arguments:

> Every national of a Member State shall be a citizen of the Union. Citizenship of the Union shall be additional to national citizenship and shall not replace it.
>
> (Article I-10, Treaty establishing a Constitution for Europe, 2004)

This rhetorical approach seems to further corroborate the idea that EU discourse resorts to elements of persuasion: the substantial use of politeness strategies attending to the *national face* of Europeans reveals that the texts analysed are constructed in a way that seems to anticipate Europeans' national concerns and, above all, in a way that seek to persuasively appease such concerns.

# 6  Final remarks

In this chapter, I provided an account of empirical research conducted on a range of EU-produced multimodal texts and from a variety of analytical perspectives. The studies show numerous modes though which EU discourse contributes to establishing a sense of European collective belonging. My goal was to reflect on the way EU discourse constructs new social meaning that may affect Europeans' perceptions of the EU, and of themselves in relation to the EU. I argued that this perception-shaping meaning is mostly constructed through cultural images and participatory channels and points to the consolidation of a salient European dimension both in the emotional sphere and in the everyday practice of Europeans. I add to this argument that the use of strategies of appeal and politeness, as well as the inherent claims for legitimacy highlighted by the literature, confirm the idea that identity building is not just about attributing new social meaning but also about negotiating it (Triandafyllidou and Wodak, 2003: 210). Referring to the EU context, European-identity building is not simply about attributing new EU-related meaning to Europeans' imagery but it is also about negotiating this meaning with Europeans themselves. Indeed, if it is true that establishing a sense of European belonging is about instilling a European dimension in Europeans' identity and social sphere, it is also true that, given the complex social set-up and historical inheritance of the EU community, this process must necessarily involve the negotiation of this dimension with existing dimensions that may be perceived as a ground for contention between the EU and its community members – i.e. national versus supranational.

I stated at the beginning of my discussion that the instances of EU discourse surveyed by the literature do not simply encourage the emergence of a participative and emotionally involved EU community but, most notably, they enact it. Embracing the CDA idea that discourse is a mode of social action, it becomes clear how the EU discourse discussed represents per se an act of European identity that is performed over a variety of communicative events and settings. What I am trying to emphasize is that the instances of EU discourse considered reveal a communicative practice that constructs and negotiates but, most importantly, **reproduces** new EU-related meaning. And when new meaning is consistently reproduced, it can eventually take root, be assimilated and even be willingly embraced by its recipients:

> the linguistic pattern is a clue to what is taken as simple common sense [. . .] and the repetition of this pattern means that [. . .] it will continue to be common sense.
> (Markus and Cameron, 2002: 13)

Hence, by reproducing new social meaning, this meaning eventually loses its novelty factor and becomes default meaning in the community's experience. For the European Union to become default meaning in Europeans' experience would mean, among other things, becoming rooted in Europeans' reality to the point that Europeans could not do without their European dimension and could not do without their involvement with/in the EU. Namely, the consistent evocation of new meaning in EU discourse could bring about a socio-semantic shift making the EU community, **the** community Europeans will relate to, and making identification with the EU project an indispensable dimension in Europeans' self. Europeans' *need* for the EU and for the European dimension of their self – whether such a condition is ever achieved – would represent a crucial argument to further legitimize EU authority: it would represent a crucial argument to justify the organization's right to exist, act and – using Cap's words[27] – 'be obeyed'.

# Notes

1 For an extensive discussion on CDA postulations, see in particular Fairclough (2001, 2005, 2007, 2010), Wodak and Chilton (2007), Fairclough and Wodak (1997) and Van Dijk (1997).

2 In this chapter, I shall refer to concepts such as *European identity, Europe, Europeans, European integration* and so forth. I shall use these broad labels to refer to the European Union – which does not coincide with geographical Europe – and to EU society – which only includes the population of EU Member States.

3 The notion of multimodal discourse, in this chapter, shall be limited to image, speech and writing – that is, visual, spoken and written discourse (see Kress, 2010).

4 The term *acquis communautaire* encompasses all founding treaties of the European Union and their respective amendments ratified by the EU Member States.

5 The European Convention is the EU panel that in 2003–4 was in charge of negotiating and drafting the Treaty establishing a Constitution for Europe. The European Constitution was eventually never enforced and was replaced by the Treaty of Lisbon (2009).

6 The European Neighbourhood Policy is an EU instrument that promotes foreign relations and assures economic and diplomatic cooperation with countries bordering the European Union.

**7** For further considerations on the issue of inclusion/exclusion, see Wodak (2004, 2007a), Mummendey and Waldzus (2004), Reisigl and Wodak (2001) and Stråth (2000).

**8** Fossum focused on the EU Charter of Fundamental Rights while Panebianco investigated extracts from the Treaty on European Union (Treaty of Maastricht).

**9** By discourse of the EU Administration, Delgado-Moreira meant official texts produced by the European Commission, the European Council, as well as texts produced in Intergovernmental Conferences and Reflection Groups.

**10** The EUROPA website (www.europa.eu) is the organization's official virtual access point to EU legislation and general information about the European Union.

**11** See Abèles et al.'s (1993) ethnological study on the Commission's organizational environment and its role in the construction of a European *culture*.

**12** The Committee of Permanent Representatives is the main preparatory body for the meetings of the European Council.

**13** To mention only a few, see Magistro (2013), Aydin-Düzgit (2012), Birkel (2009), Cramer (2009), Bozić-Vrbancić et al. (2008), Sidiropoulou (2004), Hansen (2000) and Muntigl et al. (2000).

**14** See also Walters and Haahr (2005), Koechlin (2003), Kostakopoulou (2001) and Larsen (2000) on the same argument.

**15** On security discourse, see also Buzan et al. (1998) and the edited collection by Armstrong and Anderson (2007).

**16** In this last conceptualization (charismatic), the concept of appeal plays an important role, which shall be discussed more in depth in Section 5.

**17** On the conceptualization of a European public sphere, see in particular Habermas (2001, 2005, 2006) and Schlesinger (2007).

**18** See, for example, Wright (2011), Díez-Medrano and Gray (2010), Krzyżanowski et al. (2009), Kraus (2008), Wodak and Weiss (2005) and Kostakopoulou (2001).

**19** About this argument, see in particular Wright (2000a, 2000b, 2011), Wodak (2007b, 2010), Kaelbe (2009), Fossum and Schlesinger (2007) and Habermas (2001).

**20** For further discussions on this view, see among others Hooghe and Marks (2009), Habermas (2006), Gerven (2005), Herrmann and Brewer (2004) and Fella (2002).

**21** The issue of EU legitimacy (and legitimization) has been discussed, for instance, in Kraus (2008), Habermas (2001) and Banchoff and Smith (1999). See also the rich edited collections on EU legitimacy and European identity by Fuchs and Klingemann (2011) and by Cerutti and Lucarelli (2008).

**22** Text extracted from a guide to EU citizenship and EU citizens' rights based on the current EU legislation, released by the Directorate General for Justice of the European Commission.

**23** Text taken from a flyer on the European Health Insurance Card, giving EU citizens access to state-run healthcare assistance throughout the Union.

**24** See also the discussion on 'securitization' in Sections 3 and 4.

**25** On the notion of *marketization* of institutional discourse, see Fairclough (1993, 1995a, 2005) and Chouliaraki and Fairclough (1999). See also Wodak and Weiss (2005) and Fairclough and Wodak (1997).

**26** There is a vast range of academic works discussing issues of Euro-scepticism and debating the utility and results of Eurobarometer surveys. See, among others, Risse (2010), Hooghe and Marks (2009), Díez-Medrano (2003, 2009), Kraus (2008), Verhofstadt (2006), Deutsch (2006), Berglund et al. (2006), Bruter (2005), Baycroft (2004) and Banùs (2002).

**27** Cap, 2005: 12–13.

# References

Abélès, M. (2000), 'Virtual Europe', in I. Bellier and T. M. Wilson (eds), *An Anthropology of the European Union: Building, Imaging and Experiencing the New Europe*. Oxford: Berg, pp. 31–52.

—— (2004), 'Identity and borders: an anthropological approach to EU institutions'. *Twenty-First Century Papers* (Online Working Papers from the Center for 21st Century Studies, University of Wisconsin – Milwaukee), 4.

Abélès, M., Bellier, I. and McDonald, M. (1993), 'Approche anthropologique de la Commission Européenne'. *Rapport pour la Commission Européenne*, December 1993. Available at: http://halshs.archives-ouvertes.fr/halshs-00374346/fr/ (accessed July 2012).

Aiello, G. (2007), 'The appearance of diversity: visual design and the public communication of EU identity', in J. Bain and M. Holland (eds), *European Union Identity: Perceptions from Asia and Europe*. Baden-Baden: Nomos, pp. 147–81.

Armstrong, W. and Anderson, J. (eds) (2007), *Geopolitics of the European Union Enlargement: The Fortress Empire*. London: Routledge.

Aydin-Düzgit, S. (2012), *Constructions of European Identity. Debates and Discourses on Turkey and the EU*. Basingstoke: Palgrave Macmillan.

Balirano, G. (2009), 'Towards a Turkish EU-entity: a semiotic approach to the reading of EUROPA's website cyber-representation of a "European Turkey"'. *Textus*, special issue *Identity Construction and Positioning in Discourse and Society* (ed. N. Vasta and C. R. Caldas-Coulthard), XXII(1), 179–98.

Banchoff, T. and Smith, M. P. (1999), 'Conceptualizing legitimacy in a contested polity', in T. Banchoff and M. P. Smith (eds), *Legitimacy and the European Union: The Contested Polity*. London: Routledge, pp. 1–23.

Banùs, E. (2002), 'Cultural policy in the EU and the European identity', in M. Farrell, S. Fella and M. Newman (eds), *European Integration in the 21st Century: Unity in Diversity?* Thousand Oaks, CA: Sage Publications, pp. 158–83.

Baycroft, T. (2004), 'European identity', in G. Taylor and S. Spencer (eds), *Social Identities: Multidisciplinary Approaches*. London: Routledge, pp. 145–61.

Berg, K. M. (2011), '"Intercultural dialogue" as rhetorical form: a Pyrrhic victory'. *CEMES Working Papers*. University of Copenhagen, 2.

Berglund, S., Ekman, J., Vogt, H. and Aarebrot, F. H. (2006), *The Making of the European Union: Foundations, Institutions and Future Trends*. Cheltenham: Edward Elgar Publishing.

Birkel, K. M. (2009), *We, Europe and the Rest: EU Discourse(s) at Work in Environmental Politics*. Enschede, NL: Drukkers B.V.

Bourdieu, P. (1991), *Language and Symbolic Power*. Cambridge, MA: Harvard University Press.

Bozić-Vrbancić, S., Vrbancić, M. and Orlić, O. (2008), 'European Media Programme: the role of "language" and "visual images" in the processes of constructing European culture and identity'. *Collegium Antropologicum*, December, 32(4), 1013–22.

Bruter, M. (2005), *Citizens of Europe? The Emergence of a Mass European Identity*. Basingstoke: Palgrave.

Busch, B. and Krzyżanowski, M. (2007), 'Outside/inside the EU: enlargement, migration policies and the search for Europe's identity', in W. Armstrong and J. Anderson (eds), *Geopolitics of the European Union Enlargement: The Fortress Empire*. London: Routledge, pp. 107–24.

Buzan, B., Wæver, O. and de Wilde, J. (1998), *Security: A New Framework for Analysis*. Boulder: Lynne Rienner Publishers.

Calhoun, C. (2003), 'The democratic integration of Europe: interests, identity, and the public sphere', in M. Berezin and M. Schain (eds), *Europe Without Borders: Remapping Europe Territory, Membership and Identity in a Transnational Age*. Baltimore: Johns Hopkins University Press, pp. 243–74.

Caliendo, G. (2009), 'The role of the new media in the promotion of identity frameworks', in G. Garzone and P. Catenaccio (eds), *Identities across Media and Modes: Discursive Perspectives*. Bern: Peter Lang, pp. 163–88.

Caliendo, G. and Magistro, E. (2009), 'The human face of the European Union: a critical study'. *CADAAD Journal*, 3(2), 176–202.

Caliendo, G. and Napolitano A. (2008), 'Communities, boundaries and new neighbours: the discursive construction of EU Enlargement'. *Journal of Contemporary European Research*, special issue *Media and Communication in Europe: Babel Revisited* (ed. A. I. Schneeberger and K. Sarikakis), 4(4), 322–45.

Cap, P. (2005), 'Language and legitimization: developments in the proximization model of political discourse analysis'. *Lodz Papers in Pragmatics*, 1, 7–36.

—— (2008a), 'Towards the proximization model of the analysis of legitimization in political discourse'. *Journal of Pragmatics*, 40(1), 17–41.

—— (2008b), *Legitimisation in Political Discourse: A Cross-Disciplinary Perspective on the Modern US War Rhetoric* (2nd edn), Newcastle: Cambridge Scholars Publishing.

—— (2010), 'Axiological aspects of proximization'. *Journal of Pragmatics*, 42, 392–407.

Castano, E. (2004), 'European identity: a social-psychological perspective', in R. Herrmann, T. Risse and M. Brewer (eds), *Transnational Identities: Becoming European in the EU*. Lanham, MD: Rowman and Littlefield, pp. 40–58.

Catenaccio, P. (2007), 'De-humanising the alien: the construction of migrants' rights in EU legislation', in G. Garzone and S. Sarangi (eds), *Discourse, Ideology and Specialized Communication*. Bern: Peter Lang, pp. 355–78.

Cerutti, F. and Lucarelli, S. (eds) (2008), *The Search for a European Identity: Values, Policies and Legitimacy of the European Union*. Oxon: Routledge.

Chilton, P. (2004), *Analysing Political Discourse: Theory and Practice*. London: Routledge.

—— (2005), 'Missing links in mainstream CDA: modules, blends and the critical instinct', in R. Wodak and P. Chilton (eds), *A New Agenda in (Critical) Discourse Analysis: Theory, Methodology and Interdisciplinarity*. Amsterdam: John Benjamins, pp. 19–51.

Chouliaraki, L. and Fairclough, N. (1999), *Discourse in Late Modernity: Rethinking Critical Discourse Analysis*. Edinburgh: Edinburgh University Press.

Cook, G. (2001), *The Discourse of Advertising* (2nd edn). London: Routledge.

Cramer, J. (2009), 'Using pronouns to construct a European identity: the case of politicians at Davos 2008'. *Studies in the Linguistic Sciences: Illinois Working Papers*, special issue *Proceedings of Illinois Language and Linguistics Society 1: Language Online* (ed. M. Garley and B. Slade), 2009, 94–109.

Dean, M. (2010), *Governmentality: Power and Rule in Modern Society* (2nd edn). London: Sage Publications.

Delanty, D. (2005), 'The quest for European identity', in E. O. Eriksen (ed.), *Making the European Polity. Reflexive Integration in the EU*. London: Routledge, pp. 127–42.

Delanty, G. and Jones, P. R. (2002), 'European identity and architecture'. *European Journal of Social Theory*, 5(4), 453–66.

Delgado-Moreira, J. M. (1997), 'Cultural citizenship and the creation of European identity'. *Electronic Journal of Sociology*, 2(3). Available at: http://www.sociology.org/content/vol002.003/delgado.html (accessed July 2012).

Deutsch, F. (2006), 'Legitimacy and identity in the European Union: empirical findings from the old member states', in I.P. Karolewski and V. Kaina (eds), *European Identity: Theoretical Perspectives and Empirical Insights*. Berlin: Logos Verlag, pp. 149–78.

Díez-Medrano, J. (2009), 'The public sphere and the European Union's political identity', in J. T. Checkel and P. J. Katzenstein (eds), *European Identity*. Cambridge: Cambridge University Press, pp. 81–108.

—— (2003), *Framing Europe: Attitudes to European Integration in Germany, Spain and the United Kingdom*. Princeton, NJ: Princeton University Press.

Díez-Medrano, J. and Gray, E. (2010), 'Framing the European Union in national public spheres', in P. Statham and R. Koopmans (eds), *The Making of a European Public Sphere*. Cambridge: Cambridge University Press, pp. 195–219.

Đurović, T. (2009), '"Unity in diversity". The conceptualisation of language in the European Union'. *Facta Universitatis Linguistics and Literature*, 7(1), 47–61.

Eckert, P. and McConnell-Ginet, S. (1992), 'Think practically and look locally: language and gender as community-based practice'. *Annual Review of Anthropology*, 21, 461–90.

Fairclough, N. (1993), 'Critical discourse analysis and the marketization of public discourse: the universities'. *Discourse and Society*, 4(2), 133–68.

—— (1995a), *Critical Discourse Analysis: The Critical Study of Language*. London: Longman.

—— (1995b), *Media Discourse*. London: Edward Arnold.

—— (2001), *Language and Power* (2nd edn). London: Longman.

—— (2005), 'Critical discourse analysis in transdisciplinary research', in R. Wodak and P. Chilton (eds), *A New Agenda in (Critical) Discourse Analysis: Theory, Methodology and Interdisciplinarity*. Amsterdam: John Benjamins, pp. 53–70.

—— (2007), 'The contribution of discourse analysis to research on social change', in N. Fairclough, P. Cortese and P. Ardizzone (eds), *Discourse in Contemporary Social Change*. Bern: Peter Lang, pp. 23–47.

—— (2010), *Critical Discourse Analysis: The Critical Study of Language* (2nd edn). London: Longman.

Fairclough, N. and Wodak, R. (1997), 'Critical discourse analysis', in T.A. Van Dijk (ed.), *Discourse as Social Interaction. Discourse Studies: A Multidisciplinary Introduction*. Vol. 2. London: Sage Publications, pp. 258–84.

Fella, S. (2002), 'Introduction: unity in diversity – the challenge for the EU', in M. Farrell, S. Fella and M. Newman (eds), *European Integration in the 21st Century: Unity in Diversity?* Thousand Oaks, CA: Sage Publications, pp. 1–14.

Forchtner, B. and Kølvraa, C. (2012), 'Narrating a "new Europe": from "bitter past" to self-righteousness?' *Discourse and Society*, 23(4), 377–400.

Fornäs, J. (2008), 'Meanings of money: the euro as a sign of value and of cultural identity', in W. Uricchio (ed.), *We Europeans? Media, Representations, Identities*. Bristol: Intellect, pp. 123–39.

Fossum, J. E. (2003), 'The European Union – in search of an identity'. *European Journal of Political Theory*, 2(3), 319–40.

Fossum, J. E. and Schlesinger, P. (2007), 'The European Union and the public sphere: a communicative space in the making?', in J. E. Fossum and P. Schlesinger (eds), *The European Union and the Public Sphere: A Communicative Space in the Making?* London: Routledge, pp. 1–19.

Foucault, M. (1977), *Discipline and Punish: The Birth of the Prison*. New York: Pantheon.

Fuchs, D. and Klingemann, H. D. (eds) (2011), *Cultural Diversity, European Identity and the Legitimacy of the EU*. Cheltenham: Edward Elgar Publishing.

Gastelaars, M. and de Ruijter, A. (1998), 'Ambivalences and complexities in European identity formation', in M. Gastelaars and A. de Ruijter (eds), *A United Europe: The Quest for a Multifaceted Identity*. Maastricht: Shaker, pp. 1–12.

Gerven, W. (2005), *The European Union: A Polity of States and Peoples*. Stanford, CA: Stanford University Press.

Habermas, J. (2001), 'Why Europe needs a constitution'. *New Left Review* 11, 5–26.

—— (2005), *Time of Transitions*. Cambridge: Polity Press.

—— (2006), 'Public sphere: an encyclopedia article', in M. G. Durham and D. Kellner (eds), *Media and Cultural Studies: Keyworks* (rev. edn). Oxford: Blackwell Publishers, pp. 73–8.

Halliday, M. A. K. (1973), *Explorations in the Functions of Language*. London: Edward Arnold.

Hansen, P. (2000), '"European citizenship", or where neoliberalism meets ethno-culturalism. Analysing the European Union's citizenship discourse'. *European Societies*, 2(2), 139–65.

Herrmann, R. and Brewer, M. B. (2004), 'Identities and institutions: becoming European in the EU', in R. Herrmann, T. Risse and M. Brewer (eds), *Transnational Identities: Becoming European in the EU*. Lanham, MD: Rowman and Littlefield, pp. 1–24.

Hooghe, L. (2001), *The European Commission and the Integration of Europe – Images of Governance*. Cambridge: Cambridge University Press.

Hooghe, L. and Marks, G. (2009), 'A postfunctionalist theory of European intergration'. *British Journal of Political Science*, 39, 1–23.

Hymans, J. E. C. (2004), 'The changing color of money: European currency iconography and collective identity'. *European Journal of International Relations*, 10(1), 5–31.

—— (2006), 'Money for Mars? The euro banknotes and European identity', in R. M. Fishman and A. M. Messina (eds), *The Year of the Euro: The Cultural, Social, and Political Import of Europe's Common Currency*. South Bend, IN: University of Notre Dame Press, pp. 15–36.

Ifversen, J. and Kølvraa, C. (2007), 'European Neighbourhood Policy as identity politics'. Paper presented at the *European Union Studies Association Tenth Biennial International Conference*. Montreal, 17–19 May 2007. Available at: http://www.unc.edu/euce/eusa2007/papers/ifversen-j-12b.pdf (accessed 3 October 2013).

Jacobs, D. and Maier, R. (1998), 'European identity: construct, fact and fiction', in M. Gastelaars and A. de Ruijter (eds), *A United Europe: The Quest for a Multifaceted Identity*. Maastricht: Shaker, pp. 13–33.

Johansson, J. (2007), *Learning to Be(come) a Good European: A Critical Analysis of the Official European Union Discourse on European Identity and Higher Education*. Unpublished PhD thesis. Linköpings Universitet. Available at: http://liu.diva-portal.org/smash/record.jsf?pid=diva2:17138 (accessed 27 August 2013).

Kaelble, H. (2009), 'Identification with Europe and politicization of the EU since the 1980s', in J. T. Checkel and P. J. Katzenstein (eds), *European Identity*. Cambridge: Cambridge University Press, pp. 193–212.

Koechlin, J. (2003), *L'Europe dans le Monde: La Politique Étrangère de l'Union Européenne comme Élément Constitutif de l'Identité Européenne.* Unpublished PhD thesis. Université de Genève. Available at: http://www.unige.ch/cyberdocuments/theses2003/KoechlinJ/these_front.html (accessed 29 August 2013).

Kølvraa, C. (2012), *Imagining Europe as a Global Player: The Ideological Construction of a New European Identity Within the EU.* Brussels: PIE-Peter Lang.

Kostakopoulou, D. (2001), *Citizenship, Identity and Immigration in the European Union: Between Past and Future.* Manchester: Manchester University Press.

Kratochvil, P. (2009), 'Discursive constructions of the EU's identity in the neighbourhood: an equal among equals or the power centre?' *European Political Economy Review*, 9, 5–23.

Kraus, P. A. (2008), *A Union of Diversity: Language, Identity and Polity-Building in Europe.* Cambridge: Cambridge University Press.

—— (2011), 'Neither united nor diverse? The language issue and political legitimation in the European Union', in A. L. Kjaer and S. Adamo (eds), *Linguistic Diversity and European Democracy.* Farnham: Ashgate, pp. 17–34.

Kress, G. (2010), *Multimodality. A Social Semiotic Approach to Contemporary Communication.* Oxon: Routledge.

Krzyżanowski, M. (2005), '"European identity wanted!": on discursive and communicative dimensions of the European Convention', in R. Wodak and P. Chilton (eds), *A New Agenda in (Critical) Discourse Analysis: Theory, Methodology and Interdisciplinarity.* Amsterdam: John Benjamins, pp. 137–63.

—— (2010), *The Discursive Construction of European Identities: A Multi-Level Approach to Discourse and Identity in the Transforming European Union.* Frankfurt am Main: Peter Lang.

Krzyżanowski, M. and Oberhuber, F. (2007), *(Un)Doing Europe: Discourses and Practices of Negotiating the EU Constitution.* Brussels: Peter Lang.

Krzyżanowski, M., Triandafyllidou, A. and Wodak, R. (2009), 'Introduction', in A. Triandafyllidou, R. Wodak and M. Krzyżanowski (eds), *The European Public Sphere and the Media: Europe in Crisis.* Basingstoke: Palgrave Macmillan, pp. 1–12.

Laffan, B. (2004), 'The European Union and its institutions as "identity builders"', in R. Herrmann, T. Risse and M. Brewer (eds), *Transnational Identities: Becoming European in the EU.* Lanham, MD: Rowman and Littlefield, pp. 65–96.

Larsen, H. (2000), 'The discourse on the EU's role in the world', in B. Hansen and B. Heurlin (eds), *The New World Order: Contrasting Theories.* London: Macmillan, pp. 217–44.

—— (2004), 'Discourse analysis in the study of European foreign policy', in B. Tonra and T. Christiansen (eds), *Rethinking European Union Foreign Policy.* Manchester: Manchester University Press, pp. 62–80.

Lave, J. and Wenger, E. (1991), *Situated Learning. Legitimate Peripheral Participation.* Cambridge: Cambridge University Press.

Leech, G. N. (1966), *English in Advertising: A Linguistic Study of Advertising in Great Britain.* London: Longman.

Levrat, N. (2011), 'Do the powers exerted by the EU need a legitimacy based on the citizens' european identity?', in S. Lucarelli, F. Cerutti and V. A. Schmidt (eds), *Debating Political Identity and Legitimacy in the European Union.* Oxford: Routledge, pp. 76–90.

Lewis, J. (2005), 'The Janus face of Brussels: socialization and everyday decision making in the European Union'. *International Organization*, 59, 937–71.

Määttä, S. K. (2007), 'The foundations of Europe: a critical discourse analysis of the EU Constitution'. *CADAAD Journal*, 1(1), 166–78.

Magistro, E. (2007), 'Promoting the European identity: politeness strategies in the discourse of the European Union'. *CADAAD Journal*, 1(1), 51–73.

—— (2010), 'The marketization of institutional discourse: the case of the European Union', in U. Okulska and P. Cap (eds), *Perspectives in Politics and Discourse*. Amsterdam: John Benjamins, pp. 155–72.

—— (2011), 'National face and national-face threatening acts: politeness and the European Constitution', in B. Davies, M. Haugh and A. J. Merrison (eds), *Situated Politeness*. London: Continuum, pp. 232–52.

—— (2012), *The Polite Voice of the European Union: A Corpus-Based Study of Politeness and Identity Formation in EU Public Discourse*. Unpublished PhD thesis. University of London, Royal Holloway, School of Modern Languages, Literatures and Cultures.

—— (2013), 'The challenges of *translating* polite discourse for the EU multilingual community'. *International Journal of Applied Linguistics*, 23(1), 60–79.

Markus, T. and Cameron, D. (2002), *The Words Between the Spaces: Buildings and Language*. London: Routledge.

Mummendey, A. and Waldzus, S. (2004), 'National differences and European plurality: discrimination or tolerance between European countries', in R. Herrmann, T. Risse and M. Brewer (eds), *Transnational Identities: Becoming European in the EU*. Lanham, MD: Rowman and Littlefield, pp. 59–74.

Muntigl, P., Weiss, G. and Wodak, R. (2000), *European Union Discourses on Un/Employment: An Interdisciplinary Approach to Employment Policy-Making and Organizational Change*. Amsterdam: John Benjamins.

Panebianco, S. (2004), 'European citizenship and European identity: from treaty provisions to public opinion attitudes', in E. Moxon-Browne (ed.), *Who Are The Europeans Now?* Aldershot: Ashgate, pp. 19–38.

Petersson, B. and Hellström, A. (2003), 'The return of the kings: temporality in the construction of EU identity'. *European Societies*, 5(3), 235–52.

Podkalica, A. and Shore, C. (2010), 'Communicating Europe? EU communication policy and cultural politics', in C. Valentini and G. Nesti (eds), *Public Communication in the European Union: History, Perspectives and Challenges*. Newcastle: Cambridge Scholars Publishing, pp. 93–112.

Polese, V. and D'Avanzo, S. (2012), 'Hybridisation in EU academic discourse: the representation of EU social actors', in S. M. Maci and M. Sala (eds), *Genre Variation in Academic Communication Emerging Disciplinary Trends*. Bergamo: CELSB, pp. 231–60.

Reisigl, M. and Wodak, R. (2001), *Discourse and Discrimination. Rhetorics of Racism and Antisemitism*. London: Routledge.

Risse, T. (2010), *A Community of Europeans? Transnational Identities and Public Spheres*. Ithaca, NY: Cornell University Press.

Sassatelli, M. (2002), 'Imagined Europe: the shaping of a European cultural identity through EU cultural policy'. *European Journal of Social Theory*, 5(4), 435–51.

Schlesinger, P. (2007), 'A cosmopolitan temptation'. *European Journal of Communication* 22, 413–26.

Schmitter, P. (1996), 'Imagining the future of the euro-polity with the help of new concepts', in G. Marks, F. Scharpf, P. C. Schmitter and W. Streeck (eds), *Governance in the European Union*. London: Sage Publications, pp. 121–50.

Schnurr, S., Marra, M. and Holmes, J. (2008), 'Impoliteness as a means of contesting power relations in the workplace', in D. Bousfield and M. Locher (eds), *Impoliteness in Language: Studies on its Interplay with Power in Theory and Practice*. Berlin: Mouton de Gruyter, pp. 211–30.

Shore, C. (1993), 'Inventing the "People's Europe": critical perspectives on European Community cultural policy'. *Man: Journal of Royal Anthropological Institute*, 28(4), 779–800.

—— (1995), 'Usurpers or pioneers? EC bureaucrats and the question of "European consciousness"', in A. Cohen and N. Rapport (eds), *Questions of Consciousness*. London: Routledge, pp. 290–315.

—— (2000), *Building Europe. The Cultural Politics of European Integration*. London: Routledge.

Sidiropoulou, M. (2004), *Linguistic Identities through Translation*. Amsterdam: Editions Rodopi B.V.

Sjursen, H. (2006), 'The European Union between values and rights', in H. Sjursen (ed.), *Questioning EU Enlargement: Europe in Search of Identity*. Oxon: Routledge, pp. 203–16.

—— (2008), 'Enlargement in perspective: the EU quest for identity'. *ARENA Working Papers*, 5, 1–15.

Stråth, B. (2000), 'Multiple Europes: integration, identity and demarcation to the other', in B. Stråth (ed.), *Europe and the Other and Europe as the Other*. Brussels: PIE-Peter Lang, pp. 385–420.

Tomkova, J. (2010), 'Toward a "direct dialogue"? Evaluation of public (e)consultations in the EU context', in C. Valentini and G. Nesti (eds), *Public Communication in the European Union: History, Perspectives and Challenges*. Newcastle: Cambridge Scholars Publishing, pp. 269–92.

Tóth, E. (2007), 'The reflection of national cultures in the organizational culture of the European Commission'. *EU Working Papers*, 2, 66–100.

Triandafyllidou, A. and Wodak, R. (2003), 'Conceptual and methodological questions in the study of collective identities. An introduction'. *Journal of Language and Politics*, 2(2), 205–23.

Valentini, C. (2010), 'The European Union, Europe Direct centres and civil society organisations: an enchanted partnership?', in C. Valentini and G. Nesti (eds), *Public Communication in the European Union: History, Perspectives and Challenges*. Newcastle: Cambridge Scholars Publishing, pp. 139–64.

Valentini, C. and Nesti, G. (2010), 'Conclusions', in C. Valentini and G. Nesti (eds), *Public Communication in the European Union: History, Perspectives and Challenges*. Newcastle: Cambridge Scholars Publishing, pp. 389–408.

Van Dijk, T. A. (1997), 'The study of discourse', in T. A. Van Dijk (ed.), *Discourse as Structure and Process. Discourse Studies: A Multidisciplinary Introduction*. Vol. 1. London: Sage Publications, pp. 1–34.

Van Leeuwen, T. (2007), 'Legitimation in discourse and communication'. *Discourse and Communication*, 1(1), 91–112.

Van Leeuwen, T. and Wodak, R. (1999), 'Legitimizing immigration control: a discourse-historical analysis'. *Discourse Studies*, 1, 83–118.

Verhofstadt, G. (2006), *The United States of Europe*. London: Federal Trust.

Wæver, O. (1995), 'Securitization and desecuritization', in R. Lipschutz (ed.), *On Security*. New York: Columbia University Press, pp. 46–86.

—— (1996), 'European security identities'. *Journal of Common Market Studies*, 34(1), 103–32.

Walters, W. and Haahr, J. H. (2005), *Governing Europe: Discourse, Governmentality and European Integration*. Oxon: Routledge.

Weber, M. (1958), 'The three types of legitimate rule' [trans. H. Gerth]. *Berkeley Publications in Society and Institutions*, 4(1), 1–11.

Weiler, J. H. H. (1997), 'The reformation of European constitutionalism'. *Journal of Common Market Studies*, 35(1), 97–130.

Weiss, G. and Wodak, R. (2000), 'Debating Europe: globalization rhetoric and European Union employment policies', in I. Bellier and T.M. Wilson (eds), *An Anthropology of the European Union: Building, Imaging and Experiencing the New Europe*. Oxford: Berg, pp. 75–92.

Wenger, E. (1999), *Communities of Practice. Learning, Meaning and Identity*. Cambridge: Cambridge University Press.

Wodak, R. (2000a), 'Recontextualization and the transformation of meaning: a Critical Discourse Analysis of decision making in EU meetings about employment policies', in S. Sarangi and M. Coulthard (eds), *Discourse and Social Life*. Harlow: Pearson Education, pp. 185–206.

—— (2000b), 'From conflict to consensus? The co-construction of a policy paper', in P. Muntigl, G., Weiss and R. Wodak (eds), *European Union Discourses on Un/ Employment: An Interdisciplinary Approach to Employment Policy-Making and Organizational Change*. Amsterdam: John Benjamins, pp. 73–114.

—— (2004), 'National and transnational identities: European and other identities oriented to in interviews with EU officials', in R. Herrmann, T. Risse and M. Brewer (eds), *Transnational Identities: Becoming European in the EU*. Lanham, MD: Rowman and Littlefield, pp. 97–128.

—— (2007a), 'Discourses in European Union organizations: aspects of access, participation, and exclusion'. *Text and Talk*, 27(5, 6), 655–80.

—— (2007b), '"Doing Europe": the discursive construction of European identities', in R. C. M. Mole (ed.), *Discursive Constructions of Identity in European Politics*. Basingstoke: Palgrave Macmillan, pp. 70–94.

—— (2009), *The Discourse of Politics in Action: Politics as Usual*. Basingstoke: Palgrave Macmillan.

—— (2010), '"Communicating Europe": analyzing, interpreting, and understanding multilingualism and the discursive construction of transnational identities', in A. Duszak, J. House and L. Kumiega (eds), *Globalization, Discourse, Media: In a Critical Perspective*. Warsaw: Warsaw University Press, pp. 17–60.

—— (2012), 'Language, power and identity'. *Language Teaching*, 45(2), 215–33.

Wodak, R. and Chilton, P. (2007), *New Agenda in (Critical) Discourse Analysis*. Amsterdam: John Benjamins.

Wodak, R. and Weiss, G. (2005), 'Analysing European Union discourses: theories and applications', in R. Wodak and P. Chilton (eds), *A New Agenda in (Critical) Discourse Analysis*. Amsterdam: John Benjamins, pp. 121–35.

Wodak, R. and Wright, S. (2006), 'The European Union in cyberspace: multilingual democratic participation in a virtual public sphere?' *Language and Politics*, 5(2), 251–75.

Wright, S. (2000a), *Community and Communication. The Role of Language in Nation State Building and European Integration*. Clevendon: Multilingual Matters.

—— (2000b), 'Communicating across divides: lingua francas in Europe', in L. Hantrais, J. Howarth and S. Wright (eds), *Language, Politics and Society: The New Languages Department*. Clevedon: Multilingual Matters, pp. 119–29.

—— (2011), 'Democracy, communities of communication and the European Union', in A. L. Kjaer and S. Adamo (eds), *Linguistic Diversity and European Democracy*. Farnham: Ashgate, pp. 35–56.

## EU official texts and documents

European Communities (2004), *A Constitution for Europe – Rome 29.10.2004*. Available at: http://bookshop.europa.eu/en/a-constitution-for-europe-pbKA6004806/

European Communities (2005), *Careers at the EU Institutions*. European Personnel Selection Office. Available at: http://bookshop.europa.eu/en/careers-at-the-eu-institutions-pbOC6304004/

European Commission (2006), *In Touch With the EU: Ask Your Questions, Have Your Say!* Directorate General for Communication. Available at: http://ec.europa.eu/europeaid/infopoint/publications/communication/8g_en.htm

European Commission (2010), *Freedom to move and live in Europe*. Directorate General for Justice. Available at: http://ec.europa.eu/justice/policies/citizenship/docs/guide_free_movement.pdf

European Commission (2012), *European Health Insurance Card*, Directorate General for Employment, Social Affairs & Inclusion. Available at: http://ec.europa.eu/social/main.jsp?catId=559

Treaty establishing a Constitution for Europe, *Official Journal of the European Union*, C310, vol. 47, 16 December 2004.

**PUBLIC POLICY**

# 19

# The Privatization of the Public Realm

# A Critical Perspective on Practice and Discourse

*Gerlinde Mautner*

Vienna University of Economics and Business

## 1 Introduction

When privatization first arrived on the political scene, in the 1980s, it referred to the sale of state assets – or 'the family silver' as these were sometimes dubbed, both jokingly and wistfully. In the UK, such giants as British Gas, British Airways and British Steel all went under the hammer, as did smaller concerns such as local bus companies. Deregulation and competition became important buzzwords in the neo-liberal agenda, heralding the dawn of a new and supposedly non-bureaucratic age. This type of privatization had and continues to have its critics, and rightly so. Yet, more recently, privatization has become a more far-reaching social and discursive phenomenon, striking at the heart of what it means to be a citizen, a student or a patient, rather than a customer; affecting values, beliefs and identities; impacting in myriad ways on how societies are organized and how life is lived in them; and, not surprisingly, heavily implicating discourse. Now more is at stake than questions of who owns and runs what, important though these are.

The issue I will be discussing in this chapter is the way the commercial domain has been encroaching on the non-commercial in more far-reaching ways, over and above the impact it has had on ownership and control. A certain degree of permeability between the domains has existed in various forms throughout the ages. But what we are looking at now is a relentless seeping of market-oriented behaviours and language into almost every nook and cranny of social life. The market is no longer merely a place, virtual or physical, where buyers and sellers meet and exchange goods and services. We have moved from a market economy to a market society, in which, as Polanyi put it (1977: 9), the market 'envelops society'.

My interest in privatization has arisen from two strands of my research, the spread of marketization to other social domains (Mautner, 2010a, 2010b; cf. Magistro, this volume), on the one hand, and public signage on the other (Mautner, 2012, 2014). The more deeply I got involved in the socio-political background to signage, and the way signs often index the shrinking of public space, the more obvious it became that the two strands were related. Privatization, broadly conceived, turned out to be the link. It also became clear that far beyond these two strands, privatization is a powerful and ubiquitous socio-political trend. Exploring all its facets and ramifications would be beyond the remit of a single chapter, and indeed of a single academic discipline, but what I am hoping to do here is to flag up the problem from the perspective of critical discourse studies.

The preceding paragraphs will have strongly suggested that my attitude towards the new, all-embracing type of privatization is predominantly negative. After all, no one who is enthusiastic about it would use words like *encroaching, relentless* and *seeping*. So my choice of words will in itself have been rather revealing. Yet standard CDA protocol, quite rightly, demands that researchers declare their stance openly rather than leaving readers to work it out from indirect clues. That is, if you are going to be 'unabashedly normative' (Van Dijk, 1993: 253), as I intend to be here, it is best to own up to it straight away.

My motive for investigating the new privatization is quite simple: I want it to stop. And if it can't be stopped (by far the likelier scenario, I will readily admit), then it would at least be some success to make it more transparent and increase language users' awareness of what is happening. Transparency and awareness are not sufficient conditions for change, but they are necessary ones. If people have to use 'marketized' language at all, then let us at least make sure that they do so self-reflexively, critically and, as a result, perhaps more sparingly. If the commons – that is, public resources, including space, freely accessible to all – really are in crisis, then let us face up to that rather than accepting it as 'the way things are'. Selling-out to market ideology is bad enough; but worse is to sleepwalk into it. Critical discourse analysis (CDA) has an important role to play here, because it is geared up to de-naturalize practices and discourses that have become so deeply ingrained as to be accepted as natural and inevitable, and are often presented not just as the best way forward but as the only one.

This clarification must be followed by another. The thrust of my argument may suggest to some readers that I am anti-business, or a dyed-in-the-wool Marxist, or both. As it happens, I am neither. Rather than 'anti-business' I am 'pro-boundaries', that is, in favour of maintaining clear dividing lines between commercial and non-commercial domains, and in favour of protecting the public realm against unwarranted incursions (another loaded term) from corporate concerns. I am quite happy to concede that market capitalism is a wonderful thing. Like many people in the Global North,[1] I enjoy its huge benefits every day. However, not everything that is great, as such, is also great everywhere, as Sandel (2012) argues very powerfully in *What Money Can't Buy. The Moral Limits of Markets*.

Like him, I would claim that there are areas of human existence where the logic of monetary exchange, competition and instrumental rationality is simply out of place – metaphorically, and in some cases even literally, as we will see during our foray into linguistic landscapes (Shohamy and Gorter, 2009). To argue that marketization should be reined in is not at all the same as arguing that markets are bad as such. Nor is it a plea for the opposite extreme, wholesale public ownership and a return to more powerful state bureaucracies. The problem is not that societies have markets operating within them, but that 'the market' has been elevated to a 'social principle' (Slater and Tonkiss, 2001: 25), creating a 'market society', in which 'a whole society [is] embedded in the mechanism of its own economy' (Polanyi, 1977: 9). It is indeed the boundaries that matter: determination and moderation in drawing them, and constant vigilance in protecting them.

The remainder of this chapter is structured as follows. The second section clarifies key concepts, explaining how the term *public realm* is to be understood here, and what is meant by subjecting it to a critical and discursive analysis. In the third section, I will summarize the argument presented in greater detail in Mautner (2010a), a longer treatise on the connections between language and the market society. Section 4 then discusses how the shrinking of public space is connected to discourse, while the conclusion identifies several theoretical and methodological issues that this type of research raises for CDA. Geopolitically, the frame of reference for my argument consists in the states, cities and societies of the Global North.

# 2  Key concepts

## 2.1  *The public realm*

The different meanings of *public* and *private* may appear straightforward, but on closer inspection the distinction is far from obvious; it is certainly not a neat dichotomy, and perhaps best captured in terms of a spectrum. At its opposite ends lie fairly clear-cut cases, it is true: most of us would probably not hesitate to call a family dinner at home a private event and a municipal park a public place. But what about the meeting of a school's parent-teacher association taking place in the school, or a book launch taking place in the members' room of an art gallery? Access in such cases is not universal, and in the latter case even conditional on the payment of a fee. Is a press conference public because the visual and verbal fallout it generates is broadcast to millions, or is it private because you need press corps ID to be admitted? And what about a shopping mall that presents us with a street-like environment? Even if it feels public in social terms, it is private in law, which means, among other things, that the owners can decide who is allowed in and who is kept out. If you are visibly poor, homeless or a political activist carrying a placard, the ostensibly 'public' mall is off limits to you. Nor is access the only issue. In public-service provision, such as transport and healthcare, outsourcing and PPPs (public-private partnerships) are now commonplace, creating a *mêlée* of interests, responsibilities and accountabilities. In fact, hybrid structures are all over the place and beginning to feel more like the norm than the exception. As a result, studies of space are now full of hyphenated creations such as *semi-public* (Carmona, 2010: 132) and *pseudo-private* (Mitchell and Staeheli, 2006).

To complicate matters even further, we have to bear in mind that the concepts of *public* and *private* are closely connected with cultural and historical settings. Their meaning cannot be defined in absolute but only in culturally relative terms. The distinction is fundamentally part of the Graeco-Roman tradition, lay dormant in Europe's pre-modern, feudal societies, was revived by modernity and consolidated by secular, liberal democracies (McKee, 2005: 34). The contemporary blurring of the spheres is very much a postmodern phenomenon.

In her treatise on public space, Margaret Kohn (2004: 11) also argues that 'today, the private and public realms are becoming increasingly intertwined'. To cope with the ensuing complexity, she proposes to treat public space as a 'cluster concept' to be captured by a set of criteria which are met to different degrees by different places, rather than trying to offer a unitary and universally applicable definition. Her three criteria are ownership, accessibility and intersubjectivity (that is, the degree to which a space encourages interaction). The present chapter is not only about space, but Kohn's ideas can be usefully applied to our concerns here. We will see later how the 'intertwining' that she speaks of is reflected in and promoted by discourse; how hybrid socio-legal structures create hybridity in discourse; and how different clusterings of ownership, accessibility and intersubjectivity define what kinds of discourses may be enacted where.

Before moving on, we need to take another moment to disentangle the following four, partly overlapping, terms: *public sphere, public realm, public domain*, and *public space*. The term *public sphere* is usually associated with the work of Jürgen Habermas, who defined it as

> a domain of our social life where such a thing as public opinion can be formed. Access to the public sphere is open in principle to all citizens . . . Citizens act as a public when they deal with matters of general interest without being subject to coercion; thus with the guarantee that they may assemble and unite freely, and express and publicize their opinions freely . . . To the public sphere as a sphere

mediating between state and society, a sphere in which the public as the vehicle of public opinion is formed, there corresponds the principle of publicness – the publicness that once had to win out against the secret politics of monarchs and that since then has permitted democratic control of state activity.

(Habermas, 2006: 103)

The public sphere is thus intimately linked to interaction between citizens and expression of opinion. Accordingly, it has come to be strongly associated with the media and popular culture. There is no need to reject these associations for my purposes here, but what I find useful about the term *public realm* is that it is a broader alternative. Unburdened by specifically Habermasian associations, the *public realm* can be taken to include state government and administration, and thus precisely that top layer of authority that he treats as distinct from the public sphere. That layer is very much affected by privatization, so it makes sense to use a cover term that includes it.

What about *public domain* and *public space? Public domain*, as Habermas' own definition above would suggest ('the public sphere is a domain . . .'), can be used synonymously with both *public sphere* and *public realm. Public space*, on the other hand, is part of, but not co-extensive with, *public realm*. I will use the former exclusively in a non-metaphorical sense, to refer to physical space. The two are connected: what happens with and in public *space* – whether it shrinks or expands, and what rules govern it – is determined by social agents in the public *realm*, that is, national, regional and local governments. Their authority to decide what happens with public space includes the right to share or abrogate the associated powers – in short, to privatize.

## 2.2 A critical discourse perspective

In a volume like this, it will become apparent how many different 'takes' on discourse there are, how many different types of discourse analysis, and how many different approaches (cf. Introduction) within any one type. For the present chapter, I am drawing on what one might call mainstream CDA – a moniker which back in the early 1990s, when the field was still in the making, would have been quite an oxymoron. In the meantime, though, CDA has become well established and institutionalized, so that it appears redundant to repeat in detail programmatic statements expounded exhaustively in many other sources (e.g., Van Dijk, 1993; Fairclough and Wodak, 1997; Wodak, 2004; Wodak and Meyer, 2009).

I will therefore restrict myself to pointing out the various ways in which the framework's key characteristics have informed the present study.

1    The initial impulse to study the discourse of the newly privatized public realm came from an interest in that social phenomenon rather than from strictly language considerations.

2    Underlying that interest was the constructivist conviction that language is
     instrumental in both reflecting and shaping the phenomenon. Privatization
     creates its own discourse, and that discourse, in turn, further consolidates
     privatization.

3    That conviction is linked to a belief in the ability of language to promote social
     change and in discourse analysts' aspiration to make change transparent.
     Specifically, they can and must help to challenge the misconception that,
     because privatization is now so ubiquitous, it is entirely natural – and so cannot
     be changed.

4    Privatization is regarded as the result of vested interests and unequal power
     relationships – between different social groups, but also between the state
     and business corporations. The resulting withdrawal of the state affects
     everyone because it redefines the fundamentals of statehood and citizenship.
     Also, the more areas of the public realm become privatized, the less power
     can be exercised by the disadvantaged over their already limited resources,
     both symbolic and material.

5    In examining discourse data, I am following standard CDA practice in
     potentially considering all linguistic levels, from lexis and syntax to text. A
     social structure or process may crystallize in one particular lexeme (witness,
     for example, my observations on the use of *loitering* below), or it may be
     played out through longer stretches of text, groups of texts and the
     intertextual links between them. If local authorities, for example, start
     adopting the discourse of branding, they are not only making an individual
     lexical choice; they are tapping into a much broader semiotic repertoire,
     including non-verbal modes of expression. Likewise, if a shopping mall
     pretends to be a public space, then labelling of that space (such as using
     the word *streets* for what are effectively corridors in a building) is only one
     element in an array of semiotic resources that are deployed to index open
     access and effortless consumption.

## 3  Market discourse in public administration

Already, privatization has reached areas that would once have been considered part of
an inviolate core of 'publicness'. In the UK, for example, there are now 14 private
prisons. Perhaps not surprisingly, the public arm of the sector, Her Majesty's Prison
Service, feels the need to stress its competitiveness, announcing on its website that
its vision is 'to provide the very best prison services so that we are the provider of
choice'.[2] However, the public sector still includes a number of organizations –
government ministries and courts among them – which have not been privatized and
are not exposed to market forces. Where the Rule of Law holds, you can't shop around

for the coolest foreign secretary, hire the most eloquent high-court judge or choose your favourite Inland Revenue official. In fact, even attempting to do so (let alone accepting such an offer) is considered bribery, an indictable offence.

Thus, there are areas of the public realm that have not been penetrated by the social practices associated with market mechanisms, and where society has put strong protective layers in place, in the shape of legal deterrents, to ensure that this does not happen. Citizens may be construed rhetorically as consumers (Clarke et al., 2007), but the metaphor seems inappropriate in the absence of choice. Nevertheless, organizations in these areas too can be seen to be adopting the discourses of the market – not everywhere and not all the time, but consistently enough to appear on the discourse analyst's radar. Arguably, nowhere is the evidence for a transition to a true market society more compelling than in those cases where there are none of the outward conditions commonly regarded as inducing market-like behaviours – such as deregulation and competition. Thus, what we see in parts of the public sector is discourse running ahead of practice.

Take the judiciary, for example. A few years ago, the Austrian Constitutional Court underwent a rebranding exercise resulting in a new logo. Whereas the old one featured the heraldic eagle, one of Austria's official state symbols, the new one merely consists of 14 purple dots and the acronym *vfgh* to represent the court's German name (**Verfassungsgerichtshof**).[3] The dots symbolize the court's 14 judges, but that is a rather opaque reference likely to be lost on most people. With the official state symbol edited out, there is nothing in the new logo to suggest the court's status and role. The plaque outside its offices in Vienna's city centre might as well be announcing any corporate headquarters.

The website of the Crown Prosecution Service for England and Wales is another case in point.[4] It displays, prominently, a brash, succinct, three-part motto – 'Fair, fearless, effective', a *Feedback and Complaints* feature – asking, 'Good or bad experience with us?' and a menu item headed *CPS Successes of the month*, with *of the month* triggering associations with *flavour* or *employee of the month*.

Government ministries now routinely make similar linguistic choices. The Austrian Ministry of the Interior calls itself 'the largest and most responsive service provider in the area of security'.[5] Similarly, the UK Department for Work and Pensions (DWP) declares on its website that it is 'the biggest public service delivery department in the UK and serves over 20 million customers'. The site goes on to list its 'operational organizations' under the heading of 'Our businesses'.[6] It also has a Customer Charter.[7] Several government departments have *business plans*, including the Home Office[8] and the Department for Education.[9] The Department of Health has a *Corporate Plan*, in which it sets out what it calls its *business priorities*.[10] Tellingly, higher education in the UK falls under the portfolio of the Department for Business, Innovation and Skills. On its website, under the heading *What we do*, ten topics are listed in alphabetical order, given equal rank by the same font size and equal amounts of text devoted to each topic. The paragraph introducing the ten topics, and in particular the purpose clause in the second sentence (*to promote trade*, . . .) leaves no doubt about the department's instrumental view of education:

> The Department for Business, Innovation & Skills (BIS) is the department for economic growth. The department invests in skills and education to promote trade, boost innovation and help people to start and grow a business.[11]

Local government, too, has adopted the language of the market. In a study of local council job advertisements, reported in Mautner (2010a), it emerged that in the period between 1978 and 2008, job ads have developed from brief, matter-of-fact announcements to elaborate PR exercises, advertising the locality and the council as much, if not more, than the job itself. In 2008, euphemisms abound (*challenges*[12] instead of problems, for example), and clusters of managerial jargon are not uncommon. In a single, two-sentence paragraph alone, a job ad by Lancashire County Council[13] included the terms *customer services, customer consultation, business plan development, performance management, continuous improvement approaches, customer care, targets, business plans, customer care methods* and *customer service performance*.

Of course, all the above examples could be evaluated much more positively than I have done: as indications of a move, long overdue, away from remote, inaccessible state bureaucracies. At last, one could argue, these institutions talk to citizens, feel a need to persuade people of their usefulness and good qualities ('fair, fearless, effective'), and reassure the taxpayer that because the public sector is doing a great job their money is well spent. Furthermore, organizations not only compete for clients, but also for potential employees; so from the point of view of what is generally referred to as 'employer branding', it can make sense even for a monopolist to deploy persuasive strategies to present itself in the best possible light. However, the crux isn't organizations' desire to persuade, as such, but the widespread conviction that the most persuasive discourse is that of the private sector. In order to sound professional, it seems *de rigueur* to speak that kind of language. Rather than developing their own, distinctive discourses, public-sector organizations often simply adopt the marketing speak typical of commercial promotion (or allow advertising and PR professionals to do so on their behalf). As a result, the discursive boundaries between the domains become blurred.

This blurring isn't merely a cosmetic problem on the linguistic surface. If one accepts the existence of a dialectic relationship between language and society, then it is obvious that the linguistic changes in the public realm are not just the result of, but also make a significant contribution to, what Clarke (2004), in his account of neoliberalism, calls 'the dissolving of the public realm'. As he explains (2004: 31):

> Neoliberalism has challenged conceptions of the public interest, striving to replace them by the rule of private interests, coordinated by markets. It has insisted that the

'monopoly providers' of public services be replaced by efficient suppliers, disciplined by the competitive realities of the market. It has disintegrated conceptions of the public as a collective identity, attempting to substitute individualised and economised identities as taxpayers and consumers.

# 4 Discourse and space

So far, we have looked at how public-sector organizations communicate new, 'privatized' institutional identities, and at how, in the process, they reframe their stakeholders' identities. Important as such communication is, people's contact with privatization is not restricted to their dealings with public administration. It also happens, mundanely but significantly, in that part of the public realm which is constituted by public space: in streets, parks, plazas, residential areas and shopping precincts. Contemporary cityscapes are dominated by commercial semiotics: billboards, neon signs, shopfronts, street furniture with advertising and so on. In a modern city, it would be difficult to find any spot from which no corporate message can be seen. But it isn't the mere ubiquity of advertising that concerns us here, but a more broadly conceived colonization of what used to be public objects and spaces by private interests.

Let us begin with a fairly obvious and straightforward case, so-called 'transit advertising'. In many cities, advertising space is sold on buses, trams and underground trains. In some cases, it isn't just space on such vehicles that is sold but their entire surface, so that the original livery of the public transport company is completely obliterated. Vienna's underground trains occasionally undergo such total colonization. The less obtrusive alternative, practised by Transport for London on its buses, involves posters which are attached to the vehicle but leave the organization's original visual identity intact. The distinctive red double-decker, a tourist icon as well as a means of transport, at least remains red. In this context, it matters little that many transport companies these days are actually private companies under the law. Irrespective of ownership structures, these companies still provide a public service.

Railway stations are another case in point. It is not so much the presence of advertising billboards that is the problem – at least billboards are set off clearly from their environment. However, increasingly in the UK, advertising messages are attached to the signs naming stations. Figure 19.1 shows an example from Clapham Junction train station, South London.

Without corporate advertising, station signs merely identify a place; with advertising, they identify a place specifically as one that is of interest to business. By being allowed to leave an imprint like that, a company is granted symbolic ownership of the place concerned. Yet places, I would argue, should not really be 'owned' by anyone except the *polis*. Once again, a boundary has crumbled.

It could be argued that these symbolic inroads into the public realm have no material consequence. People may find them irritating, but the signs confer no power on the

**FIGURE 19.1** *Station sign at Clapham Junction, South London.*[14]

companies involved to control anyone's behaviour. However, publicness can be threatened in much more tangible ways. The 'shrinking of the public realm' that Clarke referred to above has a physical parallel in the shrinking of public space, which does indeed have an impact on what we can do and say where. Take shopping malls, for example. At first sight, they may be mistaken for the contemporary city's *agora*, an open, democratic and egalitarian place in which the public can congregate (Dale and Burrell, 2008: 259; Sennett, 1994: 52).[15] But there are problems with this interpretation. In legal terms, the modern shopping mall is not public but private, which means that the owners or their representatives can refuse admission to people they do not want to be there. An example of the textual fallout of this situation can be seen in Figure 19.2. Not surprisingly, the homeless and beggars are conspicuous by their absence.

What is more, in such 'pseudo-public' spaces, free speech is restricted because again it is up to the property owner to decide who to admit and what kind of activity to allow. Campaigners, demonstrators and pickets are unlikely to be welcome, especially if the target of their protest is one of the mall's corporate residents. Thus, unlike the ancient *agora*, the mall is a space that revolves primarily around consumption.

**FIGURE 19.2** *Entrance to the Churchill Shopping Centre in Brighton, UK.*

It is fundamentally an apolitical space. The same is true of privately owned plazas and walkways in business districts, and of ostensibly communal spaces in gated communities. With these types of spaces proliferating, protest activity is marginalized, not by some draconian curtailment of civil liberties, but quite simply and subtly because there are fewer and fewer public places left where it is allowed to happen (Kohn, 2004: 69–92). 'Silencing', Mitchell reminds us (2003: 2), 'is a function of geography'.[16]

However, the privatization of public space not only affects the politically active. It also affects those who have no private space of their own to retreat to, and who simply need to *be* somewhere in public. That the new *quasi*-public spaces are not for them is made clear either non-verbally, through architectural design, or verbally, through signage (Mautner 2012, 2014), and quite often through both. Such signs appear to govern behaviour, but effectively govern people (Valverde, 2005: 37). For example, a sign outside an office building saying *Private Property/No loitering* (Figure 19.3) or one in a railway station saying *This concourse is not to be used for overnight sleeping* (Figure 19.4) does not mention who is being addressed. But because loitering and rough sleeping are activities typically associated with the dispossessed, it is quite

**FIGURE 19.3**  *Russell Square, London.*

**FIGURE 19.4**  *Victoria Station, London.*

obvious that they are the target. In this context, the word *loitering* is a particularly interesting case of how the meaning of a verb of doing can incorporate a typical doer. For, as sample sentences in several dictionaries show,[17] *loiter* is associated primarily with teenagers and the unemployed.

To sum up, privatization has both commercialized and 'sanitized' (Barber, 2001: 206) urban space. As a result, the city is, by and large, a less messy environment than it used to be. Yet it is also more homogenized, more oriented towards consumption, more redolent of corporate semiotics, and less likely to be a forum for marginalized groups and dissenting voices. It is true that in the contemporary digital world, the public realm isn't necessarily tied to physical space. Nonetheless, the latter still provides the all-important framework within which culture, community and discourse are organized. As Parkinson argues (2012: 2), online interaction notwithstanding, 'democracy depends to a surprising extent on the availability of physical, public space'.

# 5 Conclusion

The aim of the present chapter was to show how discourse is implicated in the privatization of the public realm, with *privatization* understood broadly as two concomitant processes:

- the contraction of what is shared by the community, widely and freely accessible, and subject to democratic accountability; and

- the expansion of what is based on contractual arrangements, distributed competitively and governed by market forces.

There are several connections to discourse. First, discourse both reflects and promotes the market society because the language originally associated with commercial exchange is transferred to social domains that were traditionally not organized along market principles, such as government and public administration. Second, linguistic landscapes are transformed in the process; not just through classic advertising on billboards, but through media that blur the boundaries between the public realm and commercial interests. Advertisements that completely cover public transport vehicles are one example, and ads attached to place signs in railway stations another. Both lead to an appropriation of public space by corporate interests. Third, the study of signs highlights the way in which discourse can be used to demarcate public from private space, to ban certain types of land use, and thus to exclude social groups typically engaging in those uses.

Although all of these developments are happening, quite literally, in front of our very eyes, they often go unnoticed, or at least unreflected. Perhaps this should not surprise us; the market is, after all, at the hub of a dominant grand narrative, to use Lyotard's term (Lyotard, 1984 [1979]). In that narrative, there is very little room, conceptually, for the idea of the commons (Bollier, 2003).[18] Accordingly, in the tangible environment, the amount of truly shared spaces is shrinking too.

Why are these developments of interest to critical discourse analysis? First, because they are closely connected to one of its core areas of concern, power differentials. These need not consist in asymmetries between individual social actors, between a fat cat and an underdog. More often than not, what we're up against are 'spiderless webs of power relationships' (Hardy and Palmer, 1999: 386) – complex, pervasive, elusive and all the more effective for it. The marketization of language, which we discussed in Section 3, may not be affected overtly by authoritarian decree from above, yet linguistic choices made by powerful elites can trigger discursive alignment further along the line (Mautner, 2010a, 2010b) because it makes sense for the less powerful to emulate the language of their betters. Second, control over space, too, is a question of power, mediated through the legal institution of private ownership, as well as through criminal and administrative law. Third, issues of voice, civil liberties and the marginalization of dissent are also high on the agenda of a critical and politically aware discourse analysis.

The privatization of the public realm, therefore, ticks all the right boxes as a classic arena for CDA. All the same, the argument as I have presented it here involves several difficulties. In the spirit of CDA's commitment to self-reflexive critique, I shall examine them now, beginning with that relating to the limitations of any approach focusing on discourse. In keeping with critical realism (Fairclough, 2005), I believe it is vital for discourse analysts to concede that social life isn't all about discourse, and only then to insist that social life is usually *also* about discourse. Privatization is a multi-layered phenomenon with political, social, legal and cultural dimensions. In my account, I did try to acknowledge this as much as space would allow, and on several occasions tapped into insights from other disciplines. But ultimately, eclectic inspiration and borrowing is no substitute for a genuinely interdisciplinary undertaking. I am confident that discourse analysts can actually do quite a lot, but, given the nature of privatization, it would be hubris to assume that we can sort it all out by ourselves. A more concerted effort by scholars from a range of backgrounds would not only be theoretically and methodologically fruitful, but also add clout to activism directed at reclaiming the public realm.

Even within the narrower confines of our own field, though, investigating something as complex as privatization presents a methodological challenge. Developing research designs boils down to questions of scale and scope, or indeed scale versus scope. Should one look at a small selection of phenomena in a very large corpus (scale), or look at as many different types of phenomena as possible (scope), or at one that scores high on both scale and scope? For the purposes of this chapter, I decided on the third option, taking a broad sweep of a varied datascape rather than homing in on a particular genre, medium, set of keywords or linguistic device. In this way, I was hoping to do better justice to the multi-layeredness, ubiquity and complexity of the problem, while flagging up a broad range of key issues that could be pursued further in future. Inevitably, breadth comes at the expense of depth. At the last resort, it is the analyst's judgement call, and for every critic arguing that a particular treatise has cast the net too wide, there will be another who says that it hasn't been cast wide enough. The privatization of the public realm simply strikes me as one of those issues where it makes more sense to err on the side of breadth. This isn't a proud programmatic statement, I hasten to add, but a humble and pragmatic one.

I began this chapter by making a plea in favour of clear boundaries between the public and private realms, between a freely accessible, equitable commons and a competitive world driven by market principles. Let me end it by emphasizing that the scholarly community has an important role to play as guardians of those boundaries. The role of linguists, specifically, is to show how discourse is instrumental both in building and maintaining them and in blurring and destroying them. Protecting the boundaries is not an end in itself, but ensures that values intrinsic to the public realm are preserved. Like neoliberals, I am convinced that we are all better off if business flourishes. Unlike them, I also believe that we are all worse off if business is allowed to flourish outside well-defined boundaries.

# Notes

1 Essentially, the expression *Global North* refers to wealthy parts of the world. It is not an unproblematic term (Del Casino, 2009: 26), but one frequently used and, on balance, preferable to alternatives that are more disparaging to poorer nations, such as the more traditional dichotomies *First World/Third World* or *developed/developing*.

2 http://www.justice.gov.uk/about/hmps, accessed 29 December 2012.

3 http://www.vfgh.gv.at/, accessed 20 December 2012.

4 http://www.cps.gov.uk/index.html, accessed 20 December 2012.

5 '*Das Bundesministerium für Inneres ist das größte und sensibelste Dienstleistungsunternehmen im Sicherheitsbereich*', http://www.bmi.gv.at/cms/bmi_minister/, accessed 20 December 2012, translation by the author.

6 http://www.dwp.gov.uk/about-dwp/, accessed 20 December 2012.

7 http://www.dwp.gov.uk/about-dwp/customer-delivery/, accessed 20 December 2012.

8 http://www.homeoffice.gov.uk/publications/about-us/corporate-publications/business-plan/business-plan-2012-15/, accessed 20 December 2012.

9 http://www.education.gov.uk/aboutdfe/departmentalinformation/Business%20Plan, accessed 20 December 2012.

10 http://corporateplan2012.dh.gov.uk/, accessed 20 December 2012.

11 https://www.gov.uk/government/organisations/department-for-business-innovation-skills, accessed 20 December 2012. Note also how the purpose of education is associated with entrepreneurialism (see Mautner, 2005).

12 In a 2008 job advertisement published by Lambeth Council in London.

13 Published in *The Guardian*, 10 September 2008.

14 Douglas & Gordon is an estate agent operating in London (http://www.douglasandgordon.com/about/).

**15** In its own historical context, the ancient *agora* was an open and egalitarian place. By today's standards, however, it would still be considered socially exclusive because only free citizens were admitted, which excluded slaves.

**16** For academics, the implications of this development can be quite close to home. The *Guardian Online* reported recently (12 June 2012) that security guards prevented strikers from picketing on the campus of Salford University. They were able to do so because the land concerned was privately owned.

**17** 'Unemployed young men loiter at the entrance of the factory' in the *Collins Cobuild Advanced English Dictionary*, 'Teenagers were loitering in the street outside' in the *Oxford Advanced Learner's Dictionary*, 'Five or six teenagers were loitering in front of the newsagent's' in the *Longman Dictionary of Contemporary English*, and 'There's a group of kids loitering outside the shop' in the *Macmillan Dictionary*.

**18** Bollier's definition of *the commons*, though phrased from an American perspective, can be applied more generally to industrialized democratic countries:

> The American commons include tangible assets such as public forests and minerals, intangible wealth such as copyrights and patents, critical infrastructure such as the Internet and government research, and cultural resources such as the broadcast airwaves and public spaces.
>
> *We, as citizens, own these commons.* They include resources that we have paid for as taxpayers and resources that we have inherited from previous generations. They are not just an inventory of marketable assets, but social institutions and cultural traditions that define us as Americans and enliven us as human beings – public education, community institutions, democratic values, wildlife and national forests, public spaces in cities and communications media (Bollier, 2003: 2–3; original italics).

# References

Barber, B. (2001), 'Malled, mauled and overhauled: arresting suburban sprawl by transforming the mall into usable civic space', in M. Hénaff and T. B. Strong (eds), *Public Space and Democracy*. Minneapolis: University of Minnesota Press, pp. 201–20.

Bollier, D. (2003), *Silent Theft. The Private Plunder of Our Common Wealth*. New York and London: Routledge.

Carmona, M. (2010), 'Contemporary public space: critique and classification. Part One: critique'. *Journal of Urban Design*, 15(1), 123–48.

Clarke, J. (2004), 'Dissolving the public realm? The logics and limits of neo-liberalism'. *Journal of Social Policy*, 33(1), 27–48.

Clarke, J., Newman, J., Smith, N., Vidler, E. and Westmarland, L. (2007), *Creating Citizen-Consumers: Changing Publics and Changing Public Services*. London: Sage.

Dale, K. and Burrell, G. (2008), *The Spaces of Organisation and the Organisation of Space. Power, Identity and Materiality at Work*. Basingstoke and New York: Palgrave Macmillan.

Del Casino, V. J. (2009), *Social Geography: A Critical Introduction*. Chichester, UK and Malden, MA: Wiley-Blackwell.

Fairclough, N. (2005), 'Discourse analysis in organization studies: The case for critical realism'. *Organization Studies*, 26(6), 915–39.

Fairclough, N., and Wodak (1997), 'Critical discourse analysis'. in T. A. Van Dijk (ed.), *Discourse as Social Interaction* (Discourse Studies: A Multidisciplinary Introduction, vol. 2). London: Sage, pp. 258–84.

Habermas, J. (2006), 'The public sphere', in R. E. Goodin and P. Pettit (eds), *Contemporary Political Philosophy: An Anthology.* 2nd edn. Oxford: Blackwell, pp. 103–6.

Hardy, C., and Palmer, I. (1999), 'Pedagogical practice and postmodernist ideas'. *Journal of Management Education,* 23(4), 377–95.

Kohn, M. (2004), *Brave New Neighborhoods. The Privatization of Public Space.* New York and London: Routledge.

Lyotard, J.-F. (1984 [1979]), *The Postmodern Condition: A Report on Knowledge.* Manchester: Manchester University Press.

McKee, A. (2005), *The Public Sphere. An Introduction.* Cambridge: Cambridge University Press.

Mautner, G. (2005), 'The entrepreneurial university: a discursive profile of a higher education buzzword'. *Critical Discourse Studies,* 2(2), 1–26.

—— (2010a), *Language and the Market Society. Critical Reflections on Discourse and Dominance.* London and New York: Routledge.

—— (2010b), 'The spread of corporate discourse to other social domains', in H. Kelly-Holmes and G. Mautner (eds), *Language and the Market.* Basingstoke: Palgrave Macmillan, pp. 215–25.

—— (2012), 'Language, space and the law: a study of directive signs'. *International Journal of Space, Language and the Law,* 19(2), 189–217.

—— (2014), 'Signs of the times: a discourse perspective on public signage, urban space and the law', in N. Coupland and A. Jaworski (eds), *The Discourse Reader* (3rd edn). London: Routledge, pp. 386–403.

Mitchell, D. (2003), 'The liberalization of free speech: or, how protest in public space is silenced', *Stanford Agora* 4. Available at: http://agora.stanford.edu/agora/volume4/articles/mitchell/mitchell.pdf

Mitchell, D. and Staeheli, L. A. (2006), 'Clean and safe? Property redevelopment, public space, and homelessness in downtown San Diego', in S. Low and N. Smith (eds), *The Politics of Public Space.* New York and London: Routledge, pp. 143–75.

Parkinson, J. R. (2012), *Democracy and Public Space: The Physical Sites of Democratic Performance.* Oxford: Oxford University Press.

Polanyi, K. (1977), *The Livelihood of Man.* New York: Academic Press.

Sandel, M. (2012), *What Money Can't Buy. The Moral Limits of Markets.* London: Allen Lane.

Sennett, R. (1994), *Flesh and Stone.* London: Faber and Faber.

Shohamy, E. and Gorter, D. (eds) (2009), *Linguistic Landscape. Expanding the Scenery.* New York and London: Routledge.

Slater, D., and Tonkiss, F. (2001), *Markets and Modern Social Theory.* Cambridge: Polity.

Valverde, M. (2005), 'Taking "land use" seriously: toward an ontology of municipal law'. *Law, Text, Culture* 9, 33–59.

Van Dijk, T. A. (1993), 'Principles of critical discourse analysis'. *Discourse and Society,* 4(2), 249–83.

Wodak, R. (2004), 'Critical discourse analysis', in C. Seale, D. Silverman, J. F. Gubrium and G. Gobo (eds), *Qualitative Research Practice.* London: Sage, pp. 197–213.

Wodak, R. and Meyer, M. (2009), 'Critical discourse analysis: history, agenda, theory and methodology', in R. Wodak and M. Meyer (eds), *Methods of Critical Discourse Analysis* (2nd edn). London: Sage, pp. 1–33.

# 20

# Pushed out of School

# A Critical Discourse Analysis of the Policies and Practices of Educational Accountability[1]

*Rebecca Rogers*
University of Missouri-St. Louis

## 1 Introduction

Luanne Treader, an African American adolescent living in an urban centre in the United States began ninth grade in 2004, just two years after the educational policy No Child Left Behind was signed into law. The period that marked her time in high school (2004–8) was characterized by a radically shifting educational landscape, both at national and local levels. Luanne's ninth grade class was referred to in school district documents as the '2004 school accountability cohort'. As critical discourse theorists remind us (e.g. Comber and Kamler, 2004; Fairclough, 1995; Foucault, 1977), people are constructed through discourse practices and the institutional labels of 'at-risk', 'drop out' and 'accountability cohort' are discursive manifestations of contemporary policies which, in turn, are adopted, transformed or resisted by students within educational systems. In this chapter, my concern is the impact of accountability policies, over time, from the student's point of view, something most policy studies neglect entirely.

'Are you going to graduate from high school?' I asked Luanne when she was in ninth grade. She responded, 'I always tell my mom that I am going to graduate on time, when I am supposed to graduate.' When I asked her the same question two years later she stated, 'I don't like it anymore [high school]. I just want to go get my GED [General Educational Development degree] and get it over with.'

Despite this stated commitment to graduating, Luanne eventually was listed as a 'high school non-completer' in the state's accountability report. In this chapter, I share a slice of Luanne's educational life to show her struggle and agency negotiating high school during an era of neoliberal educational policies. The following questions guided this study: how do accountability policies and practices unfold across time and impact the lived experiences of urban youth? What are the intersections of national, state and local educational policies which may, inadvertently, support practices that push students out of school? In what ways does Luanne resist and acquiesce to being pushed out of school? I begin with a broad-brush sketch of changes in the educational policy landscape of No Child Left Behind (NCLB). I consider the significance of key policy texts linked to NCLB and discuss the impacts of such texts on Luanne's lived experiences, including her interpretation of the policies.

## 2 Neoliberal educational policy and the discourses of accountability

The past twenty years of educational reform in the United States has been referred to as an era of accountability. In the 1980s, a drive for more punitive policies in criminal justice and education changed the face of public education, prompting tougher policies that would hold schools, educators and students accountable for performance. The 'War on Drugs', a set of policies designed to cut-down on criminal behaviour, expanded to schools where punitive discipline policies resulted in the school to prison pipeline (Advancement Project, 2010). Under zero-tolerance discipline policies, schools devote a large portion of their budget to security infrastructure associated with prisons including metal detectors, surveillance cameras and security guards. The corollary to this style of accountability in public education was to get tough on so-called failing schools, following the 1983 publication of A Nation at Risk. This report laid the ideological groundwork for NCLB. NCLB supports standards-based education reform based on the idea that high standards and measurable goals determined through testing can improve individual outcomes in education. Every year, schools are expected to meet Adequate Yearly Progress (AYP) as indicated through standardized test scores for every sub-group of students in their school. Any school that does not make AYP is subject to sanctions, the ultimate including management of the school by a for-profit educational company or school closure. This has created a test and punish formula for converting public schools into charter schools, ultimately laying the foundation for the privatization of public education (Carr and Porfilio, 2011; Meier, et al., 2004).

Evidence indicates these zero-tolerance policies have not been effective in improving school safety or the quality of the learning environment. The graduation rate in the United States in 2006 was 69 per cent. This was the lowest it had been before NCLB was passed. Related, in 2008, the number of people taking the GED test was at its highest level since before NCLB (Advancement Project, 2010). Additionally, there were 250,000 more students suspended in 2006–7 then there were when NCLB was signed into law (Advancement Project, 2010).

Critics of NCLB point out the contradictions that exist within the policy. At the top of the list is that while schools are expected to reach higher standards they are expected to do so with inadequate resources. And, when improvements are not made, funding is withheld from schools making it even more difficult to reach AYP (Meier et al., 2004). Others point out that teacher professionalism is undermined as decision-making is shifted from educators to large corporations, the same corporations that develop and publish the curricula that are, in turn, enforced through mandated tests (Nichols and Berliner, 2007). To comply with the demands of meeting AYP, teachers are forced to teach to the test and narrow the curriculum to focus exclusively on reading and maths at the expense of the arts, languages and history. NCLB creates the infrastructure for students to be tracked by ability, by behaviour or by vocational outlook. NCLB has a provision on 'Safe Schools' but, ironically, requires schools to let military recruiters have students' contact information for recruitment purposes. NCLB also includes provisions for heightened security in schools, including the hiring of police officers. This kind of criminalization of school grounds has been shown to heighten criminal behaviour (Advancement Project, 2010).

Schools attempt to manage these obvious contradictions through creative interpretation of policy. A number of widely used tactics for artificially inflating test scores have been documented: withdrawing students from attendance rolls, assigning students to alternative schools, telling students not to show up on the day of the test, encouraging students to enroll in General Educational Development (GED) programmes and expulsions, suspensions and referrals to alternative schools (Nichols and Berliner, 2007).

Yet, the policies remain very popular because of their discursive appeal to ideologies of competition, hard work and individual choice. Much of the effectiveness of neoliberal educational policies has to do with the discursive stronghold they have taken in the American psyche. The discourses of accountability, choice, violence-free schools and testing have gained credibility and become naturalized or seen as 'just the ways things are' (Foucault, 1977; Kumashiro, 2009). As Woodside-Jiron (2011: 163) points out 'these terms are often difficult to identify because they are presented with such authority and *ofcourseness* that we tend to pass over them'. Because discourse practices both reflect and construct social reality, we see how these frames are enacted through federal, state and local policies and which, in turn, reinforce the frames (Fairclough, 1995). As Edelman (1988: 31) wrote, 'A policy . . . is a creation of the language used to depict it; its identification is a political act, not a recognition of the fact.' As the mantras of 'accountability', 'testing' and 'choice' are used repeatedly in federal, state and local policies and media to convince the public that testing children more will result in higher test scores and better schools, silenced is the idea that the focus of educational policy should be on student learning, not the test-based outcome of (apparent) learning. This discursive stronghold paves the way for reforms that would otherwise be deemed unacceptable – for instance, policies that result in higher numbers of low income and minority students being pushed out of school – to be carried out with little resistance. Yet, we also need to keep in mind that during policy implementation, people in local contexts – what Dorner (2010: 305) refers to as 'policy agents' – enact the texts and discourses associated with policies in ways unforeseen by official policymakers. Thus, it is important to take a bottom-up approach to understanding the enactment of policies through lived experiences in local contexts (e.g. Hornberger, 2003).

# 3  Research design

My research followed a tradition of scholarship where ethnography and critical discourse analysis were integrated at every stage and level from critical framing and theorization to analysis and representation (Blommaert, 2008; Martín Rojo, 2010; Oberhuber and Krzyżanowski, 2008; Scollon and Scollon, 2004). This case study of Luanne Treader is nested within a longitudinal, ethnographic study of her family's experiences in the educational system. The original study (1996–9) was a three-year ethnographic study of literacy practices (Rogers, 2003). After 1999, I continued to stay in contact with the Treaders, staying abreast of school progress and family events. In the ethnographic restudy (Saldana, 2003), I recorded over 100 hours of participant-observation. Looked at together, the data for this project comprised a total of five years and covered over a decade in the lives and educational pathways of the Treaders.

## 3.1  Participants

The Treaders are an African American family living in Sherman Hollows, an inner city neighbourhood in upstate New York. The Treaders receive housing, income and food assistance. Luanne's mother, June, dropped out of school at the end of ninth grade. She has worked as a housekeeper at a hotel for over twenty years. Lester, the children's father, has a GED and is trained as a plumber. Luanne's older sister, Vicky, was tracked into special education and graduated with a certificate of completion (Rogers, 2011). Their younger brother Evan was labelled at an early age as ADHD and placed in special education (Rogers and Mancini, 2010). The family has an extended social network living in the neighbourhood. I describe the process of developing a relationship and gaining access elsewhere (Rogers, 2003, 2011).

### 3.1.1 Luanne

Luanne was born early in 1990, the second of five siblings. I met Luanne when she was six years old. A bright, active and happy child, she was eager to read books, play with her friends and watch her younger siblings. She attended a federally funded preschool and the local, public elementary and middle school. She received good grades on her report cards and there was rarely an incident with behaviour (June, interview, 9/09). As a pre-adolescent, Luanne cared for her younger siblings and cousins. During the summers, Luanne worked for the City at a pool, attended summer camps and performed with a dance team. She was a leader in her community, serving as the lead teacher for a dance team in a community youth group. As an adolescent, Luanne had pride in her community and was family-oriented. She also had a sense of humour, quick wit and was very attentive to her hair and dress. In ninth grade, Luanne's longtime boyfriend was sentenced to a year in prison for, according to Luanne, 'something he did not do'. Luanne regularly wrote letters to him. When she had access to a computer, she spent time on MySpace, writing emails to her friends, posting messages to her account and updating her profile. Luanne was taking classes that would lead to what was referred to as a 'local diploma' which was widely believed was the option for students who probably would not attend college. She was a relatively good student and served as the captain of her step team at school. Despite her firm conviction of wanting to graduate from high school and go to college, she stopped going to school when she was 17 years old. She had her first child six months later. Her second child arrived a year later.

## 3.2 *Context*

The neighbourhood that the Treaders live in faces homelessness, unemployment, underfunded school systems and gang violence. In 2004–5, the year that Luanne entered high school, 811 students were enrolled in the ninth grade class. In publicly available state 'Report Cards', students are referred to in terms of their 'accountability cohort' (https://reportcards.nysed.gov/). Luanne entered high school in 2004 and is referred to as part of the '2004 school accountability cohort'. For Luanne's cohort, the average size of an English class was 24 students; the average size of a Science class, 25 students. Eighty per cent of all of the students enrolled in the high school were eligible for free or reduced lunch. Sixty-four per cent of the students were African American, 24 per cent white, 9 per cent Latino, 3 per cent Asian or Native Hawaiian and 1 per cent American Indian. Four years later, 688 students were documented in the 2007–8 accountability reports. Of these students, 411 graduated from high school; 177 students did not graduate and were labelled in state accountability documents as 'high school non-completers'. 'Non-completers' are students who dropped out of school or who entered an approved high school equivalency preparation program (167 students labelled as dropouts and 10 who entered in a GED program). It is important to note that another 225 students who entered ninth grade with Luanne are unaccounted for in the final numbers of high school completers and non-completers. These are students who may have left the school district or who dropped out of school before their twelve grade year (https://reportcards.nysed.gov/).

It is also important to understand how the accountability policy works in New York State. According to the state policy, 'the federal NCLB Act requires that states develop and report on measures of student proficiency in 1) English Language Arts (ELA), in 2) mathematics, and on 3) a third indicator. In New York State, in 2005–2006, the third indicator is [. . .] graduation rate at the secondary level. Schools or districts that prove student proficiency on these measures are making Adequate Yearly Progress' (https://reportcards.nysed.gov/). Thus, test scores in ELA and Maths and graduation rates would be the measures through which the schools were held accountable. Problematically, in 2007, the state stopped requiring graduation rates to be reported as part of the accountability plan. Like the rest of the nation, schools in this state are punished if they do not meet AYP several years in a row, with the ultimate sanction being school closure. Like other urban schools, this high school has been the subject of media reports that proliferate the discourses of accountability through repeated claims about failing test scores and delinquent youth. These discourses create an anxiety and urgency amongst school personnel and parents to increase test scores and zero tolerance discipline measures.

## 3.3 *Data collection*

During the restudy, I visited with the family every several months over the course of two years (2007–9). Each visit was four days long and included spending four to six hours a day with the family. I collected data through interviews (Rubin and Rubin, 2011), participant-observations (Spradley, 1980), a community violence survey, document collection and other participatory experiences such as 'tours' of their online (e.g. MySpace) and offline communities (e.g. neighbourhood), literacy lessons and viewing and discussing popular culture (Morrell, 2007). While some of the data collection was planned before the study commenced (e.g. structured interviews, community walks, participant-observations), I called on different methods of data generation as the study progressed that responded to the emerging findings (e.g. non-structured interviews, literacy lessons, community violence survey). I carefully looked, listened and sought out fissures, moments of resistance and Luanne's analysis and critique of dominant norms and ideologies, or counter-narratives (e.g. Bamberg and Andrews, 2004; Hilliard et al., 2004; Solórzano and Yosso, 2009). As it became clear from Luanne's narratives what experiences she marked as central, I gathered publicly available educational policy documents. I obtained documents at the federal (e.g. NCLB), state (e.g. accountability reports from her high school from 2004–8) and local level (e.g. the school district's Code of Conduct policy manual).

## 3.4 Analysis

My analytic approach merges ethnography and critical discourse studies (e.g. Blommaert, 2008; Collins, 1996). This ethnographic orientation is central to understanding the chains of meaning as they unfold over time and across contexts. While critical discourse analysis has been associated with illustrating relations of dominance, control and oppression, it might also illustrate moments of hope, agency and resistance (Bartlett, 2012; Luke, 2004; Martin, 2004; Macgilchrist, 2007). Procedurally, I built a methodology that attended to both structure and agency and traversed the discourses of accountability as they were enacted across people, practices and time. Using Luanne's narratives – generated through fieldnotes and interviews – as the starting point of my analysis, I took stock of the 'cruces' or turning points that characterized her life in school during the era of accountability, tracing instances across texts and contexts. I extracted from key moments in time and the associated policy documents and practices and focused on the shifting combination of discourses within and between accountability texts, discourses and the local enactment and production of accountability. As I analysed the data sources, I asked: how are the discourses of accountability enacted through texts and experiences? Each event that Luanne narrated as important in her high school career was intertextually connected to and informed by accountability policies. For instance, her discussion of ability grouping and the curriculum could be linked to the state's 'assessment pathways' which illustrated the complex maze of credits and exams that were necessary to graduate. With her narratives side-by-side with policy texts, I drew on CDA's mix of interdiscursive and linguistic analysis as resources for describing, interpreting and explaining the relationships between the social processes of accountability and the impacts on lived experiences (Fairclough, 1995; Rogers, 2011; Scollon and Scollon, 2004).

## 4 Luanne's case

Luanne entered high school in 2004, just two years after NCLB was signed into law. In no uncertain terms she told me she would graduate from high school. Over time, however, her certainty turned to ambiguity as she struggled to navigate the translation of a changing educational policy landscape that included tougher graduation standards, an increased number of high stakes tests and punitive behavioural policies. Her institutional records illustrate her delayed progress, repeating parts of tenth grade for three consecutive years. In 2004–5, Luanne was a ninth grader and was promoted to tenth grade. In 2005–6, Luanne was listed as a tenth grader. In her 2006–7 report cards, she was also listed as a tenth grader, reflecting her retention in tenth grade for failure to pass the state mandated tests. In 2007–8, she was also listed as a tenth grader, taking some eleventh grade classes. With the new formula for higher standards, it was taking Luanne two years to successfully complete each grade. In the spring of 2007, Luanne stopped attending school. And, she was not alone. Of the students from her 'accountability cohort', 177 students were considered 'non-completers'. Luanne provided a fairly succinct analysis of the educational policies linked with the tracking, sorting and disregard of students: ability groups, alternative education and the criminalization of youth. Yet, in her final analysis she holds herself accountable, rather than the policies designed to push students like her out of school.

## 5 'The regular track': High stakes testing and graduation pathways

At the beginning of the restudy, I asked Luanne to reflect on her experiences in high school thus far. She was repeating parts of tenth grade for the second time. With her ninth grade report cards in front of us, I explained that the documents were one narrative about her as a student but it was only part of the story. 'What is missing from this report?' I asked Luanne. She noted, 'I was a good student. I listened to my teachers and got OK grades. It doesn't say that I was the captain of the step team.' Indeed, she earned an 80 in English, a 91 in Maths, a 75 in Social Studies and a 55 in Science. She was promoted to tenth grade but then was retained in tenth grade for two years. When she should have been in eleventh grade, she reported knowing that she was behind in the correct number of credits to graduate but not knowing that she was not in the correct grade. Her confusion over the simple fact of what grade she was in reflects the labyrinth of changes to high school graduation requirements that occurred during her tenure in high school.

Table 20.1 is a framework generated by the State Department of Education and outlines the assessment pathways to high school diplomas. The requirements are listed by 'accountability cohort' and differ according to the type of degree a student is working toward. Rather than call Luanne's class the '2004 cohort', the state refers to this group of students in the language of the policy, turning students into groups and sub-groups of test scores and graduation rates. The wording turns the act of the school being held accountable by the state into a noun phrase. The nominalization is ambiguous about who is held accountable to whom. Is the school

**Table 20.1** Assessment Pathways to a Regents and Local Diploma for General Education Students[2]

| Cohort | Assessment Pathways to a Local Diploma | Assessment Pathways to a Regents Diploma |
|---|---|---|
| 2004 and Prior | 1–5 Low Pass Regents Exams with a 55–64/0–4 Exams with a 65 or above (i.e. Any combination of exams with at least 1 low pass exam in the 55–64 range) | 5 Regents Exams with a 65 or above |
| 2005 | 1–3 Low Pass 55–64 Regents Exam Scores and at least 2 Exams at 65 or above or 3 Regents Exams with a 65 or above and 2 granted Appeals with a 62–4 | 5 Regents Exams with a 65 or above or 4 Regents Exams at a 65 or above and 1 granted appeal with a 62–4 |
| 2006 | 1–2 Low Pass 55–64 Regents Exam Scores and at least 3 Exams at 65 or above or 3 Regents Exams with a 65 or above and 2 granted Appeals with a 62–4 | 5 Regents Exams with a 65 or above or 4 Regents Exams at a 65 or above and 1 granted appeal with a 62–4 |
| 2007 | 1 Low Pass 55–64 Regents Exam Score and at least 4 Exams at 65 or above or 3 Regents Exams with a 65 or above and 2 granted Appeals with a 62–4 | 5 Regents Exams with a 65 or above or 4 Regents Exams at a 65 or above and 1 granted appeal with a 62–4 |
| 2008 and thereafter | 3 Regents Exams with a 65 or above and 2 granted Appeals with a 62–4 | 5 Regents Exams with a 65 or above or 4 Regents Exams at a 65 or above and 1 granted appeal with a 62–4 |

Note that:

1 Students may **NOT** combine a Low Pass Local Diploma option with an appeal to be granted a Local Diploma.

2 Students may **NOT** use the Appeals process to meet the requirements for a Regents Diploma with Advanced Designation

accountable to the students? The students accountable to the school? The state to the school? Only when the phrase is placed in the context of the accountability policy is it clear that the school is accountable to the state for the '2004 accountability cohort'. That is, the school is obliged to report on the test results for this group of students and be answerable to the state for the consequences. Yet the wording is transferred to the students themselves. They are discursively constructed – thought of, interacted with, known as – an accountability cohort versus individual students who will grow, learn and develop.

The table highlights three important points about this era of accountability. First, this table allows us to visually track the increasing standards that were required of students each year in the name of increasing accountability. Requirements are broken down by the year the 'accountability cohort' enters ninth grade. The graduation requirements grew steeper every year. Luanne was part of the '2004–5 accountability cohort' and was still eligible for a local diploma which meant that students had to pass their classes and also earn a 55 or higher on five Regents exams[3] taken across their four years in high school. The students in each successive accountability cohort were required to pass more of the standardized tests with higher scores. The local diploma was eventually phased out and all students needed to pass the required number of Regents courses.

Second, the table illustrates the semantically vague wording and the struggle to represent the massive institutional changes in testing and high school graduation requirements that were being phased in under NCLB. Higher graduation requirements, increased state standards and required state tests illustrate the core of the accountability movement, intended to strengthen the diploma and make it competitive in the world market. The wording reflects different kinds of diplomas, different expectations, and different kinds of students. The hybridity of the discourse, itself, represents a struggle over social change (Chouilaraki and Fairclough, 1999).

Third, the table allows us to see the two tracks that were created based on a student's anticipated 'pathway' toward a local or Regents diploma. Courses that aligned with the different diploma tracks were offered. While, in theory, students were given the option of taking courses across the different tracks; in practice, many were steered into either 'local' or 'Regents' level courses, as determined by pre-requisites and ability. One way for schools to comply with NCLB's requirement that all students demonstrate proficiency in test scores is to group students by ability (Meier et al., 2004).

Starting in ninth grade, Luanne was assigned to courses in what she referred to as the 'regular track' or what the policy referred to as the 'local pathway'. This pathway referred to the collection of courses taken by students who anticipate receiving the local diploma and were not expected to go to college. As Luanne pointed out, the curriculum and instruction for students in the 'Regular' track were less rigorous than for students in the 'Honors' track. About the differential instruction in the two tracks she said the following:

They don't teach me nothing in school.
I learn everything on my own.
They give you a piece of paper
and tell you to finish by the end of class.
They don't teach you nothing.
If you ain't in honors
then they ain't teachin' you stuff.
If you are in the regular class
all they do is give you a piece of paper
and tell you to have it done by the end of class.
And that's it.
I visited my friends who is in the honor class
and her teacher was explaining to her how she was supposed to do it [the problem].
So she got it.
My teacher, I ask him for help and he say 'just do it.'
'Do it on your own.'

Luanne was aware of and critiqued the differential content and quality of teaching in the courses associated with different graduation pathways. As she begins her narrative, the diploma track is unmarked and emphasis is placed on the lack of instruction in her classes. First, she states, 'they don't teach me nothing'. Second, 'I learn everything on my own'. And, third, 'They give you a piece of paper and tell you to finish by the end of class'. She uses the metaphor of 'piece of paper' to symbolize the worksheets and drill and skill curriculum that is characteristic of a curriculum structured by test preparation. To clarify her point, she explicitly marks the distinction between graduation pathways. 'If you ain't in honors then they ain't teachin' you stuff.' She concretizes her critique with first-hand observation of the honors class. She notices how the teacher was taking the time to show her friend how to do a maths problem and this resulted in her friend learning the concept. She sets up a contrastive structure with her own teacher, taking us back into the classroom of the local track to illustrate the lack of instruction provided from her teacher. Unlike her friend who asks for support and receives it, when Luanne asks for help her teacher says 'just do it. Do it on your own.' We can hear the alienation and inequity that Luanne feels when she witnesses the differential instruction in the different tracked classrooms. She senses that she is viewed as nothing other than part of an 'accountability cohort' which, as she insinuates, has a dehumanizing effect on young people. Her criticisms mirror the findings in the scholarship that notes how the high stakes testing regime narrows the curriculum, leading to student disengagement. Further, students who are placed in lower tracks often have teachers who are less qualified and more of their class time is spent on disciplinary issues than pedagogical issues (Collins, 2009; Oakes, 1985). Luanne was promoted to tenth grade. However, she was retained in tenth grade for two years because of her failure to achieve the right number of credits and passing scores on the standardized tests.

## 6 Alternative routes and choices

Luanne grew restless with her lack of progression in the school system. At the end of her second year taking tenth grade classes, Luanne knew she was not on track to graduate on time. She spoke with her guidance counsellor who told her she could pick up the credits she needed through after school activities (like the step team) and summer school. She enrolled in summer school and when the 2006–7 school year started, she went to meet with her guidance counsellor to check on her credit status. Her counsellor had retired and a new one taken her place. The new counsellor did not know Luanne, her record of good attendance and her leadership on the school's step team. Luanne describes the different advice she was given by the two counsellors:

> [My first guidance counselor] told me that she try to help me graduate on time.
> Cause like last year she said
> if I passed all my classes last year
> I be a 12th grader this year.
> And even if I don't she help me out,
> like she said if I get a job,
> that'll be 2 credits that I can get.
> If I do after school activities,
> that be an extra credit.
> Even if I don't have enough credits,
> she put me in summer school for two classes
> and that be 2 credits.
> But [the new guidance counsellor] this year said she can't do that,
> she said if she do that she get in trouble.
>
> (Interview 11/2007)

When Luanne explained the situation to her, the counsellor offered Luanne a series of alternative options: she could work on her GED, attend High's night school or go to JobCorp where she would work toward a trade and her GED. This network of alternative educational choices functions as a de facto tracking policy that removes students from the school's accountability profile. Perhaps because her first counsellor knew of her leadership in and out of school, she wanted to accommodate her desires for high school graduation. The second counsellor, new to the school, was adamant about strictly following what she understood as the school's policies. Indeed, Yonezawa, Wells and Serna (2002) point out that school personnel's expectations about abilities of students (signalled by race, ethnicity, language use and social class) sway decisions about course placement, credit allocation and graduation requirements.

I asked Luanne what she knew about each of these options and was shocked at the misinformation she had accumulated. About the GED she stated, 'I heard it was easier to get your GED, than to get your high school diploma'. The narrative that had been passed down to Luanne had not caught up with changes in educational policy. In 2002, amidst the push for higher standards, the GED was redesigned, making it more difficult to pass.[4]

I had never heard of JobCorp and asked her to explain it to me. She said, 'You go to campus and take classes and also work toward a job'. Still not understanding I said, 'I am having trouble picturing it. It is not high school and it is not college, what is it?' She explained, 'JobCorp is like high school with different stuff that you can do on the campus. You can get nursing credits in the GED program at JobCorp.' She explained that her uncle had attended JobCorp.

'Who goes there?' I asked. Luanne explained, 'Mainly people that dropped out of high school or got kicked out of high school and can't go back to school or people who are having a hard time getting their high school diploma'. Bothered by the lack of specifics the guidance counsellor had given to Luanne about JobCorp, I scheduled a visit with the local JobCorp so Luanne could learn more about the programme.

The third choice her guidance counsellor gave her was to attend night school. About night school Luanne explained, 'Night school is just like the High but smaller classes with four major subjects'. Luanne and her mother liked the option of night school because they both wanted her to be the first in the family to earn a high school diploma, not a GED. Luanne submitted an application to attend the night school version of the High. She hung on to her assertion that she would graduate from high school. She stated, 'I always tell my mom that I am going to graduate on time, when I am supposed to graduate'. Troublingly, though, her description of graduation was, for the first time, punctuated with temporal markers (e.g. 'on time'). This reflected her concern over needing to catch up on credits she had missed as a tenth grader.

## 6.1 Night classes or GED

At the beginning of the 2007 school year, Luanne believed she was enrolled in the night school version of the High School. However, Luanne explained, 'We got a letter in the mail saying that I was scheduled to go to the GED program at the adult learning center. My mom said she didn't want me to go there. She said she wanted me to go through the High's night program . . .' Luanne reiterated that she had filled out an application for the night school, not the GED program. 'So what happened?' I asked her.

I don't know.
Last year my mom signed the paper
saying that she wanted me to go to night school
instead of going to the High
and my guidance counselor said
that she probably put it in the wrong pile

and she probably put it in the GED pile by accident.
And I said 'can you look and see?'
and she said 'you're gonna have to wait.'
So she might have put it in the wrong one.
She got two piles at the school.
One is for the GED program
and one is for night school.

(11/2007)

Luanne's entire high school career, whether she received a high school diploma or a GED, hinged on a supposed error where the guidance counsellor placed her application in the pile for the GED programme instead of the High's night school. While this was a detrimental placement for Luanne who wanted to earn a high school diploma, it could result in higher average test scores for the school because it would remove her from the school's accountability profile. The only explanation her counsellor offered Luanne was in the form of a conditional 'she probably put it in the GED pile by accident'. When Luanne asked her to check so her placement could be determined, she was told 'you're gonna have to wait'.

Luanne did not wait for her guidance counsellor to check. She resisted this placement and stayed at the high school. She stated, 'I just got to stay in high school and do an extra year. I don't want to but I am going to have to.' In Luanne's case, it is clear how the rhetoric of choice and concomitant alternative educational pathways turns students and parents into consumers of alternative education programmes, shopping for a suitable programme rather than being guaranteed a high quality, equitable education. Neither Luanne nor her mother had adequate information about any of these programmes. The discourse of choice may function to give students and their parents a sense of empowerment in a system where their options for a high quality education are, in reality, very narrow (Kelly, 1996). When I asked her about her plans for high school graduation at the end of her tenth grade year, what had been very concrete plans for attending college were temporally more distant. 'I'll wait probably a year, then go to college. I want to be either an R and B dancer like Cierra or a nurse, like my uncle.'

## 7 Criminalization of youth

As a repeat tenth grader, Luanne got lost in the institutional web of credits, courses and alternative programmes and her enthusiasm for school waned. Her narratives of this time period were increasingly characterized by themes of violence at the school and the criminalization of youth, conditions that were heightened by the school's 'Safe School Policies'. Indeed, her experiences with violence and her own eventual criminalization at the school are encoded in the school's policy which, in turn, is buttressed through NCLB's zero tolerance policies which have been linked to the proliferation of the school to prison pipeline, particularly for minority students (Ferguson, 2001; Skiba, 2000; Swain and Noblit, 2011). The violence and criminalization of youth at her school was at the heart of Luanne's second criticism of the school. She said:

> It's not a good school to go to.
> They fight every day there.
> Every day there is a fight.
> It's not one day that go by.
> Just this year, they got metal detectors.
> In the four years that I have been there,
> I seen somebody get stabbed there.
> I see somebody get maced.
> I done seen somebody get hit with a lock.
> I seen girls get jumped by boys and girls.

She reported that the heightened security at the high school made the school feel like a jail. Indeed, in 2007, the school installed metal detectors that were donated by the City Police Department. All students had to go through a security checkpoint upon entering the school. The infiltration of prison practices in a school setting including increased surveillance, monitoring and discipline has been shown to increase the rates of violence (Advancement Project, 2010). She said:

> In High we got police all around the school and everything.
> You feel like it's a jail there.
> You can't just walk around the school
> and go to one or the next class without you seeing a cop,
> or a cop stopping you to ask something,
> like 'Do you know this person?'
> or 'Do you know that person?'
> it's like out in the streets or you in jail or something.
> When you inside your classroom,
> you can't go out to go to the bathroom
> or go to the nurse or nothing,
> you gotta do everything before you go to your classroom
> and you got five minutes to get to the class
> and in between, you got to do everything . . .
> I feel like I'm in jail.
> I feel like I'm locked in somewhere.

Luanne's narrative criticizes the prison-like atmosphere of her school. Having police at the school transforms a school day into a simulated prison instead of a learning environment. Clearly the presence of the police in her school was intimidating to her, with their power to arrest, to search and interrogate students. This kind of punitive environment is established in the district's extensive 36-page 'Code of Conduct' policy manual. Under the heading 'Student Searches and Interrogations' reads the following:

> The Board of Education is committed to ensuring an atmosphere on school property and at school functions that is safe and orderly. To achieve this kind of environment, any school official is authorized to impose a disciplinary penalty on a student and may question a student about an alleged violation of law or the District code of conduct. Students are not entitled to any sort of 'Miranda'-type warning before being questioned by school officials, nor are school officials required to contact a student's parent before questioning the student. However, school officials will tell all students why they are being questioned.

The policy also discusses the procedures for individual searches which can take place under the clause of reasonable suspicion:

> Searches of individual students shall only occur when school officials have a reasonable suspicion that such a search will yield evidence that a particular student or students possess contraband as defined by school policy. Reasonable suspicion may also be based on information provided to school officials by others (including other school students and staff) indicating that the student has contraband in his or her possession.

The purpose of this policy is to create 'safe and orderly' schools which are constructed through the language and practices of the penal system. The policy focuses on questioning students who are suspected to be in violation of the code of conduct. Yet, the 'reasonable suspicion' clause of the district policy opens the door for all students to be the subject of interrogations. This, in effect, turns the atmosphere into what Luanne refers to as 'the streets of a jail' where students are interrogated on their way to classes. She told me that similar to the cops on the street, while walking to and from classes, police routinely stopped students to ask them if they knew where someone is or asked them to produce their identification cards. She recalled, 'So they ask us, "did you see anyone in here that's not supposed to be here?" or they be like "do you know this person?" If you say no, or they think you're lying, they take you to the office.' She went on to describe how all of the students need to have their ID cards visibly on their body. She stated, 'If you don't got your ID, they put you in handcuffs and walk you to the office'. This reflects the heightened criminal policies implemented at the school in 2007, policies that were buttressed by NCLB's zero tolerance policies. Indeed, NCLB funds support the hiring of school-based law enforcement personnel and the law encourages the referral of students to law enforcement for a wide variety of student behaviours. Specifically, the law provides 'financial assistance to enhance drug and violence prevention resources available in areas that serve large numbers of low-income children, are sparsely populated or have other special needs' (No Child Left Behind, 2002: section 4003 D iii).

Luanne was involved in a fight on school grounds in the spring of 2008. Despite this being her first fight, she was suspended and placed in an alternative programme. She explained that the fight was necessary because she had to stick up for herself. She faced, as other girls do, a double-bind: not standing up for themselves could result in further victimization and loss of respect from their peer group while standing up for themselves often resulted in educational sanctions (Miller, 2008).

The form sent home stated that the violation was 'a minor altercation – fight'. Next to the disposition, the form stated '5 weeks at Adult Education Center 3–5:30 – Return'. There are several points worthy to note about these sanctions. First, the fight is coded as 'minor altercation' on the form. This was Luanne's first offence. We might question why Luanne was subject to sanctions at this level of severity. This experience coincides with national statistics about the inequality of discipline policies across racial lines (Children's Defense Fund, 2008). Second, she was pushed into a tutorial programme that lasted only two and a half hours per day versus eight hours of the regular school day. This is an example of what Swain and Noblit (2011) refer to as 'punitive education', which are practices that deny students the right to a full day of education. Third, school officials may assume that suspensions deter future misbehaviour but there are no data pointing to these outcomes. Instead, the policies make students feel less connected to the school, which is linked to the increased likelihood of engaging in oppositional behaviours (Advancement Project, 2010). Indeed, after several weeks, Luanne stopped attending the alternative programme. 'I just stopped going', she told me. Trying to understand how it is that students just stop attending school, I asked her 'Didn't the school try to find you?' She shook her head, 'Nope'. The school had effectively pushed her out of the school.

When I asked her why her high school education was interrupted, she gave four reasons, each indicating her internalized consent of the impacts of the accountability system. All were linked to the shame she felt for not finishing high school on time. 'I always tell my mom that I am going to graduate on time, when I am supposed to graduate.' Her next reason was similarly linked to the notion of regular timescale for finishing high school. Referring to her older sister who took five years to graduate from high school with an Individualized Education Diploma (the equivalent of a certification of attendance given to students in special education) she said, 'I don't want to do an extra year. I don't want to be like Vicky.' At another point she said, 'I don't want to be in there an extra year. I'm gonna be in there when my little sister come. I don't want to be in there when she come.' Finally, she said, 'Because I don't want to do a whole 'nother year at the High. I don't like it anymore. I just want to go get my GED and get it over with.' This phrase reflects a deep frustration with educational systems that coerced her into consenting to decisions that were not of her preference.

# 8  Discussion and conclusions

How might Luanne's case help us to understand the impact of accountability policies on the lived experiences of urban youth? Luanne's analysis of her experiences in school point to flaws in three intersecting policies: ability grouping, the system of alternative educational choices and discipline policies. Each of these structures has been cited as problematic aspects of NCLB and part of the reason for the silent epidemic of high school dropouts. Yet when asked why she dropped out of school, she holds herself accountable, not the flawed accountability system. While the school is under strict pressure to raise test scores and meet AYP, stakes are high for Luanne, too. She wanted to be the first in her family to graduate from high school with a regular education diploma. Luanne's experiences were situated at the intersection of accountability policies that position the test score outcomes of sub-groups of students as the central concern, not the student's learning and achievement.

At the federal level, the era of higher standards and high stakes testing translates into tougher graduation requirements at the state level which we saw vividly through the two graduation 'pathways'. Yonezawa, Wells and Serna (2002) point out that ability grouping can become de facto tracking by continuing to support racial, ethnic and social class stratification within schools, within low income and students of colour occupying the lowest levels. In Luanne's case we heard how this policy translated into a narrowing of the curriculum, dissatisfying learning experiences and a lack of progression through the system. Most telling is how the students are referred to as an 'accountability cohort' which positions and represents them as an object of the state. The unmarked pathway in the 'graduation pathways' chart was the alternative education track designed to funnel students out of high school entirely, off the accountability reports and into GED programmes.

And, while choice policies have been written extensively about in terms of options outside the traditional public school structure (e.g. Dingerson et al., 2008; Ravitch, 2010), less discussed is the infrastructure of choice that is established for students *within* the schools through alternative educational programmes. Luanne was offered three options – the GED programme, alternative high school or JobCorp. These programmes were shrouded in language such as 'alternative' and 'a safety net' and 'night school'. However, silenced is the fact that these routes do not lead to the high school diploma. Attending the traditional public high school and participating in high quality, engaging courses that would result in her promotion were not options for her.

We are reminded of the constitutive nature of discourse practices to both represent and construct social conditions, in this case of high school 'non-completers'. Graduation rates were an important part of the accountability formula for schools in this state, starting in 2002. That is, schools needed to show AYP in the numbers of students who graduated from school each year. After five years, the state decided to discontinue the reporting of graduation rates presumably because of the high rates of 'non-completers'.

The absence of holding the school accountable for progress in graduation rates is sanctioning the exclusion of large numbers of students from school each year. Thus, policies designed to diminish the 'achievement gap' have resulted in a landslide of what McNeil, Coppola, Raddigan and Vasquez Heilig (2008) refer to as 'avoidable losses' or students who are pushed out of school so the school can make short-term gains in test scores, mainly students living in poverty and minority students.

The implementation of educational policies happens slowly over time and across discursive contexts. Using CDA alongside ethnography allowed me to connect macro- and microdiscourses and to understand the longer-term interpretations and consequences of educational decisions (Martín Rojo, 2010; Oberhuber and Krzyżanowski, 2008). The longitudinal nature of the research provided me with a running record of how the radically shifting nature of educational policy was implemented. I tracked this implementation coded in discourses of 'tougher standards', 'choices' and 'safe schools' across federal, state, school district documents and held these narratives next to Luanne's lived experiences. Most critically, I have shared the impact of accountability policies on a student's lived experiences, something most policy studies neglect entirely. As Dorner (2010) points out, parents, teachers, children and youth in local contexts bring policies to life – not official policy makers. Thus, understanding how the texts and associated discourses that comprise policies are enacted on the ground, in schools and classrooms is an important part of studying educational policy.

Finally, it was even confusing for me to understand the discourses of accountability. I found myself asking Luanne to explain things to me again and again. Likewise, I read and reread policies trying to understand the shifting playing field. I realize the reading path through her case is, at times, circuitous. This web-like design mirrors the difficulty Luanne must have experienced trying to negotiate the discourses of the school as she was tracked into various programmes and as school personnel desperately tried to comply with punitive educational policies. While the school officials were not working together to push her out of school in any formal sense, there was a remarkable level of systemic coherence in pushing students out of school who would make the school district look poorly on the state accountability reports. Decisions carried out locally were tied to macro-contexts and the changing educational landscape, designed to silently create an underclass of students by excluding them from testing and penalizing schools and teachers for low test scores. How this happens, however, relies on spoken and unspoken narratives, as I have shown in this case.

# Notes

1 The National Council of Teachers of English supported this research through a Research Foundation Grant.

2 Accessed 20 August 2012 www.p12.nysed.gov/ciai/gradreq/assessmentpathways

**3** Regents examinations are standardized state examinations in core high school subject areas required for a Regents diploma. To graduate, students need to have earned credits in core subject areas and pass the Regents exam in this area. The examinations are administered by the New York State Education Department. Accessed 20 August 2010 www.nysedregents.org/

**4** It should be noted that in 2011, the American Council on Education and Pearson, a multinational education and testing company, bought the rights to the design and delivery of the GED test. This effectively turned the GED from a nonprofit programme to a for-profit business (Sieben, 2011). The company plans to develop two levels of tests – one for students interested in high school equivalency and job readiness; the other for people who want to go to college. This is similar to the 'pathways' of local and Regents tracks formerly implemented in high schools. As students are pushed out of school, they are pushed into the same tracks that were formerly implemented in schools.

# References

Advancement Project (2010), 'Test, punish and push out: How 'zero tolerance' and high-stakes testing funnel youth into the school-to-prison pipeline'. Available at: http://www.advancementproject.org/content/home (accessed 10 August 2012).

Bamberg, M. and Andrews, M. (eds) (2004), *Considering Counter-narratives: Narrating, Resisting, Making Sense*. Amsterdam: John Benjamins Publishing Company.

Bartlett, T. (2012), *Hybrid Voices and Collaborative Change: Contextualizing Positive Discourse Analysis*. New York, NY: Routledge.

Blommaert, J. (2008), *Discourse*. Cambridge, UK: Cambridge University Press.

Carr, P. and Porfilio, B. (2011), *The Phenomenon of Obama and the Agenda for Education: Can Hope Audaciously Trump Neoliberalism?* Charlotte, NC: Information Age Publishing.

Children's Defense Fund (2008), *The State of America's Children 2008*. Cambridge, MA: Washington Research Project.

Chouliaraki, L. and Fairclough, N. (1999), *Discourse in Late Modernity: Rethinking Critical Discourse Analysis*. Edinburgh, UK: Edinburgh University Press.

Collins, J. (1996), 'Socialization to text: structure and contradiction in schooled literacy', in M. Silverstein and G. Urban (eds), *Natural Histories of Discourse*. Chicago: University of Chicago Press, pp. 203–28.

—— (2009), 'Social reproduction in classrooms and schools'. *Annual Review of Anthropology*, 38, 33–48.

Comber B. and Kamler B. (2004), 'Getting out of deficit: pedagogies of reconnection'. *Teaching Education*, 293–310.

Dingerson, L., Miner, B., Peterson, B. and Walters, S. (2008), *Keeping the Promise? The Debate over Charter Schools*. Milwaukee, WI: Rethinking Schools, Ltd.

Dorner, L. (2010), 'English and Spanish 'para un futuro' – or just English? Immigrant family perspectives on two-way immersion'. *International Journal of Bilingual Education and Bilingualism*, 13(3), 303–323.

Edelman, (1988), *Constructing the Political Spectacle*. Chicago, IL: University of Chicago Press.

Fairclough, N. (1995), *Critical Discourse Analysis: The Critical Study of Language*. New York, NY: Longman.

Ferguson, A. (2001), *Bad Boys: Public Schools in the Making of Black Masculinity*. Ann Arbor, MI: University of Michigan Press.

Foucault, M. (1977), *Discipline and Punish: The Birth of the Prison*. New York: Pantheon.

Hilliard, A., Steele, C. and Perry, T. (2004), *Young, Gifted and Black: Promoting High Achievement among African American Students*. New York, NY: Beacon Press.

Hornberger, N. (ed.) (2003), *Continua of Biliteracy: An Ecological Framework for Educational Policy, Research and Practice in Multilingual Settings*. Clevedon, UK: Multilingual Matters.

Kelly, D. (1996), '"Choosing" the alternative: conflicting missions and constrained choice in a dropout prevention program', in D. Kelly and J. Caskell (eds), *Debating Dropouts: Critical Policy and Research Perspectives on School Leaving*. New York: Teachers College Press, pp. 101–22.

Kumashiro, K. (2009), *Against Common Sense: Teaching and Learning toward Social Justice* (2nd edn). New York: Routledge.

Luke, A. (2004), 'Notes on the future of critical discourse studies'. *Critical Discourse Studies*, 1(1), 149–152.

Macgilchrist, F. (2007), 'Positive discourse analysis: contesting dominant discourses by reframing the issue'. *Critical Approaches to Discourse across the Disciplines*, 1(1), 74–94.

Martin, J. (2004), 'Positive discourse analysis: solidarity and change'. *Revista Canaria de Estudios Ingleses*, 49, 179–200.

Martín Rojo, L. (2010), *Constructing Inequality in Multilingual Classrooms*. Berlin: De Gruyter Mouton.

McNeil L. M., Coppola, E., Raddigan, J. and Vasquez Heilig, J. (2008), 'Avoidable losses: high-stakes accountability and the dropout crisis'. *Education Policy Analysis Archives*, 16(3), 2–44.

Meier, D., Kohn, A., Darling-Hammond, L., Sizer, T. and Wood, G. (2004), *Many Children Left Behind: How the No Child Left Behind Act is Damaging our Children and our Schools*. Boston, MA.: Beacon Press.

Miller, J. (2008), *Getting Played: African American Girls, Urban Inequality and Gendered Violence*. New York: New York University Press.

Morrell, E. (2007), *Critical Literacy and Urban Youth: Pedagogies of Access, Dissent, and Liberation*. New York: Routledge.

New York State Department of Education. The New York State School Report Card. Accountability and Overview Report. Accessed 10 August 2012 from https://reportcards.nysed.gov/

New York State Department of Education. Regents Exam. Accessed 10 August 2012 from www.nysedregents.org/

New York State Department of Education. Assessment Pathways to a Regents and Local Diploma for General Education Students. Accessed 10 August 2012 from www.p12.nysed.gov/ciai/gradreq/assessmentpathways

Nichols, S. and Berliner, D. (2007), *Collateral Damage: How High-stakes Testing Corrupts America's Schools*. Cambridge, MA.: Harvard University Press.

No Child Left Behind (NCLB) Act of 2001, Pub. L. No. 107–110, § 115, *Title IV – 21st Century Schools: Part A – Safe and Drug-Free Schools and Communities*. Stat. 1738 (2002).

Oakes, J. (1985), *Keeping Track: How Schools Structure Inequality*. New Haven, CT: Yale University Press.

Oberhuber, F. and Krzyżanowski, M. (2008), 'Discourse analysis and ethnography', in R. Wodak and M. Krzyżanowski (eds), *Qualitative Discourse Analysis in the Social Sciences*. New York, NY: Palgrave Macmillan, pp. 182–203.

Ravitch, D. (2010), *The Death and Life of the Great American School System: How Testing and Choice are Undermining Education*. New York: Basic Books.

Rogers, R. (2003), *A Critical Discourse Analysis of Family Literacy Practices: Power in and out of Print*. Mahwah, NJ: Lawrence Erlbaum Associates.

—— (2011), 'Tracking educational trajectories and life pathways: the longitudinal nexuses of critical discourse analysis and ethnography'. *Critical Discourse Studies*, 8(4), 239–252.

Rogers, R. and Mancini, M. (2010), '"Requires medicine to progress academically": a critical discourse analysis of the intersections of IDEA, DSM-IV and an IEP', in C. Dudley-Marling and A. Gurn (eds), *Deconstructing the Normal Curve (and Reconstructing the Education for Students with Disabilities)*. New York: Peter Lang Press, pp. 87–103.

Rubin, H. and Rubin, I. (2011), *Qualitative Interviewing: The Art of Hearing Data* (3rd edn). New York: Sage.

Saldana, J. (2003), *Longitudinal Research: Analyzing Change through Time*. Walnut Creek, CA: Altamira Press.

Scollon, R. and Scollon, S. (2004), *Nexus Analysis: Discourse and the Emerging Internet*. New York: Routledge.

Sieben, L. (2011), American Council on Education and Pearson will redevelop GED as for-profit program. *The Chronicle of Higher Education*, 15 March. Available at: http://chronicle.com/article/American-Council-on-Education/126736/ (accessed 29 December 2012).

Skiba, R. (2000), *Zero tolerance zero evidence: An analysis of school disciplinary practice* (pp. 1–20). Indiana: Indiana Education Policy Center.

Solórzano, D. and Yosso, T. (2009), 'Critical race methodology: counter-storytelling as an analytical framework for educational research', in Taylor, E., Gillborn, D. and Ladson-Billings, G. (eds), *Foundations of Critical Race Theory in Education*. New York: Routledge, pp. 131–47.

Spradley, J. (1980), *Participant Observation*. New York: Holt, Rinehart and Winston.

Swain, A and Noblit, G. (2011), Education in a punitive society: an introduction. *Urban Review*, 43, 465–75.

Woodside-Jiron, H. (2011), 'Language, power and participation: using critical discourse analysis to make sense of public policy', in R. Rogers (ed.), *An Introduction to Critical Discourse Analysis in Education* (2nd edn). New York: Routledge, pp. 154–82.

Yonezawa, S., Wells, A. S. and Serna, I. (2002), 'Choosing tracks: "Freedom of choice" in detracking schools'. *American Educational Research Journal*, 39(1), 37–67.

**RACE AND IMMIGRATION**

# 21

# Immigration Discourses and Critical Discourse Analysis

# Dynamics of World Events and Immigration Representations in the British Press

*Majid KhosraviNik*
Newcastle University

## 1 Introduction

Migrants and issues around immigration in the UK have attracted increased press attention in the last fifty years. In academia, ample studies have been carried out on immigration from the sociological, political, journalistic and of course, discourse analytical point of view. Immigration discourses and their representation in media need to be considered in the light of new political, economic and social developments in the world, e.g. the shifts from a bipolar world order to what came to be known as new world order, the emergence of new north-south constellations along with (real and/or constructed) threats of terrorism. Recent economic crisis in the 'north', increased critique of the multiculturalism model and tensions in reconciling economic imperatives and socio-political ideologies have contributed to a tendency in the political spectrum of various European countries to shift towards more conservative orientations, identity convergence and foregrounding market orders (Wodak and Van Dijk, 2006; Wodak, 1996; Van Dijk, 1991; and Wodak et al., 2013 for the most recent overview). This, in effect, explains the increased sensitivities and debates regarding identity politics and Us/ Them distinctions in the society/media. From a purely statistical point of view as the research shows (see Figure 21.1) the British press has been increasingly replete with discourses on/about immigration, refugees and asylum seekers which in effect heightens the public sensitivities of 'the issue' of immigration. In the meantime, the rise in debates commonly correlates with increased systematic negative construction of those immigrating, i.e. entering the UK (Baker and McEnery, 2005).

Taking on a critical discourse analysis approach, this chapter attends to some studies on discourses of immigration and out-group communities in the context of Britain and reviews some of the analytical approaches in the field. The chapter reports on a research project carried out at Lancaster University on representation of refugees, asylum seekers and immigrants in the British newspapers within a ten year period. It discusses common discursive strategies in different types of British newspapers. The selected texts of this study on issues of immigration are embedded in – and affected by – various material domestic and international events from the Balkan conflict to British General Elections. The chapter attempts to contextualize various immigration representations in the context of these events while arguing that such discourses (partly) constitute the contexts of 'sense-making' in the society regarding the perception of immigration. It is argued that while different British newspapers may employ different linguistic strategies in representing immigrants due to their differences in ideological viewpoints and types, in some important ways they all seem to contribute to discursive construction of these groups of people as either an actively negative or passively neutral group. It is also argued that the process of interpretation of specific linguistics categories, e.g. metaphors is contingent upon contextual circumstances in the society, e.g. the (perceived) proximity of the events to Britain and the network of discourses which are already in place, i.e. exist in the repertoire of social old knowledge.

## 2  Approaches to CDA and immigration discourse

Discourse is both a carrier of ideologies and linguistic practice – as a type of social action – which contributes to construction of collective mentalities, e.g. ideologies. CDA is 'socially constitutive as well as socially conditioned' (Fairclough and Wodak, 1997: 258) and as such not only does it reflect a picture, perhaps incomplete, of the ideology, but it also shapes those social interpretive conditions in a dialectic way (Fairclough, 2001). A critical analysis of discourse hence is a critical engagement with opaque ways in which power is legitimated in discourse, inter alia, and attempts to account for socio-political contexts affecting the processes of production and interpretation of discourses (Wodak and Meyer, 2009; KhosraviNik, 2010b).

Jäger (2001: 43) drawing on Laclau and Mouffe's (1985) conceptualizations, maintains that meanings are all embedded within an epistemology that discourse holds and the 'values and meanings' change with the change in a discourse. Drawing on social cognitive psychology van Dijk discusses this abstract notion of discourse in terms of a set of 'mental models' via which the production and/or interpretation of discourse, as in concrete linguistic realizations, is mediated. He argues that 'the meaning of a discourse [linguistic data], compared to its mental model, is incomplete' (2001: 362). Wodak's definition of discourse, prioritizes language as the starting point of the 'demystification journey' while maintaining that language is a form of social practice. Wodak (2001: 66) defines discourse as 'a complex bundle of simultaneous and sequential interrelated linguistic acts, which manifest themselves within and across social fields of action and thematically interrelate semiotic, oral and written tokens, very often as "texts", that belong to specific semiotic types, that is genre'.

Discourses re/present power hierarchies not only through micro-linguistic choices within the text but also by control of a social occasion by means of the genre of a text (Weiss and Wodak, 2003: 13), e.g. gatekeeping mechanisms in the press. In the same vein preferential access to mass public discourses affords levels of power to symbolic elites (see Van Dijk, 1996) such as politicians, journalists, scholars, teachers and writers (Wodak and Van Dijk, 2006). Mass media are the most salient power apparatus due to their 'nearly exclusive control over the symbolic resources needed to manufacture popular consent, especially in the domain of ethnic relations' (Van Dijk, 1991: 42–3). The press have traditionally been more directly linked to political contentious issues (especially in Britain) and hence they have been analysed in terms of their capacity to exert hegemonic representations without appearing coercive. The institution of journalism is 'more skilled than any other institutions to act without being understood as powerful' (Hultman, 2001: 1).

On such a conceptual backdrop, a bulk of research in critical discourse analysis has been interested in representations of immigration and minorities. These studies can be categorized in terms of their scale, regions, comparative aspects, types of data sources or based on their theoretical approaches in addressing the interface of discourse and society.

Among some of the influential studies is van Dijk's early study in 1984 which investigates the immigrants' and refugees' representation in the context of the Netherlands and focuses on Tamil refugees as a group about whom there had been no prior knowledge among the Dutch. This quasi-laboratory condition threw some light on the role of media in producing (false) consciousness about a group along the commonly seen themes of illegality, invasion, criminality, etc. (1984: 243). In another major study, van Dijk (1987) discusses processes of formation of discriminatory immigration discourse by focusing on *how* discursive properties may reproduce a macro ideology by analysing the way ordinary people express, convey, or form ethnic beliefs in everyday conversations. The study concentrates on recall strategies as well as sources of information – personal experience vs. mass media – and illustrates the intermediary role of media in re/production of public discourses and perceptions. Adopting a discursive psychological approach, Wetherell and Potter (1992) analyse discourses which justify, sustain and legitimate those practices which maintain power and dominance of *Pakeha* New Zealanders over *Maoris*. The study maps out different interpretive repertoire strategies, through which race categories are constructed, exploited and legitimated. In line with other scholars, e.g. Barker (1981), they conclude that whereas once race seemed to be the most effective and prevalent legitimating tool, the ideological baton has now been handed to culture.

Taking on a more grounded cognitive approach in accounting for the intersection of discourse and society a younger generation of scholars working on/around CDA maintain that explication of processes of communication requires a more cognitive theorization. By postulating (some degrees of) universality in human cognitive apparatus, they endeavour to explain why 'it is still possible for discourse to be manipulative and/or misleading, ultimately leading to power abuse and discrimination' (Polyzou 2012 in Hart, 2010). Influenced by and furthering the research of Paul Chilton (2005a, 2005b), Hart (2010, 2011) attempts to provide a cognitive explanation for some commonly identified discursive strategies in immigration discourses, e.g. Wodak's referential, predicational strategies as well as the proximization strategies (Cap, 2011). Hart (2013) draws on evolutionary psychology to explicate the manipulative power of argumentation by discussing examples from the British press coverage of immigration. It is argued that the power of argumentative strategies can be viewed within natural tendencies in human cognitive apparatus when there is a deliberate confusion in the mental context of interpretation.

Other conceptually relevant scholars such as Polyzou and Oswald attempt to theorize and systematize a cognitive interface. Closely related to Hart's works but more visibly grounded in social theory is Polyzou (2013) who similarly advocates the applicability and usefulness of cognitive theorization for CDA and endeavours to propose a pragmatically oriented analytical framework for critical analysis of presupposition in discourse (Polyzou, forthcoming). Focusing on the notion of manipulation, Oswald (2010, 2011) attempts to map out the cognitive dynamics and conditions of manipulation by relying on a theory of information-processing which suggests that the possibility of manipulation (e.g. in immigration discourses) can be explained as a consequence of the inherent fallibility of human cognition.

Wodak (2006: 601) endorses cognitive conceptualization in explicating discourses of racism/anti-Semitism and as an approach which can throw some light on why such ideologies seem to have long lasting lives despite inhibitions incurred by law and other social institutions. Fairclough (2001) also acknowledges that there is a mystery in how people move from a self-conscious attempt of rhetorical deployment within a discourse to the stage of owning a discourse. Nevertheless, there is a strong impetus in CDA emphasizing the role of *the social* for explicating the interface of language and society. There is resistance against *naturalization* of the socio-political field which could downplay the social agency and responsibility of individuals. Wetherell and Potter (1992), despite emphasizing the merits of social cognitive approaches, criticize the absence of social theory in cognitive accounts and warn that 'attempts to define the content of racism on a prior global basis can be positively dangerous, and can sometimes have an ideological and theoretical effect counter to that intended' (1992: 71).

Ruth Wodak's Discourse-Historical Approach (DHA) (Reisigl and Wodak, 2009) to CDA has made large impacts on a range of studies in the fields of immigration and identity representations. For example Wodak and Matouschek (1993) look at immigration discourses in Austria in a body of data of official discourse (politicians), newspaper texts, and anonymous conversations on the street and account for the connection between specific discourses' hostile attitudes in the wider public. The study suggests that this discourse occasioned by the population migrations after the collapse of communist Eastern Europe not only targets the specific Eastern European ethnic out-groups, but is elastic enough to combine these prejudices with those against other existing traditional and functionally determined out-groups, e.g. Jews, Turks and bicycle riders. Wodak (1996) accounts for argumentative strategies of construction of a 'we' discourse and the strategies of self-justification through personal pronouns, depersonalization and generalization towards construction of a semantic macro-structure of anti-foreigner discourse about elements of difference, deviance and perceived threat.

Among studies in the context of the US, there is Santa Ana's (1999) study which provides an account of metaphoric representations of immigrants in American public discourse. By drawing on Lakoff's theoretical categorization and Chilton's political metaphors, he foregrounds the function of metaphors in construction of problematic political and moral imageries for international migration forces and a host country's ethical responsibilities to its workers. His study shows that the dominant metaphoric body for immigrants seems to be that of '*immigrants are animals*' followed by other less frequent secondary metaphors including '*immigrants are debased people, weeds, and commodities*' (1999: 198). Teo's (2000) study in the Australian press context focuses on news reports on Vietnamese immigrants in Australia and illustrates the qualities of systematic Othering in that discourse. He demonstrates that immigrant groups are systematically associated with crime and mayhem and that there is a disproportionate white majority voice in contrast to an over-lexicalized silenced minority. In another study on the Australian context, Clyne (2005) explores the role of language used by the Australian prime minister and other politicians in swaying Australian public opinions against 'boat people'. The study concludes that the constructed out-group is linguistically represented as unlawful and morally unfit to enter Australia, and referentially represented as bullies and queue jumpers who are a threat to Australia's sovereignty with an implied link to terrorism and crimes (2005: 193). Flowerdew et al. (2002) study immigration discourses in Hong Kong's leading liberal newspapers. The study proposes an interesting composite taxonomy of discriminatory discursive practices and argues that mass media, e.g. sitcoms and soap operas, play a crucial role in constructing a unique national identity in Hong Kong represented through a mixture of sophisticated local social practices and values with an eye to the West in contrast to crude, laughable mainland Chinese practices, including their accent. The study also reports on the use of tropes of influx, flood, burden, exodus for immigrants along with attributions of poverty, illiteracy, ignorance, laziness, etc. Cristian Tileaga's (2005) study on an East European context examines the particulars of an extreme Other representation for Romanies in Romanian middle class discourses and illustrates the rhetorical and interpretative resources used to talk about and legitimate the blaming of Romanies. According to Tileaga discourse about Romanies is more extreme than anti-alien, anti-immigrant discourses studied by numerous western critical researchers in the sense that the out-group here is not merely portrayed as different, but also as being beyond the moral order, nationhood and comparison. Blommaert (2001) addresses inequality in the process of asylum application in Belgium and discusses the role of such narratives as a localizing discourse. By focusing on the lack of communicative resources for asylum seekers –'not only linguistically but also normatively and stylistically' (2001: 414) – he concludes that the increasing trend in text-making-as-political-process exploits discursive resources and accessibilities to the interest of the dominant majority. There have also been pan-European studies on immigration discourses, e.g. Wodak and van Dijk (2006), which look at parliamentary discourses on ethnic and immigration issues within six European countries.

As reiterated by van Dijk (2005), in addition to the centrality of mass media in terms of impacting social perceptions of immigration, there is a common ground for qualities of the discursive strategies employed in different contexts in a way that much of what has been said about Europe and North America also applies to the contexts of Spain and Latin America. However, the emphasis on similarity in discursive practices and strategies used in various studies does not amount to overlooking the important contextual differences in terms of histories and socio-political developments in different contexts.

# 3 Analytical categories in immigration discourse

Various research structures, methodological taxonomies and analytical categories have been proposed and applied on immigration discourses as a salient topic in CDA. Major studies on Self and Other representation in discourse have been carried out by scholars such as Teun van Dijk and Ruth Wodak along with studies which derive from their approaches. These studies tackle various aspects of bifurcation of representations under a general strategy of positive self-presentation and negative other-presentation. The Discourse-Historical Approach's analytical strategies of referential, predicational, argumentation (topoi), perspectivization along with intensification/mitigation (Reisigl and Wodak, 2009) have been elaborated in different studies (e.g. KhosraviNik, 2010a). Some of the more recurring topoi found in this discourse in a wide range of contexts and data sets include: topos of usefulness/uselessness, topos of definition and name-interpretation, topos of danger and threat, topos of finances/economy, topos of burden, topos of numbers, topos of law, topos of history, etc. (summarized from Reisigl and Wodak, 2001: 75–80). Closely related to argumentation would be the analysis of metaphors as a common discursive strategy in immigration discourses (Van Dijk, 1984; Santa Ana, 1999) including: metaphors of aliens, metaphors of water, metaphors of natural disasters, metaphors of pollution and impurity, metaphors of war/fight, metaphors of house/building, metaphors of disease/infection, metaphors of animals, etc.

Wodak and van Dijk (2006) propose a combination of analytical categories of DHA and those of socio-cognitive approach at macro-topical as well as detailed local linguistic levels. Van Leeuwen's (1996) socio-semantic categorization of social actors has classically been considered for a variety of studies notwithstanding that certain numbers of categories would normally be applicable in any given context. A combination of proposed analytical categories from van Leeuwen (1996) and Reisigl and Wodak (2009) renders a set of questions to be considered in the course of textual analysis including which persons/actors (and how) are named and referred to in discourses? How are persons positioned in discourse (in what roles, etc.)? What features are ascribed to all those represented/introduced into discourse? What is the social and political function/goal of particular references/nominations and representations of social actors?

Although certain methods of textual analysis continue to be applied in several studies, it must be noted that each study bears its own uniqueness in terms of research questions, genre of data at hand, and communicative practices under analysis in addition to several wider socio-political contextual considerations. As such, modification, justification, and application of analytical categories for a specific research should be an integral part of each study. That is, chains of processes of production and interpretation of texts at hand including qualities of audiences, range of impact, modes of production and consumption, etc. should be brought into every study's account of the relevant context. To this effect, there has been an attempt in systematization and abstraction of analytical categories to project an overall CDA research structure within a three-level framework (KhosraviNik, 2010a). This three level analytical framework draws on categories, methodologies and aspects that are relevant and/or crucial in analysis of social representations of certain social actor(s) in discourse, e.g. immigrants, by drawing on the works of Wodak and van Dijk in Self and Other presentation. The overall aim is to help to systematize an analytical approach which accounts for questions of *what* (is there in the linguistic content), *how* (the linguistic contents are presented) and *why* (they are presented in that certain way) by focusing on representation of actors, actions and arguments involved in a discourse.

## 4 Immigration in the British press

An impressive critical analysis of immigration discourses has been carried out decades ago by Hartmann and Husband in 1974 in accordance with the propagated principles of critical studies of language use (Blommaert 2005). They focus on discourses on immigration in the British press and perceptions of such representations. The authors argue that the bulk of debates on race in Britain has been concerned mainly with immigration and control of entry of – what would have been referred to at the time as – 'coloured people' to the country. They compare the examples of anti-Semitic British news representation of Jewish immigration in 1920 with that of arguments against immigration at the time and argue that in both historical instances certain similar (pseudo) arguments and techniques have been devised in negative representation of immigrants. The representation of immigrants as 'ordinary members of the society' has been systematically and 'increasingly overshadowed by a news perspective in which they are presented as a problem' and that they are 'seen as some kind of aberration, a problem, or just an oddity, rather than as "belonging" to the society' (1974: 144–5). Another major research would be Van Dijk (1991) who analyses a corpus of British newspapers ranging from right to left of socio-political ideologies by looking at journalistic practices of coverage, e.g. headlines, topics, quotations and sources and provides a detailed representation of different social actors involved in editorials of different British newspapers. Lynn and Lea (2003) account for the social construction of asylum seeker identity in the UK through discursive and rhetoric analyses of letters written to British national newspapers and engage with questions of how social identities are manifested in discourse and how social relations are exercised in and through these identities. On a macro-structural level, three main discourses of differentiating the Other, differentiating Self and discourse of 'enemy in our midst' are identified which in turn result in a discriminatory classification of the population.

As a major multidisciplinary project, the RASIM[1] project was designed to look closely into representations of immigrants along with refugees and asylum seekers in the British press from two independently working research strands of critical discourse analysis and corpus linguistics. Among other outputs on findings of corpus linguistic and CDA strands,[2] a methodological synergy between the two strands has been proposed (Baker et al., 2008). The present chapter is focused on the CDA strand of the project.

## 4.1 Events and texts

Ten years of British press coverage of issues on immigrants, refugees and asylum seekers would expectedly render a colossal body of texts. These news texts were collected electronically using a set of carefully selected query words (see Gabrielatos 2007). All news articles which had at least one instance of the query words were initially selected. A rough graphic representation of the collated texts illustrates the multitude of the data at this stage (see Figure 21.1).

As the graph shows, within a general steady rise in the number of texts on immigration, there are some clear spikes in the number of relevant available articles.

Two requirements of context-sensitivity and systematicity have been proposed in sampling procedure for a large data set such as that of this project. Context sensitivity is to reiterate the connection between language and its context of use as a core principle in critical discourse analysis. Ideally speaking context explication would include audiences, distributing channels, genre of the communicative practice and issues of access as well as a socio-political account for the existing 'discourses in place' in the society. Systematicity is to foreground the desirability of rigour in analytical and methodological approach in CDA as a social scientific research.

Based on the number of article instances (Figure 21.1) five well distributed points of highest frequency of occurrence of articles have been chosen as the main focus of the research. These five one-month periods of press coverage were then related to their immediate world events that have contributed in spikes, as follows:

*Period 1*:    March 1999, NATO invasion in Kosovo and Kosovar refugees.
*Period 2*:    September 2001, 9/11 attacks and issues of asylum seekers in Britain, Australian 'boat people' case.
*Period 3*:    May 2002, second round of French presidential election Le Pen vs. Chirac, asylum seekers' children schooling, and assassination of Pim Fortuyn.
*Period 4*:    March 2004, Madrid bombing, the asylum bill, East European immigration checks, expansion of EU.
*Period 5*:    May 2005, campaigns leading to British General Elections.

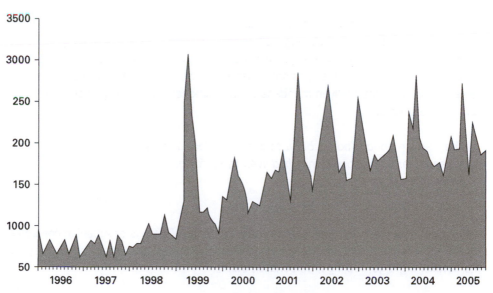

**FIGURE 21.1** *Frequency of texts on/related to immigration in the British press* (KhosraviNik, 2009).

Consequently, to do qualitative textual analysis, the texts have been sampled in terms of a) representative periods, b) representative titles and c) texts around those selected events. At the second stage a representative sample of existing socio-political perspectives of various British newspapers (left/right) has been selected. Moreover, newspapers have also been selected in terms of their 'types' (quality/tabloid). Three newspapers with their Sunday editions were selected namely: *The Guardian, The Times* and *Daily Mail.*

## 4.2  *Analytical discussion*

Expectedly perhaps, the coverage of displaced communities during the Kosovo conflict is generally sympathetic following on and feeding into dominant British (western) macro discourse on humanitarianism at the time. Such orientation is linguistically realized differently in tabloids and quality newspapers. Reflecting the paper's general journalistic/linguistic practice, the *Daily Mail*'s bulk of perspectivized (sympathetic) representations of Kosovar refugees is explicitly realized via referential strategies, e.g. referring to Albanians as 'victims of oppression'.

> The tale of these two *victims of oppression* one a survivor, one a casualty mirrors that of *thousands of others whose lives have been blackened by the Kosovo conflict.*
>
> (*Daily Mail*, 29 March 1999)

The predicational associations of what Albanian and Serbians do substantiates these frequent referential instances, e.g. 'smashing his head' in the following example. Syntactically the Serbian side is also reported in active voice in most of the negative predications. The victim Albanians are either as the patient of negative action verbs or talked about predicationally in mundane ordinary peaceful verbs, e.g. 'had lived' in the following example.

> The Serbian special police *burst through the door and handcuffed a man, a simple Albanian farmer* whose family *had lived there for generations . . . Repeatedly they smashed his head with a rifle butt.*
>
> (*Daily Mail*, 27 March 1999)

As a general trend, there is an extensivized coverage of details of Albanian characters and lives. Very frequently they are named and individualized through the coverage of life details, e.g. age, feelings, personality, etc.

> Shortly before the NATO bombing started, the family decided to make a break for freedom. With *Bajrie in her arms, Azemine Ilazi* led the way. Behind her were *her*

*other children, aged between 13 and seven, and their 65-year-old grandmother Mrs Arife Kazi.*

(*Daily Mail*, 27 March 1999)

Extensivization is also seen in the quality press coverage of the time but in comparison to the *Daily Mail*, the quality papers often resort to a balanced combination of referential, predicational and argumentative strategies with a more conservative choice of type and number of referentials.

*Mr Mita, 44, discussed the ultimatum with his wife, Atije, a teacher and his brother, Luz, who had a bakery and shared the three-storey villa built by their father.*

(*The Times*, 31 March 1999)

There is also a large presence of metaphorical expressions in representation of refugees at this period including the commonly known metaphors of large bodies and nature, e.g. floods, influx, waves of refugees, etc. along with strong emphasis of numbers.

Albania *flooded* by rising *tide of refugees* . . . a fresh exodus from the south-western town of Djakovica was reported.

(*The Guardian*, 29 March 1999)

Nato reported that *a million refugees* had crossed the border into neighbouring Macedonia and Albania, *a quarter of the Kosovan population, with up to 50,000* crossing in recent days, and at least *10,000 more expected.*

(*The Guardian*, 29 March 1999)

However, unlike a common argument in several CDA studies – that the use of metaphors of large bodies would amount to (automatic) negative representation of a group via invoking certain topoi – in this case, these freely used metaphors only contribute to construction and perception of the urgency of the situation and the need for support by emphasizing the scale of calamity. This is true unless the contexts of interpretation shift from an account of a humanitarian calamity in other parts of the world to familiar frames of 'foreigners coming to our country'. This is where the frame of representation and interpretation changes.

No government has yet announced that it is to open its doors to the displaced Kosovo Albanians. As it did during the height of the Bosnian war, *Britain is likely to operate an extremely restrictive policy, making it hard for any Albanians to reach safety in this country*

(*The Times*, 29 March 1999)

Such discourse shift, i.e. from people represented within a humanitarian frame (Entman, 2002) to people represented as immigrants entering 'our' country can be seen in other news events as well. For example a reverse order can be detected in coverage of the Madrid terrorist bombing where the force of 'victims of global terrorist' frame overcomes the mainstream immigration frame. As such discursive processes of collectivization, functionalization (Van Leeuwen, 1996) and negative representations of immigrants, e.g. as threats, burdens, etc. suddenly give way to opposite linguistic processes of individualization and extensivization of a 'terrorist victim' frame.

> For the families of *the unfortunate few who came to Spain seeking a more prosperous life* and died in Thursday's bombs *there will be some small, if bitterly belated, consolation.*
>
> (*The Times*, 13 March 2004)

> Spain announced last week that *it would give citizenship or residency to the parents, children, husbands and wives of the dead and injured in Madrid's bomb attacks. Hundreds of wounded and bereaved illegal immigrants are taking up the offer.*
>
> (*The Guardian*, 17 March 2004)

British news discourses on Muslim communities and immigration and various issues of asylum seeking in Britain have constituted a main focus of the spikes, e.g. in period two. As for the immediate backlashes of the 9/11 terrorist bombing, almost immediately the British papers engaged in making inter-discursive links with immigration whereas in the US, the terrorist attacks were not largely constructed as an immigration-related issue but as a more confrontational 'enemy from outside' frame. This could perhaps be explained with the differences in contexts of interpretations in the two countries, e.g. a relatively large percentage of British Muslims and immigration being at the heart of political discourse in Britain. In several articles, *The Times* substantiates links between immigration and (Muslim) terrorism in Britain via the frame of 'the enemy from within'. On the other hand, the liberal *Guardian* attended to news on backlashes of 9/11 and warned against attacks on Arab Americans and asylum seekers (for example on 13 September 2001 '*Arab Americans stress loyalty in face of backlash*').

As the opposition conservative newspaper at the time, *The Times* often criticizes the then-incumbent Labour government focusing on immigration. The analysis shows that as immigration becomes the focus of political debate, the immigrants are systematically backgrounded linguistically and are reduced to numbers, functions and applications at the crossfire of the political rivalry discourse in both sides of the political camp. This is a phenomenon seen in all newspapers with varying degrees during the British General Election debates. The analysis also shows that the negative representation of immigrants in the British press in the events relevant to the UK (typical immigration frame) mainly draws on a set of common topoi including topoi of numbers, economic burden (abuse of welfare system, expenditure), threat (threat to cultural identity, threat to community values), danger, and law (legality issues). For example the *Daily Mail* on 11 April 2005 taps into the topos of threat both in the form of physical violence, i.e. terrorism, and threat to British identity.

> *We face a real terrorist threat in Britain today a threat to our way of life*, to *our liberties.* Yet we have absolutely no idea who's coming into and leaving our country.

> *In addition, taking in so many people from very diverse backgrounds will transform this country's identity and character.*
>
> (*Daily Mail*, 11 April 2005)

Topos of burden:

> *Our public services are already struggling to cope with the existing numbers . . .*

> *over 30 years, that would amount to seven and a half million people or seven times the present population of Birmingham. Most of this increase would be as a result of new immigrants and their descendants.*

> *For start, where are we going to put them? They would need an extra million houses over and above existing plans for the period 1996–2021*
>
> (*Daily Mail*, 15 March 2004)

The assumption of homogeneity (for both sides; Self/British and Other/immigration identity) is pursued as a general strategy in (conservative) immigration discourses in the British press. Conservative accounts of immigrants hardly recognize immigrants by their names or other qualities and background them even when drawing on their personal narratives – which is rare in the first place. Unless immigrants can be positioned within one of the widely available negative topics, e.g. crime, violence, difference, there is no detailed coverage or individualization processes in the language used. The perception of newsworthiness of violent internal conflicts at immigration camps is a good example of such a tendency. Another example can be the naming and extensivization of three Kurdish asylum seekers who sewed their lips in protest of their rejected applications (*The Sunday Times*, 14 March 2004; 'Their "martyrdom" is just blackmail').

Liberal news reporters do make more effort to recognize diversities and generally provide more information on individual cases. Liberal accounts draw on topoi of human rights/values and international laws to support their position. These topoi are mostly used to account for asylum seekers by foregrounding the plights and fears of these people to create empathy and awareness. This is sometimes pursued by describing personal details of people involved as well.

Cases also cited include that of a *heavily pregnant asylum seeker, a 19-year-old Chinese woman with a history of severe abuse, a 65-year-old woman who is serving a sentence following conviction, and two Chinese women who claimed to have been tortured.*

Jawaid Luqmani, a solicitor and treasurer of the ILPA, said: 'It is difficult to envisage any circumstances in which someone *fleeing for their lives can arrive in the UK other than by committing an offence. The sort of people convicted of this offence won't be the gang masters and Mafioso but the naïve people* and those who feel they have *no alternative'.*

(*The Guardian*, 18 March 2005)

Next, the writer draws on a *quotation from the UNHCR's representative in Britain, Anne Dawson-Shepherd whose remarks fit well within the scheme of the article in accusing the Conservatives* and specifically relates Mr. Howard as a typical example of a political opportunist.

(*The Guardian*, 11 April 2005)

However, as far as the overall standpoint regarding immigration is concerned, the British liberal discourse lacks a clear argumentation and seems to be a defensive measure.

# 5 Concluding discussions

Extensive textual analyses of the selected texts at the micro level have led to accounts for similarities and differences in discursive strategies pursued in different newspapers. Ideally, the textual analysis of various events and news topics should be considered separately so that the relevant contextual and interdiscursive features can be integrated in the explication. On the other hand the overall and diachronic discursive characteristics and strategies could be considered as a central aim of a research project. The chapter set out to provide some of the broader trends in the British immigration discourses. Some of the micro-analytical details and findings along with several textual examples from the different newspapers are included in other project publications (e.g. KhosraviNik, 2009, 2010b and especially KhosraviNik, 2008).

Apart from the definitive impact of choice of topics and length of coverage on qualities of presence and resonance of immigration discourse in society, the research shows that one of the common strategies in constructing a supportive sympathetic representation is extensivization via which personal, emotional, circumstantial, geographical details of people and events involved are elaborated. As seen in the examples, during the Kosovo war the refugees are frequently named, and their details of age, marital status, education, personality, emotions, physical features, histories, etc. are covered. Similarly, there is a systematic preference for incorporating direct quotations from the war-stricken

Kosovars with no (negative) perspectivization through, for example, reporting verbs. This journalistic language strategy eliminates distance from the subjects as much as possible both via choice of neutral reporting verbs as well as allocations of substantial direct quotation spaces. This becomes more salient when compared to the representation of the Serbian perpetrators where there is a clear distance modalization through reporting verbs and direct quotation allocations. This extensivization (and individualization) is the exact opposite of functionalization, collectivization and aggregation processes which are the most common strategies in the representation of immigrants in British discourses, e.g. during the British election debates.

Even though there are other contextual factors influencing the scale and orientations of the coverage of these groups of people, the proximity of events/displaced populations to the UK seems to correlate with heightened levels of tension, projection of fear and a tendency towards negative representation of immigrants/refugees. Scale, content and evaluative orientations of immigration discourses seem to be determined at the intersection of a) newspapers' political perspectives (their relations to the incumbent government), b) the nature and scale of events/facts and c) the repertoire of already existing 'discourses in place' in the society. For example, amidst a supportive/ sympathetic discourse on Kosovar refugees, the conservative *Times* does not fail to also lay criticism against the then Labour government's decision to bomb the Serbian army. Similarly, the paper shows signs of alarm at the prospect of the Kosovar refugees seeking entry to UK. In contrast to its general sympathetic, supportive representation of refugees, in an article on 30 March 1999, the paper feels compelled to discuss the situation in terms of the common immigration crisis at the British borders.

In the mainstream (conservative) representation of immigration, these groups of people are systematically constructed as a homogenous group presupposing that they share similar personal characteristics, backgrounds, motivations, economic status, cultures, etc. Tapping into the discourse of fear and threat, the most typical representation of an immigrant member is a different-looking (usually via visual accompaniments if any), adult, young, single male (via predications denoting physical power) with no or little education or professional skills (via systematic absences of references). Other possible constructions, for example the elderly, children, families, educated people, and women (to a large extent) tend to be backgrounded or ignored.

What emerges from the study is that the tabloid conservative newspapers seem to directly reproduce existing layman's stereotypes while the quality conservative newspaper refrains from drawing on negative topoi directly, yet acknowledges that these topoi widely exist in society – hence communicates them as presupposed general knowledge. In other words, the quality paper's negative representation is creative and productive while the tabloid's is (quasi-) reflective and reproductive. The most common discursive strategy adopted by the tabloids is referential, followed by predicational strategies; the preferred news genre in the tabloids is narrative. In the meantime most of the references to negative topoi in the tabloids are alluded to or implemented through the use of metaphors (e.g. Britain plagued by immigrants). Such strategies together with the tabloids' mode of perspectivization help to construct a very strong 'Us vs. Them' bifurcation that, in effect, creates a 'moral panic' among its readership. The preferred discursive macro-strategy of the quality conservative newspapers is to rely on argumentation with some predicational strategies. It generally refrains from explicit negative referentials. In some instances, the distinction is simply between an explicit, lexically detectable negative Other presentation in the tabloids vs. a much more subtle and coded approach in the conservative quality papers; the latter of which relies on pragmatic devices such as insinuations, implicatures and presuppositions of a repertoire of old knowledge on the side of the readership.

There also is an argument to be made that 'meanings' and attitudes (negative or positive) are constructed at the intersection of language and society rather than by being inherent semantic properties of the language per se. The topoi of numbers and large quantities or in fact (with some reservation) any other micro-linguistic structures (except naming) do not by themselves constitute negativity or positivity. Negative evaluation is an aspect of macro structure of production and interpretation of a discourse in relation to its immediate context of audiences; in other words, it is resident or constituted at the intersection of language and society's (assumed) 'old, shared knowledge'. To understand the way a message of negativity is communicated requires an approach in which the social 'discourses in place' both synchronically and diachronically are accounted for, i.e. the emphasis on the context of audiences. Thus, it is not the micro level linguistic mechanisms (by themselves) which create positive or negative (or any other) evaluations. It is the tacit shared social macro structures which orient, regulate, and decode meanings. This is to say that real meanings are in society, rather than language, and micro mechanisms do not automatically create a macro structure of meanings even though they contribute to it and reiterate it at the micro level.

The results of this study, in line with findings of several other European studies, indicate that even the liberal press are gradually succumbing to more exclusionary rhetoric. Similar legitimation and justification strategies are increasingly employed in negative Othering processes for immigrants across Europe, albeit with different degrees and qualities. The general rise of populist discourses on immigration as seen in press discourses in this study, and the demarcation of who is the 'in' and 'out' group hint at a change towards more convergent ideologies with an implicit 'modernized' nationalist agenda which attempts to distance itself from the more traditional common discourse strategies (although the tabloids do not generally share even this attempt). These are all occasioned by the rise of more populist conservative discourses in Europe (Wodak, 1996; Reisigl and Wodak, 2001; Van Dijk, 1991; and Wodak et al., 2013 for the most recent developments) which by definition tend to over-simplify and de-historicize the current social texture of modern societies. Such strategic attempts to avoid resemblance to known prejudiced discourses (e.g. Richardson, 2013 on BNP) does not diminish the risk involved in how such macro themes of argumentation can be translated for the public and how swiftly the shifts from coded discursive practice can turn into justified material practices.

# Notes

1 'Discourses of Refugees and Asylum Seekers in the UK Press, 1996–2006', ESRC funded project carried out at the Department of Linguistics and English Language, Lancaster University. For more information, see http://ucrel.lancs.ac.uk/projects/rasim/

2 For some of these outputs see http://ucrel.lancs.ac.uk/projects/rasim/

# References

Baker, P. and McEnery, T. (2005), 'A corpus-based approach to discourses of refugees and asylum seekers in UN and newspaper texts', *Language and Politics*, 4(2); 197–226.

Baker, P., Gabrielatos, C., KhosraviNik, M., Kryzanowski, M., McEnery, T. and Wodak, R. (2008), 'A useful methodological synergy? Combining critical discourse analysis and corpus linguistics to examine discourses of refugees and asylum seekers in the UK press, *Discourse and Society*, 19(3), 273–306.

Barker, M. (1981), *The New Racism*. London: Junction Books.

Blommaert, J. (2001), 'Investigating narrative inequality: African asylum seekers in Belgium'. *Discourse and Society*, 12(4), 413–49.

—— (2005), *Discourse: A Critical Introduction*. Cambridge: Cambridge University Press.

Cap. P. (2011), 'Axiological proximisation', in C. Hart (ed.), *Critical Discourse Studies in Context and Cognition*. Amsterdam: John Benjamins, pp. 81–96.

Chilton (2005a), 'Manipulation, memes and metaphors: the case of *Mein Kampf*', in L. de Saussure (ed.), *Manipulation*. Amsterdam: John Benjamins, pp. 20–36.

—— (2005b), 'Missing links in mainstream CDA: modules, blends and the critical instinct', in R. Wodak and P. Chilton (eds), *A New Agenda in (Critical) Discourse Analysis*. Amsterdam/Philadelphia: John Benjamins, pp. 19–52.

Clyne, M. (2005),'The use of exclusionary language to manipulate opinion'. *Journal of Language and Politics*, 4(2), 173–96.

Entman, R. M. (2002), 'Framing: towards clarification of a fractured paradigm', in D. McQuil (ed.), *McQuail's Reader in Mass Communication Theory*. London: Sage, pp. 390–7.

Fairclough, N. (2001), 'Dialectics of discourse'. *Textus*, 14(2), 231–42.

Fairclough, N. and Wodak, R. (1997), 'Critical discourse analysis: an overview', in T. A. van Dijk (ed.), *Discourse as a Social Interaction* (Discourse Studies: A multidisciplinary introduction. Vol. 2). London: Sage, pp. 258–83.

Flowerdew, J., Li, D. and Tran, S. (2002), 'Discriminatory news discourse: some Hong Kong data'. *Discourse and Society*, 13(3), 319–45.

Gabrielatos, C. (2007), 'Selecting query terms to build a specialized corpus from a restricted-access database', *ICAME Journal*, 31, 5–43.

Hart, C. (2010), *Critical Discourse Analysis and Cognitive Science: New Perspectives on Immigration Discourse*. Basingstoke: Palgrave.

—— (2011), 'Moving beyond metaphor in the cognitive linguistic approach to CDA: construal operations in immigration discourse', in C. Hart (ed.), *Critical Discourse Studies in Context and Cognition*. Amsterdam: John Benjamins, pp. 171–92.

—— (2013), 'Event-construal in press reports of violence in political protests: a cognitive linguistic approach to CDA'. *Journal of Language and Politics*, 12(3), 400–23.

Hartmann, P. and Husband, C. (1974), *Racism and the Mass Media. A Study of the Role of the Mass Media in the Formation of White Beliefs and Attitudes in Britain*. London: Davis-Poynter.

Hultman, M. (2001), *Racism Discourse (Re)exploited*. MA Dissertation at Department of Cultural Studies of Linkoping University, Sweden.

Jäger, S. (2001), 'Discourse and knowledge: theoretical and methodological aspects of a critical discourse and dispositive analysis', in R. Wodak and M. Meyer (eds), *Methods of Critical Discourse Analysis*. London: Sage, pp. 32–62.

KhosraviNik, M. (2008), 'British newspapers and representation of refugees, asylum-seekers and immigrants between 1996 and 2006'. Lancaster University: Centre for Language in Social Life.

—— (2009), 'The representation of refugees, asylum seekers and immigrants in British newspapers during the Balkan conflict (1999) and the British general election (2005)'. *Discourse and Society*, 20(4), 477–98.

—— (2010a), 'Actor descriptions, action attributions, and argumentation: towards a systematization of CDA analytical categories in the representation of social groups'. *Critical Discourse Studies*, 7(1), 55–72.

—— (2010b), 'The representation of refugees, asylum seekers and immigrants in British newspapers: a critical discourse analysis'. *Journal of Language and Politics*, 9(1), 1–28.

Laclau, E. and Mouffe, C. (1985), *Hegemony and Socialist Strategy: Towards a Radical Democratic Politics*. London: Verso.

Lynn, N. and Lea, S. (2003), 'A phantom menace and the new apartheid: the social construction of asylum-seekers in the United Kingdom'. *Discourse Studies*, 4(2), 169–81.

Oswald, S. (2010), *Pragmatics of Uncooperative and Manipulative Communication*. PhD Dissertation, ms, University of Neuchâtel, Switzerland.

—— (2011), 'From interpretation to consent: arguments, beliefs and meaning'. *Discourse Studies*, 13(6), 806–14.

Polyzou, A. (2012), 'Book Review: *Critical Discourse Analysis and Cognitive Science: New Perspectives on Immigration Discourse*, by Christopher Hart, Houndmills and New York: Palgrave Macmillan, 2010'. *Critical Discourse Studies*, 9(3), 315–17.

—— (2013), *Presupposition, (Ideological) Knowledge Management and Gender in Greek Lifestyle Magazines: A Socio-cognitive Discourse Analytical Approach*. PhD Dissertation: Lancaster University, Department of Linguistics and English Language.

—— (forthcoming), Presupposition in discourse: Theoretical and methodological issues. *Critical Discourse Studies*.

Reisigl, M. and Wodak, R. (2001), *Discourse and Discrimination: Rhetorics of Racism and Anti-Semitism*. London and New York: Routledge.

Reisigl, M. and Wodak, R. (2009), 'The discourse-historical approach (DHA)', in R. Wodak and M. Meyer (eds), *Methods of Critical Discourse Analysis* (2nd edn). London: Sage, pp. 87–121.

Richardson, E. J. (2013), 'Ploughing the same furrow? Continuity and change on Britain's extreme-right fringe', in R. Wodak, M. KhosraviNik and B. Mral (eds), *Rightwing Populism in Europe: Politics and Discourse*. London, New York: Bloomsbury.

Santa Ana, O. (1999), 'Like an animal I was treated: anti-immigrant metaphors in US public discourse'. *Discourse and Society*, 11(1), 191–224.

Teo, P. (2000), 'Racism in the news: a critical discourse analysis of news reporting in two Australian newspapers', *Discourse and Society*, 11(1), 191–224.

Tileaga, C. (2005), 'Accounting for extreme prejudice and legitimating blame in the talk about the Romanies'. *Discourse and Society*, 16(5), 603–24.

Van Dijk. T. A. (1984), *Prejudice in Discourse: An Analysis of Ethnic Prejudice in Cognition and Conversation*. Amsterdam; Philadelphia: John Benjamins.

—— (1987), *Communicating Racism: Ethnic Prejudice in Thought and Talk*. Newbury Park, Calif.: Sage.

—— (1991), *Racism and the Press*. London and New York: Routledge.

—— (1996), 'Discourse, power and access', in C. R. Caldas Coulthard and M. Coulthard (eds), *Texts and Practices*. London, New York: Routledge, pp. 86–106.

—— (2001), 'Critical discourse analysis', in D. Tannen, D. Schiffrin, D. Tannen and H. Hamilton (eds), *Handbook of Discourse Analysis*. Oxford: Blackwell, pp. 352–71.

—— (2005), *Racism and Discourse in Spain and Latin America*. Amsterdam and Philadelphia: John Benjamins.

—— (2006), 'Discourse and manipulation'. *Discourse and Society*, 17(3), 359–83.

Van Leeuwen, T. (1996), 'The representation of social actors', in C. R. Caldas-Coulthard and M. Coulthard (eds), *Texts and Practices*. London and New York: Routledge, pp. 32–70.

Weiss, G. and Wodak, R. (2003), *Critical Discourse Analysis: Theory and Interdisciplinarity*. Basingstoke: Palgrave Macmillan.

Wetherell, M. and Potter, J. (1992), *Mapping the Language of Racism: Discourse and the Legitimation of Exploitation*. Hemel Hempstead: Harvester Wheatsheaf.

Wodak, R. (1996), *Disorders of Discourse*. London and New York: Longman.

—— (2001), 'The discourse-historical approach', in R. Wodak and M. Meyer (eds), *Methods of Critical Discourse Analysis*. London: Sage, pp. 63–94.

—— (2006), 'Dilemmas of discourse (analysis)'. *Language in Society*, 35(4), 595–611.

Wodak, R. and Matouschek, B. (1993), 'We are dealing with people whose origins one can clearly tell just by looking: critical discourse analysis and the study of neo-racism in contemporary Austria'. *Discourse and Society*, 4(2), 225–48.

Wodak, R. and Meyer, M. (2009), 'Critical discourse analysis: history, agenda, theory', in R. Wodak and M. Meyer (eds), *Methods of Critical Discourse Analysis* (2nd edn). London: Sage, pp. 1–33.

Wodak, R. and Van Dijk, T. A. (2006), *Racism at the Top*. Drava: Austrian Ministry of Education, Science and Culture, Austria.

Wodak, R., KhosraviNik, M. and Mral B. (eds) (2013), *Rightwing Populism in Europe: Politics and Discourse*. London and New York: Bloomsbury.

# 22

# Race and Immigration in Far- and Extreme-Right European Political Leaflets

*John E. Richardson*
Loughborough University

*Monica Colombo*
University of Milan-Bicocca

## 1 Introduction

Far-right extremism is on the rise across Europe. Demos research reports demonstrate the significant increase in hardline ethno-nationalist sentiment in many European countries, predominantly among young men (Birdwell et al., 2011; also see Bartlett et al., 2012 on Hungary; Birdwell et al., 2012 on Lega Nord, amongst others).[1] Such people are compelled by generalized fears regarding national and cultural identity, the threat they see in immigration and minority ethnic and religious communities – particularly a perceived growing power of Islam – and are simultaneously cynical about their own governments and the EU acting to address these fears/threats. This combination of (racialized) political anxiety and scepticism that established political elites will address 'popular' concerns is driving a variety of fringe and even extra-parliamentary political movements. Such groups advance their cause in a number of ways, through both online and offline media, and utilizing a wide variety of discourses and genres.

This chapter will examine multimodal discourse produced and disseminated by far- and extreme-right parties and movements in France, Germany, Italy, Spain,

Switzerland and the UK (Front National, pro NRW, Lega Nord, Democracia Nacional, Union démocratique du centre and the British National Party) and their relations to race, racialization and immigration. Our argument is that such discourse on both national identity and insecurity is functional to the ethnicization of social conflict which, in turn, may not only discursively 'work up' a sense of menace and the social construction of fear (cf. Cap, this volume; Dunmire, this volume) but also represents and facilitates a shift towards the legitimization of ethnic hate. This shift in the representation of the other (from 'alien' to 'enemy') is discursively realized through a role reversal in the relationship between in-group and out-group (cf. Koller, this volume), and specifically on the dominant-dominated dimension on which racist supremacist ideology is grounded.

## 2  Anti-immigrant discourse and 'new' racism

Discourse plays a crucial role in the reproduction and legitimation of xenophobia, racism, ethnic dominance and exclusion. There is a rich tradition of research examining the structure and function of xenophobic and racist discourse (Van Dijk, 1984; Quasthoff, 1987; Billig, 1991; Essed, 1991; Wetherell and Potter, 1992; Reisigl and Wodak, 2001), its diffusion through the mass media (Van Dijk, 1991; Wodak and Matouschek, 1993; Richardson, 2004; Hart, 2010) and its semantic organization in political discourse (Van Dijk, 1997; Wodak and Van Dijk, 2000; Van der Valk, 2003; Richardson, 2011). Reisigl and Wodak (2001: 275) define racism as follows:

> Racism is based on the hierarchising construction of groups of persons which are characterised as communities of descent and which are attributed specific collective, naturalised or biologised traits that are considered to be almost invariable. These traits are primarily related to biological features, appearance, cultural practices, customs, traditions, language or socially stigmatised ancestors. They are – explicitly or implicitly, directly or indirectly – evaluated negatively, and this judgement is more or less in accord with hegemonic views. That is, language practices, cultural traits, traditions, and customs come to represent 'race' in hegemonic discourse in an 'almost invariable pseudo-causal connection' between biological, social, and cultural traits.

Extensive research in the critical discourse analytic tradition has focused on the crucial role exerted by the political elites in the production, diffusion and legitimation of both overt and covert forms of xenophobia and racist discourse over time. In more detail: 'because of their control over public discourse, media and communication, the elites, and hence also the political elites, play a special role in the formation of public opinion about immigration and other ethnic issues' (Wodak and Van Dijk, 2000: 9).

During the past two decades, the extreme right has re-emerged as an electoral force in Western Europe; it includes many parties such as the Republikaner in Germany, the Lega Nord in Italy, the Swedish Democrats, the French Front National, the Belgian

Vlaams Blok, the Austrian Freedom Party (FPÖ), Jobbik Magyarországért Mozgalom (The Movement for a Better Hungary) and the Danish People's party.[2] These parties share a fundamental core of ethno-nationalist xenophobia (based on the so-called 'ethno-pluralist doctrine') and anti-political-establishment populism (Rydgren, 2007).

Wodak (2003, 2008) argues that the extreme right have become more and more subtle in their expression of and support for racism. At all levels of discourse, their 'new' racism is not always expressed in overtly racist terms or in the terms of neo-fascist discourse. Instead, anti-immigrant positions are generally supported and justified by arguments that concern protecting jobs, eliminating abuse of welfare benefits or cultural incompatibilities, with a particular emphasis on Muslims and the putative 'Islamization' of Europe.

This new form of racism, which Taguieff (1988) calls 'racisme différencialiste' and Wieviorka (1998) calls 'racisme culturelle', stresses the incompatible difference between ethnic groups which are described in cultural terms without specifically mentioning race or without referring to overtly racial criteria. This does not mean, however, that racialized minorities are not the targets of this new racism, merely that the grounds of their alleged incompatibility with 'Us' are expressed using 'cultural' rather than biological criteria. Schmidt (2002: 154) puts this clearly: 'A new racism has developed in recent decades in which specific cultural forms have come to signify racialised identities.' A process of racialization occurs in the discourse of elites, which ascribes to groups' certain characteristics which render them so foreign or 'alien' that it is impossible to conceive of them as equal members of the same community as the elite. As Blackledge (2006: 62) points out,

> When discussions of race as the basis of group difference are no longer politically acceptable, metaphors are sought [. . .] Symbolic representation such as this can be found in discourse about cultural practices which mark a particular group as alien from the majority. Common-sense public discourse identifies cultural practices which are different from those of the dominant group, and they become symbols of the 'Otherness' of the minority. That is, cultural practices become racialized, and come to represent a group.

These two trends – the increase in elite racism and the shift to *racisme différencialiste* – are, arguably, linked phenomena. As Krzyżanowski and Wodak (2008) point out, the move away from overt neo-fascist discourse has allowed extreme-right parties to expand their electoral support as populist nationalist parties.

The core message of the extreme right amounts to a base opposition to immigration and, frequently, settled minority ethnic communities. As Rydgren (2003) puts it, these parties use four arguments to frame immigrants as national/cultural threats: a) immigrants are a threat to ethno-national identity; b) immigrants are a major cause of criminality and other kinds of social insecurity; c) immigrants are a cause of unemployment; and d) immigrants are abusers of the generosity of the welfare states of Western democracies. Using the third and fourth of these argumentative frames, the extreme right-wing parties have promoted the idea of national preference, that is, giving 'native' communities priority when it comes to jobs, housing, health care and so on. For all these reasons, extreme right-wing parties promote an ethnic view of citizenship (*jus sanguinis*) and oppose the idea of residential or civic citizenship (*jus soli*) (cf. Brubaker, 1992).

By employing an ethno-pluralist ideology, the extreme right-wing parties claim the right of European national cultures to protect their cultural identities. According to the extreme right, there are several threats against their national identity, of which the alleged 'invasion' of immigrants is the most important. The concept of culture is naturalized and a fundamental link posited between a (ethnicized) 'culture' and its 'natural habitat'. The discursive achievement of this biologism is 'an absolute fixing of the difference between cultures' (1992.) and essentially ensures that 'culture acquires an immutable character, and hence becomes a homologue for race' (Malik, 1996: 150).

## 3 The Discourse-Historical Approach to Critical Discourse Analysis

Critical discourse analysts assume that language is a social practice that, like all practices, is dialectically related to the contexts of its use. The Discourse-Historical Approach (DHA) uses four 'levels of context' as heuristics to locate discursive practices, strategies and texts in specific socio-political contexts: first, the immediate, language or text internal co-text, which take into account issues such as textual coherence, cohesion, and 'the local interactive processes of negotiation' (Reisigl and Wodak, 2001: 41; see also Reisigl, this volume); second, the intertextual and interdiscursive relationships between utterances, texts, genres and discourses; third, the social/sociological variables and institutional frames of a specific 'context of situation'; and finally, the broader socio-political and historical contexts within which the discursive practices are embedded. These four layers enable researchers to better deconstruct the meanings of discourse and how they relate to context (see Engel and Wodak, 2013; Richardson, 2013).

In addition, the DHA seeks to identify the effect of particular discursive strategies which may serve to represent an individual or a group either positively or negatively (see Reisigl and Wodak, 2009). Specifically, the DHA offers five types of discursive strategies which underpin the justification of inclusion/exclusion of self/other, and the constructions of identities: first, referential strategies (also called nomination strategies) through which social actors are constructed and represented, for example, through the creation of in-groups and out-groups. This can be achieved through a number of categorization devices, including metaphors, metonymies and synecdoches, in the form of a part standing for the whole (*pars pro toto*) or a whole standing for the part (*totum pro parte*). Second, predicational strategies by which evaluative attributions of negative and positive traits in the linguistic form of implicit or explicit predicates are offered. Third, argumentation strategies and a fund of *topoi* through which positive and negative attributions are justified.[3] Topoi possess content-related as well as formal properties: they can be described as reservoirs of generalized key ideas from which specific statements or arguments can be generated (Ivie, 1980, cited in Richardson, 2004: 230) in addition to (explicit or inferable) premises, which connect premises in an argument (Reisigl and Wodak, 2001).[4] Fourth, perspectivization, or discourse representation. Through framing, speakers express their involvement in discourse, and position their point of view in the reporting, description, narration or quotation of relevant events or utterances. And finally, intensifying and mitigation strategies, which help to qualify and modify the epistemic status of a proposition by intensifying or mitigating the illocutionary force of utterances or the modality of pictorial representations.

Academic work on rhetoric and persuasion has recently taken a more visual turn, with a wide variety of authors examining – and demonstrating – the ways that it is possible to argue visually (Blair, 2004; Burridge, 2008; Cheles, 2010; Groarke, 2002, 2007; Richardson and Wodak, 2009). Consequently, empirical and analytic foci have been expanded from verbal discourse to include visual artefacts. In line with this standpoint, we assume that it is possible to advance and defend standpoints visually, and that if we are to understand the impact of anti-immigrant rhetoric on electorates and publics, analysing parties' visual propaganda is particularly important; visual propaganda can be regarded as a sub-genre within political discourse (Cairns, 2009) drawing strongly on emotional rhetorical appeals.

This chapter briefly examines xenophobic leaflets produced across Europe before providing a more detailed analysis of two leaflets produced by the French Front National (FN). In our analysis of all the leaflets, our focus is on how inter-ethnic conflict is discursively constructed and, specifically, how they advance xenophobic arguments through a combination of linguistic and visual elements. Our analysis of the FN leaflets, particularly, focuses on inter-discursive references which allow us to highlight the connection between two core elements in their anti-immigrant discourse: discourse on national identity and discourse on insecurity.

## 4 Xenophobic discourse in far- and extreme-right leaflets

Below, we present two leaflets (also produced as posters) which had an impact on two anti-immigrant referenda in Switzerland and the propaganda produced by extreme-right parties in other European countries. Of particular note is the first leaflet's use in the successful Swiss referendum to ban the building of minarets in November 2009, widely covered at the time by European news media.

In the past two decades the Swiss People's Party (including SVP, UDC and PPS, also known as the Democratic Union of the Centre) has established itself as one of the most powerful far-right wing parties in Western Europe. For more than two decades it has wooed an increasing number of voters with its anti-immigrant rhetoric. The leaflets, designed by Alexander Segert and used by the party during several campaigns, may well have played a significant role in this success. The SVP advertising is distinctive in the way that it uses graphic illustrations rather than the more widespread and traditional photos. The two reproduced below emulate the iconography of comics – a popular, generally understood visual language which works perfectly in political communications, due to its visual simplification. The posters/leaflets generally contain very few words; the core of the message is communicated visually, typically accompanied by a brief slogan; and as such, they can better etch themselves into collective visual memory. Indeed, despite international condemnation, in the 'anti-minarets' referendum of November 2009, 57 per cent of Swiss voters were in favour of the ban.

For all these reasons, these Swiss posters have been imitated extensively by various other European extreme-right populist parties. Perhaps not realizing the political or ideological advantage in this – essentially, acknowledging that because their fellow extreme-right European parties also position Islam as a common enemy, they should be allowed to duplicate this successful rhetorical strategy – the 'Swiss designers were not amused. At one point they went so far as to threaten to sue the Front National (FN) after the French party's youth organization had used a copy of the poster' (Betz, 2013: 74). Given this history of 'borrowing', it should come as little surprise that the posters we analyse below all contain identical elements.

On each image (see Figures 22.1–3, below), silhouettes of minarets are pictured superimposed over the national flags of Switzerland, Germany and Britain. As with other nationalist political discourse (extremist and otherwise) the flags clearly act as a metonyms for their respective nations (see Billig, 1995). The meaning potential of the minarets, on the other hand, is a little more complex. Viewed in conjunction with the veiled woman, they function, firstly, to represent Islam in a metonymic replacement of building by the faith of the people using the building. However, they also act to represent a more specific process – a process through which, in the view of these parties, their respective national spaces are gradually being taken over by Muslims. Combined with the linguistic element of the leaflets (either the imperative 'Stopp' or the 'Facts' in the BNP leaflet), it is clear that these respective parties view the presence of Islam in the(ir) national space as objectionable. Oskar Freysinger, the SVP Member of Parliament, has confirmed as much – that their campaign is directed not at minarets and Muslim buildings of worship in themselves, but against minarets as a 'symbol of a political and aggressive Islam' (quoted in Betz, 2013: 73). Political discourse, in both the news media and public policy, has constructed Islam and Muslims as a threat (Richardson, 2004) in a process which, as Fortier (2008) has pointed out, can lead to a new 'moral racism' wherein religious belief has become the primary marker of difference. The leaflet therefore recalls the widespread questioning – by both politicians and mainstream news media – of whether Muslims can, or *should*, be integrated into European society.

The placement of these fantasy minarets over the flags suggests they are either piercing *through* the flags or have been imposed, or built *on top* of them. The suggested

**FIGURES 22.1–3** *'Anti-Minaret' leaflets from Switzerland, Britain and Germany.*

violence of this process is heightened by the ways the minarets evoke spear-tips – given the wide variety of minaret designs, they didn't have to be this 'sharp ended', suggesting that this choice and its meaning potential is deliberate. Indeed, minarets, in the view of the SVP's Freysinger, have an 'imperialist connotation' (Betz, 2013: 73). This meaning is picked up explicitly in the linguistic material included on the BNP leaflet, where an overtly militaristic lexicon of war (bayonets, helmets, barracks and army) is invoked as part of a discourse of conquest – 'Islamification' being the putative goal of Turkey and, *pars pro toto*, of Muslims in general. (Otherwise this process would have been named 'Turkification', rather than the more general 'Islamification'.) The rhetoric of conquest and colonization, the negative prosody of the terms employed to substantiate the standpoint and, thereby, the threat that *They* are taken to pose to *Us*, work to substantiate and 'naturalize' the defensive stance towards 'Islamification' proposed by these various parties.

However, the leaflets do not simply suggest that 'Islamification' is a threat that will affect Us all in the same way. The presence of the second key pictorial element of these leaflets works to implicitly suggest a more specific battleground: the bodies of women. 'The Muslim woman' has become part of a visual iconography of anti-immigrant discourse in general, and anti-Muslim discourse in particular, that has been developed by European parties of the right. The leaflets position women – and the bodies of women specifically – as sites where this conflict between Islam and Us is played out. The BNP have pushed this argument to the forefront of their propaganda campaigns, to the extent that they argue, more or less explicitly, that 'we need to defend *our women*, otherwise they will end up looking *like this*' (Jiwani and Richardson, 2011; Richardson, 2011; Richardson and Wodak, 2009). That is, women's bodies are invoked, in a *pars pro totum* synecdoche, as the site for this putative process of colonization (or Islamification) and reconquest. This battle for control over (Our) women and (Our) women's bodies utilizes and subverts a liberal discourse of gender equality, apportions women's rights as the purview of nationalist men and objectifies the very women that it claims to honour. 'Nationalist' (that is, extreme-right wing) men are positioned as protectors of Our women – the passivized, embodied nation space – and ethnic managers with the power and responsibility to reject Islam.

The 'black sheep' poster on the next page (see figure 22.4), with its slogan 'For more security', was designed in 2007, on the occasion of the proposal of a new law which would authorize the deportation of foreign criminals. Of Swiss voters, 52.9 per cent approved a measure to automatically deport foreigners convicted of crimes ranging from murder to welfare fraud. In October 2007, the general elections gave the nationalist Swiss People's Party (SVP) the highest vote ever recorded for a single Swiss party. The SVP received 29 per cent of the vote (up from the already high 26.7 per cent in the 2003 election) largely on the basis of its anti-immigration stance. The same image was immediately adopted, in 2007, by the relatively minor Spanish right-wing party, Democracia Nacional (Figure 22.5), this time accompanied by the slogan '¡Compórtate o lárgate!' (Behave or get out!).

In both leaflets the key argument is advanced visually through a childlike cartoon, utilizing strong and uniform colours. Again, the flags clearly act as metonyms for their respective nations and, through the use of colour, the (significantly *white*) in-group is represented as internally homogenous. The white/black division obviously plays on the idiomatic expression 'the black sheep', though this also communicates a clear (though inherently deniable) racialized agenda. The cartoon itself is drawn with pure, smooth lines, with no distortion or expressive style. Machin (2007) argues that brightness, high saturation and purity of palette are particularly associated with ideas of intensity,

**FIGURES 22.4–5** *'Black Sheep' leaflets from Switzerland and Spain.*

excitement and simplicity. The combination of simple colours and a cartoon rendered with pure and fluid lines, results in a 'low modality world' in which 'certain kinds of actions and solutions can appear reasonable and need not be held to naturalistic everyday standards. We can remove or dilute aspects of naturalistic reality that we might dislike or that might get in the way of our plan' (Machin, 2007: 52). The inherent violence of the action depicted is therefore mitigated by being depicted as an unrealistic cartoon. The legitimization of expulsion, overtly supported through the image, is then justified by the linguistic content.

Given the context and occasion for which the UDC poster was designed, interestingly no explicit reference to migrants is made, leaving the audience apparently free to determine who the soon-to-be-excluded deviant might be. (All 'black sheep' in the Swiss case? All criminal, foreign 'black sheep' in the Spanish example?) Near the UDC logo (a smiling sun), at the bottom right side of the poster, the slogan 'My home – Our Switzerland' positions the party as the defender of the homeland. The shift from the first person singular possessive 'my' and the first person plural possessive 'our' establishes a strong continuity between the personal and the collective spheres (I/We) and fosters a strong identification with the in-group.

In the DN poster, migrants are referred to as 'foreigners' and are explicitly associated with an increasing rate of crime; their expulsion is then justified on this basis (topos of criminality). In the main slogan, a patronizing tone is adopted: indeed, the imperative

'¡Compórtate!' is generally used to address children and 'lárgarse' is a colloquial term, suggestive of a populist rhetorical move. Migrants are positioned as the addressee of the warning while the party allocates itself the role of spokesperson expressing people's attitudes and feeling towards migrants. Two different frames are at work here: the 'legal' one ('Against the increasing rate of foreign criminality') which in turn invokes issues such as public order and the role of the law in preserving such order; and, second, a moral frame which implies non-conformity to a shared set of values and rules. Both frames are utilized in service of the common xenophobic, indeed *racist*, agenda, to purify the national space of ethnic foreigners.

## 5 The Front National

Issues of security, national prosperity, national identity and safeguarding traditional cultural values have long been supported by the Front National, which regularly campaigns with arguments that presuppose the foreign 'Other' represents a threat to these areas, thereby requiring their exclusion at all social, economic and political levels. Discursive change within moderate European political parties towards regressive political policies over the last two decades has been very much influenced by the increasing voice of parties like the FN. Jean-Marie Le Pen's position for a 'national preference' was to 'become a political argument that both the moderate right and left would exploit. They started to exploit Le Pen's ideology in a less extremist, more coded rhetorical agenda' (Jugé and Perez, 2006: 204). Charlot (1986) argues that the rise of the FN made moderate French parties review their positions. The fear of losing voters to the FN was a major part of the re-emergence of the fight against illegal immigration, as well as the notion of French citizenship. As Çagatay Tekin (2008: 731) explains:

> the electoral success of FN in the presidential elections was influential: it not only increased its vote, but also extended its electoral power out of its traditional areas of influence. The strengthening of the FN electorate outside its traditional bases of influence is indicative of a particular process of extremization or droitisation of French politics (Birnbaum, 1998; Winock, 2006). On several dimensions, especially those relating to the protection of traditional values and authority, the extreme right and moderate right have come closer.

The emphasis on the national interest and a stricter control of immigration is implicit to the concept of 'immigration choisie' that Nicolas Sarkozy supported both as French Interior Minister and President. It is within the context of the regressive emphasis on controlling immigration that 'concepts of self and other, and insiders and outsiders have been rearticulated in contemporary France' (Silverman, 1999: 45), which in turn has provided the most fertile ground for the formation, legitimization and dissemination of a strong Islamophobia which should be regarded as a retreat into a cultural essentialism and racialized nationalism (Geisser, 2003; Silverstein, 2008).

Our chapter now turns to the analysis of two leaflets produced by the FN, as part of their regional election campaign, for elections held in France on 14 and 21 March 2010. The elections resulted in significant gains for the French Socialist Party (PS) and its allies, who now control 21 of the 22 regions of Metropolitan France. The FN re-emerged on the French political scene gaining almost 12 per cent of the national vote with Jean-Marie Le Pen winning 20 per cent in his south-eastern region of Provence-Alpes-Côte d'Azur and his daughter and heir Marine Le Pen claiming 18.3 per cent in the north-eastern Nord-Pas-de-Calais. Present in only 12 regions the FN consolidated, even strengthened, its position in the second round winning 17.1 per cent where present. These results have put the FN back on the political map after the setback it suffered at the last general election.

## 5.1 *Positioning*

Both leaflets (Figures 22.6–7, below) are two-page brochures and feature the same layout. The main picture and slogan function as the core argument of the whole campaign. The picture shows a (male) arm raised up, the fist clenched, holding the French flag, superimposed over the capitalized slogan reading 'Defend our colours'. The party's name is printed in a smaller font at the bottom on the left side, while the party's logo is on the right side. Flames and flaming torches are a recurring visual trope in the logos of extreme-right political parties, including the Swedish Democrats, the British National Front and Italy's La Destra (McGlashan, 2013). The visual metaphor is obvious but effective, drawing on, inter alia, 'passing the torch', 'keeping the flame alight' and 'light in the darkness' (2013). Near the logo, 'regional elections 2010' is printed in very small letters, perhaps suggesting that the issue at stake reaches far beyond the specific electoral context in which the leaflets were produced. The leaflets' colours (blue background, fonts in white) mirror those of the party's logo and of the flag itself, creating a strong sense of textual continuity and political branding.

Visual and linguistic elements jointly perform the main referential strategies adopted in the leaflets in order to discursively construct the in-group, with both the expression 'our colours' and the image of the flag standing for France and national identity. According to van Leeuwen (1995), this synecdochizing manoeuvre allows for referential inclusion. The use of pronouns, especially the first-person plural (we, our), can be used to induce interpreters to conceptualize group identity either as insiders or as outsiders (Chilton and Schäffner, 2002). The first-person plural possessive pronoun 'Our' indexes membership and establishes who is being referred to: in this case all those who identify with the nation, 'the French people'. The territorial dimension associated with the concept of nation is also evoked by the image of the flag which indexes the idea of the nation-state. As Richardson and Wodak (2009: 55) point out, debates about immigration and nationhood are crucially linked to assumptions about place, thus to deixis: '"Our" culture belongs "here" within the bounded homeland, whilst the culture of "foreigners" belongs "elsewhere" (topos of culture)'. In additional, 'our colours' is an emotionally

**FIGURES 22.6–7** *'Defend Our Colours'.*

charged expression that aims at fostering membership, a sense of belonging to a community, a shared territory and hence, implicitly, to the need to defend this community and territory from an external force (Richardson and Colombo, 2013). In this case, the threat to national identity is explicitly stated in the slogan which through the imperative mode sounds as a peremptory appeal to the electorate to rise up in this defence. The Front National is calling to the electorate to help defend national identity and the nation itself, metonymically represented through the (colours of the) flag. A frame of contest and a defensive fight is thus established (Goffman, 1974).

This argument can be regarded as a direct expression of the nationalism of the Front National. As van der Valk (2003) suggests, nationalism has played a crucial role in debates about immigration in France. Achard (1998) makes a distinction between the dimensions of *demos* and *ethnos* in national politics: '*Demos* presupposes the group, doesn't question it and poses the question of the legitimate field of political activity. *Ethnos* presupposes agreement about the activity and discusses who belongs to the group' (Achard, 1998: 20).[5] The expression 'our colours' clearly involves the dimension of the *ethnos* in that it refers to membership in a supposed homogenous collectivity.

Under this general rubric fall the interconnected arguments presented in the two leaflets. In the first leaflet, just below the picture, we read: 'Identité nationale?' (in white capital letters on a blue background) and 'Parlons-en concrètement!' (in blue capital letters on a white background). Through the use of the interrogative form, the issue of national identity is explicitly presented as a controversial one. This particular construction (interrogative/exclamative – question/answer) allows for the accomplishment of a perspectivation strategy through which the FN expresses its involvement in the debate on national identity and positions itself advancing its basic argument: the threat to (our) national identity is a matter of fact. Hodge and Kress (1988) explain that the interrogative mood is often used in place of other moods, such as declarative or imperative, because these alternatives embed role structures and relations for participants in a given speech situation that are often not acceptable, appropriate, or rhetorically effective. In this leaflet the interrogative mood serves the rhetorical function of including the audience/public into the debate ('the question') while, at the same time, positioning the participants inside a symbolic 'we' who are interested in dealing with the issue at stake in a specific way ('the answer'). This use of the interrogative therefore provides a frame in which the audience can participate in the debate. Moreover, it positions the public as looking for answers in the fierce public debate over the 'identité nationale' which has developed in France in recent years.

## 5.2 Referential and argumentation strategies

The linguistic content of both leaflets is complex. On the left side of the first page of both leaflets, a critical stance towards the government immigration policies is advanced, presented in bold. It is interesting to note that this layout supports two domains, with the problems they argue against on the left presumed to *actually* exist and examples of their actualization on the right. Further, this interplay indexes the integrated, mono-causal political ideology of the FN. Indeed, the examples of actualization appear linked because they are all, implicitly or explicitly, linked to a single cause: the presence of undesirable people in France. It is noteworthy that this argument is further supported and reinforced through a particular use of narrative.

On the second page, on the left, both leaflets display a box whose layout recalls that of a newspaper article. The use of such a diverse discursive device (combining both visual and linguistic elements) aims at providing evidence and legitimation of the Front National's arguments creating a fictional intertextual link to media discourse and, in particular, to a specific sub-genre: news stories. In this way, the public direct experience is evoked and assumed as a source of validation/legitimation of the Front National's arguments. In the first leaflet, on the left column, immigration is framed as an ongoing process ('*Depuis des années*'), implying that the government has been unable to control it, and as the cause of actual problems ('*grâce à une immigration massive*'). The qualifier 'massive' in this argumentative context is a well-known predicational strategy involving a negative qualification via intensification, suggesting that they (the many) cannot be contained. The out-group is referred to without any explicit reference to specific groups through the use of the indefinite article 'des' as a quantifier and they are qualified as jointly 'political-religious' ('*des groupes politico-religieux*'). This not only links two distinct spheres, which are not necessarily connected (the religious and the political), it implicitly politicizes the presence of Islam in France, thus entailing that opposition to France's Muslims can be approached as a matter of political debate rather than a straightforward case of prejudiced antipathy towards a religious minority. The use of indefinite articles such as 'des' when the referent has not been made explicit in an earlier sentence can be regarded as a negative referential strategy. The source of negativity may become apparent if one questions the author's preference for '*des groupe politico-religieux*' over other simpler and more accurate expressions such as 'Muslims'. These groups are allocated an active role ('*font pression*'), a process of social and cultural change is evoked ('*afin que les lois françaises s'adaptent à leur religion, à leur moeurs, à leur costumes, à leur mode de vie*'). The verb 's'adaptent' is in the active form but it may imply a passive role: the in-group is undergoing change and forced to accept it. In this way, in-group/out-group relations are discursively constructed as involving inter-ethnic conflict through the use of the antithetical 'leur'. It is noteworthy, that a reversal is suggested here (minorities usually have to adapt to the host culture, not the opposite).

The French president is portrayed not only as inactive in the defence of national identity against the threat represented by the out-group ('*Nicolas Sarcozy ne fait rien!*') but he is represented as an (imagined) antagonist (see Atkin and Richardson, 2005) ('*Bien au contraire, il encourage ces atteinte à la laïcité, et à notre unité et laisse quotidiennement violer nos valeurs répubblicaines*'): by qualifying him as 'encouraging these threats to the *laïcité* and to our unity' and as 'allowing our republican values to be violated every day' he is excluded from the 'We-group' who are concerned about national values.

Discourse on national values and national self-glorification is a straightforward and typical form of positive self-representation in political discourse (see Van der Valk, 2003; Van Dijk, 1997). As Çagatay Tekin (2008) remarks, 'the discourse of French speakers, especially those on the right of the political spectrum, is replete with references to French national identity and traditions. [. . .] Positive references praising France, [. . .] French culture [. . .], French republicanism [. . .] are all found to be quite common in the discourse of the speakers of almost all political convictions' (739). In this case, the routine practices of glorifying French national identity and values allow for the construction of a strong sense of belonging to the in-group on the one hand, and to neglect the other political actors: '*Quant à la gauche . . . PS/Verts/PC . . . Ils se taisent!*' on the other hand. In this way, the Front National positions itself in the public debate as the exclusive defender of national values in general, and 'laïcité' specifically.

The key argument is then introduced: '*La laïcité s'écroule et le communautarisme gangrène notre société. Jugez-en!*'. We find it interesting to pay attention to the following aspects. The verb 'gangrèner' is employed in the negative predicational qualification of the out-group and of the alleged effects of immigration: the verb clearly evokes a process of corruption of society and it implies the idea of national community as a living organism. Metaphors of racial, national and ethnic 'bodies' recruited from naturalizations are very common in discourses about immigrants. Moreover, the term 'communautarisme' has a particular meaning in the French context: it refers to the political or cultural claims of minority groups and it is generally used in a derogatory way by their opponents. It is important to emphasize that, according to Taguieff (2005), in the last 15 years the term 'communautarisme' has generally functioned as an 'opérateur d'illégitimation' (illegitimization device) in French political discourse where it is often opposed to 'individualism' and 'cosmopolitism'. Moreover, the term 'communautarisme' has relevant ideological implications: it legitimizes the construction of social groups on the basis of their origins within the framework of the idea of the nation-state which is grounded on the normative principle of cultural and ethnic homogeneity. In the leaflet, with regard to the construction of the out-group, the term is clearly connected to the label 'groupes politico-religieux' previously used and thus to the referential strategies adopted, of which it constitutes a further specification. The term is used by the Front National in the leaflet to refer to Islamic extremists ('les islamistes').

The Front National calls up the electorate to take into careful consideration their arguments ('*Jugez-en!*'). Again, this construction (imperative/exclamative) has the rhetorical function of discursively implicating the audience in the representation of the reality which the Front National is offering. At the same time, this inclusion should be understood as an attempt to shape the public's representation of it. On the one hand, the use of the imperative at the second-person plural (instead of the first-person plural as discussed above) in a mental process clause (the verb to judge) positions the public as holding their own convictions and capable of their own evaluation, on the other hand a privileged (and one-sided) representation of reality is then constructed. The leaflet is constructed such that the Front National arguments are seen as the only legitimate and rational ones in the debate on national identity and insecurity. Thus, while the text may appear at a superficial level to be dialogic, it is, in fact inherently monologic: in its entirety, the lexical, syntactic, and modal structure plays a significant role in the discursive process of establishing the Front National position, of implicating the public in that position, and of undermining the possibility and legitimacy of any other positions.

In the text on the right a list of examples of the ongoing process of change occurring in French society in various contexts (i.e. schools, hospitals, workplaces) is offered. Ethonyms and religionyms are highlighted in yellow and thus given a particular relevance. The use of such a marker can be regarded as a non-verbal means of intensification aiming at emotionally and cognitively engaging the audience. Again, the out-group, which is referred to through the antithetical pronoun 'Ils', is allocated an active role and is predicated as successfully demanding ('*Ils ont exigé et obtenus . . . Ils exigent*'); the particular past-present construction adopted is functional to support the argument of a longstanding process of corruption of 'our' society and to suggest the idea of the progressive and supposed inevitable Islamification of France as a consequence of immigration.

As mentioned above, on the second page a box is displayed on the left. In the first leaflet, the picture shows a group of (Muslim) people kneeling down in a very long – apparently endless – line while they are praying in the street. It is noteworthy that they are wide-shot from behind and from above so that it is not possible to see where the line ends. The headline reads 'Le scandale de la rue Myrha' and the term 'scandale' clearly implies the idea of something which is unacceptable and/or immoral. The subtitle adds further information to locate the event (18th arrondissement in Paris). The practice of praying in the street (thus illegally invading the public space), is described as an habitual one ('*tous les vendredis*').

The use of the term 'islamiste' is noteworthy. It appeared in France at the end of the 1970s and in public discourse has become specifically associated with political groups advocating Islamic fundamentalism and attempting to implement Islamic values in all spheres of life. The use of this term allows for a very negative presentation of the out-group. The overall argumentative strategy is to give support to the idea of an 'invasion' of public space, implicating that this invasion is illegal, explicitly stating that this invasion is legitimated by those who impose it in a way that disregards the rights of residents, implicitly assuming that these residents are French citizens.

The second leaflet offers many examples illustrating the racialization of the social space: the association between immigration and insecurity is realized by the Front National through the reference to the people living in the *banlieues* who are assumed to be unassimilated and inassimilable (Hailon, 2010). In the leaflet, social actors are referred to with negative terms as *voyous, eméutiers, delinquants étrangers, bandes ethniques, casseurs* (thugs, rioters, foreign delinquents, ethnic gangs, busters) and so are the places where they live: *zones de non-droit, quartiers sensibles* (no-rights zones, sensitive neighbourhoods). Here, 'bandes ethniques' implicitly refers both to black and Arab young people.

The continuity between discourses on national identity and insecurity emerges here, for instance in the use of the term 'tribalisé' (tribalized): behaviours and acts which could be embraced in the sphere of criminality and deviance (such as 'aggréssions') are connected to the opposition between Us (civilized, evolved) and Them (uncivilized, barbarian, primitive). The opposition is enforced by the explicit reference to 'anti-French and anti-white racism' ('racisme anti-français et anti-blanc') which allows the Front National to present itself as free of prejudice and to include all the French people in an indifferentiated 'we-group' which, as a whole, can be victim of so-called 'reverse' prejudice. It is noteworthy, that in referring to the alleged racist attitudes of the out-group members, an explicit reference to skin colour is made: social conflict is not only reduced to ethnic conflict (as in the box on the left, where the out-group are referred to as 'les barbares'), it is explicitly racialized.

# 6 Conclusion

Discourse on national identity and insecurity jointly contributes to the justification and continuation of a variety of prejudicial positions vis-à-vis migrants and minority communities – rejection, avoidance, discrimination and expulsion. Such hateful discourses are increasingly driven by the agendas of far-right political parties, who utilize a variety of media, genres and strategies to bolster populist support.[6] The political leaflets examined at the start of the chapter associate Islam and social/cultural threat, invoking an imperialist discourse of conquest and reconquest; the second grouping associates (ethnic and racial) difference with insecurity and criminality, and proposes an ethnic cleansing of the national space to rectify this predicament. The semantic macro-structure of the Front National's anti-immigrant discourse incorporates elements of difference, deviance and perceived threat. All these leaflets, and their arguments, assume, 'first, an image of a national space; secondly, an image of the nationalist himself or herself as master of this national space and, thirdly, an image of the 'ethnic/racial other' as a mere object within this space' (Hage, 1998: 28). They are based on a 'white fantasy' regarding the rights and abilities of right-wing extremists to regulate the ethnic and racial parameters of society, to tolerate or proscribe, to include or exclude, both physically and verbally.

However, it is the manner in which such racist arguments are advanced which interested us. As controls on the free expression of racist speech become tighter – through both legal proscription and wide acceptance of social taboos against expression of racism – such parties invent and adopt increasingly creative ways to communicate their racist political programmes. As Orwell (2004 [1946]: 114) pointed out many years ago, such inherently violent political ideologies *can* be advanced and supported in discourse, but 'only by arguments which are too brutal for most people to face, and which do not square with the professed [democratic] aims of the political parties. Thus political language has to consist largely of euphemism, question-begging and sheer cloudy vagueness'. To these rhetorical strategies we also add: coded language, wherein the ostensible semantic content of linguistic terms doesn't square with their actual meaning (and decoding requires contextual understandings of their diachronic use); allusionism and insinuation, wherein two concepts or categories are connotatively tied together through reiteration and historic ties, and so through invoking one (immigration) the speaker can insinuate others (race; crime; insecurity); and the visual enthymeme – a truncated syllogism in which one or more argumentative premise is unstated in the linguistic portion of a text, but instead depicted visually. Elsewhere, we have examined the ways that political parties have advanced visual enthymemes through the use of photographs (Richardson and Colombo, 2013; Richardson and Wodak, 2009). The cartoons used in the leaflets analysed in this chapter represent a further rhetorical development. Their low modality removes aspects of naturalistic reality, material consequence and ethical responsibility which, in so doing, allows these political parties to support policies that would be too brutal (and, arguably, illegal) to vocalize, or even represent with photographs. The success of these leaflets – indicated by their imitation and reproduction across the EU – suggests that such cartoon racism will be a feature of extremist discourse for the foreseeable future.

# Notes

1  Demos are in the process of completing a series of country-specific reports on the growth of the extreme-right and nationalist populism in Europe. For details, and publications, see http://www.demos.co.uk/projects/populismineurope (accessed 24 June 2013).

2  To take only one example: in May 2013 Tamas Gaudi-Nagy, an MP for Jobbik, argued in a Parliamentary debate that Hungarian teenagers should not be 'forced' to visit the Auschwitz concentration camp museum since it 'may not reflect real facts' about the Holocaust. Jobbik is Hungary's third largest party and won 17 per cent of the vote in the 2010 elections. See http://www.ibtimes.co.uk/articles/471826/20130528/hungary-s-far-right-jobbik-mp-auschwitz.htm, accessed 24 June 2013.

3  The work of Rubinelli (2009: 23) demonstrates that, in classic argumentation scholarship, 'the value of a topos rest[ed] on its having two functions, namely a selective function (a topos is a device to find arguments) and a guarantee function (a topos is a kind of inference link that grants the plausibility of the step from certain premises to controversial claims)'.

4  Typically, in prejudicial or discriminatory discourse, topoi of burdens, costs and irreconcilable differences are employed in quasi-rational arguments to justify the exclusion of migrants (see Krzyżanowski and Wodak, 2009; Reisigl and Wodak, 2001; Wodak and Van Dijk, 2000).

5  As Van der Valk (2003) remarks, the French naturalization system since the Revolution is predominantly based on *ius soli* although, as Achard has pointed out, the distinctions of *ius soli* and *ius sanguinis* are neither exclusive nor really opposed but analytical, and each system represents a specific mixture (see also De Cillia et al., 1999). The composition of

this mixture is an important dimension of debates on nationality in European countries. In November 1997 changes in the nationality laws were discussed in the French parliament. More particularly there was a discussion about whether children born to migrant parents would automatically obtain French nationality or whether they would obtain it after a voluntary declaration of intent at the age of 16 or 18.

**6** See http://searchlightmagazine.com/news/international-news/political-parties-drive-hate-in-eu,-commission-says (accessed 31 January 2013).

# References

Achard, P. (1998), 'Nations, nationalismes: l'approche discursive'. *Langage et Societé*, 86, 9–63.

Atkin, A. and Richardson, J. E. (2005), 'Constructing the (imagined) antagonist in advertising argumentation', in F. H. van Eemeren and P. Houtlosser (eds.), *The Practice of Argumentation*. Amsterdam: John Benjamins, pp. 163–80.

Bartlett, J., Birdwell, J., Krekó, P., Benfield J. and Gyori, G. (2012), *Populism in Europe: Hungary*. Available for free download: http://www.demos.co.uk/files/Demos_Hungary_Book_web-1.pdf?1327923915 (accessed 24 June 2013).

Betz, H.-G. (2013), 'Mosques, minarets, burqas and other essential threats: the populist right's campaign against Islam in Western Europe', in Wodak, Mral and KhosraviNik (eds), *Right Wing Populism in Europe: Politics and Discourse*. London: Bloomsbury Academic, pp. 71–87.

Billig, M. (1991), *Ideology and Opinions: Studies in Rhetorical Psychology*. London: Sage.
—— (1995), *Banal Nationalism*. London: Sage.

Birdwell, J., Bartlett, J. and Littler, M. (2011), *The New Face of Digital Populism*. Available for free download: http://www.demos.co.uk/files/Demos_OSIPOP_Book-web_03.pdf?1320601634 (accessed 24 June 2013).

Birdwell, J., Bartlett, J. and McDonnell, D. (2012), *Populism in Europe: Lega Nord*. Available for free download: http://www.demos.co.uk/files/Lega_Nord_-_web.pdf?1349354875 (accessed 24 June 2013).

Blackledge, A. (2006), 'The racialization of language in British political discourse'. *Critical Discourse Studies*, 3, 61–79.

Blair, J. A. (2004), 'The rhetoric of visual arguments', in C. A. Hill and M. Helmers (eds), *Defining Visual Rhetorics*. Mahwah, NJ: Lawrence Erlbaum Publishers, pp. 41–62.

Brubaker, R. (1992), *Citizenship and Nationhood in France and Germany*. Cambridge, MA: Harvard University Press.

Burridge, J. (2008), 'The dilemma of frugality and consumption in British women's magazines 1940–1955'. *Social Semiotics*, 18(3), 389–401.

Çagatay Tekin, B. (2008), 'The construction of Turkey's possible EU membership in French political discourse'. *Discourse Society*, 19, 727–63.

Cairns, J. (2009), 'Politics? Fear not! The rise of The Average Superhero in the visual rhetoric of Bill Davis' 1971 election pamphlet', in G. Allen and D. J. Robinson (eds), *Communicating Canada's Past: Approaches to the History of Print and Broadcast Media*. Toronto: University of Toronto Press, pp. 80–98.

Charlot, M. (1986), 'L'émergence du Front national'. *Revue française de science politique*, 36(1), 30–45.

Cheles, L. (2010), 'Back to the future. The visual propaganda of Alleanza Nazionale (1994–2009)'. *Journal of Modern Italian Studies*, 15(2), 232–311.

Chilton, P. and Schäffner, C. (eds) (2002), *Politics as Text and Talk: Analytic Approaches to Political Discourse.* Philadelphia: John Benjamins.

De Cillia, R., Reisigl, M. and Wodak, R. (1999), 'The discursive construction of national identities'. Discourse & Society, 10, 149–73.

Engel, J. and Wodak, R. (2013), '"Calculated ambivalence" and Holocaust denial in Austria', in R. Wodak and J. E. Richardson (eds) (2013), *Analysing Fascist Discourse: European Fascism in Talk and Text* London: Routledge, pp.73–96.

Essed, P. (1991), *Understanding Everyday Racism: An Interdisciplinary Theory.* London: Sage.

Fortier, A.-M. (2008), *Multicultural Horizons: Diversity and the Limits of the Civil Nation.* London: Routledge.

Geisser, V. (2003), *La Nouvelle Islamophobie.* Paris: La Découverte.

Goffman, E. (1974), *Frame Analysis: An Essay on the Organization of Experience.* New York, NY: Harper and Row.

Groarke, L. (2002), 'Towards a pragma-dialectics of visual argument', in F. H. van Eemeren (ed.), *Advances in Pragma-Dialectics.* Amsterdam: Sic Sat, pp. 137–52.

—— (2007), 'Four theses on Toulmin and visual argument', in F. H. van Eemeren, J. A. Blair, C. A. Willard and B. Garssen (eds), *Proceedings of the Sixth Conference of ISSA.* Amsterdam: Sic Sat, pp. 535–40.

Hage, G. (1998), *White Nation: Fantasies of White Supremacy in a Multicultural Society.* Annandale, NSW: Pluto Press.

Hailon, F. (2010), 'Resémantisation de faits d'altérité des corpus de presse français', in M. Abecassis (ed.), *Les voix du français: usages et représentations.* Oxford: Peter Lang, pp. 319–30.

Hart, C. (2010), *Critical Discourse Analysis and Cognitive Science: New Perspectives on Immigration Discourse.* Basingstoke: Palgrave.

Hodge, R. and Kress, G. (1988), *Social Semiotics.* Cambridge: Polity.

Jiwani, Y. and Richardson, J. E. (2011), 'Discourse, ethnicity and racism', in T. A. Van Dijk (ed.), *Discourse Studies: A Multidisciplinary Introduction.* London: sage, pp. 241–62.

Jugé, T. S. and Perez, M. P. (2006), 'The modern colonial politics of citizenship and whiteness in France'. *Social Identities*, 12(2), 187–212.

Krzyżanowski, M. and Wodak, R. (2008), *The Politics of Exclusion. Debating Migration in Austria.* New Brunswick, NJ: Transaction.

Machin, D. (2007), *Introduction to Multimodal Analysis.* London: Arnold.

Malik, K. (1996), *The Meaning of Race: Race, History and Culture in Western Society.* New York: Palgrave.

McGlashan, M. (2013), 'The branding of European nationalism: perpetuation and novelty in racist symbolism', in R. Wodak and J.E. Richardson (eds), *Analysing Fascist Discourse: European Fascism in Talk and Text.* London: Routledge, pp. 297–314.

Orwell, G. (2004 [1946]), 'Politics and the English language', in Orwell, *Why I Write.* London: Penguin Books, pp. 102–20.

Quasthoff, U. (1987), 'Linguistic prejudice/stereotypes', in U. Ammon, N. Dittmar, K. J. Mattheier (eds), *Sociolinguistics. An International Handbook of the Science of Language and Society.* Berlin: de Gruyter, pp. 785–99.

Reisigl, M. and Wodak, R. (2001), *Discourse and Discrimination. Rhetorics of Racism and Antisemitism.* London: Routledge.

—— (2009), 'The discourse-historical approach', in R. Wodak and M. Meyer (eds), *Methods of Critical Discourse Analysis.* London: Sage, pp. 87–121.

Richardson, J. E. (2004), *(Mis)Representing Islam: The Racism and Rhetoric of British Broadsheet Newspapers.* Amsterdam: John Benjamins.

—— (2011), 'Race and racial difference: the surface and depth of BNP ideology', in Copsey, N. and Macklin, G. (eds), *British National Party: Contemporary Perspectives*. London: Routledge, pp. 38–61.

—— (2013), 'Racial populism in British Fascist discourse: the case of COMBAT and the British National Party (1960–1967)', in R. Wodak and J. E. Richardson (eds), *Analysing Fascist Discourse: European Fascism in Talk and Text*. London: Routledge, pp. 181–202.

Richardson, J. E. and Colombo, M. (2013), 'Continuity and change in populist anti-immigrant discourse in Italy: an analysis of Lega leaflets, Special Issue: "Discourse and politics about migration in Italy"'. *Journal of Language and Politics*, 12(2), 180–202.

Richardson, J. E. and Wodak, R. (2009), 'The impact of visual racism: visual arguments in political leaflets of Austrian and British far-right parties'. *Controversia: An International Journal of Debate and Democratic Renewal*, 6(2), 45–77.

Rubinelli, S. (2009), Ars Topica. *The Classical Technique of Constructing Arguments from Aristotle to Cicero*. Dordrecht: Springer.

Rydgren, J. (2003), 'Meso-level reasons for facism and xenophobia: some converging and diverging effects of radical right populism in France and Sweden'. *European Journal of Social Theory*, 6(1), 45–68.

—— (2007), 'The sociology of the radical right'. *Annual Review of Sociology*, 33, 241–62.

Schmidt, R. (2002), 'Racialization and language policy: the case of the U.S.A.' *Multilingua*, 21, 141–61

Silverman, M. (1999), *Facing Postmodernity: Contemporary French Thought on Culture and Society*. London: Routledge.

Silverstein, P. A. (2008), 'The context of antisemitism and Islamophobia in France'. *Patterns of Prejudice*, 42(1), 1–26.

Spektorowski, A. (2003), 'Ethnoregionalism: the intellectual new right and the Lega Nord'. *Ethnopolitics*, 2(3), 55–70.

Taguieff, P.-A. (1988), *La Force du Préjugé. Essai sur le Racisme et ses Doubles*. Paris, France: La Découverte.

—— (2005), *La République Enlisée*. Paris: Éditions des Syrtes.

Van der Valk, I. (2003), 'Right-wing parliamentary discourse on immigration in France'. *Discourse & Society*, 14, 309–48.

Van Dijk, T. A. (1984), *Prejudice in Discourse. An Analysis of Ethnic Prejudice in Cognition and Conversation*. Amsterdam: Benjamins.

—— (1991), *Racism and the Press*. London: Routledge.

—— (1993), *Elite Discourse and Racism*. London: Sage.

—— (1997), 'Political discourse and racism', in S. Riggins (ed.), *The Language and Politics of Exclusion: Others in Discourse*. Thousand Oaks, CA: Sage, pp. 31–64.

—— (2008), *Discourse and Context. A Sociocognitive Approach*. Cambridge: Cambridge University Press.

Van Leeuwen, T. (1995), 'Representing social action'. *Discourse & Society*, 6(1), 81–107.

Wetherell, M. and Potter, J. (1992), *Mapping the Language of Racism*. New York: Columbia University Press.

Wieviorka, M. (1998), *Le Racisme: Une Introduction*. Paris: La Découverte/Poche.

Wodak R. (2003), 'Populist discourses: the rhetoric of exclusion in written genres'. *Document Design*, 4(2), 132–48.

—— (2008), 'The contribution of critical linguistics to the analysis of discriminatory prejudices and stereotypes in the language of politics', in R. Wodak and V. Koller (eds), *Handbook of Applied Linguistics. 'The Public Sphere'* (Volume IV). Berlin: de Gruyter, pp. 291–316.

Wodak, R. and Matouschek, B. (1993), '"We are dealing with people whose origins one can clearly tell just by looking": critical discourse analysis and the study of neo-racism in contemporary Austria. *Discourse & Society*, 4(2), 225–48.

Wodak, R. and Van Dijk, T. (eds) (2000), *Racism at the Top: Parliamentary Discourses on Ethnic Issues in Six European States*. Klagenfurt: Drava.

# HEALTH

# 23

# Critical Studies of Health and Illness Discourses

*Nelya Koteyko*

Queen Mary University of London

## 1 Introduction

This chapter examines the role and function of language in representing and making sense of health and illness by drawing on insights from Critical Discourse Studies that interrogate language use in order to understand its social and political import. Adopting a standpoint that health and illness are given meaning through text and are inextricably linked to the cultural and social context, it calls for greater attention to language use, and metaphors in particular, in the analyses of representations circulating in modern Westernized societies. The approach recognizes that the ways scientific and medical 'truths' are reformulated and recontextualized in the media, policy documents, and promotional materials can have consequences for how we as individuals understand ourselves and the world around us.

Following the 'linguistic turn' in humanities and social sciences (Silverman, 1987), anthropologists and medical sociologists have demonstrated the paramount role of language in the delivery of healthcare, clinical encounters, and people's experiences of health and illness (Mishler, 1984; Frank, 1995; Sarangi, 2004). Studies examining socio-cultural meanings of illness draw attention to the fact that the different ways in which we define and categorize disease, the causes of ill health, and ways of treatment can influence societal responses to health risks (Briggs and Nichter, 2009; Brown et al., 2009). This view of health risk as an inherently social and discursive phenomenon has exposed the ways illnesses can get negative meaning stemming from particular cultural contexts, and the implications such stigmatizing or contested conditions can have for afflicted individuals (Conrad and Barker, 2010). In parallel, a growing body of interdisciplinary health promotion studies has demonstrated that communication about health and illness is far more than a one-way dissemination of information, highlighting the social dynamics involved in defining, negotiating and understanding the causes and solutions to ill health. In this context, the crucial role of language in public health discourse is stressed by Turner (1995), who points out that 'We can no longer regard diseases as natural events in the world which occur outside the language in which they are described' (11). In a similar vein, earlier studies of AIDS have shown how communication about control or prevention of disease can be shaped by written and visual narratives (Harvey and Koteyko, 2012).

However, while acknowledging the importance of language, studies looking at print media and Internet-based representations of health and illness still pay limited attention to the structures of text and talk, and the specific ends to which they are deployed. In particular, research on risk reporting that examines how the complexity of the media environment and the relationship between the journalists and news sources may impact the framing of risk (Cottle, 1998; Kitzinger et al., 2003) would benefit from a systematic study of the types of rhetorical strategies used by claims makers within news media (Anderson, 2006). Here I therefore want to discuss the advantages of using linguistic and discourse analytical tools and categories to examine representations in different media. Further demonstrating that it matters how we talk and write about health and disease, the analyses presented below draw attention to pragmatic functions of language, as well as the cultural, cognitive and political context in which statements about health risks and, conversely, promissory statements about health benefits are made. I will first introduce language-focused studies examining the UK print media coverage of infectious diseases, and then proceed to discuss discursive structures employed in the online advertising of functional foods.

In theoretical and methodological terms, the studies discussed below are situated at the intersection of two domains. The first is concerned with discourse understood as social practice (Fairclough, 2003; Bhatia, 2002). Grounded in linguistics (Fowler et al., 1979), discourse studies in this tradition are concerned with the rhetorical organization of texts and examine how specific discourse structures are deployed in the constitution of particular ways of knowing (Wodak et al., 1999). This concept of discourse is linked to the broader constructivist view of social reality postulating that social texts do not merely reflect phenomena and processes pre-existing in the social and natural world, such as health risks and health benefits; rather, they actively construct them (Lupton, 1998). The social constructionist strand in medical sociology emphasizes 'how the meaning and experience of illness is shaped by cultural and social systems' (Conrad and Barker, 2010: 67). Critical studies in this tradition therefore explore different ways in which discourses around disease can promote particular ideologies and help maintain identities of public health institutions (Jones, 2012; Harvey and Koteyko, 2012).

The second is that of cognitive linguistics studies, where the Lakoffian theory of conceptual metaphor (Lakoff and Johnson, 1980) and more recent CDA approaches to metaphor can be situated (Charteris-Black, 2006; Hart, 2008; see also contributions in this volume). Proponents of the discourse-based approach to metaphor emphasize that 'participants of discourses on topics of social life tend to incorporate new events by interpreting them metaphorically as some culturally salient phenomenon, and not via projection of knowledge schemata abstracted from universal aspects of body experience' (Zinken, 2003: 508). Consequently, this strand of work investigates metaphors both as cognitive and social devices embedded in shared cultural, political and discursive formations (Nerlich et al., 2002; Zinken et al., 2008). It recognizes that metaphors can 'contribute to a situation where they privilege one understanding of reality over others' (Chilton, 1996: 74) as in Schön and Rein's (1994) classical example from the social policy context where politicians from opposing camps referred to the state of older project housing as either 'urban blight' or 'natural community'. Examples of studies in this tradition include the seminal work of Sontag (1979) on 'master illness' metaphors, such as those concerned with cancer or tuberculosis, as well as more recent work of Segal (2005) on the role of metaphors in biomedical discourses and the impact such use bears for practices of diagnosis and treatment.

## 2  Print media representations of infectious disease outbreaks

One of the central objectives underlying critical analyses of language use is to reveal how institutions produce and reproduce implicit and explicit social norms. Here the media's role as an arena where various definitions and redefinitions of public issues take place, and where members of society encounter and share metaphor and other cognitive structures, is paramount (Harvey and Koteyko, 2012). Media representations of health and illness are *recontextualizations* of specialized knowledge (Calsamiglia and Van Dijk, 2004), and in order to study how such knowledge is recreated in a different communicative situation, we need to pay attention to the detailed structures of text and talk. A number of studies have already explored the ways in which journalists can position their texts in order to conceptualize the possibility of certain health risks, such as, for example, a construction of a link between MMR vaccines, inflammatory bowel disorder, and autism (Rundblad et al., 2006). Wallis and Nerlich (2005) examined the framing of severe acute respiratory syndrome (SARS) as a 'killer', whereas studies done on discourses around foot and mouth disease (Nerlich et al, 2002), avian flu (Nerlich and Halliday, 2007), and MRSA infection (Koteyko et al., 2008a) have demonstrated further that different language choices can have important implications for the control of infectious diseases. As the recent swine flu outbreak has shown once again, crisis communication is far from a straightforward act of raising public awareness and transmitting information. Rather, it is an inherently political and discursive process based on a complex negotiation, where certain actions and groups of people can get priority over others (Larson et al., 2005).

Koteyko et al. (2008b) built on this work to examine the uses of metaphors in discourses around avian influenza. The authors focus on two events in the story of a predicted UK avian flu epidemic – 'the dead parrot' in October 2005 and 'the dying swan' in April 2006. Avian flu, especially the highly pathogenic H5N1 strain, is an emergent disease or zoonotic that can be passed from animals, whether wild birds or domesticated (poultry), to humans. In August 2005, after bird flu had appeared in Siberia and Kazakhstan, many newspapers speculated about the possibility that migratory birds could bring bird flu to Britain in the winter. What had, until then, been a far-flung illness (Joffe and Haarhoff, 2002) became a more national and individual concern. The UK government published a full version of its pandemic preparedness plan on 19 October 2005, occasioning a good deal of press coverage. By coincidence, this was the month when a parrot in a UK quarantine centre died of H5N1. On 1 November 2005 President Bush outlined Pandemic Influenza Preparations and Response plans. This again increased media attention dramatically. The beginning of 2006 was marked by outbreaks of H5N1 in wild and domestic birds elsewhere in Europe. In April 2006 a dead swan found in Scotland was diagnosed with the virus. However, there were no outbreaks of H5N1 in British poultry until spring 2007.

The authors examined the role and use of three interconnected metaphor scenarios related to the notions of *journey, war* and *house* in the UK press coverage of these events. Musolff (2006) defines a metaphor scenario as 'a set of assumptions made by competent members of a discourse community about "typical" aspects of a source-situation' (28). Such narrative-based 'scenarios' correspond to clusters of individual terms or concepts in the texts (Musolff, 2004: 18) and allow the speakers 'to not only apply source to target concepts but to draw on them to build narrative frames for the conceptualisation and assessment of socio-political issues and to "spin out" these narratives into emergent discourse traditions that are characteristic of their respective community' (2006: 36). In the context of disease, the war or battle scenario is well-entrenched (Sontag, 1979; Gwyn, 2002) and can be superimposed onto the fight that a nation or farm fights against a virus. The war scenario is an overarching scenario which subsumes other scenarios or mini-narratives and incorporates concepts of *battle, fight, attack, defence, killer, enemy, frontline* and *fortress* (Koller, 2003). Each of the sub-scenarios involved can inform metaphors that exploit aspects of the situation. Both the house scenario and the journey scenario are based on more basic conceptual metaphors or image schemata: the container metaphor (Chilton, 1996, 2004; Charteris-Black, 2006) and the SOURCE-PATH-GOAL schema respectively (Lakoff and Johnson, 1980).

In examining the activation of these parts of the metaphor field in the UK media discourse through a quantitative analysis of metaphor tokens and a qualitative study of how they cluster into scenarios, Koteyko et al. (2008a) found that the journey scenario dominated the coverage, as the virus was regularly depicted as being on its way to the UK, and for the most part was not depicted as being endemic in the poultry or human populations. The metaphor scenario evoked by a virus on a journey is linked to the image schema designated as SOURCE-PATH-GOAL, in which the personification of the virus as a moving agent is superimposed. The source in this instance is the Far East where the virus, H5N1, originates. The path is the spread of the virus from East to West, carried by real agents, such as people trading or moving animals or migratory birds. This path leads the virus ever closer to the goal that is the UK:

Virus reached the edge of Europe

(*Daily Mail*, 17 October 2005)

The Minister's stark warning [Sir Liam Donaldson saying that at least 50,000 people will die] came as scientists revealed the disease continued its march across the globe.

(*Daily Mail*, 18 October 2005)

As the UK as a nation is conceptualized as a house, the virus is seen as approaching the house and knocking on the door or as approaching the gate ('Bird flu's deadly knock is at our very door', *Daily Mail*, 17 October 2005). Defence against the virus is conceptualized as stopping it from travelling, i.e. escaping from the source (containment) or, once it has started to travel, stopping it from coming through the door or gate, that is preventing it from reaching its goal. This type of defence against a virus can then be couched in terms of war, fight or battle, in which case the house becomes a fortress. For example, the death of a parrot from the H5N1 virus triggered numerous announcements in both tabloids and broadsheets on 22 and 23 of October 2005 that the virus 'has arrived', 'has reached the shores', 'has reached the country', that is according to the SOURCE-PATH-GOAL schema the trajector had reached its final destination. The image of the UK not just as a house but a fortress to be defended against foreign invaders, which had been also exploited during the FMD epidemic (Nerlich et al., 2002), came to the fore. The following quote from an interview with a consultant in public health combines the house and the war scenarios: 'Importing exotic animals as pets offers a Trojan horse of infection for recipient nations' (*The Telegraph*, 23 Oct 2005).

The analysis by Koteyko et al. (2008b) suggests that the further along the path a virus travels and the closer it gets to its goal, the more war metaphors one might find in the media coverage. Examples cited by the authors include the *Express* headline on 22 October: BIRD FLU: IT IS IN BRITAIN; TWO MILLION UNDER THREAT AS THE KILLER VIRUS ARRIVES . . . The article described Tamiflu as the weapon of choice 'to combat bird flu' and then quoted microbiologist Professor Hugh Pennington warning that bird flu is 'very good at killing'. When a dead swan was found on a beach in Fife, Scotland in April 2006, the headlines used the journey and house scenarios, and as during FMD outbreaks, various imaginary doors were 'locked'. The *Daily Mail*, for example, described police roadblocks as follows: 'Their mission was to "lock down" the alert zone to prevent any movement of birdlife, forming a cordon 1.8 miles from the harbour where the H5N1 dead swan was found' (7 April). As in the coverage of the parrot incident, quotes from scientific experts in the *Daily Mail*, *The Guardian* and the

*Sun* contained journey and war scenarios where Tamiflu was evoked again as a frontline defence.

Overall, the authors found differences in the framing of disease management options depending on whether the crisis was seen as a national or global event. Once the virus has reached its goal, the nationalistic invasion scenario appeared to be triggered and war metaphors became a seemingly natural way of talking about disease management. Following Lakoff's (2004) suggestions, the framing of political issues and the kinds of metaphors they deploy give us apparently reasonable and natural courses of action. This was reflected in the media coverage of bird flu-related events in the UK in 2005 and 2006 which appear to have activated a reassuringly familiar range of discourses and associated precautions. Thus, amid warnings that the parrot represented a kind of Trojan horse, the practices of locking down, sealing off, closing, disinfecting and so on were reported. The precautions were made immediately intelligible as threats literally 'at the door', whereas the work undertaken by the police or government officials became a natural 'front line' response – despite the fact that none of these practices could affect wild bird movements. Based on culturally or phenomenologically salient objects or experiences, the metaphor scenarios used in the coverage allow reducing the complexity of the threat posed by a disease and engaging in infection control and risk management strategies that appear to make intuitive sense to journalists, experts and arguably the public.

This study brings attention to the political and social significance of metaphors and equips us with a better understanding of how these essential communicative devices can lead to particular ways of thinking and acting in relation to health and illness. Metaphor scenarios provide important discursive material for journalists but also, as we have seen, for scientists and policy makers to conceptualize health risks, attract attention, and structure their stories. In this way, the study also highlights the important role of sources in the processes underlying the framing of health risks. Whereas the journalists are often accused of irrationality and sensationalist coverage in relation to matters of risk, the priorities that guide different stakeholders in debates about health risks tend to be less under scrutiny. Yet, sources, and their relations with journalists, have a significant impact on the definition and framing of risks and their coverage over time therefore have to be given equal attention in the analyses of media content (Hughes et al, 2008; Anderson, 2006).

## 3 Promissory rhetoric on the Internet

In addition to studying conceptualizations of health risks, recent sociological work on the medicalization of everyday life pays attention to discourses around various enhancements, such as sexual performance drugs (Conrad, 2007) and wakefulness drugs (Williams, 2005; Coveney et al., 2009). The research lens has therefore expanded beyond the clinical setting to biotechnology and the consumer industry (Dumit, 2012), and promissory statements became a popular topic in the social study of biomedicine (Waldby, 2002; Rose, 2007). At the beginning of the 1990s, as the issues of diet and health were becoming increasingly interlinked, a new product became widely associated with hopes and promises rather than fears and risks: probiotics. Probiotics are live micro-organisms generally known as 'good bacteria' and have an uncertain status between food and drugs and between 'natural' and 'engineered' foods. Despite the fact that their benefits for healthy people are highly uncertain (Walker and Buckley, 2006), probiotic drinks have become one of the most successful products in the category of functional foods as corporations were capitalizing on the symbolic value of health 'to accumulate finance capital' (Dixon and Banwell, 2004: 126). Below I provide an overview of a study that uses the framework of discourse analysis to examine just how these values were being built into the functional food products on company websites, and explore how such advertising discourse functions within a wider context of the cultural politics of health and illness (Koteyko, 2009).

To analyse the content of promissory statements, four websites of probiotics producers (Yakult, Danone Activia, Actimel and Müller) listed as market leaders (Sloan, 2004) were selected, focusing on 36 webpages in total. Drawing on Wodak and Reisigl's framework (2001), the analysis centred on referential strategies (what terms or concepts are being used when introducing or referring to probiotics?) and predication, or evaluative attributions of negative and positive traits (what traits, characteristics and features are attributed to probiotics?). In this study I also adopted the methods of critical genre analysis (Bhatia, 2002; Fairclough, 2003) to reveal the textualization processes of the Internet advertising genre and relate them to the broader context of discursive and social practices. According to Bhatia (2002: 7), genre analysis aims to understand the realities of the world of texts rather than seeing them as a fixed entity with established boundaries – an approach that is particularly apposite for the study of malleable and fragmented Internet-based discourses.

Using Bhatia's framework, I assigned the following structural description of the websites in terms of rhetorical moves used to achieve their communicative purposes:

1   establishing credentials (menu section: 'Company profile' or 'Company history' or 'About Us' or 'Company');

2   introducing the product: information about the brands (menu section: 'What is Actimel?'/'About Activia'/'Product'/subsection 'What?'/'Products'); specification of the product characteristics, including demonstrations with images and trailers ('How it works?', 'What are probiotic bacteria?'); indicating value of the product ('Product'/subsection 'Why?', 'What's the evidence?', 'Why Activia'), drawing on scientific reports;

3   offering health information, advice, and entertainment ('Advice and tips', 'Healthy Living', 'Health', 'Staying Healthy');

**4**    establishing the relationship between the company and consumer (sections: 'Further Contact', 'More Information', 'Share your experience', 'Receive some news').

At the time of analysis,[1] the first section introduced the companies to potential visitors of the websites and was therefore dominated by the presentational aspect of the website design (Fleming, 1998) that conveys how the companies want to be perceived by the public. Here the style of informational writing followed the expository text structure typical of company brochures, where facts, events or concepts are given in order of occurrence. In this section the producers of probiotics stressed their long history, and normally there was a 'grandfather' figure – a figure of trust and wisdom – who pioneered production of dairy products with probiotics. In particular, the Müller website said the company dated back to 1896 'when yoghurt-loving Ludwig Müller first established his little Bavarian village dairy', projecting an image of a pastoral or rural idyll, whereas Yakult stressed the scientific credentials by referring to research by the microbiologist Dr Shirota back in 1930.

The next section contained product descriptions and sample print and media adverts, combining informational and entertainment website designs in order to introduce the brands in the most favourable light. In particular, Yakult and Actimel websites gave priority to the eclectic, experience-oriented design as they provided numerous games for children and interactive tests for adults. The switch to the entertainment design also entails register consequences: the style is informal and conversational, and form of address is direct and straightforward as evident from ellipses on the Yakult website ('The ingredients? Only what needs to be in. Enough bacteria to keep your belly happy. Enough taste . . . to taste'), short and punchy 'personal stories' on the Müller website. These typical advertising devices, aimed at establishing proximity with the audience (Goddard, 1998; Fairclough, 2003), also included the wide use of second person pronouns on all the websites. Two naming strategies can be observed from the introduction of the brands: creating names by using existing words (including proper names, compounds, foreign words) such as Müller Vitality, or inventing new words with recognizable links to existing words such as Danone Actimel and Activia (active, activity); and coinage of pseudo-scientific names such as Bifidus Essensis (essence) and Bifidus ActiRegularis (regulate). Here name creators attempt to combine originality with multiple cultural references, in this way associating probiotics with values of good health, the well-known paths to which include exercise and nutrition. These links between health, happiness, 'élan vital' or vital force and probiotics are further strengthened through lexical choices in slogans (the alliterative expression 'lick the lid of life!'), personal stories (purportedly 'shared' by an elderly lady: 'I am a very lucky, happy lady – and I am full of Vitality!') and images of smiling individuals.

Having indicated the needs of potential consumers in general terms in the introductory section, the next strategic move is to point to the value of the product in terms of these perceived needs by detailing the product's characteristics as well as by bringing in the evidence for their 'effectiveness'. Here the use of predication served to emphasize the 'uniqueness' of particular probiotic strains to claim the exclusiveness of their potential health benefits. Different strains were said to be 'uniquely designed' to offer (the hope of) energy and vitality to different groups: students, the elderly or women (for example, strains in Actimel products appear to be particularly suitable for the elderly and children, Danone Activia seems to work best at alleviating bloating in women, etc.). The emphasis on 'long tradition' and 'naturalness' is also brought into the picture in order to counterbalance the 'engineered' side of probiotic yoghurts – for example, the Activia brand is introduced as a 'natural way of regulating the digestive system' and Actimel emphasizes 'your body's natural defences'. As a result, probiotics seem to offer consumers an opportunity to shape their immune system in a 'natural way' just as it has become common to shape one's body through diet and exercise. The 'unique' probiotic products were also referred to as human 'helpers' in the modern struggle for health – in other words, the struggle either to prevent the loss of or to regain energy and vitality. Here the 'helping' role of 'good bacteria', as opposed to 'bad bacteria' that cause illness, comes to the fore, as probiotics are said to 'supplement', 'aid' or 'balance' digestion:

> Yakult is a probiotic. What is a probiotic? Good bacteria that supplement the natural bacteria in your gut.
> Staying as healthy as possible is important but you can also give your body a helping hand by drinking Actimel. It's a good way to help support your body's defences.

The use of the transitive verbs 'top up' (existing bacteria) and 'maximize' (one's own natural defences) augments the sense of individual agency and suggests that potential consumers are assumed to be already healthy and thus require advice on how to increase the effectiveness of their self-improvement behaviours (and this advice is readily provided further on the website). Finally, such sections as 'What is the evidence?' (Actimel) or 'Publications' (Yakult) were replete with references to microbiology articles and excerpts, making frequent use of terms such as 'research shows' and 'experts suggest', e.g. 'Stress – research shows this can upset your gut' (Danone Actimel). Appropriating the voice of science by using the factual language of the scientific reporting genre where numbers speak for themselves, the Activia website 'informed' the readers about the results of the 'Activia trial', in which '82 per cent of people with digestive discomfort said they felt better after eating Activia every day for 14 days'.

The analysis of lexico-grammatical choices and the generic structure of the websites in this study showed how the websites were corporately designed to persuade their visitors about the values of probiotics through 'informing' them about the company, 'educating' them about medical and 'scientific' properties of probiotic bacterial strains whilst also entertaining them along the way. The websites' focus on 'vitality' and 'responsibility' is indicative of the changing cultural politics of health noted in the research on other forms of media (Lupton, 1998) and leads to questions about social and cultural aspects of the discourses around functional food products.

Specifically, the linguistic structures in these online promotional texts reflect a conceptual shift undergone by the term 'immune system'. Conceptualizations of the immune system are based on different uses of the metaphor ILLNESS IS WARFARE discussed in a preceding section, which include various correspondences between infection and war, where our bodies are conceptualized as states that are at war or as a fortress (Martin, 1994). The body is therefore conceived as having borders or boundaries as well as an 'army' and/or a 'defence system'. During the mid-twentieth century, the boundary between environment and body was placed on the body's surface, e.g. 'germs' and 'chills' penetrated via unprotected body parts such as abrasions, wet hair and so on (Greenhalgh and Wessely, 2004). Later, the boundary became more internal as it was believed that the body may be weakened from within, for example, through viruses, stress or unhealthy diets (Wood, 2007). These more recent imaginaries draw on metaphors of flexibility and adaptability implicating the immune system in the neo-liberal regime of governance (Martin, 1994). The above analysis shows that the online advertising discourse, containing numerous claims that probiotic bacteria can help the consumers improve their health through 'strengthening' of the immune system and managing their 'vitality', typifies this increasingly naturalized ethics of self-care and self-improvement. By framing 'friendly bacteria' as a means of 'shaping' or 'balancing' one's immune system to achieve 'vitality' in the general struggle for health and wellbeing, the websites prioritize a political potential to mobilize the capacity of audiences to become responsible, pro-active and self-directed citizens (Rimke, 2000).

# 4  Conclusion: Critical linguistic analysis of health and illness discourses

This chapter has made the case for a language-based approach to the study of health and illness representations in the print media and on the Internet. While the crucial role of social and cultural context is now well recognized in the study of public health communication and its impact, it has been argued that such studies should put an equally strong emphasis on the empirical analysis of language choices shaping these discourses. Interrogating the persuasive effects of verbal and structural nuances in a text enhances our understanding of the ways health and illness discourses are formulated and reproduced in different media environments. From this perspective, research carried out by the author and colleagues, based on discourse and metaphor analysis, has shown how attention to discursive strategies used by different stakeholders to advocate risk management or self-care can help us examine political and ethical implications in public health communication that may not be directly apparent.

Unlike most sociological enquiries, analyses discussed above do not only focus on the emerging themes, but also examine the textual structures employed in the recontextualizations of medical and scientific knowledge. Thus, Koteyko et al. (2008b) demonstrate the value of understanding risks and the actions they prompt in the policy arena in terms of metaphor scenarios. Although similar metaphor scenarios may be used over time, the kinds of reporting they are associated with differ depending on the perceived proximity of the disease threat (Brown et al., 2009). Here the metaphors used by journalists and scientists do not only render medical knowledge intelligible to the public but also create a sense of urgency and drama. Adopting the same perspective, the study of metaphors and discursive strategies in Koteyko (2009) shows how promises surrounding the products with uncertain, future-oriented benefits are created on the companies' websites, and help construct new cultural logic around health, according to which good health and 'vitality' can be engineered, and ageing is 'fixable' if not preventable. Here attention to the lexico-grammatical choices further reveals the ways in which probiotics are promoted as a means of maintaining, enhancing and 'managing' one's physical health and 'vitality'.

By investigating how medical and scientific knowledge is linguistically defined by various claims-makers we can bring greater critical awareness to processes underlying public engagement with science and medicine. Communication during an infectious disease outbreak particularly stands to benefit from such scrutiny as political and ethical decisions regarding human travel restrictions, animal transportation, distribution of antivirals and immunization procedures can be critically examined within the framework of discourse analysis. As Powers and Xiao (2008) remind us with reference to the SARS outbreak, 'we communicate ourselves into a particular way of thinking and acting' and therefore need to study both the linguistic means and the broader political and social environment that shape such communication. As the above study of discourses on bird flu has shown, close attention to metaphors may help us shed light on policy responses; in this case by illuminating why policies that promote authoritarian and security-driven options make sense and seem a 'natural' way of addressing the political dilemmas we face (Lakoff, 2004).

Whereas traditional media sources such as newspapers, television and magazines have been well researched as outlets in which diverse statements and recommendations about health risks and benefits are made, the amount of discourse analytic work done on web-based sources has so far been relatively small (e.g. Charteris-Black et al., 2006; Richardson, 2005; Harvey, 2013). Although new types of media may reconfigure or diversify processes of communication and interpersonal interaction, they also become institutionalized, highlighting the fact that online communication remains politically and socially situated and motivated. Seale (2005), for example, found that cancer representations in popular websites are 'less fluid than is suggested by hyperbole about internet-facilitated democratisation of medical knowledge' (518). As online interfaces are increasingly implicated in the representation of biomedical advances, we need the tools of critical discourse analysis to examine the political and social uses of particular textual practices in the online environment. In this context, the above study of web-based rhetorical structures within the framework of critical genre analysis (Koteyko, 2009) demonstrates how applied linguistics can contribute to the field of 'critical Internet studies', answering Seale's (2005) call for research focused not only on production and reception in relation to health and illness, but also cultural representations.

Despite the emphasis on linguistic techniques, I hope it is by now apparent that critical linguistic study of health and illness representations does not mean a narrow focus on particular texts but takes into consideration the socio-cultural, political and historical contexts. Studies pursuing such enquiry therefore incorporate techniques and methods from different schools of linguistics, sociology or anthropology and further adapt them to suit the demands of different research sites and research questions (Jones, 2012). As a result, they are also well equipped to take into account the visual effects that had to be omitted from this discussion, and the relationship between text and image characterizing the complex multimodal environments of the print media and the Internet. Such flexible combination of micro and macro approaches to textual analysis is our best tool for a critical interrogation of discourses on emerging health risks and benefits, particularly within the emerging forms and modes of communication with which they are increasingly associated.

## Acknowledgements

The support of the ESRC is gratefully acknowledged (research grant no. RES-000-23-1306 and RES-000-22-2289). Some of the material in section 2 in this chapter is a revised version of the article previously published in *Metaphor and Symbol* (issue 23: 4) and section 3 contains updated material from the article previously published in *Critical Discourse Studies* (issue 6:2). I would like to thank the publishers for permission to reprint these materials.

## Note

1   The pages were stored on a computer during the analysis phase in 2008. As is often the case with Internet-based data, many pages may have been altered or removed since then.

## References

Anderson, A. (2006), 'Media and risk', in Sandra Walklate and Gabe Mythen (eds), *Beyond the Risk Society*. Milton Keynes, UK: Open University/McGraw Hill, pp. 114–31.

Bhatia, V. (2002), 'Applied genre analysis: a multi-perspective model'. *Iberica*, 4, 3–19.

Briggs, C. and M. Nichter. (2009), 'Biocommunicability and the biopolitics of pandemic threats'. *Medical Anthropology*, 28(3), 189–98.

Brown, B. Nerlich, B., Crawford, P., Koteyko, N. and Carter, R. (2009), 'Hygiene and biosecurity: the language and politics of risk in an era of emerging infectious diseases'. *Sociology Compass*, 2, 1–13.

Calsamiglia H. and Van Dijk T.A. (2004), 'Popularization discourse and knowledge about the genome'. *Discourse and Society*, 15(4), 2004, Special issue *Genetic and genomic discourses at the dawn of the 21st century*, guest edited by B. Nerlich, R. Dingwall, P. Martin, pp. 369–89.

Charteris-Black, J. (2006), 'Britain as a container: immigration metaphors in the 2005 election campaign'. *Discourse & Society*, 17(5), 563–81.

Charteris-Black, J., Seale, C. and Ziebland, S. (2006), 'Gender, cancer experience and internet use: a comparative keyword analysis of interviews and online cancer support groups'. *Social Science & Medicine*, 62, 2577–90.

Chilton P. (1996), *Security Metaphors: Cold War Discourse from Containment to Common House*. New York: Peter Lang.

—— (2004), *Analysing Political Discourse*. London and New York: Routledge.

Conrad, P. (2007), *The Medicalization of Society: On the Transformation of Human Conditions into Treatable Disorders*. Baltimore, MD: Johns Hopkins University Press.

Conrad, P. and Barker, K. (2010), 'The social construction of illness: key insights and policy implications'. *Journal of Health and Social Behavior*, 51(S), S67–S79.

Cottle, S. (1998), 'Ulrich Beck, risk society and the media: a catastrophic view'. *European Journal of Communication*, 13(1), 5–32.

Coveney, C. M., Nerlich, B. and Martin, P. (2009), 'Modafinil in the media: metaphors, medicalisation and the body'. *Social Science and Medicine*, 68(3), 487–95.

Dixon, J. and Banwell, C. (2004), 'Re-embedding trust: unravelling the construction of modern diets'. *Critical Public Health*, 14(2), 117–31.

Dumit, J. (2012), *Drugs for Life: How Pharmaceutical Companies Define Our Health*. Durham, NC: Duke University Press.

Fairclough, N. (2003), *Analysing Discourse Textual Analysis for Social Research*. London: Routledge.

Fleming, J. (1998), 'Web navigation'. *Designing the User Experience*. Sebastopol, CA: O'Reilly & Associates.

Fowler, R., Hodge, B., Kress, G. and Trew, T. (1979), *Language and Social Control*. London: Routledge.

Frank, A. W. (1995), *The Wounded Storyteller: Body, Illness, and Ethics*. Chicago: University of Chicago Press.

Goddard, A. (1998), *The Language of Advertising: Written Texts*. London and New York: Routledge.

Greenhalgh, T. and Wessely, S. (2004), '"Health for me": a sociocultural analysis of healthism in the middle classes'. *British Medical Bulletin*, 69, 197–213.

Gwyn, R. (2002), *Communicating Health and Illness*. London: Sage.

Hart, C. (2008), 'Critical discourse analysis and metaphor: toward a theoretical framework'. *Critical Discourse Studies*, 5(2), 91–106.

Harvey, K., (2013), *Investigating Adolescent Health Communication: A Corpus Linguistics Approach*. London: Bloomsbury.

Harvey, K. and Koteyko, N. (2012), *Health Communication*. London: Routledge.

Hughes, E., Kitzinger, J. and Murdock, G. (2008), *Media Discourses and Framing of Risk*. SCARR Working Paper. 27.

Joffe, H. and Haarhoff, G. (2002), 'Representations of far-flung illnesses: the case of Ebola in Britain'. *Social Science & Medicine,* 54(6), 955–69.

Jones, R. (2012), *Health and Risk Communication. An Applied Linguistic Perspective.* London: Routledge.

Kitzinger, J., Henderson, L., Smart, A. and Eldrige, J. (2003), *Media Coverage of the Social and Ethical Implications of Human Genetics.* Final report to the Wellcome Trust. London: The Wellcome Trust.

Koller, V. (2003), 'Metaphor clusters, metaphor chains: analyzing the multifunctionality of metaphor in text'. *Metaphorik.de,* 5, 115–34.

Koteyko, N. (2009), '"I am a very happy, lucky lady, and I am full of Vitality!" Online promotional strategies of probiotic yoghurt producers'. *Critical Discourse Studies,* 6(2), 111–25.

Koteyko, N., Brown, B. and Crawford, P. (2008b), 'The dead parrot and the dying swan: the role of metaphor scenarios in UK press coverage of avian flu in the UK in 2005–2006'. *Metaphor and Symbol,* 23(4), 242–61.

Koteyko, N., Nerlich, B., Crawford, P. and N. Wright (2008a), '"Not rocket science" or "no silver bullet"? Media and government discourses about MRSA and cleanliness'. *Applied Linguistics,* 29, 223–43.

Lakoff, G. (2004), *Don't Think of an Elephant: Know your Values and Frame the Debate.* White River Junction VT: Chelsea Green Publishing.

Lakoff, G. and Johnson, M. (1980), *Metaphors We Live By.* Chicago: Chicago University Press.

Larson, B., Nerlich, B. and Wallis, P. (2005), 'Metaphors and Biorisks'. *Science Communication,* 26, 243–68.

Lupton, D. (1998), *Risk.* London: Routledge.

Martin, E. (1994), *Flexible Bodies: Tracking Immunity in American Culture from the Days of Polio to the Age of AIDS.* Boston: Beacon Press.

Mishler, E. (1984), *The Discourse of Medicine: Dialectics of Medical Interviews.* Norwood, NJ: Ablex.

Musolff, A. (2004), *Metaphor and Political Discourse: Analogical Reasoning in Debates About Europe.* Basingstoke: Palgrave Macmillan.

—— (2006), 'Metaphor scenarios in public discourse'. *Metaphor and Symbol,* 2(1), 23–38.

Nerlich, B. and Halliday, C. (2007), 'Avian Flu: the creation of expectations in the interplay between science and the media'. *Sociology of Health and Illness,* 29(1), 46–69.

Nerlich, B, Hamilton, C. and Rowe, V. (2002), 'Conceptualising foot and mouth disease: the socio-cultural role of metaphors, frames and narratives'. *Metaphorik.de,* 2: http://www.metaphorik.de/02/nerlich.htm

Powers, J. H. and Xiao, X. (eds) (2008), *The Social Construction of SARS: Studies of a Health Communication Crisis.* Philadelphia: John Benjamins.

Reisigl, M. and Wodak, R. (2001), *Discourse and Discrimination: Rhetorics of Racism and Antisemitism.* London: Routledge.

Richardson, K. (2005), *Internet Discourse and Health Debates.* New York: Palgrave Macmillan.

Rimke, J. (2000), 'Governing citizens through self-help literature'. *Cultural Studies,* 14(1), 6 1–78.

Rose N. (2007), *The Politics of Life Itself: Biomedicine, Power, and Subjectivity in the Twenty-first Century.* Princeton, NJ: Princeton University Press.

Rundblad, G., Chilton, P. and Hunter, P. (2006), 'An enquiry into scientific and media discourse in the MMR controversy: authority and factuality'. *Communication and Medicine,* 3(1), 69–80.

Sarangi, S. (2004), 'Towards a communicative mentality in medical and healthcare practice'. *Communication & Medicine*, 1(1), 1–11.

Schön, D. and Rein, M. (1994), *Frame Reflection: Toward the Resolution of Intractable Policy Controversies*. New York: Basic Books.

Seale, C. (2005), 'New directions for critical internet health studies: representing cancer experience on the web'. Sociology of Health and Illness, 27, 515–40.

Segal, J. Z. (2005), *Health and the Rhetoric of Medicine*. Carbondale: Southern Illinois UP.

Silverman, D. (1987), *Communication and Medical Practice*. London: Sage.

Sloan, A. (2004), 'Top 10 functional food trends 2004'. *Food Technology*, 58(4), 28–51.

Sontag, S. (1979), *Illness as Metaphor*. London: Allen Lane.

Turner, B. (1995), *Medical Power and Social Knowledge*. Thousand Oaks, CA: Sage.

Waldby, C. (2002), 'Stem cells, tissue cultures and the production of biovalue'. *Health*, 6, 305–23.

Walker, R. and Buckley, M. (2006), *Probiotic Microbes: The Scientific Basis*. Washington, DC: American Academy of Microbiology.

Wallis, P. and Nerlich, B. (2005), 'Disease metaphors in new epidemics: the UK media framing of the 2003 SARS epidemic'. *Social Science & Medicine*, 60, 2629–39.

Williams, S. (2005), *Sleep and Society: Sociological Ventures into the (Un)known*. New York: Routledge.

Wodak, R., de Cillia, R., Reisigl, M. and Liebhart, K. (eds) (1999), *The Discursive Construction of National Identity*. Edinburgh: Edinburgh University Press.

Wood, F. (2007), 'Health messages get through but fail to change lifestyles'. *The Edge*, 25, 4.

Zinken, J. (2003), 'Ideological imagination: intertextual and correlational metaphors in political discourse'. *Discourse & Society*, 14(4), 507–23.

Zinken, J., Hellsten, I. and Nerlich, B. (2008), 'Discourse metaphors', in R. M. Frank, R. Dirven, T. Ziemke and E. Bernárdez (eds), *Body, Language and Mind: Vol. 2. Sociocultural Situatedness*. Amsterdam: John Benjamins, pp. 363–86.

# 24

# Public Health in the UK Media

# Cognitive Discourse Analysis and its Application to a Drinking Water Emergency

*Olivia Knapton and Gabriella Rundblad*

King's College London

## 1 Introduction

While rainy school holidays are nothing new for the UK, the summer of 2007 was the wettest on record (The Environment Agency, 2007). Particularly hard hit was the county of Gloucestershire and its neighbouring Midlands areas, where the equivalent of two months of rain (125mm) fell on 19–20 July (Pitt, 2008).

The resulting crisis was the largest natural disaster experienced in the UK. In addition to widespread surface water flooding of homes and businesses, fluvial flooding from the River Severn and the River Avon inundated the Mythe water treatment works, rendering the provision of mains water impossible. Approximately 350,000 residents lost their drinking water supply for up to 17 days. Alternative supplies had to be made available through bottled water and bowsers (static water tanks). When the mains water was returned, residents were issued a Do Not Drink notice followed by a Boil Water notice seven days later. The loss of mains water and sourcing of temporary supplies represented the UK's largest peacetime emergency since World War II (Pitt, 2008). An emergency response unit, known as Gold Command, was initiated under the control of the local police. While the provision of drinking water remains the legal responsibility of the water company (in this case Severn Trent Water), over 25 different agencies – including the military – were involved in the disaster response (Gloucestershire Constabulary, 2008).

This study explores the representations of the various authorities and the general public in the UK media coverage of the drinking water crisis. We analyse the clarity with which the different authorities' responsibilities were portrayed and discuss the implications for public understandings of authority roles. We also analyse how the language of the drinking water advice reported by the media may have reduced the affected public's comprehension of and obligation to comply with that advice.

# 2  The media and natural disasters

During natural disasters, the affected public typically turn to media sources for up-to-date information and advice. Regardless of whether the information is transmitted via television (Piotrowski and Armstrong, 1998; Spence et al., 2007), radio (Cretikos et al., 2008), email or mobile phone (Hayden et al., 2007), it is imperative that the advice is timely, accurate, clear and delivered by a trustworthy source (Glik, 2007). Failure to fulfil these criteria will result in a lack of public comprehension of the advice, which ultimately increases confusion and anxiety, reduces compliance levels and can risk public health and safety (Glik, 2007).

During this drinking water incident, affected consumers showed a preference for local media sources rather than the official health leaflets (Rundblad et al., 2010). The local radio was the most consulted information source and those who used local newspapers reported higher levels of clarity. Yet compliance with the advice was low (Rundblad et al., 2010), which suggests that the consulted media sources did little to aid public comprehension of the advice.

## 2.1  Human responsibility in disasters

Reflecting a wider belief upheld by society, natural disasters are often represented by authority figures as acts of God that are inevitable and resistant to human intervention (Steinberg, 2000). Perhaps due to this belief or perhaps due to lack of clarity over human responsibility, media coverage of natural disasters can be prone to an absence of human agency (Harwell, 2000). However, during and after a disaster, it is likely that the affected public will seek answers to many questions about the causes of that disaster (Koenig, 2007).

Due to a belief in the unfailing protection of society and government (Kumagai et al., 2006), disaster victims look for human agency when constructing explanations. Reporting styles in the media often adjust to reflect this search for responsibility. For example, after Hurricane Katrina, the media showed an apparent shift in the portrayal of authorities from efficient to inefficient as the disaster response progressed (Littlefield and Quenette, 2007). Similarly, after the Westray coal mine tragedy in Nova Scotia in 1992, initial reports represented the explosion as a natural disaster with loss and suffering yet later reports emphasized human agency and accountability as the public sought answers (O'Connell and Mills, 2003). It has also been found that the damage caused by earthquakes is attributed to the earthquake itself in immediate reports yet attributed to building structures (and therefore human agency) in reports one year later (Cowan et al., 2002). Kumagai and colleagues (2006) argue that this seeking to blame behaviour can highlight the features of the disaster that could have been avoided by human intervention. While this may help to avoid repeat incidents, it can lead to lower public trust in the authorities that are actively working to solve the current problems.

## 2.2 *Media coverage of Hurricane Katrina*

In 2005, Hurricane Katrina and the ensuing floods claimed the lives of almost 1,900 people. In New Orleans, Louisiana, a disastrous failure of the levee system caused the vast majority of the city to become flooded. Since the disaster, the media coverage has been heavily criticized for interpreting the events through frames of criminality that only served to reinforce the pervasive, yet unproven, belief that crime levels rise during disasters such as this one (Berger, 2009; Tierney et al., 2006). It has been argued that the media used crime frames to represent African American victims as looters and violent criminals (Tierney et al., 2006), and to build upon existing stereotypes of black, poor populations as dangerous (Berger, 2009). The media continually favoured the noun *looter* over the verb *to loot*. Thus the victims were portrayed as belonging to a 'looter class' rather than carrying out 'looting' as necessary for survival (Berger, 2009).

The media's exclusion of certain groups of victims throughout the disaster has also been criticized. For example, the focus on issues of race may have detracted from other groups that required aid, such as the elderly (Garnett and Kouzmin, 2007). However, it has been argued that the proportion of coverage dedicated to African Americans accurately reflected the racial distribution of the local population (Voorhees et al., 2007). Rather, it was male victims and those in poverty who were greatly over-represented.

The use of crime frames also had implications for the portrayal of the involved authorities. Firstly, some reports criticized an absence of authority and government response (Stock, 2007; Berger, 2009). This reporting has faced criticism for boosting negative public perceptions of the capabilities of authorities to respond to disasters (Littlefield and Quenette, 2007; Garnett and Kouzmin, 2007). Secondly, it has been argued that crime and war frames justify and strengthen the power of the military and law enforcement agencies (Tierney et al., 2006; Stock, 2007). This can further entrench the public perception that only the military can effectively restore 'normality' after a disaster. Crime frames may also have bolstered the authority of state power and legitimized jail as a necessary route to restoring order (Berger, 2009).

# 3 Cognitive Discourse Analysis

To explore the conceptualizations inherent in the media's reporting of the UK's drinking water crisis, this study performs discourse analysis using a recently developed method known as Cognitive Discourse Analysis (CogDA) (Rundblad, 2007). This method fuses elements from Critical Discourse Analysis (CDA) and Cognitive Linguistics.

Cognitive Linguistics claims that the mind is organized by representational conceptual structures that are experienced as real and evidenced in language (e.g. Lakoff and Johnson, 1980). Therefore by tracking the semantic and grammatical patterns in language use, we can find evidence for the mental conceptualizations that organize information and experience. In recent years, several researchers have advocated the integration of Cognitive Linguistics and CDA in order to uncover the pervasive, underlying conceptual structures within texts that can influence audiences (e.g. Hart, 2008; Charteris-Black, 2006; Wodak, 2006).

CogDA employs a functional approach for the backbone of the analysis, for example, by exploring noun and verb phrases in terms of communicative function rather than parts of speech, breaking the texts down to clausal level and highlighting techniques such as passive constructions. It also emphasizes the effects of language choice; for example creating a clause with the modal verb *should* (e.g. *you should have a drink now*) will give rise to different interpretations of the same clause created with the modal verb *can* (e.g. *you can have a drink now*). To unearth the conceptual structures within the text, CogDA merges these functional considerations with the cognitive approaches of frame semantics (Fillmore, 1982), localist semantics (Anderson, 1971), and conceptual metaphor and metonymy (Lakoff and Johnson, 1980).

## 3.1 *Frame semantics and localist semantics*

Frame semantics posits that a frame is a system of related concepts that fit together within a structure (Fillmore, 1982; Lakoff, 2010). Comprehension of one of the concepts in that structure can only occur if the structure as a whole is understood. For example, we cannot understand the concept of A CAR without understanding the entire frame of MODE OF TRANSPORT. Hence, concepts can never be understood in isolation. Furthermore, when one concept is used in language, it evokes the whole structure to which it belongs. Through careful choice of words, a writer/speaker can evoke frames that may not normally be used within the given context or can provide existing frames with new meanings.

Localist semantics (Anderson, 1971) explores how the participants/entities are portrayed in relation to one another by examining the semantic roles they fulfil (e.g. agent, theme, receiver). For example, a localist semantics analysis might consider how different agents operate within the text and what other participants they affect.

CogDA combines these approaches by focusing on the interplay between the semantic roles and frames activated in the text. By analysing which frames repeatedly appear in which semantic roles, overarching linguistic patterns can be discovered that provide evidence for the conceptual structures through which the information in the text is organized.

## 3.2 *Conceptual metaphor and metonymy*

Since Lakoff and Johnson's work in the 1980s (Lakoff and Johnson, 1980), metaphor has come to be seen as a conceptual system that maps features from a concrete source domain (e.g. WAR) onto features from an abstract target domain (e.g. ARGUMENTS) in order to aid comprehension. Evidence for these conceptual metaphors (e.g. ARGUMENT IS WAR) can be found in linguistic realizations such as *he's defending his position* and *he won the argument*.

Metonymy, like metaphor, is a way of conceptualizing one thing in terms of another. However, the mappings for metonymy occur within the same domain rather than across different domains (Lakoff and Johnson, 1980). For example, when we do not know or do not wish to reveal a specific individual's identity, we may use metonymy, such as *the council sent me a letter* or *the police arrested the thief*.

By breaking the clauses down into their semantic roles, CogDA allows for the rapid identification of metonyms and the roles they fulfil. In addition, by pinpointing repeated combinations of roles (in particular agents) and actions, CogDA easily recognizes metaphorical patterns.

# 4 Aims

Using CogDA, we explore the conceptualizations of the different authorities and the general public in the national and local UK media coverage of the drinking water crisis in 2007. By analysing a variety of linguistic techniques, we aim to show how different authorities were represented with varying degrees of reliability, effectiveness and clarity over their responsibilities. We discuss how these representations may have obscured the roles of the various authorities, which may have led to blurred public conceptualizations of those authorities. We also aim to show how the representation of the affected public throughout the incident may have reduced their understanding of and obligation to comply with the drinking water advice, which potentially put themselves and others in their care at risk.

# 5 Methods

## 5.1 Article selection

An Incident Corpus of articles published between 23 July and 10 August 2007 was compiled from local newspapers (*The Citizen Gloucestershire, The Gloucestershire Echo, The Stroud News & Journal*), local television websites (*BBC Gloucestershire*), national broadsheets (*The Guardian, The Independent, The Times, The Telegraph*), national tabloids (*Daily Mail, Express, The Mirror, The Sun, The Star*) and national television websites (*BBC, ITV, Sky*). All articles reporting on the incident were downloaded directly from each source's website or from the HighBeam Research online library (www.highbeam.com). Search terms were *Gloucestershire, drinking water, Severn Trent, Mythe, Health Protection Agency, flood* and/or *advice*. This yielded a total of 788 articles across the four incident stages (Table 24.1).

As our focus is on drinking water, all articles in the Incident Corpus were read to determine if the content considerably related to the drinking water aspects of the incident. An article was deemed as being considerably related to drinking water if at least one sizeable paragraph was devoted to the topic. Notably, one source, the national tabloid *The Star*, had no drinking water related articles. The relevant articles were compiled into a separate Drinking Water Sub-Corpus, totalling 142 articles.

To allow manual CogDA, half of the articles from the Drinking Water Sub-Corpus were selected per source and per incident stage using the online Research Randomizer (www.randomizer.org) (e.g. of the six articles published by *Daily Mail* during the Do Not Drink stage, three were randomly selected). Due to the low numbers of articles for the

**Table 24.1** Incident timeline

| Incident stage | Inclusive dates | Incident Corpus | Drinking Water Sub-Corpus | CogDA Sub-Corpus |
|---|---|---|---|---|
| Water Loss | 23–26 July | 288 | 57 | 30 |
| Do Not Drink | 27 July–2 August | 284 | 56 | 29 |
| Boil Water | 3–6 August | 93 | 10[a] | 10 |
| Water Safe | 7–10 August | 123 | 19 | 11 |
| | | **788** | **142** | **80** |

[a]Four articles continued to report Do Not Drink advice; even so, these were categorized in the Boil Water stage because they still represented the advice that was available after the Boil Water notice had been issued.

Boil Water stage, all ten articles were selected. This yielded 80 articles for the CogDA Sub-Corpus.

## 5.2 *Cognitive Discourse Analysis*

As aforementioned, CogDA is a linguistic analysis method that incorporates localist semantics and frame semantics in a functional approach to communication. In accordance with Rundblad (2007), we distinguish between nominal frames (which are sub-divided into (living) participants and (non-living) entities) and action frames. An example of the nominal frames discerned within the texts can be found in Figure 24.1.

Similarly, we distinguish between different action frames (e.g. GIVING and INGESTING). As Figure 24.2 shows, each action frame contains several verbs with related meanings (e.g. INGESTING contains the synonyms *drink* and *sip*).

As is shown in Figure 24.2, antonyms such as *give* and *receive* belong to the same action frame. For example, in the clause *the patient received advice from the doctor*, the patient cannot receive advice unless the doctor simultaneously gives advice; thus, the one and only real world action that is performed is GIVING but by alternating between *give* and *receive*, we can portray that action from different points of view. The choice of different verbs from the same conceptual frame combined with the participant/entity positioned as grammatical subject will give rise to different interpretations.

In our analysis, firstly we tagged each noun phrase and verb phrase into their nominal and action frames. Secondly, the phrases were labelled by the semantic role they performed in each clause using an approach taken from localist semantics. The semantic roles discerned were:

Agent – the participant performing the action

Theme – the participant/entity upon which the action is performed

Receiver – the participant/entity which receives/benefits from the theme

Source – the participant/entity from which the theme originates

Instrument – the participant/entity which aids the action.

Thirdly, the grammatical subject and predicate of each clause were marked. The combination of classifying both semantic agent and grammatical subject allowed us to distinguish between active voice (i.e. the agent is the subject) and passive voice (i.e. the agent is not the subject). In the examples in Table 24.2, bold marks grammatical subject; thus, we can see that the first example is active and the second is passive. The third example uses active voice yet the agent is not the subject; this type of construction is discussed in detail in subsequent paragraphs.

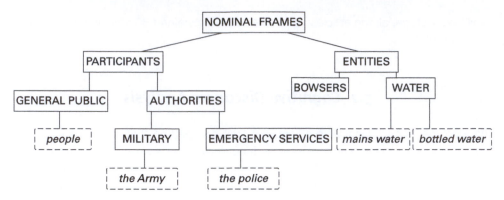

**FIGURE 24.1** *Example of classification tree for nominal frames. Frames are in capitals and their related linguistic expressions are in italics.*

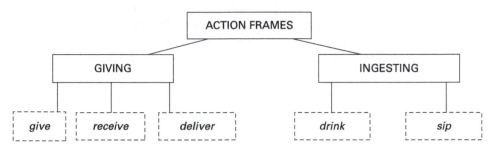

**FIGURE 24.2** *Example of classification tree for action frames.*

In addition to those participants/entities and actions that were explicitly stated in the texts, we also assigned implied and ellipted participants/entities and actions to their relevant frames. In Table 24.2, square brackets mark implication and italics mark ellipsis. Ellipsis is very common in English (Nariyama, 2004), and in the first example we see that the word *people* is ellipted from the second clause. Similarly, the context of examples 2 and 3 reveals that the implied agent is the military and the general public, respectively.

In examples 1, 2 and 3, we find instances of the following nominal frames: GENERAL PUBLIC, WATER, MILITARY, INFORMATION and EMERGENCY SERVICES. In example 3, *we* (=EMERGENCY SERVICES) is the subject of the clause; however, the verb *get* signifies that another participant must be performing a GIVE action. Therefore, in accordance with localist semantics (Anderson, 1971), *we* is assigned to the receiver position, the verb *get* is assigned to the action frame GIVING and we can infer an implied agent from the GENERAL PUBLIC frame.

The strengths of CogDA lie in its capacity to unveil the participants/entities and actions that are not explicit within the text. Therefore, in addition to addressing the roles and actions of the authorities and the general public, the analysis emphasizes

**Table 24.2** Examples of grammatical subject, implication and ellipsis

| ID | Clause | Agent | Predicate | Theme | Receiver |
|----|--------|-------|-----------|-------|----------|
| 1 | people panic and stockpile | **people** | panic | | |
| | | **_people_** | stockpile | [WATER] | |
| 2 | bottled water was delivered | [MILITARY] | was delivered | **bottled water** | |
| 3 | we get reports of crime and disorder | [GENERAL PUBLIC] | get | reports of crime and disorder | **we** |

which participants/entities are highlighted and downplayed through the use of implication and ellipsis. Metonyms, metaphors and passive voice, as established techniques for hiding participant agency, are also explored. In addition to qualitative analysis, semantic and grammatical tags were entered into SPSS 16 to allow descriptive quantitative analysis.

# 6 Results and discussion

Throughout the incident, the media used a range of linguistic devices to represent the central agents and their actions. We work through those linguistic devices to unravel, in particular, the portrayal of the authorities and the general public. We demonstrate how the language used may have obscured the authorities' responsibilities and reduced the public's obligation to comply with the drinking water advice. We discuss the implications for public understandings of both authority roles and health advice issued in times of emergency.

## 6.1 Overview

The drinking water crisis resulted in a large amount of media coverage at both the national and local level. As CogDA breaks the texts down to clause level, all frequencies represent the number of clauses unless otherwise stated. In total, the analysed articles contained 5,525 clauses. Unsurprisingly, the total amount of media coverage tailed off as the incident progressed. Therefore the Water Loss stage represents 46.4 per cent of the analysed clauses and the Do Not Drink stage represents 37.1 per cent. Following this, the coverage dropped dramatically. The Boil Water stage represents 7.2 per cent of the coverage and the Water Safe stage represents 9.3 per cent.

## 6.2 Agents

Looking at which participants fulfil the role of agent, it is clear that there are three agent frames performing the majority of actions: THE GENERAL PUBLIC, THE WATER COMPANY and the other MAJOR AUTHORITIES (Table 24.3). This latter group includes THE MILITARY, THE EMERGENCY SERVICES, POLITICIANS, GOVERNMENT DEPARTMENTS, COUNTY COUNCILS, HEALTH AUTHORITIES and CHARITIES. There is also a group of UNSPECIFIED AUTHORITIES; these are clauses in which there is an authority action yet there is not enough information to discern which authority is intended.

We now turn to look at how these agents are represented through implied and ellipted references rather than explicit references, and metaphor and metonymy rather than literal references.

### 6.2.1 Implied, ellipted and explicit agency

One technique for hiding the agent is to omit it from the clause entirely. In these cases, the grammatical subject represents other pieces of information relevant to the clause's meaning. For example, the writer may use a dummy subject (e.g. *there is no water*), place the theme or receiver in subject position (e.g. *this water is not for drinking*), use a dependent clause as the subject (e.g. *drinking this water is a health hazard*) or use a passive construction (e.g. *water was cut*). The reader therefore only has the surrounding context from which to infer the agent.

Throughout the coverage, THE WATER COMPANY and THE GENERAL PUBLIC are persistently omitted from the clauses in which they are the agent (Table 24.4). For THE WATER COMPANY, 56.2 per cent (n=773/1376) of their actions are represented with an implied agent and for THE GENERAL PUBLIC's actions, this stands at 47.4 per cent (n=826/1744). For example, clauses such as *there is no water* refer to the water

**Table 24.3**   Clauses per agent

| Agent | n | % |
|---|---|---|
| GENERAL PUBLIC | 1744 | 31.6 |
| WATER COMPANY | 1376 | 24.9 |
| MAJOR AUTHORITIES | 863 | 15.6 |
| UNSPECIFIED AUTHORITIES | 408 | 7.4 |
| No agent/non-human agents/all other agents | 1134 | 20.5 |
|  | 5525 | 100.0 |

**Table 24.4** Implied, ellipted and explicit positioning of agents

|  | General public | | Major authorities | | Water company | |
|---|---|---|---|---|---|---|
|  | n | % | n | % | n | % |
| Implied | 826 | **47.4** | 177 | **20.5** | 773 | **56.2** |
| Ellipted | 440 | **25.2** | 190 | **22.0** | 162 | **11.8** |
| Explicit | 478 | **27.4** | 496 | **57.5** | 441 | **32.0** |
|  | **1744** | **100.0** | **863** | **100.0** | **1376** | **100.0** |

company's inability to provide water; yet their agency, and hence responsibility, can only be found through inference. Likewise, clauses such as *this water is not for drinking* mean that the general public should not consume the current supply even though they are not signalled in the text.

While an implied agent can mostly be discovered through inferences from the semantic context, an ellipted agent normally arises from the syntax of the English language. As the agent can be retrieved from preceding clauses, it has higher visibility in the text than an implied agent (Rundblad, 2007). In the reports, THE GENERAL PUBLIC and THE MAJOR AUTHORITIES are often ellipted agents in dependent clauses (e.g. '... experts warning residents not to consume [mains water]'(*The Times*, 2007)/'police and council officers were on hand at each of the sites, marshalling the long queues' (*The Gloucestershire Echo*, 2007a)).

Agents cannot simultaneously be implied, ellipted and explicit within the same clause. As THE WATER COMPANY and THE GENERAL PUBLIC have high levels of implication and ellipsis, it follows that they have low levels of explicit agency. THE WATER COMPANY and THE GENERAL PUBLIC are the explicit agents of their actions in only 32.0 per cent (n=441/1376) and 27.4 per cent (n=478/1744) of clauses, respectively. Contrasting this, THE MAJOR AUTHORITIES are explicit agents in 57.5 per cent (n=496/863) of their clauses (e.g. 'Gold Command, the county's emergency response team, has issued a health and safety notice' (*The Gloucestershire Echo*, 2007e)).

Throughout this crisis, the involvement of so many different authorities in the provision of temporary water supplies may have left affected consumers unsure of which authority was tasked with which responsibility. This is despite the fact that the provision of safe drinking water in the UK is the water company's legal responsibility. The lack of visibility of the water company is incredibly worrying as it signifies an indistinguishable role for the water company throughout the incident. Rather than clarifying the situation, the opacity with which the water company was represented by the media may have obscured public conceptualizations of the water company's role. This may have diminished the affected public's confidence in the water company, contributed to widespread confusion and rendered people unaware to whom to turn for water advice. Moreover, the lack of clarity hints at a widespread gap in public knowledge about the responsibilities that the water company are obliged to fulfil in times of supply failure.

The media's portrayal of the other major authorities (such as the military and the police) as visible and prominent, overshadows the actions of the water company. Previous studies have also found that, after disasters, the military and law enforcement agencies are often represented as the only authorities capable of restoring the normal way of life (Tierney et al., 2006; Stock, 2007). Since the drinking water crisis, several official reports have stressed that the emergency services were inundated with non-emergency calls that wasted valuable time (Fire and Rescue, 2007) and that the police were expected to be 'everything to everyone' (Gloucestershire Constabulary, 2008). It would therefore appear that public conceptualizations of the police, fire and rescue, and ambulance services (i.e. the emergency services available by dialling 999) are comprised of an excessively expansive range of responsibilities whereas the conceptualizations of responders such as water companies (and potentially other utilities) are relatively restricted. As a larger part of this project, perceptions of the water company were probed in focus groups with members of the affected public (Rundblad et al., 2010). The findings confirmed that public knowledge of the water company's role was relatively limited and that they perceived the military and the police as having the most control over the incident. Media portrayals that continually favoured the emergency services over the water company would only have served to reinforce this perception of all-encompassing emergency services.

In addition, the frequent absence of clear agency for the general public may have concealed the public's own responsibility for taking actions to keep themselves and others safe. Without an overt role in the incident, the general public may have lacked motivation to comply with the health advice. This has implications for future events as previous studies have found that public responsibility for advance mitigation can be diminished if the media focus on authority accountability rather than community and individual accountability (Barnes et al., 2008).

## 6.2.2 Metaphors and non-human agency

Non-human agents (which can be either living participants or inanimate entities) constitute only a small proportion of agents (11.8 per cent, n=653/5525). Of these non-human agents, there are three main groups: THE FLOOD WATER (33.2 per cent, n=217/653), THE CRISIS (22.1 per cent, n=144/653) and CONTAMINANTS (15.6 per cent, n=102/653). While many non-human actions are unremarkable (for instance, *rivers run, contaminants pollute* and *the crisis continues*), certain non-human agents are afforded active agency through metaphorical representations.

**Table 24.5** Metaphorical clauses per agent

| Agent | n | % |
|---|---|---|
| CRISIS | 86 | **48.0** |
| FLOOD WATER | 39 | **21.8** |
| FLOODING EVENT | 14 | **7.8** |
| RAINWATER | 11 | **6.1** |
| Other agent | 29 | **16.3** |
| | **179** | **100.0** |

Considering the abundance of metaphors that have been found in previous media discourse analysis of health issues (e.g. Larson et al., 2005; Chiang and Duann, 2007), overall use of metaphors in this corpus is surprisingly low (3.2 per cent, n=179/5525). However, of those metaphors, it is THE CRISIS and THE FLOOD WATER that are the dominant metaphorical agents (Table 24.5). In fact, as metaphors, both THE CRISIS and THE FLOOD WATER are frequently personified. Thus, the resulting metaphors are those of THE CRISIS IS A LIVING ENTITY (e.g. 'last weekend's flooding crippled the county' (*The Citizen Gloucestershire*, 2007b)) and THE FLOOD WATER IS A LIVING ENTITY (e.g. 'it was forced out of action by the floods' (*The Gloucestershire Echo*, 2007e)). Moreover, the metaphorical agents perform CAUSE actions in 43 per cent (n=77/179) of all metaphorical clauses (e.g. 'the ensuing water shortage resulted in the police guarding bottled water in supermarkets' (*The Times*, 2007)). THE CRISIS and THE FLOOD WATER are therefore more than just living entities; they are living entities with force and purpose.

Metaphors allow certain aspects of a situation to be highlighted or downplayed. Therefore, assigning causality to the crisis and the flood water is one way to tone down human responsibility for the crisis. This method of evading human accountability is in fact quite common after disasters; the crisis is often represented as the most active agent with a life of its own (Harwell, 2000; Cowan et al., 2002).

## 6.2.3 Metonymy

Metonymy is particularly common in situations where the exact actor cannot be identified. Across various contexts, authority figures are frequently represented via metonyms (Rundblad, 2007). Throughout the media coverage, when authorities are written into the agent position, they are expressed as metonyms in 40.6 per cent (n=381/939) of clauses (Table 24.6). For example, 'Gloucestershire County Council . . .

**Table 24.6** Metonyms per participant in agent position

| Agent | Explicit | Of which are metonyms | |
|---|---|---|---|
| | n | n | % |
| MILITARY | 39 | 23 | **59.0** |
| ENVIRONMENT AGENCY | 36 | 21 | **58.3** |
| HEALTH AUTHORITIES | 50 | 25 | **50.0** |
| WATER COMPANY | 441 | 207 | **46.9** |
| CHARITY | 41 | 14 | **34.1** |
| EMERGENCY SERVICES | 155 | 49 | **31.6** |
| COUNCIL | 69 | 19 | **27.5** |
| POLITICIANS | 108 | 23 | **21.3** |
| | **939** | **381** | **40.6** |

welcomed the news' (*Daily Mail*, 2007)/'The Army was drafted in to distribute millions of bottles of water . . .' (*Express*, 2007). However, the different authorities vary in their level of metonymy when in agent position. THE MILITARY, THE ENVIRONMENT AGENCY and THE HEALTH AUTHORITIES all have particularly high levels.

Seeing as the Army very rarely acts as individuals, the high proportion of metonymy for the military is not a surprising finding. Similarly, individual politicians are relatively straightforward to pinpoint and so this accounts for the lower proportion of metonyms for this group. Yet the fact that over 40 per cent of authority agents are represented via a metonym raises questions about the ability of the media to form a clear, unobstructed representation of the authorities. Hiding individuals within metonyms contributes to the overarching finding that the conceptualizations of the authorities' roles in this incident were extremely indistinct.

## 6.3 *Actions*

Table 24.7 shows the actions that represent more than 3 per cent of the total clauses. As this was a crisis about provision and loss of water, the GIVE frame includes all verbs related to water provision, such as *restore, supply, deliver*, as well as the opposite of provision, namely *cut* and *interrupt*. All in all, GIVE actions account for 15.7 per cent

**Table 24.7**   Clauses per action

| Action | n | % |
|--------|------|-------|
| GIVE | 866 | 15.7 |
| SAY | 843 | 15.3 |
| CAUSE | 437 | 7.9 |
| USE | 394 | 7.1 |
| THINK | 277 | 5.0 |
| HYGIENE | 274 | 5.0 |
| INGEST | 235 | 4.3 |
| CHANGE | 211 | 3.8 |
| TAKE | 179 | 3.2 |
| EXIST | 165 | 3.0 |
| Other actions | 1644 | 29.8 |
| | **5525** | **100.0** |

(n=866/5525) of clauses. In the majority of these (54.7 per cent; n=474/866), the GIVE action is performed by THE WATER COMPANY. The similarly high frequency of SAY actions (15.3 per cent; n=843/5525) includes all verbs of speech and is driven by the amount of advice reported from authority groups.

We now look at how these actions are represented with passive voice rather than active voice, epistemic modality rather than deontic modality and ambiguous rather than specific terms. We also explore the interplay between various actions, agents and linguistic devices.

## 6.3.1 Passive voice

Passive voice is a well-known technique for hiding the agent of an action. Across all clauses, passive verb constructions represent 17.8 per cent (n=981/5525), with significantly higher use in national (20.0 per cent; n=681/3406) than local sources (14.2 per cent; n=300/2119).

Many actions carried out by authorities are represented by an UNSPECIFIED AGENT (7.4 per cent; n=408/5525). These are actions that could have been performed by a range of authorities of which the intended one is unidentifiable from the context. Agentless passives are used in 45.3 per cent (n=185/408) of these clauses (e.g.

'residents are being warned that the water is undrinkable . . . ' (*The Citizen Gloucestershire*, 2007c)), again reflecting a lack of specificity over which authorities were tasked with which responsibilities.

As described by Rundblad (2007), in medical contexts, passive voice and agent metonymy are rarely used in the same clause. In this media coverage, we see the same pattern; the two techniques infrequently occur together. The preference for either technique is dependent upon the agent; when authorities are agents, they are more likely to be hidden by metonyms than by passives. When the general public are agents, they are more likely to be hidden by passives than by metonyms (Tables 24.8–10). For example, the following two clauses both employ the GIVE action frame:

1   'Emergency services are issuing bottles of water on the streets . . .'
(*The Gloucestershire Echo*, 2007d)

2   '. . . the Echo has been inundated with complaints from readers . . .'
(*The Gloucestershire Echo*, 2007c)

Example (1) has an AUTHORITY as agent, uses active voice and represents the agent through metonymy. Example (2) has THE GENERAL PUBLIC as agent, uses passive voice and states the agent explicitly. This use of passive voice pushes the general public further into the background, which may have weakened their sense of purpose and agency within the incident. This is an issue to which we later return.

## 6.3.2 Modality

Perhaps the most worrisome aspect of the media coverage is the language used to advise the general public about the actions that are dangerous and safe to perform with both the temporary water supplies and the restored mains water.

**Tables 24.8–10**   Passive voice and metonymy for THE GENERAL PUBLIC, THE MAJOR AUTHORITIES and THE WATER COMPANY as agent

| | General public (n=1744) | | Major authorities (n=863) | | Water company (n=1376) | |
|---|---|---|---|---|---|---|
| | No metonym | Metonym | No metonym | Metonym | No metonym | Metonym |
| | n (table %) | n (table %) | n (table %) | n (table %) | n (table %) | n (table %) |
| **Active** | 1420 (81.4) | 41 (2.4) | 520 (60.3) | **241 (27.9)** | 902 (65.6) | **271 (19.7)** |
| **Passive** | **283 (16.2)** | 0 | 81 (9.4) | 21 (2.4) | 191 (13.9) | 12 (0.9) |

When the general public are the agent, 18.4 per cent (n=321/1744) of their actions are modified by a modal verb. As the incident progresses, the general public's actions with epistemic modality increase whereas their actions with deontic modality decrease (Figure 24.3). This pattern is created by the fact that epistemic and deontic modality are employed differently within the reports. Deontic modals are frequently coupled with negatives in order to instruct the public *not to do* something (e.g. 'people should not try to hose down flooded areas' (*The Telegraph*, 2007)). These instructions primarily occur in the early stages of the incident in relation to both the flood water and mains water. In contrast, epistemic modals are used in positive verb phrases that advise the public what they *can do* with their mains water (e.g. 'the boiled tap water can be used for drinking, cleaning teeth, washing dishes, preparing food and ice-making' (*The Citizen Gloucestershire*, 2007a)). The frequency of epistemic modality therefore increases as the water becomes safe to use for various activities.

However, the significant problem with the use of epistemic modals (such as *can*) is that the water instructions are presented as a choice rather than a necessity. This may have eroded the public's obligation to comply with the advice and thus made them more likely to put themselves at risk by following unsafe procedures. Previous studies have highlighted that public compliance to health advice improves when it is constructed with deontic modals (such as *should*) rather than epistemic modals (Edworthy et al., 2004). Thus, drinking water advice presented with deontic modals (example (3) would be more effective at creating a sense of obligation and ensuring public compliance (and thus public safety) than advice presented with epistemic modals (example (4)):

3   *you should not drink the tap water*

4   *you cannot drink the tap water.*

## 6.3.3  USE actions

When THE GENERAL PUBLIC are the agent, 37.5 per cent (n=654/1744) of their actions are performed upon WATER (e.g. *drink, boil*). This is not a surprising finding considering the nature of the disaster. What is surprising is that 36.8 per cent (n=241/654) of their actions performed upon WATER are USE actions (e.g. '. . . bottled water can be used as an alternative' (*The Gloucestershire Echo*, 2007b). This is compared to 20.6 per cent (n=135/654) for DRINK actions and 12.2 per cent (n=80/654) for BOIL actions.

USE actions are problematic in that they are incredibly vague and mask the specific action that is the intended target of the instruction. Take the examples:

5   *use boiled water for drinking*

6   *boiled water can be used for drinking.*

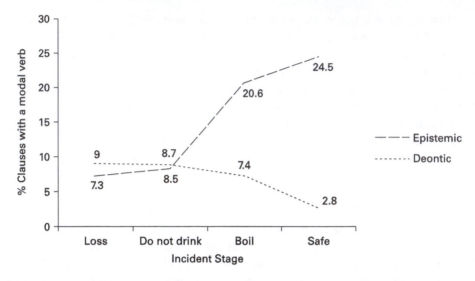

**FIGURE 24.3** *Modal verbs per incident stage when the general public are agent.*

In both examples (5) and (6), the key action DRINK is sidelined into a dependent clause and the key action BOIL is hidden within a noun phrase. Public comprehension of the advice may have been hindered by this indirect and vague style of delivery. In contrast, simple clauses with imperatives or deontic modals express the instruction much more directly by placing the target action BOIL as the main verb and thus as the focus. For example:

**7**   *boil the water*

**8**   *you should boil the water.*

A linked problem is that the verb *use* requires a qualifying dependent clause that creates a dense reporting style. In the Do Not Drink and Boil Water stages, independent clauses with the verb *use* were often succeeded by lengthy dependent clauses, for example 'tap water can now be used for cleaning teeth, washing dishes, preparing food and infant formula and ice-making' (*Stroud News and Journal*, 2007). For people with weak literacy skills, this complex style may have rendered the advice difficult to understand.

In fact, USE actions were not only widespread in the media coverage. They were also omnipresent in the water notices, the daily press conferences and the radio interviews given by the water company and other authorities. Of the 394 instances of USE in the media reports, 27.4 per cent (n=108/394) are pasted from advice leaflets, 34.5 per cent (n=136/394) are part of direct reported speech and 19.8 per cent (n=78/394) are part of indirect reported speech. Thus, only 18.3 per cent (n=72/394) are the journalists' own voices. It therefore appears that USE for water actions is pervasive throughout all areas of public life. Thus the media cannot be held solely accountable for its extensive presence; however, the inclusion of these ambiguous actions may have further cemented the public's vague conceptualizations of safe water actions.

The unselective inclusion of USE actions also points to a wider problem. Do Not Drink and Boil Water notices are in fact two separate water notices that entail different safe and dangerous water activities. If issued a Do Not Drink notice, then boiling the water will not make it safe for human ingestion. This distinction was shrouded by the USE actions that were ubiquitous throughout every stage of the incident. The key information that boiling the water offers no health protection, was implied at best, totally omitted at worst. During the Do Not Drink notice, consumers did indeed boil their tap water and then ingest it (Rundblad et al., 2010). We suggest that this low compliance was driven by the folk belief that boiling the water will always remove all contaminants. The media reports may have reinforced this belief through indiscriminate reporting of USE actions and thus the absence of a clear-cut distinction between water notices.

## 6.3.4 The interplay of USE actions, modality and passive voice

Adding to the problems of ambiguity inherent in USE, USE actions performed upon water are also expressed with high levels of epistemic modality (32.0 per cent; n=77/241). Moreover, clauses with both epistemic modality and USE actions are nearly always constructed using the passive voice (96.1 per cent; n=74/77). In fact, passive voice represents 58.9 per cent (n=142/241) of all USE actions performed on water by the general public. Within these constructions, the general public are frequently an omitted agent. Putting this all together results in sentences such as:

9  '. . . tap water can now be used for cleaning teeth, washing dishes, preparing food and infant formula and ice-making'

(*Stroud News and Journal*, 2007)

10  'Unboiled tap water can also continue to be used for flushing the toilet, washing, bathing and washing clothes'

(*Sky News*, 2007)

In summary, these sentences repeatedly adhere to the following formulaic structure:

Implied GENERAL PUBLIC agent + vague USE action + passive voice + epistemic modal + dependent participles

When broken down into these basic components, it becomes apparent that the water advice was not delivered with language that would have encouraged the affected public to comply. The public have no obvious agency, the actions they are advised to perform are not brought to the fore and the instructions are frequently presented as a choice rather than an obligation. On top of all of this, the reporting style uses an embedded clause structure that creates unnecessary complexity. Public comprehension of and compliance to the drinking water advice could have been enhanced through the use of a clearer linguistic style in communication from both the media and the authorities.

# 7 Conclusions and implications

The drinking water crisis of summer 2007 was the UK's largest peacetime emergency since World War II (Pitt, 2008). The flooding of the Mythe water treatment works due to heavy rain caused 350,000 residents to lose their drinking water supply for up to 17 days. When mains water was returned, residents were issued a Do Not Drink notice followed by a Boil Water notice. Due to the scale of the emergency, over 25 agencies were involved in the disaster response. Using CogDA, this study has examined the conceptualizations of the different authorities and the general public in the UK media reports of the incident.

## 7.1 *Authorities*

In times of mains water supply failure in the UK, it is the legal responsibility of the water company to provide temporary supplies and to restore mains water as quickly and as safely as possible. Thus, throughout this incident, the water company were arguably the most important authority. However, the media representations of the water company did not reflect nor reinforce this fact. Throughout the coverage, the water company were constantly backgrounded by use of linguistic devices such as implication and ellipsis. In fact, their agency was only explicitly stated for just over a quarter of the actions of which they were the agent. This lack of visibility may have obscured the public's conceptualizations of the water company and their responsibilities. If the public were not fully aware of the water company's role, then they may not have known to whom to turn for water advice. This may have added to the sense of confusion among much of the affected public and led to higher levels of non-compliance with the advice. Furthermore, the media's consistent omission of the water company suggests that there is a large gap in the public's knowledge of the water companies' duties in times of emergency.

In contrast, the other major authorities (such as the military and the emergency services) were highly visible within the media reports. After the incident, the emergency services reported that the public had turned to them with many requests that were outside their remit and would certainly not be classed as an emergency. This raises the problem of tying up the emergency services' resources with responding to non-life-threatening situations. The media's focus on a narrow range of major authorities rather than a broad range of responders may have reinforced the apparent public conceptualization that the emergency services can and should deal with a vast array of problems, even those that do not pose an immediate threat.

In times of emergency, it is vital that the affected public are aware of which authorities are tasked with which responsibilities. It is thus essential to improve public understanding of the water companies' duties and roles in times of supply failure. This would decrease public confusion, increase public trust in the water company and raise compliance levels to drinking water advice. In a similar vein, it is also necessary to improve public knowledge of the wide range of responders and their respective roles. This would help the affected public to make an informed choice about which authority to consult in non-life-threatening situations and thus reduce the strain on the emergency services.

## 7.2  *The general public and drinking water advice*

While the authorities have a responsibility to keep people safe in times of emergency, the affected public also have to be able to help themselves as far as possible. By issuing clear advice, authorities can ensure that the public are aware of dangerous behaviours and can take steps to protect themselves against injury or illness. However, this communication will not be successful if the language used in the health advice obscures the key messages and fails to encourage the affected public to comply.

Throughout the drinking water crisis, the media continually hid the general public in their reports through implication and agentless passives. Similarly to the water company, these linguistic devices masked the role of the general public, which could have contributed to a lack of motivation to act or take on any personal responsibilities. Moreover, the most important actions that the general public needed to take were those related to their drinking water (both temporary and mains supplies). Yet it is within the drinking water advice that the general public were hidden to the largest extent.

As well as this backgrounding of the general public through implication and passives, the drinking water advice was constructed and reported using additional linguistic devices that would not have encouraged public compliance. The advice was consistently reported with epistemic modals that presented the advice as a choice rather than a necessity, with ambiguous actions such as *use* rather than specific actions such as *drink* and with key actions sidelined into dependent clauses rather than as the focus in independent clauses. Additionally, the sentence structure of the advice tended to include chains of dependent clauses, which led to a complex style that can be difficult to understand.

**Table 24.11**   Recommendations for health advice

| Include | Avoid |
| --- | --- |
| Explicit public agency | Implied or hidden public agency |
| Deontic modals or imperatives | Epistemic modals |
| Active voice | Passive voice |
| Specific words (e.g. *drink*) | Ambiguous words (e.g. *use*) |
| Key actions in independent clauses | Key actions in dependent clauses |
| Short sentences with independent clauses | Long sentences with dependent clauses |

In future water incidents, public compliance could be enhanced by ensuring that instructions (whether directly from authorities or reported by the media) are as easily comprehensible as possible. We conclude by presenting a set of recommendations that could help authorities to construct clear, easy to follow health advice (Table 24.11).

These recommendations would improve the clarity of the language and thus increase public comprehension of the risky and safe behaviours. As a result, public compliance to the advice may also increase. It may also be worthwhile for health officials' training to include language courses that outline how specific linguistic constructions can clarify or obscure the intended message, and how this can impact public understanding and compliance.

Public health education should also target the false belief that boiling water *always* makes it safe to ingest. In this incident, a Do Not Drink and a Boil Water notice were issued one after the other. However, across both of these notices, the media and the authorities favoured the vague verb *use* instead of specific verbs (such as *drink* and *boil*). The distinction between the two notices was therefore blurred. This may have led the public to conceptualize the risky and safe behaviours as the same for both of these notices. In future Do Not Drink notices, the risks of ingesting boiled tap water need to be emphasized even further.

# Acknowledgements

This study was part of a larger project entitled *The Impact of Language and Cognition on Compliance during a Natural Disaster*. The project was funded by a grant from The Leverhulme Trust, awarded to Gabriella Rundblad (King's College London) and Paul R. Hunter (University of East Anglia). Grant reference: F/070 40/AM.

# References

Anderson, J. M. (1971), *The Grammar of Case: Towards a Localist Theory,* Cambridge: Cambridge University Press

Barnes, M. D., Hanson, C. L., Novilla, L. M. B., Meacham, A. T., McIntyre, E. and Erickson, B. C. (2008), 'Analysis of media agenda setting during and after Hurricane Katrina: implications for emergency preparedness, disaster response, and disaster policy'. *Government, Politics, and Law 2008*, 98, 604–10.

Berger, D. (2009), 'Constructing crime, framing disaster: routines of criminalization and crisis in Hurricane Katrina'. *Punishment and Society*, 11, 491–510.

Charteris-Black, J. (2006), 'Britain as a container: immigration metaphors in the 2005 election campaign'. *Discourse and Society*, 17, 563–81.

Chiang, W. and Duann, R. (2007), 'Conceptual metaphors for SARS: war between whom?' *Discourse and Society*, 18, 579–602.

Cowan, J., McClure, J. and Wilson, M. (2002), 'What a difference a year makes: how immediate and anniversary media reports influence judgements about earthquakes'. *Asian Journal of Social Psychology*, 5, 169–85.

Cretikos, M., Eastwood, K., Dalton, C., Merritt, T., Tuyl, F., Winn, L. and Durrheim, D. (2008), 'Household disaster preparedness and information sources: rapid cluster survey after a storm in New South Wales, Australia'. *BMC Public Health*, 8, 195–203.

*Daily Mail* (2007), 'Flood hit homes can now use tap water again'.

Edworthy, J., Hellier, E., Morley, N., Grey, C., Aldrich, K. and Lee, A. (2004), 'Linguistic and location effects in compliance with pesticide warning labels for amateur and professional users'. *Human Factors,* 46, 11–31.

*Express* (2007), 'Panic in the shops as water runs out'.

Fillmore, C. J. (2006), 'Frame semantics', in Gerraerts, D. (ed.), *Cognitive Linguistics: Basic Readings.* Berlin: Mouton de Gruyter, pp. 373–400.

Fire and Rescue (2007), 'Flooding review emerging issues: a report by the Chief Fire and Rescue Adviser'.

Garnett, J. L. and Kouzmin, A. (2007), 'Communicating throughout Katrina: competing and complementary conceptual lenses on crisis communication'. *Public Administration Review* December, special issue.

Glik, D. C. (2007), 'Risk communication for public health emergencies'. *Annual Review of Public Health*, 28, 33–54.

Gloucestershire Constabulary (2008), 'Operation outlook narrative and analysis: Chief Constable's report to the Gloucestershire Police Authority'.

Hart, C. (2008), 'Critical discourse analysis and metaphor: toward a theoretical framework'. *Critical Discourse Studies*, 5, 91–106.

Harwell, E. (2000), 'Remote sensibilities: discourses of technology and the making of Indonesia's natural disaster'. *Development and Change*, 31, 301–40.

Hayden, M. H., Drobot, S., Radil, S., Benight, C., Gruntfest, E. C. and Barnes, L. R. (2007), 'Information sources for flash flood warnings in Denver, CO and Austin, TX'. *Environmental Hazards*, 7, 211–19.

Koenig, H. G. (2007), 'Psychological needs of disaster survivors and families'. *Southern Medical Journal*, 100, 934–5.

Kumagai, Y., Edwards, J. and Carroll, M. S. (2006), 'Why are natural disasters not "natural" for victims?' *Environmental Impact Assessment Review*, 26, 106–19.

Lakoff, G. (2010), 'Why it matters how we frame the environment'. *Environmental Communication: A Journal of Nature and Culture*, 4, 70–81.

Lakoff, G. and Johnson, M. (1980), *Metaphors We Live By.* Chicago: University of Chicago Press.

Larson, B. M. H., Nerlich, B. and Wallis, P. (2005), 'Metaphors and biorisks: the war on infectious diseases and invasive species'. *Science Communication*, 26, 243–68.

Littlefield, R. S. and Quenette, A. M. (2007), 'Crisis leadership and Hurricane Katrina: the portrayal of authority by the media in natural disasters'. *Journal of Applied Communication Research*, 35, 26–47.

Nariyama, S. (2004), 'Subject ellipsis in English'. *Journal of Pragmatics*, 36, 237–64.

O'Connell, C. J. and Mills, A. J. (2003), 'Making sense of bad news: the media, sensemaking, and organizational crisis'. *Canadian Journal of Communication*, 28, 323–39.

Piotrowski, C. and Armstrong, T. R. (1998), 'Mass media preferences in disaster: a study of hurricane Danny'. *Social Behaviour and Personality,* 26, 341–46.

Pitt, M. (2008), *The Pitt Review: Lessons from the 2007 Floods: What People Need.* London: Cabinet Office.

Rundblad, G. (2007), 'Impersonal, general, and social: the use of metonymy versus passive voice in medical discourse'. *Written Communication*, 24, 250–77.

Rundblad, G., Knapton, O. and Hunter, P. R. (2010), 'Communication, perception and behaviour during a natural disaster involving a "Do Not Drink" and a subsequent "Boil Water" notice: a postal questionnaire study'. *BMC Public Health*, 10, 641.

Sky News (2007), 'Floods victims told boiled tap water safe'.

Spence, P. R., Lachlan, K., Burke, J. and Seeger, M. W. (2007), 'Media use and information needs of the disabled during a natural disaster'. *Journal of Healthcare for the Poor and Underserved,* 18, 394–404.

Steinberg, T. (2000), *Acts of God: The Unnatural History of Natural Disaster in America,* Oxford and New York, Oxford University Press.

Stock, P. V. (2007), 'Katrina and anarchy: a content analysis of a new disaster myth'. *Sociological Spectrum*, 27, 705–26.

*Stroud News and Journal* (2007), 'Tap water safe to drink at last'.

*The Citizen Gloucestershire* (2007a), 'Boiled tap water is safe to drink'.

—— (2007b), 'Drip, drip, hooray!'

—— (2007c), 'Oh water relief!'

The Environment Agency (2007), 'Review of 2007 summer floods'.

*The Gloucestershire Echo* (2007a), '3m litres of water to be distributed'.

—— (2007b), 'Bowser facts'.

—— (2007c), 'Bowsers run dry across the county'.

—— (2007d), 'Just who are these wasters?'

—— (2007e), 'The water is coming back – but not to drink'.

*The Telegraph* (2007), 'Swamped town told to conserve water'.

*The Times* (2007), 'Water back on in Tewkesbury, but don't drink it'.

Tierney, K., Bevc, C. and Kuligowski, E. (2006), 'Metaphors matter: disaster myths, media frames, and their consequences in Hurricane Katrina'. *The ANNALS of the American Academy of Political and Social Science*, 604, 57–81.

Voorhees, C. C. W., Vick, J. and Perkins, D. D. (2007), '"Came Hell and High Water": the intersection of Hurricane Katrina, the news media, race and poverty'. *Journal of Community and Applied Social Psychology*, 17, 415–29.

Wodak, R. (2006), 'Mediation between discourse and society: assessing cognitive approaches in CDA'. *Discourse Studies*, 8, 179–90.

**ENVIRONMENT**

# 25

# Ecolinguistics and Erasure

# Restoring the Natural World to Consciousness

*Arran Stibbe*
University of Gloucestershire

## 1 Introduction: Ecolinguistics

One of the ways that disciplines evolve and new sub-disciplines are formed is through a declaration by certain scholars that something of great importance has been overlooked, or *erased*, by the discipline. For instance, Ferber (2007: 265) claims that whiteness studies, in its concentration on race and privilege, has 'erased' gender; Barnet (2003) argues that technology has been 'erased' in cultural critique; Lutz (2009: 611) that women's writing is 'erased' in socio-cultural anthropology, and Frohmann (1992: 365) that the social dimension is 'erased' in cognitive information science. The declaration is accompanied by a demand that what has been erased is considered and incorporated in the discipline.

Closer to home, William Labov declared that the linguistics of his time had overlooked the embeddedness of language in society (although he did not use the term 'erased'). He demanded that social aspects were incorporated into the discipline, and founded the new sub-discipline of socio-linguistics (see Labov, 2001). Two things arose from this. Firstly, the discipline of linguistics could better explain language, since variation in language can only be understood with reference to social variables. But secondly, and equally importantly, it meant that linguistics could be applied practically to a range of social issues of pressing importance, such as ethnic discrimination in schools, and play a role in addressing these issues, something that Labov was evidently passionate about (see Labov, 1987).

Ecolinguistics recognizes that language is embedded in society, but goes further than that. It recognizes, like Lakoff and Johnson (1999), that language is embodied, i.e., embedded in beings who have bodies. But it goes further than that too, in recognizing that humans, human bodies, and human society are all embedded in larger natural systems – the complex interactions of humans, plants, animals, and the physical environment. The claim is that linguistics, or specifically Critical Discourse Studies, has been so focused on power relations between people, on sexism, racism and the multitude of other ways that some humans oppress other humans, that it has overlooked, or erased something of importance. And the relations of humans with other species and the physical environment are of great importance, since the continuation of all life depends on these ecological relationships. The environment *is* mentioned occasionally in passing – Fairclough (2004: 104) wrote that 'The unrestrained emphasis on growth also poses major threats to the environment' – but ecological issues have rarely been taken up and analysed in a sustained way within mainstream CDS.

Ecolinguistics is part of a larger ecological 'turn' within social science which includes ecopsychology (Fisher, 2002), ecofeminism (Pandey, 2011), ecocriticism (Garrard, 2011), ecopoetry (Bryson and Elder, 2002), and ecosociology (Stevens, 2012). All of these sub (or super) disciplines incorporate ecological aspects partly to better understand the phenomenon in question and partly to enable the academic discipline to play an active role in addressing key socio-ecological issues. For ecolinguistics, some theorists (e.g., Boguslawska-Tafelska, 2013) claim that an ecological perspective can help the discipline of linguistics come to a better overall understanding of how language works: that ecolinguistics can 'orchestrate all we observe about language and communication into one theory of language' (2013: 13). Others, writing from a 'language ecology' perspective (e.g., Bastardas-Boada, 2003, 2005), claim that ecolinguistics can improve the theoretical understanding of how languages relate to each other and the place in which they are spoken. However, of most relevance to Critical Discourse Studies are studies which apply an ecolinguistic perspective to practical issues of pressing importance in the twenty-first century such as environmental justice, water scarcity, energy security, and, in general, the gradual destruction of the ecological systems that support life. This is not a separate and distant goal from mainstream CDS, since when ecological systems fail the ones who are hit first and hardest are the already oppressed groups that are a key focus of CDS. Ecological destruction, then, is part of oppressive relations between humans and other humans, influencing others at the most basic level of the ability to continue living. There is no need for the term 'ecolinguistics', in fact, since it should be a matter of course that linguistics considers the embedding of human societies in larger natural systems, but it exists because of the erasure of nature in mainstream linguistics, as a movement to remind linguists of something important which has been overlooked.

A large part of the ecolinguistics literature focuses the discourses of environmentalism and scientific ecology, treating these discourses critically and exposing hidden messages which may work against the goals of the institutions or disciplines which employ them (e.g., Alexander, 2010; Harré et al., 1999; Stibbe, 2005). However, ecolinguistics is primarily about the *impact* that discourses have on the systems which support life, and so also analyses discourses such as those of consumerism, advertising or economic growth which have an impact, even if they are not specifically 'about' the environment or ecology at all (e.g., Halliday, 2001; Hogben, 2008; Slater, 2007). Indeed, the failure to consider the environment in neoclassical economics *is* the problem with this discourse, and what makes it so ecologically destructive. Beyond critiquing destructive discourses, however, is the search for alternative discourses which are based on very different assumptions from the mainstream discourses of industrial civilization. Bringhurst (2006), for instance, looks at Native American discourses, and Stibbe (2012) explores traditional Japanese discourses. The hope is to find ways of talking and thinking about the world that are useful in the current predicament that the world faces, either through adapting discourses from cultures around the world or creating new ones. This is a form of Positive Discourse Analysis (Martin, 2006), since the aim is to find discourses that are positive and argue for their promotion rather than seeking out discourses to resist.

Ecolinguistics, then, is a discipline that arises out of erasure – the perception that mainstream linguistics has forgotten, or overlooked, the embedding of humans in the larger systems that support life. It analyses discourses such as consumerism which are destructive in encouraging people to consume too much, destroy resources and produce waste. It analyses discourses such as those of environmentalism which attempt to deal with the ecological destruction but often contain hidden assumptions which may reduce their effectiveness. And it seeks alternative ways of thinking and talking about the world that are useful in addressing the overarching issues that humans face as the ecological systems which support life are damaged.

The concept of 'erasure', however, goes far beyond the founding of the sub-discipline of ecolinguistics. The erasure of the natural world is something that occurs widely across a large number of the discourses that structure industrial civilization. Detailed linguistic examination of erasure is a potentially useful, though underdeveloped, tool for Critical Discourse Studies in general, and ecolinguistic ones in particular. This chapter firstly contributes to the development of the concept of 'erasure' and then applies it across a wide range of discourses from those of neoclassical economics to haiku poetry. The aim is to illustrate what an ecolinguistic approach to CDS looks like in practice, and also to develop the analytic tool of erasure for future use in ecolinguistics and beyond.

## 2 The nature of erasure

The concept of discursive erasure is frequently used in social science to denote the absence of something important – something that is present in reality but is overlooked or deliberately ignored in a particular discourse. Namaste (2000) uses the term to describe how transsexual people are represented as figurative tokens in the media rather than as embodied people living their lives, and how they are made invisible by social policies that have no recognition of their existence. In addition, she states:

> Finally, and most powerfully, 'erasure' can refer specifically to the very act of nullifying transsexuality – a process whereby transsexuality is rendered impossible. As Ros and Gobeil elucidate, the use of 'men' and 'women' undermines the very possibility of a TS/TG [transsexual/transgender] position. Within this site, transsexuals cannot exist at all.
>
> (Namaste, 2000: 52)

Young and Meyer (2005: 1144) use erasure in this third sense in their analysis of the 'erasure of the sexual-minority person in public health discourse':

> Men who have sex with men (MSM) and women who have sex with women (WSW) are purportedly neutral terms commonly used in public health discourse. However, they are problematic because they obscure social dimensions of sexuality; undermine the self-labelling of lesbian, gay, and bisexual people; and do not sufficiently describe variations in sexual behaviour.

It is not just forms of sexual identity that are analysed using the concept of erasure – French et al. (2008) consider the 'material, discursive and political erasure of bank and building society branches in Britain', arguing that government discourses have ignored the issue of physical access to financial services despite its importance in financial exclusion. In a very different field, Everett and Neu (2002: 5) examine the discourse of ecological modernization and argue that 'the intersection of ecological and social realms is ignored and issues of social justice are effectively erased . . . in other words "ecological modernisation" is a discourse of the status quo'.

The term 'erasure' then, is used in a variety of ways to indicate that something important has been ignored, sidelined or excluded from consideration within a discourse. Erasure, however, is something intrinsic to the very nature of discourse. In representing and constructing areas of social life discourses will always be partial, will always bring certain elements together into a configuration, while leaving out a whole universe of other elements. The concept of erasure only becomes meaningful when combined with its counterpart, which could be called *re-minding*. Re-minding is a linguistic act where an actor surveys the universe of elements that have been excluded from a particular discourse, declares that one of these elements is important, that the discourse is 'erasing' it from consciousness, and demands that the discourse brings it back to mind. Erasure, then, is not so much a property of discourse, or a conscious act of exclusion and marginalization by the group responsible for the discourse, but part of a discursive struggle where actors attempt to create discursive change by declaring that something of importance has been excluded. What that 'something of importance' is depends on the goals and interests of those who are doing the 're-minding'.

There are a variety of forms that erasure can take, and this chapter will focus on three main forms. The first, which will be called 'the void', is the most obvious and the one most frequently described in social science: 'something important' is entirely absent and not mentioned in a discourse at all. The second type draws from the work of Baudrillard, who describes the following hierarchy of representation:

- The image is the reflection of a profound reality.

- The image masks and denatures a profound reality.

- The image masks the *absence* of a profound reality.

- The image has no relation to any reality whatsoever: it is its own pure simulacrum.

(adapted from Baudrillard, 1994: 6)

The first of these levels assumes a pre-discursive reality that is represented in a direct way – with no erasure. The third and fourth levels are of great interest for ecolinguistics, given that so much of what occurs in political and institutional discourse bears no relation to anything that exists within physical reality, but are not specifically erasure. It is the second level that is most useful here – 'The image masks and denatures a profound reality' since it suggests a form of erasure where 'something important' is represented in discourse, but in a distorted way as a 'mask' which erases its true nature. This second type of erasure, then, we will call 'the mask'.

Baudrillard's top level of representation, where discourses transparently and directly reflect a pre-existing reality, is problematic, since the complexity of pre-discursive reality is far greater than the representational resources of humans. Instead, it is useful to think of discourses as always erasing what they are describing, but doing so to a greater or lesser extent. When discourses include mention of 'something important' but still manage to erase it by representing it in a vague, weak or abstract way, then this is the third type of erasure, which we will call 'the trace'. The image is of pencil marks being erased while a trace of their former presence remains in the indentations in the page. The 'trace' can be stronger or weaker depending on how vividly the expressions in the discourse evoke 'something important'.

Erasure happens at multiple levels. At the lowest level, 'something important' is erased from sentences and clauses through a range of linguistic devices including metaphors, metonymies, nominalizations and hyponyms (as will be described shortly). If 'something important' is erased from multiple sentences then this starts to build up to erasure from the text as a whole. Texts, in turn, draw from discourses (characteristic ways of speaking and writing the world in particular areas of social life), and it is the erasure of 'something important' from the discourse that is the key concern, since discourses are what shape the society we live in. Analysis therefore starts on the lowest level, examining the sentences and clauses in a specific text, but also looks for larger patterns across the text as a whole and the discourse as a whole. As an illustration, analysis may start by looking at the erasure of the natural world in specific sentences in a neoclassical economics textbook, discover patterns of erasure across the book, then look at other books, reports and economics news articles and eventually gain insights into the erasure of the natural world within the discourse of neoclassical economics in general.

The relevant elements of erasure, then, are a) an area of social life such as economics or environmentalism, b) a discourse, which is a typical way of speaking about the world in that area which encodes a particular worldview, c) 'something important', which is entirely missing from the worldview, or present only as a faint trace, or present in a distorted version, and d) an actor who declares that 'something important' has been erased and insists that it be brought back into the discourse.

# 3 The erasure of nature

A large body of evidence (e.g., GEO, 2012; MEA1, 2005) reveals the increasing material erasure of the natural world by humans – forests are clear cut, rivers and oceans are polluted, species are made extinct, coral reefs destroyed, vast expanses of ice are melted. At the same time, and by no means coincidently, those who are causing the most destruction are finding themselves distanced from the natural world, living increasingly within the discursively constructed world of the internet, television, games, books, reports, newspapers and museums. Discourses can erase the natural world not materially, but from consciousness. Not all discourses erase to the same degree though – some provide vivid images which encourage people to respect and protect the natural world, some provide just a faint hint of the natural world, while some omit it all together.

The analyses in this section put the model of erasure described in the previous section into action through exploring the discursive erasure of the natural world – the animals, plants and physical environment that interact together to form the ecological systems that life depends on. A full methodology would consist of discourse analysis of a large range of texts that are characteristic of a discourse, examining the forms of erasure across the texts, and revealing overall patterns of significance. This chapter, however, aims to give enough depth of analysis to reveal the technical workings of erasure in discourse but with enough breadth to reveal the erasure of the natural world in a range of discourses.

## 3.1 The void: Traditional economics

The first kind of erasure is 'the void', where the natural world is completely omitted by a discourse. Traditional neoclassical economic discourses are frequently accused of failing to consider the ecological embedding of human economies (e.g., Williams and McNeill, 2005). The standard textbook, *Microeconomics* (Estrin and Dietrich, 2012), for instance, contains no discussion of the dependence on and effect of human economic activity on the environment, animals, plants or ecology in its 554 pages, aside from occasional mention of externalities and a brief discussion of what it calls the 'so-called problem of pollution' (491). The following extract from the textbook illustrates the erasure of the natural world:

> It hardly needs pointing out that the goods and services that consumers purchase do not simply materialise out of the blue. In large measure they have to be produced . . . The essential fact about production is so obvious that it hardly needs stating: it involves the use of services of various sorts to generate output . . . Clearly the manner in which production is organised has important social and political as well as economic aspects.
>
> (Estrin and Dietrich, 2012: 169)

In this extract the 'working up of facticity' (Potter, 1996) is extremely high: 'it hardly needs pointing out . . . essential fact . . . obvious . . . hardly needs stating . . . clearly', as if the discourse was merely pointing out pre-existing truths rather than playing a role in constructing social reality. Something important is missing in this social construction though: goods are described as produced by 'services' without mention of what is destroyed, harmed or disturbed to make the goods, i.e., the animals, plants and ecosystems used in or affected by production. The term *production* is nominalized from 'x produces y', which even in its verbal form does not include what is destroyed to make y. It is only in the form 'x produces y out of z' that 'z' appears, although in this slot 'z' is most likely to be a mass noun like 'wood' rather than a count noun like 'trees'. The nominalized expression *production*, then, can erase the natural world without a trace. Williams and McNeill (2005: 8) confirm that the above text is not just an isolated example:

> Raw materials used as inputs in the production process, and any other services provided by the natural environment, were omitted from consideration altogether. Amazingly, they still are. First year economics students are still taught in almost all of the currently popular textbooks that businesses manufacture their products using only labour and machines!

The list that the microeconomics textbook gives of the important aspects of how production is organized consists of 'social and political as well as economic aspects'. This erases, by total omission, the ecological aspects of production. If the ecological systems that support life are erased from economic discourse then they cannot be taken into account in economic decisions, with significant implications for how the natural world is exploited.

Ecological economics, on the other hand, is a discipline which explicitly challenges the discourse of conventional economics. The textbook *Ecological Economics: Principles and Applications* states that:

to the extent that nature and the environment are considered at all [in conventional economics], they are considered as parts or sectors of the macro-economy . . . Ecological economics, by contrast, envisions the macroeconomy as part of a larger enveloping and sustaining Whole, namely the Earth, its atmosphere and its ecosystems.

(Daly and Farley, 2004: 15)

The discourse of ecological economics is an attempt at 're-minding' – bringing animals, plants and ecosystems back into consideration through statements such as the following:

we cannot make something from nothing hence all human production must ultimately be based on resources provided by nature.

(Daly and Farley, 2004: 67)

Ecological economics is still based on the discourse of economics though, and tends to bring the natural world into an economic frame (using Lakoff's 2009 concept of 'frame') rather than placing economics within an ecological frame. The following example is typical:

The structural elements of an ecosystem are stocks of biotic and abiotic resources (minerals, water, trees, other plants, and animals) which when combined together generate ecosystem functions, or services. The use of a biological stock at a nonsustainable level in general also depletes a corresponding fund and the services it provides.

(Daly and Farley, 2004: 107)

The terms *stocks, resources, depletes, services* and *funds* combine together to strongly activate the economic frame. The terms *biotic, abiotic, ecosystem* and *biological* activate an ecological frame. However, the economic frame is primary since the economic words form the head of noun phrases while the ecological terms are merely modifiers (*biotic* resources, *ecosystem* services, and *biological* stock).

Treating the living world in the same discursive way as a stock of objects removes (from consciousness) what is unique about life such as interaction and interdependence, which ironically is what ecology is all about. This could be considered a form of the second type of erasure, 'the mask', where animals and plants have been erased and replaced with a distorted version of themselves (the stock of biological resources).

## 3.2  The mask: Animal product industries

Intensive animal agriculture and the discourses which justify, sustain and construct it, is of particular interest to ecolinguistics because of the scale of negative environmental impacts caused by factory farming (see WSPA, 2008). To create a system which treats animals inhumanely and is environmentally destructive requires work to be done by discourse to erase animals as living beings and focus narrowly on economic factors instead (Stibbe, 2001, 2003). A key device is metaphor, and the following are stark examples from the 1970s:

> The breeding sow should be thought of as, and treated as, a valuable piece of machinery whose function is to pump out baby pigs like a sausage machine.
>
> (Walls Meat Company manager in Singer, 1990: 126)

> If the sow is considered a pig manufacturing unit then improved management at farrowing on through weaning will result in more pigs weaned.
>
> (US Department of Agriculture in Singer, 1990: 126)

These metaphors explicitly encourage the reader to think of pigs as machines and manufacturing units, creating conceptual blends (Turner and Fauconnier, 2002). The resulting pig-machine blend or pig-manufacturing-unit blend can be thought of as a 'mask' – a distorted version which erases actual pigs as living beings.

The pork industry no longer uses strong metaphors like those above, perhaps because they are so frequently quoted by activists such as Singer in denouncing the industry. Instead the Pork Industry Handbook uses expressions like *structurally sound*, *boar power*, *water intake*, or *sow breakdown* referring to the animals, which more subtly establishes a pig-is-machine metaphor (Stibbe, 2003: 384). Another metaphor that works towards erasing pigs is the following example from the Pork Industry Handbook, which entirely redefines the 'health' of a pig:

> Health is the condition of an animal with regard to the performance of its vital functions. The vital functions of the pig are reproduction and growth. They are vital because they are major contributors to the economic sustainability of the pork production enterprise.
>
> (*Pork Industry Handbook* in Stibbe, 2003: 380)

In this example, individual pigs as beings are erased by the metaphorical construct of the 'pork production enterprise'. The term 'vital functions' which would usually be functions like circulation and an immune system that are essential for the life of an individual animal has been redefined narrowly as the functions that keep the enterprise profitable. The metaphorical creation of the 'pork production enterprise' as a living being with vital functions obscures or 'masks' the individual animals.

The following examples are from other intensive animal industries and illustrate how metonymy is used to erase animals:

**(a)** Catching *broilers* is a backbreaking, dirty and unpleasant job.

**(b)** [There is] susceptibility to ascites and flipover . . . in the female *breeder*

**(c)** There's not enough power to stun the *beef* . . . you'd end up cutting its head off while the *beef* was still alive.

**(d)** Exciting times for *beef* practitioners

(examples of industry discourse from Stibbe, 2001: 153)

In (a) live birds are named and referred to by a cooking method, in (b) by their function, in (c) cows are referred to by their dead flesh, and in (d) veterinarians specializing in bovine medicine are called 'beef practitioners' rather than 'cow practitioners' (Stibbe, 2001: 154).

There is also a range of ways that industry discourse erases animals by using vocabulary that is typically used for objects and applying it to living beings: *damage* instead of *injury* in the expression 'bird damage', *product* instead of *bodies* in 'product is 100% cut-up', *destruction* and *batch* in 'Isolation of salmonella will result in the destruction of the flock slaughter of the batch' and *harvest* in 'an automatic broiler harvesting machine' (Stibbe, 2001: 155). This results in an animal-object blend that acts in the same way as machine metaphors to distract attention away from animals as living beings.

Glenn describes how advertising is used in the external discourse of the animal product industry to erase from consumers' minds the grim conditions that animals are kept in at factory farms:

Advertisements' representations of 'speaking animals' who are selling the end 'products' of the brutal processes they endure in the factory farm system serve . . . a dual discursive purpose. The first purpose is to sell products, and the second role is . . . to make the nonhuman animal victims disappear.

(Glenn, 2004: 72)

In general, the creation of 'masks' to disguise the nature of animals in the meat industry could help those involved distance themselves from the impact of intensive confinement methods of farming on animal wellbeing and the environment, and focus only on economic aspects instead.

## 3.3 *The trace: ecological discourse*

Ecological discourse is, of course, all about animals, plants and the physical environment. It would seem strange at first to analyse how it erases the natural world, but erasure is not a binary all/nothing phenomenon and can occur to different degrees. Of particular importance is 'the trace' – when discourses represent the natural world but do so in a way which obscures, leaving a faint trace rather than a vivid image. This section briefly examines five reports that are characteristic of a particular type of ecological discourse – public facing summaries of the state of ecosystems for policymakers. The reports are *Ecosystems and Human Well-being: General Synthesis* (MEA1, 2005); *Ecosystems and Human Well-being: Biodiversity Synthesis* (MEA2, 2005); *The UK National Ecosystem Assessment* (NEA, 2011); *The Economics of Ecosystems and Biodiversity* (TEEB, 2010) and the *Impacts of Climate Change on Biodiversity, Ecosystems and Ecosystems Services* (NCA, 2012). For convenience these will be referred to simply as MEA1, MEA2, NEA, TEEB and NCA respectively.

The reports were selected as representing an influential discourse that potentially shapes how scientists, policy-makers and the general readers of the reports respond to major issues that humanity is facing. The focus of the analysis is the degree to which animals, plants and the natural world are erased in the discourse of the reports. To understand why this is important it is useful to give quotes from three of the reports themselves:

1   birds of all kinds, butterflies, trees such as oak, beech and birch, mammals such as badgers, otters and seals . . . are of great cultural significance and . . . undoubtedly have a huge hold over the popular imagination.

(NEA: 19)

2   Recognizing value in ecosystems, landscapes, species and other aspects of biodiversity . . . is sometimes sufficient to ensure conservation and sustainable use.

(TEEB: 11)

3   Ultimately, the level of biodiversity that survives on Earth will be determined not just by utilitarian considerations but to a significant extent by ethical concerns, including considerations of the intrinsic values of species.

(MEA1: 58)

In other words, people are more likely to respect the natural world and work towards preserving it if they value it deeply for its own sake at an ethical level, and they feel strongly about things they can concretely imagine such as butterflies, oak, badgers and seals. We would therefore expect the outward-facing discourse of ecology to try to encourage this respect by vividly representing the myriad species of plants and animals in ways which capture people's imagination and stimulate an ethical response.

This section will argue that despite the quotations above and some explicit statements such as 'biodiversity and ecosystems also have intrinsic value' (MEA2), the discourse of the reports erases animals and plants and the natural world, turning them into a faint trace that is unlikely to arouse people's imagination or care. The question is whether the discourse paints a picture of humans as part of a living world teeming with a diversity of animals and plants, or a lonely world where humans are surrounded only by 'natural capital', 'biological stock' and 'biomass'; by trees or 'cubic meters of timber'?

Returning to the discourse of the reports, it is possible to describe a number of linguistic ways that animals and plants are erased and describe a hierarchy of erasure, from the most vivid to the most obscuring. The most vivid representations of nature are the photographs – birds (TEEB, NEA), butterflies (NEA, MEA2), bees (NEA), fish (MEA2), trees (TEEB, NEA) and a hippo (TEEB), all close-up and personal, with animals sometimes looking out at the viewer in a 'demand' picture (one which demands a relationship between viewer and subject). The images are two-dimensional and static, so erase some features of the actual animals and trees (as all representations do), but still provide detailed images of individual animals and trees in a photorealistic way, forcing them into the minds of viewers.

The statement 'trees such as oak, beech and birch, mammals such as badgers, otters and seals' (NEA: 19) also represents the trees and animals quite vividly since the species are concretely imaginable (the 'basic' level in Lakoff's 1987 terms). Still, nothing about the word 'oak' conveys the myriad shapes of the actual trees, their colours, smells, textures or the complexity of their forms, so there is (as always) some erasure. These two forms of representation (photographs and specific species names) show the minimum amount of erasure, but are actually rare within the documents – the primary ways that animals, plants and the natural world are represented consist of much stronger forms of erasure.

The first stronger form of erasure occurs when superordinates replace the names of species: *birds* (NEA: 23), *mammals* (NEA: 23), *amphibians* (MEA2: 4) and *fish* (MEA1: 4); then *plants* (MEA2: 11) and *animals* (MEA2: 11); then *species* (NCA: 1); then *flora* (NEA: 48) and *fauna* (NEA: 48), right up to *organisms* (MEA2: 1). These progressively get more abstract and less imaginable – from *badger* which brings to mind many characteristics of a particular kind of animal to *organism* which erases all but the feature of being alive. Still higher up the ladder of erasure/abstraction are the terms *biodiversity* (MEA2: 1), *components of biodiversity* (MEA2: 2), *assemblages of species* (NCA: 1), *ecological complexes* (MEA2: 2) and *ecosystems* (TEEB: 7). These represent the coming together of a diversity of animals and plants but the imaginable individuals are buried deeply within the abstractions.

Terms such as *badger*, *mammal*, *species*, *organism*, *fauna* and *biodiversity* still remain within the semantic domain of living beings, however, which is as expected since the hyponymy relations between them are part of the semantics of the words themselves. However, as Fairclough (2003: 130) describes, texts can set up their own relations of hyponymy 'on the fly', and in doing so can place living beings as co-hyponyms of inanimate objects. The expression 'extraction of timber, fish, water and other resources' (NCA: 2) sets up timber, fish and water as equivalent co-hyponyms under the superordinate category of 'resources' – a category which includes both living beings and non-living materials. This erases the distinctiveness of living beings – draining the life out of them by including them in a list of resources along with inanimate objects. The expressions 'soils, air, water and biological resources' (TEEB: 10), 'terrestrial, marine and freshwater resources' (NEA: 20), and 'trade in commodities such as grain, fish, and timber' (MEA1: 59) carry out a similar function. Even biodiversity is set up as a resource in 'biodiversity and other ecological resources' (NCA: 1). The expression 'our ecological resources' (NCA: 1) uses the pronoun 'our' to erase the other lifeforms we share the planet with by turning them into human possessions rather than beings in their own right.

The complex noun phrase 'provisioning services such as food, water, timber and fibre' (MEA2: 1) erases animals and plants firstly by turning them into co-hyponyms of 'provisioning services', and secondly by burying them within mass nouns (food, timber and fibre). They are still there, but only as a trace. The process of 'massification' is a strong form of erasure, so trees become 'timber' (NEA: 7), then 'fuel wood' (TEEB: 17), then 'cubic meters of timber' (TEEB: 12), then 'wood biomass' (NEA: 18), and at the top level of erasure '27 million tonnes per year of . . . biomass imports' (NEA: 38). When trees, plants and animals are represented in mass nouns, they are erased, becoming mere tonnages of stuff.

Another massification term is 'natural capital'. The expression 'forests and living coral reefs are critical components of natural capital' (TEEB: 7) starts off with the concretely imaginable forests and reefs but then turns them into the unimaginable mass term 'capital', which later becomes 'stocks of natural capital' (TEEB: 7). TEEB is explicitly about the economics of ecosystems, so it is not surprising that it draws from the discourse of ecological economics mentioned above. However, the other documents also contain similar expressions, e.g., 'the value of the UK's natural capital is not fully realised' (NEA: 47), 'ecosystem assets' (NEA: 73), 'natural capital assets' (MEA2: 6), 'biological resources' (MEA2: 7), and 'stocks of natural ecosystem resources' (NEA: 4).

There are also representations which contain traces of animals and plants by mentioning the places where they live, but not the dwellers themselves: 'urban greenspace amenity' (NEA: 51) includes trees and plants as the merest of traces in the 'green' of 'greenspace'. The terms 'living and physical environments' (NEA: 4) and 'environmental resources' (TEEB: 20) represent animals and plants as part of an all-encompassing environment surrounding humans rather than existing in their own right. The expressions 'a biome's native habitat' (MEA2: 2) and 'the diversity of benthic habitats' (MEA2: 8) represent what Chris Philo and Chris Wilbert (2000) call 'beastly places', though without the beasts. Likewise 'seasonally grazed floodplains' (NEA2: 23) contains a trace of animals, for who else is doing the grazing? And a hint of plants, for what else is being grazed? The word 'types' takes the erasure up a level in expressions such as 'aquatic habitat types' (NEA: 10).

Another way that animals and plants are erased is through being referred to metonymically by the function they are serving within an ecosystem: 'pollinators', 'primary producers', 'dispersers', or the slightly more vivid 'pollinating insects' (NEA: 19). Fish are erased through taking the place of a modifier in noun phrases such as 'fish catch' (MEA1: 103), 'fish stocks' (MEA1: 6), 'fishing technology' (NEA: 55), 'fish consumption' (MEA1: 103) and 'fish production' (MEA1: 17). When fish are modifiers of other nouns, they have been pushed to the periphery, the clause being about something else. And the erasure is taken even further with the expression 'fisheries' (MEA2: 5), where the fish themselves remain in the morphology of the word, but just a trace within a large commercial operation. Fish are also erased by metaphor in the expression 'commonly harvested fish species' (MEA2: 3) or 'The fish being harvested' (MEA1: 15), since they are made equivalent to plants rather than being treated as animals.

The overall pattern across the reports is clear: there are visual illustrations and vivid expressions towards the top of the hierarchy of erasure (e.g., badgers, oaks, otters) but these are few and far between. For the most part the reports erase the animals, plants, forests, rivers and oceans even though they are what the reports are all about, and even though four of the five reports acknowledge that people are encouraged to protect the natural world if they find intrinsic value within it. An expression like 'ecosystem structural elements such as biomass' (NCA: 1) is still referring to animals and plants, but they remain only as the faintest of traces, and certainly not as something of intrinsic value.

# 4  Re-minding

Re-minding is the opposite or counterpart of erasure – if erasure pushes 'something important' out of consciousness then re-minding is an attempt to bring it back into consciousness. Critical Discourse Studies can themselves be a form of re-minding. By critiquing the erasure of 'something important' in a particular discourse they draw attention to what is missing, and by detailing the linguistic ways that it has been erased they provide those who produce the discourse with ways to un-do the erasure. The following quotation comes from an animal products industry journal *Poultry Science* and is a response to critical discourse analysis of industry discourse:

Scholars (Stibbe, 2003; Linzey, 2006) have suggested that industry discourse characterizes animals in ways that objectify them and obscure morally relevant characteristics such as animal sentience . . . Although an analysis of discourse may seem odd and irrelevant to animal and poultry science, this type of examination is illuminating . . . It may be necessary to reconsider several aspects of animal production relative to ideology, discourse, and practice . . . a real ethic of care and respect for animals must be embodied not just in our practices but also in the internal and external discourse of animal agriculture.

(Croney and Reynnells, 2008)

In this case, the discourse analysis reminds the industry of the erasure of animals in its own discourse and prompts a response calling for changes not only in the language used by the industry but also in its practices.

Similarly, there has been a positive reaction to discourse analysis of ecological reports by conservationists and ecologists. A leading author of the Millennium Ecosystem Assessment, on receiving a critical discourse analysis of the assessment, commented that 'I very much appreciate this type of analysis and also think that the conclusions are quite correct . . . ideally in the future assessments might be able to provide a better balance' (in Stibbe, 2012: 100). The balance in question is between making a case for politicians and finance ministers in the language they are most familiar with and representing the natural world vividly in ways that inspire people to value it for its own sake.

Another form of re-minding consists of seeking out alternative discourses which represent animals, plants and nature in vivid and direct ways with the minimum of erasure. The conservationist Wain (2007: 1) shows concern about the erasure of nature in conservation discourse, describing 'the invasion of misguided targets and measurement in conservation, and the associated vacuous management culture which can sever the link with real wildlife and real places'. Instead, he recommends a specific book which draws from an alternative discourse:

Cue another recent book which makes the real thing vivid – Jim Crumley's *Brother Nature*. Crumley takes us up-close to ospreys, kites, wild swans, beavers, and even bears. He reveals the savage beauty of nature in the landscapes of his beloved Highland edge.

(Wain, 2007: 1)

Recommending particular books could be considered a form of ecocriticism (Garrard, 2011) – the branch of literature that provides ecological criticism of books and other cultural artefacts. Of more interest for a discourse analysis approach, however, is analysis of the wider discourses that specific books draw from, revealing the linguistic techniques which enable the discourse to represent animals, plants and the natural world vividly in ways that encourage people to care about them.

Another place to search for alternative discourses is traditional cultures from around the world. Stibbe (2007), for instance, analyses the discourse of nature haiku and describes a range of discursive devices which bring animals, plants and the natural world strongly into the consciousness of readers and encourage respect and consideration. The devices include avoidance of metaphor, giving plants and animals agentive roles, using the adverb 'also' to draw out identities between humans and animals, and using specific species names (e.g., sparrow) rather than abstractions. It is worth comparing probably the most famous haiku of all by Basho:

| | | |
|---|---|---|
| furuike ya / | kawazu tobikomu / | mizu no oto |
| an old pond / | a frog leaps in / | sound of the water |

with a made-up equivalent in environmental discourse:

an old freshwater habitat / a biotic component leaps in / sound of the aquatic resource

The first strongly brings nature into consciousness by using the highly imaginable basic level (frog), making the frog the agent of an active material process, and creating multisensorial images (both visual and audial). The second erases – pushing nature out of mind through metaphor and abstraction. That is not to say that economic textbooks or environmental reports should be written in haiku, rather that some of the patterns of linguistic features used in the discourse of haiku could be adapted and applied to create a better balance between abstraction and imaginable specifics.

One final way of 're-minding' is to go beyond critiquing existing discourses, and beyond searching for currently existing alternative discourses, and instead creating new alternative discourses. David Abram's work attempts to do that. Abram is concerned with the impact of written language in severing our connection with (i.e., erasing) the natural world. He states:

There can be no question of simply abandoning literacy, of turning away from all writing. Our task, rather, is that of taking up the written word, with all of its potency, and patiently, carefully, writing language back into the land. Our craft is that of releasing the budded, earthy intelligence of our words, freeing them to respond to the speech of the things themselves – to the green uttering-forth of leaves from the spring branches.

(Abram, 1996: 273)

This writing carries out a dual purpose of calling for writing to reflect and evoke rather than erase the natural world, and demonstrating what one form of this kind of writing might look like.

# 5 Conclusion

Discourses are ultimately limited in their power to represent and construct the social world. The models at their heart are simplifications which leave out a whole universe of possibilities in their construction of a narrow part of social life. There are many discourses which focus on humans as they interact with other humans but entirely ignore the interaction of humans with other animals, plants and the physical environment. For some of those discourses, the narrow focus is appropriate and necessary, but for some it is dangerous. If economic discourses overlook the embedding of humans in the natural world then this is dangerous because certain forms of economic activity undermine the conditions necessary for the continuing survival of human societies (as well as their economies, of course). But there are deeper and more complex types and forms of erasure, which this chapter just began to explore. There is erasure when the natural world is mentioned in a discourse but in a distorted way which draws attention from its true nature, opening it up for exploitation. When animals, plants, forests and rivers are turned into machines, objects, biological resources or stocks of natural capital then this shuts down ethical considerations of the intrinsic value of what is being destroyed. Then there is erasure where a trace remains, a subtle hint, rather than a strong and vivid image – animals are still there in abstract terms like *biotic component* or *fauna*, and trees and plants are still there in *timber* and *flora*, but only in a faded form.

Re-minding is the task of bringing the natural world back into consciousness – seeking out the key discourses where the erasure of the ecological embedding of humans is dangerous, and seeking to intervene in those discourses. This cannot rely just on conscientization – on making people aware that assumptions in dominant discourses are oppressing them and encouraging them to resist. Ecological issues are somewhat different to those typically analysed in Critical Discourse Studies because there is a time and space gap between oppressive acts (overconsumption, ecological destruction and waste) and the suffering caused to groups of humans. Also many of those harmed first from ecological destruction are not human at all but other animals and life forms without a voice. However, those responsible for destructive discourses *are* human, which means that there will be some with a sense of ethics who do not want to cause harm to other animals, forests, rivers and to humans in the future. A well evidenced argument for why it would be beneficial for a particular discourse to stop erasing the natural world, together with detailed linguistic description of how the erasure takes place in the discourse, could help persuade and provide practical help to those who are in a position to change the discourse. Encouraging destructive discourses to erase the natural world a bit less is only a starting point, however. Ideally the aim is to lead to greater discursive change where a wide range of discourses begin vividly representing the natural world in ways which inspire people to take actions which protect and preserve it.

Ecolinguistics, then, is an attempt to re-mind linguists that human language is embedded in human society, and that human societies are embedded in, and entirely dependent on, larger natural systems. Practically this leads to a range of lines of enquiry, the primary one being a form of Critical Discourse Studies that aims towards the goal of protecting the systems that support life. One useful tool within Critical Discourse Studies is the framework of *erasure* and *re-minding*, and this chapter has developed these concepts and applied them illustratively to a range of discourses from an ecolinguistic perspective. Overall, it is time to consider the natural world across the whole range of activities that we, as humans, take part in, because if the natural world is ignored, is erased from discourse, it will be physically erased, and so, ultimately, will we.

# References

Abram, D. (1996), *The Spell of the Sensuous*. New York: Vintage.

Alexander, R. (2010), *Framing Discourse on the Environment: A Critical Discourse Approach*. London: Routledge.

Barnet, B. (2003), 'The erasure of technology in cultural critique'. *Fibreculture*, 1. http://journal.fibreculture.org/issue1/issue1_barnet.html

Bastardas-Boada, A. (2003), 'Ecology and diversity: a comparative trip from biology to linguistics'. in A. Boudreau et al. (eds). *Colloque International sur l'Écologie des Langues*. Paris: L'Harmattan, pp. 33–43.

——(2005), 'Linguistic sustainability and language ecology'. *Language and Ecology*. www.ecoling.net/articles

Baudrillard, J. (1994), *Simulacra and Simulation*. Ann Arbor: University of Michigan Press.

Boguslawska-Tafelska, M. (2013), *Towards an Ecology of Language, Communication and the Mind*. Frankfurt: Peter Lang.

Bringhurst, R. (2006), *The Tree of Meaning: Language, Mind and Ecology*. Berkeley: Counterpoint.

Bryson, J. and Elder, J. (eds) (2002), *Ecopoetry: A Critical Introduction*. Salt Lake City: University of Utah Press.

Croney C. C. and Reynnells R. D. (2008), 'The ethics of semantics: do we clarify or obfuscate reality to influence perceptions of farm animal production'. *Poultry Science*, 87: 387–91.

Daly, H. and Farley, J. (2004), *Ecological Economics: Principles and Applications*. Washington, DC: Island Press.

Estrin, S. and Dietrich, M. (2012), *Microeconomics*. London: Pearson.

Everett, J. and Neu, D. (2002), 'Ecological modernization and the limits of environmental accounting?' *Accounting Forum*, 24(1), 5–29.

Fairclough, N. (2003), *Analysing Discourse: Textual Analysis for Social Research*. London: Routledge.

——(2004), 'Critical discourse analysis in researching language in the new capitalism: overdetermination, transdisciplinary and textual analysis' in C. Harrison and L. Young (eds), *Systemic Linguistics and Critical Discourse Analysis*. London: Continuum, pp. 103–22

Ferber, A. (2007), 'Whiteness studies and the erasure of gender'. *Sociology Compass*, 1(1), 265–82.

Fisher, A. (2002), *Radical Ecopsychology: Psychology in the Service of Life*. State University of New York Press.

French, S., Leyshon, A. and Signoretta, P. (2008), '"All gone now": the material, discursive and political erasure of bank and building society branches in Britain'. *Antipode*, 40(1), 79–101.

Frohmann (1992), 'The power of images: a discourse analysis of the cognitive viewpoint'. *Journal of Documentation*, 48(4), 365–86.

Garrard, G. (2011), *Ecocriticism*. London: Routledge.

GEO (2012), *Global Environment Outlook*. United Nations Environment Programme. Available at: http://www.unep.org/geo/geo5.asp (accessed 1 January 2014).

Glenn C. (2004), 'Constructing consumables and consent: a critical analysis of factory farm industry discourse'. *Journal of Communication Inquiry*, 28(1), 63–81.

Halliday, M. (2001), 'New ways of meaning: the challenge to applied linguistics' in Alwin Fill and Peter Mühlhäusler (eds), *The Ecolingusitics Reader*. London: Continuum 175–202.

Harré, R., Brockmeier, J. and Mühlhäusler, P. (1999), *Greenspeak: A Study of Environmental Discourse*. London: Sage.

Hogben, S. (2008), 'It's (not) easy being green: unpacking visual rhetoric and environmental claims in car, energy and utility advertisements in the UK (2007–08)1'. *Language & Ecology*, 3(1), www.ecoling.net/articles (accessed 1 January 2014).

Labov, W. (1987), *How I Got into Linguistics, and What I Got Out of It*. Available at:www.ling.upenn.edu/ wlabov/Papers/Howlgot.html (accessed 1 January 2014).

——(2001), *Principles of Linguistic Change Vol 2: Social Factors*. New York: Wiley-Blackwell.

Lakoff, G. (1987), *Women, Fire and Dangerous Things: What Categories Reveal about the Mind*. Chicago, IL: University of Chicago Press.

——(2009), *The Political Mind: A Cognitive Scientist's Guide to your Brain and its Politics*. London: Penguin.

Lakoff, G. and Johnson, M. (1999), *Philosophy in the Flesh: The Embodied Mind and its Challenge to Western Thought*. New York: Basic Books.

Lutz, C. (2009), 'The erasure of women's writing in sociocultural anthropology'. *American Ethnologist*, 17(4), 611–27.

Martin, J. (2006), 'Positive discourse analysis: power, solidarity and change'. *Journal of English Studies*, 4(14), 21–35.

MEA1 (2005), *Ecosystems and Human Well-being: General Synthesis*. Millenium Ecosystem Assessment. Available at: http://www.unep.org/maweb/en/Synthesis.aspx (accessed 1 January 2014).

MEA2 (2005), *Ecosystems and Human Well-being: Biodiversity Synthesis*. Millenium Ecosystem Assessment. Available at: http://www.unep.org/maweb/en/Synthesis.aspx (accessed 1 January 2014).

Namaste, V. (2000), *Invisible Lives: The Erasure of Transsexual and Transgendered People*. Chicago, IL: University of Chicago Press.

NCA (2012), *Impacts of Climate Change on Biodiversity, Ecosystems and Ecosystem Services: Technical Input to the 2013 National Climate Assessment*. United States Global Change Research Program. Available at: http://downloads.usgcrp.gov/NCA/Activities/Biodiversity-Ecosystems-and-Ecosystem-Services-Technical-Input.pdf (accessed 1 January 2014).

NEA (2011), *UK National Ecosystem Assessment: Synthesis of the Key Findings*. Available at: http://uknea.unep-wcmc.org/ (accessed 1 January 2014).

Pandey, S. (2011), *Emergence of Eco-feminism and Reweaving the World*. Springfield: MD Publications.

Philo, C. and Wilbert, C. (2000), *Animal Spaces, Beastly Places: New Geographies of Human-animal Relations*. London: Routledge.

Potter, J. (1996), *Representing Reality: Discourse, Rhetoric and Social Construction*. London: Sage.

Singer, P. (1990), *Animal Liberation* (2nd edn). New York: New York Review.

Slater, P. (2007), 'The gadgeteer: sex, self and consumerism in *Stuff* magazine'. *Language and Ecology*, 2(1), www.ecoling.net/articles

Stevens, P. (2012), 'Towards an ecosociology'. *Sociology*, 46(5), 579–95.

Stibbe, A. (2001), 'Language, power and the social construction of animals'. *Society and Animals*, 9(2), 145–61.

——(2003), 'As charming as a pig: the discursive construction of the relationship between pigs and humans'. *Society and Animals*, 11(4), 375–92.

——(2005), 'Counter-discourses and harmonious relationships between humans and other animals'. *Anthrozoös*, 18(1), 3–17.

——(2007), 'Haiku and beyond: language, ecology and reconnection with the natural world'. *Anthrozoös*, 20(2), 101–12.

——(2012), *Animals Erased: Discourse, Ecology and Reconnection with the Natural World*. Middleton: Wesleyan University Press.

TEEB (2010), *The Economics of Ecosystems and Biodiversity: Mainstreaming the Economics of Nature*: A synthesis of the approach, conclusions and recommendations of TEEB. http://www.teebweb.org/teeb-study-and-reports/main-reports/synthesis-report/

Turner, M. and Fauconnier, G. (2002), *The Way We Think. Conceptual Blending and the Mind's Hidden Complexities*. New York: Basic Books.

Wain, G. (2007), 'Feral feelings'. *ECOS: A Review of Conservation*, 28(2), 1.

Williams, J. and McNeill, J. (2005), *The Current Crisis in Neoclassical Economics and the Case for an Economic Analysis Based on Sustainable Development*. U21 Global 001. Available at: http://www.u21global.edu.sg/PartnerAdmin/ViewContent?module=DOCU MENTLIBRARY&oid=14094 (accessed 1 January 2013).

World Society for the Protection of Animals (2008), *Eating our Future: The Environmental Impact of Industrial Animal Agriculture*. Available at: http://www.eathumane.org/ download/140_eating_our_future_nov_08_.pdf (accessed 1 January 2013).

Young, M. and Meyer, H. (2005), 'The trouble with "MSM" and "WSW": erasure of the sexual-minority person in public health discourse'. *American Journal of Public Health*, 95(7), 1144–9.

# 26

# Values, Assumptions and Beliefs in British Newspaper Editorial Coverage of Climate Change

*Cinzia Bevitori*

University of Bologna

## 1 Introduction: Aims and scope

In his influential book *Why We Disagree about Climate Change*, the distinguished climatologist Mike Hulme argues that climate change cannot be merely portrayed as a physical phenomenon, but first and foremost as a social one. In other words, according to Hulme, climate change would best be regarded as an 'idea' which, by meeting new cultures and new worlds on its way, particularly through the intermediary role of the media, 'takes new meanings and serves new purposes' (Hulme, 2009: xxvi). Hence, any representation of scientific knowledge, let alone climate change, far from being stable or 'fixed' in any unproblematic way (see also Latour, 1987), may rather be seen as being closely intertwined with specific imaginaries, as well as political and social concerns, carrying with them distinct *values, assumptions* and *beliefs*.

This of course begs the question of where and how these values, assumptions, beliefs and imaginaries are socially, politically and culturally built and shaped. Although far from straightforward, it may be claimed that the media play a crucial role in this process, as well as in shaping public understanding of science, as has been largely documented (inter alia Wilkins, 1993; Bell, 1994; Nelkin, 1987). Indeed, media representations, as Boykoff (2011: 2) suggests, are 'critical links between people's everyday realities and experiences, and the ways in which these are discussed at a distance between science, policy and public actors'.

The aim of this chapter is thus to empirically and critically explore what and how assumptions, beliefs and values on the issue of climate change are construed in British quality newspaper discourse, by focusing on one subset of opinion discourse; i.e. British editorials. As such, it builds and chronologically extends previous work analysing how climate change, one of the most emblematic and controversial issues of global environmental discourse shaping our new century, is represented in both opinion and news discourse (Bevitori, 2010a, 2010b, 2011a, 2011b), as well as across new forms of journalism (2012), with the purpose of illuminating the connection between their typical rhetorical aims and patternings of resources that are used to achieve them within this specialized domain.

Despite extensive literature on media coverage of climate change, scant attention has been paid to editorials or leading articles on the topic (but see Bevitori, 2010a, 2010b). Quintessentially argumentative and persuasive, editorials may in fact be regarded as crucial sites which are worth bringing to attention for several reasons. Beyond being purposefully aimed at formulating opinions (Fowler, 1991; Van Dijk, 1996), they can be seen to contribute to enhancing certain value positions, which can in turn encourage certain forms of social behaviour.[1] This, of course, is not in any way meant to suggest that the 'apparently neutral' news reporting may not be as effective as opinion pieces in 'naturalizing' ideologies (Fowler, 1991; White, 1997, 2004). Rather, while agreeing that all texts are in principle discursive constructions of some kind, what makes newspaper editorials distinctive is precisely the fact that specific textual strategies are employed 'which foreground the speech act of offering values and beliefs' (Fowler, 1991: 208–9). The following extract will provide an illustration of the point made:

> The *Independent on Sunday* does not presume to advise its readers on how to vote, but we are obliged to set out the factors that we believe should determine the nation's choice. Each reader, even if broadly in sympathy with this newspaper's editorial views, will weigh the factors differently and may view his or her choices differently according to the situation in particular constituencies. But our priorities are clear.
>
> ('Election Special: The Prime Minister must feel the lash of accountability', *Independent on Sunday* 2005)

Although the data shows that the *Independent*'s editorial voice tends to generally advance its own arguments in a more straightforward way than the other newspapers in the corpus, it can nonetheless be claimed that leading articles may be (and often are) used to establish the political identity of a newspaper. In particular, they do so by setting out concerns or making direct calls for action through the use of linguistic and discursive resources that are strategically different from the ostensibly 'objective' news coverage (Fowler, 1991).

This chapter is organized as follows; section 2 provides some background on key issues around climate change and its reporting. In section 3, the analytical tools and methodologies employed will be outlined. Details of the corpus and rationale for this study will then be provided in section 4, while section 5 discusses some of the major findings, focusing in particular on how ways of knowing and believing shape our understanding of climate change and how this does impinge on our vision(s) of the future. Some concluding remarks will finally follow in the last section.

## 2 Climate change and the press: An overview

Despite its long history and ancient roots (see, for example, Weart, 2008), media accounts of climate change did not appear in the public arena until the late years of the 1980s, when they saw a dramatic increase (Carvahlo and Burgess, 2005; Boykoff, 2011). Among the reasons contributing to this rise, as Boykoff (2011: 48–9) argues, there are ecological, political and scientific interweaving factors. As far as the first is concerned, the 'ecological' factor points to some extreme meteorological events, such as the extraordinary heatwave hitting North America in 1988, whose great physical impact was highly influential in fostering public concerns (see also Ungar, 1992; Demeritt, 2001). A noteworthy warning was also issued by a top NASA climate expert to the US Congress declaring that warmer temperatures were very likely caused by the burning of fossil fuels and were not only a result of natural variation (Dr Hansen, cited in Boykoff and Roberts, 2007: 6). As regards the second factor, a number of events hint to the fact that it was in this same year that climate change began to emerge as a political issue. For example, the then Prime Minister Margaret Thatcher's speech in September 1988 to the leading British academy of science, The Royal Society, mentioning the potential impacts of climate change, is often cited as an early example of a 'green', albeit not uncontroversial, speech.[2] Throughout the following decade, in the 1990s, an increasing politicization of climate science at the interface between science, policy-making and media has been observed (see Trumbo, 1996; Boykoff and Boykoff, 2004; Carvahlo, 2005). This was partly attributed to a small group of influential scientists, the so-called climate 'sceptics', or 'contrarians' (Boykoff, 2011), who strongly contested scientific findings regarding human contributions to climate change. Despite being a minority, these groups managed nonetheless to gain increased attention. As Antilla (2005) argues, these climate sceptics are often 'primary definers' (Hall, 1978), i.e. official sources of information, enjoying privileged access to the media in some news outlets (see also Wilkins, 1993). In an influential article by Max and Jules Boykoff (2004), the US prestige press was starkly criticized for adhering too faithfully to journalist conventions, and in particular to the critical notion of 'balance'. In other words, according to Boykoff and Boykoff (2004), the concept of 'balance-as-bias' refers to the fact that by providing a balanced set of views leading to competing points of view on a scientific issue, when actually they are not, tends to create the ideal condition to delay action. Finally, as far as the third, or 'scientific' factor is concerned, since the creation of the Intergovernmental Panel on Climate Change (henceforth IPCC) in 1988 by the World Meteorological Organization (WMO), scientific news stories began to regularly appear in mainstream media. Since the mid 1990s, IPCC reports began to represent what have fittingly been defined as 'critical discourse moments' (Carvahlo, 2005, after Chilton, 1987; Gamson, 1992), succeeding in gaining widespread media attention. This is because the credibility of the science of climate change hinges primarily on the Panel, which has also a leading role in influencing the UN Framework Convention on Climate Change (UNFCCC), the main international treaty providing the plan scheme for negotiating specific international treaties (such as the Kyoto Protocol) with the aim of setting binding limits on greenhouse gases. The consensus on anthropogenic climate change provided by the IPCC, however, is at the heart of much controversy; in particular, one of the key issues regards the degree of likelihood about causes and effects (Weingart et al., 2000; Zehr, 2000; Boykoff, 2011: 62–70 for an overview).

# 3 Tools, methods and procedure

In order to set out the goals and objectives that will frame my analysis, the tools and techniques of corpus linguistics and critical discourse analysis are used, and a corpus-assisted discourse analysis approach is proposed. Since the pioneering works on corpus investigation techniques in the analysis of discourse (e.g. Hardt-Mautner, 1995; Stubbs, 1994, 1996; Gerbig, 1997), much recent research, from a variety of perspectives, has attempted to reconcile corpus data with discourse analytical methods, with a growing concern with how to avoid potential biases arising from ad hoc selective use of evidence (inter alia Partington, 2004; Koller and Mautner, 2004; Orpin, 2005; Baker, 2006; Baker et al., 2008), as well as with the no less important matter of what texts 'mean' within specific cultural contexts (Partington, 2004; Coffin and O'Halloran, 2005; Thompson and Hunston, 2006; Miller, 2006; Morley and Bayley, 2009).

As far as the first point is concerned, criticism has chiefly been raised regarding the arbitrary selection of linguistic and discursive features in order to meet the analyst's specific interpretation (e.g. Widdowson, 1995). However, in spite of the usefulness of corpus approaches in enhancing objectivity in critical discourse analysis research, Baker (2012) has cautioned about overstating the capacity of corpus linguistics to diminish researcher bias. As I have argued elsewhere (see, for example, Bayley and Bevitori, 2009; Bevitori, 2010a, b), while the role of the analyst is still crucial and cannot be detached from her/his socio-political positioning, applying a rigorous methodology grounded in scientific principles can however be helpful in redressing the problem of selective interpretation.

A challenge to CDA has also been recently made by Carvahlo (2008), who argues that, despite the objectives that CDA has set itself, some aspects still lack satisfactory inspection. In particular, according to Carvahlo, attention should be focused on the diachronic dimension, the role of sources, along with some critical reflection on the influence of specific fields of action upon the practices and products of journalism. Although some of Carvahlo's points raised are certainly worth considering, empirical evidence, as I will argue, might also be brought into play.

The perspective endorsed here relies on the analytical framework of Systemic Functional Linguistics (SFL) (Halliday, 1978, [1994] 2004) as well as on the appraisal systems, a development of the interpersonal system at the level of discourse semantics, dealing with the way in which writers express evaluation, attitude and emotions through language (Martin and White, 2005). Drawing on the crucial notion that a corpus is not merely a 'repository' of practical examples, but 'a treasury of acts of meaning which can be explored and interrogated from all illuminating angles' (Halliday, [1994] 2004: 406), the corpus-assisted approach proposed in this study entails a blend of quantitative and qualitative dimensions in the analysis, alongside the use of different research procedures, or, by borrowing a term from the social sciences, 'triangulation' of data; a notion which implies the gathering of data through different strategies (Bryman, 2003, see also Baker, 2006). The interface between quantitative and qualitative aspects can have many advantages, as meaning encompasses both aspects. As Halliday (2005: 76) crucially notes:

> Qualitatively, there will be certain key discourses which carry special value, either intrinsically, because they somehow distil the semiotic essence of their moment in space-time, or extrinsically because they played a critical part in the ongoing material events [. . .]. Quantitatively, on the other hand, dominant semiotic motifs emerge more or less gradually over time; to access and evaluate these one needs a corpus of contextualized discourses that can be examined and interpreted as a whole.

From a corpus-assisted perspective, this is seen to work at different levels of analysis. The quantitative analysis of statistically salient words through and examination of both frequency lists and keywords lists provide the basis to more qualitative investigations of concordances in their widened context of occurrence. The purpose is to identify patterns of (ideological) meaning across texts and contexts, as well as to assess their combined effects to best capture their significance as 'an ensemble of discursive events' (Foucault, [1966] 1971: 231).

A constant tension is thus created between the quantitative dimensions of the data produced by the software (Scott, 2008) and the qualitative readings of the data in their complete textual form, embedded within larger contextual processes of interpretation. In sum, a cross-fertilization of analytical and methodological linguistic and discursive approaches, which are further complemented with the analysis of how meaning is produced, reproduced and negotiated within social practices over time (inter alia Halliday, 1978; Fairclough, 1992; Chouliaraki and Fairclough, 1999).

# 4 Corpus and rationale

The climate change diachronic editorial corpus (henceforth CCDE corpus) was collected through an online searchable database. It consists of all editorial articles published in three selected British 'quality' newspapers, *The Guardian, The Independent* and *The Times*, containing either the search phrase 'climate change' or 'global warming' within a time span of ten years, in alternate years between 2001, when the Third Report of the IPCC was released, and the year 2011, at the threshold of Kyoto's expiration date. As global climate change is an increasingly important political and social issue, a few words on the reasons for the selection of these newspapers are pertinent in order to facilitate understanding of the debate. To begin with, the decision stems from the interest in covering a wider range of arguments and perspectives of the political spectrum of the quality press (see also Carvahlo, 2005; Bevitori, 2010a, b). As far as the political leanings of the newspapers are concerned, while *The Times* has been traditionally considered as a 'moderately' centre-right newspaper (generally backing the Conservative Party), it endorsed the Labour Party both in the 2001 and 2005 General Elections. However, a possible shift in support has occurred when it backed the Tories at the European elections in June 2009 as well as the London mayoral race. *The Guardian* has generally been regarded as tending towards left (or centre-left) wing views of the British political opinion, with a readership largely split between Labour and Lib Dem voters. Finally, despite its non-affiliation with any of the political parties, *The Independent* is generally considered a left-leaning newspaper. Due to the complex and dynamic nature of climate change policy-making process, the diachronic dimension would allow keeping track of the major events in climate change science and policy over the period. Details on the data of the corpus are provided in Table 26.1.

One immediate observation is that *The Independent* accounts for a significantly higher number of leading articles than *The Guardian* and *The Times*, which in turn seems to suggest a higher degree of interest in the topic at issue by *The Independent*'s editorial voice. Since the number of texts may be a good indicator to gauge the scale of attention and significance given by media outlets to a specific issue (Carvahlo, 2005;

**Table 26.1** Number of articles and running words in the UK CCDE (2001–11) corpus

| UK All | Number of articles | Running words |
|---|---|---|
| Guardian | 182 | 105,809 |
| Times | 118 | 68,723 |
| Independent | 312 | 184,968 |
| Overall | **612** | **359,500** |

see also Bevitori, 2010a ,b), a quick glance at the breakdown across newspapers in the corpus over time may be helpful. As Figure 26.1 shows, in 2007 – a key year in the history of climate change – the volume of editorial coverage was about double in *The Times* and three and four times greater in *The Guardian* and *The Independent* respectively than that at the beginning of the new century. However, attention decreases significantly soon after.

This is in line with much research on media reporting on climate change, which has compellingly demonstrated that coverage of climate change is typically cyclical (Trumbo, 1996; McComas and Shanahan, 1999; Carvahlo and Burgess, 2005), as there appears to be a marked tendency to 'ebb and flow' depending on how media respond to particular events. The year 2007 may in fact be considered a turning point, coinciding with an upsurge of media attention due to various intersecting factors (Bevitori, 2010a, b). First of all, in 2007 both the IPCC and Al Gore were jointly awarded the Nobel Peace Prize for their commitment to reduce climate change; moreover, the *Bali Roadmap*, which came to light after strenuous negotiations at the 13th session of the United Nations Convention of Climate Change (COP 13) held in Bali in December 2007, marked a milestone in the process of consensus building. Finally, the publication of the Stern Report (Stern, 2007) at the end of the previous year set up room for ensuing discussions throughout 2007. However, after a period of stagnation, attention was revived in 2009 by the next round of negotiations under the United Nations Convention on Climate Change (COP 15), held in Copenhagen in the month of December. The Conference, which was defined by the Norwegian environment minister as 'the most difficult talks ever embarked upon by humanity',[3] gave birth to the highly controversial 'Copenhagen Accord'. Despite widespread expectations following the new US presidential election of Barack Obama, the accord fell short of the ambitious targets agreed in Bali, by failing to provide a new binding agreement to lessen carbon emissions. Another event to date,

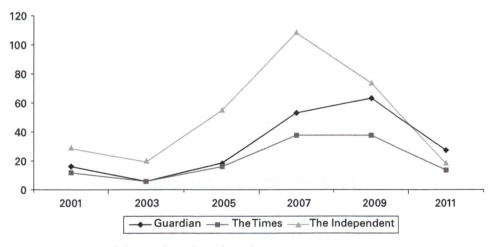

**FIGURE 26.1** *Breakdown of number of articles across newspapers over time.*

which attracted considerable media attention in 2009, was the 'Climategate' affair; a term used to describe the scandal triggered by leaked private email communications of academics of the University of East Anglia's Climatic Research Unit suggesting omissions and flawed data in the science of climate change (see also Nerlich, 2010). However, as Boykoff (2011) argues, although the 'Climategate' was a hot topic during this time, 'it still remained a relatively weak "signal" over this period amidst the "noise" of overall climate change or global warming coverage' (36). In the following couple of years, at the time when the Kyoto Protocol was drawing close to its expiry date, attention decreased rapidly, reaching in 2011 its initial levels.

# 5 Analysis and discussion: Ways of *knowing* and *believing*

Drawing insights from broader philosophical and psychological research, in his seminal article on opinions and ideologies in editorials, van Dijk (1996: 4) argues that 'opinions are a type of *belief*, as also knowledge, attitudes, ideologies and other mental representations consist of beliefs'. While a useful distinction can thus be made between 'factual' beliefs, or knowledge, as justified or uncontroversially accepted principles, and 'evaluative' beliefs, as a concept better associated with one's values, ideals, or norms than with rationalization and the observations of reality, according to Hulme (2009), there appears to be a deep tension between knowledge and beliefs running through much of the discussion of climate change. An investigation of the editorial voice(s) across newspapers can thus fittingly provide a lens through which *discourses* around climate change can be examined. In fact, although in the latest years a high degree of scientific consensus has been reached, the 'climate imperative'[4] does not seem to translate into common shared goals, nor does it have the same configurations.

The following analysis will thus set out to explore how ways of *knowing* and *believing* can shape our understanding of climate change and how this may affect our vision(s) of the future. It will make a quantitative and qualititative investigation of the mental verbs *know* and *believe* across newspapers by looking in particular at which projecting sources are typically represented by the editorial voice, as well as at the nature of what is projected. As noted, the constant move back and forth between quantitative configurations produced by the software combined with close readings of textual instances within considerations of the wider context will thus guide the analysis.

## 5.1 *Frequency and distribution*

A preliminary quantitative analysis of *know** and *believ***[5] in the corpus indicates that the former occurs more frequently with a relative frequency of 0.049 per hundred words compared to 0.031 for the latter (Figure 26.2).

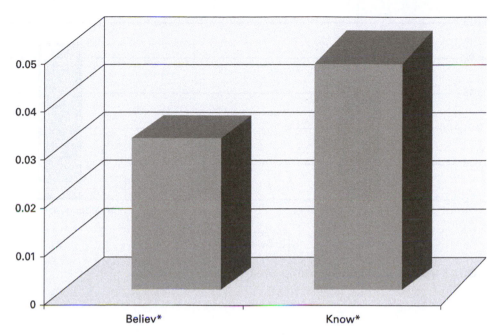

**FIGURE 26.2** *Relative frequency of* know* *and* believ* *in the CCDE corpus.*

However, a closer look at the breakdown of each newspaper in the corpus (Figure 26.3) reveals that while the lemma *know** occurs more frequently both in *The Guardian* and in *The Independent* with a relative frequency of 0.017 and 0.022 per hundred running words respectively, in *The Times*, in contrast, the lemma *believ** is slightly more frequent with a relative frequency of 0.012 per hundred running words.

This is all the more remarkable in light of the fact that the word form *know*, which occurs with a higher frequency, tends to be typically co-selected with the personal pronoun 'we' especially in *The Independent*. In contrast, the word form *believe* tends to be typically co-selected with a human collective, such as 'people', 'public' and 'respondents', which seems to suggest that *believe* is most typically used to represent perceptions of the public opinion, or the *vox pop* (Hall, 1978). As I have argued elsewhere (see Bevitori, 2010a: 50–51), besides its key role in providing the empirical basis for the analysis, frequency may also be regarded as an expression or 'symptom' of something that is worth exploring further. In order to get closer to an understanding of similarities and differences in the way newspapers make use of these mental processes, I shall now move on from the quantitative analysis of their frequency and distribution across texts to a more qualitative interpretation of the data. The questions I shall thus attempt to tackle are the following: what kind of and whose *knowledge* and *beliefs* do the different newspapers in the corpus tend to represent? And what kind of *values* are typically attached to them?

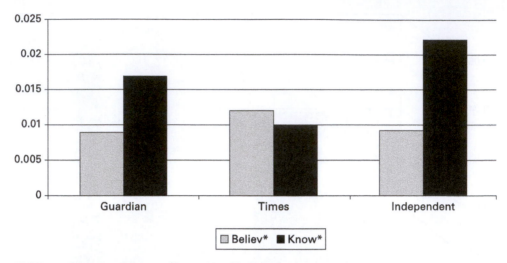

**FIGURE 26.3** *Breakdown of* know* *and* believ* *across newspapers.*

## 5.2 *What* we know

The lexical verb *know* has been extensively discussed in a number of different ways in linguistics: as a 'factive' verb in the truth-functional tradition (Lyons, 1977), or as a mental process construing 'sensing', according to the systemic functional approach (Halliday, [1994] 2004); at a more delicate level, *know* (as well as *believe*) are classified as process of cognition construing a person or persons involved in conscious processing. There are two participants in the clause, the Senser and the Phenomenon. Moreover, from a topological perspective, the verb is also seen to realize meanings of epistemic modality (Fuller, cited in Martin and White, 2005: 16); similarly, in his corpus-based analysis of commitment and subjectivity in newspaper opinionated discourse, Marín-Arrese (2007: 91), drawing on Langacker (1991), discusses the verb *know* as an evidential marker, which in co-selection with the pronoun 'we' indicates an 'explicit shared responsibility'.

Moving from the analysis of the collocates that are typically associated, or co-selected, with the lexical verb *know*, findings reveal that the Senser is typically realized by the first person pronoun 'we' in all newspapers, although, as has already been noted, with a significantly higher degree in *The Independent*, in which the two words co-occur in more than 70 per cent of all instances. Thus, the projecting phrase 'we know' may be seen as strongly implying issues of affiliation and alignment. By proposing shared knowledge, in fact, the writer invites the reader to co-participate and agree (and thus be-aligned) with the newspaper's point of view. However, differences as regards the nature of what is projected, or the Phenomenon, emerge.

To begin with, in both *The Independent* and the *The Guardian*, appeals to shared, accepted knowledge relates to questions of human-induced temperature rises, their dramatically negative consequences, in which matters of urgency aimed at averting a catastrophic or 'apocalyptic' future are typically foregrounded, as well as proposed solutions to counter them. The following extracts will provide an illustration:

1   **WE KNOW** that the world is heating up. **We know** that mankind's reckless use of fossil fuels **is responsible. But** just how hot does it **need** to get before some of the **terrible consequences** of global warming – rising sea levels, droughts, agricultural failure – manifest themselves? An international report, released tomorrow, argues that the world **could** reach that **'danger'** temperature in as little as 10 years' time. **We** ignore these warnings at **our peril**. This report confirms that tackling climate change is not something we can defer. It **requires** an **immediate response**. Otherwise, **we will** reap the **dire consequences** within **our** own lifetimes.

('No delay', *The Independent*, 24 January 2005)

2   Reports from the IPCC due later this year will analyse the impact of climate change in further detail. But **we already know** well enough what this **will** be. **Unless we** reduce greenhouse gas emissions, we **will** face a world **of resurgent disease, famine and drought**. Water supplies **will dry out;** agriculture **will fail;** entire ecosystems **will collapse** and millions of environmental refugees will be created. War and geopolitical **collapse are likely** to follow. **We also know** what **needs** to be done. There **must** be a global treaty on reducing emissions that **will** put a high price on carbon emissions and it **must** be enforced through taxation and fines. The problem is not one of information, but action. Not enough is being done. Negotiations on a successor to the Kyoto protocol have stalled.

('Now it is up to the world's political leaders to deliver more than hot air', *The Independent*, 3 February 2007)

As is evident, in *The Independent* the consequences of unrestrained use of carbon emissions are largely construed through resources of negative 'affect' in Martin and White's terms (2005), aimed at triggering emotional reactions ('terrible', 'dire', 'danger', 'at our peril') which, in association with the use of the predictive 'will' ('will face [. . .] resurgent disease, famine and drought', 'will dry out', 'will fail', 'will collapse') tends to create a doomsday scenario. The attitudinal values thus operate in combination to set up a negative prosodic environment, which reverberates across very loaded stretches of text. Moreover, as examples (3) and (4) suggest, what 'we know' seems to revolve around the idea that dangers are not remote or uncertain, and therefore, decision-making processes should involve taking measures urgently in order to prevent further harm:

3    What **we do know** is simple: that climate change is **most likely** caused by carbon emissions. The answer is to cut those emissions. **The time to do so is now**. Even if there is nothing that can be done for the **damage** already taking place, that should only cause policy makers to redouble their efforts.

('Climate Change: no more excuses', *The Guardian*, 3 February 2007)

4    **We still need to know** much more about the planet, but even when **we do know,** it seems, **we fail to act**.

('Natural disasters: Shocks that shouldn't surprise', *The Guardian*, 29 December 2011)

Thus what is at stake is the central 'paradox' of climate change politics, as the sociologist Anthony Giddens argued (2009), which, in essence, states that in spite of the enormous dangers posed by climate change, their apparent invisibility in people's daily life results in delaying action until it is too late. This may also be seen as closely interrelated to questions of 'future discounting' (see Caney, 2009), a concept based on the notion of 'social discounting rate', which has been discussed by several economists, among which is Sir Nicholas Stern. The concept refers to the extent to which resources should be allocated to people's interests in the present in preference to people's interests in the future. Interestingly, a closer analysis of instances of the lemma *consequence/s* across newspapers over time reveals that the word not only has a considerably higher frequency in *The Independent* (57 instances, corresponding to 0.06 per hundred running words, compared to 0.01 (18 instances) and 0.007 (5 instances) in *The Guardian* and *The Times* respectively), but also a third of all its occurrences shows a highly negative collocational profile, co-occurring with intensifying lexis, such as the adjectives *disastrous, catastrophic, dire, terrible, horrifying*, or the nouns *disaster, alarm*.

Concordance 1 provides a sample of 18 instances of this.

owed a range of **potentially catastrophic**     consequences if we adopt a 'business as
skirt over the **potentially catastrophic**     consequences of warming, nor the costs
t rate, the world will reap **catastrophic**     consequences. Sea levels will rise, imp
ed for 2100. This would have **devastating**     consequences for the hundreds of millio
sponse. Otherwise, we will reap the **dire**     consequences within our own lifetimes.
. We are beginning to recognise the **dire**     consequences of this warming of the ear
s for the world even than the **disastrous**     consequences of the Iraq war.       Last
ect of the world avoiding the **disastrous**     consequences of climate change are look
maintain yields, despite the **disastrous**     consequences of bottom-dredging for the
e to heat up with **potentially disastrous**     consequences. It concerns the climate c

likely that we are seeing another **malign** consequence of climate change. Bluetong
es and droughts. This will have **terrible** consequences for millions of species of
need to get before some of the **terrible** consequences of global warming – rising
during the summer. For animal life, the consequences will be **even more severe**.
s to focus on an unfolding **disaster.** The consequences of collective failure to a
te to become dominated by **alarm** over the consequences of temperature rises and f
people, as it has done with such **tragic** consequences over the past 12 months.

**Concordance 1** *Sample of 'consequences' in* The Independent

The analysis therefore points to the fact that discourses of 'fear and danger' around human-induced global climate change, as well as its apocalyptic consequences, are the underlying dominant motif in *The Independent*; moreover, this tends to be consistent over time. It may thus be claimed that *The Independent*'s authorial stance tends to reproduce an 'alarming'[6] assessment of the problem and, accordingly, to 'naturalize' a reading position which is one of disturbing prospects. However, although representations of climate change tend to generally come, as Giddens (2009: 28) would put it, 'with a doomsday literature attached', and despite the fact that negative events are more likely to gain attention from the media,[7] this strikingly contrasts with associations found in *The Times*, as it will be shown later.

As far as proposed solutions are concerned, the writer typically makes use of resources of modals of necessity, or deontic modality, (e.g. 'needs to be done', 'must be', 'must be enforced'), expressing the cogent need to urgently tackle the problems of emissions, as well as providing a guide for action. As a matter of fact, data in the corpus show that both *The Independent* and *The Guardian* are strongly supportive of the emissions trading system set out by the Kyoto mechanism. Under the Protocol, the UK, as well as other European nations, are deeply committed to controlling greenhouse gas emissions. What is more, the European Union created financial incentives and penalties in order to encourage each member state to meet its target.

If the question of meeting targets in British newspapers discourse(s) on climate change is indeed crucial, as also confirmed in previous research (see Bevitori 2010a: 119), a strong criticism of the government's failure to provide an adequate response is seen to feature prominently, especially as regards the question of timing, effective strategies, goals and objectives. This can be illustrated by the following example, in which one of the most significant and controversial pieces of the UK national legislation on climate change, the Climate Change Bill, is debated. The Bill was introduced in March 2007 by the former Environment Secretary, Hilary Benn, as a result of numerous review and debating stages, with the aim of achieving a mandatory reduction of 60 per cent in carbon emissions by 2050.[8] The Bill was strongly criticized by environmental organizations as well as by some political parties due to two main reasons. First of all, the proposed 60 per cent target was considered as not ambitious enough; secondly, the inclusion of aviation and shipping sectors in the Draft Bill was also strongly encouraged. The Bill eventually became law the following year, in November 2008, setting the targets to an 80 per cent cut overall by 2050. As extract (5) suggests, despite a positive 'appreciation' of the proposed measures in order to mitigate climate change ('a step in the right direction', 'right approach'), which, in concurrence with adverbs such as 'obviously' acts to construe a reader as sharing this particular set of values, what clearly emerges is a negative 'judgement' of the government's failure to perform a coherent and effective energy policy ('perfectly capable of [. . .] when they become inconvenient', 'anything like discipline', 'ambitious rhetoric'):

5     All this would **obviously** constitute a step in the **right** direction. But the **fundamental flaw** in the Bill would remain: where is the guarantee that these pledges will be met? **We know** that the Government is **perfectly capable** of dropping targets when they **become inconvenient.** This is what happened when it became clear that the longstanding Labour manifesto commitment to cut the UK's emissions by 20 per cent by 2010 would not be attained. Making such targets legally binding is the **right** approach in theory. **But** five-year 'carbon budgets', as set down in the Bill, **will not** provide **anything like enough discipline** for governments. Only annual binding targets can achieve that. **Unfortunately**, we are still in the realm of **ambitious rhetoric, rather than action**, from the Government when it comes to climate change.

('Does the left hand know what the right is doing?',
*The Independent*, 31 October 2007)

If the analysis so far has suggested that both in *The Independent* and *The Guardian*, the editorial voice tends to construe a reader sharing concerns about domestic problems, in *The Guardian*, issues regarding a more global perspective are also frequently raised. In the following excerpt (6), the question of human development and equality in a globalized world is advanced by the editorial voice. Through the projecting phrase 'we know', as well as formulations of denial/countering ('not only . . . but'), the reader is thus positioned to accept that lifestyles and behaviours of the developed world play a significant role in determining the choices available for the developing countries:

6     **We know,** for instance, that the **problem** is **not only** deprivation, *but* that our **way of life** is **environmentally unsustainable**. Climate change, for which the poor are **least responsible** and to which they are **most vulnerable**, is one reason why new goals **must** apply to the whole world, **not just** the poor parts of it. *But* the effort to set global goals **needs** to involve **much more reflection as well as more action**.

('Global development: Reimagining the goals',
*The Guardian*, 31 December 2011)

As has been noted, this clearly contrasts with *The Times*'s attitude towards the impact of climate change, where a different set of values, assumptions and beliefs are voiced.

First of all, a deep tension between the 'facts', on the one hand, and 'predictions', on the other, can be observed. For example, in contrast to the 'hot air' metaphor, employed by *The Independent*'s editorial voice (see, for example, the headline of excerpt (2) discussed earlier) in order to negatively appraise politicians as a result of their inability to deliver, in *The Times* (see example (7)), 'hot air' is used to metaphorically describe the unreality of frightening predictions. The issue is in fact typically addressed in terms of binary opposition between what 'we know' about changing global climatic conditions, i.e. the 'real' facts, and expectations of how this will impact in the future, i.e. predictions, which are typically construed as unreal ('hot air', 'pure fantasy', 'fanciful'):

7    Predictions are **so much hot air. All <u>we know</u> with any certainty** is that **<u>we really do not know</u> how** the world **will** appear this time next year.

    ('Into the unknown', *The Times*, 30 December, 2007)

8    Some of the more **apocalyptic visions** of climate change are **pure fantasy and scare-mongering**, but the planet does deserve **the benefit of the doubt**.

    ('A very political Climate', *The Times*, March 2007)

9    The planet deserves **the benefit of the doubt.** Climate change is **serious and must** be a **political priority. But** the arguments **must** be subject to **free and rigorous** debate and the facts separated from **fanciful predictions** – the environment is **too important** to be bequeathed to **the hysterical**.

    ('A Climate of Intolerance', *The Times*, 7 April 2007)

As a large number of instances in *The Times* show, belief and scepticism about climate change strongly tie in with political and ideological views, and much less so with the science. In other words, as a term which is commonly employed to describe positions of those who are unconvinced by the science,[9] scepticism does not seem to fully nor adequately describe the newspaper's stance. However, sceptical objections are raised by *The Times*'s editorialist voice as regards the high dramatization of the events by those advocating an 'alarmist' view. Extract (9) is the last paragraph, or the 'coda', of an editorial piece whose headline reads: 'A Climate of Intolerance'. Interestingly, the nominalization 'intolerance' in the title manipulatively functions to construct an assumed consensus over the unwillingness or refusal to accept differences in opinions or beliefs by environmental lobbies in their attempt to overstate and amplify the scale of the problem. Nominalization is, according to Halliday ([1994] 2004: 656), a very powerful grammatical 'resource', through which a semantic category, such as a process, is reclassified metaphorically as a noun, thereby obfuscating agency (see also Kress, 1995). Despite agreeing on the reality that climate change is happening, the reader is positioned to accept the facts but to distrust predictions. What follows (10) is the opening of the same leading article, in which the reality and significance of climate change is projected through unspecified authoritative sources ('few scientists or rational politicians'). However, at the same time, a stark criticism is directed towards environmental lobbies though resources of negative 'judgement':

10   Few scientists or rational politicians **doubt** that global warming **is a serious** issue that poses **long-term dangers** to the planet. The scientific evidence that the world's climate has changed and that this change is accelerating is **convincing.** *But* it is **also beyond doubt** that the world is **in danger of** being **held captive** by **powerful** lobby groups that have **distorted** data, made **unjustified** extrapolations and attempted to **stifle** debate on one of the most important issues of our time.

('A Climate of Intolerance', *The Times*, 7 April 2007)

One of the critical aspects lying at the very heart of the tension between facts and predictions in *The Times* are some climate-related concerns about the 'future', which, in particular, revolve pre-eminently around the energy issue. In the following extract, the appeal to shared, accepted knowledge relates to both questions of carbon dioxide emissions and their harmful effects on people's health, as well as to the shortage of fuels supplies. However, both arguments are posited as rationales for supporting the development of nuclear power:

11   **We know** from our own past experience that factories and homes that burn coal and spew out pollution **severely damage** health. That is the situation in China now. **We also know** that hydrocarbon fuels **will** become more scarce in the future and that it makes sense to diversify into **nuclear**.

('Copenhagen's hot air may help cool the planet', *The Times*, 6 December 2009)

This is even more interesting in light of the fact that a keyword analysis of *The Times* subcorpus against the rest of the corpus reveals the word *nuclear* is 'key', occurring with a relative frequency of 0.15 per hundred compared to 0.06 per hundred running words.[10] The heuristic device may be valuable in providing the analyst with new paths to follow. Although words such as 'energy' and 'power' emerge as the strongest collocates of the adjective *nuclear*, a more systematic look at the semantic patterns arising from the widened co-text and context of each concordance line also indicates that the word is also typically associated with the word 'future'. What is more, instances indicate that the need to turn to nuclear energy as a way to ensure a viable alternative to fossil fuels is advocated by the editorial's stance. An illustration is provided by the following extract of a leading article titled, 'The future is green, the future is nuclear' (12). Through the parallelism between 'nuclear' and 'green',[11] based on the assumption that nuclear power is free of greenhouse gases (which is of course highly controversial), the reader is manipulatively invited to acknowledge that nuclear is ecologically, and economically, sustainable:

12   Professor David MacKay, the government's chief scientific adviser on climate change, has said what many people have long believed. You cannot meet

Britain's **future energy needs** and reduced carbon emissions without a big expansion of **nuclear power**.

('The future is green, the future is nuclear',
*The Times*, 4 October 2009)

Crucially, the presupposed assumption on the necessity to develop nuclear power in order to satisfy the energy demands of the future is projected through a multiplying of external voices. Here the Senser ('many people') engaged in the mental process ('have [long] believed') is in fact embedded within a main verbal clause, projected by an authoritative source, ('the government's chief adviser'). This leads us nicely into the analysis of the next section in which the analysis of 'what people believe' will be now briefly focused on.

## 5.3 *What* people *believe*

As has been noted, a close reading of instances of the verb *believe* reveals that, in contrast to *know*, the Senser is typically realized by a human collective such as 'people', as well as 'the public' and 'the respondents'; in other words, the *vox populi*. According to Fowler (1991: 46–8), the use of the 'public idiom', as defined by Hall (1978), is inherently ideological. It is a 'discursive norm', which helps engaging readers in an illusory conversation, and, in turn, helps in building consensus among them by appealing to a shared 'stock of knowledge'. Opinion polls act in this sense as persuasive devices in leading articles (see also Virtanen, 2005).

Both 'knowledge' and 'belief' about climate change are construed though a number of resources, which act to engage the reader to experience different visions of the future. However, while in *The Times*, the 'sustainability' of nuclear energy is at the heart of the debate, concerns relating to the science of climate change and its anthropogenic causes surface and are revived again in 2009 on the eve of the Climategate scandal (example (13)):

13   On the subject of climate change, there appears to be plenty of people who have discovered a hobbit. The poll in *The Times* today reveals that **only 41 per cent of respondents <u>believe</u>** that climate change is happening and that human causation is an established fact. **A third of the public <u>believes</u>** in the fact of climate change but remains unpersuaded that it is the work of human hands. **Nearly one in ten people <u>believes</u>** that climate change is a purely natural phenomenon and blaming humans is propaganda put about by environmentalists. **Fifteen per cent of the country simply <u>do not accept</u>** that climate change is happening at all. There has **clearly** been a **serious failure** of political communication *but* the last group at least **should be easy to convince**.

('Changing the climate', *The Times*, 14 November 2009)

As extract (13) illustrates, in 'Changing the climate', the editorial voice addresses public opinion by basing its claim on negative bias of political communication, through resources of negative 'judgement' ('serious failure'). However, sceptical positions as regards the science of climate change are once again challenged by the institutional voice. In contrast, representations of people's beliefs in both *The Independent* and *The Guardian* lie in the discrepancies between beliefs and behaviours, which, according to many scholars, is one of the critical factors in fostering inaction:[12]

14   The opinion survey by the Energy Saving Trust is **encouraging** in parts.
     **Around 80 per cent of the public believe** that climate change is a major
     problem and want the Government to let them know what they can do to save
     energy. **A similar proportion believes** that climate change **will** have an
     **adverse effect** on them and their families. This is **heartening** because it
     shows that the message about the scale of the threat is getting through; so
     too is the message about how we can reduce the impact of global warming.
     According to the survey, **a majority** regard reducing energy use in the home
     as a '**virtuous**' activity.

     ('The green gap between concern and action,
     *The Independent*, 2 April 2007)

15   But as today's Guardian/ICM poll shows, the **now universal public belief** that
     climate change exists has not yet transformed into support for the sort of
     individual action that could tackle it. While **89% in Britain believe** climate
     change is a threat, most people have done only a little or nothing at all to
     respond to it. There is clear opposition (61%) to an environmental tax on air
     travel and scepticism too about road pricing. Only **26% believe people** should
     pay a charge per mile to drive. There is a lingering sense that voters see
     climate change as someone else's problem.

     ('Global warming: The message hits home',
     *The Guardian*, 23 June 2005)

The findings, as both extracts show, point to an authorial voice which sets forth the necessity to mobilize change through a concerted effort of both citizens and governments alike, in a combination of bottom-up practices and top-down practices, where the focus is on individual lifestyles and behaviours, as far as the former is concerned, alongside processes of institutional and/or governmental decision making. This seems to be in line with a systematic longitudinal study of trends in public opinion about global warming over twenty years (Nisbet and Myers, 2007), in which it is observed that poll results tend to be cited by journalists as 'reflective of a public demanding action on global warming' (2007: 2). In sum, the unresolved conflict between what 'we know we ought to do' and 'what we actually do' seem to crucially emerge in many representations of 'what people believe' about climate change.

# 6 Concluding remarks

The role of media as key players in shaping public perceptions and opinions on contentious issues, such as climate change, has been long and amply recognized. In this complex and dynamic arena, opinion leaders may be seen to play an even more crucial role in shaping the multifarious, politicized realm in which meanings are constructed, negotiated and contested between competing points of view. In particular, through the combined use of methods and techniques, the study has attempted to shed light on how ways of 'knowing and believing' are socially constructed in editorial opinion discourse, and how readers are positioned to value different aspects of the debate surrounding climate change. Media of course is one among the many actors on the world global stage; however, its mediating role between the science, governance and society is indeed crucial. It is in this complex relationship that the 'idea' of climate change may be better understood as a socio-political phenomenon rather than a physical one; a privileged site of struggle between different interests and different visions of the future.

# Notes

1  For a useful discussion on the communication of climate change in the public arena, see Moser and Dilling 2007.

2  Thatcher's speech to the Royal Society on 27 September 1988 is available online at http://www.margaretthatcher.org/speeches/displaydocument.asp?docid=107346 (accessed August 2009).

3  See Reuters by Alister Doyle, Environment Correspondent OSLO, Friday 4 Dec 2009, at: http://www.reuters.com/article/2009/12/04/idUSGEE5B31HG (accessed 1 June 2014).

4  See for example, R. K. Pachauri, 'The Climate Imperative', at http://www.project-syndicate.org/commentary/the-climate-imperative (accessed August 2009). Rajendra Pachauri has been designated as the chairman of the Intergovernmental Panel on Climate Change since 2002.

5  The asterisk indicates that all verb forms of the lemma are included.

6  See Risbey 2008 for a discussion of 'alarming' versus 'alarmist' perspectives on climate change.

7  'Negativity' is in fact one of the 'news values' identified by Galtung and Ruge (1965) in their pioneering work on news discourse (see also Bell, 1991). Although this study focuses on editorials, the influence of what is covered/not covered in the news by the same media outlets is still of importance.

8  The Climate Change [HL] Act 2007–08 is available at http://services.parliament.uk/bills/2007–08/climatechangehl.html (accessed 1st November 2013).

9  A lengthy discussion on the notion of scepticism with reference to the climate change debate is found in Boykoff, 2011: 159–64.

10 A keyword analysis helps identify words which are statistically more frequent, and therefore with a higher degree of saliency, in a given corpus against a reference

corpus. As far as this study is concerned the frequency lists of each newspaper editorial corpus has been compared to the whole editorial corpus.

**11** For more discussion on how the lemma 'green' is discursively constructed in newspaper discourse as well as news blogs, see Bevitori 2012.

**12** The conflict has been generally defined as 'attitude-behaviour' and 'action-value' gap; see Ungar, 1992; Boykoff, 2011: 151 for a discussion.

# References

Antilla, L. (2005), 'Climate of scepticism: US newspaper coverage of the science of climate change'. *Global Environmental Change*, 15, 338–52.

Baker, P. (2006), *Using Corpora in Discourse Analysis.* London: Continuum.

—— (2012), 'Acceptable bias? Using corpus linguistics methods with critical discourse analysis. *Critical Discourse Studies*, 9(3), 247–56.

Baker, P., Gabrielatos, C., KhosraviNik, M., Krzyzanowski, M., McEnery T. and Wodak, R. (2008), 'A useful synergy? Combining critical discourse analysis and corpus linguistics to examine discourses of refugees and asylum seekers in the UK press'. *Discourse and Society*, 19, 273–306.

Bayley, P. and Bevitori, C. (2009), '"Just war" or Just "war": Arguments for doing the "Right Thing", in J. Morley and P. Bayley (eds), *Corpus-Assisted Discourse Studies on the Iraq Conflict. Wording the War.* London: Routledge, pp. 74–107.

Bell, A. (1991), *The Language of News Media.* Oxford: Blackwell.

—— (1994), 'Climate of opinion: public and media discourse on the global environment'. *Discourse and Society*, 51(1), 33–64.

Bevitori, C. (2010a), *Representations of Climate Change. News and Opinion Discourse in UK and US Quality Press: a Corpus-Assisted Discourse Study.* Bologna: Bononia University Press.

—— (2010b), 'Climates of meaning: the rhetorical functionality of *should* in UK and US editorials on climate change'. Paper given at the 22nd European Systemic Functional Linguistics Conference and Workshop. University of Primorska 9–12 July 2010.

—— (2011a), 'The meanings of RESPONSIBILITY in the British and American press on climate change: a corpus-assisted discourse perspective', in S. Goźdź-Roszkowski (ed.), *Explorations across Language and Corpora.* Frankfurt/Main: Peter Lang Series: Łódź Studies in Language (ed. B. Lewandowska-Tomaszczyk), pp. 243–59.

—— (2011b), '"Imagine, if you will . . .": Reader positioning on climate change in US op-ed articles', in G. Di Martino, L. Lombardo and S. Nuccorini (eds), *Challenges for the 21st Century: Dilemmas, Ambiguities, Directions.* Vol. II, Language Studies, Rome: Edizioni Q.

—— (2012), 'How green is "green"? A corpus-assisted analysis of environmental discourse across forms of journalism'. *Occasional Papers, Quaderni del Centro di Studi Linguistico-Culturali.* Bologna: CeSLiC e AlmaDL, pp.1–30.

Boykoff, M. T. (2011), *Who Speaks for the Climate? Making Sense of Media Reporting of Climate Change.* Cambridge: Cambridge University Press.

Boykoff, M. T. and Boykoff, J. (2004), 'Balance as bias: global warming and the US prestige press'. *Global Environmental Change*, 14, 125–36.

Boykoff, M. T. and Roberts, T. (2007), 'Climate change and human development – risk and vulnerability in a warming world: media coverage of climate change – current trends, strengths and weaknesses'. *United Nations Development Program Human Development Reports.*

Bryman, A. (2003), 'Triangulation', in M. S. Lewis-Beck, A. Bryman and F. T. Liao (eds), *Encyclopedia of Social Science Research Methods.* London: Sage, pp. 1142–3.

Caney, S. (2009), 'Climate change and the future: discounting for time, wealth, and risk'. *Journal of Social Philosophy*, 40(2), 163–86.

Carvahlo, A. (2005), 'Representing the politics of the greenhouse effect. Discursive strategies in the British media'. *Critical Discourse Studies*, 2(1), 1–29.

—— (2008), 'Media(ted) discourse and society: rethinking the framework of Critical Discourse Analysis'. *Journalism Studies*, 9(2), 161–77.

Carvahlo, A. and Burgess, J. (2005), 'Cultural circuits of climate change in UK broadsheet newspapers, 1985–2003'. *Risk Analysis*, 25(6), 1457–69.

Chilton, P. (1987), 'Metaphor, euphemism, and the militarization of language'. *Current Research on Peace and Violence*, 10, 7–19.

Chouliaraki, L. and Fairclough, N. (1999), *Discourse in Late Modernity. Rethinking Critical Discourse Analysis.* Edinburgh: Edinburgh University Press.

Coffin, C. and O'Halloran, K. A. (2005), 'Finding the global groove: theorising and analysing reader positioning using appraisal, corpus, and a concordancer. *Critical Discourse Studies*, 2(2), 143–63.

Demeritt, D. (2001), 'The construction of global warming and the politics of science', *Annals of the Association of American Geographers*, 91(2), 307–37.

Fairclough, N. (1992), *Discourse and Social Change.* Cambridge: Polity Press.

Foucault, M. ([1966] 1971), *The Discourse on Language.* New York: Harper Colophon.

Fowler, R. (1991), *Language in the News. Discourse and Ideology in the Press.* London and New York: Routledge.

Galtung, J. and Ruge, M. H. (1965), 'The structure of foreign news: the presentation of the Congo, Cuba and Cyprus crises in four Norwegian newspapers'. *Journal of Peace Research*, 2, 64–90.

Gamson, W. (1992), *Talking Politics.* Cambridge: Cambridge University Press.

Gerbig, A. (1997), *Lexical and Grammatical Variation in a Corpus. A Computer-assisted Study of Discourse on the Environment.* Bern: Peter Lang.

Giddens, A. (2009), *The Politics of Climate Change.* Cambridge: Polity Press.

Hall, S. (1978), 'The social production of the news', in S. Hall, C. Crichter, T. Jefferson, J. Clarke and B. Roberts (eds), *Policing the Crisis: Mugging, the State, and Law and Order.* London: Macmillan, pp. 53–77.

Halliday, M. A. K. (1978), *Language as Social Semiotic: The Social Interpretation of Language and Meaning.* London: Edward Arnold.

—— ([1994] 2004), *An Introduction to Functional Grammar.* London: Edward Arnold.

—— (2005), 'On matter and meaning: the two realm of human experience'. *Linguistics and the Human Sciences*, 1(1), 59–82.

Hardt-Mautner, G. (1995), 'Only connect. Critical discourse analysis and corpus linguistics'. University of Lancaster, online, at http://www.comp.lancs.ac.uk/computing/research/ucrel/tech_paperHardt Mautner (accessed 5 April 2005).

Hulme, M. (2009), *Why We Disagree about Climate Change: Understanding Controversy, Inaction and Opportunity.* Cambridge: Cambridge University Press.

Koller, V. and Mautner, G. (2004), 'Computer applications in critical discourse analysis', in C. Coffin, A. Hewings, and K. O'Halloran (eds), *Applying English Grammar.* London, Arnold, pp. 216–28.

Kress, G. (1995), 'The social production of language: history and structures of domination', in P. H. Fries and M. Gregory (eds), *Discourse in Society: Systemic Functional Perspectives*. Norwood, NJ: Ablex, pp. 169–91.

Langacker, R. (1991), *Foundations of Cognitive Grammar*. Vol. 2. Standford: Standford University Press.

Latour, B (1987), *Science in Action*. Cambridge, MA: Harvard University Press.

Lyons, J. (1977), *Semantics*. Cambridge: Cambridge University Press.

Marín Arrese, J. I. (2007), 'Commitment and subjectivity in the discourse of opinion columns and leading articles'. *RAEL*, Vol. 1, 82–98, online at http://dialnet.unirioja.es (accessed January 2009).

Martin, J. R. and White, P. R. R. (2005), *The Language of Evaluation: Appraisal in English*. London, Palgrave Macmillan.

McComas, K. and Shanahan, J. (1999), 'Telling stories about global climate change: measuring the impact of narratives on issue cycles'. *Communication Research*, 26(1), 30–57.

Miller, D. R. (2006), 'From concordance to text: appraising "giving" in Alma Mater donation requests', in G. Thompson and Hunston (eds), *System and Corpus: Exploring Connections*. London, Equinox, pp. 248–68.

Morley, J. and Bayley, P. (eds) (2009), *Corpus-Assisted Discourse Studies on the Iraq Conflict. Wording the War*. London: Routledge.

Moser, S. and Dilling, L. (eds) (2007), *Creating a Climate for Change: Communicating Climate Change and Facilitating Social Change*. Cambridge: Cambridge University Press.

Nelkin, D. (1987), *Selling Science: How the Press Covers Science and Technology*. New York: Freeman.

Nerlich, B. (2010), '"Climategate": paradoxical metaphors and political paralysis'. *Environmental Values*, 19, 419–22.

Nisbet, M. C. and Myers, T. (2007), 'The polls – trends: twenty years of public opinion about global warming'. *Public Opinion Quarterly*, 71(3), 1–27.

Orpin, D. (2005), 'Corpus linguistics and critical discourse analysis'. *International Journal of Corpus Linguistics*, 10(1), 37–61.

Partington, A. (2004), 'Corpora and discourse, a most congruous beast', in A. Partington, J. Morley and L. Haarman (eds). *Corpora and Discourse*. Bern: Peter Lang, pp. 11–20.

Risbey, J. S. (2008), 'The new climate discourse: alarmist or alarming?' *Global Environmental Change*, 18, 26–37.

Scott, M. (2008), *WordSmith Tools – Version 5.0*. Oxford: Oxford University Press.

Stern, N. H. (2007), *The Economics of Climate Change: The Stern Review*. Cambridge: Cambridge University Press.

Stubbs, M. (1994), 'Grammar, text, and ideology: computer-assisted methods in the linguistics of representation'. *Applied Linguistics*, 15(2), 201–23.

—— (1996), *Text and Corpus Analysis*. Oxford: Blackwell.

Thompson, G. and Hunston, S. (eds) (2006), *System and Corpus: Exploring Connections*. London: Equinox.

Trumbo, C. (1996), 'Constructing climate change: claims and frames in US news coverage of an environmental issue'. *Public Understanding of Science*, 5, 269–73.

Ungar, S. (1992), 'The rise and (relative) decline of global warming as a social problem'. *Sociological Quarterly*, 33, 483–501.

Van Dijk, T. A. (1996), 'Opinions and ideologies in editorials'. Paper for the 14th International Symposium of Critical Discourse Analysis: Language, Social Life and Critical Thought.

Athens, 14–16 December 1995, Second Draft, March 1996, at: www.hum.uva.nl/teun/editoria.htm (accessed April 2007).

Virtanen, T. (2005), '"Polls and surveys show": public opinion as a persuasive device in editorial discourse', in H. Halmari, T. Virtanen (eds), *Persuasions across Genres. A Linguistic Approach*. Amsterdam/Philadelphia: John Benjamins, 153–80.

Weart, S. R. (2008), *The Discovery of Global Warming*. Cambridge: Cambridge University Press.

Weingart, P., Engels, A. and Pansegrau, P. (2000), 'Risks of communication: discourses on climate change in science, politics, and the mass media'. *Public Understanding of Science*, 9, 261–83.

White, P. R. R. (1997), 'Death, disruption and the moral order: the narrative impulse in mass-media hard news reporting', in F. Christie and J. R. Martin (eds), *Genres and Institutions: Social Processes in the Workplace and School*. London: Cassell, pp. 101–33.

—— (2004), 'Subjectivity, evaluation and point of view in media discourse', in C. Coffin, A. Hewings and K. O'Halloran (eds), *Applying English Grammar*. London: Edward Arnold.

Widdowson, H. (1995), 'Discourse analysis: a critical view'. *Language and Literature*, 4(3), 157–72.

Wilkins, L. (1993), 'Between facts and values: print media coverage of the greenhouse effect, 1987–1990'. *Public Understanding of Science*, 2, 71–84.

Zehr, S. (2000), 'Public representations of scientific uncertainty about global climate change'. *Public Understanding of Science*, 9, 85–103.

# Index

Africa 327–8, 331–2, 385, 388–405, 479,
    482–3, 499, 517
accountability policies 479–80, 485, 496–7
agency
    ellipted 568–9
    explicit 568–9
    implied 568–9
alliteration 143, 354
AntConc 215, 234, 277
Anthony, L. 215
argument
    from authority 34
    from necessity 37
    *see also* digital argument deconstruction
argumentation
    analysis of 10, 67–70, 72, 74–5, 77–9,
        81, 86, 88, 91–4
    fallacious 68–9, 72, 74, 79, 91, 107–8
    *see also* fallacy
    scheme
    *see* topos
asylum *seekers* 12–13, 118, 235, 279, 502,
    506, 509, 512–13, 517–18, 622
audience design 365, 377, 383

Baker, P. 213, 221, 223
Bakhtin, M. 348, 350, 357–8
bias 5, 38, 42, 56, 95, 115, 119, 130, 213,
    235, 353–6, 361, 363, 605–6, 620,
    622–3
body politic 45–6, 48–52, 54–7, 62, 64–6,
    162–3, 355, 361
Bourdieu, P. 50, 363–4, 435–6,
British National Corpus (BNC) 223, 277
British press 55, 211–12, 214, 223, 225,
    229, 233–5, 403, 501–2, 504, 508–9,
    512–13
Bush, G.W. 191–6, 202–3, 206, 208, 321,
    326–7, 329–31, 333, 335–9, 342, 546

capital
    natural 594–5, 599
    cultural 361
    social 361
    symbolic 142, 361
categorization 6, 145, 174–5, 399–400, 505,
    524
cherry-picking 212
Chilton, P. 98, 190, 207, 447, 504–5
choice policies 496
Cicero 19, 24–5, 74, 77, 90
climate change 185, 189, 200–3, 205–6,
    209, 287, 423–4, 429, 593, 601,
    603–6, 608–10, 613–25
Clinton, H. 348, 359–60
Clinton, W. 326–7, 329–31, 335–6, 338–9,
    342
Cognitive Linguistic Approach (CLA) 5–6, 9,
    13, 163, 167–70, 174, 183–4, 187, 517
    *see also* cognitive linguistics
cognitive linguistics 6–8, 15, 63–6, 107, 163,
    167–9, 177, 186–7, 207, 209–10, 544,
    562, 581
cognitive pragmatics 5–8, 11, 115, 119
    *see also* critical cognitive pragmatics
coherence 6, 38, 65, 116, 126, 128, 131,
    134–5, 140–1, 143, 388–9, 400, 497,
    524
Cold War 21, 117, 186, 321–5, 328–34,
    336–40, 342, 344, 436, 555
collocation 5, 57, 218–20, 253–5, 264, 266,
    278, 280, 614
colonial discourse 391, 401
    *see also* Africa
community of practice 433, 443–5
conceptualization 9–10, 13, 21, 53, 137,
    169–72, 183–5 187, 373, 447, 451,
    454, 503, 505, 546, 562–3, 578
    *see also* construal

Conceptual Metaphor Theory (CMT) 52–3
concordance 213, 219–22, 225, 228–9, 234, 265, 275, 607, 614–15, 618, 624
construal 107, 151, 172, 176, 178, 185, 190, 196, 199, 202, 204–6, 210
    forced 189, 191, 203
    operation 13, 163, 167, 169–70, 181, 183, 187, 517
context
    linguistic 234
    intertextual 10
    historical 10, 22–3, 55, 150, 213, 322, 554
    social 15, 146, 148, 151, 153, 155–6, 161, 543
    situational 282
contextual selection constraint 105
Conversation Analysis (CA) 2, 12, 14, 122, 134–5, 149, 375
Corpus Assisted Discourse Analysis 213
    see also corpus linguistics, Corpus Linguistic Approach
Corpus Linguistic Approach 5, 7–8, 11, 555
corpus linguistics 5, 12, 14, 64, 212–13, 235, 241, 253, 278–80, 509, 517, 606, 622–4
criminalization of youth 486, 492–3
critical cognitive pragmatics 5–8, 11
Critical
    Metaphor Analysis 7–8, 12, 167, 186, 279
    Metaphor Studies 5–6
    see also Critical Metaphor Analysis
    Linguistics 3–4, 7–8, 11, 15, 97, 106, 281, 382
    Theory 2, 81, 435

deception 98–108, 115–18
deixis 6, 145, 157, 177, 531
    see also indexical
deictic centre 170, 200–1, 207, 447
democratic peace 323, 338–41, 343–4
Derrida, J. 238, 242–4, 261, 278
Dialectical-Relational Approach 3–4, 7–8, 11
digital argument deconstruction 237–44, 260–2, 264–6, 278
discourse
    community 57, 148, 155, 546
    ecological 593
    see also ecolinguistics
    institutional 365, 367–70, 381, 408, 416–17, 448, 451, 457, 587

interventionist 189, 191, 197–8, 200, 203, 208
marketization of 293, 448, 451, 454, 457
media 9–10, 13–14, 45, 52, 58, 128, 163, 187, 204, 206, 209, 363, 365–78, 381–7, 389, 397–400, 403, 424, 426–7, 454, 534, 546, 556–7, 571, 622–3, 625
    of environment 203, 598, 601, 604, 622
    of health 543–4, 552, 586, 602
    of illness 543, 552
    of immigration 13, 118, 163, 187, 191, 209, 279, 501, 503–8, 513–15, 517–18, 540
    of legitimization 196, 199, 204
    professional 365, 367–8, 370–1, 381
    state political 189–92, 196, 199–200, 208
    structures 10, 121–2, 124, 126–7, 131–4, 137–9, 143–4, 544
Discourse-Historical Approach (DHA) 3, 7–9, 11, 40, 45, 67–9, 78–81, 85–90, 92, 148, 151, 184, 213, 322, 408, 426, 505, 507
Discourse Space (DS) 190–1, 199–200, 207
    Theory (DST) 190, 209
Discursive Psychology (DP) 122
Dispositive Analysis 7–8, 55, 518
Duisburg School
    see Dispositive Analysis
Dylan, B. 351

Ecolinguistics 583–5, 587, 591, 599, 601
ecological turn 584
editorial 135–44, 238, 287, 508, 603–4, 608–10, 616–18, 620–2, 624–5
educational policy 479–80, 482, 485–6, 491, 497, 499
erasure 583–8, 590, 594–7, 599–602
European
    Council (EC) 451
    Commission (CEC) 409, 412, 416, 420, 423, 427–8, 439, 446, 448, 451, 455
    Parliament (EP) 409, 412, 415, 417, 420, 427, 439
    Public Sphere 412, 414, 417, 423, 428–30, 451, 454, 456
    Union (EU) 37, 343, 407–9, 411–12, 414–15, 420, 422–32, 434–6, 442–3, 446–7, 450–9, 615
Europeanization 369, 410, 428, 430, 443

Fairclough, N. 9, 67, 69–70, 72, 88–91,
     213–14, 287, 367, 388, 505, 584, 594
fallacy 5, 28, 78–9, 82–4, 89, 93, 111,
     116–17
  straw man 106, 110, 119
far-right
  extremism 521
  parties 14, 525, 537, 541
figure/ground (relation) 180
film music 297, 316
Foucault, M. 323, 361–2, 367, 387, 433
Fowler, R. 98, 619
framing 169–70, 174–5, 291, 326–30,
     371–2, 425, 454, 482, 517, 525,
     544–5, 548, 556–7, 581, 600
Frankfurt School 2, 94
free speech 470, 477
Front National 48, 522, 525–6, 530, 533–7,
     539

genre 2, 5, 12–14, 41, 55, 70, 95, 132, 138,
     144, 294, 382–3, 417, 429, 438, 457,
     503, 625
  analysis 286, 549, 554–5
  discourse 128, 130, 136, 363, 370–1, 373
  policy 424
  political 191, 358–9
Goffman, E. 374–5, 417

Habermas, J. 38, 68–71, 73, 81–3, 92, 97,
     464–5
Habermas's Discourse Ethics 85
habitus 50, 64, 95, 434
Halliday, M.A.K. 2–4, 281–3, 298, 433, 617
  see also Systemic Functional Grammar,
     Systemic Functional Linguistics
Hardt-Mautner, G. 213
health advice 567, 570, 575, 579–80
high school dropout 496
high stakes testing 486, 489, 496, 500
Hodge, R. 98, 283, 533
Hoey, M. 214
Hunston, S. 218
Hurricane Katrina 560–2
Hussein, S. 20, 28–9, 192–5

identity
  collective 9, 20, 148, 151–5, 160–1,
     444–5, 455, 469
  ethno-national 523

European 417, 435–40, 443–4, 448–57,
     460
  national 25, 42, 68, 77–8, 87, 96, 206,
     210, 281, 439, 448, 506, 519, 522,
     524–5, 530–1, 533–7, 557
  personal 151
  supra-national 437, 439
  trans-national 439
ideological square 172
implicature 107, 117, 194, 208, 516
indexical 125–6, 131, 135, 343, 356–7, 359,
     362–4
  entailment 357
  presupposition 357
in-group 20–1, 28–9, 31, 34–9, 150, 152,
     157, 172, 180–1, 186, 207, 347, 437,
     446–7, 522, 524, 528–9, 531, 534–5
inside-deictic-centre (IDC) 191, 194–6,
     198–9, 203, 205
  see also deictic centre
intentionality 77, 99–100
intertextuality 155, 213, 344, 348, 357,
     363–4, 369, 415
interview 135, 147, 156–61, 374–7, 379,
     383, 386, 419–20, 431, 437–9, 459,
     484–5, 500, 556
intratextual 354
Iraq war 21, 25, 27, 41, 190, 192, 194–6,
     202, 208
Islamization 523

keyword
  analysis 241–2, 264–6, 278, 555, 618,
     621
  mining 241
Kress, G. 98, 180, 281, 283–5, 414, 533,
     594
Krishnamurthy, R. 223

Lakoff, G. 52, 54, 282, 505, 544, 548, 563,
     584, 590, 594
legitimation
  see legitimization
legitimization 9, 12, 102, 162, 186, 189–95,
     208–9, 223, 422, 435, 441–2, 444,
     447, 451, 453, 516, 522, 530
  see also discourse of legitimization
legitimization-proximization model 5–8
  see also legitimization, proximization
Lisbon Treaty 410

macrostructure 134, 139
manipulation 6, 13–15, 40, 42, 102, 105,
        116–18, 505, 517, 519
marketization 462–3
        *see also* discourse, marketization of
Marx, K. 2, 23, 246–7, 251, 278, 283, 462
mass media 134–5, 139, 365–71, 378–82,
        407, 503–4, 506, 517, 522, 582,
        625
        *see also* social media
memory
        episodic 124, 126, 139, 144, 146
        long term 122, 124, 128
        working 122, 144, 168
mental representation 101, 122–3, 129,
        131, 134–5, 139, 141, 145, 167, 610
metonymy 53, 64–6, 185, 562–3, 568,
        571–2, 574, 582, 592
modality 6, 75, 154–6, 158, 170, 177, 283,
        372, 525, 529, 538, 573–5, 577
        deontic 82, 154, 158, 615, 573, 575,
        577
        epistemic 119, 154, 573, 575, 577, 612
model
        context 125–31, 133, 137–8, 142,
        188
        mental 123–31, 133, 135, 139–41, 143,
        145, 151, 162, 184, 503
        situation 123–4, 126–8, 130, 139,
        143
modernization theory 323–4, 333, 344
multimodal analysis/studies 282–3, 285,
        293–5, 316, 351, 359, 540
multimodality 11, 15, 281–3, 285, 287,
        292–5, 316, 366, 382, 456
Muslims 512, 523, 526, 528, 534
mutual information 218

national security 191, 321–6, 328–34,
        336–45
NATO 29, 201, 509–11
natural disaster 507, 559–61, 580–2, 614
Nazi Germany 27–8
Neoliberalism 455, 468, 498
Nexis UK 214–15
nine eleven (9/11) 30, 192, 194, 203–4, 249,
        342–3, 363, 509, 512
No Child Left Behind 479–80, 495, 499–500
nominalization 12, 106, 186, 379, 486, 587,
        617

Obama, B. 30–1, 62, 64, 321, 326, 328–31,
        335–40, 342, 347–52, 354, 356–64,
        498, 609
Open Door (OD) 322–4, 337, 341–2
optimal relevance 62–3
other (re)presentation 19, 26, 40, 506–7,
        508
        negative 133, 141–3, 507, 516
        *see also* out-group, the other
out-group 20, 26, 28–9, 142, 150, 152,
        155, 162, 172, 180–1, 186, 207, 502,
        505–6, 522, 524, 534–7
outside-deictic-centre (ODC) 191, 194–6,
        198–200, 203, 205, 208
        *see also* deictic centre

panning 177–8
Partington, A. 213
passivization 106
pitch 158, 298, 300–3, 305, 307, 309
        high 301–3, 309–10, 313, 315
        low 301–2
        meaning of 301–2, 305
        movement 301–3
        range 298, 300, 305–8
pop culture 356
positioning 169–70, 176–8, 180, 182,
        184–5, 207, 209, 214, 226, 531, 533,
        569, 622–3
pragma-dialectics 4, 7, 69, 72–3, 79, 81–2,
        94, 240, 266, 540
Press Complaints Commission 212, 228
presupposition 56, 107, 119, 134–5, 200,
        357, 386, 398, 505, 516, 518
privatization 161, 461–2, 465–6, 469, 471,
        473–5, 477, 480
production format 374–5
proximization 6, 12–13, 189–209, 447, 453,
        504
        axiological 191, 193–6, 209, 453
        STA model of 191, 199, 203
        spatial 181, 191, 193–5, 202–3, 206
        temporal 191, 193, 202–3, 206
        theory 189–92, 195–7, 199–200, 202,
        206–8
perlocutionary 99–100, 102, 105, 108, 184,
        372
political protests 167–8, 182–4, 187
positive discourse analysis 386, 397, 404,
        498–9, 585, 601

post-foundational 385–6, 388–9, 400, 402, 404
powerless Other 237–9, 261–3, 266
prestige advertising 446–8
processing effort 63, 104, 115
promissory statements 544, 549
public
    compliance 575, 579–80
    health communication 552–3
    realm 461, 463–70, 473–6
    space 189–90, 196, 208, 443, 462–6, 469–71, 473, 476–7, 536
    sphere 50, 52, 237, 266, 280, 369, 378, 443, 453–9, 464–5, 477
    *see also* European Public Sphere

racism 119, 130, 132–5, 137, 141–4, 146, 188, 206–7, 290–1, 347, 372, 389, 505, 522, 526, 537–8
Rasmussen, A.F. 27, 201–3
reception format 372, 374–5
reference corpus 213, 241, 277, 622
Reisigl, M. 9, 22, 24–5, 35, 77, 89, 149, 184, 213, 549
Relevance Theory (RT) 6, 62–3, 103, 119
re-minding 586–7, 590, 596–600
rhetorics
    of judging 20–2, 26–7, 29, 31, 35, 38–9
    of failing 20–2, 26, 29–31, 38–9
    of penitence 20–2, 26, 32–5, 38–9
    of judge-penitence 20, 22, 26, 35–6, 38–9, 41
rhythm 298–301, 313–14
rules for rational dispute 79

self (re)presentation 87
    positive 88, 106, 133, 141–2, 144, 442, 507, 535
    *see also* in-group
schematization 169, 173
school-to-prison pipeline 498
semantics
    frame 186, 562, 565, 581
    localist 562–3, 565–6
signage 462, 471, 477
slogan
    campaign 347, 358
    political 347–8, 351, 353–7, 359–62

social
    actor 3, 7–9, 15, 28, 69, 122–3, 127, 136, 154–8, 160, 170, 174, 182, 292, 354, 379, 434, 474, 507–8, 524, 536
    cognition 123, 127, 129, 147–8, 152, 161–3
    *see also* personal cognition
    knowledge 129, 131, 557
    media 238, 277, 365, 367, 379–82, 384
    psychology 123, 151, 161, 163, 382, 403, 581–2
    structures 1, 122, 129, 131, 133–4, 136, 138, 144, 168, 388
Socio-Cognitive
    Approach 3, 7–8, 15, 121, 148–52, 184, 507
    Analysis (CGA) 9, 134, 136, 148
    Representation (SCR) 148, 150–2, 154–5, 158–61
sound qualities 298–300, 306–7, 310, 312–13
Standpoint of the Criticized (SotC) 241–4, 249, 252, 264–5
source domain 63, 175, 563
speech act 7, 21, 70–2, 82, 89–91, 93, 125–8, 131, 134, 138, 355, 361, 437, 604
Sperber, D. 6, 51, 62, 116, 125
surrogate subjectivity 237, 239, 250, 253, 265–6
Systemic Functional
    Grammar (SFG) 4, 239, 266, 278
    Linguistics (SFL) 607, 622

target domain 63, 175–6, 563
technology
    of agency 444
    of involvement 444
terrorism 204, 288, 295, 316, 332, 501, 512–13
    *see also* war on terror
text mining 241, 248–9
theoretical attractor 3–4, 6
the other 25–6, 28–9, 36–7, 39, 238, 261–3, 266
topos 68–9, 75–7, 85–9, 91, 93, 538
    formal classes of 76
    of burden 78, 507, 513
    of history 19, 21–2, 24–6, 29–31, 35, 37–9, 507

transit advertising 469
triangulation 55, 150, 161, 213, 607, 623

validity claim 22, 69–71, 73, 82, 93
Van Dijk, T. 9–11, 184, 239, 418–19, 462,
    503–4, 506–8
Van Eemeren, F. 5, 84, 117
Van Leeuwen, T. 175, 180, 283–5, 292, 298–9,
    306, 310, 314, 372, 507, 531, 594
viewing frame 181–3, 185
virtuous circle 323, 337–9

war on terror 192, 199, 202–3, 205, 316, 363

weapons of mass destruction (WMD) 27,
    192–6, 208, 331–2
wildcard 216
Wilson, D. 62, 101, 104, 116, 119, 125
WMatrix 248, 265, 277, 280
Wodak, R. 3, 5, 7, 11, 22, 24–5, 35,
    77, 89, 91, 149, 184, 213, 239,
    287–8, 402, 415–18, 420–2,
    427, 437, 439, 444, 503–8,
    523, 531
world-systems theory 341

Žagar, I. 68, 85–8